C000319228

The Good Sk
& Snowboarc
Guide **2002**

SKI CLUB OF GREAT BRITAIN
HALF-PRICE
MEMBERSHIP OFFER
(see page 11)

The Good Skiing & Snowboarding Guide **2002**

Edited by
Peter and Felice Hardy

CONSUMERS' ASSOCIATION

Which? Books are commissioned by
Consumers' Association and published by
Which? Ltd, 2 Marylebone Road, London NW1 4DF
Email address: books@which.net
Resort reports to: goodskiandsnowguide@which.net

Distributed by The Penguin Group:
Penguin Books Ltd, 80 Strand, London WC2R 0RL

First edition of *The Good Skiing Guide*: 1985
This edition September 2001

The views expressed herein are those of the Editors, and not necessarily those
of the Ski Club of Great Britain.

Editors	Peter and Felice Hardy
Researchers	Jane Blount, Bryony Deacon, Kate Parker
Contributors	Minty Clinch, Doug Sager, Arnie Wilson, Virginia Wallis
Cover design	Price Watkins Design
Cover photo	J Stock-Stockshot
Maps	Holmes Linnette

British Library Cataloguing-in-Publication Data:
A catalogue record for this book is available from the British Library

ISBN 0 85202 869 5

For a full list of Which? books, please write to:
Which? Books, Castlemead, Gascoyne Way, Hertford X SG14 1LH
or access our web site at www.which.net

Editorial	Joanna Chisholm, Alethea Doran, Vicky Fisher
Production	Joanna Bregosz
Typeset by	Saxon Graphics Ltd, Derby
Printed and bound in Spain by	Bookprint, S.L., Barcelona

Contents

Euro Converter

The table below gives the exchange rate on changeover day, 1 January 2002, between the euro and the 'old' currencies of Austria, France, Germany, Italy and Spain. The pound/euro figure is only an approximate guide.

Pound	Euro	Schilling	Mark	Fr/Franc	Lira	Peseta
£0.60	1	13.76	1.96	6.56	1,936	166
£3	5	68.80	9.78	32.80	9,681	832
£6	10	137.60	19.56	65.60	19,363	1,664
£9	15	206.40	29.38	98.39	29,044	2,496
£12	20	275.21	39.12	131.19	38,725	3,328
£18	30	412.81	58.67	196.79	58,088	4,992
£24	40	550.41	78.23	262.38	77,451	6,655
£30	50	688.02	97.79	327.98	96,814	8,317
£36	60	825.62	117.35	393.57	116,176	9,983
£42	70	963.22	136.91	459.17	139,411	11,647
£48	80	1,100.82	156.57	524.77	154,902	13,311
£54	90	1,238.43	176.02	590.36	174,264	14,975
£60	100	1,376.03	195.58	655.96	193,627	16,639
£120	200	2,752.06	391.17	1,311.91	387,254	33,277

International dialling codes

Andorra	00376	Norway	0047
Austria	0043	Spain	0034
Canada	001	Sweden	0046
France	0033	Switzerland	0041
Italy	0039	USA	001

This year, we have included hotel and apartment telephone numbers in *The Guide*. For reasons of space, we have omitted country codes (although these can be found under the *Tourist Information* details for each resort). We have also omitted the '0' which proceeds most European numbers when dialled locally, but which is not part of the international dialling code. For example, Chamonix Reservations Centre is listed as (450 53 23 33). From the UK, however, you would dial (0033 450 53 23 33). From France you would dial (0450 53 23 33). Please note that the initial '0' in Italian numbers is not omitted when dialling from outside the country.

		PISTES	EUROPE	NORTH AMERICA
	Cable-car	———	Beginner	Easy
	Gondola	———	Easy	Intermediate
	Chair-lift (inset figure denotes number of seats)	———	Intermediate	
		———	Difficult	
	Drag-lift	◆		Difficult
	Funicular	◆◆		Very difficult
	Mountain railway	··········	Unpisted itinerary	Unpisted itinerary

Introduction

This is your alarm call . . .

The time has come for skiers and snowboarders to face the facts of global warming. Not that the winter sports holiday as we know it is in immediate danger of disappearing – but its future is finite. Like all those directly involved in reporting the sport that we love, it would be easy to bury our heads in the snow and ignore what is happening around us. However, anyone who has regularly visited the Alps over the past 20 years cannot fail to have noticed climatic change. In half a lifetime on skis we have seen major glaciers shrink by hundreds of metres and the pattern of seasonal precipitation edge forward by a full fortnight. December snowfall is increasingly uncertain, while the deepest cover is to be found in late spring at a time when most resorts have already closed their lift systems.

Nonetheless, in winter 2000–1 the largest amounts of snow accumulated on 3,500-m peaks across the French and Swiss Alps since records began over 60 years ago. For example, on Pic Blanc above Alpe d'Huez we skied in thigh-deep powder in the middle of April. And we could have done the same three weeks later. So what's the problem?

The fact is that this increased precipitation is falling as snow only at higher altitudes. The low-lying runs of these same resorts suffered from less cover than usual. In 2000–1 the Tyrol and other parts of Austria suffered from nominal snow cover during the first half of the winter. When the snow did arrive it was too late to form a satisfactory base. Rain and high winds – even in February and at altitudes of up to 2,500m – were alarming features of strange winter weather throughout Europe. Rain threatened to wash out the Alpine World Championships in St Anton and tested the technical properties of skiers' clothing across the Alps. For low resorts with no access to high-level skiing, this volatile weather pattern is of far greater concern.

Professor Martin Beniston, co-author of the latest UN report on climate change and head of geosciences at Fribourg University in Switzerland, has said that the Alps are warming up faster than the rest of the globe. He has warned that the snowline in the main Swiss–French Alpine chain will rise from 1,200m to 1,800m. In Austria, where the snowline is lower, this would mean no cover beneath 1,200m and would leave resorts such as Zell am See (750m) and Kitzbühel (760m) marooned in green fields.

It may be tempting to dismiss this as scare-mongering, but we must recognise what is happening on those glaciers that are still covered. Some 25 years ago a fad for year-round skiing led to the development of a dozen high-altitude lift systems in Austria, France, Italy and Switzerland. Loss of interest has led to a steady decline in the number of summer skiers over the past decade, and major resorts such as Tignes, Zermatt and Kaprun now choose to shut their lifts for at least part of the 'closed' season. Despite this trend, however, other resorts are busily trying to develop or expand summer ski areas. Val Thorens, Engelberg, Alpe d'Huez, the Stubai, Sölden and Alpe d'Huez have all built – or are seeking to build – new lifts, while Alagna has spent billions of lire on developing a brand new summer ski area. The reason? Not to offer entertainment for that shrinking band of August piste-hounds, but to provide at least a modicum of snow-sure skiing throughout future uncertain winters.

Although the Alpine ski holiday is unlikely to disappear in the near future, tour operators will have to adjust to changing conditions, with a greater emphasis on the end than on the start of the season. The unseemly scrabble for beds in 'safe' resorts such as Val d'Isère and Obergurgl becomes more and more competitive each year. It is clear that in the future we will have to venture higher up the mountains to enjoy shorter runs. Meanwhile, resort-level snow at Christmas – an essential festive ingredient – could become a thing of the past in lower-lying resorts. Regardless of whether Professor Beniston's warning is accurate, you won't find us below 1,800m on 25 December.

The euro

The conversion to the euro throughout much of Europe takes place during the course of the 2001–2 ski season. The changeover period is short and sharp. The euro comes into street usage on 1 January 2002. French francs, Austrian schillings and the other affected currencies will be withdrawn almost immediately, and they cease to be legal tender on 28 February. The skiing countries that have adopted the euro in the first phase are Austria, Finland, France, Germany, Greece, Italy and Spain. Andorra, which until now has used both the peseta and French franc, will also become a 'euro-zone'.

For the visitor from Britain all this will require some mental adjustment. While the price of a package holiday will be paid in the UK in pounds, in participating countries the costs of in-resort extras, such as lift passes, tuition, childcare and equipment rental, must be paid in euros. Resorts in these countries have published their lift prices in euros and, in theory, the transition should for the first time give us the chance to compare prices not just from resort to resort, but from country to country. In reality, however, a number of factors such as different age limits for children and seniors, and different types of pass, make comparisons complicated.

After considerable debate, we have decided to leave prices for this edition in the more familiar old currencies. No doubt we will soon be familiar with euros, but for this winter 100F will mean more to regular visitors to France than 15-plus euros. We have provided a ready-reckoner currency converter on page 6.

Air rage

Readers of *The Good Skiing & Snowboarding Guide* complain bitterly that standards of service provided by both charter and scheduled airlines now seriously detract from the enjoyment of their ski holidays.

Airports too do not escape censure – Lyon's charter terminal comes in for particular criticism: 'We spent three hours at the end of our holiday in this soulless hangar and most of it was spent waiting for the BA charter check-in to open. Our reps had to meet the incoming flights and were forced to leave us to battle with harassed airline officials on our own to secure seats beside our young children'.

Passengers to Geneva fared no better: 'With little available information we spent six hours waiting for a Britannia flight at a massively overloaded airport, having been dumped by our reps who were anxious to be rid of us. The charter flight itself was pretty basic, with unacceptable leg-room for anyone over 5ft 9ins tall. The food was barely adequate and we had to pay for a glass of sparkling water and a lemonade on a flight that was delayed by five hours'.

One regular skier who uses Heathrow said: 'The falling standard of Swissair since its merger with Sabena is now a complete joke. The directors of the airline should be forced to queue in the cattle-pen at 7am every Monday morning for inevitably delayed flights to Geneva and Zurich. There are never enough ground staff to cope'.

Most transatlantic carriers received similar criticism, with readers unanimously complaining about lack of room. 'Standards on scheduled flights have dropped to the kind of level you might have expected to find on a charter 15 years ago. On my expensive Air Canada flight to Vancouver I experienced new heights of discomfort, sandwiched as I was between two large people. The steward barely managed to be civil, while the stewardesses rarely managed a smile between them'.

Only the low-cost airlines were singled out for praise. EasyJet received much applause from a number of readers: 'What a treat,' wrote one reporter, 'to leave an airport a happy man at having just experienced excellent value for money. My return flight to Geneva cost less than my train fare home from Gatwick'.

These comments mirror the results of a *Holiday Which?* survey of over 31,000 readers, published in spring 2001, which showed that the budget airlines' cheap and cheerful approach was winning hearts and minds. Three no-frills airlines, including easyJet, came in the top ten, soaring ahead of charter airlines and short-haul scheduled services. On average, over half the members who had flown with a budget airline would recommend it to a friend, compared with only 20 per cent who would say the same about charter airlines.

Downwardly mobile

The mobile phone is a permanent fixture (some might say a ubiquitous intrusion) in our lives – and the ski slope is no exception. While riding a chair-lift in quiet contemplation, nothing is more annoying than being an unwilling eavesdropper on somebody else's banal conversation. However, gone are the days when a wrong turning or an untimely fall could result in friends losing each other for the whole day. Calls from mobiles alert the rescue services to injured skiers or snowboarders and undoubtedly have saved lives. On a more mundane level mobiles are also useful for arranging lunch or après-ski rendezvous. 'A table for four at 1pm?' *Pas de problème*' (if only resorts would print restaurant numbers on piste maps . . .).

Important dates

Easter 2002 falls on Sunday 31 March, the earliest date in recent years. For once, the festival does not coincide with the Paris school holidays, so both the surrounding weeks in the French Alps should be relatively quiet at a time when snow conditions should still be excellent.

Expect to pay the highest prices at New Year, during high-season February and at British half-term. The UK school break for winter 2001–2 is divided fairly evenly between the weeks beginning 9/10 February and 16/17 February. The second week coincides with President's Weekend (the week beginning 16/17 February) when US and Canadian resorts will be at their busiest. The French February and spring school holidays are staggered by zones, but this does not eliminate overcrowding on the slopes in the French Alps. It is advisable to avoid the Paris winter holidays (16 February to 4 March). The Paris spring holidays do not begin until 13 April. Visitors to the French Dauphiné (including Alpe d'Huez and Les Deux Alpes), resorts in the French Pyrenees (including Barèges) and Andorra should be aware of the Grenoble and Toulouse school holiday dates (9–25 February and 6–22 April).

How you can help

We need your help to update *The Guide* accurately each year. Together with our team of researchers, we try to visit as many resorts as possible, but it is not feasible to visit over 600 in a 20-week season. Lifts are constantly being upgraded, the standards and service of hotels and restaurants rise and fall, and the tuition given at ski and snowboard schools can vary from season to season. Please tell us about your ski holiday experiences – both the good and the bad – typed or printed in as much detail as possible. Readers who send the best letters will receive a free copy of *The Good Skiing & Snowboarding Guide*. Further details on how you can help can be found in *Reporting on the resorts*, on page 586. Remember, too, that you can email your report to:
goodskiandsnowguide@which.net

Ski Club of Great Britain and *The Good Skiing & Snowboarding Guide*

The Ski Club of Great Britain has enjoyed a strong association with *The Good Skiing Guide*, now *The Good Skiing & Snowboarding Guide*, for many years. Founded in 1903, it is the largest and most active club for British skiers and snowboarders in the UK. Catering for snow-users of all ages, it offers members services and benefits unavailable elsewhere.

Information and web site

The Club's information department provides members with impartial advice and information on over 500 resorts around the world. The Club's award-winning web site (*www.skiclub.co.uk*) contains information on Club matters, the most up-to-date snow reports, and hosts a tour-operator search engine where users can select certain criteria for their ideal holiday and then link to the most appropriate tour operator.

Reps in resorts

The Ski Club's reps – unpaid volunteers, trained and experienced in leading groups of skiers and snowboarders in search of the best snow – now operate in 40 resorts in Europe and North America.

Holidays

The Ski Club's holiday programme covers 30 resorts in 8 countries. Holidays are organised by skiing standard and run by Ski Club reps/leaders. A wide range of ski instruction trips is offered, together with off-piste and advanced tours.

Events and other member benefits

Members receive four free copies per year of the Club magazine, *Ski and Board*, and details of the companies that offer Club members discounts on holidays, travel and accommodation, equipment and resort rental prices.

The Golden Ski Awards 2002

The Golden Ski Awards are judged annually by the editors, contributors and reporters of *The Good Skiing & Snowboarding Guide*. These prestigious 'White Oscars' go to those resorts, establishments and facilities that we consider have provided an outstanding level of service to skiers and snowboarders during the 2000–1 season. Two winners have been selected for each category: one in Europe and the other in North America (chalets are an exception).

Resort of the Year
Winners: Val d'Isère (France), Whistler (British Columbia)
Also nominated: St Anton (Austria), Park City (Utah)

Most Improved Resort of the Year
Winners: Mayrhofen (Austria), Kicking Horse (British Columbia)
Also nominated: Tignes (France), Big White (British Columbia)

Small Resort of the Year
Winners: Baqueira Beret (Spain), Solitude (The Cottonwood Resorts, Utah)
Also nominated: La Tania (France), Alta (The Cottonwood Resorts, Utah)

Family Resort of the Year
Winners: Lech (Austria), Deer Valley (Park City Resorts, Utah)
Also nominated: Vaujany (France), Smugglers' Notch (Vermont)

Hotel of the Year
Winners: Auberge de la Maison (Courmayeur),
Fairmont Chateau Whistler (Whistler)
Also nominated: Alex Schlosshotel Tenne (Zermatt), Le Hameau Albert 1er (Chamonix), Amangani (Jackson Hole), Weisses Rössl (Kitzbühel)

Tour Operator Chalet of the Year
Winner: Chalet Rubis – Val d'Isère (Scott Dunn Ski),
Also nominated: Domaine de la Baronne – Crans Montana
(Oxford Ski Company)

Resort Restaurant of the Year
Winners: Tivoli (Cortina d'Ampezzo), Zoom (Park City)
Also nominated: Hus No.8 (Lech), Pas de l'Ours (Crans Montana),
Sushi Village (Whistler)

Mountain Restaurant of the Year

Winners: Chalet Alti-Bar (Alpe d'Huez), The Lookout Cabin (The Canyons, Park City Resorts, Utah)
Also nominated: Upstairs at L'Arbina (Tignes), Alta Lodge (Alta, The Cottonwood Resorts)

Ski School of the Year

Winners: Stoked The Ski School (Zermatt), Deer Valley Ski School (Park City Resorts, Utah)
Also nominated: Rote Teufel (Kitzbühel), Perfect Turn (Sunday River, Maine)

Ski Shop of the Year

Winners: Precision Ski (Val d'Isère). Summit Ski & Snowboard (Whistler). Also nominated: Ski In (Courmayeur), Alba Sports (St Anton), Freeride.fr (Méribel), Glacier Sports (Zermatt), Base Mountain Sports (Vail), Steamboat Ski Rentals (Steamboat, Colorado)

Best Mountain Loo

Winners: Riffelberg ('pink and scented – men and women') and Findlerhof ('toilets so sterile clean you could eat your lunch off the floor')(both Zermatt)
Also nominated: Aeroplanstadl (Bad Hofgastein)

Readers are invited to submit their nominations for The Golden Ski Awards 2003, together with a short explanation. Please send them to: Dept CD, Consumers' Association, FREEPOST, 2 Marylebone Road, London NW1 1YN. No stamp is needed.

Alternatively, you can email them to us: *goodskiandsnowguide@which.net*

Simply the best

The resorts listed below are those considered by the editors and contributors to the Guide to be the best in a variety of categories. The ten entries in each category are listed in alphabetical order, rather than by ranking.

Skiing/boarding for all standards

Les Arcs
Aspen
Courchevel
Flaine
Keystone
Mammoth
Méribel
Tignes
Vail
Whistler

Beginners

Les Arcs
Beaver Creek
The Canyons
Cervinia
Flaine
Geilo
Livigno
Mayrhofen
Soldeu–El Tarter
Wengen

Intermediates

Alpe d'Huez
Bad Gastein
Courchevel
Park City
La Plagne
Selva Gardena
Serre Chevalier
Sestriere
Vail
Wengen

Advanced

Alpe d'Huez
Chamonix
Jackson Hole
Park City
Snowbird and Alta
St Anton
Val d'Isère and Tignes
Verbier
Whistler
Zermatt

Moguls

Avoriaz
Breckenridge
Davos and Klosters
Killington
Mürren
Red Mountain
St Anton
Taos
Telluride
Verbier

Off-piste

Alagna
Alyeska
Chamonix and Argentière
Fernie
La Grave
Snowbird and Alta
Val d'Isère and Tignes
Verbier
Whistler
Zermatt

Snowboarding

Avoriaz
Axamer Lizum
Chamonix
Davos
Red Mountain
Serre Chevalier
Squaw Valley
St Anton
Vail
Whistler

Families

Les Arcs
Beaver Creek
Deer Valley
Lech
Obergurgl
Smugglers' Notch
Solitude
Vaujany
Villars
Whistler

Non-skiers

Aspen
Bad Gastein
Cortina d'Ampezzo
Innsbruck
Kitzbühel
Lake Tahoe
Megève
Seefeld
St Moritz
Zermatt

Close to an interesting city

Bad Gastein (Salzburg)
Chamonix (Geneva)
La Clusaz (Geneva)
Cortina d'Ampezzo (Venice)
Isola 2000 (Nice)
Park City (Salt Lake City)
Sauze d'Oulx (Turin)
Seefeld (Innsbruck)
Whistler (Vancouver)
Winter Park (Denver)

Airport convenience

Avoriaz
Chamonix
La Clusaz
Crans Montana
Innsbruck
Megève
Sauze d'Oulx
Verbier
Wagrain
Winter Park

Luxury accommodation

Aspen
Courchevel 1850
Crans Montana
Deer Valley
Gstaad
Lech and Zürs
Méribel
St Moritz
Vail and Beaver Creek
Zermatt

Value for money

Barèges
Big Sky
Livigno
Madesimo
Passo Tonale
Red Mountain
Schladming
Serre Chevalier
Soldeu-El Tarter
Söll and the SkiWelt

Eating out

Aspen
Cortina d'Ampezzo
Courchevel
Courmayeur
Kitzbühel
Megève
Park City
Tremblant
Whistler
Zermatt

Outstanding mountain restaurants

Alpe d'Huez
Cervinia
Cortina d'Ampezzo
Courchevel
Courmayeur
Klosters
Megève
La Plagne
St Moritz
Zermatt

Après-ski

Baqueira–Beret
Chamonix
Cortina d'Ampezzo
Courmayeur
Ischgl
Kitzbühel
Sauze d'Oulx
Soldeu–El Tarter
St Anton
Zermatt

Ski and shop

Aspen
Breckenridge
Cortina d'Ampezzo
Courmayeur
Jackson Hole
Mammoth
Megève
Park City
Whistler
Zermatt

Small attractive villages in big ski areas

Arabba (Sella Ronda)
Champéry (Portes du Soleil)
Dorf Gastein (Bad Gastein)
Haus-im-Ennstal (Schladming)
Montchavin (La Plagne)
Samoëns (Flaine)
St Christoph (St Anton)
St-Martin-de-Belleville (Trois Vallées)
Vaujany (Alpe d'Huez)
Venosc (Les Deux Alpes)

Romantic/charming resorts

Alpbach
Courmayeur
Jackson Hole
Kitzbühel
Megève
Mürren
Saas-Fee
Stowe
Telluride
Zell am See

Purpose-built convenience

Alpe d'Huez
Les Arcs
Courchevel 1850
Flaine
Isola 2000
Obertauern
La Plagne
Snowbird
Tignes
Valmorel

Snow-sure resorts

Cervinia
Kaprun
Mammoth
Obergurgl–Hochgurgl
Obertauern
Saas-Fee
Val d'Isère and Tignes
Val Thorens
Whistler
Zermatt

Austria

In recent winters, Austria has clawed its way back to a position of power and influence in European skiing. It has been helped by the apparent invincibility of its national ski teams and, rather more importantly, by a favourable rate of exchange. Despite this, Austria no longer holds the title of premier destination for British skiers, a position that it cherished throughout most of the second half of the twentieth century. Indeed, it is unlikely to do so ever again, being safely entrenched in second place behind France. The immutable Austrian holiday formula is still synonymous with snow fun: rolling, tree-lined slopes above charming villages, jolly inns, foaming tankards of beer, lively bars and discos, and liberal sound-bites of accordion music. But the harsh reality is that its delightfully atmospheric resorts – with a couple of notable exceptions – are unable to satisfy the increasingly voracious demands of the accomplished snow-users of today.

Of course, Austrian destinations continue to provide excellent skiing and snowboarding for beginners and intermediates in an enjoyable environment. However, today's shortened learning curve for skiers – and an even shorter one for riders – has resulted in an increased number of more proficient snow-users. Those who absconded elsewhere in the late 1980s, when the sterling exchange rate plunged, are not all keen to return – even though the rate is back up to over ATS21 against the pound in the countdown to Euro-Day. They have come to demand steeper ski terrain than is typically found in the pastureland of the Tyrol and Salzburgerland. Indeed, St Anton and its Arlberg neighbours stand almost alone as Austrian resorts that satisfy this requirement.

What skiers and snowboarders can no longer take for granted is snow, a substance that was significantly lacking across a giant swathe of Austria for most of the 2000–1 season. In late January, we skied in the low-lying Tyrol on the kind of grass-studded slopes you might expect to find in early April. When the eyes of the world were focused on St Anton for the World Alpine Skiing Championships, it poured with rain. When the snows finally arrived, the winter was far too advanced for a proper, safe base to form above the low-altitude villages that make up the majority of Austria's skiing portfolio.

However, despite the uncertainties of snow cover and the mainly benign quality of the skiing, Austria's biggest plus point is the superlative standard of accommodation. Reporters constantly express their surprise at finding spotless pensions as well as lavish hotels in the tiniest of villages, and as one commented: 'all I want from a skiing holiday is plenty of easy piste-cruising and a first-class hotel that doesn't cost a fortune. That is why I return to Austria year after year'.

Alpbach

ALTITUDE 1,000m (3,280ft)

Beginners ✱ Intermediates ✱✱✱ Advanced ✱ Snowboarders ✱✱

If your Tyrolean holiday is not complete without lads in leather breeches and girls in puff-sleeved *dirndl*, then Alpbach is the place for you. Tradition, quality skiing and an intimate relationship with British skiers over the past 40 years have set this resort apart from other Tyrolean destinations.

✔ Attractive village
✔ Alpine charm
✔ Lack of queues
✔ Ideal for non-skiers
✔ Long vertical drop
✔ Family skiing
✘ Poor access to slopes
✘ Limited number of pistes
✘ Unexciting nightlife

Alpbach is a small, sunny village on a steep hillside. The compact centre is dominated by a pretty green-and-white church surrounded by old wooden chalets and the buttressed walls of the two medieval inns. It is a strikingly attractive resort, far removed from the commercial influences of mainstream Tyrol.The hotels and restaurants tend to be owned and staffed by locals rather than seasonal employees, so the hosts have a genuine interest in the welfare of their guests.

The ski area is limited in size but offers a variety of terrain, best suited to intermediates. The inconvenience of having to take a five-minute bus ride from the village to the main mountain, the Wiedersberger Horn, and back again each day is a drawback, particularly for families with small children confined to the village-centre nursery slope. However, the bus service is efficient.

On the snow
top 2,025m (6,643ft) bottom 830m (2,722ft)

Apart from the nursery slopes and the Böglerlift, with its south-facing red (intermediate) run, all of Alpbach's skiing is on the Wiedersberger Horn. Mountain access from Alpbach is via the two-stage Achenwirt gondola across the wooded, north-facing slopes to Hornboden at 1,850m. Queuing is not a problem, although weekends are busier.

Alpbach has 19 lifts and some long runs, but it is still stuck with the unfair reputation of being a beginners' resort. Mountain access is also possible by chair-lift from **Inneralpbach** along the valley. Snowmaking on the lower, rocky meadows beneath the first stage of the gondola has made it possible to ski down to the bottom for most of the season. The next-door village of **Reith** shares a lift pass, has three lifts and a new eight-person gondola for 2001–2, which replaces the main chair-lift.

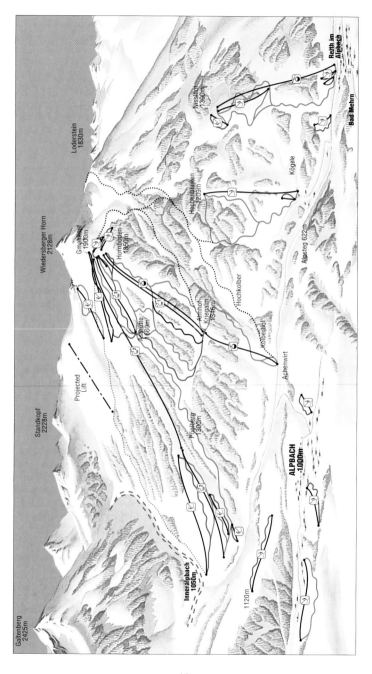

This is the first phase of a plan to provide a link to Alpbach, which in turn is exploring the viability of an on-mountain connection to the **Wildschönau** area.

Beginners

Complete novices need not stray from the village. Easy nursery runs are served by a drag-lift in the centre beside the Böglerhof and the shorter Lukaslift. Once the basics have been mastered, skiers progress to the *Familienabfahrt* on the Hornboden via the gondola. This is a long path from Gmahbahn to Kriegalm, which reporters claim is often icy.

Intermediates

With the exception of a couple of moderately challenging black (difficult) runs, 70 per cent of the mountain is given over to intermediate skiing. The small number of trails (ten) marked on the local lift map belies the actual size of the groomed area, and the pistes are extremely wide. The Hornbahn 2000 quad chair-lift allows some challenging intermediate skiing. The standard of piste preparation is high. The red (intermediate) piste 8 is 'a beautiful run down to Inneralpbach'.

> **WHAT'S NEW**
>
> Brandegg quad-chair replaces T-bar at Wiedersberghorn
> Eight-person gondola replaces Reith chair-lift

Advanced

From Hornboden, a couple of wide trails run back down to the Kriegalm mid-station, including an FIS (International Ski Federation) racecourse, which is one of the two black runs on the mountain; the other is Brandegg. From here a red (intermediate) run to the bottom creates a good, fast course of over 1,000m vertical.

Off-piste

Alpbach is ideal for 'lazy powder skiers'. According to one reporter you can lie in bed after a night of new snow until 10.30am and still cut fresh tracks. To the west of the main ski area is an interesting range of off-piste bowls. The long, red itinerary route from Gmahkopf down to Inneralpbach is not pisted, although it is usually well-skied. Some fairly challenging off-piste can be found around the Wiedersberger Horn.

Snowboarding

The undulating topography is a dream for riders and boasts two terrain parks and a half-pipe.

Tuition and guiding

One reporter described Skischool Alpbach as 'friendly and traditional, absolutely not *avant garde*'. We have positive reports of the Alpbach Skischool Aktiv, and Reith has its own ski school.

Mountain restaurants

The Hornboden restaurant is situated 50m below the top stage of the gondola, which is fine for skiers but inconvenient for the many non-skiers, who have to walk down a steep stretch of piste to reach it. The lower section is self-service while upstairs is a restaurant serving Tyrolean food. The Gmahstuben is cheap and cheerful. The Böglalm farmhouse contains a self-service restaurant, but is criticised for being 'incredibly inefficient'. Gasthof Wiedersberger Horn at Inneralpbach is one of the best restaurants in the region.

Accommodation

Most of Alpbach's accommodation is in hotels and guesthouses, ranging from basic B&Bs to the very comfortable. Three of the most luxurious hotels are the Böglerhof (☎ 5336 52270), Alpbacherhof (☎ 5336 5237) and the Alphof (☎ 5336 5371) ('a ten-minute stroll from the centre but the cheapest four-star in Alpbach').

Eating in and out

Recommended eateries include Gasthof Jakober, Alpbacher Taverne, Gasthof Wiedersberger Horn and the Reblaus pizzeria. The Böglerhof's restaurant is the smartest. The Rossmoos and Zottahof restaurants, both up the mountain, are popular in the evening.

Après-ski

If drinking and dancing until dawn are an integral component of your ski holiday, you should consider other, livelier resorts. Outside the main holiday weeks the resort is dead by 11pm, except at weekends when an influx of visitors gives it much-needed cheer. Achenwirt, at the foot of the mountain, is 'good for a couple of beers on the way home'. The Jakober Bar is an early-evening rendezvous point. The Hornbeisl bar is next to the lifts in Inneralpbach. The Waschkuch'l is good for a quiet drink, while the Birdy Pub in the village centre is noisier. The Alpbacher Weinstadl provides late-night music.

Childcare

The care of children at the ski school is more American-style than European: 'we were told not to worry about the children if we were late or the weather was bad. The instructors would take care of them, which they did. When the weather was bad the children were taken into a restaurant to get warm'. The ski kindergarten, Frosty's Schneewelt, operates from a leisurely 10am to 3.15pm and even has an American-style 'magic carpet' lift. Alpbach Kindergarten takes children from three years old.

TOURIST INFORMATION
Tel 43 5336 6000
Fax 43 5336 600200
Email info@alpbach.at
Web site www.alpbach.at

Bad Gastein

ALTITUDE 1,100m (3,608ft)

Intermediates ✳✳✳ Advanced ✳✳ Snowboarders ✳✳

The Gasteinertal, a long closed valley flanked by the Hohe Tauern mountains, offers a higher class of skiing than the lowland pastures of the Tyrol and an altogether more cosmopolitan atmosphere. Bad Gastein, the main resort in the valley, is a collection of once-grand hotels painted mostly in the imperial yellow of Vienna's Schönbrunn Palace and stacked dramatically up a steep hillside around a waterfall that plunges into the River Ache. The resort's elegant casino harks back to the days when this was one of the greatest spas of Europe. Franz Schubert and Johann Strauss both composed here, and the guest list never failed to include at least a couple of crowned heads. However, the medical spa business is not what it was, although winter sports have given the region an injection of new life.

- ✔ Large ski area
- ✔ Tree-level skiing
- ✔ Variety of après-ski
- ✔ Thermal baths
- ✔ Choice of mountain restaurants
- ✔ Easy rail access
- ✔ Reasonable prices
- ✘ Lack of skiing convenience
- ✘ Unconnected ski areas
- ✘ Heavy traffic
- ✘ Poor piste-marking
- ✘ Awkward for families with small children

Some 23 million litres of hot water per day bubble up from 17 natural springs and are piped into all the main hotels. The public indoor and outdoor pools at the Felsenbad by the Bahnhof (railway station) are a popular rendezvous where you can wallow in the waters and, through a haze of steam, watch skiers in action just a few metres away. About 4.5 million litres of this hot water are also piped down the road to Bad Gastein's sister spa of **Bad Hofgastein**. This is a spacious and comfortable resort that is popular with families.

Dorf Gastein, at the entrance to the Gasteinertal, is a sleepy and unspoilt village with its own attractive ski area that extends over the 2,027-m Kreuzkogel to the resort of **Grossarl** in a neighbouring valley. **Sport Gastein**, at the head of the valley, is a separate ski area based around an abandoned gold-mining village. In the Middle Ages the area was responsible for ten per cent of the world's gold and silver output.

The Gastein resorts are included in the new Skiverbund Amadé lift pass, which covers 30 resorts in this corner of Austria. It gives access to 276 lifts serving 865km of piste. In practice, this means that the visitor with a car can also ski in **Schladming** or join the giant **Altenmarkt–Zauchensee** circuit for a day from nearby **St Johann im Pongau**. This includes both **Flachau** and **Wagrain**.

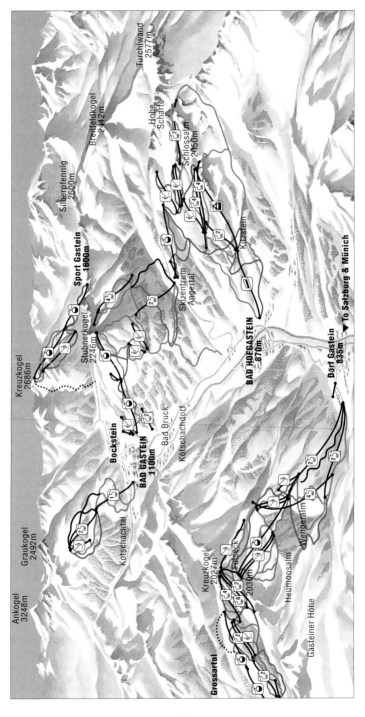

Ankogel
3248m

Turchlwand
2577m

Hohe
Scharte

Schlossalm
2050m

Kürstein

Breitfeldkogel
2412m

Silberpfennig
2600m

Kreuzkogel
2686m

**Sport Gastein
1600m**

Stubnerkogel
2246m

Skizentrum
Angertal

**BAD HOFGASTEIN
870m**

**Dorf Gastein
835m**

▼ To Salzburg & Münich

Bockstein

**BAD GASTEIN
1100m**

Bad Bruck

Kötschachdorf

Graukogel
2492m

Kötschachtal

Kreuzkogel
2027m

Fulseck
2030m

Wengeralm

Heumoosalm

Gasteiner Höhe

Grossartal

On the snow
top 2,686m (8,810ft) bottom 850m (2,788ft)

The lift company is midway through a £20-million upgrade of its system, but first you have to get to the lift. If you are accustomed to clicking into your bindings outside your hotel door and skiing home at the end of the day, then Bad Gastein is not for you. It was built on a steep hillside as a spa, not a ski resort, and a considerable amount of walking is unavoidable. The main Stubnerkogel ski area is situated on the western side of the valley and is reached by a modern, two-stage gondola from the top of the town near the railway station. In theory, you can leave your equipment in the ski-and-boot store, which avoids the necessity to lug skis up tough gradients from the town centre. However, you may not finish here at the end of the day.

WHAT'S NEW

Skiverbund Amadé lift pass covers 30 resorts
Weitmoser twin drags replaced by six-person chair-lift

At the top of the Stubnerkogel a choice of beautifully manicured runs takes you 1,100 vertical metres down to the floor of the Anger Valley. From here a gondola whisks you up the Schlossalm above Bad Hofgastein. A funicular followed by the choice of cable-car or chair-lift provides alternative access to Schlossalm from Bad Hofgastein. However, the best piste skiing lies a few minutes by car further down the valley above the village of Dorf Gastein.

The ancient double chair-lift gives the initial impression that skiing is restricted to the benign rolling meadows immediately above, yet the lift in turn gives access to a modern gondola that brings you swiftly up to the summit of the Fulseck. A series of demanding red (intermediate) and token black (difficult) runs take you either back down to Dorf Gastein or over the top to Grossarl.

Sport Gastein, at the head of the valley, is another separate ski area. It is an icy place when the weather closes in. However, on a fine day the piste skiing is varied, and the off-piste can be quite exceptional. If snow conditions are poor elsewhere in the valley, Sport Gastein can become crowded. The small Graukogel area above Bad Gastein on the far side of the valley completes the skiing possibilities with a few satisfying descents that include a World Cup course.

An improved ski bus service links the separate resorts and ski areas, but is still oversubscribed in high-season weeks. Taxis are plentiful, but, in order to explore the area fully, a car is a necessity. Reporters praised the lift map for its clarity and accuracy.

Beginners

The area has five nursery slopes served by drag-lifts, but overall it cannot be recommended for beginners. From Bad Gastein, the main novice slopes are a bus ride away at Angertal. Most blue (easy) runs are a pinkish-red in comparison with similar-sized Austrian resorts.

Intermediates

The entire valley is best suited to strong intermediates looking for a combination of mileage and challenge. Graukogel has superb tree-level skiing and is the place where the locals go on a snowy day. Confident snow-users will be interested mainly in the long run around the back of the mountain, which is reached either from Hohe Scharte at 2,300m or from Kleine Scharte at 2,050m. In good snow conditions it is possible to ski 1,450m vertical over 8km, all the way to the bottom of the railway. The fall-line run beneath the Gipfelbahn Fulseck at Dorf Gastein is also highly recommended.

Advanced

The north-facing runs down into the Angertal area provide some of the best skiing in the region. From Jungeralm, a long, undulating black (difficult) run drops directly through the woods. Laireiteralm at Grossarl is a long black run that provides considerable challenge. Schöneck at Sport Gastein is a short, but steep, bump run.

Off-piste

Untracked opportunities abound above the Schlossalm next to Hohe Scharte. Both the north and south faces of Sport Gastein can provide excellent powder runs after a new snowfall. In good conditions the 2.2-km Tiefschneeabfahrt (deep snow run), reached from the top of the Graukogelbahn, is just what it says, and most enjoyable.

Snowboarding

Bad Gastein, Bad Hofgastein and Sport Gastein all have commendable half-pipes, but most freestyle riders congregate in the terrain park at Dorf Gastein. The nightlife at Bad Gastein is considered too staid by riders, with Bad Hofgastein a preferable lodging base.

Tuition and guiding

We have positive reports of the Ski School Luigi in Bad Gastein. The size of classes seems to vary between four and 12 pupils, and the standard of the instructors' English is high. Ski School Bad Gastein and the Bad Hofgastein Ski and Racing School both have fine reputations. Ski School Holleis in Dorf Gastein is described as 'small and friendly with useful instruction'.

Mountain restaurants

The area is plentifully served with both pleasant huts on the slopes and self-service cafeterias at the lift stations. Prices are no higher than in the valley, where they are low by Austrian standards. Aeroplanstadl, on the home run to Bad Hofgastein, houses some of the finest WCs in the Alps. 'Both the Damen and the Herren bear witness to the fact that this whole valley is obsessed with waterworks. Together they form an underground ablutionary palace decorated with granite cattle troughs, giant boulders and ancient cast-iron village pumps'.

The Jungerstube and the Wengeralm were warmly recommended. The Waldgasthof in the Angertal earned praise for its 'roaring log fire, cosy dining booths and the best *Gulaschsuppe* we have ever tasted'.

Accommodation

The position of your accommodation in Bad Gastein is crucial because of the steep layout of the resort, which also has an annoyingly complicated one-way system, heavy traffic and difficult parking. The old hotels are flanked by smart boutiques and expensive jewellers, who set their sights on Bad Gastein's wealthy German visitors, here for health treatments, rather than the skiers and boarders.

The modern Elizabethpark (☎ 6434 2551) beside the waterfall is said to be 'comfortable but a bit characterless and a long walk from the snow'. Hotel Wildbad (☎ 6434 3761), conveniently situated near the top of the town, is warmly recommended: 'unbelievably good food for Austria, a true gastronomic treat'. Hotel Mozart (☎ 6434 2686) is spacious and well-positioned. Hotel Grüner Baum (☎ 6434 2516), built in 1831 by Archduke Johann as a hunting lodge, is 5km out of town in a rural setting and has a justified reputation as one of the great hotels of Austria.

Eating in and out

The choice of restaurants is limited mainly to the hotels, but the Bahnhof restaurant is particularly recommended as good value for money. The Mozart is praised for its fondue. The Restaurant am Wasserfall is 'inexpensive and cheerful', as is the Felsenbad. The Chinarestaurant, according to one reporter, 'makes a pleasant change from *Wienerschnitzel*'. Hotel Rader and Gasthof Radhausberg in Böckstein are recommended, while Villa Solitude's brasserie and the restaurant in the Grüner Baum provide the best gourmet fare in town.

Après-ski

The Felsenbad, opposite the Bahnhof restaurant, boasts thermal indoor and outdoor pools as well as a bar, and attracts the crowds as they come off the slopes. The Austrians see nothing unhealthy in the marriage of beer and Bad, and a promotional video shows spa patrons happily imbibing. No visitor should miss the chance to improve his or her health by taking a train ride to the Healing Galleries, 2km inside the mountain near Böckstein. The combination of a 90°C temperature, relative humidity and low doses of rare radon gas can allegedly cure respiratory and muscular ailments.

The Gatz Music Club and Hägblom's are the hot-spots at teatime and again much later in the evening. Their late-night rival is the Central Park Entertainment near the waterfall. Eden's Pub is said to be usually crowded 'not least because a giant moose head takes up most of the room'. Ritz in the Salzburgerhof Hotel has live music and is more sophisticated. The casino is worth a visit, and the Manfreda and Kir Royal bars are ever popular. Other late bars to check out include Oslag, Hexn-Häusl, Weinfassl, Highlife, Pub am Wasserfall and the

Zirbenstube. The bar at the British-owned Hotel Tannenburg offers the cheapest drinks in town.

Childcare

As with all resorts with a disparate ski area, it is difficult to recommend Bad Gastein for children. All the villages have ski and non-ski kindergartens that take three- to five-year-olds. Hotel Grüner Baum runs a crèche for its small residents, which includes lunch.

Linked or nearby resorts

Bad Hofgastein
top 2,686m (8,810ft) bottom 870m (2,854ft)

Bad Hofgastein has neither the inconveniently steep, dark setting nor the faded grandeur of its neighbour. Although smaller, it is still sizeable, with 50 hotels and guesthouses built around a pedestrianised centre and spread along the broadest part of the valley. The Kitzstein funicular is a hearty walk or a free bus ride away. Bad Hofgastein is a good base for winter walking and cross-country skiing, and busy ice-rinks complete the winter scene. There are indoor and outdoor thermal swimming-pools as well as a modern sports centre. Reporters complained that morning queues for the funicular can be annoying. It holds 100 people while the cable-car above it has a capacity for only 80. Wise people take the chair from the top of the train.

The ski kindergarten takes children from three years old. The most convenient hotels are the more recently built ones lining the road from the centre to the river. The four-star Österreichischer Hof (☎ 6432 62160) is described as 'delightful', and the palatial Grand Park Hotel (☎ 6432 6356) boasts its own spa. There are five discos and more than a dozen bars.

TOURIST INFORMATION
Tel 43 6432 7110
Fax 43 6432 711032
Email info@badhofgastein.com
Web site www.badhofgastein.com

Dorf Gastein
top 2,686m (8,810ft) bottom 835m (2,739ft)

Dorf Gastein is the first of the settlements you reach on entering the Gasteinertal. Too many visitors to the area drive through without stopping. What they miss is a delightful little village with a charming main street lined with arcades. It remains untouched by the slightly depressing health-conscious image of its bigger sisters. Horses and carts clatter along the narrow street past the old church, more often taking local folk about their business than taking tourists for joy rides. There are several friendly hotels in the centre: Hotel Römerhof (☎ 6433 7777) has a swimming-pool and spa; while Gasthof Steindlwirt (☎ 6433 7219) and Hotel Kirchenwirt

Skiing facts: Bad Gastein

TOURIST INFORMATION
Kaiser-Franz-Josef-Strasse 27, A–5640 Bad Gastein
Tel 43 6434 2531
Fax 43 6434 253137
Email fvv.badgastein@aon.at
Web site www.badgastein.at

THE RESORT
By road Calais 1,232km
By rail station in resort
Airport transfer Salzburg 1½hrs
Visitor beds 6,700
Transport free ski bus with lift pass

THE SKIING
Linked or nearby resorts Bad Hofgastein (l), Dorf Gastein (n), Sport Gastein (n), Grossarl (n)
Number of lifts 52 (276 in Skiverbund Amadé lift pass)
Total of trails/pistes 201km (30% easy, 58% intermediate, 12% difficult). 865km in Skiverbund Amadé lift pass area.
Beginners 5 lifts and pistes, points tickets available

LIFT PASSES
Area pass Skiverbund Amadé (covers 30 resorts) ATS1,960–2,065 for 6 days
Pensioners no reductions
Credit cards yes

TUITION
Skiing Ski School Bad Gastein (☎ 6434 2260), Ski School Luigi (☎ 6434 4440), Ski and Racing School Bad Hofgastein(☎ 6432 6339), Ski School Schlossalm (☎ 6432 3298), Ski School Fuchs (☎ 6432 8485), Ski School Holleis in Dorf Gastein (☎ 06433 7538)
Snowboarding as ski schools
Other courses cross-country, race camps, telemark
Guiding through ski schools and L. Kravanja (☎ 6434 2941), F. Sendlhofer (☎ 6434 2879), Hans Zlöbl (☎ 6434 5355)

CHILDREN
Lift pass 6–14yrs ATS980–1,035 for 6 days, free for 5yrs and under
Ski & board school as adults
Kindergarten (non-ski) at Hotel Grüner Baum (☎ 6434 2516)

OTHER SPORTS
Curling, ice-climbing, indoor golf and tennis, parapente, riding, rifle shooting, skating, sleigh rides, snowshoeing, squash, swimming

FOOD AND DRINK
Coffee ATS27–35, glass of wine ATS30–45, small beer ATS22–30, soft drink ATS25–27, dish of the day ATS100–190

(☎ 6433 7251) were both recommended by reporters. Gasthof Mühlbachstüberl (☎ 6443 7367) is 'very friendly with good food'. Evenings are said to be livelier than you might expect in a village of this size.

TOURIST INFORMATION
Tel 43 6433 7277
Fax 43 6433 727737
Email info@dorfgastein.com
Web www.dorfgastein.com

Innsbruck

ALTITUDE 575m (1,886ft)
RESORTS COVERED Axamer Lizum, Fulpmes, Igls, Neustift and the
Stubai Glacier, Seefeld

Beginners ✱✱ Intermediates ✱✱✱ Advanced ✱ Snowboarders ✱✱✱

Innsbruck enjoys a reputation as a minor ski resort in its own right, but its true significance for the skier and snowboarder is as a jumping-off point for a host of big-name resorts in the Tyrol and even the Arlberg. These can be reached daily by bus, although a hire car adds both convenience and flexibility.

- ✔ Attractive town
- ✔ Short airport transfer
- ✔ Variety of skiing in area
- ✔ Summer skiing on Stubai Glacier
- ✔ Extensive cross-country
- ✔ Activities for non-skiers
- ✗ Small, separate ski areas
- ✗ Weekend lift queues

Austria's third most important city has twice hosted the Winter Olympics and enjoys the advantage of its own international airport, which is enclosed by dramatic towering mountain ranges on either side of the Inn Valley. Innsbruck is strategically positioned for road links in western Austria and is well-served by a network of motorways. The Ötztal and the snow-sure skiing of **Obergurgl** and **Sölden** can be reached in less than 90 minutes by car. The journey to **Kitzbühel** and the **SkiWelt** takes an hour. As an additional incentive to stay in the city, a single ski pass called the Innsbruck Glacier Skipass covers the seven main local areas of **Igls**, **Axamer Lizum**, **Fulpmes**, **Neustift** and the **Stubai Glacier**, **Tulfes**, **Hungerburg** and **Mutters**; it gives access to a total of 62 lifts serving 130km of piste and offers three days' skiing out of a total four or six days. (**Seefeld** is not covered by the pass.)

The two versions of the more expensive Innsbruck Super Skipass also allow you to ski or ride Kitzbühel and/or the Arlberg for a day as well as the Innsbruck area, thus providing 210 lifts and 520km of piste. It is as flexible as the Innsbruck Glacier Skipass, and bus travel is included in the price.

The cost of staying in the city is lower than in a conventional ski resort. The choice of restaurants is wide, and the nightlife is lively. Because Innsbruck is a real city rather than a ski resort, a lot more than just winter sports is on offer. The city has a dozen museums, a wealth of cultural sights, such as the famous Golden Roof and the Imperial Palace, a zoo, and from the end of November each year a colourful Christmas market is set up in the Old Town.

The city's smartest hotel is the five-star Europa-Tyrol (☎ 5125 9310), which is attractively wood-panelled and boasts the well-respected Europastüberl restaurant. The 14 four-star hotels include Hotel-Restaurant Goldener Adler (☎ 5125 71111) and Romantikhotel Schwarzer Adler (☎ 5125 87109), both of which have recommended restaurants. Hotel Maximilian (☎ 5125 9967) is a family-run hotel on the edge of town. Hotel Bierwirt (☎ 5123 42143) has been owned by the same family for 300 years. At the lower end of the price scale are many pensions, including Gasthof Koreth (☎ 5122 6262), in a rural position ten minutes' drive from the city centre, and Weinhaus Happ (☎ 5125 82980) in the Old Town. The local Hungerburg plateau has five hotels and pensions, including the three-star Hotel-Pension Zur Linde (☎ 5122 92345).

In recent years Innsbruck has become a snowboarding headquarters, with the offices of both Burton, the board manufacturer, and the International Snowboard Federation in the city. This has proved to be a magnet for riders. Innsbruck's 'own' skiing is to be found just outside the city above Hungerburg on the south-facing slopes of the Hafelekar. The black (difficult) Karrine and the red (intermediate) Langes Tal runs are both challenging. The area above Tulfes on the other side of the valley consists of two blue (easy) runs and two reds.

Axamer Lizum
top 2,343m (7,687ft) bottom 874m (2,867ft)

This is a somewhat characterless ski station comprising four hotels and a huge car park at 1,553m beneath the peaks of the Hoadl and Pleisen mountains, but nevertheless it offers the best range of skiing and boarding within immediate reach of Innsbruck. Weekend lift queues can be a problem, but the ten lifts provide extensive and varied pistes. This was the main Alpine venue for both the 1964 and 1976 Innsbruck Olympics, and the Olympic Museum is worth a visit. Axamer is one of the top snowboarding resorts in Austria, with freeriding a particular strength. Gullies form natural half-pipes, and riders can sometimes even outnumber skiers here. The 6.5-km Axamer run – graded black (difficult), but red (intermediate) by most resorts' standards – takes you all the way down to the quiet village of **Axams** at 874m.

The pick of the skiing is accessed by a fast quad chair-lift from the car park or by a funicular that climbs the ridge to the summit of the Hoadl, the high point of the area. From here the Olympic women's downhill course provides a demanding return route to the ski school meeting place. Across the narrow valley, a long chair-lift serves either a black run back to Axamer Lizum or gives access to a sunny, easy piste that takes you back down the valley to the little village of **Götzens**.

There is one mountain restaurant, the Gipfelhaus at the top of the train at Hoadl, which has panoramic views, home cooking and the names of the former Olympic medal winners (from the two Innsbruck Winter Olympics) engraved on the wall. The four-star Lizumerhof (☎ 5234 68244) and Hotel Kögele (☎ 5234 68803) are both

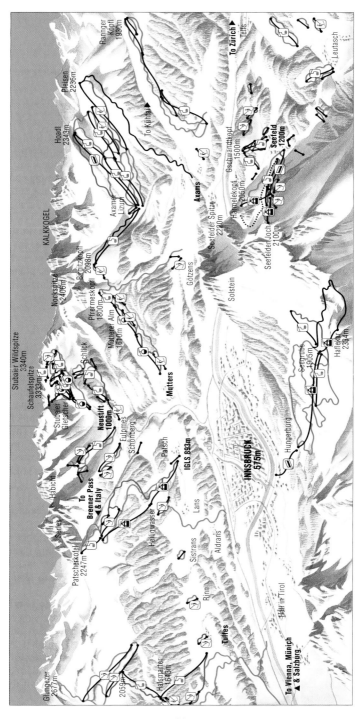

recommended. Off Limits is the main bar, but most snowboarders will head for the brighter lights of Innsbruck.

Fulpmes
top 2,200m (7,218ft) bottom 937m (3,074ft)

Slightly further away, but still within easy reach by post bus, the Stubai Valley offers a range of easy meadow skiing. **Mieders**, **Telfes**, Fulpmes and **Neustift** all share a lift pass. Above Fulpmes there is good skiing, branded as **Schlick 2000**, in a sheltered bowl on the 2,230-m Sennjoch. Some of the runs are tough and unpisted, but the majority are easy and confidence-building, and ideal for lower intermediates. The small, sunny nursery area received favourable reports.

The Alpenhotel Tirolerhof (☎ 5225 62422), Hotel Alte Post (☎ 5225 62175), and Haus Sonnegg (☎ 5225 64062) are all recommended. Restaurants include the Leonardo Da Vinci ('popular and good value') and the Gasthaus Hofer, which serves 'simple, plain Austrian farmhouse fare'. The Café Corso, the Ossi-Keller, Platzwirt and Dorfalm discos make the resort a lively place by night.

Igls
top 2,247m (7,372ft) bottom 893m (2,930ft)

Igls, 5km from Innsbruck up towards the Europabrücke and the Italian border, is a fine example of a traditional Tyrolean village but with limited skiing. The four blue (easy) and red (intermediate) runs on the Patscherkofel have been greatly enhanced by the addition of a fast quad chair-lift to mid-mountain, and a second chair up to the Schutzhaus has been planned for some time but has so far not been installed. The top of the mountain is accessed by cable-car from above the village centre. The red Olympic downhill presents the biggest challenge. It was here in 1976 that Franz Klammer threw caution to the wind and hurled himself down the mountain to win the most memorable Winter Olympics gold of all time. Considerable snowmaking allows skiing to continue through March. There are four mountain restaurants, most of them criticised for their high prices, although the one at the top of the cable-car received substantial praise.

The resort supports two ski schools, Schigls and Igls 2000, both with instructors who speak good English. The two nursery slopes are covered by snow-cannon and are a five-minute walk from the village centre. Non-skiing children can attend Bobo's Children's Club from Monday to Friday, and there is a children's ski school.

The village is small and uncommercialised, with sedate hotels and coffee houses, excellent winter walks and the Olympic bob-run, which is open to the public. The Sporthotel Igls (☎ 5123 77241) is singled out for its cuisine, while the five-star Schlosshotel (☎ 5123 77217) is warmly praised. Hotel Batzenhäusl (☎ 5123 8618) is recommended for both comfort and cuisine. Nightlife is not the resort's strongest point, but the bars at the Bon Alpina and the Astoria are the livelier spots. The Sporthotel disco is open until late.

Neustift and the Stubai Glacier
top 3,200m (10,499ft) bottom 1,000m (3,281ft)

The main community of the broad and lush Stubaital (Stubai Valley), Neustift is a large, sprawling village that has expanded greatly in recent years. Nevertheless, it remains very much the traditional Tyrolean village at heart, centred around a magnificent and ornately decorated church, which is the landmark of the valley.

Recommended hotels include the Jagdhof (☎ 5226 2666) ('wonderful five-star with great atmosphere'), the Tirolerhof (☎ 5226 3278) ('excellent food and a warm welcome') and the Sporthotel Neustift (☎ 5226 2510). Nightlife is lively in the Romanastuben. Neustift has its own gentle ski area on wooded north-facing slopes but it is also the main base for the Stubai Glacier, 20 minutes' drive away at the end of the valley.

The Stubai Glacier is one of the most extensive summer ski areas in Europe, with 21 runs open throughout the summer months. Twin gondolas take you up to the first stage at Fernau. From here you can continue by gondola or chair-lift to a network of lifts. When snow is scarce elsewhere the slopes can become unbelievably crowded, and German bank holidays are to be avoided. The glacier is often closed in January.

Keen skiers and riders stay in the comfortable Alpenhotel Mutterberg (☎ 5226 8116) at the base of the lifts. It has its own swimming-pool and disco. The Gamsgarten restaurant has a good choice of reasonably priced food. Separate ski schools operate in both Neustift and on the glacier and each has a kindergarten. The Stubai Superskipass also covers a small area at **Milders** and the assorted lifts in the valley.

Seefeld
top 2,100m (6,890ft) bottom 1,200m (3,937ft)

Seefeld, with its frescoed medieval architecture, is a smaller version of Innsbruck, Kitzbühel and the other beautiful towns of Austria. The resort is stylish and sophisticated and has seven luxury hotels, a casino, an extensive health centre and horse-drawn sleighs. The village centre is pedestrianised. Seefeld's main winter activity is cross-country skiing, but it also has three small, alpine ski areas: Geigenbühel for beginners, Gschwandtkopf, a low peak next to the cross-country loipe used mainly by the ski school, and Rosshütte, the more extensive area with steeper runs and a long off-piste trail. All three areas are reached from the village centre by the free bus service.

The town boasts no fewer than seven five-star hotels including the Klosterbräu (☎ 5212 26210), a former sixteenth-century monastery complete with indoor and outdoor swimming-pools and a Roman sauna with steam grotto. Others recommended are the Creativhotel Viktoria (☎ 5212 4441), Aparthotel Schönruh (☎ 5212 2447) and the less pricey Hotel Bergland (☎ 5212 2293) The four-star Karwendelhof (☎ 5212 2655) is in the pedestrian precinct. The Kaltschmid (☎ 5212 2191) is 'handy for the nursery slope with a nice pool on the fourth floor'. The luxury Gartenhotel Tümmlerhof (☎ 5212 2571) is set in its own park and offers daycare and a children's playground. The resort kindergarten is in the Olympia Sport and Congress Centre.

Gourmets can try the Alte Stube in the Hotel Karwendelhof. Café Nanni and Café Moccamühle are popular for après-ski. The Big Ben bar is as English as you would expect, and the Brittania Inn is another popular pub. Monroe's disco-bar attracts the late-night crowd, as do the Miramare and the popular Postbar in the Hotel Post. The Kanne in the Hotel Klosterbräu, the centre of the village's social life, has live music. Reporters recommended the Lammkeller in Hotel Lamm. The bar Fledermaus has live jazz. Other activities include SnowCarting (go-karts on snow), tubing down the bob-sleigh run, a vast curling centre, a grotto 'saunarium' and indoor swimming-pool in the Olympia Sport and Congress Centre.

Snowboarding

Innsbruck is a popular base for riders, with a wide choice of resort destinations within easy reach. Axamer Lizum is the highlight, with a terrain park and a half-pipe, but freestylers are even better served by the area's large number of natural obstacles. The small resort has a good atmosphere for snowboarders, and on some days they even outnumber the skiers. Fulpmes, the Stubai Glacier and Hungerburg all have recommended terrain parks.

Cross-country

Cross-country skiing started as a recreational sport in 1964 when Seefeld hosted the Winter Olympics Nordic events. The resort then went on to host the events in the 1976 Winter Olympics and in the 1985 Nordic World Championships. The excellent facilities include a team of specialist cross-country instructors at the Nordic Ski School in Seefeld's Olympia Sport and Congress Centre. The 200km of loipe are mechanically prepared, and a cross-country trail map is available from the tourist information office. The Innsbruck area has a total of 12 cross-country resorts covering 500km of loipe.

TOURIST INFORMATION
Innsbruck
Tel 43 5125 9850
Fax 43 5125 98507
Email info@innsbruck.tvb.co.at
Web site www.innsbruck-tourismus.com

Ischgl

ALTITUDE 1,400m (4,529ft)

Intermediates ✱✱✱   Advanced ✱✱   Snowboarders ✱✱✱

Ischgl is the focus of the Silvretta ski area on the Austrian–Swiss border, a long-established resort with some of the best skiing in Austria. In February 1999 it was painfully branded on the world's memory, when extraordinary snowfalls, coupled with hurricane-force winds, isolated Ischgl, while avalanches devastated neighbouring **Galtür** and nearby villages at the cost of 40 lives. As part of its attempt to overcome the resulting bad publicity, Ischgl has introduced a compensation scheme for holiday-makers unable to get in or out of the resort as a result of road closures. After the first 24-hour period, Ischgl will pay for the accommodation of snowed-in or snowed-out guests until the road re-opens.

For most visitors, duty-free **Samnaun** (covered on the area lift pass together with Galtür, **Kappl** and **See**) on the Swiss side of the frontier is the principal attraction of the Silvretta ski region. Alcohol at competitive prices, rucksacks for sale

✔ Extensive intermediate cruising
✔ Large ski area
✔ Off-piste and ski-touring
✔ Biggest terrain park in Europe
✔ Reliable snow record
✔ Wide choice of nightlife
✔ Beautiful scenery
✗ Lack of easy runs
✗ Crowded home pistes
✗ Poor choice of mountain restaurants

to transport it back over the mountain and the allure of a Swiss lunch make it an irresistible day-trip. The return journey involves a ride on the Pendelbahn, the world's first double-decker cable-car, which is handsomely engineered and fitted with escalators for easy access.

Although Ischgl is only a few kilometres as the crow flies from **St Anton**, it remained largely unknown in Britain until the 1999 avalanches. The first lift was not installed in Ischgl until 1963. Since then, the resort has developed from a small farming village into a bustling community on a hillside to the south of the main road. It is compact, if somewhat overgrown, with some 9,800 beds. Wealthy young Germans still dominate what has always been an expensive resort, but the British are gradually discovering it. Many of the regulars consider Ischgl to be the second-best resort in Austria (after St Anton) – an assessment that takes both the skiing and the nightlife into account. Ischgl is famous for its end-of-season concerts; Sting performed here on the piste in April 2001.

On the snow
top 2,864m (9,394ft) bottom 1,377m (4,517ft)

The spine of this ski area is the long ridge that forms the Austrian–Swiss border, with Ischgl's slopes facing north-west and west and Samnaun's facing south-east and east. The rapid Fimbabahn gondola, connected by a tunnel to the centre of town, and the Funitel Silvrettabahn provide comfortable and rapid access to Idalp, an open, mid-mountain plateau, while a third lift – the Pardatschgratbahn – ends 300m higher. From this focal point the pistes fan out over the upper slopes, with extensive and well-linked opportunities for fast cruising.

Two chair-lifts provide a choice of routes to the run down to Samnaun, with the much longer, covered chair from Gampenalp as a third alternative. After eating and shopping, snow-users can take a short roadside descent below the village to Ravaisch, the departure point for the 180-person double cable-car, which arrives at Alp Trida Sattel, a sun trap with spectacular views but no direct link back to Ischgl. Instead, snow-users must descend to Alp Trida, the starting point for parallel drag-lifts and a chair to Idjoch on the top of the ridge for the journey back to base. A six-person chair-lift gives a speedy connection between Alp Trida and Alp Trida Sattel. Once back in the Ischgl area, there is a choice of two long paths through woods to the resort; in high season, however, both are dangerously crowded.

Beginners

With only one resort-level lift and no blue (easy) runs leading back to the resort, Ischgl is neither cheap nor particularly user-friendly for first-timers, who have no sensible choice but to return to the village by gondola. Idalp's sunny nursery slopes are inviting, although frequently crowded with ski school classes. The next stage in the learning curve is also tricky, as blue runs are interrupted on occasion by short sharp red (intermediate) stretches. This is true of the adventurous blue descent from Inneres Viderjoch back to Idalp, though advanced beginners should have the skills to tackle it. The six-person Velilleckbahn chair-lift from Idalp is a better option for the less confident.

Intermediates

Ischgl has a number of long, challenging red runs, which makes it ideal for aspiring intermediates. On the extreme edge of the skiing, the descent from Palinkopf (the highest point in the lift system) to Gampenalp attracts relatively few skiers. On the other side of the ridge the lovely valley run to Samnaun is a real thigh-burner, especially as conditions are often more icy on the south-facing side. Those who complete it without stopping will have earned their lunch. The Palinkopfbahn chair takes skiers to the start of an equally testing red run all the way down to Bodenalp.

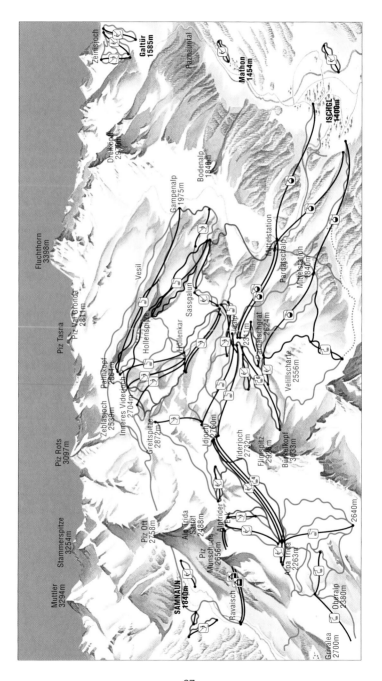

Advanced

Ischgl is short of genuine black (difficult) runs. The best ones are found between the Inneres Viderjoch and the Paznauner Taya. From the top of the Pardatschgrat there is a mild black descent to the bottom of the Velilleckbahn chair, at which point it turns into a challenging itinerary back to the resort. This is marked as a red dotted line but, as it is narrow and popular with advanced skiers and riders, it provides a stern and bumpy workout. The six-person chair that has replaced the old Schwarzwand and Palinkopf drag-lifts gives access to a steep and challenging black run.

Off-piste

Although the Paznaun Valley is famous for its spring ski-touring, Ischgl itself is not known as a resort for advanced skiers and off-piste enthusiasts. In consequence, the powder is not skied out the moment the lifts open, as it would be in St Anton. The most favourable terrain is off the Gampenalp chair. Touring with a guide is a popular pastime but the greatest care should be taken at all times.

Snowboarding

The Silvretta area has established itself as a major snowboard centre, with the Boarders Paradise Funpark at Idjoch, which is claimed to be the largest and one of the best in Europe and has a vertical drop of 350m. It is divided into separate areas for different disciplines such as freeride, mogul and new school (not just for riders but also for those on extreme carving skis and snowblades), and contains a good half-pipe and 30 obstacles. Samnaun has its own half-pipe.

Tuition and guiding

The Ischgl-Silvretta Ski and Snowboard School (SSS) offers tuition in English for groups of about 10–12 people. With 100 qualified instructors on its books, the school can arrange off-piste tours on demand.

Mountain restaurants

Why have an Austrian lunch when you can have a Swiss one? That is the question they trade on in Samnaun, but the reality is that it is quite difficult to find that great Swiss staple of Rösti with bacon, cheese and fried egg among the pizzerias and Austrian taverns that jostle for space among the duty-free shops in Samnaun. On the Swiss side, the Samnaunerhof and the Schmuggler Alm are recommended. The best options on the Austrian side include the restaurant in the hotel at Bodenalp and the Restaurant Idalp.

Accommodation

Ischgl's popularity with German skiers and snowboarders has resulted in quality hotels in each category, many of them with a degree of solid Alpine charm. One reporter considered Ischgl to be 'the quintessential Alpine ski town'. However, the recent building boom has produced

Skiing facts: Ischgl

TOURIST INFORMATION
Postfach 9, A–6561 Ischgl, Tyrol
Tel 43 5444 5266
Fax 43 5444 5636
Email info@ischgl.com
Web site www.ischgl.com

THE RESORT
By road Calais 1,017km
By rail Landeck 30km, frequent buses from station
By air Innsbruck 1½hrs
Visitor beds 9,800
Transport free bus service links Ischgl, Kappl and Galtür

THE SKIING
Linked or nearby resorts Galtür (n), Kappl (n), Samnaun (l)
Number of lifts 42 in Ischgl, 67 in Silvretta area
Total of trails/pistes 200km in area (27% easy, 63% intermediate, 10% difficult)
Beginners 2 lifts

LIFT PASSES
Area pass Silvretta (covers Ischgl, Samnaun, Galtür, Kappl and See) ATS2,195–2,560 for 6 days. VIP (covers Ischgl–Samnaun) ATS1,995-2,185
Pensioners 60yrs and over, Silvretta ATS2,050 for 6 days. VIP ATS1,730
Credit cards no

TUITION
Skiing Ischgl-Silvretta Ski and Snowboard School (☎ 5444 5257)
Snowboarding as ski school
Other courses Big Foot, cross-country, telemark
Guiding through ski school

CHILDREN
Lift pass 7–16yrs Silvretta ATS1,455 for 6 days. VIP ATS1,310; family passes available
Ski & board school as adults
Kindergarten as ski schools

OTHER SPORTS
Indoor climbing wall, indoor tennis, para-pente, skating, sleigh rides, SnowCarting (Samnaun), swimming

FOOD AND DRINK
Coffee ATS28, glass of wine ATS35, small beer ATS35, soft drink ATS30, dish of the day ATS140–80

ugly extensions and overcrowding as the demand for more beds tempts hoteliers to outgrow their sites.

Negotiating the hilly terrain on foot can be hazardous, but progressive thinking has led to indoor public staircases linking the various resort levels. As you can walk through the village from end to end in 15 minutes, almost any hotel makes a convenient base for at least one of the three lifts up to the mid-station. The exception is the Hotel Antony (☎ 5444 5427), which is isolated near the Madlein drag-lift on the hillside opposite the village, but is highly recommended in other respects. The curved bulk of the Hotel Elisabeth (☎ 5444 5411) dominates the Pardatschgratbahn, while the Goldener Adler (☎ 5444 5217) is close to the Silvrettabahn at the opposite end of the village. The family-run

Hotel Solaria (☎ 5444 5205) is central and comfortable, if somewhat quirky in its reception arrangements. Hotel Olympia (☎ 5444 5432) is recommended by reporters for 'cost, location, accessible parking, as well as a small spa'.

Eating in and out

Hotel restaurants predominate, which means a wide choice of typically Austrian meals that lack individuality or merit. One reporter complained: 'there appeared to be few restaurants that were not part of a hotel'. The Goldener Adler is praised for its ambience and its fresh trout, and the Trofana Alm bar-restaurant for its pizza. The Buffalo Western Saloon provides a limited American alternative; the menu in the cocktail bar is impressive. The Heidelberger Hütte specialises in fondue evenings, with transport by snowcat or horse-drawn sleigh.

Après-ski

The international clientèle creates a real buzz when skiing finishes for the day, with the bars in the central area near the church overflowing into the streets when the weather is fine. In the early evening the crowds move on to the Kitzlock and Nicki's Stadl, *ancien régime* establishments that specialise in Austrian politesse and tea-dancing to the strains of Strauss. The Kuhstall by the Silvrettabahn attracts a young crowd in the early evening.

A rowdier scene is on offer at the Trofana Alm, where high spirits can lead to dancing on the tables but stop short of lager loutishness, which is not welcome in this upmarket resort. For clubbing, the best places are the Wunderbar in the Hotel Madlein and the bar in the Hotel Post. The Allegra Bar also has impromptu dancing, and the Hotel Elisabeth has dancing girls.

The Silvretta Centre has an adventure swimming-pool, bowling alley and pool tables. The farming museum in Mathon on the road to Galtür is also popular.

Childcare

Three-year-olds can learn the basics in the ski kindergarten then graduate to the children's ski school from four years of age, according to ability. The meeting point is beside the adventure garden, and lunch is served in the youth centre. There is also a kindergarten in the Silvretta cableway building on Idalp.

Linked or nearby resorts

Galtür
top 2,300m (7,546ft) bottom 1,585m (5,200ft)

In comparison with Ischgl, Galtür is an oasis of calm tucked away round a bend in the valley near the head of the Paznaun Valley, but sadly this image was temporarily obscured by the avalanche tragedy of

February 1999. Rebuilding has taken place, and any scars that remain are not physical. The resort is connected to neighbouring Ischgl by free shuttle buses during the day. Although it has more than 3,000 beds and a large modern sports centre, it has the feel of a genuine Alpine village. It is easy to imagine Ernest Hemingway strolling into the local pub after climbing on skins from the neighbouring Montafon Valley in the spring of 1925.

Galtür's skiing is at **Wirl**, an outpost reached in five minutes by a free shuttle bus that runs frequently at peak times. For those who prefer ski-in ski-out arrangements, Wirl has several hotels. The skiing is open, uncrowded and well-suited to beginners and families. Galtür is a notable centre for ski-touring, especially in spring, with a wide choice of climbs at all levels.

Unlike Ischgl, Galtür is quiet at night, but there are several bars where both locals and visitors meet. The most popular are La Tschuetta, just off the main square, and s'Platzli in the cellar of Hotel Rössle. Others include the Iglu in the village centre, along with Weiberhimmel and the Huber-Stadl at the ski area. The family-run Flüchthorn Hotel (☎ 5444 55550) offers a warm welcome in a central location. The Post (☎ 5444 5232) is also convenient. As in Ischgl, most dining takes place in hotel restaurants, with the Rössle and the Alpenrose recommended. Galtür has night-skiing and night-boarding, and a modern sports centre offering tennis, squash and swimming. The village also boasts a hang-gliding and parapente school, a toboggan run and a skating-rink with curling.

TOURIST INFORMATION
Tel 43 5443 8521
Fax 43 5443 852176
Email galtuer@netway.at
Web site www.galtuer.com

Samnaun
top 2,864m (9,394ft) bottom 1,840m (6,035ft)

Lost in an inaccessible pocket in the mountains on the Austrian–Swiss border, Samnaun lives off its duty-free status and its ski links with Ischgl. Although the links are now very swift, it is hard to imagine anyone choosing to spend a holiday in a place that is as lacking in atmosphere as this resort. The Gästekindergarten takes potty-trained children all day Monday to Friday. Hotels include Chasa Montana (☎ 81 861 9000), Hotel Post (☎ 81 861 9200) and Hotel Silvretta (☎ 81 868 5400).

TOURIST INFORMATION
Tel 41 81 868 5858
Fax 41 81 868 5652
Email info@samnaun.ch
Web site www.samnaun.ch

Kitzbühel

ALTITUDE 760m (2,493ft)

Beginners **✱✱** Intermediates **✱✱✱** Advanced **✱** Snowboarders **✱✱**

Kitzbühel is a walled, medieval settlement of heavily buttressed buildings painted with delicate frescoes, which survives the relentless battering of a nine-month tourist season with measured aplomb. Throughout the season the town positively buzzes with excitement. Wealthy fur-clad Germans mix with younger and often more financially challenged skiers from Britain, Holland and Italy to form an alpine social melting-pot with few equals. Serious shoppers will be disappointed, for Kitzbühel lacks the designer retailers you might expect in such an upmarket resort. The town centre is mercifully traffic-free, and a bus service ferries skiers to and from the Hahnenkamm and the Kitzbüheler Horn mountains.

✔ Large ski area
✔ Beautiful architecture
✔ Alpine charm
✔ Lively après-ski
✔ Wide range of activities for non-skiers
✔ Short airport transfer
✘ Low altitude and poor snow record
✘ Heavy traffic outside pedestrian centre
✘ Lack of skiing convenience

Kitzbühel's world renown as a ski centre is based largely around the annual Hahnenkamm downhill race, the Blue Riband event of the World Cup calendar. Despite this, Kitzbühel's skiing is largely intermediate, with few pisted challenges for experts. Apart from **Innsbruck**, this is the one destination in the Tyrol that is really appropriate for skiers and non-skiers alike.

Kitzbühel's insuperable problem is its lack of altitude. It is far too early to suggest that this might be one of the first major resorts to fall victim to global warming, but outside the mid-winter weeks you must be prepared to contend with patchy snow and/or slushy conditions as the norm – at least at lower levels. Artificial snowmaking covers 30km of piste including the Streif, as well as the pistes down to the village of **Kirchberg**.

On the snow
top 2,000m (6,562ft) bottom 760m (2,493ft)

The main skiing is divided between two mountains: the Kitzbüheler Horn and the more challenging Hahnenkamm, which is easily accessed from near the centre of town by a six-person gondola. Reporters complained of having to hike uphill for 100m to the start of the piste ('we have never had to pole so far before and after lifts'). From here an

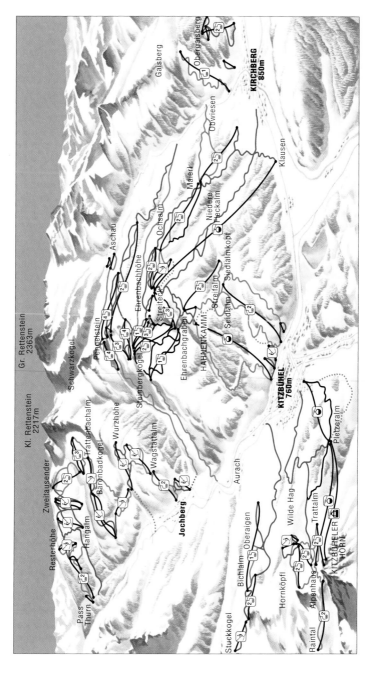

interesting network of mainly red (intermediate) and blue (easy) cruising runs spreads out down three faces of the mountain to form the largest and most challenging sector. Even though the area is confined, the variety of runs and scenery gives you the pleasant impression that you are going somewhere rather than skiing the same slopes over and over again.

Kitzbühel's second ski area, the Kitzbüheler Horn, is to the east of town, across the main road and the railway tracks. Towering above the resort, it is a distorted but beautiful pyramid of rock and ice. A cable-car takes you up to 2,000m, the highest point in the area, where the views are spectacular. The skiing is pleasant and gentle, but experienced skiers will quickly find the Horn a disappointment.

Aurach, a ten-minute ski bus ride away from Kitzbühel, is a third separate area with three gentle blue runs and a marginally steeper reddish alternative.

Beginners

Kitzbühel has four good nursery slopes near the town and plenty of easy skiing for second-weekers. The blue Pengelstein run takes you all the way down to Kirchberg and is one of the best in the resort. Over on the Kitzbüheler Horn, the long Hagstein blue run (No. 3 on the resort's piste map) is a gentle but interesting cruise from top to bottom. However, nervous skiers should beware of the Pletzerwald variation through the trees, which turns into a choice between an awkward red and the steep black (difficult) Horn Standard.

Intermediates

Kitzbühel is essentially for cruisers. Pengelstein-Süd is a long, flowing red that starts at the top of the Pengelstein chair and is the gateway into the Ski Safari (see below). It brings you down to the hamlet of **Trampelpfad**. The Hochsaukaser red at Pengelstein is a wide, fast piste with wonderful lips and rolls – one side is usually left entirely unprepared and becomes a challenging mogul field. The long Fleckalm, Seidlalm and Streifalm are excellent cruising runs over varied summer pastures.

The celebrated Ski Safari, marked by elephant signposts, is an enjoyable pisted itinerary that takes you from the Hahnenkamm up the Kitzbühel Valley to **Jochberg** and **Pass Thurn**. Anyone with a couple of weeks' ski experience can manage the outing, which consists of a series of blue and gentle red runs linked by lifts along the east-facing slopes of the valley. The wooded skiing on the Wurzhöhe above Jochberg is always uncrowded, and it is worth spending some time here before moving on up the valley. Pass Thurn is cold and isolated, but it holds the best snow in the region. The downside is that the Safari is no circuit – it can only be fully skied in one direction. To return to Kitzbühel you have to queue for a bus for the 19-km road journey from Pass Thurn. Plans to build the crucial link lift from Jochberg back up the Hahnenkamm are unlikely to be realised in the near future, despite promises.

Advanced

The best of the steep skiing is reached via a network of lifts in the Ehrenbach sector of the Hahnenkamm. Try the Sedlboden and Ochsenboden. The black variation of Oxalm-Nord is part of the otherwise long red run down to Kirchberg. Rettenstein at Pass Thurn is a short, sharp black, which ends up at the bottom of the Zweitausender double-chair.

Snowboarding

Riders tend to congregate on the Horn, which has a well-equipped terrain park with a half-pipe and boardercross course. There are many natural obstacles as well as some good off-piste for freeriders.

Off-piste

Those who are new to off-piste skiing can find plenty of easy powder skiing close to the pistes in the Hahnenkamm area after a fresh snowfall. Pass Thurn is particularly recommended. Bichlalm is another enjoyable spot for powder. Kitzbühel's specialist off-piste ski school is called Ski Alpin.

Tuition and guiding

Kitzbühel has six separate ski schools including the famous Rote Teufel (Red Devils). Competition is keen and all work hard to produce a good service to customers. The Rote Teufel, which has been the subject of mixed reports in recent years, has clearly smartened up its act ('excellent tuition by a true professional. She taught me more in a single morning than I learned in a whole week in France last year').

Mountain restaurants

The Hoch Kitzbühel restaurant at the top of the Hahnenkamm gondola has a sun terrace as well as waiter- and self-service sections indoors: 'superb *Gulaschsuppe* and enormous veal cutlets'. Don't miss the adjoining Hahnenkamm museum. Trattenbergalm between Jochberg and Pass Thurn has some of the best simple food in the region. Panorama-Alm above Pass Thurn has a glass-walled bar outside to keep out the wind, and a roaring log fire within. The Pengelstein restaurant now has an attractive interior with an open fire ('service and food exceptionally good'). The Staudachstub'n on the main run down to the Fleckalm gondola is 'a real delight. The *Tirolergröstl* has to be tasted to be believed'. The Ehrenbachhohe is 'overcrowded and disorganised'.

Accommodation

Hotel Tennerhof (☎ 5356 6318170) heads a long list of luxury establishments. It is closely followed by the entirely revamped Weisses Rössl (☎ 5356 63472) which now has a hedonistic spa. The Goldener Greif (☎ 5356 64311), the Jägerwirt (☎ 5356 64067) and the Maria Theresia (☎ 5356 64711) are popular four-stars. Sporthotel Bichlhof (☎ 5356 64022) is centrally located and warmly recommended. The

Skiing facts: Kitzbühel

TOURIST INFORMATION
PO Box 164, A-6370 Kitzbühel, Tyrol
Tel 43 5356 621550
Fax 43 5356 62307
Email info@kitzbuehel.com
Web site www.kitzbuehel.com

THE RESORT
By road Calais 1,130km
By rail station in resort
Airport transfer Salzburg 1½hrs,
Munich 2 ½hrs, Innsbruck 2hrs
Visitor beds 8,272 in Kitzbühel, Reith
and Aurach
Transport free ski bus

THE SKIING
Linked or nearby resorts Aurach (n),
Kirchberg (l), Jochberg (l), Pass Thurn (l),
St Johann in Tyrol (n)
Number of lifts 27 in Kitzbühel,
59 in linked area
Total of trails/pistes 164km in linked
area (39% easy, 46% intermediate,
15% difficult)
Beginners 9 runs in linked area, learn-
to-ski pass available

LIFT PASSES
Area pass (covers Kitzbühel, Kirchberg,
Jochberg, Pass Thurn, includes ski bus,
swimming-pool and reduction for sauna)
ATS1,968–2,133 for 6 days
Pensioners ATS1,560–1,680 for women
60yrs and over and men 65yrs and over
Credit cards yes

TUITION
Skiing Hahnenkamm Egger (☎ 5356
71126), Kitzbüheler Horn (☎ 5356
64454), Rote Teufel (Red Devils)
(☎ 5356 62500), Reith and Ski Alpin
(☎ 5356 65496), Total (☎ 5356
72011), Aurach (☎ 5356 65804)
Snowboarding as ski schools
Other courses cross-country, skiing for
the disabled, teen skiing, telemark
Guiding through Alpinschule Kitzbühel
(☎ 5356 73323)

CHILDREN
Lift pass 6–15yrs ATS1,177 for 6 days,
free for 5yrs and under and for sized
1.2m (4ft) and under when accompanied
by an adult
Ski & board school as adults
Kindergarten (ski) through ski schools,
(non-ski) Anita Halder (☎ 5356 75063)

OTHER SPORTS
Bobsleigh, curling, floodlit tobogganing,
hang-gliding, horse-riding, hot-air
ballooning, indoor tennis and squash,
night-skiing, parapente, shooting range,
skating, ski-jumping, sleigh rides, snowshoeing, swimming

FOOD AND DRINK
Coffee ATS28, glass of wine ATS45,
small beer ATS30, soft drink ATS28,
dish of the day ATS100–140

converted hunting lodge of Schloss Lebensberg (☎ 5356 6901), on the
outskirts, has a medieval-style interior complete with four-poster beds,
and offers a very high level of pampering. This includes a health centre
with swimming-pool and free weekday babysitting. The Zur Tenne
(☎ 5356 64444) in the town centre is a comfortable designer hotel.

Eating in and out

Austrian alpine food wins few gastronomic prizes, but you can eat better and with more variety in Kitzbühel than in most resorts. The Goldener Greif is renowned for its *Salzburger Nockerl*, a kind of hot meringue soufflé. The Hotel zur Tenne specialises in fresh trout and is said to be 'outstanding, but expensive'. The revamped Weisses Rössl has a private *Weinstube* for small parties. The Landeshäusl and Huberbräu are both reasonably priced and cheerful. Lois Stern has sushi, Thai and other Far Eastern cuisine ('by far the most exciting menu in town'). The existence of a McDonald's seems a shame in such beautiful surroundings, but thankfully its presence is muted.

Après-ski

Nightlife in Kitzbühel is extremely vibrant with groups of happy people touring the bars and clubs in the pedestrianised streets of the Vorderstadt until dawn. Two British-style pubs, The Londoner and Big Ben, attract the lion's share of the youth business along with Highways, which offers live music. The locals congregate in Stamperl and Fünferl, while the Goldener Gams is a modest restaurant and bar with live music and a sophisticated Tyrolean atmosphere that attracts all ages. S'Lichtl, also in the Vorderstadt, is a bar decorated with light bulbs, which draws a more sophisticated crowd. Late-night revellers head for Royal, the most popular disco. Take Five, Olympia and Roses are the other night-clubs. The Waschkuchl and the Schirmbar in the Sporthotel Reisch are for discerning drinkers. The Casino is 'large, comfortable and sophisti-cated with security checks at the door and a dress code.' The Aquarena health centre has a 25-m pool and entry is free with a ski pass.

Childcare

Although for skiing convenience Kitzbühel gets a heavy minus mark, beginner children are well catered for, with five lifts that make up the extensive nursery area on the golf course at the foot of the Hahnenkamm. All the ski schools accept children.

Linked or nearby resorts

Kirchberg
top 2,000m (6,562ft) bottom 850m (2,788ft)

Once upon a time Kirchberg was the no-frills dormitory village that gave you a back door into Kitzbühel's skiing at knockdown prices, but without its medieval charm. This once poor relation, only 6km around the shoulder of the Hahnenkamm at the head of the Brixen Valley, still gives alternative access to Kitzbühel's main ski area, but circumstances have changed and it now has 8,000 tourist beds. The resort has its own small beginner and intermediate lifts on the Gaisberg, and offers access to the Hahnenkamm by a two-stage chair and the Klausen gondola.

It has a kindergarten, Kinderclub Total, and two ski schools, Skischool Total and Skischool Kirchberg.

The town's layout is not designed for ski convenience; distances are considerable, and the ski bus service is seriously over-subscribed. Choose where you stay with care in relation to both price and where you want to ski. The Tiroler Adler (☎ 5357 2327) is neither particularly convenient nor cheap, but is one of the best hotels in town. Hotel Alexander (☎ 5357 2222) and Hotel Metzgerwirt (☎ 5357 2128) are both recommended. The nightlife is just as busy as in Kitzbühel but less sophisticated. Charley's Club and Le Moustache are among the main centres of activity. The 3.5-km toboggan run on the Gaisberg is floodlit in the evenings.

TOURIST INFORMATION
Tel 43 5357 2309
Fax 43 5357 3732
Email info@kirchberg.at
Web site www.kirchberg.at

Lech and Zürs

ALTITUDE Lech 1,450m (4,756ft), Zürs 1,720m (5,642ft)

Beginners ✳✳ Intermediates ✳✳✳ Advanced ✳✳ Snowboarders ✳

Every skiing nation has at least one ultra-smart resort that lures the 'beautiful people' to its manicured slopes, and **Lech** and neighbouring **Zürs** are the most exclusive resorts in Austria. Not only do these villages attract the rich and famous to their portfolio of six five-star hotels but they also quite literally exclude skiers from the slopes when they consider these to be full. As soon as 14,000 tickets have been sold the tills are closed. Priority is given to those skiers who are staying in the resort, although Arlberg lift passes issued in **St Anton** and **St Christoph** are still valid. The result is that even on the busiest weekends of the year queues are never longer than ten minutes.

- ✔ Alpine charm
- ✔ Beautiful scenery
- ✔ Long intermediate runs
- ✔ Efficient lift system
- ✔ Varied off-piste skiing
- ✔ Efficient piste signposting
- ✔ High standard of hotels
- ✔ Lack of queues
- ✔ Facilities for families
- ✘ Difficult road and rail access
- ✘ High prices

Lech was first inhabited by Swiss immigrants in the fourteenth century, and this corner of Austria still looks more towards Switzerland, its nearest neighbour, than to the main part of Austria. Despite the presence of luxury hotels, Lech is a traditional village with an onion-domed church and a river. More than 100 hotels and businesses now receive their heating and hot water from a communal eco-friendly plant that is fuelled by wood-pulp. During construction the opportunity arose to improve the main street. Pavements and pedestrian zones have been widened, and three new bridges now give better access across the river.

Over the years, the biggest expansion has been in **Oberlech**, a satellite 200m up the mountain, which was once the summer home of herdsmen and shepherds. The collection of hotels here is ideally placed for the skiing and provides a safe and car-free centre for families with small children. The network of underground tunnels beneath the top cable-car station and the hotels means that visitors arriving by cable-car do not have to lug suitcases across the piste.

Zürs is little more than a collection of four- and five-star hotels in an isolated position astride the Flexen Pass. The village lacks much of the charm of Lech, although resort-level snow is guaranteed for most of a long season, which continues to the end of April.

Zug, 3km by road through the woods from Lech and fully integrated into the lift system, also offers rural tranquillity. An evening journey from Lech through the star-lit woods by horse-drawn sleigh is a delightful and romantic experience.

The resorts share a varied and extensive ski area, although advanced skiers might be more interested in the abundant off-piste and ski-touring opportunities. St Anton, with its larger choice of advanced piste terrain, is 40 minutes' drive away and is included in the same hands-free lift pass, along with the free bus service to the car park and lifts at **Alpe Rauz** on the perimeter of the St Anton ski area. For the present, the only access is via the Flexen Pass from **Stuben**, which is liable to closure owing to avalanche danger in extreme weather conditions. Plans have been formulated to build a tunnel from Stuben, below St Christoph, to Zug, which would open up Lech and Zürs to a new and much larger market.

On the snow
top 2,450m (8,036ft) bottom 1,450m (4,757ft)

The Lech/Zürs circuit of 110km of prepared pistes, spread over three mountains and served by 34 lifts, provides mainly intermediate skiing of the highest quality. The circuit can be skied only in a clockwise direction, and pistes are particularly well signposted. The steady upgrading of the lifts and the limitation on the number of skiers have alleviated any queuing problems; most of the older chair-lifts have been speeded up and have 'moving carpet' conveyor belts to enable skiers to progress on to the lift more quickly.

Mountain access to the circuit is via the twin Rüfikopf cable-cars, which scale an impressive wall from the centre of Lech. Long and challenging itineraries lead down off the shoulder in either direction through the woods to the road by Zürs, or back to Lech via a scenic itinerary through the Wöstertäli. Alternatively, you can enjoy the lengthy and benignly beautiful pistes towards Zürs, where a 'moving carpet' on the bridge over the main road connects you with the second half of the circuit.

Lech's main skiing area, on the sunny side of the valley, is contrastingly open and mostly gentle, although the slopes immediately above the village are of a more challenging gradient. Mountain access on this side is via an assortment of four lifts – including a detachable quad-chair – from different points in or near the village. Above Oberlech, lifts and pistes spread throughout a wide, fragmented basin below the peaks of the Kriegerhorn and the Mohnenfluh. The two are linked by a cable-car with spectacular views.

Beginners

First-timers can use a beginner's ticket and should not buy the expensive Arlberg Ski Pass. Lech has excellent nursery slopes behind the church as well as at Oberlech. Beginners should quickly progress to a whole range of blue (easy) runs on the Oberlech side of the valley. One of the attractions of the resort for second-week skiers is that they should be able to negotiate the blue Rüfikopf run from the top of the cable-car, which in turn links into the *Familienabfahrt* to bring them all the way to Zürs.

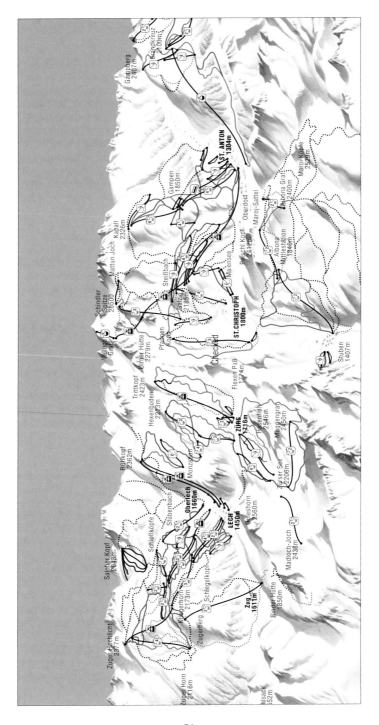

Intermediates

Confident skiers head up the Rüfikopf cable-car for the choice of red (intermediate) pistes down the Hexenboden and Trittkopf. Follow the local lift map with care: appropriately coloured circles indicate pisted runs, while ski routes are marked by diamonds. It is easy to think that a red-diamond with a thin black border is a hard intermediate run. In fact it is an extreme itinerary that is neither patrolled nor pisted, although some are so well skied that they become pistes. From Zürs you can either take the scenic Zürsertäli or choose more direct routes down to the Zürsersee and on via the Madloch towards Lech.

Advanced

Zürs has the steeper skiing of the two main resorts, including a couple of short, sharp black (difficult) pistes, notably the Hexenboden Direkte. Langerzug and Tannegg are two challenging runs down the shoulder of the Rüfikopf, and Kriegerhorn Südhang is another recommended piste. The ski routes marked on the lift map offer a considerable challenge.

Off-piste

When fresh snow falls, both Lech and Zürs are a delight. Experts can try the various descents of the 2,173-m Kriegerhorn and the Zuger Hochlicht beyond it. The long run down from the top to the village of Zug via the narrow Zuger Tobel can be spectacular in powder snow conditions. Langerzug and Tannegg, around the shoulder of the Rüfikopf, are dramatic in the extreme. For environmental reasons, it is strictly forbidden to ski off-piste through the trees – anyone caught doing so risks having their lift pass confiscated. Ski-touring and heli-skiing are popular.

Snowboarding

Lech's Boarderland terrain park on the Schlegelkopf is 300m long, with a half-pipe, a quarter-pipe and a series of obstacles. Zug has myriad gullies and drops, as well as a natural half-pipe when snow conditions allow. However, the resort is too expensive to attract substantial numbers of young riders.

Tuition and guiding

The Austrian Ski School in Lech, Oberlech and Zürs received mixed reports this year. At the ski school meeting area, instructors' names are nailed to the class boards – the same instructors teach the same level all season. This means that classes do not suffer from a change of instructor mid-week or even daily, as is the case in many resorts. However, one reporter said that his instructor spoke poor English ('we didn't feel we learnt very much'). Eighty per cent of ski teachers in Zürs and more than 50 per cent in Lech are booked for private rather than group lessons each day, but reporters complain that it is impossible to book a teacher for less than a full week during high season.

Skiing facts: Lech and Zürs

TOURIST INFORMATION
A–6764 Lech/A–6763 Zürs, Am Arlberg
Tel Lech 43 5583 2161
Zürs 43 5583 2245
Fax Lech 43 5583 3155
Zürs 43 5583 2982
Email lechinfo@lech.at
zuersinfo@zuers.at
Web sites www.lech.at/www.zuers.at

THE RESORT
By road Calais 975km
By rail Langen 17km, frequent buses daily
Airport transfer Innsbruck 2hrs, Zurich 2½ hrs
Visitor beds 8,450 (with Zürs)
Transport free ski buses between Lech, Zürs and Rauz. Shuttle bus at weekends, Lech–Zurich Airport ATS800 return

THE SKIING
Linked or nearby resorts Rauz (I), St Anton (n), Stuben (n), St Christoph (n), Zug (I), Sonnenkopf–Klösterle (n)
Number of lifts 34 in Lech/Zürs, 85 on Arlberg Ski Pass
Total of trails/pistes 110km in Lech/Zürs (40% easy, 40% intermediate, 20% difficult). 260km on Arlberg Ski Pass
Beginners 1 free lift, points tickets available

LIFT PASSES
Area pass Arlberg Ski Pass (covers Lech, Oberlech, Zürs, Rauz, St Christoph, St Anton, Stuben, Sonnenkopf–Klösterle)

ATS2,120–2,360 for 6 days
Pensioners Senior ticket for women 60yrs and over, and men 65yrs and over, ATS1,802–2,006 for 6 days. 75yrs and over ATS100 for whole season
Credit cards no

TUITION
Skiing Austrian Ski School: Lech (☎ 5583 2355), Oberlech (☎ 5583 200), Zürs (☎ 5583 2611)
Snowboarding as ski schools
Other courses cross-country, heli-skiing, race training, snowshoeing, telemark
Guiding through ski schools, Wucher Heli-skiing (☎ 5583 2950)

CHILDREN
Lift pass (covers resorts and linked area) 7–15yrs ATS1,280–1,420 for 6 days. 6yrs and under ATS140 for whole season
Ski & board school as adults
Kindergarten Lech: Miniclub (☎ 5583 21610), Oberlech: Kindergarten (☎ 5583 3236), Zürs: Kinder & Skikindergarten (☎ 5582 224515), Little Zürs Kindergarten (☎ 5583 2245)

OTHER SPORTS
Curling, floodlit tobogganing, helicopter rides, indoor golf, indoor squash and tennis, paragliding, skating, sleigh rides

FOOD AND DRINK
Coffee ATS35, glass of wine ATS50, small beer ATS40, soft drink ATS38, dish of the day ATS120–250

Mountain restaurants

Most of the hotels on the slopes in Oberlech and Zürs serve lunch, so there is no need for other restaurants. Two exceptions are the atmospheric Alte Goldener Berg above Oberlech and the simple Flexen Pass on the piste near Zürs. Hotel Montana (☎ 5583 24600) in Oberlech is owned by the family of the former Olympic downhill champion Patrick Ortlieb and is recommended for its food. Hotel Burg (☎ 5583 2291), also in Oberlech, has a gourmet restaurant that needs to be booked a few days in advance at weekends and during high season. The Seekopf at Zürs is also recommended, while the Rote Wand in Zug is 'quite superb, but moderately expensive'.

Accommodation

Lodging is mostly in comfortable and expensive hotels, plus some spacious apartments. The village is fairly compact, and location is not particularly important. The smartest hotel – indeed one of the most celebrated five-stars in Austria – is the sumptuous Gasthof Post (☎ 5583 22060). It has only 38 rooms, including ten suites with private steam baths, and you need to book a year in advance. Hotel Kristiania (☎ 5583 2561), set in a quiet position 500 metres from the centre, numbers Boris Becker among its annual clients.

The Arlberg (☎ 5583 2134), Gotthard (☎ 5583 3560), Krone (☎ 5583 2551) ('an exotic spa with a Moroccan flavour') and the Schneider-Almhof (☎ 5583 3500) ('the height of luxury') are all warmly recommended by regulars. The Tannbergerhof (☎ 5583 3313) is popular with the British and is the centre of Lech's social life. Hotel Elizabeth (☎ 5583 2330) is said to be very comfortable, as is the Monzabon (☎ 5583 2104), and there are numerous less formal hotels and plenty of pensions, but nothing is cheap. It is worth noting that even the best hotels do not generally accept credit cards.

In Oberlech, the four-star Sonnenburg (☎ 5583 2147) is 'delightfully convenient and much the best hotel in the hamlet'. Bergkristall (☎ 5583 2678) has 'excellent food and service with easy access to the slopes'. In Zug, the four-star Rote Wand (☎ 5583 3435) is 'wonderfully peaceful'. It also has a new annexe of apartments: 'modern design and perfect for families'. Zürs has three five-star hotels including Thurnhers Alpenhof (☎ 5583 21910). The four-star Arlberghaus (☎ 5583 2258) receives glowing reports and has a curling-rink on its roof. Regular ski buses connect Lech, Zug and Zürs to the St Anton ski area, and post buses run to the railhead at Langen.

Eating in and out

Good restaurants abound, as you might expect in resorts of this calibre, but most are in the hotels and none is cheap. Gasthof Post is 'outstanding but a bit formal'. Hus No. 8 in Lech, opposite the Post Hotel, is 'quaint Austrian – the only real non-hotel gourmet restaurant in town'. The Brunnenhof is strongly recommended, together with Bistro s'Casserole, Rudi's Stamperl and the Dorf Stüberl. Don Enzo serves pizzas and pasta. Oberlech boasts the Goldener Berg, which is famous for fondues. In Zürs, the Chesa Verde is an award-winning restaurant, while in Zug the Rote Wand is highly recommended.

Après-ski

The average age of the clientèle in Lech and Zürs is higher than that in other Alpine resorts. Wherever you look you will see bronzed and fit 60-year-olds wearing the latest in designer ski suits, as well as thirty-somethings who might, perhaps, aspire to look like this in the autumn of their lives. Consequently, après-skiers at these resorts prefer to put their hair up, rather than let it down.

The ice-bar outside the Tannbergerhof in Lech is where, weather permitting, the evening begins in earnest as the slopes close. Guests filter inside to join in the tea-dancing, which swings into action as night falls. The hotel also hosts a disco with a good atmosphere later on in the evening. The Sidestep Bar in the Hotel Krone attracts the over-25s for dancing, and the Klausur Bar in the Schneider Almhof is popular. The s'Pfefferkörndl bar has youth appeal. At 5.30pm each Thursday the Rüfikopf cable-car is transformed into a bar, and the restaurant at the top becomes the highest casino in the Alps. For ATS350 each you are given a glass of champagne on the way up to the blackjack and roulette tables. Places must be reserved in advance for a minimum of 15 people.

The floodlit toboggan run is the quickest way to travel down from Oberlech to Lech at the start of the evening's entertainment. Sleigh rides to Zug for dinner are a treat, and you can take the cable-car up to Oberlech and toboggan down afterwards. Die Vernissage in Zürs is recommended, and the Zürserl in the Hotel Edelweiss is the biggest disco in town, while the Rote Wand and the Sennkessel in Zug are both lively.

Public transport comes to a halt in the early evening. Taxis are expensive, but a collection service called 'James', which runs until 4am, will return you to wherever you are staying in Lech, Zürs and Zug for a reasonable set fee of ATS50 for the evening.

Childcare

The area lends itself well to family skiing, particularly at Oberlech, the site of the main nursery slopes. A number of hotels run their own crèches. We have positive reports of the Oberlech kindergarten. Children under six years old ski for ATS140 for the whole season. The ski school takes children all day and supervises lunch (parents must remember to provide lunch money each day). The Lech Miniclub is for children from three years of age. The Little Zürs kindergarten takes children from three years old and provides ski instruction for children from four years of age.

Mayrhofen

ALTITUDE 630m (2,066ft)

Beginners ✱✱ Intermediates ✱✱✱ Snowboarders ✱

More than 9 per cent of skiers and 20 per cent of summer tourists who make their way by coach up the beautiful Ziller Valley to Mayrhofen come from Britain. The consistent annual figures clearly belie its discouraging reputation as a low-budget resort for beginners, where poor and unchallenging skiing is compensated by a frenetic nightlife that burns until breakfast time. Only the lively nightlife is a fact.

✔ Competent ski teaching
✔ High standard of accommodation
✔ Summer skiing on Hintertux Glacier
✔ Extensive ski pass region
✔ Focus on children's activities
✘ Low-altitude skiing
✘ No skiing to village from main mountain
✘ Crowded slopes

Mayrhofen has taught generations of British skiers to love low-lying Tyrol. Many remain intensely loyal to a destination that somehow manages to combine the opposing images of family resort and raucous party venue. At the top of the broad Ziller Valley, Mayrhofen's own skiing on the Penken, Ahorn and **Finkenberg** has now been extended over the back of the Wanglspitz to link up with Lanersbach and Vorderlanersbach in the Tuxer Valley. The project involved the construction in summer 2001 of a 150-person cable-car from Moosboden to Wanglalm, which should be completed in time for the start of the 2001–2 season. Skiers and snowboarders in Mayrhofen this winter will have access to 141km of piste served by 48 lifts, the biggest ski area in the Ziller Valley. Two six-seater chairs serving new pistes in the Gerent area are also under construction. Local passes are sold, but, if you want to ski further afield, the regional Zillertal Superskipass allows access to a total network of 151 lifts and 470km of piste – including the **Hintertux** Glacier as a supplementary option.

Despite the steady growth of tourism, Mayrhofen still clings to its agricultural origins and large green areas are preserved. You can stroll across town in ten minutes. Buses and trains (apart from the valley sightseeing steam train) are free provided you have your Superskipass. All lift stations in the region have free parking, except for the Penkenbahn in the centre of Mayrhofen.

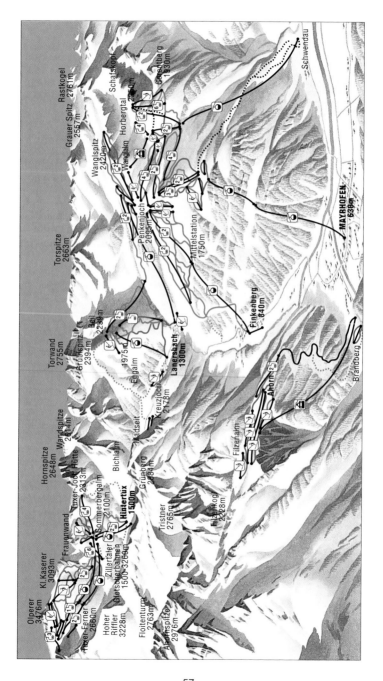

On the snow
top 2,250m (7,382ft) bottom 630m (2,066ft)

Mayrhofen's main mountain is the Penken, to which gondolas rise from the town centre as well as from the outlying hamlets of Finkenberg and **Schwendau**. There is no route whatsoever back down to Mayrhofen, and reporters complain of high-season queues to ride the Penkenbahn out of Mayrhofen every morning and similar queues to get down again to town at the end of the day. However, the upgrading of the Horbergbahn gondola at Schwendau from four to eight seats provides swift alternative mountain access.

Mayrhofen's second mountain on the other side of the valley is best-suited to beginners, although the 5.5-km black (difficult) Ebenwald piste from the top – the only village-run in Mayrhofen – attracts more accomplished skiers and riders. The ski bus service runs between the town and the limited capacity cable-car that provides the only access. Grooming is good, and electronic boards tell you which lifts have queues.

Beginners
Babies are better catered for than adult beginners. The former have their own play areas, whereas the latter are forced to ride awkward drag-lifts for all the blue (easy) runs on Ahorn and in most cases on Penken, which at least has one ultra-flat, long, beginner itinerary – the 'Horberg Baby Tour'. Reporters criticised the ski schools for teaching their beginner classes on the Penken instead of on the more suitable Ahorn: 'standing in the beginners area was like being in a football crowd, with different classes converging into each other and not enough room for any of them to learn properly'.

Intermediates
Many Penken runs are graded red (intermediate), not because they are steep but because they are narrow – often less than 20m wide. This creates difficulties for skiers and riders when descending together. The long cruising terrain served by the Katsenmoos double-chair is some of the best in the resort. The new cable-car and six-seater chairs should add some important red terrain.

Advanced
As one reader put it: 'experts are better off in another resort'. Their greatest challenge is avoiding collisions with aimlessly wandering schools of novice skiers and boarders. The black run from the top of Ahorn can provide some amusement.

Off-piste

The ingenious will find short, steep descents through rocks and woods on Penken and Gerent. Peter Habeler, who climbed Everest without oxygen in 1978, has a school that also offers off-piste tours with overnight stops in a mountain hut.

Snowboarding

The terrain park has a 150-m half-pipe and an assortment of jumps and rollers. Highlight is a mega-spine leading to a triple-kicker tabletop with a 30-m landing. The Ahorn is a good learning area, although there are still too many T-bars in the whole area for comfort. Hintertux has a large terrain park open all year round, and the 120-m Olperer is Europe's highest half-pipe.

Tuition and guiding

Mayrhofen has more than 100 instructors from three competing schools. Despite typical classes of 12, most students give the teaching high marks, although crowded slopes are a problem. Manfred Gager's school offers carving courses. Max Rahm's SMT provides video analysis. Peter Habeler's Mount Everest school is the third option. All three schools teach snowboarding, although SMT is the only one to have a separate department for riders – the Mayrhofen Snowboard School.

Mountain restaurants

Numerous 'umbrella bars', some open-air and others weatherised, serve quick snacks, schnapps and beer – generally to the accompaniment of raucous accordion music, but without the ear-splitting drinking games of Hilde's Skitenne (priciest in the region) and Vroni's Skialm (al fresco barbecue chicken). One reader said that lunch in the Sunnalm restaurant was 'a frightening example of Austrian hillbilly cuisine at its most unpalatable'.

Accommodation

The general standard of accommodation is superlative, with many hotels featuring swimming-pools, saunas or Turkish baths. The five-star Elisabethhotel (☎ 5285 6767) sets the pace in luxury. Hotel Strass (☎ 5285 6705) is next door to the Penken lift and home to both the Ice Bar and Sports Arena disco. Just up the road is the Waldheim (☎ 5285 62211), which has comfortable rooms with views. Most tour operators feature the Neuhaus (☎ 5285 6703) along the main road ('excellent, with a high standard of food'). The impeccable Hotel Berghof (☎ 5285 62254) has its own indoor tennis courts. The Alpenhotel Kramerwirt (☎ 5285 6700) is recommended.

Eating in and out

Most guests choose half-board, but several reporters complained that the portions in the hotels are inadequate. Mayrhofen has fewer independent dining venues than one might expect. Among them is the

Wirthaus zum Griena, which is a listed 400-year-old building and provides what one reporter described as a menu of 'local mountain food'. Singapore is an average Chinese restaurant, Mo's serves Cajun burgers, and Mamma Mia is a bright Italian. Grill Kuchl has a good, inexpensive menu. Café Dengg has the best pizza. The Sports Bar Grill in Hotel Strass serves Mexican food.

Après-ski

The Ice Bar at the foot of Penken gondola becomes a seething mass of humanity at the end of the day and claims to be Europe's biggest sales point for Grolsch beer. Uli Spiess' Happy End is a quieter alternative. The Lolly and the Speakeasy are both popular bars. The Sports Arena is one of the more hi-tech discos in the Alps. The Scotland Yard Pub is a popular hang-out for riders and has darts, a working red telephone box and British beer. The Garage attracts the younger set, while Schlusselalm is 'the best disco in town for the over 25s'. Erlebnis Mayrhofen, a swimming pool complex with a 101-m chute, ranks as one of the top five waterparks in the Tyrol.

Childcare

The mother of Uli Spiess, the former Austrian racer, pioneered the idea of the ski kindergarten in Mayrhofen, a formula that has since been adopted around the world. She has now retired and her son has sold his ski school, but the standard of childcare is still exemplary. Wuppy's Kinderland minds children from three months to seven years of age. SMT and Gager both run ski- and non-ski kindergartens, while Peter Habeler takes children from five years of age. If you register your child at the tourist office, he or she will receive a birthday gift in the post.

Linked or nearby resorts

The Zillertal lift-pass region covers 11 different local areas stretching down to the River Inn and the Germany–Innsbruck autobahn, and up the valley sides east as far as **Königsleiten** and **Gerlos** and west as far as Hintertux. Individually, none offers much more than a single day's interesting skiing, but bus transport is free and generally efficient, and a free train goes from Mayrhofen down the valley to **Zell am Ziller**, and on to **Fügen** and the mainline junction at **Jenbach**.

After Mayrhofen, Zell am Ziller is the second most substantial valley resort. The name should not be confused with Kaprun's twin resort near Salzburg, Zell am See. In fact, Zell am Ziller is the antithesis of a ski resort. Sitting in the Ziller river valley at 570m, Zell is a bustling, commercialised market town. Counting the lift systems of its neighbours, **Ramsau-im-Ziller** and **Hippach**, Zell am Ziller claims a regional area with 47km of pistes and 22 lifts. Neither of Zell's own two areas, Kreuzjoch or Gerlosstein, is within walking distance of the town. Kreuzjoch's centrepiece is a swift eight-person gondola, and Gerlosstein has twin cable-cars – testimony to the crowds that flock in from Germany each weekend.

Skiing facts: Mayrhofen

TOURIST INFORMATION
Postfach 21, A-6290 Mayrhofen, Zillertal
Tel 43 5285 6760
Fax 43 5285 676033
Email mayrhofen@zillertal.tirol.at
Web site www.mayrhofen.com

THE RESORT
By road Calais 1,159km
By rail Jenbach station in resort
Airport transfer Innsbruck 1hr, Munich
and Salzburg 2½hrs
Visitor beds 8,680
Transport free day-time bus service
around Zillertal included in lift pass

THE SKIING
Linked or nearby resorts Finkenberg (l),
Fügen (n), Fügenberg (n), Gerlos (n),
Hintertux (n), Hippach (n), Juns (n),
Kaltenbach (n), Kramsach (n),
Lanersbach (l), Madseit (n), Ramsau-im-
Ziller (n), Schwendau (l),
Vorderlanersbach (l), Zell am Ziller (n)
Number of lifts 48 in Mayrhofen and
linked area. 148 in Zillertal
Total of trails/pistes 141km (44% easy,
48% intermediate, 8% difficult),
462km in Zillertal
Beginners 3 runs and lifts
Summer skiing 18km of piste on
Hintertux Glacier

LIFT PASSES
Area pass Zillertal Superskipass
(includes glacier), ATS2,130 for 6 days

Pensioners no reduction
Credit cards no

TUITION
Skiing Manfred Gager (☎ 5285 63800),
Peter Habeler (☎ 5285 62839), Max
Rahm's SMT (☎ 5285 63939)
Snowboarding Mayrhofen Snowboard
School (SMT) (☎ 5285 63939)
Other courses cross-country,
race training, ski-touring, teen skiing
Guiding Peter Habeler

CHILDREN
Lift pass Zillertal Superskipass (includes
glacier), 6–15yrs ATS1,300–1,720 for
6 days, 16–20yrs 20% discount, free for
5yrs and under
Ski & board school as adults
Kindergarten (ski) Peter Habeler,
(non-ski) Wuppy's Kinderland (☎ 5285
63612), (ski/non-ski) Manfred Gager,
Max Rahm's SMT

OTHER SPORTS
Curling, hang-gliding, horse-riding,
ice-climbing, indoor tennis and squash,
night-skiing/boarding, parapente,
skating, sleigh rides, snowmobiling,
snowshoeing, swimming, tubing

FOOD AND DRINK
Coffee ATS25–30, glass of wine ATS30,
small beer ATS25, soft drink ATS25,
dish of the day ATS80–200

Tux im Zillertal
top 3,250m (10,663ft) bottom 1,500m (4,920ft)

Hintertux, or the Tuxer Glacier as the locals call it, boasts the steepest
glacier skiing in Austria and, snow permitting, is open 365 days a year
(20km of the piste is open all summer). It also offers the most advanced
skiing and snowboarding on the otherwise strictly low-altitude Zillertal

Superskipass. Skiing at this end of the Zillertal extends to 120km of piste served by 33 lifts.

Hintertux consists of a handful of modern four-star hotels including Hotel Bergfried (☎ 5287 87239), which has a swimming-pool surrounded by rock walls with stone leopards looking on. The hotels are little frequented by British skiers, who find more life at less cost down the valley in Lanersbach. The Tuxer Valley winds steeply southwest for 17km from Mayrhofen, requiring a 45-minute free shuttle transfer from Mayrhofen to Hintertux. Buses run every 15 minutes during the morning peak hours.

The glacier attracts such vast numbers that, as a result, 2-m high metal cattle pens welcome skiers and snowboarders at the Hintertux base-station. Hotel residents in Hintertux with six-day lift passes enjoy their own separate entrance. Lower glacier lifts and pistes are very crowded. Higher lifts are less crowded, with the more testing top runs often empty in less-than-ideal weather.

From Hintertux a four-person gondola and a double chair-lift take you up to the foot of the glacier at Sommerbergalm, site of a comfortable self-service cafeteria and an outdoor umbrella bar blaring schmaltzy folk tunes. From here, two drag-lifts and a covered quad-chair branch to the right towards the Tuxer Joch. Branching to the left and up to the Tuxerfernerhaus restaurant complex is the two-stage Gletscherbus Funitel gondola, carrying up to 24 skiers and snowboarders in sit-down comfort to the top of the glacier, at 3,250m, and Austria's highest privately-owned mountain hut. The Funitel provides considerably greater stability and allows the lift to operate even in moderately high winds.

Nowhere on the glacier is the skiing overly challenging, with most runs groomed and free of bumps. However, the pistes are considered to be the best year-round downhill training ground in Europe, and national teams spend much of their summer here. The home run to Sommerbergalm is narrow and can be dangerously overcrowded in places. The only marked off-piste itinerary, the Schwarze Pfanne, goes all the way down to Hintertux but is frequently closed. Hintertux has its own ski and snowboard school. The regular pitch of the glacier is ideal for beginner riders.

TOURIST INFORMATION
Tel 43 5287 8506
Fax 43 5287 8508
Email info@tux.at
Web site www.tux.at

Obergurgl–Hochgurgl

ALTITUDE 1,930m (6,330ft)

Beginners ✷✷ Intermediates ✷✷ Advanced ✷ Snowboarders ✷✷

The charming village of Obergurgl provides snowsure, high-altitude skiing from November until Easter, a fact that has endeared it to generations of British families whose skiing is restricted to school holiday periods when sufficient snow cover elsewhere in Austria is by no means a foregone conclusion.

Obergurgl is situated at the head of the remote and beautiful Ötz Valley, which is a 90-minute drive from **Innsbruck**. Building in Obergurgl has reached capacity within the avalanche-safe area and, despite the large number of luxury hotels, it remains a small village, set around the church and a handful of shops on the lower level and around an open-air ice-rink on the upper level. The Edelweiss und Gurgl Hotel is the four-star hotel around which much of village life rotates.

✔ Ideal for families
✔ Extensive ski-touring
✔ Late-season skiing
✔ Resort charm
✔ Magnificent scenery
✗ Lack of tough runs
✗ Limited facilities for non-skiers

The wealth of luxury hotels in the village attracts an upmarket clientèle, predominantly from Germany but traditionally bolstered by British families. However, prices are reasonable compared to larger resorts such as **Ischgl**. Guests confess to being bowled over by the natural, unspoilt beauty of the resort, which instils unfailing loyalty. As one reader put it: 'I almost didn't want to send in this report in case too many others discover this lovely resort'.

Cars are banned from the village between 11pm and 6am, and parking is not easy. Most Obergurgl visitors are more than content to remain in their elegant eyrie at the head of the valley: only limited **Vent** and mass-market **Sölden** are within easy reach for a day out from Obergurgl, but lift passes are not compatible.

Hochgurgl is little more than a collection of modern hotels perched by the side of the road leading up to the Timmelsjoch Pass, which is closed in winter. In the past Obergurgl and Hochgurgl were seen as entirely separate destinations – while Obergurgl drew families like a moth to a searchlight, Hochgurgl had a more serious skiing image. However, the resorts are now linked across the König and Verwall valleys by an eight-person gondola.

Obergurgl first made its mark on the European skiing map on 27 May 1931, when the Swiss aviation pioneer Professor Auguste Piccard made a forced landing in his hot-air balloon on the Gurgler-Ferner

Glacier after achieving the world altitude record of 16,203m. A local mountain guide, Hans Falkner, spotted the balloon landing in the last light of the day. The following morning he carried out a triumphant rescue of the explorers leading them between the crevasses to Obergurgl and glory for all concerned.

On the snow
top 3,080m (10,104ft) bottom 1,793m (5,881ft)

The slopes of both Obergurgl and Hochgurgl occupy a northwest-facing area at the southern end of the Ötztal on the Italian border. These are linked via the 3.6-km gondola, which runs from the bottom of the Wurmkogl lift at Hochgurgl to the bottom of the blue (easy) Run No. 3, halfway up the Festkoglbahn. Most of the skiing is above the tree-line, and runs are intermediate. Not all of the handful of black (difficult) runs justify their gradings, and advanced snow-users will soon tire of the limited pistes – unless they are interested in ski-touring, for which the area is outstanding.

The skiing takes place over three small areas, naturally divided by the contours of the terrain. Hochgurgl offers the greatest vertical drop off the glacier but also the most severe weather conditions: even on a sunny day in February, extreme cold can be the price you pay for high-quality snow. The wide, wooded hillside leads down to **Untergurgl**, which is little more than a roadside lift station and car park.

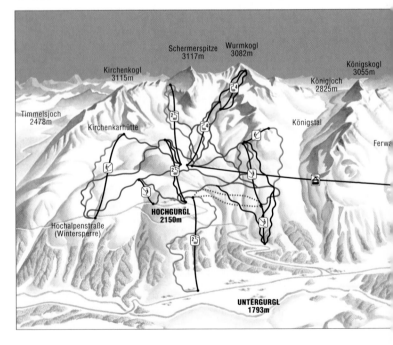

Obergurgl's two sectors, properly linked in one direction only, generally comprise more interesting terrain, with the steeper runs at the top and some good off-piste alternatives. Easy access to the Festkogl area is provided via a four-seater enclosed chair, which starts from directly behind the Hotel Edelweiss und Gurgl. Alternative access is via a gondola on the outskirts of Obergurgl, while Gaisberg is reached by a chair-lift, which rises lazily over gentle slopes from the village centre. Reporters noted that the area's piste grooming and signposting are excellent.

Beginners

Complete novices start on nursery slopes set well away from the village near the cross-country track. While Obergurgl has easy skiing in both its main sectors, Hochgurgl has a far more comprehensive selection of blue pistes. The top of the long glacier is served by two chairs – one a high-speed covered quad, which affords some protection against the elements, often quite severe at this altitude.

Intermediates

The Festkogl gondola rises steeply to a sunny plateau with a restaurant and a couple of drag-lifts. The area of mainly red (but not difficult) intermediate runs is served by a modern quad-chair, which takes you up to the highest point of Obergurgl's skiing at 3,035m. Less confident

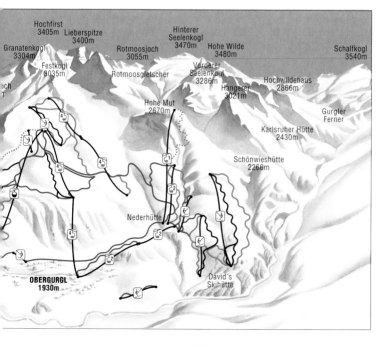

skiers and snowboarders will enjoy the blue run from the gondola station down to the bottom of the Rosskar double-chair.

While Hochgurgl's skiing is generally less challenging, the Schermer-Spitz chair, with conveyor-belt entry, gives access to a wide and easy red piste, which is the start of nearly 1,500m vertical all the way down to Untergurgl. A two-stage covered quad-chair takes you up to the summit of the Wurmkogl, which offers an exciting descent for strong intermediates. The drag-lift on the southern side of the ski area serves a long and varied red run with moguls.

Advanced

The pistes offer little serious challenge or scope. In the Gaisberg sector a long, antique single-chair goes up to the Hohe Mut at 2,670m. The first part of the only official run down is a ski route, which in turn becomes a black piste, but the 1.8-km descent is not difficult when snow cover is deep, and one suspects that the grading is designed to reduce traffic and avoid bottlenecks at the outdated lift. Accomplished snow-users will enjoy the black itinerary down the Ferwalltal from the top of the Festkogl gondola. However, the run is prone to avalanche danger, and great care should be taken.

Off-piste

Obergurgl, with its 21 glaciers, is one of the great ski-touring centres of Europe. More limited opportunities also exist for those who prefer to take their powder by lift rather than on skins. An off-piste run in good powder conditions off the back of the Hohe Mut takes you on a glorious descent that ends up near the Schönwieshütte.

Snowboarding

This is a good place for riders of all levels, with some excellent carving opportunities on the gentle slopes. Wurmkogl has a half-pipe and a terrain park with a small range of obstacles in the Festkogl ski area.

Tuition and guiding

Obergurgl is one of the homes of the Austrian Instructors' Ski School, and the standard of teaching and organisation here should therefore be among the highest in Austria. However, we have received considerable criticism of both the Obergurgl and Hochgurgl schools, with lack of motivation being the main complaint. One reporter said that his teacher 'was simply not interested in improving the standard of the class. You got the impression that he was only going through the motions in return for his meal ticket. It may have been a long season for him, but for us it was our precious one-week holiday'. Other reporters complained of as many as 15 pupils per class, and criticised division into language groups (not always well organised): 'the ski school seemed to allocate children mainly by height'). Gripes include a lack of English-speaking instructors, poor group selection and 'almost non-existent tuition skills'.

Mountain restaurants

'Lunch in Obergurgl is a treat', said one reporter. The Hohe Mut Hütte, at the top of the single-chair at Gaisberg, provides magnificent views of the Ötztal and the Dolomites. Although you can make the return journey by chair-lift, the alternative post-prandial prospect of the black ski route down acts as a deterrent to those wanting lunch and means that the old wooden chalet is the least crowded restaurant in the area. On fine days there is an ice-bar and barbecue on the terrace. The Schönwieshütte, a 15-minute walk from the Sattellift piste, is a touring refuge, which serves simple meals ('best *Gulaschsuppe* and *Kaiserschmarren* ever').

David's Schihütte at the bottom of the Steinmannlift is recommended for its *Tirolergröstl* (potato with bacon), although the service can be 'so slow as to be non-existent, with Serbian waiters who speak no English or German'. The Festkogl mountain restaurant is described by a number of reporters as 'indifferent'. The Nederhütte is warmly recommended for 'good food and an excellent atmosphere'.

In Hochgurgl, the Wurmkogl (by the top of the Wurmkogl quad-chair) is the best of the three altitude restaurants. Toni's Almhütte – a rustic wooden hut owned by the Sporthotel Olymp – is highly praised. The sun terrace of the Hotel Riml has great views.

Accommodation

Most of the accommodation is in smart hotels and, to a lesser extent, in guesthouses and pensions. It is also possible to rent attractive and spacious apartments by contacting the resort directly. The resort's five-star is Hotel Hochgurgl (☎ 5256 6265), which has luxury suites and apartments, as well as a crèche and a health club. Hotel Crystal (☎ 5256 6454) is a monster of a building, completely out of keeping with resort character, but extremely comfortable inside. The Deutschmann (☎ 5256 6594) takes its name from the old Obergurgl family that owns it. The Bergwelt (☎ 5256 6274) ('art-deco furniture and a great pool') and the Austria (☎ 5256 6282) are both highly recommended. Hotel Gotthard (☎ 5256 6292) is also warmly praised.

In the centre, Hotel Edelweiss und Gurgl (☎ 5256 6223) is highly thought of, although its bedrooms are not as large or as well-equipped as those in the new four-stars. The Jenewein (☎ 5256 6203) is praised for its friendly service and 'quite exceptional demi-pension food'. Hotel Alpina de Luxe (☎ 5256 600) was described as 'outstanding, with wonderful hospitality'. Haus Schönblick (☎ 5256 6251) has 'helpful owners, large rooms and excellent buffet breakfasts'.

In Hochgurgl we have good reports of the Hotel Riml (☎ 5256 6261) and the less expensive Sporthotel Ideal (☎ 5256 6290) ('it is, as the name implies'). The three-star Alpenhotel Laurin (☎ 5256 6227) is highly recommended for its first-rate food.

Skiing facts: Obergurgl

TOURIST INFORMATION
Hauptstrasse 108, A-6456 Obergurgl, Ötztal
Tel 43 5256 6466
Fax 43 5256 6353
Email info@obergurgl.com
Web site www.obergurgl.com

THE RESORT
By road Calais 1,102km
By rail Ötztal 54km, regular buses from station
Airport transfer Innsbruck 1½hrs
Visitor beds 4,000
Transport free ski bus

THE SKIING
Linked or nearby resorts Hochgurgl (l), Sölden (n), Vent (n)
Number of lifts 23
Total of trails/pistes 110km (32% easy, 50% intermediate, 18% difficult)
Beginners 4 lifts, 1 is free, points tickets available

LIFT PASSES
Area pass Gurgl (covers Obergurgl/Hochgurgl) ATS1,960–2,230 for 6 days

Pensioners 60yrs and over, as children
Credit cards no

TUITION
Skiing Obergurgl (☎ 5256 6305), Hochgurgl (☎ 5256 6265–99)
Snowboarding as ski schools
Other courses cross-country, extreme skiing/boarding, monoski, seniors, ski-touring, skwal, snowblading, telemark
Guiding through Obergurgl ski school

CHILDREN
Lift pass 8–16yrs ATS1,360 for 6 days
Ski & board school as adults
Kindergarten Bobo's Kinderclub (☎ 5256 6305)

OTHER SPORTS
Horse-riding, ice-climbing, night-skiing/boarding, shooting, skating, sleigh rides, snowshoeing, squash, swimming

FOOD AND DRINK
Coffee ATS27–32, glass of wine ATS25, small beer ATS35, soft drink ATS25–32, dish of the day ATS100–130

Eating in and out

Dining is largely confined to the main hotels, most of which have separate à la carte restaurants. Pizzeria Romantika in the Hotel Madeleine provides some respite from the ubiquitous rounds of Wienerschnitzel. The Edelweiss has a comfortable candlelit *stübli* with an atmosphere of 'relaxed elegance'.

The Bergwelt is recommended for its nouvelle cuisine. Pizzeria Belmonte in Haus Gurgl has 'the best pizzas in town'. Restaurant Pic-Nic is also recommended. A reporter spoke warmly of fondue evenings organised up the mountain at the Nederhütte. One small supermarket in Obergurgl looks after the needs of self-caterers. Reporters warned that restaurants in Hochgurgl itself are nearly all attached to the smart hotels and are expensive.

Après-ski

Non-skiing activities are limited in this small resort, but Obergurgl is surprisingly active in the evenings. The Nederhütte at the top of the Gaisberg lift becomes crowded as the lifts close for the day. Dancing to the owner's three-piece band and copious measures of gluhwein prepare you for the gentle run down to the village at dusk. The outdoor bar of the Edelweiss at the foot of the Gaisberg lift continues to attract customers until dark. Its cellar disco is said by most reporters to be the best in town. The Joslkeller has a cosy atmosphere and good music, which gets louder with dancing as the evening progresses. You will find the odd person in ski suit and ski boots still here in the early hours. The Krump'n'Stadl is noisy, with yodelling on alternate nights. Hexenkuch'l has live music, as does Toni's Almhütte in Hochgurgl.

Childcare

In a move to attract more families, the resort allows children aged seven years and under to ski for free – a higher age limit than in many other resorts in the Alps. Bobo's Kinderclub takes non-skiing children from three years old. A number of hotels operate their own crèches, usually free of charge. These include the Alpina, Austria, Bellevue, Bergwelt, Crystal, Hochfirst, Hochgurgl and Olymp. The minimum age accepted varies from hotel to hotel. Obergurgl Ski School takes children from five years old, and Hochgurgl accepts children as young as three years old for lessons.

Linked or nearby resorts

Vent

top 2,680m (8,793ft) bottom 1,900m (6,234ft)

Vent is a small resort with just four lifts, 15km of piste and a total of 900 beds. However, what it does have is some good off-piste skiing. The resort has one ski and snowboard school for adults and children, called Serafin Kleon, and a mountain guiding company. Small non-skiers are cared for in the kindergarten in the Familyhotel Vent (☎ 5254 8102).

TOURIST INFORMATION
Tel 43 5254 8193
Fax 43 5254 8174
Email info@vent.at
Web site www.vent.at

Obertauern

ALTITUDE 1,740m (5,707ft)

Beginners ✱✱ Intermediates ✱✱✱ Snowboarders ✱

Obertauern is Austria's best shot at a purpose-built resort and is as far removed as possible from the popular image of a cute Austrian ski resort based around an onion-domed church and the village inn. Instead, it consists of a long straggle of roadside hotels and bars and looks more like a Wild West town. However, Obertauern is by no means devoid of charm, and any architectural liberties at variance with the usual perception of an Austrian ski resort are generally hidden under a reliable blanket of snow. Indeed, its renown is based largely on its reputation for guaranteed snow cover – it remained open until 6 May in 2001 – and if there is decent snow anywhere in Austria, you will find it here.

- ✔ Excellent snow record
- ✔ Reliable resort-level snow
- ✔ Superb piste-grooming
- ✔ Skiing convenience
- ✔ Interesting off-piste
- ✘ Late-season queues
- ✘ No bus system
- ✘ Lack of non-skiing activities
- ✘ Quiet après-ski
- ✘ Spread-out village

The resort lies on a high pass in the Niedere Tauern mountains, 90km south of Salzburg. This does make the lift system susceptible to closure in high winds. The main cluster of buildings, which constitutes the centre, is around the village nursery slope and the tourist information office. Obertauern is one of Austria's top-five winter destinations, although it was discovered by British skiers only in the mid-1980s. The impressive peaks of the Niedere Tauern mountain range surround the road around the resort, allowing the construction of lifts from a central point to fan out into a natural ski circus. The ski area is not particularly extensive but provides an interesting variety of gradient and terrain.

On the snow
top 2,313m (7,587ft) bottom 1,640m (5,379ft)

The circus of 29 lifts covers 95km and can be skied in both directions, but the skiing is concentrated on the north side of the resort, spread around a broad, undulating and mainly treeless bowl ringed by rocky peaks. Four main lifts rise from around the bowl to points near the rim. Two of them ascend to approximately 2,000m from almost the same point as each other at Hochalm (1,940m); the Seekareckbahn quad chair-lift takes you up over a steep, east-facing slope, and the Panorama quad-chair takes you over a more varied south-facing one.

A clockwise circuit of this northern part of the area need not involve any of the higher, more difficult runs. On the south side of the resort the mountains rise more dramatically, keeping the village in shade for much of the day in mid-winter. The local lift map fails to show either piste names or numbers, but the signposting of the clockwise and anti-clockwise circuits is generally sufficient.

Beginners

The nursery slopes are excellent, with a short, gentle drag-lift in the heart of the village, just north of the main road, and another longer one on the lower slopes at the eastern end. Another runs parallel to and just south of the road. The high Gamskarlift, at the top of the steep Schaidberg six-person chair, also affords gentle skiing.

Intermediates

The entire circuit is geared towards intermediates, with some truly superlative long, but not over demanding, red (intermediate) descents from the lip of the bowl. Some of the best are accessed from the Panorama and Hundskogel lifts. The top of the Plattenkarbahn quad-chair is the starting point for a challenging run of over 400m vertical.

Advanced

There is enough to keep advanced skiers happy here for a week, although the more adventurous will want to explore the other resorts in the region (such as **St Johann im Pongau** and **Schladming**). Pistes can become heavily mogulled around the edge of the bowl.

Off-piste

In powder conditions the off-piste skiing is spectacular, with long runs both above and below the tree-line. To find the best and safest runs you need the services of a local guide. Vertical is the off-piste mountain guiding company.

Snowboarding

The freeriding here is first-rate, but not so the half-pipe, which is said to be 'unexciting'. Beginners have some good tame trails to learn on.

Tuition and guiding

Obertauern has six ski and snowboard schools, including the Krallinger Obertauern-Süd, which has a higher than average number of female instructors and is much favoured by tour operators. The others are CSA (known as Schischule Willi Grillitsch), Schischule Top and Schischule Frau Holle. Christian and Werner Schmidt run their dedicated Snowwave Snowboardschule from the Hotel Solaria, and Gerfried Schuller runs the Obertauern Snowboardschule. The Frau Holle school also gives snowboarding lessons.

Mountain restaurants

Because of the ski-in ski-out nature of Obertauern, it is quite easy to return to the village for lunch. Alternatively, the choice of mountain restaurants is more than adequate. The Dikt'nalm has table service. The Lurzeralm is 'piste-side, rustic and pleasant'. The Seekarhaus at Kringsalm has been rebuilt as a four-star hotel. The Sonnhof restaurant is equally busy, and one reporter warned that at weekends you need to lunch before noon to be sure of obtaining a table at the smaller mountain restaurants.

Accommodation

Nearly all the accommodation is in hotels and guesthouses, few of them cheap. Location is not particularly critical unless you have small children (choose a hotel within easy walking distance of one of the kindergartens). Sporthotel Edelweiss (☎ 6456 7245), Hotel Römerhof (☎ 6456 72380) and Alpenhotel Perner (☎ 6456 7236) are all recommended four-stars along with Sporthotel Cinderella (☎ 6456 7589) and Hotel-Restaurant Montana (☎ 6456 7313). Haus Kärntnerland (☎ 6456 7250) is said to be 'clean, comfortable and friendly, with exceptional food'. The Alpenrose apartments in the village centre are described as 'cosy and well-appointed'. The lavish Sportinghotel Marietta (☎ 6456 7262) remains a favourite with reporters.

Eating in and out

Most of the restaurants are in hotels. The Stüberl restaurant in the Hotel Regina is reported to be extremely good value ('quiet, candlelit, and serves enormous portions'). The Lurzeralm requires reservations and serves 'well-presented, good food'. The Latsch'n'Stüberl has friendly service and well-prepared food.

Après-ski

The nightlife is centred on the main hotel bars, of which more than 15 offer music and dancing. The Edelweisshütte is the place to go at the end of the day, along with the Gamsmilch Bar and the Achenrainhutte. Later on the action moves to La Bar and Premillos, next to the Hotel Steiner. The Gasthof Taverne reportedly has the liveliest disco later in the evening.

Childcare

Non-skiing children from two to six years of age are cared for all day in the Petzi-Bar crèche or in the CSA Mini Club. All the ski schools run ski kindergartens, with lunch provided on request.

TOURIST INFORMATION
Tel 43 6456 7252
Fax 43 6456 7515
Email info@ski-obertauern.com
Web site www.ski-obertauern.com

Saalbach–Hinterglemm

ALTITUDE 1,000m (3,280ft)

Beginners ✱✱✱ Intermediates ✱✱✱ Advanced ✱✱ Snowboarders ✱✱✱

Saalbach–Hinterglemm is the collective marketing name of two once-separate villages in the pretty Glemmtal valley near **Zell am See**. The narrow valley, with uniform 2,000-m peaks on either side, lends itself to a natural ski circus, which can be skied as happily in one direction as in the other. It provides some of the best intermediate and advanced skiing in Austria, second only to that in the Arlberg region.

The two villages, a five-minute drive apart, have grown so much over the years that they now stretch along the valley and almost meet. The steep and thankfully pedestrianised main street of Saalbach, with its smart hotels and high-priced fashion boutiques, gives one the distinct feeling of having strayed on to the set of a twenty-first-century sequel to *The Sound of Music*. The Alpine charm is positively Disneyesque. Old it may appear, but most of the village dates from the 1980s. Hinterglemm is little more than a collection of stolid Austrian hotels, which acts as an alternative base at the far end of the ski system. Both used to be extremely popular with the British, but these days the principal foreign tourists in Saalbach are German, while Hinterglemm is known locally as 'Little Holland'. A third village, **Leogang**, provides a back door into the ski area and is a quieter, more attractive alternative.

> ✔ Short airport transfer
> ✔ Reliable snow cover
> ✔ Traffic-free village centres
> ✔ Wide selection of accommodation
> ✔ Good child facilities
> ✔ Large choice of ski schools
> ✔ Extensive ski area
> ✗ Lift queues
> ✗ Sprawling villages
> ✗ High prices
> ✗ Noisy at night

On the snow
top 2,096m (6,877ft) bottom 1,000m (3,280ft)

Both sides of the valley are lined with a network of 52 lifts, which also links to neighbouring Leogang. Much of the system has been upgraded to provide an easy traffic flow around the 200-km circuit of prepared pistes. From the bottom of Saalbach, the Schattberg-Ost cable-car gives direct and easy access (in good snow conditions) to the southern half of the circuit. The 100-person lift is prone to serious queues when the sunny side of the valley opposite has scarce snow cover. A triple-chair at the top end of the village is the starting point for the northern half of the ski area. Chair-lifts on the sunny side of the mountain have been systematically upgraded; they include two six-seaters and two quads. From **Vorderglemm**, the two-stage Schönleitenbahn gondola takes you up to Wildenkarkogel and into the Leogang ski area. You can also find your way here from Saalbach via a gondola, which feeds a network of gentle, south-facing runs. The picturesque Glemmtal offers considerable langlauf opportunities.

Beginners

Both villages have their own nursery slopes, and the north side of the valley is dotted with T-bars serving an unusual variety of beginner terrain. When you feel capable of graduating to the main circus, the gentler southern side offers a vast area of blue (easy) runs. In patchy snow conditions, take either gondola to the 1,984-m Zwölfer; the long *Familienabfahrt* back to the valley usually holds the snow well. From Schattberg-Ost the 7-km *Jausernabfahrt* is a gentle cruise down to Vorderglemm, where you can take the Wildenkarkogel gondola up the other side of the valley for the easiest of cruises back to Saalbach.

Intermediates

Anyone who can ski parallel will enjoy the full circuit, although it is possible to shorten the outing by cutting across the valley at four separate points. Those seeking confidence-building slopes will have a field day here, as most of the southern side of the valley is an easy blue playground. Challenging exceptions to this are the Schönleiten Talstation from the Wildenkarkogel Hütte, the women's downhill from Kohlmaiskopf and a few shorter red (intermediate) runs above Hinterglemm. The Leogang sector has some usually uncrowded terrain that is well worth exploring at weekends when the main slopes are busy.

Advanced

Schattberg-Ost, Schattberg-West and Zwölferkogel make up the more challenging north-facing slopes. The north face of the Zwölfer is a classic, harsh black (difficult) run, which can be heavily mogulled at times. The home run from Schattberg-Ost can be extremely icy and crowded. A far more interesting route begins with the Westgipfel triple-chair to Schattberg-West, from where you can take a steep black to the bottom and, after another chair ride, follow the challenging itinerary to Bergstadl.

Off-piste

The north side of the valley offers some outstanding powder runs, but a local guide is necessary to discover which slopes are safe, and when. Sepp Mitterer, as well as all the regular ski and board schools, can arrange off-piste guiding.

Snowboarding

Saalbach has devoted 13km of slopes to riders of all levels and is now recognised as a major resort for snowboarders. The vast 12-km

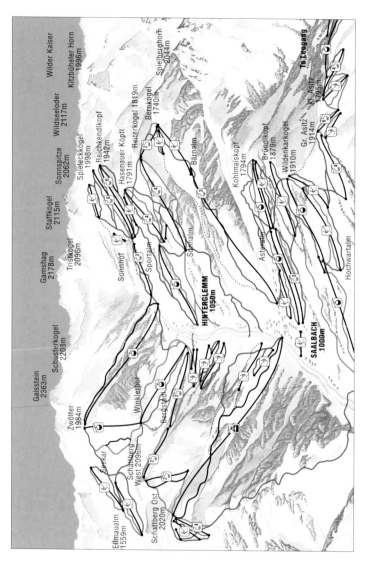

snowboard-only terrain park at Hinterglemm includes a boardercross course. Saalbach has a half-pipe accessed by the Bernkogel chair and there is a second one served by the Poltenlift quad in the Leogang sector. Off-piste snowboarding opportunities can be wonderful, with good riding down to the main valley road, which is served by a regular, free shuttle bus.

Tuition and guiding

Since deregulation permitted the establishment of alternative ski and
snowboard schools in Austria, no less than nine now compete for the
resort's big business. Schischule Wolf, based in Hinterglemm, attracts
a disproportionate number of Anglo-Saxon guests. The smaller
Mitterlengau (also known as Activ) in Hinterglemm has a sound reputation. Schischule Fürstauer in Saalbach is particularly recommended
for children's tuition. Snowboardschule Saalbach is the resort's
specialist school for riders.

Mountain restaurants

As one reporter put it: 'there are almost as many restaurants and
delightful huts as there are runs. The Pfefferalm above Hinterglemm is
the most picturesque old farmhouse we have ever encountered'.

The Goasstall is equally rustic and is recommended for its glühwein.
The good-value Rosswaldhütte, beside the Rosswald lift in the
Hochalmspitze area, is an attractive chalet where the friendly staff wear
traditional costume. The rather twee Wildenkarkogel Hütte at the top
of the Vorderglemm gondola is also accessible for non-skiers.

Accommodation

The Saalbach-Hinterglemm area has a total of 31 four-star hotels. In
Saalbach these include the Alpenhotel (☎ 6541 6666), the Ingonda
(☎ 6541 6262), the Kristiania (☎ 6541 6253) and the Saalbacher Hof
(☎ 6541 7111). In Hinterglemm, the Dorfschmiede (☎ 6541 7408) is
recommended ('delicious food and helpful staff') along with the
Glemmtalerhof (☎ 6541 7135) ('ideally situated and comfortable') and
the friendly Blumenhotel Tirolerhof (☎ 6541 6497). Hotel Hasenauer
(☎ 6541 6332) in Hinterglemm is convenient for the lifts. The resorts
also have some less expensive alternatives. Three-star Hotel Sonnblick
(☎ 6541 6408) at Hinterglemm is said to have 'excellent food and a
pleasant bar', while Landhaus Wolf (☎ 6541 7226) is said to be 'clean
and very friendly'.

Eating in and out

Bäckstättstall is the most exclusive restaurant in Saalbach. The Hotel
Bauer is said to be 'good value, with a much more varied menu than you
would expect in Austria'. The Guter Stube in the Hotel Dorfschmiede
has 'the best gourmet food in the region', and the Knappenstube is also
recommended. Hotel Hasenauer in Hinterglemm is 'cheaper than
anywhere else', while the Bärenbachhof is 'not as expensive and better
than most'. Two reporters spoke warmly of Hotel Gollingerhof's restaurant in Hinterglemm.

Après-ski

The endearing feature of Saalbach is the immutable, jolly Austrian
formula. True, the folk dancers now save their thigh-slapping and
yodels for the more appreciative lakes-and-mountains clientèle in the

Skiing facts: Saalbach–Hinterglemm

TOURIST INFORMATION
Glemmtaler Landesstrasse 550,
A–5753 Saalbach
Tel 43 6541 680068
Fax 43 6541 680069
Email contact@saalbach.com
Web site www.saalbach.com

THE RESORT
By road Calais 1,193km
By rail Zell am See 19km
Airport transfer Salzburg 1½hrs
Visitor beds 16,360
Transport free ski bus with lift pass

THE SKIING
Linked or nearby resorts Bad Gastein
(n), Bad Hofgastein (n), Grossarl (n),
Kaprun (n), Leogang (l), Zell am See (n)
Number of lifts 52
Total of trails/pistes 200km (45% easy,
47% intermediate, 8% difficult)
Beginners 5 lifts, points tickets available

LIFT PASSES
Area pass (covers Saalbach-
Hinterglemm and Leogang)
ATS1,845–2,070 for 6 days
Pensioners reductions for women 60yrs
and over, men 65yrs and over
Credit cards yes

TUITION
Skiing Saalbach: Aamadall (☎ 6541
668256), Fürstauer (☎ 6541 8444),
Hinterholzer (☎ 6541 7607),

Heugenhauser (☎ 6541 8300),
Zinc (☎ 6541 8420). Hinterglemm:
Gensbichler (☎ 6541 7511), itterlengau
(or Activ) (☎ 6541 7255), Wolf
(☎ 6541 6346)
Snowboarding as ski schools and
Snowboardschule Saalbach
(☎ 6541 20047)
Other courses cross-country, race-
training, telemark
Guiding Sepp Mitterer (☎ 6541 7008),
or through ski schools

CHILDREN
Lift pass 7–15yrs ATS1,100–1,240,
16–19yrs ATS1,660–1,865, both for
6 days. Free for 6yrs and under
Ski & board school as adults
Kindergarten (ski), Fürstauer, Wolf
(non-ski) Gartenhotel Theresia
(☎ 6541 7415–40),
Hotel Glemmtalerhof (☎ 6541 7135),
Hotel Lengauerhof (☎ 6541 7255),
Partnerhotels (☎ 6541 7408)

OTHER SPORTS
Curling, hang-gliding, ice-hockey, indoor
tennis and squash, parapente, skating,
sleigh rides, swimming

FOOD AND DRINK
Coffee ATS26–30, glass of wine
ATS25–60, small beer ATS32–38,
soft drink ATS26–30,
dish of the day ATS110–120

summer, but the waitresses still wear their *Dirndl* dresses and genuine smiles of welcome as they pocket your money. Après-ski starts with a drink at the Bäckstättstall Umbrella Bar with 'a disco/band and striking views over Saalbach; they also do a potent glühwein to add some challenge to the very short run down to the street'. The Schirmbar is also recommended. Hinterhagalm has a huge copper pot of glühwein on the bar, and it is on draught at Bauer's Schialm by the church in Saalbach. In Hinterglemm, the snow-bar outside the Hotel Dorfschmiede is always crowded. The Hexenhäusl attracts crowds as they leave the slopes, and Lumpi's Bla Bla has a good atmosphere. The Pfeiffenmuseum Café in the Glemmtalerhof houses a quite enormous collection of pipes and smoking paraphernalia, while the Road King is a popular late-night bar. After 11pm you can dance at no fewer than 20 bars and discos. These include Barbarella Dancing in Saalbach and Tanzhimmel in Hinterglemm. A regular bus service for night-owls now runs up and down the valley from 8pm to 3am.

Childcare
Schischule Wolf and Fürstauer both operate their own ski kinder-gartens every day except Sunday for children from four years of age. Hotels including Gartenhotel Theresia, Hotel Glemmtalerhof, Partnerhotels and Hotel Lengauerhof care for non-skiing children from two-and-a-half or three years of age.

Linked or nearby resorts

Leogang
top 2,096m (6,875ft) bottom 800m (2,625ft)
Leogang – an amalgamation of ten farming hamlets spread out along a main road – claims the title of longest village in Europe. A smart, modern gondola takes skiers and snowboarders up to Berghaus Asitz at 1,758m, from where a quad-chair and a six-seater chair link you into the Saalbach circuit. Accommodation is in a mixture of hotels and chalets. The four-star Salzburgerhof (☎ 6583 7310) is 'definitely the most convenient place to stay'. Others nearby include Gasthof Rupertus (☎ 6583 8466) Asitz Stub'n (☎ 6583 8556) and Fortshofgut (☎ 6583 8545). The St Leonhard (☎ 6583 8542) is an eight-minute walk from the lift. The two ski schools have a shortage of English speak-ers ('my girlfriend had to rely on the kindness of a Dutchman to trans-late everything'). Five cross-country trails total more than 40km, and snow rafting is also available. The kindergarten in Hotel Krallerhof takes children from two years of age. Nightlife centres on the Outback Bar at the bottom of the gondola.

TOURIST INFORMATION
Tel 43 6583 8234
Fax 43 6583 7302
Email office@sale-touristik.at
Web site www.leogang-saalfelden.at

Schladming

ALTITUDE 745m (2,224ft)

Beginners ✱✱✱ Intermediates ✱✱✱ Snowboarders ✱✱

Schladming is essentially an ordinary Austrian town that derives much of its income from industries other than tourism and skiing. Not much happens here. Indeed, during its entire 680-year history – unless you count a little bloodshed in the sixteenth century and the birth of Arnold Schwarzenegger – you would be hard pushed to find any single event of international significance. Day-to-day life in this attractive provincial town, with its onion-domed church and magnificent eighteenth-century town square, continues at a rhythm that is not dictated solely by tourism. The resort also has the country's smallest brewery. The linked skiing has its own local lift pass but is also included in the new Skiverbund Amadé lift pass, which covers 276 lifts serving 865km of piste in 30 ski areas.

All these contributory factors make Schladming an utterly charming and unspoilt base from which to explore huge tracts of mostly linked intermediate skiing and snowboarding that are entirely unknown to the majority of British snow-users. Anyone looking for *Lederhosen-und-oompah Gemütlichkeit* will discover that it still thrives here.

✔ Large ski area
✔ Lively après-ski
✔ Tree-level skiing
✔ Excellent for cross-country
✔ Short airport transfer
✔ Summer skiing on Dachstein Glacier
✔ Variety of mountain restaurants
✔ Recommended childcare
✗ Poor skiing convenience
✗ Lack of challenging runs

On the snow
top 2,015m (6,609ft) bottom 745m (2,224ft)

Schladming lies in the centre of a long and beautiful valley, with the main slopes spread disparately across the mountains on the southern side. Planai at 1,894m and Hochwurzen at 1,850m are the mountains closest to Schladming. The lift pass is hands-free. The easiest access to Planai is via a two-stage gondola from the edge of Schladming, which is a comfortable walk from the centre. The Kessleralm mid-station of the gondola can also be reached by car. Planai is somewhat precariously linked at valley level to the next mountain, Hochwurzen, by a series of chair-lifts. It offers several long red (intermediate) runs, which are served by two steep drags, a jumbo gondola and a double-chair. A gondola from the village of **Pichl** to the bottom of the Hochwurzenbahn gives access to the Reiteralm, which offers a variety of red and blue (easy) tree-lined runs served by a double chair-lift and a gondola.

Above Schladming, on the eastern side of Planai, two chair-lifts link up with the Mitterhaus double drag-lift to provide a gateway to Hauser Kaibling, a 2,015-m peak that towers over the pretty village of **Haus-im-Ennstal**. A replacement eight-person gondola built in summer 2000 at the Pruggern end of the village greatly improved mountain access and reduced queues for the other gondola at the Schladming end.

Still further to the east along the valley, the Galsterbergalm at 1,976m offers a few (mainly gentle) slopes reached by cable-car from the village of **Pruggern**. This in turn gives access to a couple of further lifts for skiing above the tree-line. The small, separate **Fageralm** area is also included in the local lift pass.

On the other side of the valley from Schladming, the commune of **Ramsau-Ort** at 1,200m has no less than 19 lifts scattered around the hills on either side of the village. All are short and easy slopes. **Turlwand**, outside Ramsau, is the starting point for the cable-car up to the **Dachstein Glacier**; the village is served by a chair-lift and three drag-lifts, and has limited year-round skiing that is too gentle to be of much more than scenic interest for alpine skiers.

The Schladming area has some of the best cross-country skiing in Austria, with 250km of trails against a dramatically scenic backdrop and plenty of small huts to call in at for refreshments.

Beginners

At this low altitude, the functioning of the 25 listed nursery slopes is heavily dependent on the weather. The gentle **Rohrmoos** meadows on the lower slopes of Hochwurzen provide the best arena for first turns when snow cover permits, with plenty of easy alternatives on the higher slopes of the main mountains. However, one reporter said that the Planai nursery slopes were 'short and overcrowded' and 'the gentle high-altitude runs on Fageralm provided a better alternative'.

Intermediates

Despite the lack of variety, the red (intermediate) and blue (easy) cruising terrain is plentiful enough to keep any skier busy for a week. The World Cup racecourses on both Planai and Hauser Kaibling should please fast intermediates, and the long downhill course on Hochwurzen is thigh-burning. The usually uncrowded Reiteralm piste also gives plenty of opportunity for high-speed cruising.

Advanced

Advanced piste-skiers will quickly tire of the limited terrain, where only one short run is graded black (difficult). However, Schladming is an attractive base from which to explore a huge range of skiing, including

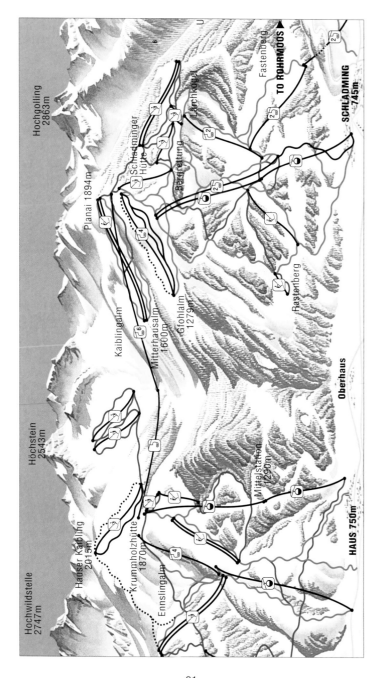

Obertauern and the Sportwelt Amadé, which is centred on **St Johann im Pongau**. The new giant regional lift pass, the Skiverbund Amadé, gives access to plenty of more challenging terrain in this corner of Austria. However, a car is essential.

Off-piste

Skiing outside the marked pistes is discouraged on the main mountains, except on the ski routes. In good snow conditions the north face of Hauser Kaibling offers great scope, and the runs through the trees from Bergstallalm on Planai are recommended.

Snowboarding

Schladming is great for beginner and intermediate riders, with the Planai and Dachstein Glacier having the best terrain. A terrain park and two half-pipes add to the attractions. Snowboarding has been a commercial success in Schladming, not least because it is the home of the former European champion Gerfried Schuller, who has his own school here. He also runs the Blue Tomato snowboard shop as well as Snowboardschule Dachstein-Tauern.

Tuition and guiding

The Plania Hochwurzen and the rival Franz Tritscher Ski School both cheerfully provide the full range of lessons and courses. Snowboardschule Dachstein-Tauern is the alternative for riders.

Mountain restaurants

'The mountain restaurants are tremendous,' said one reporter. 'Service was invariably friendly and efficient with large helpings. I put on seven pounds in a week'. The Seiterhutte below the summit of Hochwurzen is singled out for particular praise. The Krümmelholze at Haus is recommended too. Panorama Alm on Reiteralm and Kessleralm on Planair are 'pleasant self-services with reasonable prices and friendly staff'. Onkel Willy's Hütte ('buzzing with atmosphere') has live music and a sunny terrace. The Eiskarhütte on Reiteralm is also popular.

Accommodation

The Sporthotel Royer (☎ 3687 200) receives rave reviews. The Alte Post (☎ 3687 22571) ('small bedroom, but good food with Strauss, Mozart and Haydn in the background') is recommended. Haus Stangl (☎ 3687 22150), a simple B&B, is also praised. Hotel Zum Stadttor (☎ 3687 24525) has 'large rooms and excellent food'.

Eating in and out

The restaurants are mainly in the hotels. We have good reports of the Rôtisserie Royer Grill in the Sporthotel Royer. The Alte Post is recommended for 'excellent trout and other dishes in a pretentious but friendly atmosphere'. Its *Postreindl* (pork fillet with creamed mushrooms and gnocchi) is 'not to be missed'. The Neue Post has two recommended à la carte restaurants, the Jägerstüberl and the Poststüberl. Le Jardin is a warmly commended French restaurant. The Gasthof Kirchenwirt is 'unmatched for quality of food, price, atmosphere and service'. Charly Kahr's Restaurant is also praised for its outstanding Salzburg cuisine.

Après-ski

Après-ski starts early at Onkel Willy's Hütte on Planai before filtering down to the Siglu in the Hauptplatz. Later on the action moves to The Pub, La Porta, the Hanglbar and – still later – to the Sonderbar disco. The Schwalbenbrau brewery is worth a visit, although the intentionally cloudy beer it produces is not to everyone's taste and may explain why it is the smallest brewery in Austria. The Planaistub'n, also known as Charly's Treff, draws large crowds. Café-Konditorei Landgraf and Niederl are both praised. One reporter favoured Ferry's Pub in the Steirergasse, another the Hanglbar; the bowling alley behind the latter is said to offer a good night out. The Beisl bar is 'intimate and lively with good music'. La Porta is 'small, crowded, with a great atmosphere'.

The 7-km toboggan run from the top to the bottom of Hochwurzen down the hairpin road can be used only at night (when the road is closed) and is claimed to be the longest in Austria ('the bruises are well worth the experience. It was as much fun as the skiing'). Schladming has a large swimming-pool and leisure complex.

Childcare

Few resorts receive such resounding reviews for both their ski and non-ski kindergarten. 'Outstanding facilities for very young children,' commented one reader. 'There were 40 small children in the ski kindergarten, and the facilities were brilliant; this is definitely the area to bring small children to be well looked after and to learn to ski,' said another. Frau Ladreiter and Meine Kleine Schule are the resort's two non-ski kindergartens.

Linked or nearby resorts

Haus-im-Ennstal
top 2,015m (6,611ft) bottom 750m (2,460ft)

Haus is a quiet village with its farming origins still in evidence, although it has a considerable amount of holiday accommodation in guesthouses and apartments. There are cafés, one of which has jazz nights, and a couple of shops. The four-star Hauser Kaibling hotel (☎ 3686 23780) has a swimming-pool and is recommended for its cuisine. Dorfhotel Kirchenwirt (☎ 3686 2228) is a traditional hotel in the village centre, the Gasthof Reiter (☎ 3686 2225) is a fine old chalet much cheaper than most of the accommodation, and the Gürtl (☎ 3686 2383) is a quiet family-run hotel well situated for the cable-car.

Skiing facts: Schladming

TOURIST INFORMATION
Erzherzog-Johann-Strasse 213, A-8970
Schladming
Tel 43 3687 22268
Fax 43 3687 24138
Email touristoffice@schladming.com
Web site www.schladming.com

THE RESORT
By road Calais 1,221km
By rail station in resort
Airport transfer Salzburg 1hr,
Munich 2½hrs
Visitor beds 3,500
Transport free ski bus with lift pass

THE SKIING
Linked or nearby resorts Haus-im-
Ennstal (l), Obertauern (n), Rohrmoos (l),
Ramsau/Dachstein (n), St Johann im
Pongau (n)
Number of lifts 24 in Schladming, 86 in
linked area, 276 in Skiverbund
Amadé area
Total of trails/pistes 53km in
Schladming,167km (29% easy,
59% intermediate, 9% difficult,
3% very difficult) in linked area,
856km in Skiverbund Amadé area
Beginners 25 lifts in area, lift pass
reductions available
Summer skiing nearest on
Dachstein Glacier

LIFT PASSES
Area pass Skiverbund Amadé
ATS1,920–2,065
Pensioners no reductions
Credit cards Amex and Diners only

TUITION
Skiing Planai Hochwurzen
(☎ 3687 23582), Franz Tritscher
(☎ 3687 22647)
Snowboarding Snowboardschule
Dachstein-Tauern
(☎ 3687 24223)
Other courses cross-country, moguls,
race-training, seniors, snowblading,
telemark
Guiding through ski schools, Helli Team
Bedarfsflug (☎ 3687 81323)

CHILDREN
Lift pass Ski Verbund Amadé 6–15yrs
ATS960–1,035, 3–5yrs ATS100,
free for under 3yrs. All for 6 days
Ski & board school as adults
Kindergarten (ski) through ski schools,
(non-ski) Frau Ladreiter (☎ 3687 61313),
Meine Kleine Schule (☎ 3687 24407)

OTHER SPORTS
Climbing wall, curling, hang-gliding,
horse-riding, hot-air ballooning,
ice-climbing, indoor climbing wall, indoor
tennis and squash, night-skiing,
8-km night-tobogganing run, parapente,
skating, snowbiking, snowrafting,
snowshoeing, sleigh rides, swimming

FOOD AND DRINK
Coffee ATS28, glass of wine ATS23,
small beer ATS27–30, soft drink ATS25,
dish of the day ATS100–130

A gentle nursery slope lies between the village and the gondola station, and snowboarders are catered for with a half-pipe. Skischule Brandner, WM-Ski und Snowboardschule and Snowboardschule Dachstein-Tauern all offer tuition.

TOURIST INFORMATION
Tel 43 3686 2234–0
Fax 43 3686 2234–4
Email haus-ennstal@aon.at
Web site www.haus.at

Rohrmoos
top 1,850m (6,070ft) bottom 870m (2,854ft)
This diffuse satellite has easy skiing to and from many of its hotel doorsteps. Among the choice of good-value hotels and guesthouses are the Austria (☎ 3687 61444) and the Waldfrieden (☎ 3687 61487). Both are well-placed at the point where the lower, gentle slopes of Rohrmoos meet the steeper slopes of Hochwurzen. The smarter Schwaigerhof (☎ 3687 61422) boasts an excellent position on the edge of the pistes and is one of the few places with a swimming-pool. The Schütterhof (☎ 3687 61205) is also warmly recommended. Après-ski is informal and centres on the hotel bars. The Tauernalm is the main meeting point. Café Perner is a tea-time favourite, and Knappenkeller in Rohrmoos is busy later on. Both Schladming ski schools operate here. Max and Moritz Club is the non-skiing kindergarten for children aged two to five years. Hotel Seiterhof (☎ 3687 61194) is highly praised ('wonderful apartments that are much cheaper than any tour operator's if booked direct').

TOURIST INFORMATION
Tel 43 3687 61147
Fax 43 3687 6114713
Email info@rohrmoos.at
Web site www.rohrmoos.at

Söll and the SkiWelt

ALTITUDE 703m (2,306ft)

Beginners ✱✱✱ Intermediates ✱✱✱ Snowboarders ✱

Once the top package resort in Austria, with a reputation in the 1980s for excessive drinking, Söll is now focusing on family values. Anyone unimpressed by purpose-built, ski-in ski-out concrete buildings, who wants a reasonable amount of easy skiing at modest cost, and who does not mind a bit of accordion music, should consider Söll as a destination. It is a quiet, modern town of family homes, set back from the highway in open fields, and has minimal claims to Tyrolean charm. At the same time it is the hub of one of Austria's largest networks of interconnected pistes. Söll was a summer resort for walkers until skiing offered its 3,000 inhabitants winter work, hosting some 4,300 guests per week. Söll's car-free main street runs for less than 100m and is largely devoid of the overly cute, wooden architecture that is typical of the Tyrol. Shopping is limited to supermarkets and ski and souvenir shops. A free bus runs every 30 minutes to the gondola station.

✔ Short airport transfer
✔ Friendly, low-key atmosphere
✔ Value-for-money
✔ Westendorf recommended for families
✗ Low-altitude skiing
✗ Short season
✗ Bus ride from town to lifts

Officially dubbed the SkiWelt Wilder Kaiser-Brixental, the region counts 93 lifts and 250km of pistes spread around an oval of nine resorts measuring 150 sq km, sandwiched between the Kitzbüheler Alps to the south and the craggy Wilder Kaiser peaks to the north. It is only 70km from Innsbruck and within easy reach of the German border. Although skiing began here as early as 1948, when Europe's longest chair-lift was built in **Hopfgarten**, Söll's own lifts were not seriously developed until the 1960s, and links to the SkiWelt were not finished before the 1970s. All the skiing in the region is well below 2,000m but an extensive range of 250 snow-cannon cover most of the lower slopes, allowing skiing into April when temperatures permit.

The British make up 20 per cent of what is a youngish clientèle, in which influxes of Scandinavians and Dutch outnumber the Germans. Nightlife at weekends is hectic, with several bars hosting live music. However, there is only one disco of note.

Children under seven ski free, and those 16 and under receive discounts of more than 40 per cent, as do women of any age on Wednesdays from January onwards each season.

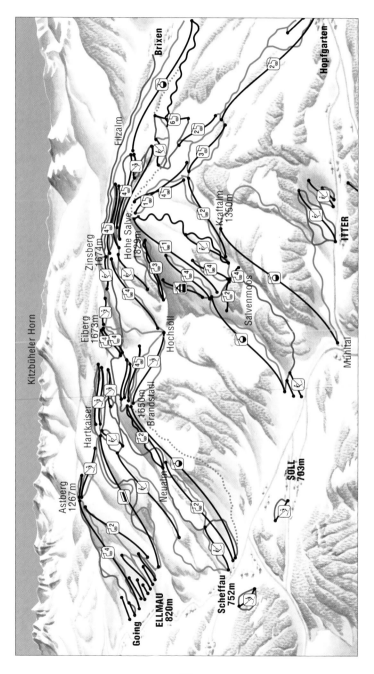

On the snow
top 1,829m (6,001ft) bottom 622m (2,040ft)

Söll's skiing starts with a free, 15-minute bus ride across the resort to a modern eight-person gondola. The ancient single chair above this has now been replaced by a second eight-person gondola that takes you swiftly up to Hohe Salve, which at 1,829m is the highest point in the Main Skiwelt circuit (although Westendorf has higher skiing).

Thanks to a lift capacity of more than 123,000 skiers per hour, SkiWelt queues seldom exceed 20 minutes. Additional snowmaking now covers the run down to the village. Grooming standards are ensured by 45 snowcats, which run all night. *Pistenhilfe* security patrols have been introduced with the aim of eliminating 'piste rowdies' and aiding lost tourists.

From Hohe Salve it is possible to ski to seven of the SkiWelt resorts; Westendorf requires a short bus transfer from **Brixen**, and **Kelchsau** a less frequent and longer bus trip from the village of Hopfgarten. Advanced terrain is often limited by a lack of respectable snow depth. The SkiWelt is primarily suited to beginners and undemanding intermediates who do not mind short runs and uphill traverses. There is no ski bus itinerary connecting the resorts, so care must be taken when skiing far afield.

Beginners
The SkiWelt has more than 100km of blue (easy) runs. Most beginner areas are at the base of the ski area, where the snow often melts away. **Scheffau** is the only resort with a top-to-bottom blue piste. Söll has a simple, wooded run from mid-mountain. Zinsberg and Brandstadl offer ample easy terrain.

Intermediates
More than half the pistes in the SkiWelt are graded intermediate, but short runs down to lifts, rather than long itineraries from village to village, are the rule. The red (intermediate) trail in the sun down to Hopfgarten, and the less exposed run down to Söll from Hohe Salve, are good cruisers, as is the 7.5-km Kraftalm run to **Itter**.

Advanced
From Hohe Salve the Lärchenhang is one of the unmarked local runs on the north side, where a bowl region called Mulde (now marked on the piste map) presents some challenge and a reasonable pitch.

Off-piste
Short, steep sections that require ducking under warning ropes do appear in Westendorf and are regularly skied by locals. The SkiWelt offers a wealth of guided ski-tours, for example Brechhorn, which demands little uphill effort when there is enough snow to make powder skiing possible.

Snowboarding

Brixen, Westendorf and Scheffau have official freestyle pistes, while Söll has a well-maintained terrain park above Salvenmoos with a half-pipe and some jumps. The mainly gentle and undulating terrain of the SkiWelt is ideal for first-timers.

Tuition and guiding

More than 450 ski teachers in 16 SkiWelt ski schools specialise in making skiing fun for beginners. The standard of English is high. Söll's three schools promise – but do not guarantee – that, by the end of their first week, pupils will make it all the way from the very top to the very bottom of the area.

Mountain restaurants

The SkiWelt lists a total of 63 mountain eateries, six of which are above Söll, and most suffer from peak-season lunchtime crowds. Schernthannstuberl is praised for its 'fairly large choice, big portions and hot food'. Self-service and simple meals abound. Stöcklalm, Kraftalm and Gründalm are typical, unexceptional inns, all with terraces and wide panoramas. Hochschwendt is said to be the cheapest. The glass-walled Siglu Bar at **Hochsöll** is popular with children.

Accommodation

Four of Söll's 70 hotels are rated four-star and the remainder are reasonably priced inns and guesthouses. The main hotel is the four-star Postwirt (☎ 533 5081) with its distinctive stuccoed exterior and an outdoor heated swimming-pool. The Alpenschlössl (☎ 533 6400) is even more luxurious, with an indoor waterfall, but it is a 30-minute walk from the centre. Other hotels include the lively Christophorus (☎ 533 5264) as well as the out-of-town Agerhof (☎ 533 5340).

Eating in and out

Most visitors are on hotel half-board packages. For Austrian coffee-and-cakes it is worth making the hike to Panorama for the view (and the food), and the modest Söller Stube on the main street merits a visit. Schindlhaus is advertised as a gourmet restaurant. Venezia and Don Giovanni ('pizzas the size of car wheels') serve cheap Italian fare.

Après-ski

At the Whisky Mühle, scantily clad go-go girls (and boys) kick away each Friday night until 3am. The Dorfstadl in the Hotel Tyrol comes a poor second. Salvenstadl is a new bar with live music. Buffaloes has a Wild West theme.

Childcare

The Söll-Hochsöll Ski School has the most extensive programmes for children of all ages. Bobo's Children's Club is part of this school and accepts children from five to 14 years of age. Bobo the Penguin is the symbol of an Austrian association that guarantees English-speaking, certified teachers. The Mini-Club takes children from three to five years.

Linked or nearby resorts

Brixen im Thale
top 1,829m (6,001ft) bottom 800m (2,624ft)

At the far end of the SkiWelt is the last fully connected resort of the area. It boasts 2,700 beds but as yet no British tour operators come here. A six-person gondola and covered high-speed chair lead up to Hohe Salve. The Parade Pub next to the lift station is unique in the SkiWelt, if not in the Alps: a computer monitors demand for specific drinks, then raises or lowers prices to provide the ultimate in 'demand economy' drinking. Gustl's Treff is a favourite hangout for snowboarders.

TOURIST INFORMATION
Tel 43 5334 8433
Fax 43 5334 8332
Email brixen@skiwelt.at
Web site www.brixenimthale.at

Ellmau
top 1,829m (6,001ft) bottom 820m (2,690ft)

With 4,900 beds, Ellmau is the biggest SkiWelt resort. Its 20 lifts include what is advertised as the fastest, most modern funicular in Austria. Toboggan runs are floodlit at night. Hotel Christoph (☎ 5358 3535), a five-minute walk from the funicular, is described as 'excellent, with helpful staff and good food'. Sporthotel Ellmau (☎ 5358 3755) is a four-star with an indoor swimming-pool. Most luxurious of all is the five-star Relais & Chateaux Hochfilzer (☎ 5358 2501), which has a fitness and beauty centre. Ellmau's nightlife rivals that of Söll, with Pub Memory, Ellmauer Alm, Heldenbar and the Tenne all lively destinations. For children there are the Kaiserbad water chutes and adventure swimming-park. Adult activities include hang-gliding, ice-climbing, an indoor climbing wall and parapente.

The Ellmauer Skischule teaches cross-country and telemark. Children up to four years old can be cared for at the Krabbelstube.

TOURIST INFORMATION
Tel 43 5358 2301
Fax 43 5358 3443
Email ellmau@netway.at
Web site www.ellmau.com

Going
top 1,829m (6,001ft) bottom 800m (2,624ft)

Fully linked into the SkiWelt, with the best views of the Wilder Kaiser and a large nursery slope, Going is beginning to be noticed by the

British, not least because of the exceptional five-star Hotel Stanglwirt (☎ 5358 2000), which has indoor swimming, tennis and a Lipizzaner riding school. Going has its own ski and snowboard school.

TOURIST INFORMATION
Tel 43 5358 2438
Fax 43 5358 3501
Email going@netway.at
Web site www.going.at

Hopfgarten
top 1,829m (6,001ft) bottom 622m (2,040ft)
Few British skiers take advantage of the 2,000 beds in Hopfgarten, which has become a favourite with young Australian package tourists. Access to the top of Hohe Salve requires three chair-lift rides. There is floodlit tobogganing, and the quiet chalet-style village is dominated by the twin yellow towers of the impressive local church. Spirited nightlife and dancing can be found at the 02 disco and the Cin-Cin. Accommodation includes Sporthotel Fuchs (☎ 5335 2420) and Aparthotel Hopfgarten (☎ 5335 3920).

TOURIST INFORMATION
Tel 43 5335 2322
Fax 43 5335 2630
Email info@hopfgarten.tirol.at
Web site www.hopfgarten.com

Itter
top 1,829m (6,001ft) bottom 703m (2,306ft)
Itter has only 850 visitor beds, but a fast gondola with no queues for the uphill journey, plus the longest run in the SkiWelt (8km), make it a quieter, cheaper alternative to Söll. The Schidisco in Gasthof Schusterhof (☎ 5335 2681) and the Dorfpub are perhaps not up to the decibel level of Söll but sufficient for most. Sporthotel Tirolerhof (☎ 5335 2690) has a bowling alley. Leo Fuchs is the ski school for adults and children.

TOURIST INFORMATION
Tel 43 5335 2670
Fax 43 5335 3028
Email tvb-itter@netway.at
Web site www.tiscover.com/itter

Scheffau
top 1,829m (6,001ft) bottom 752m (2,467ft)
Scheffau has only 2,200 beds and 15 lifts serving 23km of pistes, which begin at a gondola situated awkwardly across the main road from the sprawling village. Scheffau's hotel guests have their own queue-free

Skiing facts: Söll

TOURIST INFORMATION
Postfach 21, A-6306 Söll, Tyrol
Tel 43 5333 5216
Fax 43 5333 6180
Email info@soell.com / info@skiwelt.at
Web site www.soell.com /
www.skiwelt.at

THE RESORT
By road Calais 1,108km
By rail Kufstein 15km, St Johann 25km,
Wörgl 15km
Airport transfer Munich 2hrs,
Salzburg 1hr, Innsbruck 45mins
Visitor beds 4,000
Transport free bus between village and
ski area

THE SKIING
Linked or nearby resorts Brixen (l),
Ellmau (l), Going (l), Hopfgarten (l), Itter
(l), Kelchsau (n), Kirchberg (n), Kitzbühel
(n), Scheffau (l), Westendorf (n)
Number of lifts 12 in Söll, 93 in SkiWelt
Total of trails/pistes 34km in Söll,
250km in SkiWelt (43% easy,
51% intermediate, 6% difficult)
Beginners 8 lifts and 22 runs in area

LIFT PASSES
Area pass SkiWelt (covers all lifts in
area) ATS1,686–1,968 for 6 days
Pensioners 10% reduction for 60yrs
and over
Credit cards no

TUITION
Skiing Söll–Hochsöll (☎ 5333 5454),
Austria Söll (☎ 5333 5005),
Ski & Snowboard School Pro Söll
(☎ 5332 72610)
Snowboarding Freaks on Snow
(☎ 664 341 8409), and as ski schools
Other courses cross-country, extreme
skiing, freestyle, moguls,
race training, skiing for the disabled,
ski safari, ski-touring, snowblading,
telemark
Guiding through ski schools

CHILDREN
Lift pass 6–16yrs SkiWelt
ATS963–1,115
Ski & board school as adults
Kindergarten (ski) Bobo's Children's
Club, (non-ski) Mini-Club Söll–Hochsöll
(for both ☎ 5333 5454)

OTHER SPORTS
Curling, floodlit toboggan run, hang-
gliding, horse-riding, night-skiing,
parapente, skating, ski-touring,
squash, sleigh rides, swimming

FOOD AND DRINK
Coffee ATS25–30, glass of wine
ATS28–55, small beer ATS26–35,
soft drink ATS23–30,
dish of the day ATS120–140

VIP lift access. The Brandstadl bowl keeps its snow cover better than
the sunnier slopes across in Söll, and Scheffau has more than its share
of the SkiWelt's snowmaking. CC-Pub, Conny's Corner and the Pub
Royal are the only nightspots.

TOURIST INFORMATION
Tel 43 5358 7373
Fax 43 5358 73737
Email info@scheffau.com
Web site www.scheffau.com

Westendorf
top 1,892m (6,001ft) bottom 800m (2,624ft)

Westendorf's broad shoulder of open pistes looks steep from the valley floor. It is more snow-sure than elsewhere in the SkiWelt, and skiing on the 45km of pistes goes up to a higher altitude and can be more challenging. However, flat roads between lifts are an irritating feature, as is the 1-km distance between the modern gondola and the town. The resort is not connected by lift to the rest of SkiWelt, but a regular ski bus plies between Brixen and the resort.

Westendorf is one of the most attractive of all the SkiWelt villages and has a genuine Tyrolean atmosphere coupled with a vigour lacking in some of the others. Its substantial accommodation base of 3,775 beds, almost equal to Söll's, makes for lively entertainment, with 'acid house' at Gerry's Inn, 'techno' at the Wunderbar, and 'jello' shots at the Mosquito Bar. Four-star Hotel Jakobwirt (☎ 5334 6245) is praised for its 'friendly staff, good food, good facilities and a central location'. The other four-stars are the Glockenstuhl (☎ 5334 6175) and the Schermer (☎ 5334 6268). Hotel Post (☎ 5334 6202) is recommended as a family hotel and described as 'well located, the staff were friendly, and the atmosphere at the bar was terrific. The owner, George, kept giving the youngsters lollipops and chocolates.'

Pistes in the Brechhorn area are said to be 'an absolute dream, anyone could negotiate them'. The resort boasts three ski and board schools. Reporters recommended Ski School Top for its more personal service. Ski School Westendorf is warmly praised: 'we were a group of three families all in different classes and all of us were satisfied. The instructors spoke great English.' Westendorf's other ski and board schools are Skischule/Snowboardschule Ideal and Schischule Top. Courses on offer include cross-country, skiing for the disabled, snowblading and telemark.

TOURIST INFORMATION
Tel 43 5334 6230
Fax 43 5334 2390
Email westendorf@netway.at
Web site www.westendorf.com

St Anton

ALTITUDE 1,304m (4,278ft)

Intermediates ✳✳✳ Advanced ✳✳✳ Snowboarders ✳✳✳

St Anton is to skiing what St Andrews is to golf. The Arlberg region, of which St Anton is the capital, is the birthplace of modern technique and in part responsible for the way in which we ski today. The awesome quality of the mountains means that St Anton's star has never faded. Other resorts have since risen to dominate the world stage, but St Anton still ranks among the top five for truly challenging skiing. In 2001 St Anton was the venue for the World Ski Championships. Six years of hard work were blighted by unprecedented rain that delayed the races, but considerable improvements have been made to both the town and the lifts as a lasting legacy. The resort's hands-free 'smart card' lift pass works efficiently.

- ✔ Extensive off-piste
- ✔ Large ski area
- ✔ Ski-touring opportunities
- ✔ Efficient lift system
- ✔ Lively après-ski
- ✗ Few activities for non-skiers
- ✗ Crowded pistes

The percentage of snowboarders here is lower than in most European resorts, largely because the steep and usually heavily-mogulled main pistes are suitable only for the extremely proficient rider. However, the freeriding in the powder and among the trees is quite sensational. St Anton is twinned with the ski resort of Mount Buller in southern Australia, and attracts a large number of Australians who work here.

Skiing came to the Arlberg in the late nineteenth century. St Anton became accessible to the outside world in 1884 when the railway tunnel under the Arlberg Pass was completed. As early as 1895 the pastor of Lech visited his parishioners on skis. In 1921 Hannes Schneider opened the Arlberg Ski School. Generations of Europeans grew up with the distinctive Arlberg technique – skis clamped together, shoulders facing down the hill – a contrived yet elegant style that dominated the sport until the French, and in particular Jean-Claude Killy, declared stylistic war during the 1960s.

St Anton is as easy to get to from Zurich as from Munich or Innsbruck. One major drawback has been that the village was bisected by the railway line. However, in preparation for World Ski Championships, the railway line was shifted 200m to the south side of the valley.

The giant reception centre built on the former site for the games has been turned into a sports hall and greatly enhances the resort's amenities. The new station has been built underground, which has

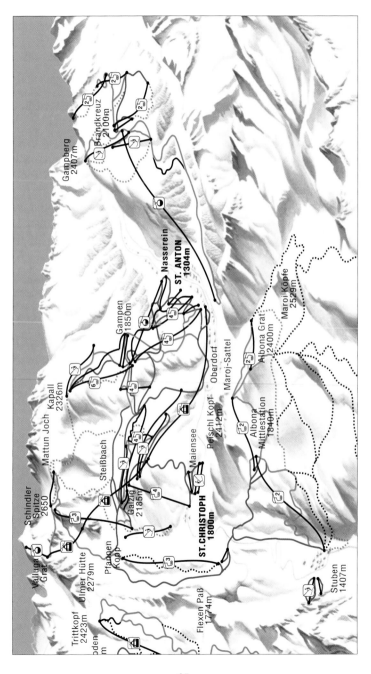

transformed the village centre. Skiers no longer have to cross over or under the tracks to reach the slopes.

The undistinguished village architecture is a blend of old and new that owes little to planning and much to those who recognised an opportunity and seized it before the current strict zoning regulations came into force. A fierce policy of no outside ownership, no holiday homes and no expansion in the number of guest beds has saved St Anton from otherwise inevitable blight.

The centre is a relatively peaceful pedestrian zone lined with shops, cafés and St Anton's handsome traditional hotels. The rest of the town straggles along the road in both directions, towards Mooserkreuz to the west, and towards the satellite villages of **Nasserein** and **St Jakob** to the east. Nasserein is now fully accessible from St Anton, with a new chair-lift from the village to Gampen. But it is an isolated place in which to stay. The shuttle bus does not run in the evening, and the nightlife is limited to local bars unless you are prepared for a 20-minute walk.

On the snow
top 2,811m (9,222ft) bottom 1,304m (4,278ft)

The Arlberg Ski Pass covers the linked area of St Anton, **St Christoph** and **Stuben**, as well as **Klösterle** and the more famous villages of **Lech** and **Zürs**. A free ski bus links the ski areas.

St Anton's skiing takes place on both sides of the valley, but the most challenging area is on the northern slopes dominated by the 2,811-m Valluga. The old lifts on the Galzig and in St Christoph have been systematically replaced by covered quad-chairs, which have done much to improve mountain access.

The high-speed quad-chair to Gampen takes the morning strain off the Galzig cable-car. The new Nasserein gondola was also a major improvement. However, the predictable result is that the volume of people has not been reduced but simply moved from the lift queue to the piste. The large number of snow-users – even in January – can be frightening. In the afternoon skiers and boarders jostle for position on the home run like Parisian taxi drivers. Anyone lacking in courage or technique feels wholly intimidated. However, a new blue (easy) run down from Galzig has gone some way towards alleviating the problem.

At mid-mountain level, the ski area splits into two, separated by a valley. Gampen, at 1,850m, is a sunny plateau with a six-person chair-lift rising to the higher slopes of Kapall at 2,333m. Galzig is the focal point of the serious skiing and riding. From Galzig you can ski down to St Christoph at 1,800m, a small hamlet crowned by the Hotel Arlberg-Hospiz. Above Galzig lie the more sublime challenges of the Valluga and the Schindlergrat at 2,650m. The Valluga is reached by a second and oversubscribed cable-car from Galzig, which has a confusing and unsatisfactory numbered-ticket system. You take a ticket and ask the lift attendant to translate it into a time so that you know when to return. The alternative is to ski down into the valley behind Galzig and take the quad up to the Schindlergrat. The skiing from here is some of the best in St Anton.

The Rendl at 2,100m is a separate ski area on the other side of the St Anton valley and is reached by the Rendlbahn gondola, a short ski bus ride from town. It offers interesting and often uncrowded skiing and catches so much sun that its local nickname is Rendl Beach.

Beginners

St Anton is not a beginner's resort, and anyone less than a confident intermediate would be well-advised to avoid it. The few blue slopes would nearly all be classified as intermediate elsewhere ('some of the blues would be enough to put beginners off for life'). Even the crowded main run back into the village is seen as a challenging red (intermediate) by most skiers.

Three learner pistes with their own T-bars are spread between Nasserein and the funicular railway. The Gampen has a children's ski area and a gentle T-bar. St Christoph has its own beginner piste and lift. Those with a little experience may also find some of the runs on the Rendl negotiable.

Intermediates

Confident intermediates head for Galzig. The sunny slopes below are served by the Osthang high-speed quad, and the main runs are sufficiently self-contained to encourage confidence but vary considerably in degree of difficulty. A delightful and easy blue run takes you down into St Christoph, and a quad-chair has been built to replace the old cable-car for the return journey. The Osthang, a fearsome bump run with a hostile camber, takes you back down towards St Anton, but there are other, less extreme, options. Timid skiers should note that St Anton has dispensed with black (difficult) runs in favour of unpisted ski routes, in what some critics see as a negation of responsibility. These appear on the map as either plain red or black-bordered diamonds. For red read black, for black-bordered read double-black.

Advanced

Depending on the snow conditions, almost all of St Anton's skiing can be considered advanced. From the Vallugagrat, three of St Anton's finest long runs lead back to the broad flat valley of the Steissbachtal, a corridor between the Valluga runs and those on the adjoining Kapall.

The toughest of the three is the Schindlerkar, a wide 30-degree mogul marathon that seems to go on for ever. Strong skiers can repeat it continually by riding the Schindlergratbahn triple chair-lift, but its south-facing aspect makes it vulnerable to early-morning ice and late-afternoon slush. The Mattun is a series of mogulled bowls linked by a traverse; it is less steep in pitch but more interesting because of the variety of its challenges. The third, much easier, option – the long dog-leg via the Ulmerhütte – opens up the Valluga to confident intermediates. It is also the starting point for the run to Stuben.

Off-piste

The off-piste possibilities are limitless, and a guide can find fresh powder a week after the last fall. An experienced skier wanting to enjoy St Anton to the full should view the services of a local guide as part of the basic cost of the holiday, along with accommodation and food. However, St Anton's mainly south-facing slopes harbour an extremely high avalanche risk.

The patio-sized top of the Valluga is accessed by a final six-person cable-car confined to sightseers, or skiers accompanied by a qualified guide. From the top it is possible to ski down the Pazieltal into Zürs and Lech. The valley itself is not difficult to ski, but the first few metres of the north face of the Valluga are terrifying, with a cliff ready to take away anyone who falls. The Malfon Valley over the back of the Rendl is a wide, enjoyable off-piste run which, when there is sufficient snow, ends on a road at the base of the lift. Above Stuben, a 20-minute walk up the Maroi Kopfe gives entry to the Maroi Valley.

Snowboarding

St Anton has some of the best snowboarding terrain in the whole of Austria, with a seemingly endless choice of natural obstacles and gullies, as well as steep powder fields and drop-offs. Gampen, Kapall and Rendl are particularly good areas to ride. Beginners will find the area steep, although Nasserein has some easier slopes. The Rendl has a terrain park with an obstacle course and a half-pipe.

Tuition and guiding

The Arlberg Ski School has 250 instructors, half of whom teach group ski-school classes at any one time while the other half are hired out as private guides. The rival St Anton Ski School, run by Franz Klimmer, has 60 instructors. Competition between the two is fierce, which helps to maintain standards, with class sizes usually restricted to ten. We have encouraging reports of both ski schools.

Alpine Faszination is a small, off-piste guiding service, which is strongly recommended by reporters. The rather pretentious-sounding St Anton am Arlberg Snowboard Academy is run under the banner of the Arlberg Ski School.

Mountain restaurants

According to reporters, most restaurants in the area offer reasonable fare at high-altitude prices. The Albonagrat seats only about 25 but is highly rated ('superb, great atmosphere, cheap food'). The bleak self-service at Galzig has panoramic views over the slopes and inevitably gets overcrowded, but it does have an adjoining table-service rest-aurant. The Sennhütte, Kaminstube and the Rodelhütte are all recommended. Stoppl's at St Christoph is popular. The terrace of the Arlberg-Hospiz-Alm is a particular favourite, with lunch served by waiters in traditional dress. The Hotel Post in Stuben and the Maiensee

Stube in St Christoph are both praised for 'warm, wood-panelled atmosphere and good food'.

Accommodation

The area has two five-star hotels: the historic and expensive Arlberg-Hospiz (☎ 5446 2611) at St Christoph and the modern St Antoner Hof (☎ 5446 2910) near the bypass. The four-star options are headed by the Neue Post (☎ 5446 2213) ('accommodation excellent') and the Hotel Alte Post (☎ 5446 2553), both much richer in tradition and closer to the lifts. St Anton has an abundance of chalets, as well as a large number of pensions and apartments.

Hotel Karl Schranz (☎ 5446 25550), owned by the former world champion, is said to be 'a very comfortable four-star with good food but quite far from the centre'. Hotel Arlberg (☎ 5446 22100) has 'excellent food and rooms, and friendly, helpful, English-speaking staff'. Those who find themselves uncomfortably far away from the ski slopes can leave their skis and boots overnight in the storage at the bottom of the Galzig cable-car.

Eating in and out

The standard of restaurants has greatly improved in recent years. The Arlberg Hospiz-Alm in St Christoph is transformed by night from mountain pit-stop to gourmet restaurant: 'the giant wine bottles in the cellar have to be seen to be believed'. The Hospiz itself is even more impressive, but more formal. The family-run Floriani is warmly recommended along with the Museum ('great food and an interesting collection of ski pictures and artefacts'). Regular St Anton visitors will be pleased to know that the old station building and its adjoining buffet, which was one of the best restaurants in town, have survived the railway's move intact. The Funky Chicken and Australian-run Pomodoro are both snowboarders' haunts, the latter offering 'fine pizzas and idiosyncratic Eastern Pacific music'. Sportcafé Schneider and the 60s-style Café Aquila are both praised. The Brunnenhof in St Jakob has 'some of the best food in the region'. Ferwall is a delightful restaurant reached by horse-drawn sleigh.

Après-ski

St Anton's undeniably vibrant après-ski scene starts to warm up from lunch-time in the Sennhütte before snow-users make their way down to the Mooserwirt just above the final descent to the resort. The Australian-inspired and Swedish-owned Krazy Kanguruh just above it is equally popular. A 4.5-m high yellow inflatable marsupial perched on the roof beckons thirsty skiers as they make their way home. Long before the lifts close for the day the bar is packed tighter than Bondi Beach. However, not all reports were favourable: 'we loathed the Krazy Kanguruh – I think we were too old'.

In the après-ski world of twenty-first century St Anton, the sedate tea-dancing of old has become 'beer-dancing' – with a pretty waitress administering Red Bull and vodka at £2 a shot. Most guests, after dancing in their ski boots and consuming copious amounts of alcohol, still manage to negotiate on skis the final 800m home in the dark. Down in the resort the action continues until sundown on the terrace of the Hotel Alte Post before switching to the Postkeller or to the Underground, which has live music. The St Antoner Hof bar is recommended for 'a quiet, sophisticated drink'. Scottie's Bar in the Hotel Rosanna is a rendezvous for Brits. After midnight the youth scene switches to the Piccadilly and Jonathan Verney's Kartouche, while the over 25s head for his revamped Kandahar. Only ten per cent of bars and clubs are now owned by Austrians.

Childcare

St Anton has done much to improve its previously inadequate facilities for small children. The Arlberg Ski School runs Kinderwelt, a kindergarten with four 'campuses': at the ski school meeting place, on the Gampen, in Nasserein and in St Christoph. Small skiers are accepted from two-and-a-half years of age as long as they are out of nappies. Kiki Club, run by the St Anton ski school, runs ski classes for children.

Linked or nearby resorts

Stuben
top 2,811m (9,222ft) bottom 1,407m (4,616ft)
The village was named after the warm parlour – or *stube* – of a solitary house on the Arlberg Pass where pilgrims used to shelter in the eighteenth century. Only 32 houses have been added since then, and Stuben has a mere 104 residents and 650 guest beds. The Post (☎ 5582 7610), now a four-star hotel, was where mail-coach drivers changed horses for the steep journey up the pass. With its small collection of hotels and restaurants, Stuben is an ideal base for the Arlberg. Stuben Ski School has a pedigree that goes back to the beginning of alpine skiing.

TOURIST INFORMATION
Tel 43 5582 399
Fax 43 5582 3994
Email info@stuben.at
Web site www.stuben.com

St Christoph
top 2,811m (9,222ft) bottom 1,800m (5,906ft)
Further up the Arlberg Pass, St Christoph was the last dwelling place for the pilgrim making his way into the mountains. In 1386 a shepherd called Heinrich Findelkind von Kempten built a hospice on the pass with his own savings and manned it in the winter with two servants. The Brotherhood of St Christoph (a charitable foundation of locals inspired by von Kempten) still exists, but the hospice burned

Skiing facts: St Anton

TOURIST INFORMATION
A-6580 St Anton am Arlberg
Tel 43 5446 22690
Fax 43 5446 2532
Email st.anton@netway.at
Web site www.stantonamarlberg.com

THE RESORT
By road Calais 1,092km
By rail station in resort
Airport transfer Innsbruck 1hr,
Zurich 2–3hrs, Munich 3–4hrs
Visitor beds 8,900
Transport free ski bus

THE SKIING
Linked or nearby resorts St Christoph
(l), Klösterle (n), Lech (n), Pettneu (n),
Stuben (l), Zürs (n)
Number of lifts 41 (85 on Arlberg
Ski Pass)
Total of trails/pistes 260km of prepared
pistes (25% easy, 40% intermediate,
25% difficult, 10% very difficult)
Beginners 8 lifts, points cards available

LIFT PASSES
Area pass Arlberg Ski Pass (covers St
Anton, St Christoph, Stuben, Lech, Zürs,
Klösterle) ATS2,120–2,360 for 6 days
Pensioners ATS1,802–2,006 for 6 days
for women 60yrs and over and men 65yrs

and over. Over 75yrs ATS100 for whole
season
Credit cards no

TUITION
Skiing Arlberg Ski School (☎ 5446 3411),
St Anton Ski School (☎ 5446 3563),
Stuben Ski School (☎ 6682 217)
Snowboarding as ski schools
Other courses cross-country, heli-
skiing, off-piste, ski-touring, telemark
Guiding Alpine Faszination
(☎ 5447 5105) and through ski schools

CHILDREN
Lift pass Arlberg Ski Pass, 7–15yrs,
ATS1,280–1,420 for 6 days. 6yrs and
under, ATS140 for whole season
Ski & board school as adults
Kindergarten (ski/non-ski) Kinderwelt
(☎ 5446 2526), Kiki Club (☎ 5446
3563)

OTHER SPORTS
Curling, floodlit tobogganing, indoor
tennis and squash, paragliding, sleigh
rides, swimming

FOOD AND DRINK
Coffee ATS25, glass of wine ATS50 ,
small beer ATS35, soft drink ATS30,
dish of the day ATS130–250

down in 1957. The five-star Arlberg-Hospiz hotel (☎ 5446 2611) was
built on the site. St Christoph has five other hotels as well as the
Bundessportheim Ski Academy.

TOURIST INFORMATION
Tel/fax as St Anton

Wildschönau

ALTITUDE 830m (2,722ft)

Beginners ✱✱ Intermediates ✱

The Wildschönau, its name dating from the twelfth century and roughly translated as 'wild beauty', is a quiet corner of the Tyrol within sight of the ski slopes of both **Alpbach** and **Söll**, about 70km from Innsbruck on the edge of the Kitzbüheler Alps. The region is made up of four resorts – **Niederau**, **Oberau**, **Auffach** and **Thierbach** – which sprawl for kilometres along the highway, each with its own small centre. Niederau is the best known but it has neither the best skiing nor is it the biggest village in the Wildschönau. However, it is the most popular with British skiers, who make up a significant proportion of an otherwise predominantly German market (the border is only 20km away).

- ✔ High standard of accommodation
- ✔ Short airport transfer
- ✔ Reasonable prices
- ✘ Lack of long runs (Niederau)
- ✘ Exceptionally limited skiing network
- ✘ Low altitude
- ✘ Short ski season

The appeal of Wildschönau, with its 29 lifts and 42km of low-altitude pistes, seems to be its very benign slopes (56 per cent of them are classified as easy). Skiing began here in 1947, with the first chair-lift built in the Tyrol. Oberau (3km from Niederau) is the Wildschönau's regional centre and has an impressive Benedictine church and a year-round population of 1,850. Apart from a kitsch woodcutter's chalet, Auffach is a village of non-descript modern buildings.

Niederau, Auffach and Oberau are linked by 13 free buses per day. The old silver-mining village of Thierbach has only two drag-lifts and 500 beds among a local population of 200, but boasts an elevation of 1,150m.

On the snow
top 1,903m (6,243ft) bottom 830m (2,722ft)

From Niederau's gondola station, it is only seven minutes to the top at Markbachjoch (1,500m), where traversing uphill left or right leads to a total of three pisted runs back to the bottom. Niederau has ten lifts, eight of which are drags, and Oberau has a further seven short drag-lifts. Auffach offers the region's best skiing, with slopes rising to 1,903m, but it is not featured in any British tour operator's brochure. The resort's modern four-person gondola rises in two stages through woods to a series of five parallel drag-lifts that are all high (between 1,500m and 1,900m).

Beginners

Despite being touted by tour operators as a resort for beginners, the Wildschönau is exceptionally limited even in relatively snow-sure beginner terrain. It has three drag-lifts serving nursery slopes near the gondola and two more beginner drags that are a 15- to 20-minute hike away. There is no blue (easy) route down to Niederau from the mountain top, and only three very short blues at the top for those who do commute up and down from the village.

Intermediates

An experienced intermediate who happens to find him- or herself in the Wildschönau will enjoy the Lanerköpfl International Ski Federation (FIS) downhill course. Auffach's four drag-lifts to the skier's left of the gondola serve exclusively red (intermediate) pistes, with some areas left unpisted. Auffach has the longest, most satisfying intermediate run in the region, with 1,000 vertical metres of enjoyable cruising.

Advanced

Niederau has two ski routes down the fall-line to the skier's right of the gondola, and the black (difficult) racecourse Lanerköpfl, which would challenge any advanced skier provided it is taken in a tuck from top to bottom. Day trips are possible to **Mühltal** and **Roggenboden**.

Off-piste

The Wildschönau's rounded, low-lying hills make for easy ski-tours when snow conditions allow for powder skiing. A black (difficult) itinerary route from the summit of the Schatsberg that takes you down to the valley floor beyond Auffach can be entertaining in the right conditions.

Snowboarding

There is nothing much to recommend the resort to riders, although Auffach does have a basic terrain park and a half-pipe.

Tuition and guiding

Niederau has two schools, Activ and Wildschönau, with the former the better prepared of the two for ski-touring. Both have ample experience with beginners, and English is widely spoken. Oberau has the Happy Schischule and Auffach's is called the Hochtal.

Mountain restaurants

The Wildschönau region has a total of seven mountain restaurants. At the top of Niederau, Rudi's Markbachjoch is cosy with its blue curtains and sanded pine tables, and is celebrated for its plum pancakes. Auffach's Schatbergalm and Koglmoos are large self-service inns. The Anton Graf Hütte in Niederau is an authentic touring hut.

Accommodation

Hotel Sonnschein (☎ 5339 8353) in Niederau is 'in a class of its own: indoor pool, excellent half-board meals and sumptuous rooms'. The older Hotel Austria (☎ 5339 8188) also offers an indoor swimming-pool but is criticised for its standard of accommodation ('disappointing for four-star rating, with the half-board food rather plain and uninter-esting'). The Hotel Silberberger (☎ 5339 8407) in Oberau is warmly praised along with the Angerhof (☎ 5339 8402). Oberau accommo-dates some 2,500 tourists in its central hotels, guesthouses and farms, including the Tirolerhof (☎ 5339 83160), which has a swimming-pool, and Gasthof Kellerwirt (☎ 5339 8116), an old monastery. Auffach's Gasthof Weissbacher (☎ 5339 8934) is popular, as is the three-star Gasthof Schatzbergalm (☎ 5339 8835).

Eating in and out

Most dining is done in hotels and guesthouses. In Niederau, Café Lois provides extremely filling pizzas, while Hotel Sonnschein provides 'good food in agreeable surroundings'. Sport Café-Pub displays antique radios and TVs and serves cheap sausage and chips. Gasthof Kellerwirt in Oberau serves appetising cuisine.

Après-ski

Zither and harp evenings, with Tyrolean costume, are regular hotel events. Sean plays the guitar at the Hotel Vicky, which now boasts a number of British and Irish brews on tap. Serious drinking takes place at the Cave Bar, while the Dorfstuben is more salubrious. Others include Bobo's, Sport Café-Pub and Treff. Almbar provides a disco. The Avalanche Pub in Auffach slides from afternoon to early morning (3pm to 3am), and Carlie's Pub is the other après-ski venue. Oberau's SnoBlau Pub is quite active. Sports available include hang-gliding, horse-riding, night-skiing, parapente, skating, sleigh rides, snowbiking, snowshoeing, swimming and floodlit tobogganing.

Childcare

All four ski schools give lessons to children from four years of age, and the Wildschönau school minds children from two years of age indoors. Children under six ski for free.

TOURIST INFORMATION
Tel 43 5339 8255
Fax 43 5339 2433
Email info@wildschoenau.tirol.at
Web site www.wildschoenau.com

Zell am See

ALTITUDE 750m (2,460ft)

Beginners ✳✳   Intermediates ✳✳✳   Snowboarders ✳✳

Zell am See is an attractive medieval town at the gateway to Austria's highest mountain, the Grossglockner. It is just one hour by road from Salzburg and is bypassed by a 10-km tunnel, which takes all the through-traffic underground from the satellite of **Schüttdorf** to the northern end of the lake. The town was first settled by a monastic order in the eighth century. Its medieval guest-houses and shops cluster around a smart pedestrianised centre with a tenth-century tower.

Zell am See's summer trade is almost as important as its winter trade, and the resort's huge international popularity rests on its hard-to-beat geographical setting at the foot of the 2,000-m Schmittenhöhe.

The mountain provides an ample amount of easy intermediate skiing, and the towering presence of the Kitzsteinhorn above neighbouring **Kaprun** means that snow is guaranteed in winter. Kaprun has one of the best developed glaciers in Austria. When winter cover is sparse elsewhere, its slopes become a daily point of pilgrimage for thousands of tourists from other resorts in Salzburgerland, and overcrowding here can be unacceptable. Access to and from the mountain is now restricted to the gondola since the tragic train fire of November 2000, in which 155 skiers died. The train tunnel is likely to remain permanently closed as a memorial to the dead.

The glacier used to offer year-round skiing on the upper slopes. However, in recent years the ice has shrunk alarmingly and its summer snow record is now by no means reliable. In June 2001 the glacier was closed for ten days as well as for a further ten days in September.

Kaprun and Zell am See market themselves jointly as the Europa Sport Region. The shared ski pass provides a total of 130km of skiing and access to 55 lifts. Mountain facilities have improved, although Zell prides itself on its 'green' image and has vowed to replace old lifts but not to build any new ones. The focus on uphill transport has switched from the slow and overcrowded Schmittenhöhe cable-car to Schüttdorf. From here, the Areitbahn gondola has been extended so that the summit can now be reached in just 20 minutes.

> ✔ Facilities for non-skiers
> ✔ Short airport transfer
> ✔ Extensive cross-country skiing
> ✔ Attractive pedestrian centre
> ✔ Lively nightlife
> ✔ Year-round skiing on Kitzsteinhorn Glacier
> ✘ Overcrowding at peak periods
> ✘ Lack of skiing convenience

From Schmittental, 2km from the centre of Zell, the old Schmittenhöhe cable-car rises sedately to the summit, or a second cable-car takes you into the Sonnalm area on the sunny, south-facing side of the bowl, which is served by two more chairs and a drag-lift. A considerable number of skiers prefer to start the day on the Areitbahn gondola at Schüttdorf. The free bus runs every 20 minutes.

The pretty village of Kaprun, a five-minute journey by road, also has its own ski area above the village comprising mainly blue (easy) runs. The best of Kaprun's skiing is on the Kitzsteinhorn Glacier, 20 minutes by bus from Zell. A gondola, followed by a quad-chair, take you up to the Alpincenter at 2,450m, where lifts whisk you on up to the top of the ski area at 3,029m. The glacier offers good but exposed blue and red runs.

Beginners
The main novice slopes at Zell are on the top of the Schmittenhöhe, and you will need to take the lift down again at the end of the day. There are also nursery slopes at the bottom of the cable-car and at Schüttdorf. Kaprun has its own winter nursery slope on the edge of the village as well as extensive easy runs on the glacier.

Intermediates
On the south side of the Schmittenhöhe, a succession of gentle, broad and sunny pistes descend along the ridge and on down to Schüttdorf. A right fork takes you to Areitalm, which is the arrival point for the first stage of the gondola from Schüttdorf; the cruising piste down from here to the bottom does not keep its snow in warm weather. The Sonnalm area also provides plenty of easy cruising.

Advanced
The two black (difficult) runs that branch off over the southern lip of the bowl provide the best advanced terrain. These soon steepen into testing, but not intimidating, long runs with the occasional pitch of almost 30 degrees. The other two runs to the base-stations are less severe but receive more sun.

Off-piste
Zell's environmental policy means that off-piste skiing is restricted to the point of being almost forbidden. After a fresh fall, a number of tree-line runs look particularly enticing, but the protection of saplings is a priority, and you risk confiscation of your lift pass if you ski them.

Snowboarding
Zell am See is excellent for beginner riders and has a permanent half-pipe. However, boarders should note that the small amount of off-piste on the Schmittenhöhe is not open to riders. Kaprun, with its glacier, is the more attractive destination, and its terrain is well suited to intermediate freeriders. The terrain park has a half-pipe, which is in operation (snow permitting) all year round.

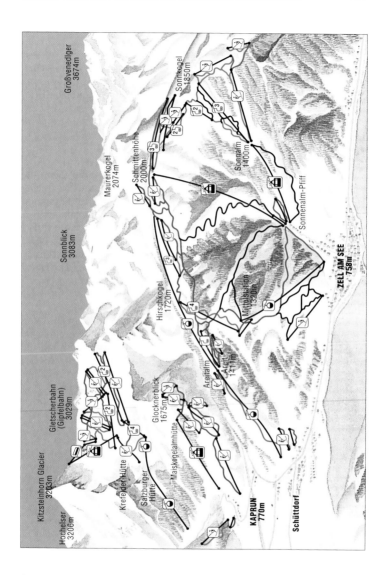

On the snow
top 1,965m (6,445ft) bottom 750m (2,460ft)

In winter 2000–1 the region was blighted by insufficient early snow from which it never recovered. In a normal season, the Schmittenhöhe's moderate slopes provide long, gentle red (intermediate) runs both back down to the village and along the southern flank to Schüttdorf. Steeper slopes drop from a bowl and provide the resort's most challenging skiing.

107

Tuition and guiding

Ski and snowboard schools in the valley seem to vary in quality, and we have mixed reports of the schools in the region. None of them has priority in the lift lines, so it is not worth taking lessons just to jump the queues. The Wallner-Prenner ski school is no more and has been replaced by Schischule Zell am See. The Schmittenhöhe receives considerable praise. The Kitzsteinhorn Ski School in Kaprun operates all year round and has a high standard of instruction.

Mountain restaurants

Zell am See has a good choice of mountain eating-places (the Schmittenhöhe alone has nine); although these are crowded during busy weeks, prices are reasonable. The black run down from Sonnalm has a pleasant hut for those who can get to it. The Sonnenalm-Pfiff is praised for its 'delicious hot chocolate'. Schmiedhofalm has amazing views from its sunny terrace. The mid-station restaurant serves 'huge and excellent *Kaiserschmarren* (chopped pancake with stewed plums). Glocknerhaus, on the way down to Schüttdorf, is also popular. Hans' Schnapps Bar on the summit has a live rock band two days a week.

Accommodation

The luxurious Grand Hotel (☎ 6542 788), jutting out over the lake, and the five-star Salzburgerhof (☎ 6542 765) are the most comfortable hotels in town. The four-stars are the Alpin (☎ 6542 769) and the Sporthotel Alpenblick (☎ 6542 5433). Hotel Bellevue (☎ 6542 73104) is a recommended three-star, and Hotel St Georg (☎ 6542 768) has smart, pine-panelled rooms and views of the lake. Hotel Berner (☎ 6542 779), set above the town, has a heated outdoor swimming-pool and is popular with reporters ('decorated in a rather grand style, but the owners and staff are friendly').

Eating in and out

The Steinerwirt is considered the best value for money, along with the Kupferkessel and the Saustall. Hotel St Georg has a pleasant restaurant with good-quality food. The Ampere, Landhotel Erlhof and the Salzburgerhof are also recommended for their high standard of cuisine. The Baum-Bar in Kaprun has a large restaurant in a conservatory.

Après-ski

Zell am See is lively by any standards. Once the lifts have closed for the day the first stop is a choice of the Kellerbar of the Hotel Schwebebahn near the lifts, Café Feinschmeck, with its vast variety of pastries, and the Mösshammer in the main square, which also serves coffee and cakes. Tea-dancing still exists in Zell, and a number of reporters have enjoyed watching major-league ice-hockey matches. The Crazy Daisy bar is a focal point for Anglo-Saxon visitors. The Kellerbar of the Hotel zum Hirschen is bustling, and you can relax in the main bar of the Tirolerhof

Skiing facts: Zell am See

TOURIST INFORMATION
Brucker Bundesstr. 3, A-5700
Zell am See
Tel 43 6542 770
Fax 43 6542 72032
Email est@gold.at
Web site www.zellkaprun.com

THE RESORT
By road Calais 1,184km
By rail station in resort
Airport transfer Salzburg 1hr
Visitor beds 13,800
Transport free ski bus

THE SKIING
Linked or nearby resorts Kaprun (l),
Maria Alm (n), Saalbach-
Hinterglemm (n)
Number of lifts 28 in Zell am See,
27 in Kaprun
Total of trails/pistes 75km in Zell am
See (38% easy, 50% intermediate,
12% difficult), 130km in linked area
Beginners 2 lifts in Zell am See, 2 lifts in
Kaprun, points tickets available
Summer skiing 15 lifts on
Kitzsteinhorn Glacier

LIFT PASSES
Area pass Europa Sport Region (covers
Zell am See, Kaprun, Saalbach-
Hinterglemm) ATS1,880–2,050
for 6 days
Pensioners ATS1,850 for women 60yrs
and over, men 65yrs and over
Credit cards yes

TUITION
Skiing Zell am See: Schmittenhöhe
(☎ 6542 732070), Skischule Zell am
See Areitbahn (☎ 6542 56020), Sport
Alpin (☎ 664 4531417), Thumersbach
(☎ 6542 73579). Kaprun: Hartweger
(☎ 6547 7766), Kaprun (☎ 6547
8070), Kitzsteinhorn (☎ 6547 8621 363),
Professional (☎ 6547 7562),
Oberschneider (☎ 6547 8232)
Snowboarding as ski schools, FOT
Snowboard Academy (☎ 6547 7760)
Other courses cross-country, moguls,
race camps on Kitzsteinhorn, skiing for
the disabled, telemark
Guiding Safari in Austria (☎ 6643
361487)

CHILDREN
Lift pass 6–15yrs ATS1,145–1,200 for
6 days, free for 6yrs and under if
accompanied by parent
Ski and board school as adults
Kindergarten (ski/non-ski) Play & Fun
(☎ 6542 56020)

OTHER SPORTS
Curling, hang-gliding, horse-riding,
hot-air ballooning, ice-climbing, ice-
driving, ice-hockey, indoor tennis and
squash, luge, parapente, shooting range,
skating, ski jumping, sleigh rides, snow-
rafting, snowshoeing, swimming, tubing

FOOD AND DRINK
Coffee ATS28–30, glass of wine
ATS28–30, small beer ATS28–32, soft
drink ATS25, dish of the day ATS90–280

and at the same time hear yourself think. Late-night action switches to
the Viva nightclub, which swings on until dawn, Evergreens for the
over 25s, and the Diele Bar, which attracts a young crowd.

Childcare

The children's facilities here are generally favourable, with a kindergarten taking children from 12 months and the ski kindergarten from two years. Ski lessons are given at all the ski schools from the age of four. The Grand Hotel and the Feriendorf Hagleitner both run crèches.

Linked or nearby resorts

Kaprun
top 3,029m (9,938ft) bottom 770m (2,526ft)

This is a delightful, typical Austrian holiday village, set a few kilometres back into the mountains from the lakeside and connected to Zell am See by a free day-time bus service. Although this is a thriving resort with new hotel and apartment developments, Kaprun has managed to retain its essential village atmosphere. However, it will take a generation for the village to recover fully from the tragic train fire of November 2000 in which so many locals – particularly teenagers – died.

The four-star Orgler Hotel (☎ 6547 8205) has comfortable accommodation and one of the best restaurants. The Sonnblick (☎ 6547 8301) and the Kaprunserhof (☎ 6547 7234) cater for families. We have good reports of the Salzburgerhof B&B (☎ 6547 8601) and Pension Heidi (☎ 6547 8223). The village has a handful of shops and restaurants. A decent attempt has been made at providing nightlife for visitors, who range from holiday skiers to racers in training during the summer months. Kitsch and Bitter has a live band mid-week. Mandy's Music Bar, Take Two, the Pavillon and the Yeti Klinikbar are all lively. The Baum-Bar has a late-night disco, while the Austrian Pub attracts snowboarders. The Optimum sports centre contains an indoor swimming-pool with a giant water-slide.

TOURIST INFORMATION
Tel 43 6547 8643–0
Fax 43 6547 8192
Email kaprun@kaprun.net
Web site www.europa-sport-region.com

Round-up

Bad Kleinkirchheim
top 2,000m (6,560ft) bottom 1,080m (3,543ft)

Bad Kleinkirchheim – or BKK as it is usually known – is the home resort of the Austrian super-hero Franz Klammer. As one reporter put it: 'what is good enough for Franz is good enough for me'. These days the greatest of all Austrian downhill champions spends more time in Colorado than in Carinthia, but the old spa town and thriving summer resort continues to develop its skiing in his absence.

The ski area is linked to the neighbouring village of **St Oswald**, and together the two provide 85km of mainly intermediate pistes served by 32 lifts. BKK is quite spread out and has a wide choice of hotels: these include the stylish Thermenhotel Ronacher (☎ 4240 282) and Hotel Pulverer-Thermenwelt (☎ 4240 744). The après-ski is limited to a few bars, discos, restaurants, and excellent spa facilities.

With the top lifts reaching 2,000m, the ski area is low; snow conditions are consequently unreliable both early and late in the season. However, some 50km of slopes are covered by a battery of 350 snow-cannon. The World Cup downhill course was designed by Klammer himself and includes a sequence of jumps that, even when prepared as a recreational run, require considerable concentration. Most runs are wide and gentle, and queues are reported during high season. The lift pass also covers the neighbouring resorts of St Oswald and **Falkert**.

Both the BKK and St Oswald ski schools give group and private tuition in skiing, snowboarding and cross-country – St Oswald's being on its 42km of loipe. Three- to six-year-olds can attend the kindergarten for full or half days, where a mixture of games and skiing is offered. BKK actively encourages snowboarders, with a floodlit terrain park and the Crazy Carving Company snowboard school. This school is part of Ski and Sportschule Krainer, which also offers the more unusual options of snowbiking, ice-tennis and ice-surfing.

TOURIST INFORMATION
Tel 43 4240 8212
Fax 43 4240 8537
Email bkaefer@bkk.at
Web site www.bkk.at

Fieberbrunn
top 2,020m (6,627ft) bottom 800m (2,625ft)

Ten kilometres up the road from **St Johann in Tirol** is the sprawling village of Fieberbrunn. Its small but attractive ski area is north-facing and is known as a *schneeloch*, or snowpocket. Mountain access should be enormously improved by the building of a gondola for 2001–2 in place of the Doischberg T-bar. The main skiing is at tree-level, with 13 lifts giving access to a small network of mainly long and easy runs totalling 35km. There are two rival ski schools – Rosenegg and Fieberbrunn – and we have favourable reports of both. The resort kindergarten takes children aged one to ten years.

TOURIST INFORMATION
Tel 43 5354 56304
Fax 43 5354 52606
Email info@fieberbrunn-tirol.at
Web site www.fieberbrunn-tirol.at

Gargellen
top 2,300m (7,546ft) bottom 1,430m (4,692ft)

Gargellen is a chalet-style village in the Montafon area. A variety of hotels include the four-star Madrisa (☎ 5557 630), which was built at the beginning of the twentieth century as a private home and opened as a hotel in the 1920s. It has 120 beds, a nightclub, swimming-pool and fitness centre. The resort itself boasts eight lifts, including an eight-person gondola due to be opened in 2002. There are 33km of pistes, extensive off-piste, and free ski buses connect Gargellen to neighbouring resorts. Ski and Snowboard Schule Gargellen offers all-day lessons as well as off-piste skiing and a children's ski school. The village kindergarten accepts children from two years old. Other activities in the resort include canyoning, curling and parapente. The further Montafon resorts of **Gaschurn** and **St Gallenkirch** are both within easy reach.

TOURIST INFORMATION
Tel 43 5557 6303
Fax 43 5557 6690
Email tourismus@gargellen.to
Web site www.gargellen.to

Serfaus
top 2,684m (8,806ft) bottom 1,427m (4,682ft)

The exclusive resort of Serfaus boasts many luxury modern hotels, which attract a mainly Austrian and German clientèle. The resort is car-free and has an unusual underground railway, which runs on air cushions rather like a hovercraft. This transports snow-users from the far end of the village to the ski lifts and contributes to the peaceful atmosphere in the resort. The Serfaus ski area is linked to the villages of **Fiss** and **Ladis**, making a total of 53 lifts serving some 160km of piste. The nursery slopes have three drag-lifts. The ski school offers daily lessons in skiing and snowboarding, with classes meeting in the Komperdell area at the top of the cable-car. Off-piste guiding and ski-touring are available, and there is also a ski kindergarten. Mini-Treff is the non-ski kindergarten. Other activities include cross-country on 60km of trails.

TOURIST INFORMATION
Tel 43 5476 62390
Fax 43 5476 6813
Email info@serfaus.tirol.at
Web site www.serfaus.com

Sölden
top 3,250m (10,663ft) bottom 1,377m (4,517ft)

Sölden is a high-altitude, and therefore snow-sure, resort that is spread out along the main road in the upper reaches of the isolated Ötz Valley. The resort stretches for more than 2km along the valley floor on either side of the road and river. Although it is an unmemorable sprawl of hotels, restaurants and bars, Sölden has considerable atmosphere and it would be uncharitable to dismiss the whole as unattractive.

The skiing is suited mainly to intermediates. The two developed glaciers, Rettenbach and Tiefenbach, have now been linked into the main ski system, ensuring complete snow security. Together with the revamped Giggijochbahn and the Gaislachkoglbahn, these bring the total to 34 lifts serving 141km of mainly easy-to-intermediate piste in this vastly expanded area. The vertical drop is substantial by Austrian standards. Sölden's ski area is in two sections linked by chairs up both walls of the narrow Rettenbachtal, which provides the toll road up to the glaciers. The Glacier Express gondola forms the link between the two. Both sectors are reached by gondolas from either end of the village, which are in turn linked by a ski bus that runs efficiently every ten minutes. **Hochsölden** is a collection of hotels set 700m up the mountainside on a shelf, giving dramatic views of the Ötztal and easy access to the slopes.

Sölden is a popular spot for riders, with three ski schools. The terrain park at Giggijoch contains a half-pipe, boardercross course and a range of interesting obstacles and jumps. A second terrain park, on the Rettenbach Glacier, is open in autumn when snow allows.

The choice of mountain restaurants is large: Gampealm, Eugen's Obstlerhütte and Löple Alm are all authentic huts with plenty of Tyrolean atmosphere. Rotkogljoch has been enlarged but is 'still totally overcrowded'. Giggi Treff is recommended along with Gampe Thaya, Huhnersteigen, Schwarzkogerl and Silbertal.

The position of accommodation is important, and a hotel near one of the two main lift stations is a must. The Hotel Regina (☎ 5254 2301), right by the Gaislachkoglbahn, is strongly recommended. Gasthof Sonnenheim (☎ 5254 2276), in the same area, is praised for being 'extremely cheap'. Hotel Stefan (☎ 5254 2237) by the Giggijoch gondola station has a good restaurant, and Alpengasthof Grüner

(☎ 5254 2214) continues to receive praise, too. Other restaurants include s'Pfandl, which has 'interesting cuisine and a grass-clad roof', and Café Elisabeth is popular with the locals. The Gruner and the Waldcafé are 'always reliable'. Dominic is said to be the best eatery in the village. The Alpina, Stefan and Hubertus à la carte restaurants are also recommended, while Hotel Liebe Sonne has a cosy stübli.

The nightlife, at least in the high-season weeks, is buzzing to the point of being raucous. Café Philip at **Innerwald** has a lively atmosphere and is a gathering point for young people. The single-chair down from here runs until 6pm. The Hinterher, Dominic and Café Heiner are always crowded. Later in the evening, Jakob's Weinfassl attracts a 30-something clientèle. Discos includes the Alibi Bar in Hotel Central, which is the most sophisticated venue.

Apart from private babysitting, Sölden has no special facilities for non-skiing children. The Sölden/Hochsölden Ski School runs a ski kindergarten, with a play area for skiers aged three years or more. The revamped swimming-pool is 'complete with foliage and swirly bits'.

TOURIST INFORMATION
Tel 43 5254 5100
Fax 43 5254 510520
Email info@soelden.com
Web site www.soelden.com

St Johann im Pongau
top 2,188m (7,177ft) bottom 650m (2,132ft)

The four valleys of **Flachau**, **St Johann im Pongau**, **Wagrain** and **Zauchensee** lie only 45 minutes from Salzburg and provide a playground for intermediates. The statistics are impressive: a dozen resorts with 350km of linked (albeit not always on the mountain) skiing, served by 130 lifts all covered by one ski pass. St Johann itself (not to be confused with St Johann in Tirol) is a cathedral town that was all but devastated by a disastrous fire in 1852; as a consequence it lacks the medieval charm of Austria's other county towns and larger resorts.

The ski area, which is known as the Sportwelt Amadé, has always boasted one of the best-value lift passes in Austria. For the 2001–2 season, the region is included in the new Skiverbund Amadé lift pass, which covers 276 lifts serving 865km of piste in 30 ski areas.

Few British tour operators feature the region in their brochures as they cannot contract enough hotel beds to make its inclusion a commercial viability. Wagrain and Flachau are the most convenient and attractive bases from which to explore the circuit. St Johann has its own small, separate ski area, and the link into the Sportwelt Amadé is via the hamlet of **Alpendorf**, a 3-km ski bus ride away. The pistes in the area are well serviced with eating places, from small huts to larger self-services.

Each of the resorts has at least one ski school, and St Johann has four. We have encouraging reports of all of these as well as of those in Flachau. St Johann has a terrain park. Vitamin B and Board Unlimited are two specialist boarding schools in Alpendorf. Cross-country skiers are well served by 160km of trails along the valleys.

Accommodation in St Johann and Alpendorf includes the four-star Dorfhotel Tannenhof (☎ 6412 52310), the luxurious Sporthotel Alpenland (☎ 6412 70210), the three-star Hotel Brückenwirt-Tennerhof (☎ 6412 42590) and Gasthof-Pension Taxenbacher (☎ 6412 4288). The resort's nightlife is limited. The inconvenient bus journey to Alpendorf means that St Johann is not ideal for families.

The small village of Wagrain has fortunately been able to develop away from the minor road from St Johann to Flachau and **Radstadt**. Hotel Grafenwirt (☎ 6413 7162) is discreetly upmarket; Hotel Enzian (☎ 6413 8502) and the Wagrainerhof (☎ 6413 8204) are also both recommended. The ski kindergarten accepts children from three years old.

Neighbouring Flachau, the home of the Austrian downhill champion Hermann Maier, has undergone considerable expansion in recent years. The main accommodation is in large chalet-style hotels and inns, as well as apartment blocks. Beginners learn to ski on a gentle piste in the village. There is a non-ski kindergarten, and the Griessenkar Ski School takes children from three years old. Flachau's recommended hotels include the four-star Vierjahreszeiten (☎ 6457 2981) and the luxurious Hotel Tauernhof (☎ 6457 23110).

The market town of **Altenmarkt** is a centre for the local sportswear and ski equipment industries. A modest ski area is linked to neighbouring Radstadt, but the main skiing is a bus ride away at Zauchensee or Flachau. The kindergarten cares for children from three years old. The pleasant village has 22 hotels, including six of a luxury standard.

Filzmoos is another small village in the Sportwelt Amadé, dating from the early twentieth century, when it was a popular holiday destination for the wealthy Viennese. Today it has a ski area served by 17 lifts, shared with neighbouring **Neuberg**. The **Dachstein Glacier** is only 18km away, and the rest of the Sportwelt Amadé is reached by bus via Flachau. The kindergarten takes children from three years old and has English-speaking staff. The choice of accommodation in 25 hotels and a selection of apartments is large in relation to the size of the village, which is famed as the hot-air ballooning capital of Austria.

TOURIST INFORMATION
Tel 43 6412 60360
Fax 43 6412 603674
Email info@stjohann.co.at
Web site www.stjohann.co.at

St Johann in Tirol
top 1,700m (5,576ft) bottom 680m (2,230ft)

St Johann in Tirol is a large, busy town with a ski area of 17 lifts. Its expansion from a pretty Tyrolean village to a sprawling light-industrial centre has done little for its charm. However, the centre, with its ornately frescoed buildings and old coaching inns, remains largely unspoilt, and the heavy traffic is confined to the outskirts. St Johann offers a pleasant setting for a lively and varied winter holiday at prices that are reasonable by Austrian standards. Queues are not usually a problem but are increased by weekend visitors from Innsbruck and Munich. In spite of this, the north-facing orientation of the slopes and competent grooming generally keep the slopes in fine condition.

The resort is particularly geared towards beginners, with six nursery-slope lifts scattered between the town and the hamlet of **Eichenhof**, which is served by ski bus. The rolling lower pastures are ideal novice terrain, with a choice of blue (easy) runs higher up, to which beginners can progress after a few days. Practically all the skiing on the top half of the mountain is graded red (intermediate), but the area is limited in size and lacks any real challenge. Another major drawback is the distance across town to the lifts – the skiing can be accessed from five different points, but all are a long walk or a bus ride away from the centre.

Both of the two ski schools offer snowboard tuition, and the resort has a terrain park with a 60-m half-pipe. Non-ski Miniclub St Johann cares for children under four years every day except Saturday. The Ski Kinderclub takes children from four years. The choice of 18 mountain restaurants is way above average for a resort of this size – almost every piste has a welcoming mountain hut at the top, bottom or part-way down. The cross-country skiing is extensive and covers 210km of prepared tracks from St Johann to **Erpfendorf**, **Going**, **Kirchdorf**, **Oberndorf** and **Waidring**.

The central feature of St Johann is the three-star Hotel Gasthof Post (☎ 5352 2230), which dates from 1225 and is beautifully frescoed. Hotel Park (☎ 5352 62226), near the gondola, is also recommended, and we have favourable reports of Hotel Fischer (☎ 5352 62332). Hotel Goldener Löwe (☎ 5352 62251) is strongly endorsed for families. St Johann's nightlife is young and vibrant: popular bars include Buny's, Max's and Café Rainer, which hosts a regular Tyrolean evening each Monday. The restaurant in the Gasthof Post is recommended, while Lange Mauer is a rare Austrian Chinese restaurant, and Masianco serves pizzas and Mexican food.

TOURIST INFORMATION
Tel 43 5352 63355
Fax 43 5352 65200
Email info@st.johann.tirol.at
Web site www.st.johann.tirol.at

Tiroler Zugspitze
top 2,964m (9,724ft) bottom 1,000m (3,280ft)

Lermoos and nearby **Ehrwald** are the principal villages of the Tiroler Zugspitze, a marketing consortium of small, separate ski areas, which share a lift pass, north-west of **Innsbruck** near the German border. The **Zugspitze**, at 2,964m is the highest and is reached by cable-cars from both Austria and Germany. **Biberwier** has installed a six-person chair-lift for the

2000–1 season, which should transform mountain access. Lermoos has nine lifts, Ehrwald eleven, Biberwier seven and **Zugspitze** ten.

Beginners can try the nursery slopes at the Lermoos base and graduate to a longer, gentle run by taking the gondola up Ehrwalder Alm. For intermediates, the Zugspitze Bowl offers wide pistes and easy red (intermediate) runs, which lead over the border into Germany. Advanced snow-users will find the area limited; there is one black (difficult) run on the Grubigstein above Lermoos. However, in good snow conditions you can ski down from the Zugspitze Glacier. The area has more than 100km of prepared loipe.

Lermooser Skischule, Ehrwalder and Total in Ehrwald are the three ski and snowboard schools, offering morning and afternoon tuition. Bergrettung is an off-piste guiding company based in Ehrwald. Bobo's is the ski kindergarten in Lermoos and Leo-Kinderhut is the crèche. Spielman's Hotel (☎ 5673 22250), on the edge of the village of Ehrwald, is a traditional, frescoed Tyrolean chalet. The owner and his son are both celebrated local climbers as well as being accomplished chefs who provide everything home-made.

In Lermoos, the Gasthof-Pension Lermooserhof (☎ 5673 2241) is said to be 'friendly, but too far out of town'. Reporters were enthusiastic about Hotel Post (☎ 5673 22810) in the centre. The Jux bar near the gondola base is the most popular meeting point at the end of the day. The post-dinner crowd move on to the Rustika Bar/Disco.

TOURIST INFORMATION
Tel (Lermoos) 43 5673 2401 / (Ehrwald) 43 5673 2395
Fax (Lermoos) 43 5673 2694 / (Ehrwald) 43 5673 3314
Email info@zugspitzarena.com
Web site www.zugspitzarena.com

Waidring
top 1,860m (6,102ft) bottom 780m (2,558ft)

This unspoilt village is less than 20km from St Johann in Tirol and is situated in the same snowpocket as Fieberbrunn. The quiet resort is known for its family skiing, with convenient nursery slopes in the village centre. It boasts 25km of piste served by ten lifts. The main skiing is at Steinplatte, 4km from the village, and is suited to beginners and intermediates.

There are five mountain restaurants on the slopes. The best hotel is the Waidringerhof (☎ 5353 5228), which has a swimming-pool and a pleasant dining-room. The central Hotel Tiroler Adler (☎ 5353 5311) is also recommended. The nightlife in Waidring is relaxed and informal, and the Schniedermann Bar and the Alte Schmiede are both popular.

TOURIST INFORMATION
Tel 43 5353 5242
Fax 43 5353 52424
Email waidring@netway.at
Web site www.tiscover.com/waidring

France

France has the best skiing in the world – the scale of the dozen top French destinations is truly stupefying – and this may explain why more British snow-users holiday here than in any other country. Myriad resorts – 319 to be exact – have been developed in France over the past 30 years, and those with international pretensions are far better equipped than their equivalents in Switzerland, Austria or Italy.

However, unlike their Alpine neighbours, most French resorts are purpose-built *stations de ski* that provide ski-in ski-out convenience often at a high cost to the ambience. The majority of accommodation provided is in apartments not hotels, and the first concrete *résidences* were built with rabbit-hutch rooms that are now considered far too cramped for the demands of today's tourists. Many reporters also complain that major French resorts are short on charm, with inadequate self-catering accommodation and overpriced restaurants and bars. They lack the overall appeal of their North American counterparts.

All that is about to change. Intrawest, the giant Canadian resort builder, is poised to bring about a revolution in the Tarentaise that will shake the French ski industry to its foundations. In partnership with Compagnie des Alpes, the largest lift company in the world (of which it owns 17.6 per cent), Intrawest is bringing North American ski know-how to Europe, complete with luxury condominiums and a level of customer care that is positively alien to the French. This should vastly improve the standard of ski and snowboard accommodation in France and a few more smiles from resort staff would be welcome. Work on the first European Intrawest village begins in Les Arcs in April 2002. Flaine is next in line for the makeover treatment and at least half-a-dozen French ski resorts should follow over the next ten years.

But can the Canadians improve French nightlife? With a few notable exceptions, such as Chamonix, Megève and Les Deux Alpes, après-ski in French resorts is subdued. In many resorts the only post-piste pastime for visitors is to prop up the neighbourhood bar or make their own entertainment in their chalets or apartments. The few discos are often grossly overpriced, underfrequented and play unrecognisable 'Euromusak'. However, none of these shortcomings seriously detracts from what the French resorts have to offer. The inescapable reason why more British now ski and snowboard in France than anywhere else in the world is because, taking every factor into consideration, there is simply nowhere better.

Alpe d'Huez

ALTITUDE 1,860m (6,100ft)

Beginners ✳✳✳ Intermediates ✳✳✳ Advanced ✳✳✳ Snowboarders ✳✳

Alpe d'Huez first opened as a resort in 1936 with a handful of tourist beds. At the time of the 1968 Olympics it was little more than a one-street Alpine village dominated by a futuristic modern church. The massive building surge that followed led to the resort spreading out in all directions in a plethora of architectural styles. Traffic remains a problem, although it must be pointed out that, as there is no through-road from the resort to anywhere else, it is more a question of overcrowded parking than busy main roads.

A bucket lift acts as the primary people-mover. A shuttle bus takes skiers up to the slopes from the lower reaches of what is a steep resort for pedestrians, although several reporters said there was no sign of a bus during their entire stay. Alpe d'Huez is one of the few resorts that can be reached directly by aircraft as it has its own altiport. **Les Deux Alpes** is several minutes away by helicopter or 45 minutes by road.

✔ Extensive ski area
✔ Sunny position
✔ Beautiful scenery
✔ Variety of mountain restaurants
✔ Widespread artificial snow
✔ Ideal for families
✔ Varied off-piste
✘ Lack of alpine charm
✘ Limited tree-skiing
✘ Weekend crowds
✘ Uninspiring nightlife

The 3,330-m summit of Pic Blanc dominates Les Grandes-Rousses, the fifth largest ski area in France and one of increasing importance to the British market. Alpe d'Huez is its capital and the hub of 230km of linked skiing served by 86 lifts. Though not a purpose-built resort, so great are the additions to the original village that it has all the convenience of one. The lower satellites of **Auris-en-Oisans**, **Oz Station**, **Vaujany** and **Villard-Reculas** have slowly developed as resorts in their own right.

Alpe d'Huez was one of the venues for the Killy Winter Olympics in 1968. For a while the village fathers toyed with the notion of cultivating the *exclusif* tag, which is attached to Megève and Courchevel 1850. In the end, the need to pay for what was then one of the most modern lift systems in the world pointed them in the direction of the mass-market. Sadly, lift upgrading has not continued at a seasonal pace, and although the gondolas are modern, a number of slow old chair-lifts are still in operation. The clientèle remains predominantly French, but Alpe d'Huez works hard at maintaining its international image.

On the snow
top 3,330m (10,922ft) bottom 1,100m (3,608ft)

Alpe d'Huez is a genuine all-round ski resort with excellent nursery slopes, good red (intermediate) runs, long black (difficult) trails and extremely serious off-piste opportunities. Mountain access is multiple: two main modern gondolas feed traffic out of the village into the Pic Blanc sector, and there are alternative routes at peak times. High-season queues for the first and particularly for the second stage of the main 25-person DMC gondola can develop into a scrum. Feeding more skiers into such a high-capacity system has an obvious downside, and the pistes immediately above the village (Les Chamois, Le Signal and Le Lac Blanc) are prone to overcrowding.

WHAT'S NEW
Four-seater chair replaces old two-seater on Sarenne Glacier
Additional snow-cannon at Villard-Reculas
Signal slope floodlit for night-skiing

The skiing as seen from Les Bergers lift station looks disarmingly mild: an open mountainside served by an array of gondolas and chair-lifts. However, skiers and snowboarders who have cut their teeth on the gentle pastures of the Tyrol will be shocked by the hidden severity of the skiing. Much of the Pic Blanc is concealed from sight by the lie of the land – from its 3,330-m summit in good snow conditions it is possible to ski more than 2,000m vertical down to well below Alpe d'Huez.

The area divides naturally into four main sectors: Pic Blanc, Signal de l'Homme/Auris, Signal/Villard-Reculas and Oz/Vaujany. The central part of the skiing takes place immediately north-east of the resort on sunny slopes and is reached via the two impressively efficient stages of the DMC gondola. Late in the season, some of the best skiing is to be in the Montfrais sector of Vaujany, which keeps its snow well.

The long-awaited second stage of the Marmotte gondola has opened up the Clocher de Mâcle area with a re-graded black piste. During the summer of 2001 the old two-person chair on the Sarenne Glacier is being replaced by a four-person chair-lift. There are plans to add a chair-lift below the chair as alternative access to the Sarenne Glacier. The Signal blue (easy) run is now floodlit three times a week throughout the winter for night-skiing/boarding.

Beginners
The first stage of the DMC gondola serves an enormous area of green (beginner) runs close to the resort. The Rif Nel piste is the gentlest of the long pistes from the base of the gondola back down to Les Bergers. All the satellites have nursery slopes, some of them more novice-friendly than others. Vaujany's ski area starts at Montfrais, a sunny balcony above the resort that is reached by gondola. Two drag-lifts give access to green and blue runs, which are ideal beginners' terrain.

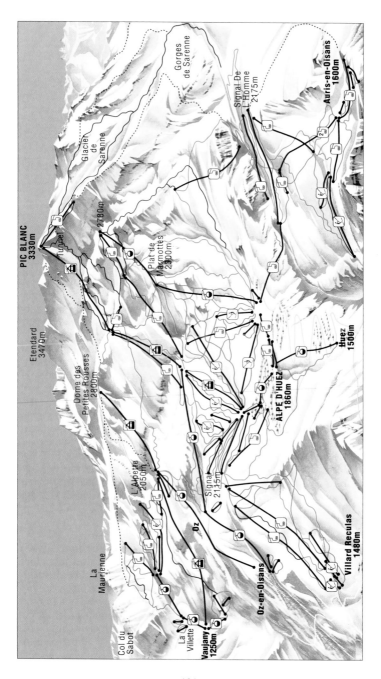

Intermediates

From the top of the DMC gondola try the long red Les Rousses. Take the usually mogulled and crowded first 100m slowly so as not to miss the path that cuts north-west beneath the cableway into the Vaujany sector. From here you can ski all the way down to Oz or Vaujany. Snow-cannon have been added along the 'wall' section. A wide and pleasant blue piste is L'Olympic from the top of Les Marmottes gondola, and the Chamois piste is a quiet alternative to the busy Couloir piste.

Signal is a rounded, snow-covered peak adjacent to Alpe d'Huez. It is reached by a four-seater chair or alternative drag-lifts and provides some varied intermediate runs, which are easily accessible from the heart of the village. Behind Signal, longer runs drop down the open slopes above the village of Villard-Reculas. A quad-chair allows mountain access from the village, regardless of snow cover.

Advanced

A largely under-used piste takes you all the way down to the hamlet of **L'Enversin d'Oz**, which is linked to Vaujany by a cluster gondola. From the summit of Pic Blanc this represents a mighty vertical of 2,330m, claimed to be the longest in the Alps (with lifts to take you back up again). The top of the Clocher de Mâcle chair-lift is the starting point for some interesting black runs. These include the beautiful Combe Charbonnière past Europe's highest disused coal mine; from here pistes lead either down into the Sarenne Gorge or back to the resort. The short run down from Clocher de Mâcle to Lac Blanc is steep, but the snow is usually good. From the top of Pic Blanc two black pistes, the Sarenne and the Château Noir, take you all the way down into the Sarenne Gorge and are claimed, at 16km, to be the longest black runs in the Alps. However, it should be pointed out that they derive most of their length from the run-out along the bottom of the gorge. Only some pitches of the Sarenne are really difficult.

The front face of Pic Blanc is accessed via a tunnel through the rock, 200m below the summit, with an awkward path at the end of it. The steep and often icy Tunnel mogul field that awaits you can be extremely daunting when no snow has fallen for some weeks. However, in fresh powder the pitch is near perfect and a new alternative path makes it viable for less accomplished skiers.

Off-piste

Opportunities for *ski sauvage* from the top of Pic Blanc are superb. Variations include the Grand Sablat, the Combe du Loup and a long and tricky descent via the Couloir de Fare. A 20-minute climb from the cable-car station takes you to the top of La Pyramide, the off-piste starting point for more than 2,000m of vertical, bringing you down through a range of gullies and open snowfields all the way to Vaujany or Oz. The top can be very icy, and ropes may be needed to negotiate the steeper couloirs in packed snow conditions. The off-piste variation from the ridge separating Oz from Alpe d'Huez is a gloriously steep powder field, which filters into the tree-studded gorge at the bottom. It is prone to avalanche and should be attempted only in the morning. There are seven itineraries in the area, all of which are marked on the piste map.

Snowboarding

The terrain park on the Signal piste has a tunnel and a fairly dramatic half-pipe which, along with a boardercross course, are open both day and night. The area has a considerable number of natural drop-offs and the entire mountain is well-suited to freeriders.

Tuition and guiding

The French Ski School (ESF) has 300 instructors based in Alpe d'Huez, Auris, Oz and Vaujany. Reports of the ESF are improving, and it now claims that two-thirds of the instructors are English-speaking. One reporter remarked that, although the initial impression of the ski school in Alpe d'Huez was one of 'total chaos, with hundreds of instructors and students jostling together', the instructors were 'always cheerful and friendly'. The International Ski School (ESI) offers ski and snowboarding classes restricted to eight, with tuition in English. The third mainstream ski and snowboarding school is Fun Evasion, and British Masterclass courses are held in Alpe d'Huez.

Mountain restaurants

Chez Patou, a stone hut below the top of the Alpette gondola on the Oz piste, offers farmhouse fare at reasonable prices. Les Airelles is a simple restaurant built into the rock at the top of the Montfrais nursery drag-lift above Vaujany. We have an improved report for La Cabane du Poutat, above Alpe d'Huez, where 'staff may be a little distant, but the menu is extensive'.

La Bergerie, on the red run down to Villard-Reculas, is an Alpine museum that doubles as a restaurant; the setting, complete with open fire and cow bells, is particularly attractive. The Chalet du Lac Besson, on the cross-country trail between the DMC gondola and Alpette, has a sunny terrace in a peaceful setting and offers some of the best mountain cuisine in the region. Equally good is the Chalet Alti-Bar next to the altiport at Alpe d'Huez. The food is delicious and you can sit on the terrace watching the private planes, helicopters and microlights take off and land.

Le Tetras in Auris serves fine pizzas and has a varied wine list. The Auberge Forêt de Maronne below Auris can usually be reached only in mid-winter via a choice of long blue or black runs through scenic Alpine meadows. Combe Haute in the Sarenne Gorge has a welcoming atmosphere and is renowned for its salads.

Accommodation

The higher up the hill you are staying, the easier it is to get to and from the skiing. The hard core of one four-star, (the Royal Ours Blanc (☎ 476 80 35 50), and eight three-star hotels is supported by numerous family-run hotels. The Christina (☎ 476 80 33 32) is friendly and charming and one of the few attractive chalet-style buildings at the top of the resort. Au Chamois d'Or (☎ 476 80 31 32) has a highly regarded restaurant. La Mariandre (☎ 476 80 66 03) is 'surprisingly good for a three-star'. Les Grandes Rousses (☎ 476 80 33 11) 'needs a complete makeover. Food is good, but there is no choice'. The best apartments include those in the Rocher Ensoleillé (☎ 476 80 62 55), which has its own outdoor heated swimming-pool and optional self-catering ('a little pokey but warm and comfortable'). Maeva's Les Bergers apartments (☎ 476 11 40 00) are recommended by reporters.

Eating in and out

Dining is an important business in Alpe d'Huez, a legacy from its more exclusive days ('this is one of our favourite pastimes, and Alpe d'Huez is an excellent place to indulge it'). There are more than 50 restaurants in the resort itself. Au P'tit Creux ('intimate atmosphere and wonderful, but avoid it at weekends') is one of the best restaurants here. Au Chamois d'Or and L'Outa vie with it as the principal centres for haute cuisine in town. Le Colporteur has a strong following. La Pomme de Pin is praised for its 'enormous helpings – a meal like this would have cost quite a lot more in the Home Counties'. Another reporter commented: 'this restaurant certainly isn't cheap but the food is absolutely first-class'. La Crémaillère and Le Génépi both offer mountain specialities. La Taverne is praised: 'the atmosphere is lively without being rowdy and the food is both first-class and reasonably priced'. Pizzeria l'Origan is 'friendly with a good range of pizzas and pasta'. The restaurant in Vaujany's Hotel Rissiou is open to non-residents and offers first-rate cuisine and wines. Supermarkets in Alpe d'Huez are adequate, and reporters recommended Les Bergers in the Centre Commercial.

Après-ski

The Cactus Café and the Underground have live music ('the Underground is small, crowded, and the floor is permanently under two inches of spilt beer'). Crowded House was 'full of severely under-age British youngsters'. Le P'tit Bar de l'Alpe has live blues every night. L'Avalanche is said to be 'lacking in atmosphere' with 'music and loud holidaymakers'. Le Sporting, which overlooks the skating rink, is 'a pleasant piano bar with an interesting and reasonably priced menu'. Smithy's Tavern screens live football matches on a giant TV screen. L'Etoile des Neiges is a typical French café. Alpe d'Huez sports four discos, including the Igloo and Crystal. Snowboarders will find the resort eminently affordable.

Childcare

The ESF ski school guarantees class sizes of no more than ten. However, one reporter said that 'we regularly saw classes of 13 or more small children during April high season'. The ESI gives lessons to children from three-and-a-half years and the ESF from four years old. Les Eterlous, next to its Club Med building, takes skiing and non-skiing chil-

Skiing facts: Alpe d'Huez

TOURIST INFORMATION
Place Paganon, BP 54, 38750 Alpe d'Huez
Tel 33 476 11 44 44
Fax 33 476 80 69 54
Email info@alpedhuez.com
Web site www.alpedhuez.com

THE RESORT
By road Calais 934km
By rail Grenoble 63km
Airport transfer Lyon 2hrs, Grenoble 1½ hrs
Visitor beds 32,000
Transport free ski bus

THE SKIING
Linked or nearby resorts Auris-en-Oisans (I), Les Deux Alpes (n), La Grave (n), Oz Station (I), Vaujany (I), Villard-Reculas (I)
Number of lifts 86
Total of trails/pistes 230km (36% beginner, 28% easy, 24% intermediate, 12% difficult)
Beginners 11 beginner lifts, 1 free at Alpe d'Huez
Summer skiing Sarenne Glacier (July–August)

LIFT PASSES
Area pass (covers linked resorts and 1 day in Les Deux Alpes, La Grave, Milky Way, Puy-St-Vincent) 1,103FF for 6 days
Pensioners 60yrs and over 780FF for 6 days, free for 70yrs and over
Credit cards yes

TUITION
Skiing ESF (☎ 476 80 31 69), ESI (☎ 476 80 42 77),

Fun Evasion (☎ 476 80 69 94), British Masterclass (☎ 01237 451099) (UK)
Snowboarding 5 Montaine (☎ 607 57 46 12), and as ski schools
Other courses cross-country, freestyle, indoor tennis and squash, moguls, mono-ski, night-skiing/boarding, race-training, ski extreme, ski and snowboard touring, skiing for the disabled, slalom, snow-blading, teen skiing, telemark
Guiding Bureau de Guides (☎ 476 80 42 55), SAF Isère Heliskiing (☎ 476 80 65 49), Stages Vallençant (☎ 476 80 98 40)

CHILDREN
Lift pass 5–16yrs 780FF for 6 days
Ski & board school as adults
Kindergarten (ski) La Garderie des Neiges (☎ as ESF), (ski/non-ski) Le Baby Club (ESI) (☎ 476 80 42 77), Les Eterlous (☎ 476 80 43 27), Les Crapouilloux (☎ 476 11 39 23)

OTHER SPORTS
Aeroclub, curling, frozen-waterfall-climbing, hang-gliding, helicopter rides, ice-climbing, ice-driving, indoor climbing wall, indoor archery and golf, indoor squash and tennis, luge, microlight, night-skiing/boarding, parapente, skating, snowcat trips, snowbiking, snowshoeing, swimming

FOOD AND DRINK
Coffee 15–20FF, glass of wine 18FF, small beer 15–25FF, soft drink 13–20FF, dish of the day 70–85FF

dren from three to eleven years of age. Les Crapouilloux is a crèche for children from two years old. Its staff will meet older children from ski school and take them to the crèche for lunch and afternoon supervision.

Linked or nearby resorts

Auris-en-Oisans
top 3,330m (10,922ft) bottom 1,600m (5,249ft)

Auris consists mainly of apartment blocks and, though somewhat isolated from the bulk of the skiing in Les Grandes-Rousses, is well positioned for outings to Les Deux Alpes, **Briançon/Serre Chevalier** and **La Grave**. The Hotel Beau Site (☎ 476 80 06 39) attracts predominantly French guests. Down the hillside in the old village is the more traditional Auberge de Forêt de Maronne (☎ 476 80 00 06) with its fine cuisine, as well as a variety of chalets and gîtes to rent.

TOURIST INFORMATION
Tel 33 476 80 13 52
Fax 33 476 80 20 16
Email auris-en-oisans@wanadoo.fr

Oz Station
top 3,330m (10,922ft) bottom 1,350m (4,429ft)

This small, purpose-built village lies above the old village of Oz-en-Oisans. It is reached by a fast all-weather road from the valley in only 20 minutes and thereby provides an excellent back door into the lift system. Two gondolas branch upwards in different directions, one to L'Alpette above Oz-en-Oisans and the other in two stages to the mid-station of the DMC gondola above Alpe d'Huez. The shopping and nightlife is limited. More accommodation is planned for the 2001–2 season. The village has an ESF ski and board school and a crèche that takes children from six months to six years old.

TOURIST INFORMATION
Tel 33 476 80 78 01
Fax 33 476 80 78 04
Email info@oz-en-oisans.com
Web site www.oz-en-oisans.com

Vaujany
top 3,330m (10,922ft) bottom 1,250m (4,101ft)

Vaujany is a sleepy farming community that would have slowly crumbled into agronomic oblivion but for a quirk of fate. Its fortunes took a turn for the better when compensation in the 1980s for a valley hydro-electric scheme made the village rich beyond its residents' wildest dreams. Oz benefited to a lesser extent from the scheme, and the two villages plunged their millions into the winter sports industry. This explains why Vaujany, an apparently impoverished mountain village, manages to own a state-of-the-art 160-person cable-car that still ranks among the top half-dozen in the world. No one has yet seen a queue here. A separate gondola provides slower alternative access to the main mountain via Vaujany's own attractive ski area of Montfrais.

Considerable, but considered, development is taking place, and a number of new chalets and apartments have been built. However, the community retains its rural atmosphere. There are four simple hotels in the village centre. The Rissiou (☎ 476 80 71 00) is under British management in winter and offers a good standard of accommodation. Nightlife centres on the bars of L'Etendard and the Rissiou. Two discos provide late-night entertainment.

Vaujany has what we consider to be one of the best-equipped crèches in the French Alps and, if you have small children, this is almost a reason in itself for choosing the resort. The age range here is from six months to six years old. The resort boasts a large indoor swimming-pool and health centre, and in the summer of 2001 a new shopping mall was being built above the cable-car station.

TOURIST INFORMATION
Tel 33 476 80 72 37
Fax 33 476 79 82 49
Email vaujany@icor.com
Web site www.vaujany.com

Villard-Reculas
top 3,330m (10,922ft) bottom 1,500m (4,921ft)

This rustic old village is linked into the ski area by a quad-chair-lift. Much has been done in recent years to renovate the village; a number of apartments now supplement the Beaux Monts (☎ 476 80 43 14) hotel and the converted cowsheds and barns. Sustenance is provided by one small supermarket and a couple of bars and restaurants, including the popular Bergerie. A blue (easy) piste from the bottom of the Petit Prince runs to the village, offering an alternative route to the steeper runs. The ESF has a branch in the village. The road to Allemont on the valley floor is wide and easily accessible in winter, but the one-track road to Huez is normally closed during the season.

TOURIST INFORMATION
Tel 33 476 80 45 69
Fax 33 476 80 45 69
Email info@villard-reculas.com
Web site none

Les Arcs

ALTITUDE 1,600–2,000m (5,249–6,560ft)

Beginners ✳✳✳ Intermediates ✳✳✳ Advanced ✳✳✳ Snowboarders ✳✳✳

In the early 1960s, during the boom years of skiing, a mountain guide called Robert Blanc had a vision of a new type of ski resort to be built above his local market town of **Bourg-St-Maurice**. In time he managed to create not one but three ski villages at different altitudes, all of them sharing one ski area. Plans to link this

✔ Large ski area
✔ Modern lift system
✔ Excellent children's facilities
✔ Skiing convenience
✔ Extensive off-piste
✔ Beautiful scenery
✘ Lack of alpine charm
✘ Limited après-ski

to neighbouring **La Plagne** to create one of the biggest ski circuits in Europe have been delayed for a year. However, work on the construction of the £10-million 200-person cable-car that will span the gorge between them has already started. For the present Les Arcs has 200km of groomed runs served by 76 lifts.

Even more exciting for Les Arcs is the development of a new North American-style village, which is likely to set the pattern for future resort development across the giant swathe of the Alps where the lifts are owned by the Compagnie des Alpes (CdA). Canadian resort-builder Intrawest, which is responsible for developing Whistler, Tremblant, Panorama, Keystone and Copper Mountain, has a 17.6 per cent share in CdA. Work starts in April 2002 on the new village – to be called **La Daille d'Arc 2000** – and is expected to take several years to complete. The finished apartments will be of the elevated standard that visitors to North America have come to expect.

The original village of Les Arcs, **Arc 1600**, opened in the winter of 1968. It consisted of one hotel and a few shops constructed on a plateau above Bourg. According to enthusiastic reporters, Arc 1600 is still the most compact and friendly place to stay.

Arc 1800, the largest and most cosmopolitan of the three villages, came on stream in 1975. Again it centred on one hotel and a collection of architecturally appealing apartment blocks. It has grown dramatically since it was first built and is now divided into three sub-villages of Le Charvet, Les Villards and Charmettoger. Arc 1800 is the heart of the three main villages and houses most of the accommodation, shops and après-ski.

The highest and bleakest centre is **Arc 2000**, which sits in its own secluded bowl at the foot of the main mountain, the Aiguille Rouge (3,226m), and is close to some of the best skiing. One reporter com-

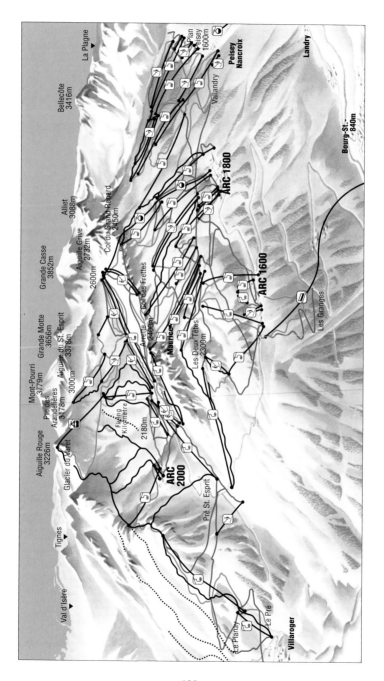

mented: 'it is to be avoided unless you want snow-sure skiing at the end of the season'. The new Intrawest village is to be situated just below it.

All three present villages are served by a road from Bourg-St-Maurice; however, the Arc en Ciel funicular takes just seven minutes to reach Arc 1600 from there. Although Les Arcs is partly car-free and the resorts are linked by bus, a car is useful to reach the other resorts available on the same lift pass.

Throughout the first half of the 1980s, Les Arcs led the way with a range of snow sports known as *les nouvelles glisses* – alternative ways of sliding down a mountain. The monoski was first seen here, and the snowboard made its European debut in the resort.

Les Arcs then fell upon troubled financial times but, under the ownership of CdA, it is now facing a considerably brighter future and is continuing to try hard after its decade out in the cold. Both the resort and the lift system are steadily being upgraded. The standard of piste marking is praised by reporters: 'every junction had signposts that would do any motorway proud'.

On the snow
top 3,226m (10,581ft) bottom 850m (2,788ft)

According to visitor surveys, the snow-users of Les Arcs want bump-free pistes – and that is what they get. Considerable time and money are spent ironing out moguls, and the result is a wealth of unusually long and smooth runs that start way above the tree-line and progress down through the woods to unspoilt villages such as **Le Pré** and **Villaroger**.

The greatest concentration of lifts, slopes and therefore skiers is above Arc 1800, where sunny and gentle pistes attract intermediates and families. The skiing above Arc 1600 is steeper and more wooded, with some rewarding off-piste opportunities. Another claim to fame of Les Arcs is its Olympic speed-skiing track on the face of the Aiguille Rouge, which can be tested by members of the public. With typical Les Arcs panache, the course has also been used to establish records for motorbikes and even mountain bikes.

Lift queues are not generally a problem, although there are a few exceptions. At the Carreley and Chantel chairs reporters came across 'huge queues until 10am and again at the end of the day'. Some found mid-afternoon crowds for the Vallandry chair-lift.

Beginners

One of Robert Blanc's legacies was *ski évolutif*, an easy means of learning that originated in America as GLM (graduated length method). As the name implies, you start on skis as short as 100cm and progress to longer skis as your technique and confidence improve. The advantage is that by learning to ski parallel from day one, you can become a competent intermediate skier by day six ('bravo for *ski évolutif* – within three days I was parallel skiing short skis'). To reach that stage, skiers have a choice of 10 green (beginner) runs. Each of the three villages has user-friendly nursery slopes close by, with the most extensive just above Arc

1800 around the altiport and Le Chantel area, and in the bowl above Arc 2000. Above Arc 1600, strong beginners and timid intermediates can enjoy the Mont Blanc trail, a 'wide, well-pisted run accessed by the Mont Blanc lift'.

Intermediates

As a rule, the bigger the ski area the more scope there is for intermediates, and Les Arcs is certainly no exception. Of the resort's 121 runs, more than half are divided between blue (easy) and red (intermediate) trails, and many of the reds are not difficult. The slopes above Arc 1800 are packed with relatively easy intermediate slopes. Good cruising runs are found between the Grand Col, Aiguille Grive and Arpette. Above **Peisey-Nancroix** and **Vallandry** there is much classic intermediate terrain. The Aigle and L'Ours reds are particularly recommended by reporters as 'nice, not too testing runs down through the trees'.

Advanced

The black (difficult) run down Comborcières to **Pré-St-Esprit** is one of the places where those who want to can still find testing moguls ('mogulled from head to foot'). But the classic run in Les Arcs is the 7-km descent from the top of the Aiguille Rouge all the way down to Le Pré and Villaroger, with a vertical drop of more than 2,000m. Among the 17 black runs, the Piste de L'Ours from Arpette is one of the most exciting descents.

Varet is a long, steep piste from the top of the Aiguille Rouge, which is a real challenge, especially in deep snow. The Robert Blanc piste is an excellent descent off the north face of the mountain. Droset, down to Pré-St-Esprit, is another testing run from the Aiguille Rouge. The Varet eight-person gondola gives easy access to a number of long black trails.

Off-piste

With so many off-piste opportunities in Les Arcs it really does pay, both in terms of safety and finding the best terrain, to hire a guide. In fresh snow conditions the most exhilarating and steepest powder skiing is below the Aiguille Rouge. Steep bowl-skiing is found beneath the Crête de L'Homme, accessed by a traverse to the right as you exit the Aiguille Rouge cable-car. Other decent off-piste is behind the Aiguille Grive and the Aiguille Rouge at the south-western edge of Arc 1800's ski area. Exciting off-piste descents start from the Grand Col to Villaroger, with the route continuing behind the Aiguille Rouge, and from the Aiguille Grive down to Peisey-Nancroix.

Snowboarding

The undulating contours of its slopes make Les Arcs ideal for snowboarding, and ever since the sport was introduced to Europe from America the resort has played an important role in establishing its popularity. The dedicated terrain park between Arc 1600 and 1800 has now been enlarged to incorporate seven jumps, a half-pipe and a boardercross course. The park is served by a chair and a shorter drag-lift, and international competitions are regularly held here. Freestylers favour the naturally wavy terrain of Les Deux Têtes black run and the red La Cachette. Hard-boot fans will enjoy Froides Fontaines, which is excellent for a carving work-out. The red Grand Renard is a natural downhill course, which is superb for big turns. The Peisey sector is well-suited to freeriders.

Tuition and guiding

Les Arcs has the French Ski School (ESF) in all three high-altitude villages ('the instructors spoke good English'), as well as Arc Aventures, and Ecole de Ski Virages, which are all based in Arc 1800. All the ski schools run snowboarding courses. Tip Top is a small specialist snowboard school operating from Arc 1600, while In Extremis is based in Arc 1800.

Mountain restaurants

Mountain eating-places are not a particular strength of Les Arcs, but we have some enthusiastic reports: 'in 13 years of skiing holidays we have never been at such a good mountain restaurant as Aiguille Grive. We had lunch there every day'. Some excellent rustic-style establishments exist in the lower hamlets, with Pré-St-Esprit, below Arc 2000, boasting two popular lunch spots. Of these, the rustic Bélliou La Fumée, a 500-year-old hunting lodge, is the more attractive.

The cosy Solliet restaurant on the way down to Villaroger receives good reports, and in nearby Le Pré the Aiguille Rouge and La Ferme attract lunchtime skiers when the long run down is open. In nearby **Le Planay**, Chez Léa is highly recommended for its wholesome food and attractive farmhouse setting. L'Ancolie at Nancroix, reached by bus from the bottom of the lift system at Peisey-Nancroix, 'serves outstanding food in an intimate atmosphere'.

Accommodation

About two-thirds of the skiers and snowboarders visiting Les Arcs stay in apartments and these are steadily improving. During the 2001–2 season the second phase of the luxurious MGM apartments (central booking service (☎ 479 07 68 00)) above Arc 1800 comes on stream along with Les Chalets des Neiges and Chalet Altitude, both in Arc 2000. Hotel du Golf (☎ 479 41 43 43) ('excellent, the food was of a high standard') is the largest and most central hotel in Arc 1800. The other three-stars are Hotel Club Latitudes (☎ 479 07 49 79) and Grand Hotel Mercure Coralia (☎ 479 07 65 00) ('bedrooms large, clean, with huge cupboards, and dinner was a tremendous experience. It was worth every franc').

La Cachette (☎ 479 07 70 50) at Arc 1600 has nurtured a reputation as one of the best family hotels in the Alps. It has been refurbished to a standard above its official three stars. Hotel Explorers (☎ 479 04 16 00) and Hotel Béguin (☎ 479 07 72 61) are both small and in 1600.

Skiing facts: Les Arcs

TOURIST INFORMATION
BP 45, F73706 Arc Cedex
Tel 33 479 07 12 57
Fax 33 479 07 45 96
Email lesarcs@lesarcs.com
Web site www.lesarcs.com

LONDON AGENT
Erna Low Consultants (see *Which tour operator?*)

THE RESORT
By road Calais 937km
By rail Bourg-St-Maurice 15km, buses and funicular to Arc 1600
Airport transfer Lyon 2½hrs, Chambéry 2hrs, Geneva 2½hrs
Visitor beds 28,000
Transport free shuttle bus between villages

THE SKIING
Linked or nearby resorts Bourg-St-Maurice (l), Peisey-Nancroix (l), La Plagne (n), Le Pré (l), Vallandry (l), Villaroger (l)
Number of lifts 76
Total of trails/pistes 200km (11% easy, 44% intermediate, 31% difficult, 14% very difficult)
Beginners 1 free lift in each centre

LIFT PASSES
Area pass Grand Domaine (covers Les Arcs, Villaroger, Peisey, Vallandry, La Plagne, and 1 day in La Rosière/The Trois Vallées/Tignes and Val d'Isère) 710–1,065FF for 6 days, 5% loyalty discount
Pensioners 60–74yrs 865FF for 6 days, free for 75yrs and over
Credit cards yes

TUITION
Skiing all centres: ESF (☎ 479 07 40 31), Optimum (☎ 01992 561085 in UK), 1800: Arc Aventures (☎ 479 07 41 28), Virages (☎ 479 07 78 82)
Snowboarding as ski schools, 1600: Tip Top (☎ 479 07 28 00), 1800: In Extremis (☎ 479 07 21 72)
Other courses cross-country, extreme skiing, heli-skiing/boarding, moguls, seniors, powder clinics, race-training, ski-évolutif, skiing for the disabled, ski orienteering, snowblading, speed skiing, teen skiing, telemark, women's clinics
Guiding Bureau des Guides (☎ 479 07 71 19)

CHILDREN
Lift pass 7–14yrs 905FF for 6 days
Ski & board school Arc Aventures, ESF, In Extremis, Tip Top, Virages
Kindergarten (ski/non-ski) 1600: La Cachette/ESF (☎ 479 07 70 50), 1800: Pomme de Pin (☎ 479 04 15 35), 2000: Les Marmottons (☎ 479 07 64 25), (non-ski) Bourg-St-Maurice: Pomme d'Api (☎ 479 07 59 31)

OTHER SPORTS
Climbing wall, dog-sledding, hang-gliding, horse-riding, ice-driving, night-skiing, paintballing, parapente, skating, ski-jöring, ski-jumping, sleigh rides, snowbiking, snowmobiling, snowscooting, snowshoeing, speed skiing, squash

FOOD AND DRINK
Coffee 8FF, glass of wine 12FF, small beer 12–18FF, soft drink 16FF, dish of the day 60–90FF

Les Mélèzes Hotel Club (☎ 479 07 50 50) and the popular two-star L'Aiguille Rouge (☎ 479 07 57 07) ('exceptional value') are both in Arc 2000, where there are two Club Med villages. Les Lauziers apartments in 1800 are convenient for the slopes but have their drawbacks ('a functional building with strange sloping floors; we didn't like the cramped and spartan interiors').

For those preferring to stay in the valley town of Bourg-St-Maurice, which is linked directly into the lift system and convenient for visiting other resorts such as **Val d'Isère**, the good-value Hostellerie du Petit-St-Bernard (☎ 479 07 04 32) has 'awful old soft beds', but is welcoming to families and has a 'quite superb, old-style French restaurant complete with snails and frog-legs'.

Eating in and out

The best choice of restaurants is at Arc 1800: L'Equipe is the biggest ('excellent for a posh meal, with Savoyard dishes and a fixed-price menu') but not necessarily the best. Casa Mia specialises in Italian food ('basically a pasta and pizza place, décor rustic – after a fashion – and the service was friendly and informal'), while L'Onglet and the Marmite (Le Charvet) and Le Coq Hardy (Villards) are also recommended. For value-for-money family fare the Laurus is worth visiting.

At Arc 2000, Le Red Rock is popular and informal with live music, and Le St Jacques is more intimate with higher prices. Latino Lococafé and Pierre Chaud are both praised. Les Chabottes at Pont Baudin near Peisey-Nancroix serves 'excellent local specialities at prices lower than at Arc 1800'.

Self-caterers will find a wider selection and lower prices in Bourg-St-Maurice, with its two hypermarkets on the outskirts of town. In Arc 1800 there are 'some fine bakeries, an expensive butcher and a small supermarket with limited fresh supplies'.

Visitors considering an outing to the traditional restaurants in outlying villages between Les Arcs and Bourg-St-Maurice should try the rustic Bois de Lune at Montvenix. Booking is recommended, and the restaurant will collect you and take you back. Chez Mimi at Vallandry, Chez Léa at Le Planay and L'Ancolie at Nancroix are other options.

Après-ski

Reporters are unanimous that Les Arcs suffers from a dearth of après-ski activity. When the lifts close in Arc 1800, skiers and instructors tend to divide themselves between two bars at Le Charvet (Le Gabotte and Le Thuria). At nearby Les Villards, much of the action is at the Pub Russel and the Saloon Bar, which features live music. At 2000 the Red Rock is the 'in' place for a *vin chaud*. The Hotel du Golf hosts live jazz and Le Fairway disco is in the basement. All three resorts have discos, including the Arcelle in 1600 and Rock Hill in Le Charvet, while snowboarders prefer the Carré Blanc in Les Villards.

Apocalypse at 1800 is 'wildly expensive'. The music at KL 92 in Arc 2000 is said to be sufficiently *sympa* to allow conversation. Reporters found the shopping area at Arc 1800 to be 'tacky – and smelling of chips, pizza and doughnuts'.

Childcare

Les Arcs has a three-kids grading, the highest of the Label Kid stamp of approval from the Ministry of Tourism, denoting that the resort offers children a safe environment with plenty of entertainment, toys and equipment. Babies aged four months and over are welcome in the day nurseries at La Cachette in Arc 1600 and at the Pomme d'Api in Bourg-St-Maurice. The nursery at Arc 1800 takes children from one year of age. Les Marmottons at Arc 2000 accepts children from two years. The ESF organises courses for children aged three years and over in Le Pomme de Pin club. Children from three-star level (intermediate) can enrol in Ski Nature courses to explore the mountain environment, learn map reading and discover animal tracks in the snow. All the adult ski and snowboard schools offer tuition for children.

Linked or nearby resorts

Peisey–Nancroix/Vallandry
top 3,226m (10,581ft) bottom 1,350–1,600m (4,428–5,248ft)

Snow-users in Les Arcs tend to regard this cluster of villages at the south-western end of the ski area as a useful tree-level bolt hole in bad weather. French families, who have been coming here since World War II, prefer to think of it as a peaceful, undemanding ski area of 12 lifts that is occasionally invaded by Johnny-come-latelys from Les Arcs. These villages of some 9,500 beds offer a more rural setting and a cheaper accommodation base for the region and will link by cable-car with La Plagne for the 2002–3 season. **Peisey** is a traditional farming community, and **Nancroix** is the starting point for 39km of cross-country trails. The small ski resorts of **Plan Peisey** and **Vallandry** are linked by gondola to Peisey in the valley below. Three lifts serve the nursery slopes. The resort will have a new six-person chair-lift in time for the start of the 2001–2 season.

TOURIST INFORMATION
Tel 33 479 07 94 28
Fax 33 479 07 95 34
Email info@peisey-vallandry.com
Web site www.peisey-vallandry.com

Chamonix

ALTITUDE 1,035m (3,396ft)

Intermediates ✱✱ Advanced ✱✱✱ Snowboarders ✱✱✱

Chamonix is truly different from any other ski resort in the world. Anyone who has learned the basics on the rolling pastures of the Austrian Tyrol or in the purpose-built 'ski factories' of the French Tarentaise is in for a stupendous shock. This is high Alpine territory where misjudging the severity of a run or the sudden changes of weather above 3,000m can cost a life. Someone has gone up – or down – every slope, no matter how dangerous, in what is still acknowledged as the climbing and extreme skiing capital of the world. In the past, complacency was the biggest foe of this year-round holiday destination. However, a number of new lifts have now been built in every ski area.

✔ Unsurpassed scenery
✔ Large vertical drop
✔ Extensive off-piste skiing
✔ Outstanding mountain guides
✔ Short airport transfer
✔ Wide choice of non-skiing activities
✔ Cosmopolitan atmosphere
✔ Vibrant nightlife
✘ Fragmented ski areas
✘ Lack of skiing convenience
✘ Unpredictable weather patterns
✘ Heavy traffic

Chamonix lies in the lee of Mont Blanc, the highest mountain in western Europe. It is home to the Compagnie des Guides de Chamonix, the oldest and most renowned mountain guiding service in the world. As in many other parts of the Alps, the pioneering climbers were British. The celebrated explorer Richard Pococke and his 24-year-old companion William Windham arrived in the Chamonix Valley from Geneva in 1741. Their party of 13 had expected to meet 'savages' along the way and was consequently armed to the teeth. To confuse even further the bemused but peaceful peasants they encountered, along what is now the Autoroute Blanche, Pococke was dressed as an Arab (for reasons best known to himself).

Forty-five years later, locally born doctor Michel-Gabriel Paccard and his reclusive partner Jacques Balmat conquered Mont Blanc; this was the most famous of many first ascents that have made the town pre-eminent in climbing lore.

The tallest landmark is the Aiguille du Midi, a 3,842-m granite needle above Chamonix that acts as the starting point for some of the most beautiful off-piste skiing in the Alps. From below, the Aiguille looks unassailable – a series of sheer granite pitches linked by ribbons of wind-blown snow – but not only has it been climbed, but it has also

been skied, by Yves Detry, a local guide. In 1998 a few million tons of it suddenly sheared away through natural erosion, causing an earthquake that registered 2.8 on the Richter scale. The new north face was deemed impossible to climb, but within a couple of months a Russian, who had apparently come to Chamonix only for a business conference, shinned up it in a single day.

Chamonix is not so much a single resort as a chain of unconnected ski areas set along both sides of the valley dominated by Mont Blanc. The success of a visit to Chamonix depends in part on the vagaries of the weather. On sunny days, it is glitteringly beautiful and deceptively tranquil. On stormy days, of which there are many, it is a brooding place, menaced by razor-sharp peaks and tumbling walls of ice.

The town itself is based around a core of hotels and villas built at the end of the nineteenth century and subsequently hemmed in by the neo-brutalist architecture of post-war tourism. The resort of Chamonix took shape before cars took over, and its current concerns are primarily to do with traffic management.

Most visitors to the valley consider a car to be essential ('having a car around Chamonix can be truly liberating, as most of the ski areas are a few miles apart'), the alternative being a local bus service that links the base-stations with moderate efficiency. The original village square is fully pedestrianised, and the main street is closed to traffic during daylight hours. This allows for the free flow of shoppers at the cost of considerable congestion on the outskirts, especially in the ever-expanding satellite township of **Chamonix Sud**. The shopping facilities in Chamonix are so comprehensive that one reporter commented: 'almost a range of shops that one would expect to find in any British town'.

For the past two seasons Chamonix has been estranged from neighbouring Courmayeur in Italy by the closure of the Mont Blanc tunnel following the fatal fire there in February 1999. At the time of writing, the tunnel is due to re-open in time for the 2001–2 season, but whether this will actually happen is still uncertain. Not everyone, least of all most of the Chamonix residents, is in favour of the re-opening, and this view is also reflected by the 619 inhabitants of the village of **Servoz**, below the French mouth of the tunnel. For the first time since General de Gaulle opened it in 1965, the poisonous yellow layers of diesel pollution that hung over their homes have dissipated and they can once again see the peak of Mont Blanc. However, it seems likely that Chamonix-based skiers and boarders will again be able to tour into Italy this winter for a lazy lunch without having to make the long detour home by the Grand St Bernard tunnel.

On the snow
top 3,842m (12,605ft) bottom 1,035m (3,396ft)
The Chamonix Valley caters for all levels of skier and rider but not in the same place, making it difficult for mixed-ability groups to ski on the same mountain. With **Les Houches** (not included in the Cham'Ski lift pass), there are five main base-stations, most of which are a bus ride from the town centre. The closest mountain access point is the celebrated Aiguille du Midi cable-car, which takes skiers and snowboarders up on to the shoulder of Mont Blanc for the descent down the Vallée Blanche. The combined area of Le Brévent and La Flégère provides the bulk of the skiing, a sunny and often underrated circuit with excellent terrain for all levels of intermediate and advanced skiers and snowboarders. However, the toughest and easiest skiing lies further up the valley at **Argentière** and **Le Tour** respectively. A chair-lift off the back of Le Tour at Tête de Balme gives access to some delightful skiing down towards **Vallorcine** in Switzerland.

Les Houches has broken away from the Chamonix umbrella and to the chagrin of its former ally has established itself as a go-ahead resort in its own right, with modern lifts and a highly rated FIS downhill course. It now seeks to align itself with its other big-name neighbour, **St-Gervais/Megève**. A much-discussed gondola would make it part of a separate 350-km linked ski circus centred on Megève, but this is still far off in the pipeline. In bad weather the best sheltered skiing in the valley can be found here.

The lift pass situation is 'messy and confusing'. The main choice lies between no less than 12 permutations of the Cham'Ski pass and the Ski Pass Mont Blanc. You can also buy a whole range of half-day and one-day passes valid only for certain areas. The Ski Pass Mont Blanc is slightly more expensive but covers Les Houches and a number of other outlying resorts.

Beginners

Learn to ski in Chamonix if you must but do not expect to like it. The worst part is that the ski areas are so separate and spread out. The town has small training areas for absolute beginners at Les Planards and Le Savoy, but don't expect to link up before nightfall with more experienced family or friends.

Once you have mastered the basics, the best practice slopes are at Le Tour, the most far-flung of the valley's outposts. As Le Tour is tree-free, the light is often hostile, but on a clear day you can take the high-speed quad that has replaced the slow old gondola to access Charamillon and the wide, empty slopes that fan out across the Col de Balme above it. The best-protected area from bad weather is the small network of blue (easy) runs at the top of Prarion in Les Houches. The Brévent/Flégère area is south-facing, and therefore the sunniest place to learn, with Brévent boasting a green (beginner) run. Les Chosalets, located at the foot of the Grands Montets lift in Argentière, is another beginner area.

Intermediates

Such is the diversity of pistes that skiers and snowboarders with the skills to tackle a red (intermediate) run with confidence can spend a week in the valley without going to the same place twice. The most convenient starting point is Le Brévent, where the six-seater gondola to Planpraz gives access to a choice of inviting blue runs down to the Col Cornu chair. This in turn opens up several moderately challenging reds, the longest of which goes to the bottom of La Charlanon drag-lift. Planpraz is also the launch point for the dramatic cable-car ride up to Le Brévent itself, a 2,525-m crag with unsurpassed views of Mont Blanc. From this point, the return to the mid-station is via a sweeping red piste or a bumpy black (difficult) trail. Only genuinely confident intermediates should attempt the return to Chamonix down the black run from the bottom of La Parsa chair.

La Flégère is reached from the suburb of **Les Praz**, a ten-minute bus ride from the town centre. The terrain is similar to that of Le Brévent, to which it is linked by cable-car, with long red and blue runs from the top of L'Index to the mid-station and a black descent back to base.

No visit to Chamonix is complete without a ride up the two-stage Aiguille du Midi cable-car, the highest in Europe. This is the departure point for the 22-km glacier run down the Vallée Blanche, which, depending on the route your guide takes, is either a gentle cruise through some of the most awesome mountain scenery in the world or a character-building encounter with ice-screws, karabiners and the other ironmongery of ski mountaineering. The easiest route can be attempted (and, once you start, there is no alternative but to finish it) by any intermediate who can ski parallel – you can even ski it in the light of the full moon. The Vallée Blanche provides thousands of snow-users with their first unforgettable taste of high-mountain off-piste adventure. The trickiest part comes early on in the shape of the infamous steps cut into the spine of the ridge from the cable-car station and the skiing start-point. The only unnerving bit is the five-minute stroll down the ice steps at the top.

Chamonix guides now routinely rope up their clients and issue them with crampons. The kind guides carry your skis, and a fixed rope on the left gives added security against a slide into the 2,000-m abyss. To avoid yawning and hidden crevasses you must follow your guide's tracks, but the gradient is gentle enough for intermediates – so slight at times that freshly waxed skis are needed to cross the lower section of the glacier without continuous poling. The return to Chamonix is either by rack-and-pinion railway from Montenvers or via a short climb and a long (and at times inevitably uncontrolled) descent down a narrow path and short piste into the centre of Chamonix.

Advanced

When enthusiasts talk of Chamonix, they really mean the Grands Montets at Argentière. This is a truly magnificent mountain for expert skiers and riders – steep, complex and dramatic with seemingly unlimited possibilities. It is accessed either by the 80-person cable-car to Lognan or by the high-speed quad-chair to Plan Joran from the Argentière base-station. When the cognoscenti arrive at Lognan, they join the rush – and almost invariably the queue – for the Grands Montets cable-car.

The huge popularity of this lift is undiminished by both the 30FF supplement payable on top of the Mont Blanc lift pass and the 200 slippery metal steps leading from the top-station to the start of the skiing. This reveals itself to be a bumpy defile divided into two black (difficult) runs, Les Pylones (under the cable-car) and the awkwardly cambered Point de Vue which, as its name suggests, provides stunning views of the glacier as it tracks down its edge. The Bochard gondola opens up another huge section of the mountain, including the 4.5-km Chamois descent to the Le Lavancher chair.

Off-piste

On powder mornings the rush for the Grands Montets is fierce, but the area is so enormous that skiing it out quickly is beyond even the powers of Europe's most dedicated first-track pack – they take at least a couple of hours to do this. Although open snowfields, bowls and gullies abound between the marked pistes, this is wild and dangerous terrain. The glacier is a web of crevasses and seracs that change position from season to season. Although the more macho of the temporary residents claim to know the mountain well enough to ski it alone, the truth is that to ski here without a qualified guide is to court death. From a skiing point of view, the most challenging descent is the Pas de Chèvre, a run from the top of Bochard via one of several extreme couloirs down the Mer de Glace to the bottom of the Vallée Blanche. Another classic is the Grand Envers route down the Vallée Blanche, reached from the top of the Aiguille du Midi cable-car, but far removed from the regular run in terms of degree of difficulty.

Snowboarding

Most riders here are out to shred some of the steepest and most demanding powder in the world ('a hot venue for boarders – unbelievably sheer faces, narrow chutes and huge cliffs have attracted a new breed of enthusiasts bent on pushing the sport to new horizons'). However, the Grands Montets also houses an impressive terrain park that is managed by the Chamonix Snowboard Club. There is also a terrain park at Charamillon, the mid-station at Le Tour, and a half-pipe near the Kandahar chair in Les Houches. Summits is the specialist board school in Argentière.

Tuition and guiding

The Chamonix branch of the French Ski School (ESF) and the Compagnie des Guides share an office in the downtown area ('off-piste virgins should take a lesson as Chamonix contains extreme terrain suitable only for people with proper equipment and training'). The less traditional Sensation Ski Ecole International takes a wilder approach to the learning curve, which is said to be popular with British clients. The ESF also has an office in Argentière, while Les Houches is served both by the ESF and Evolution 2.

Mountain restaurants

The Chamonix Valley is not generally recommended for those who like to lunch seriously on the mountain ('non-descript food served in small quantities at inflated prices'). However, the new Bergerie above the top of the Brévent cable-car is a welcome addition: 'excellent food in a warm atmosphere'. Plan Joran at Lognan is probably the best mountain restaurant in the valley. La Crèmerie du Glacier in the woods at the bottom of the Grands Montets is the only one that is independently owned and is warmly praised for its special menu of *croûte fromage* ('cheese and wild mushrooms – one of the best dishes I have ever eaten'). Those who ski the Vallée Blanche have little choice but to eat at the spectacularly sited Requin refuge, while Les Marmottons was described as 'a good place to stop for a drink on the way home'.

Accommodation

Chamonix offers the full spectrum, from dormitory-style youth hostels to four-star hotels (there are 70 hotels in all), plus a wide choice of chalets and apartments, many of them newly renovated. All bookings should be made through the Chamonix Reservations Centre (☎ 450 53 23 33). The most luxurious hotels are Le Hameau Albert 1er and L'Auberge du Bois Prin, owned by brothers Denis and Pierre Carrier. Hotel Mont-Blanc is the third four-star. Le Hameau Albert 1er includes a renovated complex called Les Fermes, which consists of two eighteenth-century farmhouses containing 12 wood-panelled suites, a swimming-pool and health centre, and a rustic restaurant. In the three-star category, the Sapinière recalls the heyday of the British Empire, both in its furnishings and its clientèle ('some rather loud and rich'). It has now upgraded its annexe. The pleasant Hotel Richemond also trades on the faded glories of yesteryear, but from a more central location. Hotels Alpina and Gustavia are both central, quality three-star hotels. Reporters staying at Hotel Le Chamonix complained of 'a bruisingly narrow bath, but the hotel location was ideal'.

Eating in and out

No one denies that the Michelin-rated Le Hameau Albert 1er has the best food in Chamonix, but prices have risen to such a level that even the seriously wealthy hesitate to visit the restaurant except on special occasions, when they can enjoy Chef Pierre Carrier's innovative cuisine and a cellar containing some 20,000 bottles of fine wine. The hotel's second restaurant, Les Fermes, is much more relaxed ('highly enjoyable mountain dishes in a convivial atmosphere'). L' Auberge du Bois Prin follows Le Hameau Albert 1er closely in both quality and price, and the food at the Hotel Eden in Les Praz is also recommended. La Bergerie serves Savoyard specialities, while the Bistro de la Gare is known for its cheap daily special. Le Sarpe in **Les Bois** is praised for quality combined with good value. L'Impossible, the ancient barn in Chamonix Sud converted by extreme skier Sylvain Saudan, is a winner for atmosphere. Other recommendations include La Cantina for Mexican cuisine, Satsuki for sushi and Le Cafeteria, which is said to provide 'very reasonably priced, wholesome food'. Les Calèches ('possibly overdid the rustic beams a bit') is a typical Savoyard bistro, and La Flèche d'Or is an inexpensive brasserie. Self-caterers are well served by specialist food shops and supermarkets.

Après-ski

'Night-time activities are every bit as frenzied as the day-time skiing,' noted one reporter. The ski- and board-mad early evening trade starts at 5pm at bars such as the Chambre Neuf. The video bars of Le Choucas

Skiing facts: Chamonix

TOURIST INFORMATION
85 Place du Triangle de L'Amitié,
F-74400 Chamonix, Haute Savoie
Tel 33 450 53 00 24
Fax 33 450 53 58 90
Email info@chamonix.com
Web site www.chamonix.com

THE RESORT
By road Calais 900km
By rail station in resort
Airport transfer Geneva 1½ hrs
Visitor beds 63,000
Transport free ski bus included in
lift pass

THE SKIING
Linked or nearby resorts Argentière (n),
Courmayeur (n), Les Houches (n),
Megève (n), St-Gervais (n), Le Tour (n)
Number of lifts 49
Total of trails/pistes 150km (52% easy,
36% intermediate, 12% difficult)
Beginners 12 lifts, reductions available

LIFT PASSES
Area pass Cham'Ski (covers valley
except Les Houches) 999FF, Mont Blanc
(covers Argentière, Chamonix,
Courmayeur, Les Houches, Megève)
1,180FF, both for 6 days
Pensioners 60yrs and over 849FF for
6 days
Credit cards yes

TUITION
Skiing ESF Chamonix (☎ 450 53 22 57),
ESF Argentière (☎ 450 54 00 12),
Sensation Ski Ecole International
(☎ 450 53 56 46).

ESF Les Houches (☎ 450 54 42 96),
Evolution 2 Les Houches (☎ 450 54
31 44)
Snowboarding as ski schools, Summits
(☎ 450 54 05 11)
Other courses cross-country, heli-
skiing, ski-touring
Guiding Compagnie des Guides de
Chamonix (☎ 450 53 00 88),
Association Internationale des Guides
(☎ 450 53 27 05), Stages Vallençant
(☎ 450 54 05 11), Mont Blanc Ski Tours
(☎ 450 53 82 16), Sensation Ski Ecole
International Stages Bernard Muller
(☎ 450 55 94 26), Roland Stieger
(☎ 450 54 43 53), Yak & Yeti (☎ 450
53 53 67)

CHILDREN
Lift pass Cham'Ski 4–11yrs 699FF,
12–15yrs 849FF. Ski Pass Mont Blanc
12yrs and under 826FF. Both for 6 days
Ski & board school as adults
Kindergarten (ski) Panda-Ski (☎ 450
54 04 76), (ski/non-ski) Panda Club
(☎ 450 54 04 76), (non-ski) Halte
Garderie (☎ 450 53 36 68)

OTHER SPORTS
Curling, hang-gliding, helicopter rides,
ice-driving, indoor tennis and squash,
parapente, skating, ski-jumping,
SnowCarting, snowshoeing, swimming

FOOD AND DRINK
Coffee 10–15FF, glass of wine 20FF,
small beer 15–20FF, soft drink 20FF,
dish of the day 75FF

and Driver are fashionable, and there is no shortage of alternative entertainment along the Rue du Docteur Paccard. The bars empty out at
about 7.30pm when snow-users return to their chalets or apartments
for dinner. From about 10.30pm the partying starts up again at Arbat,
which has the best live music in town. Wild Wallabies, inspired by St
Anton's Krazy Kanguruh, is a top choice for riders, as is Jekyll and
Hyde, while real late-nighters end up at the Blue Night, which stays
open until 5am.

The Bumble Bee, Bar du Moulin, La Cantina and the Mill Street Bar
in Chamonix are all popular, as is The Office Bar in Argentière. Le Pub
and The Ice Rock Café in Chamonix Sud are well frequented; the latter
is a large basement bar incorporating half a truck and various motorbikes and is packed until the early hours. Dick's Tea Bar, of Val d'Isère
fame, has a branch here.

Childcare

The ESF schools in Chamonix and Argentière have classes for children
aged between four and 12 years. They also have a crèche with full daycare. The Panda Club in Argentière provides care every day of the week
for children aged six months to three years. For three- and four-year-
olds, Panda-Ski offers daily sessions in the Jardin des Neiges near the
Lognan lift station. In addition, a municipal crèche, Halte Garderie,
provides entertainment for children aged between 18 months and six
years, but this is available only through tour operators.

Linked or nearby resorts

Argentière
top 3,275m (12,605ft) bottom 1,240m (4,067ft)

In winter, Argentière's main street becomes 'Ski Bum Alley', with a
large proportion of its rooms let out cheaply for the season. After dark,
the bars hum with macho talk of the day's achievements. The Office Bar
is the favoured British watering-hole. The Stone Bar is popular; the
Rusticana more cosmopolitan. Hotel Le Dahu (☎ 450 54 01 55), a
prominent landmark on the congested road from Chamonix to
Martigny, is recommended both for comfort and food. La Ferme d'Elise
(☎ 450 54 00 17) ('a well-kept secret') is a renovated farmhouse run as
a small hotel.

TOURIST INFORMATION
Tel 33 450 54 02 14
Fax 33 450 54 06 39
Email info@chamonix.com
Web site www.chamonix.com

Les Deux Alpes

ALTITUDE 1,650m (5,412ft)

Beginners ✱ Intermediates ✱✱✱ Advanced ✱✱ Snowboarders ✱✱✱

This efficient and only partly purpose-built resort lies between Grenoble and **Briançon**, within easy reach of **Alpe d'Huez** in one direction and **Serre Chevalier** in the other. Its primary asset is the height of the skiing, which means that snow is assured at any stage of the season, and the glacier is also open during the French summer holidays. Les Deux Alpes began as a ski resort shortly before the outbreak of World War II. Pride of place was a Heath-Robinson-style rope-tow, which fell down 15 minutes after the opening ceremony. It was not until the late 1950s that a new gondola and one of France's first ski passes – costing 2.50FF per day – paved the way for Les Deux Alpes to develop into a proper ski area. Today it resembles a large ski factory, but with fresh air and impressive scenery.

- ✔ Snow-sure slopes
- ✔ Modern lift system
- ✔ Long vertical drop
- ✔ Excellent child facilities
- ✔ Beautiful scenery
- ✔ Lively après-ski
- ✔ Summer skiing
- ✗ Large and spread-out village
- ✗ Disjointed bus system
- ✗ Crowded home runs
- ✗ Heavy traffic during peak season

Although the town itself is visually unappealing, it is by no means the worst example of modern French architecture. Both village and ski area are long and narrow, and there is less skiing terrain than one would imagine for such a long vertical drop. However, the skiing links with **La Grave**, which is one of the most dramatic off-piste ski areas in Europe. The shuttle bus is said to be a disaster: 'the two distinct circuits are in no way timetabled to coincide, so you can easily be left waiting for some considerable time if you wish to go from one area to the next'.

A quieter, alternative base is the quaint old hamlet of **Venosc** in the Vénéon Valley below Les Deux Alpes. Its ancient cobbled streets are lined with craft shops and studios, and it has three extremely pleasant and inexpensive restaurants. The village is linked by an efficient, modern gondola that you have to take down again at the end of the day as you cannot ski back to the resort.

On the snow
top 3,600m (11,808ft) bottom 1,600m (5,249ft)

The chamois hunters and shepherds who once roamed what are now the ski slopes would scarcely recognise their traditional haunts today. Indeed, it is easy for skiers to be confused by such a multitude of lifts and 220km of piste within a relatively confined area. Apart from a smaller, uncrowded sector to the west of the village, between Pied Moutet at 2,339m and the Alpe du Mont de Lans, the bulk of the skiing is between the village and La Toura (2,600m) to the east. Reporters commented on the 'sameness' of the pistes: 'a huge array of blue (easy) and green (beginner) runs, all of which are rather dull'. The piste grooming was criticised, too: 'in some places only half a piste had been groomed – this made skiing especially difficult in poor visibility as you could be surprised by skiing from groomed piste to thick snow on the marked piste'.

The principal lift is the Jandri Express jumbo gondola, which deposits skiers on the glacier in 20 minutes. It is prone to rush-hour queues, and the alternative Jandri 1 or the Diable gondola from the other end of the village followed by the Jandri 2 cable-car may provide less irksome, but not necessarily quicker, mountain access. Above the 2,600-m mid-station the terrain narrows down to a bottleneck, and Le Jandri pistes have 'too many skiers of too many ability levels thrown together'. The broad glacier plateau offers easy slopes and even a sub-glacial funicular for novice skiers, who find wind-blown drag-lifts extremely daunting.

Beginners

The most extensive nursery slopes are at the top of the ski area on the Glacier du Mont de Lans. A compensation is the excitement of being able to experience your first slither on skis high up the mountain with magnificent views. The slopes immediately above the village are steep, and learners can either download by gondola or take a green path, Chemin Demoiselles, from 2,200m to return to the village. However, this is 'only a narrow track, very crowded, icy in places, tiring and not at all enjoyable'. Another reporter pointed out: 'there is no getting away from that awful green run to the resort or queuing for the gondolas to return to the valley'.

Intermediates

Competent cruisers can enjoy themselves on most of the upper slopes at Les Deux Alpes, although less experienced skiers may find themselves somewhat overwhelmed by the steep homeward-bound runs, which can become crowded at the end of the day. One way to escape from the mainstream skiing is to try one of the rare runs through the trees. There is an enjoyable piste down to the village of Bons at 1,300m, while Mont de Lans can be reached from both ski areas. La Breche was enjoyed by reporters: 'could have skied this all week if it were not for the fact that it is only accessible via cable-car with constant queues'.

Advanced

Experienced skiers inevitably gravitate towards the Tête Moute area, which provides some of the steepest terrain on the mountain. They will be tempted to go straight from the Venosc end of the village by gondola

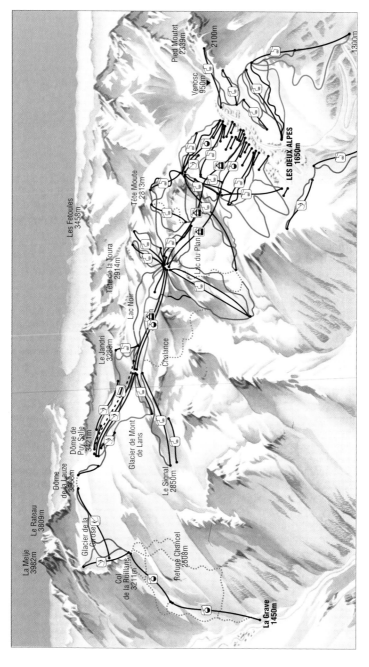

to Le Diable at 2,400m. From here, the Grand Diable chair reaches the Tête Moute itself, where steep, north-facing runs lead to Lac du Plan and onwards towards the Thuit chair. Le Diable ('a rare enjoyable black') offers a challenging and often mogulled 1,200-m descent to the village. Another reporter noted that 'the last section just drops away into icy, inky blackness'. There are seven other black (difficult) runs.

Off-piste
Les Deux Alpes has enclosed bowl-skiing, which is ideal for those wanting to try off-piste for the first time. For seasoned deep-snow skiers there are a number of easily accessible (but not so easily skiable) couloirs. La Grave, one of the most exciting and scenic off-piste ski areas in the Alps, is on the doorstep – the 'over-the-top' link from Les Deux Alpes via the Glacier du Mont de Lans involves a 20-minute walk. Alternatively, you can take a bus between the two villages. A wonderful descent takes you 'off the back' towards the unspoilt climbing village of **St-Christophe-en-Oisans**.

Snowboarding
Riding takes pride of place in Les Deux Alpes each October as an apéritif to the winter ski season. The resort is the venue for the World Snowboard Meeting, which claims to be 'the highest and biggest exhibition of snowboarding on the planet'. Due to the layout of the pistes, riders need never take a drag-lift, which is a huge advantage. The terrain park is on La Toura piste in winter and moves to the glacier in the summer. The park includes boardercross and a half-pipe, plus a barbecue and sound system.

Tuition and guiding
The main ski schools are the French Ski School (ESF) and the rival International Ski School St-Christophe (ESI). The British-run European Ski School offers tuition (in English) to classes of up to four pupils ('I cannot speak highly enough of the teachers, who explained everything fully and taught with a high degree of understanding and patience,' said one reporter). Courses are for two hours each day and include video analysis and computerised ski simulators. Primitive Snowboard School is the specialist for wannabe riders.

Mountain restaurants
Les Deux Alpes receives few bouquets for its eight mountain restaurants, and, if it were not so inconvenient, more skiers might consider lunching in town or downloading by gondola to Venosc. 'Uninviting' and 'over-priced' were two comments from reporters. The Panoramic ('friendly and efficient') is a convenient meeting-point. The highest restaurant, Les Glaciers, is as its name suggests on the glacier and 'left us cold'. Chalet de La Toura over the back of the mountain is 'in an excellent location with very good food', and La Fée Refuge is 'attractive and friendly but the menu choices are pedestrian'. La Meije offers a

'friendly, efficient service of local specialities at very reasonable prices,' while La Patache and La Petite Marmite are both recommended, too.

Accommodation
Most of the accommodation is in apartments, with the remainder in the resort's 40 hotels and pensions. The top end of the market boasts two four-star hotels, the Bérangère (☎ 476 79 24 11) and La Farendole (☎ 476 80 50 45), which both have indoor swimming-pools. There are ten three-star hotels and 16 two-star ones. The Edelweiss Hotel-Club (☎ 476 79 21 22) is warmly recommended for its 'wonderful gourmet dinners, with local produce properly cooked and well presented; the staff were patient and helpful and the bedrooms large, if a little spartan'. Hotel Les Marmottes (☎ 476 79 2191) is 'superb, with a five-course dinner and large bedrooms'. Le Souleil'or (☎ 476 79 24 69) has 'friendly owners and decent accommodation', and Hotel Chalet Mounier (☎ 476 80 56 90) was praised for its 'wonderful feminine touch'. Several reporters complained of the standard of the budget accommodation: 'we spent the first evening and night cleaning it and complaining about the lack of facilities such as light bulbs, beds and chairs'.

Eating in and out
L'Abri and La Spaghetteria are warmly recommended for pizza and pasta. Blue Salmon Farm specialises in fish dishes and Il Caminetto is a much-praised Italian restaurant. Le P'tit Polyte is 'smart, expensive and worth every centime'. Le Four à Bois is renowned for its regional specialities, while Le Saxo serves Tex-Mex cuisine and La Papate is reputed to have 'a good atmosphere'. Les Deux Alpes appears to have a higher turnover of restaurants than any other major resort. As one reporter said: 'We marvelled at the value of more than one restaurant – only to find it had closed down by next season'. Hotel Chalet Mounier Restaurant served 'high-quality French cuisine at reasonable prices, with attentive service, sumptuous and romantic surroundings'. 'Fantasic food shops' makes life easy for the many self-caterers.

Après-ski
Les Deux Alpes scores highly for après-ski among those who like lively, noisy bars and discos and do not mind bumping into lots of other British people (more than 25 per cent of non-French visitors are British). GoGo Café Bar is a 'cosy wooden chalet-type coffee bar with a log fire, English newspapers and entertaining French cartoon books for children', and Pub Windsor remains an enduringly popular haunt. Rodéo Saloon, at the Venosc end of town, displays a bizarre mechanical bull, which inevitably attracts the wilder element of après-skiers. The Asterix Bar, in the hotel of the same name, is 'not very pretty, but offers friendly service'. Le Pressoir and Le Tonic are described as 'useful watering-holes'. The four discos are La Casa, Le Club 92, L'Avalanche and L'Opéra Music Temple. The ice grotto is well worth a visit.

Skiing facts: Les Deux Alpes

TOURIST INFORMATION
BP 7, F–38860 Les Deux Alpes, Dauphiné
Tel 33 476 79 22 00
Fax 33 476 79 01 38
Email les2alp@les2alpes.com
Web site www.les2alpes.com

THE RESORT
By road Calais 953km
By rail Grenoble 70km
Airport transfer Grenoble 1½ hrs,
Lyon 2hrs
Visitor beds 35,000
Transport free ski bus

THE SKIING
Linked or nearby resorts La Grave (l),
Alpe d'Huez (n), Serre Chevalier/
Briançon (n), St-Christophe-en-
Oisans (l), Venosc (l)
Number of lifts 61 including La Grave
Total of trails/pistes 220km with La
Grave (24% easy, 44% intermediate,
16% difficult, 16% very difficult)
Beginners 10 lifts, of which 4 are free
Summer skiing mid-June–Sept, 16 lifts

LIFT PASSES
Area pass 865–960FF for 6 days
(includes 1 free day in Alpe d'Huez, Serre
Chevalier, Puy-St-Vincent or The Milky
Way)
Pensioners 25% reduction for 60yrs and
over, free for 75yrs and over
Credit cards yes

TUITION
Skiing ESF (☎ 476 79 21 21),
ESI (☎ 476 79 04 21), European Ski

School (☎ 476 79 74 55),
Ski Privilège (☎ 476 79 23 44)
Snowboarding ESF, ESI, European Ski
School, Primitive Snowboard School
(☎ 476 79 09 32)
Other courses cross-country, extreme
skiing/boarding, moguls, powder clinics,
race camps, skiing for the disabled,
ski-jumping, ski-touring, slalom,
snowblading, telemark
Guiding Bureau des Guides ESF
(☎ 476 79 21 21), Vénéon 2 Alpes
(☎ 476 80 52 72)

CHILDREN
Lift pass 5–13yrs, 569–632FF for
6 days
Ski & board school ESF, ESI, European
Ski School
Kindergarten (ski) ESF, ESI, (non-ski)
Crèche du Clos des Fonds (☎ 476 79 02
62), Le Bonhomme de Neige (☎ 476 79
06 77)

OTHER SPORTS
Bungee-jumping, climbing wall, curling,
helicopter rides, ice-climbing, ice-driving,
ice-gliding, inflatable bob-run,
night-skiing, parapente, quad-karting on
ice, skating, snowbiking, snowmobiling,
snowshoeing, squash, swimming,
tobogganing, tubing

FOOD AND DRINK
Coffee 9–12FF, glass of wine 15–18FF,
small beer 20FF, soft drink 15FF,
dish of the day 85FF

Childcare

Among the bridges, tunnels and animal characters at the Espace Loisirs playground are a trampoline, a small slalom course, toboggan run, ski-biking, tubing and an inflatable bob-run, with organised races most days. Bookings can be made through the tourist information office. Qualified staff welcome children from six months to two years old at the slope-side La Crèche du Clos des Fonds, and Le Bonhomme de Neige caters for two- to six-year-olds.

The ESF operates a kindergarten slope in the centre of town close to the Jandri Express, and the ESI has its own kindergarten. Both ski schools offer half- or full-day courses for children over four years of age who wish to ski or snowboard. We have positive reports of the ESF children's ski school: 'the French instructors spoke adequate English and even in the worst of the weather they took the wee souls out for at least part of the three-hour lesson. When they got cold, wet and fed up they returned to the ESF chalet to dry out and watch videos'. The European Ski School received mixed reports: 'our kids enjoyed ski school with friendly English-speaking instructors,' and 'lack of technical tuition'.

Linked or nearby resorts

La Grave
top 3,550m (11,647ft) bottom 1,450m (4,757ft)

A 20-minute hike over the back of Les Deux Alpes brings you into the ski area of La Grave. The ancient, rugged village straggling the road up to the Col du Lauteret has in the past earned its reputation as a climbing centre rather than as a ski resort. It crouches in the shadow of the 3,982-m La Meije, which in 1876 was one of the last great European peaks to be conquered. La Grave's reputation is founded on the fact that it has just one short piste and two lifts. This may sound insignificant until you realise that one of those lifts takes you up over 2,000m vertical. It does not normally open until late January, although the ski area can be reached from Les Deux Alpes. The steep, unpisted routes down provide some of the most challenging advanced skiing and riding in Europe. As the glacial area is heavily crevassed and the couloirs are steep, skiers are strongly advised to use the services of a local guide at all times. La Grave has a three-star and couple of simple hotels but little to offer anyone who does not climb or ski off-piste.

TOURIST INFORMATION
Tel 33 476 79 92 46
Fax 33 476 79 91 24
Email dominique.ferrero@wanadoo.fr
Web site www.la_grave.com

Flaine

ALTITUDE 1,600m (5,248ft)

Beginners ✱✱✱ Intermediates ✱✱✱ Advanced ✱✱✱ Snowboarders ✱✱✱

Flaine, a purpose-built resort much loved by the British in general, and the Scots in particular, is the focal point of the Grand Massif, France's fourth biggest ski area. Its proximity to Mont Blanc gives it a favourable micro-climate.

The first view down into the village from the approach road is an unexpected one; Flaine sits ostentatiously in an isolated bowl where you would not expect to find any habitation at all. The grey concrete of the resort matches the grey rock formation. Reporters' opinions of Flaine varied from 'mindblowingly ugly – I work in Harlow New Town and Flaine wouldn't look out of place here' to 'a stunning architectural achievement in the true spirit of the Bauhaus school of design'. Two enclosed people-mover lifts operate day and night between the higher and lower villages, Forêt and Forum. Le Hameau de Flaine area is served by a free bus, which runs from the chalets to the nursery slopes every 15–30 minutes (from 8.30am until midnight).

✔ Large ski area
✔ Excellent family facilities
✔ Skiing convenience
✔ Short airport transfer
✔ Car-free resort
✔ Reliable resort-level snow
✔ Lack of queues
✔ Variety of off-piste skiing
✗ Tired apartments
✗ Lack of alpine charm
✗ Limited nightlife

Flaine connects with the three lower and more traditional resorts of **Samoëns**, **Morillon** and **Les Carroz**, and a piste takes you down to the charming village of **Sixt**.

When Flaine opened in 1968 it was hailed as the showpiece of the French Alps – a unique resort where culture and skiing combined to produce what was described as a leisure environment. The celebrated American architect Marcel Breuer was commissioned to design the original buildings to blend in with the rocky surroundings of this extraordinarily beautiful valley.

The former world champion Emile Allais, the grandmaster of ski resort design, laid out the pistes, and winter tourists arrived in their thousands. Low-cost ski-in, ski-out rental apartments attracted budget skiers from all over the world. But in the 1980s the slide from grace began, and, like a ruptured slab avalanche, its only path was an accelerating downhill decline. Most of the works of art by Picasso, Vasarely and Dubuffet that adorned the resort's museum and open spaces were sold off and many of its self-catering apartments fell into a state of disrepair.

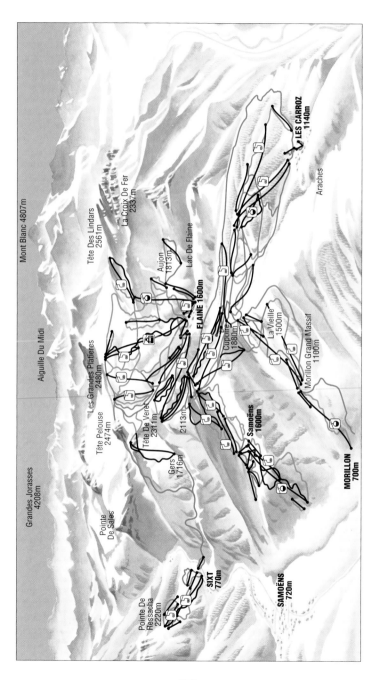

However, all that is poised to change. The resort is now owned by the giant Compagnie des Alpes, which now runs a string of resorts in France, Italy and Switzerland. One of its major shareholders is the Canadian resort developer Intrawest. The North American company is concentrating its first efforts in the Alps on a pilot ski village in Les Arcs. However, Flaine is widely tipped for its first serious top-to-bottom makeover, which is expected to push the resort up to the premier league of European ski destinations. If the current plans to increase the size of the resort by a third get the go-ahead, we can expect to see the rapid development of a second North American-style resort in Europe.

At present 74 lifts serving 265km of piste make up this vast area. Many are in serious need of replacement but the new owners have a £20-million five-year investment plan. During the 1999–2000 season three new chair-lifts were built to take skiers up to the highest point of the ski area. In 2000 a new eight-seater detachable chair-lift was added in Les Grands Vans area to replace an old three-seater. During a week in high season 2001, however, reporters complained that it was 'hardly ever operative'. A further two six-seaters have been added, as well as a four-seater chair that links the Combe de Vernant into the Grand Massif. Future plans include a programme of snow-cannon that will give cover to a quarter of the entire area.

WHAT'S NEW

Gondola from Samoëns to Verclan 1600m

Additional accommodation at Samoëns

£400,000 investment in piste improvements

On the snow
top 2,480m (8,134ft) bottom 700m (2,296ft)

The area divides naturally into separate segments. Flaine's own skiing is ranged around the north-facing part of its home bowl, with lifts soaring to nearly 2,500m around the rim. Most of the skiing is open and un-sheltered. The main mountain access from the village centre is by gondola up to Grandes Platières, a high, wide plateau with panoramic views. A large number of runs go from here down to the resort; most are graded red (intermediate) or blue (easy). In general, the skiing in the enclosed Flaine bowl is somewhat limited, and its real attraction lies in its link with the remainder of the Grand Massif area; this is via the Grands Vans chair-lift, which was upgraded to an eight-person detachable for the 2000–1 season ('extremely comfortable and fast with no queues'). The resort's drag-lifts receive criticism: 'Some of the drag-lifts are very fierce – especially the Bois and the Aujon. The blue runs up here would otherwise be excellent for inexperienced skiers'.

The Tête du Pré des Saix is the central point of the entire Grand Massif system. From here, north-facing runs drop down steep mogul slopes towards Samoëns ('most enjoyable, challenging blacks up top, opening up to fast cruising lower down'). On the other side of the valley, the parallel easier pistes towards Morillon comprise long and gentle trails in the tree-line.

The runs to Les Carroz are short but offer a wide variety of trails, including more difficult sections at the top of the red runs and some good off-piste. Sixt, along the road from Samoëns, has its own small ski area. The resort is directly linked into the Grand Massif via a piste, but ski buses provide the only return.

Beginners

Flaine has extensive novice slopes in the middle of the village. Improvers can try wide, snaking blue runs on the bowl's west-facing slopes. Crystal and Serpentine are long runs around the shoulder of the mountain that beginners can tackle by the end of their first week.

Intermediates

The whole area is designed for intermediates. Day-long forays into the far corners of the Grand Massif are well within the capabilities of most snow-users with a few weeks' experience. However, it is important to allow plenty of time for the return journey. The Tourmaline blue from the Grands Vans down to Le Forêt is usually well-groomed.

Advanced

The more difficult skiing sections of the Flaine bowl are in the middle, graded black (difficult) under the gondola and red to each side. The black Diamant Noir is an enjoyable mogul slope ('the highlight of a week's skiing') with 'a narrow gully to negotiate under the scrutiny of those going up the chair'. The Agate piste from the Tête des Lindars is 'an interesting black with a couple of awkward bits that get the adrenaline going a little'. There are plenty of steep runs and a good variety of terrain, making Flaine a suitable destination for advanced snow-users.

Off-piste

Flaine and the Grand Massif area offer outstanding off-piste possibilities. The rocky terrain means that powder hunts can all too easily end on a cliff, and the services of a local guide who really knows the region are essential. Mont Blanc Helicopters can be booked to pick you up from the end of an off-piste trip and return you to the resort.

Snowboarding

Flaine is home to one of the best terrain parks in Europe. The 3km-long section offers enough jumps and obstacles of all varieties to keep even the most hardcore freestyler happy. Fantasurf has a designated kids' half-pipe. At the bottom of the park is a well-prepared half-pipe. Combe des Gers bowl is popular with freeriders, and heli-boarding is available near the resort. Flaine is also popular with Alpine riders, or carvers.

Tuition and guiding

Flaine has two main ski schools and three independent ones. We have mixed reports of the French Ski School (ESF): 'large classes, but our instructor was extremely helpful'. Flaine Superski offers half-day improvement courses. Ski Action-Ski Passion was set up by two former members of the French ski team and has a growing reputation. ESF Instructors at Fantasurf, the dedicated terrain park, provide equipment and two hours of lessons per day for kids.

Mountain restaurants

Those in the immediate Flaine vicinity are limited, especially in the Aujon area, but there is a wide choice further afield. Close to the resort the Blanchot is recommended ('excellent French onion soup and exceptionally tasty vin chaud'), and Chalet Bissac is 'busy, but has quick hot food'. Bar L'Eloge, by the Flaine gondola, has a simple choice of food and friendly service. La Combe, in the Morillon area, has 'terrific ambience'. The Oréade, at the top of the Kédeuse gondola, is praised for its food and large, sunny terrace. The restaurant on the Chariande piste at Samoëns has reasonable prices and an excellent view from the terrace.

Accommodation

The heart of the resort is Flaine Forum, where the few shops and restaurants and the ski school meeting-place are located. Le Totem (☎ 450 90 80 64), with Picasso's statue of the same name standing outside, is the main piste-side hotel. In the past the hotel has enjoyed a sound reputation, but in recent years the standard of both cuisine and service have been criticised. One reporter commented: 'the kitchen just could not cope. My food arrived long after everyone else had finished eating'. Another said: 'chambermaids showed surly dissatisfaction when we did not want the rooms cleaned at 8.30am'. Les Lindars (☎ 020-7348 3333 UK), once Flaine's most famous, family hotel, is now a Club Med. The other family hotel is Hotel-Club Le Flaine (☎ 450 90 47 36). The two-star Aujon (☎ 450 90 80 10) is a popular alternative.

Flaine Forêt, on a shelf above Flaine Forum, has mainly self-catering accommodation and its own shops ('a very limited range') and bars. The apartments received mixed comments. The Andromedes block (☎ 450 90 80 01 for all self-catering accommodation) is said to be 'surprisingly spacious and clean, but decidedly tired. The cooking facilities were the best that I've seen in a French apartment. The décor was authentic 70s with liberal use of wood-effect formica'. The Doris block is 'as far from the slopes as you can get. It was small with two electric rings, one of which didn't work properly, and it was for six people'. However, some of the rental apartments have been refurbished. The apartments are small, even by French standards, but cheap compared with the more fashionable resorts. Le Hameau de Flaine, on the mountain at 1,800m, is a later development of attractive Scandinavian-style chalets inconveniently situated for the ski area.

Eating in and out

Chez La Jeanne is 'small and friendly with excellent pizzas and good house wine'. Also in Flaine Forum, the White Grouse Pub serves snacks, pizzas and fondues. La Perdrix Noire in Flaine Forêt serves

Skiing facts: Flaine

TOURIST INFORMATION
Galerie des Marchands, F-74300 Flaine
Tel 33 450 90 80 01
Fax 33 450 90 86 26
Email welcome@flaine.com
Web site www.flaine.com

LONDON AGENT
Erna Low Consultants (see *Which tour operator?*)

THE RESORT
By road Calais 890km
By rail Cluses 25km, frequent bus service to resort
Airport transfer Geneva 1½hrs
Visitor beds 9,500
Transport free ski bus

THE SKIING
Linked or nearby resorts Les Carroz (l), Morillon (l), Samoëns (l), Sixt (n)
Number of lifts 26 in Flaine, 129 in Le Grand Massif
Total of trails/pistes 140km in Flaine (12% easy, 42% intermediate, 37% difficult, 9% very difficult), 260km in Le Grand Massif
Beginners 7 runs, 4 of them are free. Points tickets available

LIFT PASSES
Area pass Grand Massif (covers Flaine, Les Carroz, Morillon, Samoëns and Sixt) 970FF for 6 days
Pensioners 60–74yrs 776FF, free for 75yrs and over. Both for 6 days
Credit cards yes

TUITION
Skiing ESF (☎ 450 90 81 00), ESI (☎ 450 90 84 41), Ski Action-Ski Passion (☎ 450 90 80 97), Flaine Superski (☎ 450 90 82 88), Ski Global (☎ 450 90 42 26)
Snowboarding as ski schools
Other courses cross-country, extreme skiing, heli-skiing and heli-boarding, race camps, seniors, snowblading, teen skiing, telemark
Guiding Mont Blanc Helicopters (☎ 450 90 80 01), and through ski schools

CHILDREN
Lift pass Grand Massif 5–11yrs 679FF, 12–15yrs 728FF. Both for 6 days
Ski & board school as adults
Kindergarten (ski) Rabbit Club (ESF), La Souris Verte (ESI), as adults. (non-ski) Les Petits Loups (☎ 450 90 87 82)

OTHER SPORTS
Dog-sledding, hang-gliding, helicopter rides, horse-riding, ice-diving, ice-driving, indoor climbing wall, parapente, skating, snowmobiling, snowshoeing, swimming

FOOD AND DRINK
Coffee 10–18FF, glass of wine 15FF, small beer 15–20FF, soft drink 18FF, dish of the day 50–75FF

regional specialities and is voted best restaurant by a number of reporters. La Pizzeria in the Forum is said to be 'excellent and reasonably priced,' and Le Grain de Sel replaces the former Trattoria and serves traditional food. There are well-stocked supermarkets on both Forum and Forêt levels. L'Auroch in the Forum shopping centre serves traditional French cuisine.

Après-ski

People do not come to Flaine for the nightlife and many tend to opt for quiet evenings in, especially those with small children. The Cîmes Rock Café in Flaine Forum has karaoke. The White Grouse Pub, that little piece of France that is forever Scotland, has raised its standards. The Perdrix Noire has wooden table-top games. Ski Fun disco has been completely renovated.

Childcare

All five ski schools offer lessons for children. La Souris Verte at the ESI takes children all day, as does the ESF Rabbit Club, which is the more French-oriented of the two. Both collect children from their accommodation each morning and return them at the end of the day. Non-skiing children are cared for at Les Petits Loups kindergarten, but priority is given to the families of resort workers and you need to book at least two months in advance. Hotel-Club Le Flaine and Club Med have kindergartens for their residents.

Linked or nearby resorts

Les Carroz
top 2,480m (8,134ft) bottom 700m (2,296ft)

Les Carroz is large, and, in the view of most correspondents, more pleasing to the eye than Flaine. Its drawback is its low altitude. The resort spreads across a broad, sunny slope on the road to Flaine and attracts many families and weekend visitors.

The gondola and chair-lift are a steep walk from the centre of the village, but within easy reach of some attractive, simple old hotels including Les Airelles (☎ 450 90 01 02) and the Croix de Savoie (☎ 450 90 00 26). Most of the self-catering accommodation is much less conveniently placed. The bus is not included in the lift pass and runs intermittently to Flaine; late-night taxis between the two resorts are hard to find.

The resort boasts two ski and snowboard schools for adults and children: the ESF and Nouvelle Dimension. Both offer cross-country skiing, snowblading and telemark among their list of special courses. La Souris Verte cares for small non-skiers from three months to five years old, and Les Loupiots accepts skiing and non-skiing children from four months to 12 years old. Heli-skiing and heli-boarding is available through the local Bureau des Guides. Ecole d'Alpinisme des Carroz also offers off-piste guiding.

TOURIST INFORMATION
Tel 33 450 90 00 04
Fax 33 450 90 07 00
Email carroz@carroz.com
Web site www.lescarroz.com

Morillon
top 2,480m (8,134ft) bottom 700m (2,296ft)
The old village of Morillon is centred around a sixteenth-century church and linked by road or gondola to Morillon 1100. Together they have some 10,000 visitor beds and make a popular second-home resort for the French. The resort has seven of its own lifts and is linked into the Grand Massif ski area. Morillon has its own ESF for adults and children, and the local Bureau des Guides takes clients off-piste. The children's village accepts little ones from six months up to ten years of age. Most of the accommodation is in chalets, apartments and gites. Le Morillon, a two-star hotel (☎ 450 90 10 32), has a recommended restaurant.

TOURIST INFORMATION
Tel 33 450 90 15 76
Fax 33 450 90 11 47
Email otmorill@ot-morillon.fr
Web site www.ot-morillon.fr

Samoëns
top 2,480m (8,134ft) bottom 700m (2,296ft)
The beautiful old town of Samoëns in the Giffre Valley has been a ski resort since 1912 and is the only one in France to be listed as a historical monument. It was once a thriving stone-cutting centre, and twice a week the tourist information office organises guided tours. Traditional-style bars and restaurants abound in what is a resort largely undiscovered by other nationalities. The three-star Neige et Roc (☎ 450 34 40 72) is recommended, together with the two-star Les Sept Monts (☎ 450 34 40 58) and Les Drugères (☎ 450 34 43 84). The resort has two new B&Bs – Chez Bobo (☎ 450 34 98 95) and Les Gîtes de Plampraz (☎ 450 34 95 98) – as well as two dozen restaurants, of which Le Pierrot des Neiges is highly praised.

Samoëns has an ESF with 95 instructors and eight mountain guides, a crèche for children from three months old and a ski kindergarten for children from three to six years of age. It also has 90km of loipe and a cross-country ski school. Dog-sledding, indoor climbing and skating are all offered in the resort, plus the more unusual activities of archery in the forest for adults and children over seven years of age (on snowshoes if necessary), caving, winter bivouac weekends, and snowshoeing rambles with accommodation in mountain refuges.

TOURIST INFORMATION
Tel 33 450 34 40 28
Fax 33 450 34 95 82
Email samoens@wanadoo.fr
Web site www.samoens.com

Megève

ALTITUDE 1,100m (3,608ft)

Beginners ✱✱✱ Intermediates ✱✱✱ Snowboarders ✱

In 1916, Baroness Noémie de Rothschild decided to find a resort in her home country to rival St Moritz. On advice from her Norwegian ski instructor she visited the tiny village of Megève. So impressed was she that five years later she built the Palace Hotel Mont d'Arbois, which helped transform Megève into an international resort. As a result, Megève was later able to boast that at the height of the season it was home to more crowned heads of state than any other ski resort in Europe. But its reputation slowly faded. The stars migrated to brighter galaxies that offered more certain snow and more challenging skiing.

✔ Large linked ski area
✔ Attractive medieval town centre
✔ Excellent child facilities
✔ High standard of restaurants
✔ Sophisticated après-ski
✔ Range of non-skiing activities
✔ Short airport transfer
✔ Tree-line skiing
✘ Unreliable resort-level snow
✘ Heavy traffic outside pedestrian area
✘ Lack of steep slopes

But Megève is back as a serious contender for the most stylish resort in the Alps. A combination of extensive gentle skiing, excellent children's facilities, lavish hotels and superlative restaurants, all set in a village that oozes ambience, acts as the lure for a new generation of snow-users. The village heart is built around a fine medieval church and carefully restored old buildings set in a traffic-free main square where you can hire brightly painted sleigh-taxis driven by local farmers. The four streets branching off it are lined with designer boutiques that attract many non-skiers. Free buses link the mid-town with the lifts, and coaches run to other nearby resorts covered on the Evasion Mont Blanc lift pass.

On the snow
top 2,350m (7,708ft) bottom 850m (2,788ft)

The skiing takes place on smooth and well-groomed pistes. Two of the three areas, Mont d'Arbois and Rochebrune, are connected at their bases by cable-car. Mont d'Arbois is the most extensive and in turn is accessed by separate gondolas from La Princesse outside **Combloux**, **Le Bettex** above St-Gervais, and **St-Nicolas-de-Véroce**. The skiing around Mont d'Arbois is mainly gentle, although some more challenging runs are to be found higher up on Mont Joux.

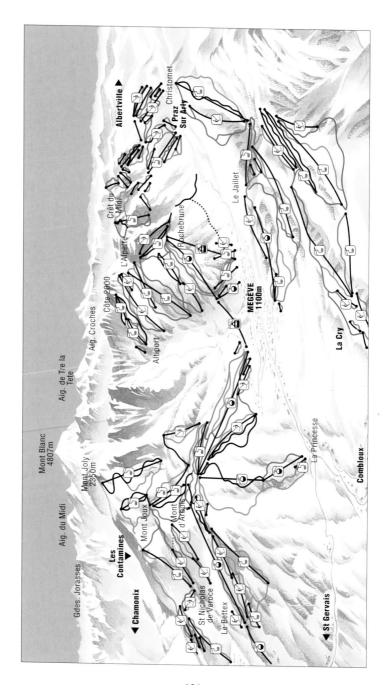

The access to the Rochebrune area is by a swift modern gondola that starts from the town centre. Rochebrune offers arguably the most attractive runs in the area in a delightful tree-lined setting and it is usually less crowded than Mont d'Arbois.

Megève's third skiing area is Le Jaillet – self-contained and reached by gondola only after a lengthy walk or bus ride from the middle of town. Its runs are mainly gentle and do not hold their snow well.

Beginners

The nursery slopes at Mont d'Arbois are easily accessible by cable-car or ski bus. The resort also abounds in green (beginner) slopes and gentle blues (easy). From Mont Joux, long blue runs descend to Les Communailles near Le Bettex, with drag-lifts back up to the ridge. The runs into Megève itself are mostly wide and easy and include a long green piste. There is a drag-lift in the trees at the top-station of Le Jaillet for novices, and the runs in this area are both mild and pleasant.

Intermediates

The skiing at Mont d'Arbois rises to its highest point of the area at Mont Joly at 2,350m. A choice of long and fairly gentle red (intermediate) runs takes you down into the attractive little village of St-Nicolas-de-Véroce as well as to St-Gervais. The large ski area is well suited to intermediates, although the low altitude makes the season a short one. The Evasion Mont Blanc lift pass covers all the resorts in the Chamonix Valley, making this a vast area.

Advanced

Provided you have a car, Megève is the most pleasant resort in the Mont Blanc area in which to base yourself to enjoy the 13 resorts (including **Chamonix** and **Argentière)** covered by the Evasion Mont Blanc ski pass. The pistes on the north-facing La Princesse side of the mountain are wooded, but the black (difficult) grading is not altogether justified. From the top of the gondola at Rochebrune, further lifts take you on up to Alpette. The highest point and the start of Megève's downhill course is Côte 2000, which provides some of the toughest skiing in the area and the best snow.

Off-piste

The area through the trees towards La Princesse provides superlative powder skiing after a fresh snowfall, as does Côte 2000. The off-piste is far less skied than in most of the other Mont Blanc resorts and is therefore likely to remain untracked for longer. A 90-minute walk up Mont Joly takes you to a point where you can ski down to the village of **Les Contamines**. Mont Blanc Helicopters (based in Annemasse) will pick up skiers and snowboarders from off-piste trips and return them to the pistes in Megève.

Snowboarding

As Megève has such a vast area, riders will be able to find plenty of suitable terrain. The gentle slopes make the resort particularly good for novice riders. The terrain park is at Mont Joux.

Cross-country

Langlaufers have a choice of four circuits totalling 75km, including a long, tricky but wonderfully scenic track from the Mont d'Arbois cablecar to Le Bettex and St-Nicolas-de-Véroce. Another links with the resort of **Praz-sur-Arly**. Unusual activities for cross-country enthusiasts include guided day-tours between Val d'Arly and Beaufortain.

Tuition and guiding

Megève's ski schools have fine reputations, particularly for beginners, who progress speedily from the nursery areas to the long and flattering easy and intermediate slopes. 'I can't praise the ESI enough,' said one reporter, 'my father, who is in his 70s and not very fit, felt very confident after three lessons'. The long-established Bureau des Guides de Megève is warmly recommended.

Mountain restaurants

Megève certainly has no shortage of lunch venues, adding to its gourmet attraction. The ski area is home to about 30, most of which are marked on a special walker/cross-country skier lift map. However, reporters noted that eating on the mountain can be expensive. Particularly recommended is the Auberge du Côte 2000, owned by the Rothschild family and serving some of the finest food in a resort where you are spoilt for choice. A trip to the Alpette restaurant is a must; the restaurant runs a snowcat service from the lift station for non-skiers. Radaz Ferme Auberge has 'a great atmosphere but slow service, so go early'.

In the Mont d'Arbois sector, Le Rosay is a 'reasonable self-service with an excellent balcony'. Chalet Idéal Sport, another Rothschild-owned eatery, is popular with those who want to see and be seen. Les Mandarines has 'some of the most inventive and delicious puddings we have ever eaten'. L'Igloo has a sunny terrace with magnificent views of Mont Blanc.

Accommodation

Megève has more than 40 hotels, as well as both sumptuous and more utilitarian private chalets. The standard of its six four-stars and some of its ten three-stars is outstanding. Chalet Relais et Châteaux du Mont d'Arbois (☎ 450 21 25 03) used to be the Rothschild family home and is located some distance from the town near the Mont d'Arbois cablecar. We also have good reports of Hotel Coin du Feu (☎ 450 21 04 94) and La Chauminé (☎ 450 21 37 05). Au Vieux Moulin (☎ 450 21 22 29) is said to be 'warm, spacious and tastefully decorated. Only a short stroll from the hustle and bustle, and the food was excellent'.

Jocelyn and Jean-Louis Sibuet own a collection of charming hotels in the resort. The Mont Blanc (☎ 450 21 20 02) is in the centre of the pedestrian zone and is one of the finest hotels in Europe. Les Fermes de Marie (☎ 450 93 03 10), a ten-minute walk from the town centre, is based around a sixteenth-century cowshed with vaulted ceiling; a collection of farm buildings in the grounds has been converted into luxury suites. The hotel has a fitness and beauty centre, which is one of the best in the Alps. The four-star Lodge Parc (☎ 450 93 05 03) has also been restored by the Sibuets; it boasts 53 bedrooms and is decorated in eclectic style, with the atmosphere of a private club.

Simpler accommodation includes three-star Le Fer à Cheval (☎ 450 21 30 39) and the Gollet (☎ 450 47 3 34) and Richmond (☎ 450 21 43 25) self-catering apartments.

Eating in and out

One reporter commented on the 'extensive quantity and variety of eating places to suit all budgets'. This is certainly true; Megève has more than 70 restaurants and is one of the gourmet dining centres of the Alps. At the top of the range, the Hotel Mont Blanc's Les Enfants Terribles has 'delicious but expensive food'. The Chalet Relais et Châteaux du Mont d'Arbois has a high-quality restaurant. Le Fer à Cheval serves a fine dinner but is also recommended for its English breakfast. At Jacques Megean fresh truffles are the speciality. Flocon de Sel, with its inventive cuisine prepared by Emmanuel Renaut, has recently been given a Michelin star. La Ferme de Mon Père is an imaginative restaurant with three Michelin stars. It is built as an old-style farmhouse complete with sheep, cows and goats outside the window. Le Bar du Chamois is a lively and less expensive bistro serving fondue and local white wines.

Après-ski

This is taken almost more seriously here than the skiing, and the choice of venues is enormous, ranging from the simplest of bars to the most exotic of nightspots. Le Prieuré is recommended for tea and cakes.

Later on the après-ski revolves largely around Megève's piano bars and nine nightclubs. Club de Jazz Les Cinq Rues is one of the most popular evening venues, set in cosy surroundings complete with open fire; during the ski season it attracts some of the big international names in jazz. Bar St Paul is 'cheap and frequented by locals'. The casino, originally a 1930s bus station, also houses a restaurant. Rosie Crève Coeur is an unusual bar that looks as if it has stepped out of a 1940s US air-force base. Le Palace Café is popular with a young crowd, while Le Cave de Megève attracts the forty-somethings.

The Palais des Sports contains an Olympic-size skating-rink and a vast swimming-pool. Electric-powered ice bumper-cars are an unusual sport available on the skating-rink. Shopping is a major pastime here ('a window-shopper's paradise'), headed by the original Aalard department store, antiques and jewellery shops, designer clothing boutiques, and some delightful household and interior decoration outlets.

Childcare

In keeping with its family values, Megève has some of the most extensive nursery slopes and comprehensive childcare facilities of any resort in France. The non-ski kindergarten, Meg'Loisirs, is housed in a well-equipped two-storey building next to the Palais des Sports. Creative children who want to take a break from skiing can attend Megève Matériaux on the outskirts of town. Here, six- to 13-year-olds can try their hand at stencilling, fabric painting and lots more.

Linked or nearby resorts

Les Contamines-Montjoie
top 2,500m (8,202ft) bottom 1,164m (3,818ft)

This unspoilt village is near the head of the narrow Montjoie Valley, just over the hill from Megève. It has a keen following despite the fact that the whole set-up is awkward. The long village is on one side of the river, the ski area on the other, and Le Lay base-station is a long, 1-km uphill walk from the centre. However, a regular shuttle bus runs between the village and the gondolas. Prices are below average for this area of France ('excellent value, with cheap lift passes'), and accommodation is modest.

The east-facing bowl, which makes up the ski area, holds its snow well and offers a good alternative when neighbouring resorts have none. Off-piste enthusiasts can find virtually untouched powder all over the area after a fresh snowfall. Two efficient gondolas, Auberge du Télé and Le Pontet (the latter is further down the valley and therefore less busy) take snow-users up to a plateau at 1,470m, where a further gondola takes them on to Le Signal and the start of the skiing.

Almost half of the 44 runs are intermediate, with the higher runs towards Mont Joly steeper and more testing. The Col du Joly at 2,000m separates the main bowl from a smaller but open area.

Ski, snowboard and telemark lessons are given by the ESF ('an excellent instructor') and Snowsession, and the Bureau des Guides is for off-piste guiding. Garderie Croc'Noisettes offers daycare and lessons for children from one to seven years old. The Jardin des Neiges is open only in the mornings during the French school holidays. Auberge de Colombaz is on an off-piste itinerary towards the village. The six mountain restaurants include 'a lovely little restaurant at the top of the Ruelle lift on the Belleville side' and 'a fairly large, pleasant restaurant at Etape'. Le Signal is rather basic.

The village runs along a single street with a Baroque church, old-fashioned chalet-style hotels and a few shops and cafés. The best location is on the east side of the river near the gondola. La Chemenaz (☎ 450 47 02 44) is the only three-star hotel; the rest are two-star. A wide variety of self-catering apartments is available. The 15 eateries include a couple of crêperies, a pizzeria, and restaurants serving local specialities. Nightlife is limited to a skating-rink, two discos, a cinema and concerts in the village church.

Skiing facts: Megève

TOURIST INFORMATION
BP 24, F-74120 Megève, Haute Savoie
Tel 33 450 21 27 28
Fax 33 450 93 03 09
Email megeve@megeve.com
Web site www.megeve.com

THE RESORT
By road Calais 890km
By rail Sallanches 12km, regular bus service to resort
Airport transfer Geneva 1hr
Visitor beds 40,500
Transport free ski bus with lift pass (links centre with access lifts)

THE SKIING
Linked or nearby resorts Argentière (n), Chamonix (n), Combloux (l), Flumet (n), Le Bettex (l), Les Contamines-Montjoie(n), Les Houches, Les Saisies (n), Notre-Dame-de-Bellecombe (n), Praz-sur-Arly (n), St-Gervais (l), St-Nicolas-de-Véroce (l)
Number of lifts 79 in resort, 121 in region
Total of trails/pistes 300km in resort, 450km in linked area (30% easy, 45% intermediate, 25% difficult), 729km in Mont Blanc ski area
Beginners 5 lifts, points tickets available

LIFT PASSES
Area pass Evasion Mont Blanc 890FF (covers 121 lifts in region), Mont Blanc 1,180FF (also covers all Chamonix and Courmayeur lifts), both for 6 days
Pensioners 60yrs and over 490–792FF
Credit cards yes

TUITION
Skiing ESF (5 centres) (☎ 450 21 00 97), ESI (☎ 450 58 78 88)
Snowboarding as ski schools
Other courses cross-country, freestyle, moguls, seniors, snowblading, skiing for the disabled, skwal, race-training, telemark
Guiding Bureau des Guides et Accompagnateurs (☎ 450 21 55 11), Mont Blanc Helicopters (☎ 450 92 78 21), and through ski schools

CHILDREN
Lift pass Evasion Mont Blanc 634FF, Mont Blanc 452FF, both 4–12yrs for 6 days
Ski & board school as adults
Kindergarten (ski/non-ski) Caboche (☎ 450 58 97 65), Princesse (☎ 450 93 00 86), Meg'Loisirs (☎ 450 58 77 84)

OTHER SPORTS
Climbing wall, curling, dog-sledding, hang-gliding, hot-air ballooning, ice-bumper cars, ice-climbing, ice-hockey, indoor tennis, light-aircraft flights, night-skiing, parapente, skating, sleigh rides, snowmobiling, snow polo, snowshoeing, swimming

FOOD AND DRINK
Coffee 12–16FF, glass of wine 10–14FF, small beer 18–23FF, soft drink 15FF, dish of the day 75–120FF

TOURIST INFORMATION
Tel 33 450 47 01 58
Fax 33 450 47 09 54
Email info@.lescontamines.com
Web site www.lescontamines.com

St-Gervais

top 2,350m (7,708ft) bottom 860m (2,821 ft)

As a spa resort, St-Gervais has attracted tourists since 1806 and today is popular with families wanting a cheaper alternative to Megève. Spa treatments are available in the hot springs. Nearby **Le Bettex** at 1,400m is a quieter village with a few comfortable hotels and some cross-country skiing.

The main ski area of St-Gervais is on the slopes of Mont d'Arbois and is linked with that of Megève. It has a terrain park with a half-pipe, and the area is accessed by a fast, 20-person jumbo gondola from the edge of the resort to Le Bettex. The second stage goes up to St-Gervais 1850. This is a popular and often crowded entrance to Megève's pistes. Skiing on the Mont Blanc side of St-Gervais is served by the Tramway, a funicular that climbs slowly to the Col de Voza at 1,653m, where it links to the skiing above **Les Houches**. Hotel-Restaurant Igloo and the Terminus in **Le Fayet** area both have good reputations for their cuisine.

St-Gervais has three nursery-slope lifts and two kindergartens. The ESF at St-Gervais and the ESI at Le Bettex both teach cross-country, slalom, snowblading, snowboarding and telemark. The two local mountain guiding companies are Compagnie des Guides de St-Gervais and Guides des Cimes, and both can organise heli-skiing.

Hotels here include three-star Le Carlina (☎ 450 93 41 10), with an indoor swimming-pool, Chalet l'Igloo (☎ 450 93 05 84) and the quiet Arbois Bettex (☎ 450 93 12 22): all three at the edge of the piste. A reporter recommended the Regina (☎ 450 47 78 10), with its reasonable prices and friendly staff. La Flèche d'Or (☎ 450 93 11 54) is mentioned. St-Gervais has a moderate range of restaurants, with 4 Epices and L'Eterle both good value. Le Four and Le Robinson serve a variety of local specialities, while La Tanière and La Chalette are traditional. La Nuit des Temps is the only disco.

TOURIST INFORMATION
Tel 33 450 47 76 08
Fax 33 450 47 75 69
Email welcome@st-gervais.net
Web site www.st-gervais.net

La Plagne

ALTITUDE 1,250–2,100m (4,100–6,889ft)

Beginners ✱✱✱ Intermediates ✱✱✱ Advanced ✱✱ Snowboarders ✱✱✱

Skiers and snowboarders expecting to visit France's newest ski circuit, which has been billed as a genuine rival to the Trois Vallées, will have to wait another year. The 200-person cable-car that will link La Plagne with Les Arcs at a cost of £10 million is unlikely to be completed before the 2002–3 season.

✔ Large integrated ski area
✔ Skiing convenience
✔ Beautiful scenery
✔ Extensive off-piste
✔ Geared to family skiing
✔ Summer skiing on the glacier
✖ Limited nightlife
✖ Some villages lacking in atmosphere

After a decade of debate, the two resorts (now under the same ownership) have finally agreed to build the link that will create one of the largest winter playgrounds in the world – 190 lifts and over 500km of groomed pistes designed to suit every category of skier from complete beginner to expert. The new link across the mile-wide gorge between the satellite villages of **Montchavin** (La Plagne) and **Peisey Vallandry** (Les Arcs) is scheduled to open in time for Christmas 2002. But even the most optimistic figures suggest that less than 30 per cent of visitors to either resort will actually use it.

Some would argue that La Plagne is already too big. From the air you get the impression that you are descending on to the jotting pad of a trainee town planner. Its ten separate villages, which are joined by lift pylons and ribbons of white, resemble a suburban sprawl of outstandingly dubious architectural merit. The resort's signature on the landscape is the giant battleship apartment block of **Aime-la-Plagne**, which, depending on your viewpoint, is either monstrous or magnificent ('nowhere near as ugly as I had been led to believe – a pleasant surprise'). Under the dynamic ownership of the Compagnie des Alpes, La Plagne has been undergoing a renaissance in recent years. The company, which already owns 11 resorts in France as well as Courmayeur in Italy and a significant interest in Verbier and Saas Fee in Switzerland, is now systematically upgrading La Plagne's 111 lifts serving 215km of groomed piste, of which 67 per cent is classified as easy to intermediate.

The British make up 37 per cent of all foreign visitors, and all the mass-market tour operators offer holidays here in villages and accommodation of varying character, so it is vital to choose carefully.

La Plagne's six high-altitude villages lie in the central area at altitudes ranging from 1,800m to 2,100m. As far as modern architecture is concerned, the later the better: imaginatively designed **Belle**

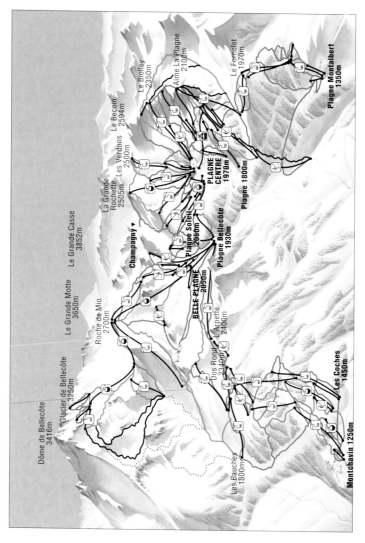

Plagne is the firm favourite, with its attractive village centre and integrated arcs of apartment buildings, while the low-rise wood-clad complexes at **Plagne 1800** and **Plagne Villages/Plagne Soleil** are inspired by Savoyard tradition.

Aime 2000's apartments have been redecorated. **Plagne Bellecôte's** semi-circle of high-rise reddish blocks is an acquired taste.

The four lower villages, **Montchavin**, **Montalbert**, **Les Coches** and **Champagny-en-Vanoise**, lie on different access roads in far-flung parts of the mountain but all are connected with the central complex by lift. Although the farming village of Montchavin was adapted to become part of La Plagne in the early 1970s, a rural smell still lingers in the air. It has a gondola link to neighbouring Les Coches, which is a modern ski complex with its own wooded slopes.

Champagny-en-Vanoise, at the base of the south-facing back side of the mountain, consists of a series of hamlets in a quiet valley linked to the ski area by an efficient gondola. Montalbert and its satellite holiday centre have snow-cannon on their west-facing slopes.

All ten villages are self-sufficient, with their own selection of shops, bars and restaurants. The six high villages are connected by bus or covered lifts from 8am to 1am. As its name suggests, Plagne Centre has the lion's share of essential services – banks, a post office, police, doctors and 'a fairly good range of shops' – in the environs of its bleak, subterranean commercial precinct. Aesthetic it is not, but it scores highly for convenience, as does Bellecôte, which also has banks and a post office.

On the snow
top 3,250m (10,660ft) bottom 1,250m (4,100ft)

La Plagne represents the ultimate in ski-in ski-out convenience. To point your skis in any direction from the nexus in Plagne Centre is to lock into the network of lifts on the shallow gradients of La Grande Rochette, Les Verdons and Le Biolley. The old Grande Rochette lift was replaced for the 2000–1 season by a Funitel gondola. The Bellecôte gondola provides the most efficient connection with Roche de Mio, a steeper mountain with more challenging terrain; from here you can take the lift up to the Bellecôte Glacier, which is the highest point in the entire resort.

The Montchavin/Les Coches area is connected to the high-altitude area through Arpette, a direct quad-chair ride from Bellecôte. The predominantly wooded Montalbert–Longefoy pistes lie on the other side of the resort below Aime-la-Plagne. Access to Champagny-en-Vanoise is via Les Verdons, the midway point on the rim of the main bowl, or Roche de Mio.

La Plagne has few queues in good weather, but the links to the outlying areas close down rapidly in stormy weather, causing congestion in the centre. Reporters praised the ski area: 'the signposting is good and the pistes are well groomed'. La Plagne has 100km of marked cross-country trails in the lower villages but only 11km spread between the high-altitude satellites.

Beginners
With the exception of Champagny-en-Vanoise, all parts of the mountain have extensive beginner slopes. Those staying in the other three

low-altitude villages of Les Coches, Montchavin and Montalbert gain in visibility by being below the tree-line, but this advantage used to be balanced by less reliable snow conditions, especially in spring. However, the area's recent investment in new snow-cannon has improved this.

The slope in Plagne Centre below the Marie-Chantal piste is 'supposed to be green (beginner), but it is too difficult for complete beginners. There are easier runs but you have to buy a lift-pass to use them'. The pistes on either side of the Arpette ridge above Bellecôte offer gradients so gentle that even the most fearful novice should gain in confidence, while the web of blue (easy) runs between Belle Plagne and Plagne Centre make for a natural second-week progression.

Intermediates

As befits a state-of-the-art ski area, La Plagne offers most to those snow-users dedicated to racking up the kilometres. This can be done most readily on the red (intermediate) runs on the eastern side of the bowl above Aime-la-Plagne. However, Roche de Mio has more varied terrain, with the run back to Belle Plagne via a long tunnel particularly recommended. An adventurous alternative is the Crozats piste down to Les Bauches 1800, which has a link back to the main circus via two exposed chair-lifts.

The summer ski drag-lifts at the top of the glacier are not usually open in winter, but La Combe and Le Chiaupe runs to the Bellecôte gondola base-station hold no terrors for committed motorway cruisers. Enterprising intermediates will enjoy the exhilarating Mont de la Guerre run from Les Verdons to Champagny-en-Vanoise, but check conditions first as the descent is extremely rocky when snow is sparse.

Advanced

The resort has a general lack of black (difficult) runs, with most pistes described as 'fairly intermediate'. One reporter commented: 'this is definitely a family resort – tough runs are scarce'. Although glaciers are not generally known for steep skiing, La Plagne's is one of the exceptions. The disadvantage is the 45-minute trek to the top from the centre of the resort, but once in place advanced skiers and snowboarders will find plenty to test them. The other steep area is off Le Biolley ridge above Aime-la-Plagne. When conditions are good, the Morbleu piste is a compellingly direct drop to Le Fornelet cross-country area. On the east-facing side of the ridge, the Emile Allais descent to the bottom of the outlying Charmettes chair is the longest black run in the resort.

Off-piste

As with the advanced pistes, the best areas of off-piste are on the fringes of the resort, including the long, sweeping descent from the top of the glacier down to Les Bauches. From here, the choice lies between an easy blue piste to Montchavin, a return to Arpette via the Bauches chair or, more dramatically, an itinerary down to Peisey-Nancroix in the adjacent valley. The other prime off-piste area lies on the western slopes of Le

Biolley; it is especially enjoyable towards the end of the season, when spring snow is at its best. The back of the Bellecôte Glacier offers the demanding Col du Nant run into the remote valley of Champagny-le-Haut, followed by a return to Champagny-en-Vanoise by shuttle bus.

Snowboarding

If La Plagne is not a favourite among dedicated freeriders, it is because of its lack of ambience rather than lack of opportunity, since there is plenty of excellent off-piste. Riders congregate at the Col de Forcle terrain park between Plagne Bellecôte and Plagne Villages. Montchavin also has a terrain park. The wide pistes and the lift system are ideal for Alpine snowboarders or carvers.

Tuition and guiding

The French Ski School (ESF) is based in each of the ten villages of the resort, employing more than 500 instructors. However, reporters complained of their large size: 'I saw a couple of ESF groups of 20, which is much too large to learn anything'. The volume of business means that the ESF has been able to introduce teenage ski classes for greater peer-group pleasure. It also has guided off-piste courses in La Plagne and the surrounding outposts of the Tarentaise Valley.

We have good reports of Oxygène at Plagne Centre, where instructors are said to be 'friendly and professional'. Elpro, based in Belle Plagne, and Evolution 2 in the village of Montchavin are the alternative ski and snowboard schools. La Plagne has a ski school called Antenne Handicap, which offers private lessons for people with physical and mental disabilities.

Mountain restaurants

In an area increasingly well known for its mountain restaurants, there are three outstanding choices. The Au Bon Vieux Temps, just below Aime-la-Plagne, is recommended for its sunny terrace, traditional Savoyard dishes and efficient service. La Soupe au Schuss, also at Aime-la-Plagne, is another excellent venue. The Petit Chaperon Rouge, on the edge of the nursery slope just above Plagne 1800 ('quiet, pleasant, with nice food for a reasonable price') is the wiser choice on a snowy day because of its open fires.

Good value is represented by La Rossa at the top of the Champagny gondola. The Dou du Praz above Plagne Villages received mixed reports, including 'the staff were rude and impatient'. Reporters favoured Chez Pat du Sauget, an old summer farm on the pastures above Montchavin, which has recently been elevated to *auberge* status, with the addition of simple bedrooms. Polly's, next to the skating rink at Plagne Bellecôte, is said to have 'wonderful food – the Salad Blue is fantastic and it is reasonably priced in general'. Le Loup in Plagne 1800 is recommended for lunch. Le Bec Fin in Plagne Centre is described as 'value-for-money'. The Plan Bois, above Les Coches, has 'rustic charm and is a great spot for lunch'.

Accommodation

Two-thirds of La Plagne's 50,000 beds are in the high-altitude villages, and one-third are in the lower villages. In Belle Plagne, Hotel Eldorador (☎ 479 09 12 09) ('small rooms but food to die for') offers ski-in ski-out convenience. The Centaur (☎ 479 09 79 79 for all self-catering) is a well-equipped three-star *résidence*, while Les Balcons de Belle Plagne (☎ 479 55 76 76) is a high-quality *résidence*/hotel. Also in Belle Plagne, the luxurious chalet/hotel Les Montagnettes (☎ 479 55 12 00) represents a welcome wind of change with its chalets and apartments that can be rented for self-catering or with full hotel services. The newer Paladien Terra Nova (☎ 479 55 79 00) in Plagne Centre runs its own crèche and mini club. Aime-la-Plagne has a four-star MGM apartment complex built around a swimming-pool.

Self-caterers in search of a taste of rural France can rent one of 200 *gîtes* on the lower slopes of La Plagne. They are rated as normal, comfortable or luxurious and cost about half the price of the higher, purpose-built accommodation.

In Champagny-en-Vanoise the four-star *résidence*, Les Chalets du Bouquetin (☎ 479 55 01 13), is said to be 'the most beautiful in La Plagne'. Also in Champagny, two-star Club Alpina (☎ 479 55 04 59) is a chalet-style building containing a restaurant, and a sports centre with a swimming-pool. Champagny's Le Centaure apartments (☎ 479 09 12 09) were praised by reporters: 'very clean and well equipped, with direct lift access and a good-sized south-facing balcony'.

Eating in and out

La Soupe au Schuss in Aime-la-Plagne is an expensive restaurant serving specialities from the Périgord region. Le Matafan in Belle Plagne offers a range of medium-priced Savoyard dishes including raclette and fondue. Le Loup Garou, a short sleigh ride (or walk) down the path from Plagne Centre to Plagne 1800, serves similar dishes in a festive atmosphere. Le Bec Fin in Plagne Centre is 'homely', and Le Loup in 1800 is praised: 'served the best pizza I have ever tasted. Pleasant surroundings – lots of old copper and cow bells'. Le Terrasse in 1800 is also recommended. Les Coches and Montchavin have half-a-dozen restaurants each, while Champagny and Plagne Montalbert have more than ten each. All the villages have supermarkets and delicatessens for the self-catering brigade.

Après-ski

By comparison with its Tarentaise neighbours, **Val d'Isère** and **Courchevel**, La Plagne's nightlife is quiet. The six discos and four late-night bars are mainly in Plagne Centre and Bellecôte. The current favourite in Plagne Centre is Le King Café, which has live music most nights and a weekly karaoke ('turns into a national competition of pride, usually started by loud Brits who eventually get overwhelmed by the French'). Le Mat's Pub is a faithful re-creation of a British pub, making it a winner among Brits staying in Belle Plagne ('popular with

Skiing facts: La Plagne

TOURIST INFORMATION
BP 62, 73211, Aime Cedex
Tel 33 479 09 79 79
Fax 33 479 09 70 10
Email bienvenue@la-plagne.com
Web site www.la-plagne.com
UK Agent Erna Low (see *Which tour operator?*)

THE RESORT
By road Calais 930km
By rail Aime 18km
Airport transfer Lyon 2hrs, Geneva 3hrs
Visitor beds 46,000
Transport free bus service

THE SKIING
Linked or nearby resorts Les Arcs (n), Peisey-Nancroix (n), Tignes (n), Trois Vallées (n), Val d'Isère (n), Vallandry (n)
Number of lifts 111
Total of trails/pistes 215km (9% easy, 58% intermediate, 28% difficult, 5% very difficult)
Beginners nursery slope with free drag-lift in each of 10 resorts
Summer skiing Bellecôte Glacier

LIFT PASSES
Area pass 1,070FF for 6 days (covers 10 centres, Les Arcs and 1 day in L'Espace Killy or Trois Vallées)
Pensioners 60yrs and over 870FF for 6 days, free for 72yrs and over
Credit cards yes

TUITION
Skiing ESF in all 10 centres (☎ 479 09 00 40), Belle Plagne: Elpro (☎ 479 09 11 62), Montchavin: Evolution 2 (☎ 479 07 81 67), Plagne Centre: Oxygène (☎ 479 09 03 99), Antenne Handicap (☎ 479 09 13 80)

Snowboarding ESF, Elpro, Evolution 2, Oxygène
Other courses cross-country, extreme skiing, freestyle, heli-skiing/heli-boarding, moguls, monoski, powder clinics, seniors, skiing for the disabled, ski-touring, snowblading, speed skiing, Skwal, teen skiing, telemark, women's clinics
Guiding ESF, Evolution 2

CHILDREN
Lift pass 5–13yrs 805FF (covers 10 centres) for 6 days
Ski & board school ESF, Elpro, Evolution 2, Montchavin/Les Coches: Formule Ski (☎ 479 07 82 82), Oxygène
Kindergarten (ski) through ski schools, (non-ski) Aime-la-Plagne: Maison des Lutins (☎ 479 09 04 75), Belle Plagne: Garderie (☎ 479 09 06 68), Mini-Eldo at the Eldorador (☎ 479 09 12 09), Champagny: Cabris (☎ 479 55 05 37), Montalbert: Bambins (☎ 479 55 54 40), Montchavin: Formule Ski (☎ 479 07 82 82), Club Garderie (☎ 479 07 82 82), Plagne Bellecote: Maison de Dorothée (☎ 479 09 01 33), Plagne Centre: Crèche Municipal (☎ 479 09 00 83), Garderie Marie Christine (☎ 479 09 11 81), Terra Nova (☎ 479 55 79 00), Plagne Villages/Plagne Soleil: Foret des Enfants (☎ 479 09 04 40)

OTHER SPORTS
Bob-rafting, bobsleigh, climbing wall, hang-gliding, luge-ing, night-skiing, parapente, skating, sleigh rides, snowmobiling, snowshoeing, squash, swimming, taxi-bob, tubing

FOOD AND DRINK
Coffee 8–10FF, glass of wine 18–20FF, small beer 16–18FF, soft drink 16FF, dish of the day 55–90FF

holiday-makers and workers alike. I have seen people in there at 1am still in ski gear and ski boots'). Le Saloon is also popular. The watering-hole of choice in Bellecôte is Le Show Time Café/Le Jet Discothèque, while the Lincoln is the winner in Plagne Soleil ('British-run, so don't go here for French atmosphere. All the staff were British except one. But it had good food'). Aime-la-Plagne has Totobrix, while Le Galaxy is the night-spot in Champagny, and Oxygène disco is in Montchavin.

The most exhilarating non-skiing activity in La Plagne is the Olympic bob-run, which is open to the public whenever conditions permit. The Taxi-Bob is the genuine experience, with two rookies sandwiched between a professional driver and a brake-man for a breathtaking 50-second descent at speeds of up to 100kph. The softer option is the bob-raft, a four-person, foam-rubber cocoon that hurtles down in gravity-propelled mode at 80kph. Reporters complained about a shortage of non-skiing activities in Champagny: 'lack of things to do, especially for children, in the early evenings. It would not suit teenagers or young couples'.

Childcare

'An excellent ski area for our intermediate children, and very cheerful lift operators – especially towards the children' was the comment from one reporter. Certainly the villages each have their own nursery slopes and children's ski school. However, ski school classes in high season 'sometimes contained up to 15 children'. The ESF has learn-to-ski programmes for children aged two to seven in specially designed snow gardens in all of the villages. 'We found the Belle Plagne kindergarten to be both friendly and flexible. However, in practice the one at Bellecôte involves less walking for toddlers'. The Oxygène ski school at Plagne Centre was recommended: 'The instructors' English is excellent and they are always friendly and caring too. Other parents tell me they are far better than the ESF who appear to have no patience with children'. The Club Garderie Montchavin–Les Coches has a mixed programme of skiing and other learning activities for children aged three and upwards.

La Plagne has ten nurseries for toddlers and older; Marie Christine in Plagne Centre accepts babies as young as three months old, while Belle Plagne and Montalbert accept little ones from 18 months. The Eldorador Hotel has its Mini-Eldo children's club (four- to 12-year-olds), plus a supervised children's table in the hotel restaurant and babysitting by arrangement in the evening. Hotel Paladien Terra Nova has a mini-club for little ones from 18 months old. Garderie Marie Christine is for non-skiing children aged two to six.

Portes du Soleil

ALTITUDE Avoriaz 1,800m (5,904ft), Morzine 1,000m (3,280ft)

Beginners ✳✳✳ Intermediates ✳✳✳ Advanced ✳ Snowboarders ✳✳✳

The Portes du Soleil might be considered to be one of Europe's greatest overall ski areas were it not for one major fault: it is too low. With a top height of only 2,350m and the villages mostly below 1,200m, snow cover is by no means guaranteed and the links are liable to rupture at any time. However, its proximity to Mont Blanc does to some extent confer its own micro-climate.

✔ Vast ski area
✔ Ideal cruising territory
✔ Extensive cross-country trails
✔ Good childcare facilities
✔ Car-free resort (Avoriaz)
✔ Short airport transfer
✔ Tree-level skiing (Châtel and Morgins)
✘ Low altitude (except Avoriaz)
✘ Overcrowded pistes (Avoriaz)

The circuit straddles the French–Swiss border close to Geneva and is an uneasy marketing consortium of a dozen ski villages, ranging from large, internationally recognised resorts to the tiniest of unspoilt hamlets.

The published statistics refer to 650km of piste (although how this figure is arrived at is best not examined) served by 206 lifts (more than half of them are drag-lifts) to create a well-linked circus covering vast tracts of land bordered by Lac Léman. In reality, the Portes du Soleil consists of a series of naturally separate ski areas. Most are joined by awkward and often confusing mountain links, while a few, such as **St-Jean d'Aulps/La Grande Terche** and **Abondance**, are entirely independent.

While it is possible to complete a tour of the main resorts in one day, this actually involves limited enjoyable skiing and a considerable amount of time spent on lifts, although the new hands-free lift pass eases passage. To explore the region fully you need four weeks, at least two bases, a car and exceptional snow conditions such as the region has recently been enjoying.

Out of the 12 resorts, only **Avoriaz** can be recommended as a snow-sure base and, when cover is poor or non-existent elsewhere, the overcrowding here becomes a complete misery. However, keen skiers and snowboarders should base themselves at this end of the circuit, where the slopes are the most challenging.

Signposting has improved but is still desperately confusing, as is the overall Portes du Soleil piste map. The introduction of suggested itineraries, each illustrated by a different bird or animal for different standards of skiers, has not been voted a great success by reporters. As one commented: 'when trying to find my way back down to **Châtel** at the end of the day, a picture of a running rabbit is of little help'. Snow-users

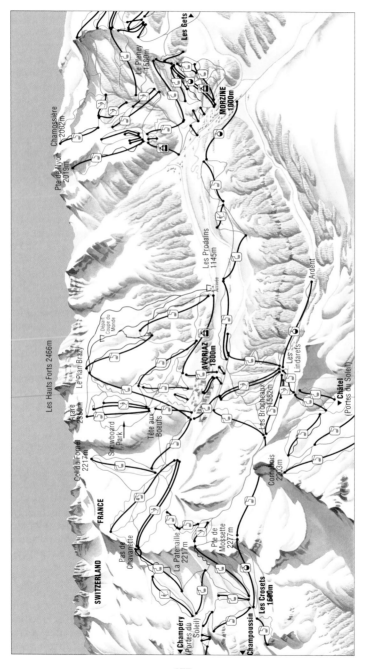

are advised to carry passports as well as two sets of currency. Although Switzerland will no doubt accept euros in border areas, the rate may not be advantageous to visitors. Avoriaz is mainly a collection of apartment blocks perched on the edge of a cliff far above **Morzine** and built in what for the 1960s was a truly futuristic style. Unfortunately, many of the older blocks are showing their age, and no amount of face-lifts can improve the lack of space in their interiors. The resort is reached from the valley either by a narrow, winding road or by cable-car from Les Prodains. A vehicle has no useful purpose in car-free Avoriaz, and the charges in the car park are iniquitous. Transport to your apartment block or hotel is via horse-drawn sleigh, piste machine or on foot. When not on skis, moving around is made easier by public lifts within the apartment blocks to different levels of this steep resort. The busiest area is around the foot of the nursery slopes by the shops, bars and restaurants.

Morzine is a market town and long-established resort on the lower section of the road to Avoriaz. It has all the appeal of an old-style chalet resort set in charming, wooded surroundings. The biggest drawback is its lack of altitude (1,000m), which means that resort-level snow can be scarce. The town covers a large area on both sides of a river gorge and is on several levels. It has a serious traffic problem, but a high foot-bridge over the river makes getting around less tortuous for pedestrians than for motorists. The main congested shopping street climbs from the old village centre beside the river to more open ground at the foot of Le Pleney, where the resort has developed, with hotels and shops around the tourist information office.

Such is the diffuse nature of the resort that the free buses and a miniature road train are an essential form of transport. Horse-drawn taxis are an alternative means of getting around. As Morzine is a proper working town, it boasts a better range of shops than in most ski resorts.

On the snow
top 2,350m (7,708ft) bottom 1,100m (3,608ft)

The skiing around Avoriaz is ideal for all standards of snow-users. Above the village is an extension of the main nursery slopes, with a variety of drag-lifts serving a series of confidence-building green (beginner) runs, which link with the lifts coming up from Morzine.

The best of the Avoriaz skiing is to be found in the Hauts Forts sector above the resort (from where you can descend 1,300m vertical to the cable-car station at Les Prodains) and on the Swiss border at Pas de Chavanette. From here the Chavanette black (difficult) run – better known as The Wall – takes you down towards **Les Crosets**, **Champéry** and the rest of the Portes du Soleil.

Les Crosets sits above the tree-line surrounded by abundant wide pistes, some of them north-facing but most of them sunny. From here there are connections with **Champoussin** and **Morgins**. Morgins has little skiing on the approach side from Champoussin, but it includes an excellent north-facing red (intermediate) run cut through the woods above the village. Those who wish to continue skiing the circuit must

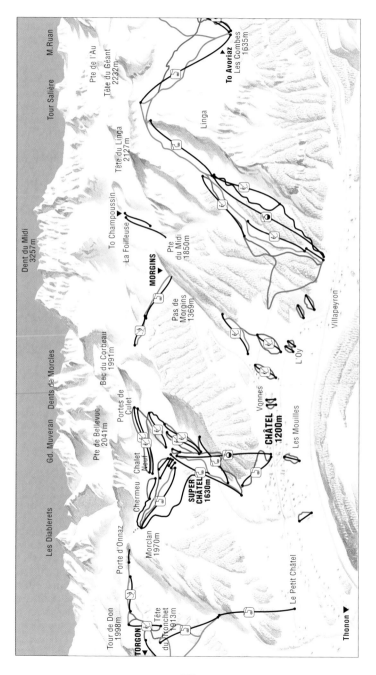

walk across the village or take a short bus ride to the nursery slopes and the lifts for **Super-Châtel** and France. In strong contrast to the sometimes bleak ski-fields of Avoriaz, the pistes here wind through the trees and are connected by a series of short drag-lifts.

The Morclan chair from Super-Châtel up to 1,970m serves the most challenging slope – a moderately difficult mogul field. The top of this chair is the departure point for **Torgon**, one of the further extremities of the Portes du Soleil, back across the border in Switzerland. The remainder of the skiing around Super-Châtel is mostly blue (easy) and red, on wide areas both above and below the lift station.

The Portes du Soleil circuit breaks down at Châtel and, whichever way you are travelling, the link cannot be made on skis. You have to take a bus across the village to the gondola up to Linga; this is the first of a long chain of lifts and pistes towards Avoriaz and provides one of the best intermediate playgrounds in the region with a seemingly endless variation of terrain and gradients.

From Avoriaz you can also ski down to Les Prodains and Morzine, which has its own extensive ski area linking to **Les Gets**. Most queuing problems in the Portes du Soleil are in the Avoriaz sector.

Beginners

Given acceptable snow conditions, it does not really matter which end of the circus you choose. Châtel and Morgins both have easy nursery slopes and plenty of tree-level skiing to which novices can graduate after a few days. Morzine, and in particular the runs around **Super-Morzine**, are well-suited to first-timers.

Intermediates

The whole of the Portes du Soleil ski area is ideal cruising territory. Less confident snow-users will prefer the long, sweeping runs at the Châtel end of the circuit. Linga and Plaine Dranse have entertaining slopes that keep their snow well. Stronger skiers and boarders will look towards the greater challenges of Champéry and Avoriaz. Les Gets is also an ideal base from which to explore the intermediate skiing.

Advanced

Accomplished snow-users should base themselves at the Avoriaz end of the circuit, although Champéry and Châtel are also delightful. Thanks to lift improvements, all are within easy reach of one another. It is perfectly possible to make a leisurely start from Châtel, explore Avoriaz and Les Crosets, and return to Châtel within three hours. The Wall is the most notorious run in the area; a sign at the top warns that it is to be attempted only by experts, yet it is usually crowded with intermediates. Certainly the initial angle of descent is such that you cannot see what lies ahead. After the first 50m the run flattens out considerably, though the moguls tend to be poorly cut by the high intermediate traffic. However, there are plenty of other equally challenging pistes in the region, including the World Cup run from Le Plan Brazy above Avoriaz all the way down to Les Prodains.

Off-piste

The best powder runs are to be found within easy reach of the piste above Châtel and Avoriaz on both sides of the Swiss border. After a fresh snowfall various itineraries parallel to The Wall can be exhilarating. The area is prone to considerable avalanche danger, and the services of a qualified guide are essential. Other off-piste opportunities include the Crêtes, Le Fornet and La Suisse.

Snowboarding

Avoriaz was the first resort in Europe to appreciate the importance of snowboarding when the sport was in the early stages of development. It was also the first (in 1993) to build a half-pipe and is now recognised as one of the world's major snowboarding centres. The terrain park has recently been improved with the addition of a permanent boardercross course and a separate section with gaps, tables and rails. It provides a micro-park for children with mini-boardercross and smaller obstacles. For alpine riders, the Arare piste is hard to beat for high-speed carving. Les Crosets, Morgins, Super-Châtel, Torgon and Les Gets all have terrain parks.

Tuition and guiding

Avoriaz has the International Ski School (ESI) and the French Ski School (ESF) ('too serious and boring for most of the week, with a ridiculous emphasis on final day tests'), whereas the ESF in Morzine is recommended for its 'friendly instructors'. Both the ESF and ESI also teach snowboarding, in healthy competition with Emery Snowboard School, Free Ride and the much-praised British Alpine Ski and Snowboarding School. The last, in both Morzine and Avoriaz, was set up by a couple of BASI instructors, and was described by one reporter as 'everything the ESF is not – small classes and good technical advice in one's mother tongue'. You need to book well in advance, especially during school holidays. Ski Snowboard et Aventures is Morzine's specialist board school, while Bureau de la Montagne and Maison de la Montagne are this resort's mountain guiding companies.

Mountain restaurants

The Portes du Soleil offers a mixed bag of eateries, ranging from overcrowded self-services to wonderful old huts off the beaten track. Prices are generally high on both sides of the border, and there are simply not enough restaurants. Coquoz at Planachaux enjoys a circular open fire and offers wonderful local Swiss specialities. **Les Lindarets**, the hamlet just north of Avoriaz, has the best concentration of eating-places with competitive prices, and La Chanterelle at the foot of the Chéry Nord chair is warmly recommended, too. La Cabushe near Le Ranfoilly is 'simple, but brilliant value', while Plaine Dranse is said to be 'a great find – this is where the locals eat, so prices must be fair'.

Les Prodains, at the bottom of the Vuarnet run from Avoriaz, is much praised, not least for its reasonable prices. The two restaurants at the top of Le Pleney are said to be 'always busy, but the wait is worth it', and the Perdrix Blanche at Pré-la-Joux is good value and recommended for its warm atmosphere. Les Portes du Soleil at Super-Châtel is praised, together with Chez Gaby in Champoussin. Le Corbeau above Morgins is said to be rustic, with reasonable prices.

Accommodation

The accommodation in Avoriaz is nearly all in apartment blocks, which vary in quality according to their age. The advertised maximum occupancy of each apartment is usually grossly overstated – a flat for four people sleeps two in comfort and a flat for six actually sleeps four. Bookings should be made through Pierre & Vacances (☎ 143 22 22 22), Maeva Latitudes (☎ 472 56 92 92) and Les Fontaines Blanches (☎ 450 74 28 00). The two hotels are Les Dromonts (☎ 450 74 08 11) and La Falaise (☎ 450 74 26 00). Location within the resort is of no significance for skiing purposes, although some of the village streets, which are also pistes, may prove difficult for novices.

Morzine has a plentiful supply of hotels in each price bracket; most are chalet-style and none is luxurious. In the central area, Les Airelles (☎ 450 74 71 21) is one of the more comfortable, while Hotel Fleur des Neiges (☎ 450 79 01 23) is a reasonable two-star built in chalet-style. Hotel Le Tremplin (☎ 450 79 12 31) ('delightful family-run establishment') is on the edge of the piste with a grandstand view of the night-skiing and -snowboarding arena. We continue to receive rave reports of the Hotel Le Dahu (☎ 450 75 92 92) ('excellent and friendly').

Eating in and out

Avoriaz boasts a choice of about 30 restaurants, most of which are rather overpriced. Les Intrets is a favourite with reporters for its raclette, fondue and pierrade, and Le Petit Vatel serves rustic fare. The Bistro opposite Le Village des Enfants is 'good, but expensive', while Les Fontaines Blanches is 'reasonably priced, with a wide range of excellent food'. Le Savoyard provides plenty of local flavour.

In Morzine, the Neige Roc at Les Prodains and Le Tremplin are also highly rated by reporters. L'Etale serves regional specialities in a 'wonderful, authentic mountain atmosphere', and La Chamade and La Grange are both highly rated for a special night out.

Après-ski

The Place in Avoriaz has live, non-French music and an 'excellent atmosphere'. Les Ruches and Le Choucas are hangouts for riders; the latter offers live music and is usually not too crowded. Pub Le Tavaillon was described by one reporter as 'the nerve centre of Avoriaz'. The nightclubs are said to be generally overpriced and empty, except on striptease nights, when audience participation is invited. Le Festival and Midnight Express discos both charge entrance fees, and Midnight Express offers a free 'bucking bronco'. Morzine abounds with civilised tea-rooms and bars. Inside the Wallington complex are a bowling alley, pool hall, bar and disco. L'Opéra and Le Paradis de Laury's are the nightclubs.

Childcare

Le Village des Enfants/Le Village Snowboard in Avoriaz has a justified reputation as one of the better childcare establishments in France. Children from three years old are taught in the centre of the village, using methods developed by the celebrated French ski champion Annie Famose. Younger non-skiing children are looked after in Les P'tits Loups day nursery, of which we have good reports.

Morzine's L'Outa crèche takes infants from two months to six years, while Pingouins Malins provides daycare for children from four to 12 years with ski lessons.

Linked or nearby resorts

Abondance
top 1,800m (5,906ft) bottom 930m (3,050ft)

This tiny, historic village lies 7km from **La Chapelle d'Abondance** and is not linked into the main Portes du Soleil system. A bus service runs from Châtel and La Chapelle d'Abondance. It has its own small ski area with a dedicated children's area on the slopes beneath the Col de l'Ecuelle, served by a gondola and a series of drags.

TOURIST INFORMATION
Tel 33 450 73 02 90
Fax 33 450 73 04 76
Email ot@valdabondance.com
Web site www.valdabondance.com

Champéry
top 2,350m (7,708ft) bottom 1,053m (3,455ft)

This traditional Swiss village is set in dramatic surroundings within easy skiing distance of Avoriaz. The one-way main street is lined with attractive wooden chalets, hotels, shops and restaurants. The 125-person cable-car up to Planachaux is on the hill down to the valley road that skirts the village; the lift is served by a free minibus. Both Swiss Ski School and Freeride Company give snowboarding lessons.

Champéry's accommodation includes two long-established hotels – Hotel Suisse Golden Tulip (☎ 244 79 07 07) and Hotel et Résidence de Champéry (☎ 244 79 10 71) – which are comfortable and welcoming. Auberge du Grand-Paradis (☎ 244 79 11 67) is also recommended, while Hotel la Rose des Alpes (☎ 244 79 12 18) gives value for money.

One of the best restaurants in the area, the Grand-Paradis, is 2km outside the village at the foot of the slopes and is reached by bus from Champéry. It has an atmospheric, wood-panelled interior with an open fire. Restaurant du Nord offers traditional Swiss specialities, while Les

Pervenches and Le Centre serve Far Eastern specialities. Popular bars include Mitchell's, the Bar des Guides, Le Levant, Le Pub, La Crevasse and Les Mines d'Or. The comprehensive sports centre boasts indoor and outdoor ice-rinks, swimming-pools and a fitness centre.

Champéry has a gentle nursery slope with a rope-tow in the middle of the village; snow permitting, this provides an ideal beginners' area for small children. The ESS takes children from three years.

TOURIST INFORMATION
Tel 41 244 79 20 20
Fax 41 244 79 20 21
Email champery-ch@portesdusoleil.com
Web site www.champery.ch

Champoussin
top 2,350m (7,708ft) bottom 1,680m (5,512ft)

Champoussin is a mini-resort of new, rustic-style buildings that are almost all apartments ('highly recommended') and a main hotel, the Résidence Royal Alpage Club (☎ 244 76 83 00) ('better value than it used to be'). The hotel boasts a sauna, swimming-pool, games room and disco, and runs its own kindergarten and mini-club. Après-ski is limited to the hotel and two restaurants: Le Poussin bar/restaurant and Chez Gaby, which runs a snowcat service from the village in the evening. Floodlit skiing takes place here on Wednesday evenings, and the thermal baths 10km away at **Val d'Iliez** are worth a visit.

The small ski school does not receive impressive reports, and reporters have mixed views on the resort: 'great for family holidays, but singles, extreme skiers and snowboarders should look elsewhere' and 'Champoussin is so small and remote that just looking at it could give you cabin fever'.

TOURIST INFORMATION
Tel 41 244 76 83 00
Fax 41 244 76 83 01
Email hotel.royal.alpage@portesdusoleil.com
Web site www.portesdusoleil.com

La Chapelle d'Abondance
top 1,700m (5,577ft) bottom 1,010m (3,313ft)

This old farming community, 6km down the valley from Châtel, straddles both sides of the road without any defined centre. On one side, two long chairs take you up to Crêt Béni at 1,650m, from where a series of drags serves a choice of mainly easy runs through the pine forest. On the other side of the road a gondola and a chair-lift link into Torgon and Châtel. Hotels Les Cornettes (☎ 450 73 50 24) and the Alti 1000 (☎ 450 73 51 90) both have swimming-pools and fitness centres. Les Cornettes also houses one of the best restaurants in the region.

TOURIST INFORMATION
Tel 33 450 73 51 41
Fax 33 450 73 56 04
Email ot-chapelle@portesdusoleil.com
Web site www.portesdusoleil.com\station\chapelle

Châtel

top 2,350m (7,708ft) bottom 1,200m (3,936ft)

Châtel is still a pleasant farming village, but caring for livestock and tilling the fields take a poor second place to the more lucrative business of tourism. Unfortunately, precious little planning has gone into the development of the village, which consists of a straggle of buildings up towards the Morgins Pass and Switzerland, and down the hillside and along the valley towards the Linga lift and the connection with Avoriaz. The valley lifts are linked by free ski buses, which are crowded in the afternoon and have to fight their way through a village centre that is often choked with traffic. The diffuse nature of the resort makes a car an advantage for reaching the out-of-town lift stations.

Châtel has a wide choice of hotels, most of them chalet-style and simple. Location is important and it is well worth checking out the distance from a main lift before booking. Hotel Fleur de Neige (☎ 450 73 20 10) is praised for the quality of its food: 'more like a restaurant with rooms than a hotel'. Hotel Castellan (☎ 450 73 20 86) is 'simple, but with excellent food', while Hotel Les Rhododendrons (☎ 450 73 24 04) is 'perfectly located and typically French'.

Restaurants include Le Monchu on the Swiss border ('absolutely the best food and atmosphere in town'), La Bonne Ménagère, which is popular, and the Vieux Four ('slow service but food is good, basic French'). The resort provides a bowling alley and an ice-rink, but otherwise the after-slopes entertainment is limited to a handful of bars.

Châtel offers a total of six ski schools. The ESF has a solid reputation, although some reporters experienced classes of up to 20 pupils. Ski Surf Ecole. is warmly praised ('tuition is excellent, imaginative, clear, technical and given with fun and enthusiasm'). Ecole de Ski Francis Sports is an alternative ski school, while Virages Snoways specialises in off-piste. Les Mouflets caters for children from ten months to six years, but the number of places is limited. Le Village des Marmottons is for children from two to eight years old, with a mixture of games and skiing for the older ones. Ian and Jane McGarry's ski courses (see *Skiing by numbers*) in the resort are highly rated.

TOURIST INFORMATION
Tel 33 450 73 22 44
Fax 33 450 73 22 87
Email touristoffice@chatel.com
Web site www.chatel.com

Skiing facts: Avoriaz

TOURIST INFORMATION
Place Central, F–74110 Avoriaz
Tel 33 450 74 24 24
Fax 33 450 74 24 29
Email info@avoriaz.com
Web site www.avoriaz.com

THE RESORT
By road Calais 902km
By rail Thonon les Bains 43km,
Cluses 40km
Airport transfer Geneva 2hrs
Visitor beds 16,000
Transport traffic-free resort

THE SKIING
Linked or nearby resorts Abondance
(n), Champéry (l), Champoussin (l),
La Chapelle d'Abondance (l), Châtel (l),
Les Crosets (l), Les Gets (l), Montriond
(l), Morgins (l), Morzine (l), St-Jean
d'Aulps/La Grande Terche (n), Torgon (l)
Number of lifts 38 in Avoriaz, 206 in
Portes du Soleil
Total of trails/pistes Avoriaz 150km
(8% beginner, 55% easy,
27% intermediate, 10% difficult),
650km in Portes du Soleil
Beginners 15 lifts, lift pass 485FF for
6 days

LIFT PASSES
Area pass Portes du Soleil (covers 12
resorts) 998FF for 6 days
Pensioners 60yrs and over 798FF for

6 days
Credit cards yes

TUITION
Skiing British Alpine Ski/Snowboarding
School (☎ 01237 451099 in UK),
ESF (☎ 450 74 05 65),
ESI (☎ 450 74 02 18)
Snowboarding as ski schools, Emery
Snowboard School (☎ 450 74 12 64),
Free Ride (☎ 450 74 00 36)
Other courses cross-country, telemark
Guiding Mont Blanc Helicopters
(☎ 450 74 22 44)

CHILDREN
Lift pass 5–16yrs Portes du Soleil 669FF
for 6 days
Ski & board school as adults, Le Village
Snowboard (☎ 450 74 04 46)
Kindergarten (ski) Le Village des Enfants
(☎ 450 74 04 46), (non-ski) Les P'tits
Loups (☎ 450 74 00 38)

OTHER SPORTS
Dog-sledding, floodlit tobogganing,
hang-gliding, parapente, skating, ski-
jöring, sleigh rides, snowbiking,
snowmobiling, snowscooting, squash,
swimming.

FOOD AND DRINK
Coffee 8FF, glass of wine 20–25FF,
small beer 15–25FF, soft drink 20FF,
dish of the day 75FF

Les Crosets
top 2,350m (7,708ft) bottom 1,660m (5,445ft)
Les Crosets is a tiny ski station in the heart of the open slopes on the
Swiss side of the Portes du Soleil. It is popular with riders and has its
own snowboard school as well as a terrain park. The hamlet is fairly
functional and, apart from a visit to the Sundance Saloon disco, has no
obvious appeal to anyone but serious snow-users who want an early

night. However, four of the slopes are floodlit for skiing and riding until 11pm each Wednesday and Saturday.

Hotel Télécabine (☎ 244 79 03 00) is simple, British-run and serves excellent food. Half a dozen eateries on the piste are also open in the evening. The ESS has a branch here, and there is also a mini-club.

TOURIST INFORMATION
Tel 41 244 77 2077
Fax 41 244 77 3773
Email info@lescrosets.com
Web site www.lescrosets.com

Les Gets
top 2,350m (7,708ft) bottom 1,175m (3,854ft)

Les Gets is situated on a low mountain pass 6km from Morzine, with lifts and pistes on both sides and good nursery slopes on the edge of the village and higher up at Les Chavannes (1,490m), which is reached by road or gondola. This attractive village, an old farming community that has expanded almost out of recognition, boasts a large and underused floodlit piste. Parts of the ski area and many of the mountain restaurants are accessible on foot. Les Gets is connected by ski lifts to Morzine.

The resort contains three ski schools, and we have generally favourable reports of them all. Ski Plus specialises in 'excellent private tuition in English', while the Ile des Enfants kindergarten ('quite Gallic but lots of fun, they don't take the skiing too seriously') receives better comments than the ESF. The non-ski Bébé Club takes children from three months old.

Much of the accommodation is in chalets. Hotel Alpages (☎ 450 75 80 88) is recommended along with the Boomerang (☎ 450 79 80 65) and the Marmotte (☎ 450 75 80 33). The limited choice of restaurants include Le Tyrol. Most of the nightlife centres on hotel bars and the two discos. The English-run Pring's is popular.

TOURIST INFORMATION
Tel 33 450 75 80 80
Fax 33 450 79 76 90
Email lesgets@lesgets.com
Web site www.lesgets.com

Montriond
top 2,350m (7,708ft) bottom 950m (3,116ft)

Montriond is little more than a suburb of Morzine, with no discernible centre and a number of simple, reasonably priced hotels. A bus links it to the resort's gondola, which provides direct access to the main lifts.

Skiing facts: Morzine

TOURIST INFORMATION
BP 23 Place de la Crusaz,
F–74110 Morzine
Tel 33 450 74 72 72
Fax 33 450 79 03 48
Email touristoffice@morzine.com
Web site www.morzine-avoriaz.com

THE RESORT
By road Calais 888km
By rail Cluses or Thonon les Bains 30km
Airport transfer Geneva 1½hrs
Visitor beds 17,000
Transport free bus service runs between Morzine and Les Prodains

THE SKIING
Linked or nearby resorts *as Avoriaz*
Number of lifts 27 in Morzine,
206 in Portes du Soleil
Total of trails/pistes Morzine 140km
(10% beginner, 44% easy,
36% intermediate, 10% difficult),
650km in Portes du Soleil
Beginners 6 lifts, special prices for some lifts

LIFT PASSES
Area pass Portes du Soleil (covers 12 resorts) 998FF for 6 days
Pensioners 798FF for six days
Credit cards yes

TUITION
Skiing ESF (☎ 450 79 13 13), British Alpine Ski and Snowboarding School Morzine (☎ 014855 72596 in UK)
Snowboarding as ski schools, Ski Snowboard et Aventures (☎ 450 79 05 16)
Other courses cross-country, race-training, Skwal, telemark
Guiding Bureau de la Montagne (☎ 450 79 03 55), Maison de la Montagne (☎ 450 75 96 65)

CHILDREN
Lift pass 5–16yrs Portes du Soleil 669FF for 6 days
Ski & board school as adults
Kindergarten (non-ski) L'Outa (☎ 450 79 26 00), (ski/non-ski) Pingouins Malins (☎ 450 79 13 13)

OTHER SPORTS
Cascade climbing, climbing wall, curling, dog-sledding, hang-gliding, heli-skiing, ice-hockey, ice-snorkelling, night-skiing/boarding, parapente, skating, ski-jumping, snowshoeing, swimming

FOOD AND DRINK
Coffee 8FF, glass of wine 15FF, small beer 14FF, soft drink 15FF, dish of the day 65FF

TOURIST INFORMATION
Tel 33 450 79 12 81
Fax 33 450 79 04 06
Email ot.montriond@valleedaulps.com
Web site www.portesdusoleil.com

Morgins
top 2,000m (7,710ft) bottom 1,350m (4,428ft)

Morgins is a few kilometres from Châtel and is the border post with Switzerland. It is a relaxed, residential resort spread across a broad valley, but it lacks any real character and, as the best skiing is elsewhere, it is not the ideal base for keen snow-users. A car is useful for visiting other resorts in the region, but traffic is a problem.

Most of the accommodation is in chalets and apartments. Pension de Morgins (☎ 244 77 11 43) is 'clean and comfortable'. The resort has a crèche, of which we have positive reports. The large nursery slope in the centre of the village is prone to overcrowding. Early-evening après-ski is limited to a skating-rink, indoor tennis and a few bars. The SAF disco provides lively late-night entertainment.

TOURIST INFORMATION
Tel 41 244 77 23 61
Fax 41 244 77 37 08
Email touristoffice@morgins.com
Web site www.morgins.ch

St-Jean d'Aulps/La Grande Terche
top 1,800m (5,906ft) bottom 900m (2,952ft)

St-Jean is the village and La Grande Terche is the name given to a tiny development of apartments at the foot of the lifts, which are a 15-minute drive from Morzine. The skiing is not fully linked into the system but it is surprisingly good and well worth a visit if you are staying elsewhere in the area. It has a combined ski area with **Bellevaux**.

TOURIST INFORMATION
Tel 33 450 79 65 09
Fax 33 450 79 67 95
Email ot-saintjean@valleedaulps.com
Web site www.portesdusoleil.com

Torgon
top 2,350m (7,708ft) bottom 1,100m (3,608ft)

Torgon is perched above the Rhône close to Lac Léman on the outer edge of the Portes du Soleil. Although it is in Switzerland, it is linked in one direction with La Chapelle d'Abondance and in the other with Châtel, both of which are in France. The distinctive and none-too-pleasing A-frame architecture contains comfortable apartments (☎ 244 81 24 14). There is little else to do here but ski. The Jardin des Neiges kindergarten takes children from three years of age.

TOURIST INFORMATION
Tel 41 244 81 3131
Fax 41 244 81 4620
Email tourisme@torgon.ch
Web site www.torgon.ch

Risoul 1850

ALTITUDE 1,850m (6,068ft)

Beginners ✱✱✱ Intermediates ✱✱✱ Advanced ✱✱ Snowboarders ✱✱✱

The purpose-built resort of Risoul 1850 has extensive and convenient family skiing and a reputation for reliable late-season snow, yet it remains an underrated destination. The main reason for its low-profile image is its remoteness from any international airport ('the long airport transfer was horrible'); it is situated at least three-and-a-half hours' drive from Turin, Lyon, Grenoble or Marseille. Risoul was first planned as a ski resort back in the 1930s but did not actually come into being until 1971. Its ski area of 56 lifts and 180km of pistes is shared with neighbouring **Vars 1850** and is known as the Domaine de la Forêt Blanche.

✔ Tree-level skiing
✔ Value for money
✔ Skiing convenience
✔ Suitable for families
✔ Lack of queues
✔ Good snow record
✔ Late-season skiing
✘ Long airport transfer
✘ Limited chalet and hotel accommodation
✘ Lack of restaurants
✘ No activities for non-skiers

Its difficult location means that the area is free of weekend over-crowding. The resort's clientèle is both family- and budget-oriented. Eastern European visitors are now arriving by the bus-load, supplanting the British among the 30 per cent of skiers who are not French.

Risoul has attractive wood-and-stone apartment complexes, but its small downtown section is blighted by illegally parked cars, a lack of proper pavements and a ghastly profusion of billboards. Reporters were impressed by the resort's convenience: 'the least amount of walking and the most amount of skiing we have ever done in the Alps'.

On the snow
top 2,750m (9,020ft) bottom 1,650m (5,412ft)

Risoul is primarily a beginner and intermediate resort, although there are also off-piste opportunities. 'A good-value resort for all differing levels,' commented one reporter. Lifts fan out from the village base, but the lift system still has a predominance of drag-lifts ('a bit of a pain'). A new chair-lift takes you from the village all the way up to Payrefolle at 2,457m. Risoul offers three slalom race-training areas, a mogul-training course and a speed-skiing piste.

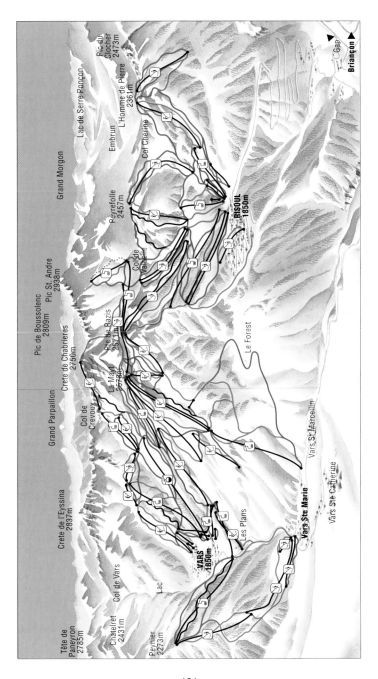

Beginners

The Plate de la Nonne quad-chair takes you over to Vars 1850, and it is possible to ski back on blue (easy) runs. The green (beginner) runs, with a children's park and snowmaking at the bottom of Risoul, are some of the most attractive in Europe. The French Ski School (ESF) beginner area has its own bucket-lift. Two chair-lifts from Risoul give access to easy terrain.

Intermediates

A number of readers have complained that the resort has arbitrarily changed some of its blue runs to red (intermediate) runs. The official explanation is that these runs can be exactingly narrow for beginners. However, more cynical observers suggest that Risoul wants to upgrade its 'too easy' image. Most interesting are the ridge-line run from Risoul's high point, Crête de Chabrières, and the return to the village from the liaisons on Razis, which requires a hike back up from below the car park. Virtually unskied are the long, wide, mogul-free reds into **Vars Sainte-Marie**.

> **WHAT'S NEW**
>
> Chair-lift from base area up to Payrefolle

Advanced

There are only eight black (difficult) runs, which readers say are graded thus more for their lack of grooming than their gradient.

Off-piste

Risoul has neither glaciers nor couloirs but it does have a lot of gladed powder skiing in fresh snow conditions. In the back bowl by Valbelle is a natural half-pipe shared by skiers and boarders. It is possible, given enough snow and the taxi fare home, to ski below the resort to the old village of Risoul. The area to the skier's left of the Chardon chair also offers reasonable challenges.

Snowboarding

Snowboarders rate Risoul as one of the best resorts in France. The Surfland terrain park on L'Homme de Pierre is regularly used for boardercross competitions. It has a Renault 16 to jump over, several quarter-pipes, an excellent half-pipe and numerous obstacles. Close to Surfland is a nursery slope that is ideal for beginner riders. Freeriders will be spoilt for choice with the resort's powder bowls.

Tuition and guiding

The ESF claims an average of ten skiers per class, but reporters have spotted groups of 15 and complain that not enough instructors are available during peak holiday periods. The rival International Ski School (ESI) guarantees no more than eight pupils per class.

Mountain restaurants

If skiing with a sandwich is ever to make a comeback it may be in Risoul, where the eating places are cheap enough but seriously lacking in both cuisine and character. La Tétras is a welcome addition. Barjo at the bottom of the Mayt chair on the Vars 1850 side offers overnight accommodation and food. Vallon and Valbelle are small, spaghetti and *steak-frites* joints. Vars L'Horizon at the top of the Sainte-Marie chairlift is 'typically French'.

Accommodation

The two-star Le Chardon Bleu (☎ 492 46 07 27) is the only hotel in Risoul 1850. Some chalet accommodation is available, but most visitors opt for self-catering apartments. Les Mélèzes (☎ 492 46 03 47) is functional but seriously lacking in space. Le Belvédère (☎ 492 46 03 47) is bigger and better. There is no shuttle bus.

Eating in and out

Most of the eateries are unambitious in price as well as menu. Cheap and plentiful are the burgers and *frites* at Snack Attack and Chez Robert. La Dalle en Pente and Le Cesier Snowboard Café have low prices and frequent special offers. L'Assiette Gourmande is the closest thing to gourmet cuisine. At La Cherine under the Mélèzes apartments 'you sit at long tables and muck in – very good value'.

Après-ski

The Grotte du Yeti is a young person's haunt for happy hour after the lifts close. According to one reporter: 'nightlife is non-existent apart from the Yeti, which was full of Scandinavians. The music varied enormously, with something for everyone.' La Dalle en Pente has live bands and is open until 2am. Readers commented that late-night noise in the resort is a serious problem: 'if you got to sleep before 2am you were woken up by revellers trying to find their way home. This contradicts the resort's family image.' Risoul has a two-screen cinema and a skating-rink but no swimming-pool. An unusual sport available here is 'ruissiling' – hiking with crampons and ice axes on frozen rivers.

Childcare

Les Pitchouns crèche is conveniently located above the ESF and takes children from six months to six years of age. A packed lunch must be provided if children are to be left all day. Both the ESF and ESI have children's learning areas.

Linked or nearby resorts

Vars 1850
top 2,750m (9,020ft) bottom 1,850m (6,068ft)

Vars 1850, with its 18,000 beds, is larger, less attractive and also less welcoming to the British than Risoul 1850. No UK tour operators currently come here. The old village is linked by drag-lift to the modern station, but

Skiing facts: Risoul 1850

TOURIST INFORMATION
Risoul 1850, F-05600, Hautes-Alpes
Tel 33 492 46 02 60
Fax 33 492 46 01 23
Email o.t.risoul@wanadoo.fr
Web site www.risoul.com

THE RESORT
By road Calais 1,024km
By rail Montdauphin 30 mins,
bus connection with Risoul
Airport transfer Grenoble 3½hrs,
Marseille 3½hrs
Visitor beds 17,600

THE SKIING
Linked or nearby resorts Vars 1850 (I),
Vars Sainte Marie
Number of lifts 56 in the Forêt Blanche
area
Total of trails/pistes 180km (17% easy,
37% intermediate, 34% difficult,
12% very difficult)
Beginners 10 lifts, 3 of them are free

LIFT PASSES
Area pass Forêt Blanche (covers Risoul
and Vars) 714–837FF for 6 days
Pensioners 65yrs and over 708FF for

6 days, free for 69yrs and over
Credit cards yes

TUITION
Skiing ESF (☎ 492 46 19 22),
ESI (☎ 492 46 20 83)
Snowboarding as ski schools
Other courses cross-country, monoski,
skwal, slalom, telemark
Guiding through ski schools

CHILDREN
Lift pass 5–11yrs 708FF for 6 days, free
for 5yrs and under
Ski & board school as adults
Kindergarten (ski) ESF and ESI mini-
clubs as adults (non-ski) Les Pitchouns
(☎ 492 46 02 60)

OTHER SPORTS
Curling, horse-riding, ice-climbing,
night-skiing, parapente, ruissiling,
skating, sleigh rides, snowmobiling,
snowshoeing

FOOD AND DRINK
Coffee 7–8FF, glass of wine 12FF,
small beer 15–18FF, soft drink 15FF,
dish of the day 55–90FF

you have to hike across town to access the Vars gondola and high-speed chair back to Risoul 1850. The local ESF offers alpine skiing and snowboarding courses, as well as carving, cross-country, race camps, snowblading and telemark. The baby club takes children from six months old, and the ski school accepts children from four years of age. Other activities include dog-sledding, parapente, skating, snowshoeing, snow-mobiling and a museum of the history of speed skiing.

TOURIST INFORMATION
Tel 33 492 46 51 31
Fax 33 492 46 56 54
Email vars.ot@pacwan.fr
Web site www.vars-ski.com

Serre Chevalier–Briançon

ALTITUDE 1,200–1,500m (3,936–4,920ft)

Beginners ✹✹ Intermediates ✹✹✹ Advanced ✹✹ Snowboarders ✹✹✹

Serre Chevalier is not a resort in its own right, but the collective name for more than a dozen villages and hamlets that line the main valley road between the Col du Lautaret and the ancient garrison town of **Briançon**. After two disastrous seasons, Nature rewarded Serre Chevalier with more snow than any other resort in Europe during 2000–1.

Chantemerle (Serre Chevalier 1350) is the closest village to Briançon. **Villeneuve–Le Bez** (marketed as Serre Chevalier 1400) is the most central and lively, and **Monêtier-Les-Bains** (Serre Chevalier 1500) is a pretty spa village that attracts the fewest tourists. Briançon is directly linked by gondola to the substantial ski area.

Having a car here is a definite asset as you can take advantage of the off-slope facilities in the various conurbations. The Grande Serre Chevalier lift pass covers five nearby resorts, including **Montgenèvre** in the extensive **Milky Way** area, 15 minutes down the road. The skiing is for all standards but is particularly well suited to the adept intermediate, who will enjoy the 250km of cruising and the well-linked, albeit rather old-fashioned, lift system.

✔ Large linked ski area
✔ Good artificial snow cover
✔ Varied off-piste
✔ Tree-level skiing
✔ Recommended for families
✔ Value for money
✘ Heavy traffic along main highway
✘ Scattered resort
✘ Weekend high season crowds
✘ Not recommended for non-skiers

On the snow
top 2,800m (9,184ft) bottom 1,200m (3,936ft)

The three main mountain access points are by gondola and cable-car from Villeneuve–Le Bez, Chantemerle and Briançon, with most of the lifts and pistes concentrated in the area above Villeneuve and Chantemerle. The Monêtier section also has its own lifts starting from the base and is the most appealing in the whole area, although the least accessible. There is a floodlit piste for night-skiing at Briançon. The bus system links all the villages and appears to have improved. However, 'the lifts need upgrading in places as we seemed to spend a long time on lifts,' commented one reporter. The area boasts an electronic and efficient hands-free lift pass.

Beginners

The Grand Alpe section above Chantemerle has a decent but some-times busy beginners' area, and Briançon has its own nursery slopes at the gondola mid-station. There are commendable starter slopes at Monêtier and Villeneuve with beginner lifts at their bases. A long green (beginner) run goes from Col Méa down to Villeneuve.

Intermediates

As one reporter noted: 'for an average skier there are few better places'. Monêtier has some enjoyable red (intermediate) pistes through the woods. The Vallon de la Cucumelle above Fréjus is a recommended red: 'a long fun run with good potential for off-piste either side'. From Bachas at 2,180m down to the valley at Monêtier there is a wide choice of intermediate runs through the woods. Le Bois is a short red run.

Advanced

Overall, Monêtier is the prime area of the mountain for advanced skiers, although the high and exposed link with Villeneuve can some-times be closed. Isolée is an exciting black (difficult) run, which starts on the ridge from L'Eychauda at 2,659m and plunges down towards Echaillon. Tabuc is a long black run through the woods with a couple of steep and narrow pitches. The Casse du Boeuf, a sweeping ridge through the trees back to Villeneuve, is, according to one reporter, 'bet-ter than sex but more tiring'.

Off-piste

The Fréjus–Echaillon section above Villeneuve provides some fine runs for experienced skiers, with short and unprepared trails beneath the mountain crest. The Yret chair gives easy access to some off-piste runs, including the testing face under the lift, which is often mogulled.

Snowboarding

Many riders consider this to be the best resort in France. Freeriders ben-efit from the great terrain with its mixture of trees, gullies, bowls and natural jumps. The original terrain park is at the bottom of the Yret chair-lift and the one at Villeneuve contains half- and quarter-pipes.

Tuition and guiding

We have generally favourable reports of the ESF in all the villages ('our instructor had good English and was very good humoured too'). Buissonnière ESI (in 1400) received immense praise: 'I have not had better lessons'. In all, Serre Chevalier has six ski schools, with three of them specialising in off-piste tours. First Tracks, which is run by the ESF, is a specialist snowboarding school in Villeneuve, and Generation Snow is in Chantemerle.

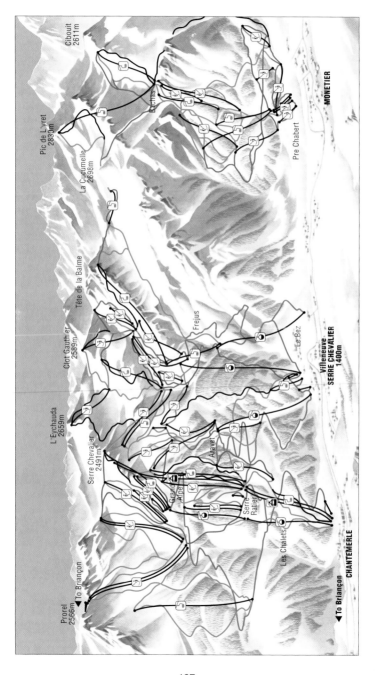

Cibouit
2611m

Pic de L'vret
2830m

La Cucumelle
2698m

Tête de la Balme

Clot Gauthier
2589m

L'Eychauda
2659m

Serre Chevalier
2491m

Prorel
2566m

▶ To Briançon

▼ To Briançon

Bachas

Frejus

Le Bez

Aravet

Grand
Alpe

Serre
Ratier

Les Chalets

Pre Chabert

MONETIER

Villeneuve
SERRE CHEVALIER
1400m

CHANTEMERLE

197

Skiing facts: Serre Chevalier

TOURIST INFORMATION
BP 20, 05240 Serre Chevalier, Hautes-Alpes
Tel 33 492 24 98 98
Fax 33 492 24 98 84
Email contact@ot-serrechevalier.fr
Web site www.serre-chevalier.com

THE RESORT
By road Calais 984km
By rail Briançon 6km, regular bus service to resort
Airport transfer Lyon 3hrs, Turin 2hrs, Grenoble 2½hrs
Visitor beds 35,000
Transport free ski bus with lift pass

THE SKIING
Linked or nearby resorts Alpe d'Huez (n), Briançon (l), Montgenèvre (n), La Grave (n), Les Deux Alpes (n), Puy-St-Vincent (n)
Number of lifts 76 in Grande Serre Chevalier area
Total of trails/pistes 250km in linked area (19% easy, 69% intermediate, 12% difficult)
Beginners 10 runs, 1-day lift pass 65FF

LIFT PASSES
Area pass Grande Serre Chevalier (covers all centres) 970FF for 6 days including 1 day in each of Les Deux Alpes, La Grave, Montgenèvre, Puy-St-Vincent and Alpe d'Huez
Pensioners free for 70yrs and over
Credit cards yes

TUITION
Skiing1350: ESF (☎ 492 24 17 41),
Evasion ESI (☎ 492 24 02 41), Montagne Aventure (☎ 492 24 05 51); **1400**: Buissonnière (☎ 492 24 78 66), ESF, Evasion ESI, Montagne à la Carte (☎ 492 24 73 20); **1500**: ESF, Montagne et Ski (☎ 492 24 46 81)
Snowboarding ESF and ESI, Generation Snow (1350) (☎ 492 24 21 51)
Other courses cross-country, extreme skiing, monoski, race training, skiing for the disabled, skwal, snowblading, teen skiing, telemark
Guiding Compagnie des Guides de L'Oisans (☎ 492 24 75 90), Montagne à la Carte, Montagne et Ski

CHILDREN
Lift pass Grande Serre Chevalier 6–12yrs 690FF for 6 days
Ski & board school as adults
Kindergarten (ski/non-ski) **1350**: Les Poussins (☎ 492 24 03 43), Jardin des Neiges (☎ 492 24 17 41); **1400**: Schtroumpfs (☎ 492 24 70 95), Jardin des Neiges (☎ 492 24 71 99), Kids de l'Aventure (☎ 492 24 93 10); **1500**: Les Eterlous (☎ 492 24 45 75), Jardin des Neiges (☎ 492 24 42)

OTHER SPORTS
Hang-gliding, horse riding, ice-climbing, ice-driving, night-skiing, parapente, skating, ski-jöring, sleigh rides, snowmobiling, snowshoeing

FOOD AND DRINK
Coffee 10–16FF, glass of wine 20FF, small beer 15–20FF, soft drink 15–20FF, dish of the day 55–80FF

Mountain restaurants

The choice of eating places is small. Café Soleil above Chantemerle is well-located and has 'very well-prepared food and a great atmosphere, the best *vin chaud*, and clean toilets, too'. Le Briance was also praised. L'Echaillon is 'pretty and off the beaten track, with friendly staff', but is also said to be the 'poorest value for money'. Le Grand Alpe serves 'big portions'. Père et Noëlle is 'good value and lively'.

Accommodation

Most of Serre Chevalier's accommodation is in apartments and all accommodation can be booked through Serre Chevalier Reservations (☎ 492 24 98 80). The Altea, Vauban and Parc hotels are Briançon's three-stars, while the Pension des Ramparts is a small and simple hotel with a loyal following. Club Hotel Yeti in Briançon is said to have 'paper-thin walls, but the food is good'. The Grand Hotel at Chantemerle is 'a modest place despite its name, and excellently placed right opposite the lift station'. L'Auberge du Choucas, also in Monêtier, is known for its gourmet cuisine. Le Lièvre Blanc in Villeneuve, a British-owned two-star, is recommended.

Eating in and out

A car is useful for visiting the many restaurants along the valley. Le Petit Duc is a friendly crêperie beside the river in the lower part of Villeneuve–Le Bez. Le Petit Lard is 'rustic, French and fantastic value – but you have to book'. Pastelli in Le Bez has been criticised for its 'unimaginative food'. Le Bidule in Le Bez has a friendly ambience and specialises in fresh fish and seafood. Le Caribou is a new restaurant in Monêtier ('a beautifully converted seventeenth-century stable with arched stone ceiling. The food in quality and presentation was delightful'). Le Passé Simple in Briançon has a historic Vauban menu with dishes from the seventeenth century.

Après-ski

'In short – if you don't ski don't come,' said one reporter. All three villages are quiet after dusk and the resort is not ideal for non-skiers. Bars include Le Sous Sol in Villeneuve. Le Yeti and the Underground are the best late-night drinking places in Chantemerle; both have live bands and stay open until 2am. Le Frog ('a very British clientèle') and La Baita discos in Villeneuve come alive at weekends. Le Cavaillou in Le Bez is highly recommended. Le Lièvre Blanc is a riders' hangout with weekly live music, and l'Iceberg is also rated cool by riders.

Childcare

Each village has its own crèche and children's ski school. In 1350, Les Poussins takes children from eight months, and the Jardin des Neiges from three years. In 1400, Les Schtroumpfs caters for children from six months, and the Jardin des Neiges from three years. Kids de l'Aventure, also in 1400, is for children from seven years; this includes activities such as dog-sledding. In 1500, Les Eterlous takes children aged eighteen months to six years, and the Jardin des Neiges from three years.

The Trois Vallées

ALTITUDE Méribel 1,450–1,700m (4,756–5,576ft), Courchevel 1,300–1,850m (4,264–6,068ft), La Tania 1,350m (4,429ft), Val Thorens 2,300m (7,544ft), Les Menuires 1,850m (6,068ft)

The time has finally come for the Trois Vallées to change its name. This winter the world's largest linked ski area becomes even larger with a new ski area opening in the fourth valley, the Maurienne. A high-speed gondola provides easy access. What puts the Trois – it must become Quatre – Vallées ski-lengths ahead of its rivals in the super-circus league is the range and sophistication of the resorts it contains, coupled with the variety of skiing on offer. Ideal topography means that even the links between each valley are serious runs in their own right. Its critics claim that 90 per cent of the skiing is geared towards intermediates, but then 90 per cent of the skiers who visit the area are intermediate. However, the Trois Vallées still provides more than adequate scope for those of greater or lesser ability. This substantial chunk of the French Alps is covered by what is considered to be the most efficient overall lift system in the world.

> **MÉRIBEL**
>
> Beginners ✶✶ Intermediates ✶✶✶
> Advanced ✶✶✶ Snowboarders ✶✶
> ✔ Large ski area
> ✔ Choice of luxury chalets
> ✔ Resort-level snow (Mottaret)
> ✔ Off-piste skiing
> ✘ Fragmented resort layout
> ✘ Skiing inconveniently located
> ✘ Heavy traffic, limited parking
> ✘ Crowded pistes at peak times
> ✘ Poor bus service

Collectively, it is the most popular French ski destination for the British, and the French, who rarely venture beyond their own mountains, claim, with dubious justification, that it is also the largest linked ski area in the world. Certainly we concede that the Trois Vallées wins a place on the international podium for best all-rounder.

At one end of this ski area, above the Bozel Valley, sits chic **Courchevel 1850**, with its less smart satellites of **Courchevel 1650**, **Courchevel 1550** and **Le Praz**, with pleasant budget-priced **La Tania** beneath it. At the other end, the pastoral Belleville Valley is dominated by functional **Val Thorens** and **Les Menuires**. In the middle is cosmopolitan **Méribel**, with its British bulldog overtones. The skiing in the Trois Vallées is reached by two winding mountain roads from Moûtiers or by an underused gondola from **Brides-les-Bains**.

A fourth valley, the Maurienne, has no road access from the other three, but the skiing is now properly linked by a new Funitel gondola for 2001–2. This twin-cable gondola, which can continue to operate in moderately high winds, starts beside the Moutière chair-lift and

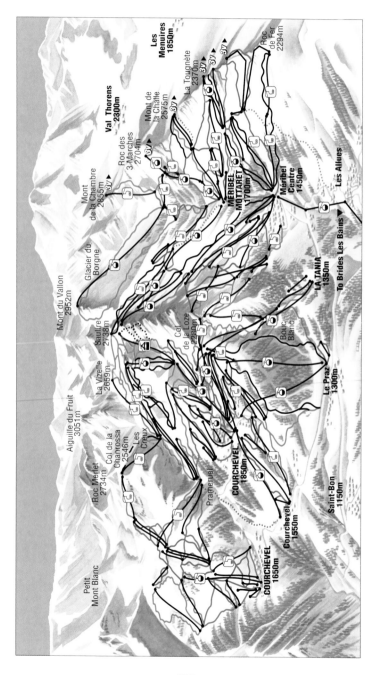

transports you to the top of the Col de La Montée du Fond. Both the existing Trois Vallées ski area and the new Pointe de Bouchet ski area can also be reached from Orelle in the Maurienne Valley. Orelle is only a two-hour drive from Turin via the Fréjus tunnel.

The network of cable-cars, gondolas, detachable-chairs and tows is of gargantuan proportions and improves each year. The Trois Vallées has 200, all of them linked by well in excess of 600km of prepared slopes and uncounted hectares of off-piste terrain. Méribel alone has an extraordinary 15 gondolas. Given a single week's holiday, a competent skier will barely scratch the surface; it takes an entire 20-week season based in at least two different resorts even to begin to get to grips with it.

WHAT'S NEW

Méribel: Plan des Mains chair-lift upgraded to six-seater
Val Thorens: Funitel gondola from Val Thorens to Montée du Fond
Maurienne: two chair-lifts from PlanBouchet to Pointe de Bouchet

However, the area is not without faults. The mountains are managed by an uneasy alliance of four separate lift companies, each of which looks after itself extremely well and pays lip service to its agreement with the others. As a result ski passes are checked at almost every lift. A hands-free lift pass is desperately needed but is unlikely to materialise for the present. The lift capacity is so high that queues are a rarity but as a result the main runs inevitably become overcrowded.

Each resort has its own character. So many British people holiday or work in Méribel during the winter months that any attempt to order a drink in French can be met with a look of blank incomprehension. It is an expensive resort, which offers more luxury-class chalets with en-suite bathrooms and large apartments than any other ski destination in the whole of Europe.

Méribel was founded by an Englishman – Colonel Peter Lindsay, a dedicated pre-war skier, built the first lift here in 1938. Amazingly, the resort has stayed faithful to his original concept of a traditional chalet village: every building has been constructed in local stone and wood in harmony with the mountain setting. Today, it has stretched with little or no long-term planning into a hotchpotch of confusingly named hamlets at different altitudes. The convenience of these hamlets for skiing, shopping and nightlife varies considerably. 'The Heart of the Trois Vallées' is Méribel's marketing slogan, but because of its diffuse layout it is devoid of a single heart and its atmosphere is accordingly muted. Reporters commented that the free bus service, which in theory runs every 20 minutes until midnight, is both irregular and overcrowded ('an absolutely awful way to end a wonderful day's skiing').

Méribel Centre (1,450m) is the commercial core – a one-street village with the tourist information centre as its focal point. It has a number of boutiques and souvenir shops beyond the usual sports shops, and one main supermarket. The bi-weekly street market provides colour and bargains.

Méribel Mottaret (1,700–1,800m) is a ski-in, ski-out satellite situated further up the valley and is also divided into individual hamlets. Brides-les-Bains, in the valley below Méribel, is connected by a 25-minute gondola ride and serves as a budget base and useful back door into the system.

Courchevel is not one but four quite separate resorts at different altitudes, linked on piste but with little else in common. A 'quick and efficient' free bus service connects the different villages. Before booking a holiday here it is crucial to ascertain exactly where you will be staying.

Courchevel 1850 is the international resort with the jet-set image. Like its stylistic rival, **Megève**, a high proportion of its designer-clad visitors come here to see and to be seen. The only exercise they take is to ferry gastronomic delights from plate to mouth at the resort's clutch of restaurants, which are among the finest in the Alps. A covered mall houses expensive boutiques, and a couple of supermarkets cater for the more mundane needs of self-caterers. Two chic boutiques are devoted entirely to the kind of lingerie that, in terms of money for weight, is matched only by rare postage stamps. The secluded Jardin Alpin sector is a Millionaire's Row of sumptuous chalets and shockingly expensive hotels tucked away in trees that provide at least an illusion of privacy.

COURCHEVEL
Beginners ✱✱✱
Intermediates ✱✱✱
Advanced ✱✱✱
Snowboarders ✱✱
✔ Big vertical drop
✔ Long cruising runs
✔ Tree-level skiing
✔ Resort-level snow (1850)
✔ Gourmet restaurants
✔ Luxury accommodation (1850)
✔ Skiing convenience
✔ Large ski area
✔ Off-piste skiing
✗ Fragmented resort
✗ High prices (1850)
✗ Crowded pistes at peak times

Courchevel 1650 is 200 vertical metres lower down both the mountain and the price scale. Many would argue that this is *le vrai* Courchevel, with its year-round population and atmosphere of the farming community it once was. One reporter commented: 'we are passionate about 1650 and would not go anywhere else. It is a completely separate resort and we have never felt we were missing out on the glitzier village above us'. The skiing here is both extensive and isolated from the main Trois Vallées thoroughfares; consequently, it remains wonderfully uncrowded. A new gondola has done much to improve mountain access. Alterations have been made to the town centre, but it still suffers from traffic on the main road, which continues up to 1850.

Courchevel 1550 is off the beaten track and away from the heart of the skiing. It is little more than an attractive cluster of apartment buildings, chalets and a few hotels. Le Praz (sometimes known as **Courchevel 1300**) is a farming village at the foot of the lift system and a popular and cheap base for Courchevel's skiing ('if the road was re-routed and the snow a little more reliable, this would be a heavenly place'). Two gondolas ('always free of queues') swiftly take you up towards the Col de la Loze or to 1850.

The modern but pleasing village of La Tania provides an alternative base for the price-conscious. It is a couple of kilometres by road from Le Praz and is linked by piste to Courchevel 1850 as well as to Méribel via the Col de la Loze. The resort, built in the 1990s, is served by a jumbo gondola and has developed its own village atmosphere. An attractive new residential sector called Le Forêt is a collection of Scandinavian-style chalets set in the woods above the village.

LA TANIA
Beginners✱✱✱
Intermediates✱✱✱
Advanced✱✱✱
Snowboarders✱✱
✔ Skiing convenience
✔ Large ski area
✔ Large choice of chalet accommodation
✔ Reasonable prices
✘ Uncertain resort snow cover

At 2,300 metres, Val Thorens is the highest ski resort in Europe. Consequently, it is one of only a handful where you are virtually guaranteed snow at resort level over both Christmas and a late Easter. On a sunny day its functional, purpose-built architecture is almost pleasing. You can ski into the centre of the car-free village, and the horseshoe of surrounding peaks is dramatic. In bad weather this far above the tree-line, you may be forgiven for thinking you have been stranded amid the mountains of the moon; few places in the Alps are colder, and a white-out is just that.

VAL THORENS
Beginners ✱✱
Intermediates ✱✱✱
Advanced ✱✱✱
Snowboarders ✱✱
✔ Resort-level snow
✔ Long season
✔ Large ski area
✔ Glacier skiing
✔ Skiing convenience
✔ Off-piste skiing
✘ Lack of tree-level skiing
✘ Exposed and cold in mid-winter
✘ Limited for non-skiers
✘ Limited nightlife

Les Menuires, down the valley from Val Thorens at 1,850m, is a budget resort that continues to work hard at changing its image. It has a reputation, only partially justified, as the ugliest resort in the Alps ('well worth a visit for the architecture alone. It reminded me of something you might see in Russia – horrible, but fascinating at the same time'). Certainly, the original centre, La Croisette, is a prime example of 1960s alpine architectural vandalism, but much has been done to smarten it up. The new church acts as a more appealing focal point and the more modern satellites of **Reberty** and **Les Bruyères** are positively attractive. You can holiday in comfort, hardly ever venturing into La Croisette. Both satellites are on the piste and have their own hotels and restaurants as well as all the shops you might need, apart from a chemist (there is one in La Croisette).

On the snow
top 3,300m (10,825ft) bottom 1,300m (4,264ft)

Each resort has its own large ski area, which is covered by a single-valley local pass. The links between the three valleys are liable to be suspended when snow cover is insufficient or in storm conditions. You should also note that the Trois Vallées lift map is printed back to front; Courchevel 1650, which appears to be the most westerly resort in the complex, is in fact the most easterly. What appear to be south-facing slopes are therefore north-facing and consequently hold the snow well.

LES MENUIRES
Beginners ✳✳
Intermediates ✳✳✳
Advanced ✳✳✳
Snowboarders ✳✳
✔ Large ski area
✔ Long cruising runs
✔ Sunny slopes
✔ Off-piste skiing
✔ Well-run children's village
✔ Budget prices
✔ Skiing convenience
✔ Extensive snowmaking
✗ Lack of tree-level runs
✗ Ugly architecture in centre
✗ Heavy traffic
✗ Limited nightlife
✗ Few activities for non-skiers

Les Allues Valley, dominated by Méribel and its higher satellite of Mottaret, lies in the middle and provides the ideal jumping-off point for exploring the whole area. However, it does not necessarily give the easiest access to the most rewarding skiing. Both sides of the open valley are networked with modern lifts. The western side culminates in a long skiable ridge, which separates it from the beautiful Belleville Valley and the resorts of Val Thorens, Les Menuires and **St-Martin-de-Belleville**. The eastern side rises to the rocky 2,738-m summit of Saulire and the Col de la Loze at 2,274m. Beyond lie the Bozel Valley and Courchevel. At the head of Les Allues Valley rises Mont du Vallon (2,952m) – the most easterly of the horseshoe of 3,300-m peaks accessed from Méribel and Val Thorens – which provides some of the most scenic and demanding off-piste in the region.

The ski area extends over the back of the Montée du Fond into the Maurienne Valley, which is now easily accessed on the Val Thorens side by the new Funitel gondola. The red (intermediate) run of 660m vertical takes you down to the Chalet Refuge de Plan Bouchet at 2,350m, from where a fast chair-lift takes you back up to the Col de Rosaël. This season sees the inauguration of a two-stage fixed chair-lift, which takes you up to the Pointe de Bouchet and a new ski area, which has blue (easy), red and black (difficult) runs as well as some exciting off-piste opportunities for experienced skiers and snowboarders.

Beginners

Facilities for beginners are good in all the major resorts, although the sheer volume of visitors here often necessitates impersonal instruction that is not conducive to the early-learning process. The runs surrounding the altiports at both Courchevel and Méribel are ideal beginner areas with enough length to help build confidence. Nursery slopes in Méribel and Mottaret are subject to the heavy traffic of more experienced skiers and snowboarders passing through at speed. Both Val Thorens and Les Menuires also have dedicated learning areas, as does La Tania. Once the basics have been conquered, the area lends itself to easy exploration. Second-week skiers will quickly find that they can cover considerable distances on green (beginner) and blue runs, an experience that greatly adds to the feeling of achievement.

Intermediates

The Trois Vallées constitutes what many skiers rightly regard as the greatest intermediate playground in the world: a seemingly endless network of moderately graded runs that provide a challenge to all levels of skier. As one reader put it: 'we have been spoilt by the Trois Vallées and now look upon most other resorts with disdain'. The Combe de Vallon is a magnificent cruise of 1,100m vertical from the top of Mont Vallon all the way down to Méribel-Mottaret.

The Cime de Caron above Val Thorens is more famous for its Combe du Caron black descent, but there is also a red variation around the shoulder, as well as the scenic Itinéraire du Lou. The blue Arondiaz from the top of Courchevel 1650 back down to the resort is a great last run of the day, and its north-facing aspect usually ensures good snow cover.

Advanced

With a maximum gradient of about 38 degrees, the couloirs of Courchevel are among the most radical black runs marked on any piste map in the world, although two of them – Télépherique and Emile Allais – have now been regraded as off-piste itineraries. Take the 150-person cable-car up from the Courchevel side of Saulire, exercising special care on the entry route, which can be dangerously icy. In most conditions, the runs are by no means as difficult as they look from below, but as one reader put it: 'actually getting to them is a life-threatening experience'.

The Courchevel side of Saulire is the starting point for a magnificent descent of 1,400m vertical to Le Praz. It is tiring rather than technically difficult, apart from the black Jockeys piste on the final section, which is shaded for most of the winter and consequently icy. La Masse above Les Menuires boasts Les Enverses and the usually icy La Dame Blanche.

Off-piste

The guided off-piste opportunities are outstanding, and one of the great charms of the Trois Vallées is that after a major snowfall the best powder runs are some of the most accessible. The long runs down to Les Menuires from the Méribel ridge are exhilarating. During a heavy snowfall, the tree-lined slopes above La Tania provide some of the most enjoyable powder skiing in the whole of the Trois Vallées, yet are always underused.

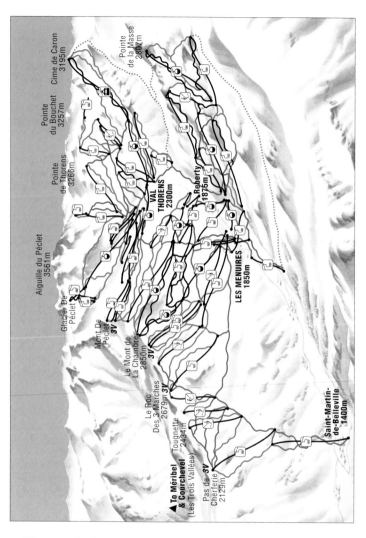

The summit of La Masse on the far side of the Belleville Valley is also the starting point for long itineraries towards St-Martin. The powder runs from the summit of Cime de Caron include the Vallon du Lou. Roc Merlet above Courchevel 1650 is the jump-off point for a glorious descent around the shoulder into the Avals Valley, which brings you back, after a short walk, to 1650. Mont Vallon and the Col du Fruit offer further thrills.

Snowboarding

There is a terrain park above Arpasson on the Tougnette side of Mottaret and a designated snowboard area below the second Plattières station above Mottaret. At Courchevel impossibly high moguls are interspersed with steep canyons on the Verdons piste for the use of skiers as well as snowboarders. Plantrey boasts a terrain park with an obstacle course as well as a dedicated trick space and a giant half-pipe. A third terrain park has been created at Biolley.

Tuition and guiding

The sheer volume of business during the main weeks of the season inevitably turns the various ski and snowboarding schools into sausage factories. Unless you feel you benefit from the 'follow-me' type of instruction, or decide that the lift priority given to a class warrants the cost, you might do better to save your money.

The French Ski School (ESF) has no less than 550 instructors in Courchevel alone, a proportion of whom spend the low-season weeks giving the evil eye to teachers from the smaller schools, who continue to find work when they do not. Magic in Motion, previously considered to be the best school in Méribel, receives less favourable reports: 'Our instructor's English was so bad that three out of seven in our class complained to the ski school manager, who said there was no one else available'. Ski Cocktail, its main rival, is no more. Ian and Susan Saunders (BASI instructors who work for the ESF in Méribel) have their own company, Ski Principles, which provides 'great instruction by sympathetic teachers'. White Abyss ('the owner seemed as short on modesty as he was on ski length') is a new ski school that concentrates on the luxury chalet market for private clients. British ski shop Freeride.Fr offers a choice of high-quality skis and boots, together with a chalet equipment-fitting service.

Supreme in Courchevel 1850 is an all-British school of which we receive mixed reports. One reporter said: 'a great lesson from an expert and really friendly instructor', while another commented: 'what was a small specialist school is in danger of becoming part of the establishment – with customary loss of service'. Le Ski School, also known as New Generation, is another British ski school that has a strong following in Courchevel 1650 ('a two-hour lesson for my son and myself was the best £140 I have ever spent').

La Tania has its own branch of the ESF as well as three independent schools: Arthur MacLean, Magic in Motion and Snow Ball.

If British skiers do take lessons in either Les Menuires or Val Thorens, they don't tell us. We have no reports of the ski schools apart from the ESF in either resort. Val Thorens does, however, have a good choice of schools and courses including Pros-Neige and Ski Safari Pepi Prager, both of which can organise heli-skiing trips. Patrick and Eric Berthon offer specialist mogul skiing courses and the Gilbert Smith International Race Camp takes place on the glacier. It is important to note that all ski lessons in the Trois Vallées must be booked in advance during high season.

Mountain restaurants

The majority of mountain restaurants in the Trois Vallées serve bland fast food at truly shocking prices. Bel-Air, at the top of the Courchevel 1650 gondola, is 'the best mountain restaurant as opposed to gourmet rip-off in the region, with friendly waiters, excellent food and great views. Sadly, it is so busy that even if you book it is hard to secure a table without a wait'. Le Petit Savoyard in Courchevel 1650 is also praised. L'Ours Blanc has 'a sunny terrace and good pizzas at reasonable prices', while Chalet de Pierres above Courchevel 1850, with liveried waiters hovering on the edge of the piste, is a gastronomic delight, but expensive. Cap Horn, just above the Courchevel altiport, has 'acceptable gastronomic fare at horrendous prices'.

Le Bouc Blanc at the top of La Tania gondola serves 'good food at acceptable (by local standards) prices but the service is abysmal', while Pub Le Ski Lodge down in La Tania offers 'the cheapest lunches in the Trois Vallées'.

Les Castors, at the foot of the Truite run in Méribel, is 'crowded but still excellent, despite a change of ownership', Roc des Trois Marches offers consistently good value, and Plein Soleil at Mottaret is 'perfect for a sunny day lunch'. Les Rhododendrons waiter-service restaurant has 'seriously improved', while Le Rond Point provides 'some of the best lunchtime fare in the region'. Le Bibi Phoque at Chaudanne makes 'excellent crêpes and galettes'.

Chalet 2000 in the Reberty *quartier* of Les Menuires is 'an undiscovered treat' with a shaded terrace and 'dangerously flamed langoustines'. Fortunately, Quatres Vents at Les Bruyères 'maintains a consistent standard'.

Accommodation

Méribel began as a chalet resort and so it remains. In the short summer months the village rings to the sounds of saw and hammer as new luxury establishments sprout in response to demand. Those who don't like walking in their ski boots are strongly advised to check out the location of their chalet before booking. Of the hotels, the four-star Grand Coeur (☎ 479 08 60 03) was one of the resort's first and remains its finest: 'the food and service are excellent; its understated luxury appeals equally to the Brits and the French'. The Marie Blanche (☎ 479 08 65 55) and Le Yeti (☎ 479 00 51 15) are also recommended. In Mottaret, the four-star Mont Vallon (☎ 479 00 44 00) is praised.

Courchevel 1850 boasts a host of four-star de luxe hotels (there are no five-stars in France), which pamper their wealthy guests. The Byblos de Neige (☎ 479 00 98 00) is the glitzy centrepiece, while Les Airelles (☎ 479 09 38 38) is more discreet. Hotel des Neiges (☎ 479 03 03 77) is an established favourite, and the Trois Vallées (☎ 479 08 00 12) is 'intimate and charming'. The family-run three-star La Sivolière (☎ 479 08 08 33) provides four-star comfort and has a health centre. The two-star Courcheneige (☎ 479 08 02 59) is popular with British families, and Le Mélèzin (☎ 479 08 01 33) is the luxurious Alpine headquarters of Amanresorts. Ducs de Savoie (☎ 479 08 03 00), Le Lana (☎ 479 08 01 10), Carlina (☎ 479 08 00 30) and La Loze (☎ 479 08 28 25) are singled out for praise, too, while Le Lodge Nogentil (☎ 479 08 32 32) is a smart British-owned chalet-hotel in a good location.

The quality of some of the luxury catered chalets here ranks alongside the smartest hotels. The Les Chalets du Forum apartment complex (☎ 479 08 27 15) is praised by reporters ('modern, with a perfect location'), although both the apartments themselves and the staircases are showing signs of wear and tear. Courchevel 1650 consists mainly of chalets. However, the ski-in ski-out Hotel du Golf (☎ 479 00 92 92) is on the edge of the piste and 'cannot be beaten for convenience'. The village of Le Praz contains the comfortable Hotel Les Peupliers (☎ 479 08 41 47) ('a delightful base from which to ski Courchevel without paying through the nose').

Many of the pleasant Scandinavian-style chalets set in the woods above La Tania are run by British tour operators. Hotel Montana (☎ 479 08 80 08) in the centre is 'excellent, modern and clean with large rooms and a small swimming-pool'.

Accommodation in Val Thorens is divided between the standard French apartments and mainly unremarkable hotels – the four-star Fitz-Roy (☎ 479 00 04 78) being the exception. The Val Thorens (☎ 479 00 04 33), Le Val Chavière (☎ 479 00 00 33) and Le Portillo (☎ 479 00 00 88) are recommended three-stars, while Le Bel Horizon (☎ 479 00 06 08) and Le Sherpa (☎ 479 00 00 70) are cheaper options. Les Montagnettes Soleil (☎ 479 00 20 51) has 'quite superb' apartments.

Les Menuires is mainly apartment territory – the older ones in La Croisette being cramped and to be avoided. Their more modern counterparts in Les Bruyères are also beginning to show signs of exhaustion. Hotel Maeva Latitudes (☎ 479 00 75 10) in Les Bruyères offers some of the best-value accommodation and five-course dinners in the region ('quite exceptional food, pleasant rooms and ideally situated on the edge of the piste. Don't tell anyone else'), while L'Ours Blanc (☎ 479 00 61 66) at Reberty and Le Menuire (☎ 479 00 60 33) are both recommended, too.

Eating in and out

Méribel has a surprisingly limited choice of recommended restaurants for a resort of its size, mainly because such a large proportion of its clientèle eat in their catered chalets. Les Enfants Terribles (formerly Le Jardin d'Hiver) is said to be 'worthy of a good night out'. La Cava is recommended for fondue, while La Taverne offers pizzas and Savoyard dishes and has established itself as one of the resort's main rendezvous. Chez Kiki specialises in charcoal grills, and the surroundings are appealing, while El Poncho is a friendly Tex-Mex at Méribel 1600 serving some of the best-value food in the resort.

In Mottaret, Ty Sable is strongly recommended, and Hotel Tarentaise, on the edge of the piste, is British-managed and popular

Skiing facts: Courchevel

TOURIST INFORMATION
BP37, La Croisette, F–73122 Courchevel,
Savoie
Tel 33 479 08 00 29
Fax 33 479 08 15 63
Email pro@courchevel.com
Web site www.courchevel.com

THE RESORT
By road Calais 968km
By rail TGV Moûtiers 25km, frequent
buses
Airport transfer Chambéry 2hrs,
Geneva 3hrs, Lyon 2½hrs
Visitor beds 32,000
Transport free ski bus

THE SKIING
Linked or nearby resorts Les Menuires
(l), Méribel (l), St-Martin-de-Belleville (l),
La Tania (l), Val Thorens (l)
Number of lifts 67 in Courchevel, 200 in
Trois Vallées
Total of trails/pistes 150km in
Courchevel (26% beginner, 27% easy,
36% intermediate, 11% difficult),
600km in Trois Vallées
Beginners 26 slopes, 11 free lifts

LIFT PASSES
Area pass Courchevel only 970FF,
Trois Vallées 1,193FF, both for 6 days
Pensioners 20% reduction for
60–69yrs, 50% reduction for 70–75yrs,
free for 76yrs and over
Credit cards yes

TUITION
Skiing 1550: ESF (☎ 479 08 21 07),

1650: ESF (☎ 479 08 26 08),
Le Ski School (☎ 01484 548996 in UK),
1850: Académie (☎ 479 08 11 99),
ESF (☎ 479 08 07 72),
Ski Supreme (☎ 479 08 27 87)
Snowboarding as ski schools
Other courses cross-country,
dog-sledding, ice-climbing, race-training,
ski-jumping (Sports Club ☎ 479 08 08
21), skwal, snowrafting, telemark
Guiding Bureau des Guides (☎ 479 01
03 66), (heli-skiing) SAF Air Courchevel
(☎ 479 08 00 91)

CHILDREN
Lift pass 5–15yrs Courchevel only
630–722FF, Trois Vallées 774–899FF,
both for 6 days
Ski & board school as adults
Kindergarten (ski) 1550:
ESF (☎ 479 08 21 07), 1650:
ESF (☎ 479 08 26 08), 1850: ESF
(☎ 479 08 07 72), (non-ski) 1650:
Les Pitchounets (☎ 479 08 33 69),
1850: ESF Village des Enfants
(☎ 479 08 08 47)

OTHER SPORTS
Climbing wall, dog-sledding, ice-climbing,
ice-driving, ice-hockey, karting, lugeing,
night-skiing/boarding, parapente, quad
bikes, skating, ski-jumping, snowmobiling, snowshoeing, squash, swimming

FOOD AND DRINK
Coffee 13–15FF, glass of wine 20–25FF,
small beer 28FF, soft drink 15FF,
dish of the day 75FF

Skiing facts: La Tania

TOURIST INFORMATION
La Tania F–73125, Courchevel Cedex, Savoie
Tel 33 479 08 40 40
Fax 33 479 08 45 71
Email info@latania.com
Web site www.latania.com

THE RESORT
By road Calais 950km
By rail TGV Moûtiers 18km
Airport transfer Chambéry 2hrs, Geneva 3hrs, Lyon 2½hrs
Visitor beds 4,000
Transport free ski bus

THE SKIING
Linked or nearby resorts Courchevel (I), Les Menuires (I), Méribel (I), St-Martin-de-Belleville (I), Val Thorens (I)
Number of lifts 67 in Courchevel area, 200 in Trois Vallées
Total of trails/pistes 180km in Courchevel area (26% beginner, 27% easy, 36% intermediate, 11% difficult), 600km in Trois Vallées
Beginners 11 lifts, points tickets available

LIFT PASSES
Area pass La Tania only 970FF, Trois Vallées 1,193FF, both for 6 days

Pensioners 20% reduction for 60–69yrs, 50% reduction for 70–75yrs, free for 76yrs and over
Credit cards yes

TUITION
Skiing ESF (☎ 479 08 80 39), Arthur MacLean (☎ 612 67 30 49), Magic in Motion (☎ 479 01 07 17), Snow Ball (☎ 479 08 24 21)
Snowboarding ESF, Magic in Motion
Other courses snowblading, teen skiing, telemark
Guiding through ESF, Olivier Houillot (☎ 479 08 39 58)

CHILDREN
Lift pass 5–15yrs La Tania only 630–722FF, Trois Vallées 774–899FF, both for 6 days
Ski & board school as adults
Kindergarten (ski/non-ski) Jardin des Neiges, Maison des Enfants (for both ☎ 479 08 80 39)

OTHER SPORTS
Dog-sledding, snowshoeing, swimming

FOOD AND DRINK
Coffee 12FF, glass of wine 20FF, small beer 20FF, soft drink 13FF, dish of the day 65–75FF

with the French for its food. The central Côte Brune is still a culinary mainstay. Pizzeria du Mottaret is 'the restaurant with the best ambience and prices'. Courchevel 1850 abounds in fine restaurants at truly stratospheric prices. The Chabichou Hotel has two coveted Michelin stars, as does Le Bateau Ivre ('much better value than London and a real gastronomic treat'). The seafood restaurant at the Byblos de Neige is a wonder to behold; however, few reporters found themselves in this envious price bracket. La Saulire (Jacques' Bar) in the square at 1850 offers haute cuisine at far wallet-friendlier prices and is without doubt the most welcoming and best-value restaurant in town: 'a resort

Skiing facts: Méribel

TOURIST INFORMATION
BP1, F–73551 Méribel, Savoie
Tel 33 479 08 69 01
Fax 33 479 00 59 61
Email info@meribel.net
Web site www.meribel.net

THE RESORT
By road Calais 962km
By rail TGV Moûtiers 18km, regular bus service to resort
Airport transfer Chambéry 2hrs, Geneva 3hrs, Lyon 2 ½hrs
Visitor beds 30,000
Transport free ski bus

THE SKIING
Linked or nearby resorts Courchevel (l), Les Menuires (l), St-Martin-de-Belleville (l), La Tania (l), Val Thorens (l)
Number of lifts 75 in Méribel, 200 in Trois Vallées
Total of trails/pistes 150km in Méribel (15% easy, 71% intermediate, 14% difficult), 600km in Trois Vallées
Beginners 3 free lifts, reduced lift pass available with instruction

LIFT PASSES
Area pass Méribel only 614–945FF, Trois Vallées 1,193FF, both for 6 days
Pensioners 20% reduction for 60–69yrs, 50% reduction for 70–75yrs, free for 76yrs and over
Credit cards yes

TUITION
Skiing ESF (☎ 479 08 60 31), Magic in Motion (☎ 479 08 53 36), Ski Principles (☎ 01803 852185 in UK), White Abyss (☎ 607 73 90 95)
Snowboarding as ski schools
Other courses cross-country, moguls, race-training, telemark
Guiding Bureau des Guides (☎ 479 00 30 38)

CHILDREN
Lift pass 5–15yrs Méribel only 630–722FF, Trois Vallées 774–899FF, both for 6 days
Ski & board school as adults
Kindergarten (ski) Méribel and Mottaret: Les P'tits Loups (☎ 479 08 60 31), (non-ski) Halte-Garderie Club Saturnin (☎ 479 08 66 90)

OTHER SPORTS
Dog-sledding, ice-hockey, parapente, skating, snowshoeing, snowbiking, swimming

FOOD AND DRINK
Coffee 13–15FF, glass of wine 20–25FF, small beer 28FF, soft drink 15FF, dish of the day 75FF

institution with a passionate following'. Le Plancher des Vaches and La Chapelle are also warmly praised.

Restaurants at Courchevel 1650 are less Parisian in price. La Montagne is recommended for 'its outstanding, mouth-watering *côte de boeuf*', while L'Eterlou is 'family-run, welcoming and reasonably priced' and La Montagne is 'extremely popular on chalet staff night off'. In Courchevel 1550 the Oeil du Boeuf is 'good, but rather smart', and La

Skiing facts: Val Thorens

TOURIST INFORMATION
F–73440 Val Thorens, Savoie
Tel 33 479 00 08 08
Fax 33 479 00 00 04
Email valtho@valthorens.com
Web site www.valthorens.com

THE RESORT
By road Calais 981km
By rail TGV Moûtiers 33km, frequent
buses to resort
Airport transfer Chambéry 2hrs,
Geneva 3hrs, Lyon 2½hrs
Visitor beds 24,000
Transport free ski bus

THE SKIING
Linked or nearby resorts Courchevel (I),
Les Menuires (I), Méribel (I), St-Martin-
de-Belleville (I), La Tania (I)
Number of lifts 30 in Val Thorens, 200 in
Trois Vallées
Total of trails/pistes 140km in Val
Thorens (40% easy, 50% intermediate,
10% difficult), 600km in Trois Vallées
Beginners 4 free lifts
Summer skiing 3 lifts and 3 runs on
Péclet Glacier

LIFT PASSES
Area pass Val Thorens only 714–905 FF,
Trois Vallées 1,193 FF, both for 6 days
Pensioners 20% reduction for
60–69yrs, 50% reduction for 70–75yrs,
free 76yrs and over
Credit cards yes

TUITION
Skiing ESF (☎ 479 00 02 86),
ESI Ski Cool (☎ 479 00 04 92),
Gilbert Smith International Race Camp
(☎ 479 00 04 24), Patrick and Eric
Berthon (☎ 479 00 06 16),
Pros-Neige (☎ 479 01 07 00),
ESI (☎ 479 00 01 96)
Snowboarding as ski schools
Other courses cross-country, extreme
skiing, heli-skiing, ice-driving, moguls,
race-training, skiing for the disabled,
Skwal, teen skiing, telemark
Guiding Bureau des Guides
(☎ 479 00 08 08), Ski Safari Pepi Prager
(☎ 479 00 01 23), Ski The 12 Valleys
(☎ 479 00 00 95)

CHILDREN
Lift pass 5–15yrs Val Thorens only
630–722FF, Trois Vallées 774–898FF,
both for 6 days
Ski & board school as adults, and Marie
Goitschel Village (☎ 479 00 00 47)
Kindergarten (ski/non-ski) ESF,
Marie Goitschel Village

OTHER SPORTS
Climbing wall, ice-driving, indoor tennis
and squash, parapente, skating, snowmobiling, snowshoeing, swimming

FOOD AND DRINK
Coffee 12FF, glass of wine 20FF, small
beer 20FF, soft drink 13FF,
dish of the day 65–75FF

Cortona and Le Caveau are warmly recommended: 'great atmosphere and food in both'. Le Praz is famed for the outrageously expensive but nevertheless compelling Bistrot du Praz and Charley, its *bon vivant* host. Hotel Les Peupliers, the original village inn, is 'a culinary hide-away that I am keeping to myself', while L'Orsonne Blanche is said to be a cheaper alternative 'with portions big enough to make your salopettes wince'.

Skiing facts: Les Menuires

TOURIST INFORMATION
BP22, F–73440 Les Menuires, Savoie
Tel 33 479 00 73 00
Fax 33 479 00 75 06
Email lesmenuires@lesmenuires.com
Web site www.lesmenuires.com

THE RESORT
By road Calais 972km
By rail TGV Moûtiers 28km
Airport transfer Chambéry 1½hrs,
Geneva 3hrs, Lyon 2hrs
Visitor beds 26,000 (including
St-Martin)
Transport free ski bus around resort

THE SKIING
Linked or nearby resorts Courchevel (l),
Méribel (l), St-Martin-de-Belleville (l),
La Tania (l), Val Thorens (l)
Number of lifts 45 in Les Menuires and
St-Martin, 200 in Trois Vallées
Total of trails/pistes 160km in Les
Menuires (30% easy, 52% intermediate,
18% difficult), 600km in Trois Vallées
Beginners 5 free lifts
Summer skiing in Val Thorens

LIFT PASSES
Area pass Les Menuires only 945FF,
Trois Vallées 1,193FF, both for 6 days
Pensioners 20% reduction for

60–69yrs, 50% reduction for 70–75yrs,
free for 76yrs and over
Credit cards yes

TUITION
Skiing ESF (☎ 479 00 61 43),
ESI (☎ 479 00 67 34)
Snowboarding as ski school
Other courses cross-country, extreme
skiing, moguls, race-training, skiing for
the disabled, teen skiing, telemark
Guiding through ESF and ESI

CHILDREN
Lift pass 5–15yrs Les Menuires only
630–722FF, Trois Vallées 774–899FF,
both for 6 days
Ski & board school as adults
Kindergarten (ski/non-ski) Village des
Schtroumpfs (☎ 479 00 63 79), Village
des Marmottons (☎ 479 00 69 50)

OTHER SPORTS
Hang-gliding, parapente, skating,
snowmobiling, snowshoeing, swimming,
tubing

FOOD AND DRINK
Coffee 12FF, glass of wine 20FF,
small beer 20FF, soft drink 13FF,
dish of the day 65–75FF

La Tania contains four reasonably priced restaurants including Pub Le Ski Lodge and La Taiga, which are described as 'welcoming and serve tasty, (relatively) inexpensive food'.

Val Thorens boasts 45 restaurants headed by the gourmet Chalet des Glaciers. Le Galoubet is recommended at lunch-time for its dish of the day, and La Joyeuse Fondue, Le Vieux Chalet and Bloopers are all praised, too. El Gringo's Café in the Péclet shopping centre is among the most popular. Chamois d'Or serves 'excellent smoked salmon and avocado salad'.

Les Menuires is no gastronomic haven, but the half-board food in Hotel Les Latitudes was described as 'much more exciting than we could have hoped for'. Better restaurants include La Mascotte and Chalet Nécou.

Après-ski

In Méribel Jack's Bar close to the piste puts on a popular après-ski happy hour, 'lively, happy atmosphere, value for money' said one reporter, but 'full of sad, middle-aged English drinking lager and playing bar billiards to the strains of old Beach Boy tapes,' commented another. Le Rond Point is equally busy as the lifts close. L'Artichaud, located above the ice-rink, has live music, a fun atmosphere and stays open late. Dick's Tea-Bar, a branch of the Val d'Isère original, is also extremely popular.

At Prends Ta Luge Et Tire-toi ('grab your toboggan and go') in the Forum complex at Courchevel 1850 you can surf the Web, buy a snowboard or get a tattoo. The 5 à 7 beneath the Hotel Albatross is popular, and L'Accord and Le Grenier are two usually crowded piano bars. La Grange and Les Caves are the main late-night but prohibitively expensive venues ('where the French glitterati buy vodka by the bottle while dancers gyrate to Euro anthems on podiums overlooking the dance floor'). Le Kalico is a much cheaper 2am alternative ('no entry fee and reminiscent of a student disco with Brits dancing ankle-deep in beer').

At Courchevel 1650, Le Bubble is the new 'in' place, while Le Signal is the bar-restaurant where the locals meet and Le Plouc is a small, smoky and busy bar. By night Le Green Club has a modest entry fee, a British DJ and 'the best music at any altitude in Courchevel'. Rocky's Bar is also always busy. At Courchevel 1550 après-ski revolves around La Taverne ('very French, very friendly') and the Glacier Bar ('full of British resort staff'). Chanrossa provides some of the best late-night action. Le Praz is not the place for raucous nightlife. Its crêperie makes 'the best *vin chaud* in the business', and the Bar Brasserie is 'the only place with any life'.

La Tania's nightlife has much improved in recent years: it boasts a handful of bars with a relaxed atmosphere.

The popular watering holes at Val Thorens are Le Tango, the Ski Rock Café, the Viking Pub and the Frog and Roast Beef. Reporters praised the swimming-pool and indoor tennis courts.

Après-ski in Les Menuires involves a wide range of sporting alternatives including skating, tubing and swimming as well as concerts in the new village hall for the less active.

Childcare

All the main resorts are well served with ESF ski and non-ski kindergarten. However, it is important to note that the facilities offered may not be conducive to the enjoyment of your holiday. The Gallic approach to childcare may seem harsh by northern European standards, with a serious emphasis on learning to ski without any accompanying element of fun. The number of children who tearfully refuse to return to these French establishments on day two of their holiday has led tour operators to set up more sympathetic crèches and even ski classes.

Reporters praised the Méribel ESF ski school: 'although the classes were large, the teachers made the lessons fun. The Marie Goitschel Village in Val Thorens attracts predominantly French children. It has its own small ski area and accepts children from three years. Reporters said that the teaching is 'excellent'. The ESF in Courchevel 1850 is criticised as being 'too serious' in its approach, and 'needs to be more organised'. Many parents staying here feel that Le Praz has a better ski school, and the instructors will come up to 1850 to collect children. The Maison des Enfants and the Jardin des Neiges non-ski and ski-kindergarten at La Tania take children from three to 12 years old. Children staying in Les Menuires are cared for at the Village des Schtroumpfs from three months and at the Village des Marmottons from two-and-a-half years of age.

Linked or nearby resorts

St-Martin-de-Belleville
top 3,300m (10,825ft) bottom 1,400m (4,593ft)
St-Martin-de-Belleville is an old village situated below Les Menuires, with its own chair-lift access to the ridge above Méribel. As one reporter put it: 'St-Martin essentially has the good features of Les Menuires without the bad'. It is a farming community at pastoral counterpoint to the hi-tech world of the ski network above it. The old cheese-making village has considerable charm and several fine restaurants; La Bouitte in nearby **St-Marcel** is a serious exercise in gastronomy.

Le Bidou has 'a Savoyarde menu in an atmospheric basement'. L'Etoile de Neige is a lunchtime favourite with ski guides, while Les Airelles offers 'excellent value, food and service'. L'Eterlou offers 'a sunny terrace and friendly staff', while La Voute is recommended for steaks and pizzas, and La Montagnarde is 'strong on cheese and potatoes in hayloft-like surroundings'. Recommended hotels include the St Martin (☎ 479 00 88 00) and Alp'Hôtel (☎ 479 08 92 82). Hotel Edelweiss (☎ 479 08 96 67) is 'pleasant with a good restaurant'.

St-Martin is linked into the system by a slow triple-chair. However, the second stage is a high-speed quad-chair that takes you directly to the top of Tougnette. Nevertheless, if you are staying in Méribel do not linger too long over lunch – allow a full 40 minutes to reach the ridge of the valley on your way home.

TOURIST INFORMATION
Tel 33 479 08 93 09
Fax 33 479 08 9171
Email lesmenuires@lesmenuires.com
Web site www.st-martin-belleville.com

Val d'Isère and Tignes

ALTITUDE Val d'Isère 1,850m (6,068ft), Tignes 2,100m (6,888ft)

Beginners ✳✳ Intermediates ✳✳✳ Advanced ✳✳✳ Snowboarders ✳✳✳

Early in December Val d'Isère traditionally hosts the first European leg of the World Cup downhill or 'Super G'. Between then and the first week of May, more British skiers visit this remote and rather unprepossessing resort at the head of the Tarentaise Valley than anywhere else.

- ✔ Large well-linked ski area
- ✔ Extensive off-piste
- ✔ Summer skiing (Tignes)
- ✔ Reliable snow record
- ✔ Excellent lift system
- ✔ Lively après-ski (Val d'Isère)
- ✔ Skiing convenience (Tignes)
- ✘ Few activities for non-skiers (Val d'Isère)
- ✘ Lack of tree-level runs
- ✘ Unattractive village (Tignes)

It is a destination for serious enthusiasts, which somehow manages to blend a cocktail of high ski-tech and mass-market tourism with a smooth topping of sophistication. The ski area is directly linked to neighbouring Tignes and is jointly marketed as L'Espace Killy, after its most revered son Jean-Claude Killy, who swept the board of gold medals at the 1968 Winter Olympics.

The quality of the skiing in the area is so varied and demanding that it has raised a whole generation of international experts who never ski anywhere else. As one reporter commented: 'Anyone who claims to be bored with Espace Killy is either lying or certifiable'. A vertical drop of 1,900m, coupled with 97 lifts, including two high-speed underground railways, seven gondolas and three cable-cars, form the hardcore infrastructure. For the expert, however, the real joy lies in the unlimited off-piste opportunities to be found in this wild region on the edge of the Vanoise National Park. Apart from the eleventh-century church, precious little remains of the old village of Val d'Isère, which became a winter sports resort in 1932. Today, it has grown into a hotchpotch of a ski town, which sprawls from the apartment blocks of **La Daille** at one end to **Le Fornet** at the other.

Val Village, a cluster of 'old-style' stone buildings around the church, and housing smart boutiques, was created in time for the 1992 Olympics. It provided the village with an attractive focal point that it had previously lacked. Much has since been done to improve the appearance of the rest of the town. Some of the original concrete apartment buildings have been resurfaced in wood and stone. The wide pavements dotted with mature trees have greatly enhanced its appeal for pedestrians.

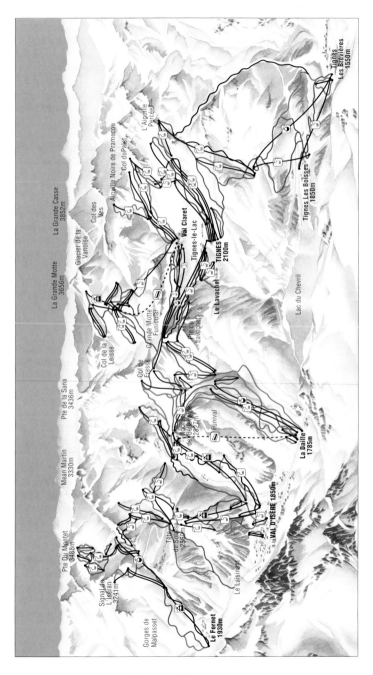

The old village of Tignes disappeared beneath the waters of the Lac du Chevril when the valley was dammed in 1952. Its replacement is synonymous with high-rise housing estates set at varying altitudes of about 2,000m and represents some of the most ghastly excesses of 1960s' French Alpine architecture. The hamlets of **Val Claret**, **Tignes-le-Lac**, **Le Lavachet**, and even the much lower community of **Tignes-les-Boisses** are all visually unattractive. Only the valley farming community of **Tignes-les-Brévières** is appealing. However, Tignes is in the process of spending £35 million in an effort to improve the resort's appearance. Many of the older buildings have been reclad and apartment owners have been given financial incentives to carry out renovations. Tignes-le-Lac has been transformed by a tunnel bypass and a people-mover lift now links the car park at Val Claret with the funicular station.

WHAT'S NEW

Upgrading of the Cascade chair on the Pissaillas Glacier
New gondola replaces Bellevarde cable-car
New four-star restaurant at Val Claret
Additional snowmaking across whole area
New mountain restaurant at Tignes

The glacier in Tignes is no longer open for 365 days of the year. In 2001, for the second successive year, it closed from 14 May until 15 June and 9–28 September. Ostensibly this was to allow the lifts to be serviced. In reality, not enough skiers and snowboarders use the glacier during these periods to justify the expensive of running the lift system.

Buses between Val d'Isère and Tignes are neither frequent nor cheap. If you have your own car and want a change of scenery, day-trips to **Les Arcs**, **La Plagne**, **La Rosière** and **Sainte-Foy** are all possible.

On the snow

top 3,456m (11,335ft) bottom 1,550m (5,084ft)

Val d'Isère alone has eight major points of mountain access including a high-speed underground train. The ski school rush hour should be avoided, and the French school holidays in February are inevitably crowded, but otherwise queuing is not a serious problem. The long valley floor is covered by an efficient free ski bus known as Le Train Rouge, and with experience you can avoid the bottlenecks. Radio Val d'Isère (96.1FM) gives up-to-date news on piste grooming, weather and snow reports.

L'Espace Killy divides naturally into six separate ski sectors. On the Val d'Isère side are Col de l'Iseran, Pissaillas, Solaise and Bellevarde, which are strung in a row along the curving road between the satellites of Le Fornet and La Daille. The first two sectors are linked by lift at altitude, but Solaise and Bellevarde join only at valley level close to the resort centre. Bellevarde links easily with Tignes via the Tovière ridge/Col de Fresse.

The skiing at Tignes is split into three areas – Tovière, the Grande Motte Glacier and Palet/L'Aiguille Percée. Tignes also has an underground railway, in which passengers are whisked at high speed up through the rock and permafrost from Val Claret at 2,100m to the Panoramic restaurant at 3,030m in just six minutes. Both Tignes and Val d'Isère trains are of a similar type to the one in which 155 skiers and snowboarders died in November 2000 in the fire at Kaprun. Extensive modifications to both tunnels have been carried out and the addition of a small fire extinguisher and a minuscule window hammer to each carriage goes some way to reassuring passengers.

An alternative lift network takes you from Tignes-le-Lac towards the dramatic rock formation of L'Aiguille Percée, in one direction, or towards Val d'Isère's more demanding ski area in the other. For most of the season there is more skiing in Tignes down to the lower lying hamlets of Les Boisses at 1,850m and Les Brévières at 1,550m.

Piste-grooming in Val d'Isère is of an exceptionally high standard that is now matched in Tignes, which spends £2.5 million each winter on running its lift system. However, the severity of the terrain makes it greatly liable to avalanches. In high winds or after a major dump, the whole area is liable to temporary closure. Those in the know take a day out on the protected pistes of Sainte-Foy.

Beginners

Val d'Isère is unfairly denigrated for its facilities for beginners. In fact, it has acceptable – and free – nursery slopes right in the centre of the village and a wide choice of ski schools. The problem stems from the fact that there is nothing for the improving beginner. Do not trust the piste map; some of the runs marked green (beginner) could frighten the daylights out of you ('so-called gentle slopes have bumps that will throw beginners into the air like rag dolls'). One solution is to ski on Solaise and take the chair-lift or cable-car back down. The new Bellevarde gondola will provide an alternative high-speed download. The Col de l'Iseran sector has some gentle runs, but here, as in other parts of the resort, it is too difficult to ski back to the valley. Tignes has a good choice of blue (easy) runs on the glacier but the usually chilly temperature is not conducive to learning.

Intermediates

Piste-grading is not Val's strongest point, and colour-coding is on the dark side – some blues would be red (intermediate) runs elsewhere, and you may find the odd red that is positively black (difficult) by Tyrolean standards. The Bellevarde sector provides plenty of variety. The L and Germain Mathis runs (check to see if they are open) off the back of Solaise take you down to the hamlet of **Le Laisinant** and both offer superb cruising, combined with beautiful scenery. The OK run around the shoulder of the Rocher de Bellevarde is the World Cup downhill course, while the long descent to Val Claret from the Grande Motte glacier is a test for even the fittest, strongest thigh muscles when taken without stopping.

Advanced

The Face de Bellevarde, reached by either the Funival funicular railway or the new gondola, was used as the men's downhill course for the 1992 Winter Olympics. The legacy is a superb black run, which leads you back to Val in rather more than the two minutes it took winner Patrick Ortlieb and his fellow competitors. Sache, a long black with fierce moguls, starts from the blue Corniche run below L'Aiguille Percée and takes you down to Tignes-les-Brévières, where it merges with the red Pavot. If you are looking for moguls, the run through the trees from the top of Le Fornet can, at times, be the best in the resort. The steepest bump run is the Epaule du Charvet.

Off-piste

The area has some of the best lift-served off-piste in the world and the starting points for the most challenging itineraries are marked on the piste map. Once you commit yourself, you are on your own and it is easy to get lost – or worse. It is imperative to have a local guide who can read the snow conditions and knows which routes are safe. In fresh powder the Charvet area is a particular favourite. One resident reporter commented: 'there is no greater thrill than cutting first tracks on the Face du Charvet or the Couloir Mont Blanc before skiing the Bec d'Aigle'. The Couloir des Pisteurs, on the north face of the Grande Motte, appears to be unskiable from the top of Bellevarde. However, a mountain guide can lead you through its superb landscape of seracs and crevasses. The Signal de l'Iseran/Pissaillas Glacier sector provides some of the most dramatic runs.

Snowboarding

Val's terrain park is situated above La Daille on the upper slopes of Bellevarde. The Combe de Palafour terrain park at Tignes has a half-pipe, a boardercross course and assorted obstacles. A terrain park operates on the Grande Motte Glacier throughout the summer. Both Val and Tignes offer some amazing freeriding as well as lots of natural cliffs and gullies.

Tuition and guiding

To get the best out of the ski area you need some expert help: the two resorts boast a clutch of rival ski and snowboarding schools. The ESF operates in both resorts ('our instructor was so old her face was lined with wrinkles deep enough for cedar trees to take root in. She was affable, capable, but holistically oriented. I did not feel the need to descend into Zen to improve my skiing'). Anglo-Saxons tend to favour the alternatives, which are more linguistically and emotionally geared towards the needs of the calibre of skier who wants to get the best out of the area. Pat Zimmer's Top Ski was the first independent ski school in France, when founded in 1976. Its supporters would still argue that it is the best. The secret of its success is that it has remained small.

Instructors take groups of six skiers off-piste in the mornings and give instruction on piste technique in the afternoons.

In the past we received only favourable reports of Snow Fun, however recent reports are not so good: 'The teacher tended to concentrate on the person at the front and back, the rest just muddled through' and 'my ski instructor didn't really make any attempt to learn our names'. We have encouraging reports of Mountain Masters. One reporter described a guide from Alpine Experience as: 'the best I have ever come across anywhere'. Evolution 2, in both Val and Tignes, is widely praised for its expertise. A reporter commended the Val branch: 'while my instructor's English was hardly English, he did teach me an incredible amount in three days. Evolution rentals also proved top-notch'. The Tignes branch offers a range of non-skiing activities including ice-diving under the lake, and the school also owns a mountain restaurant and a hotel.

Hors-Limites Surf School in Val runs free introductory snowboard lessons, with equipment included, on the nursery slopes on Sunday afternoons. It takes riders from as young as five years old in small groups. We have no reports of Billabong and Misty Fly. In Tignes, Surf Feeling, Snocool and Kébra Surfing are the specialist board schools.

Reporters continue to praise Val's equipment shop Precision Ski: 'they are so thorough and so friendly and deserve their award as the best equipment supplier. It seems as if there is nothing they don't know about skiing. The Tourist Office tried to persuade us to go to Killy, but they just hand out boots and skis with no consultation'.

Mountain restaurants

Eating out at altitude is not Espace Killy's strongest point. The better establishments are on the Val side and include Trifollet ('good pizzas'), which is halfway down to La Daille, and La Folie Douce, at the top of the La Daille gondola. Neighbouring La Fruitière is decorated as a Savoyard dairy, has some of the best food on the mountain as well as some of the best WCs, and should be booked in advance during high season. Les Tufs, at the bottom of the Funival, provides 'efficient service, friendly staff and some of the most reasonably priced food in the resort'. The new Toit du Monde restaurant, owned by the mother of the violinist Vanessa Mae, replaces the former Crech'Ouna, near the Funival station: 'cuisine best described as Savoie-Asian fusion. Sometimes it works, sometimes it most certainly doesn't' and 'the wine is ridiculously overpriced'. Bananas is a favourite among reporters – for the ambience rather than the quality of the food. Clochetons is also praised for its 'reasonably priced *table d'hôte*'.

The Ski d'Eté restaurant complex below the Grande Motte gondola was recommended for its good value: 'a large attractive eating area with plenty of choices'. Le Panoramic, at the top of the Grande Motte funicular, offers a self-service and separate waiter-service restaurant ('surprisingly good, with courteous staff'). At lunchtime many snow-users return to the valley, where restaurants are as busy as they are by night.

Upstairs at L'Arbina in Tignes-le-Lac is 'a serious but reasonably priced gastronomic experience, but you must book, even at lunchtime'. The rebuilt restaurant at the Col du Palet is described as 'very welcoming', while La Taverne at Val Claret is 'better and cheaper than most restaurants in the region'.

Accommodation

In Val d'Isère a couple of four-stars heads a choice of 35 hotels. The Christiania (☎ 479 06 08 25) is the most comfortable, while the three-star Blizzard (☎ 479 06 02 07), Savoyarde (☎ 479 06 01 55) and the Tsanteleina (☎ 479 06 12 13) enjoy a strong British following. The piste-side Hotel Brussel's (☎ 479 06 05 39) is praised by one reporter despite being 'stuck in a 1970s time warp'. Hotel Les Sorbiers (☎ 479 06 23 77) is built in a wood-and-stone chalet style. Most snow-users stay in chalets or in self-catering apartments. The Alpina Lodge Résidence (☎ 479 41 60 00) is recommended for 'location, prices, reasonable accommodation and very helpful staff'.

In Tignes, most accommodation is in self-catering apartments, which vary dramatically in quality in direct relation to their age. Hotels range from the comfortable four-star Le Ski d'Or (☎ 479 06 51 60) in Val Claret ('bright, spacious rooms') to a clutch of two-stars including the well-positioned Hotel L'Arbina (☎ 479 06 34 78) at Tignes-le-Lac, which has a health centre, and Hotel La Vanoise (☎ 479 06 31 90) ('convenient, with an excellent breakfast and five-course dinner'). Village Montana (☎ 479 40 01 44) and The Alpaka Lodge (☎ 479 06 45 30) are both said to be extremely comfortable.

Eating in and out

'The worst thing about Val d'Isère is the amount of Savoyarde restaurants,' complained a reporter, 'yes, of course, they offer specialities of the region, but there is a limit to the amount of cheese dishes you can eat in a week'. A welcome change is the Perdrix Blanche, which is unpretentious and renowned for its seafood ('amazing selection of fresh fish. It is the most expensive restaurant we went to, but it does have a lovely warm atmosphere'). Casa Strada was praised as 'our favourite restaurant. A genuine Italian restaurant off the tourist trail but centrally located opposite the church'. The Grand Ours is 'in an attractive setting with delicious food', while Chalet du Crêt is a 'wonderfully gastronomic' smart restaurant in a 300-year-old chalet. The restaurant in the Blizzard was praised: 'good atmosphere and excellent service'.

Les Clochetons in the Manchet valley provides a free minibus service as well as 'a great meal at a reasonable price in a lovely setting'. Pacific Pizzeria 'has good food, including fish at sensible prices'. Crêpe Val, close to the post office, is recommended for regional specialities as well as crêpes, and L'Arolay in Le Fornet serves 'fine food'. The Melting Pot is 'an absolute delight,' with 'very nice Asian-inspired food', while La Casserole is highly rated by reporters ('a charming chalet-style restaurant with reasonable prices'). Victor's, above the Casino supermarket,

Skiing facts: Val d'Isère

TOURIST INFORMATION
BP 228, F–73155 Val d'Isère, Savoie
Tel 33 479 06 06 60
Fax 33 479 06 04 56
Email info@valdisere.com
Web site www.valdisere.com

THE RESORT
By road Calais 1,003km
By rail Bourg-St-Maurice 30km
Airport transfer Chambéry 2hrs, Geneva 2½ hrs, Lyon 2½hrs
Visitor beds 27,700
Transport free ski bus between La Daille and Le Fornet

THE SKIING
Linked or nearby resorts Tignes (l), Sainte-Foy (n)
Number of lifts 97 in L'Espace Killy
Total of trails/pistes 300km in L'Espace Killy (15% easy, 47% intermediate, 38% difficult)
Beginners 6 lifts, one of them free
Summer skiing sometimes possible on Pissaillas Glacier

LIFT PASSES
Area pass L'Espace Killy 915–1,070FF for 6 days
Pensioners 60–69yrs 899–971FF for 6 days, 70–74yrs 537–609FF, free for 75yrs and over
Credit cards yes

TUITION
Skiing Alpine Experience (☎ 479 06 28 81), Atimanya (☎ 479 06 25 38), ESF (☎ 479 06 02 34), Evolution 2 (☎ 479 41 16 72), Mountain Masters (☎ 479 06 05 14), Oxygène (☎ 479 41 99 58), Ski Adventure (☎ 479 06 26 99),

Ski Prestige Heliski (☎ 479 06 04 53), Snow Fun (☎ 479 06 19 79), Stages Val Gliss (☎ 479 06 00 72), Top Ski (☎ 479 06 14 80), Tetra Hors-piste (☎ 479 41 97 07)
Snowboarding as ski schools, and Billabong (☎ 479 06 09 54), Hors-Limites Surf School (☎ 479 41 97 02), Misty Fly (Evolution 2) (☎ 479 41 95 77)
Other courses cross-country, extreme skiing/boarding, heli-skiing/boarding, moguls, powder clinics, race-training, skiing for the disabled, snowblading, teen skiing, telemark
Guiding through ski schools, and Bureau des Guides (☎ 479 06 94 03)

CHILDREN
Lift pass 5–12yrs 746–915FF for 6 days
Ski & board school Billabong, ESF, Evolution 2, Hors-Limites Surf School, Oxygène, Snow Fun, Stage Val Glisse, Top Ski
Kindergarten ESF (ski/non-ski) Jardin de Neige (☎ 479 06 02 34), Petit Poucet (☎ 479 06 13 97), Village d'Enfants (☎ 479 41 99 82), Snow Fun Club Nounours (☎ 479 06 16 79), Evolution 2 Yéti Courses (☎ 479 41 16 72)

OTHER SPORTS
Dog-sledding, hang-gliding, ice-climbing, ice-driving, indoor climbing wall, microlighting, parapente, skating, ski-jöring, snowmobiling, snowshoeing, swimming

FOOD AND DRINK
Coffee 10–15FF, glass of wine 15–16FF, small beer 16–25FF, soft drink 18–24FF, dish of the day 80–110FF

was said to have 'fantastic food. It's quite a noisy place as it fills up with large groups of Swedes'. Val d'Isère has four supermarkets ('the Casino supermarket is much nicer than my local Tesco – and better stocked', and several specialist food shops.

In Tignes Le Lavachet, L'Osteria is recommended for raclette and pierrade, and Le Ski d'Or is for fish. Hotel L'Arbina (upstairs restaurant) is 'outstanding, a *crêpe des escargots* to die for'. Daffy's Caffé in Val Claret serves Mexican food ('disappointingly bland with haphazard service'), while Pizza 2000 at Val Claret is 'much more than just a pizzeria – great food, service and ambience'. Le Bouf Mich in Val Claret is 'absolutely terrific, with great food and a jovial atmosphere'. L'Auberge des Trois Ourson in Val Claret is 'very cosy with lots of teddy bears', while La Côte de Boeuf in Tignes Le Lac is 'heaven for meat-lovers'. The five supermarkets in Tignes sell a wide range of food and other goods.

Après-ski

Val d'Isère buzzes with a fun-seeking après-ski crowd. Dick's Tea-Bar continues to be one of the most celebrated discos in the Alps, while Café Face and Bananas are riding high. The Moris Pub and La Taverne enjoy a lively, young following and L'Aventure is a popular club 'designed as a house, complete with double bed and bath'. Club 21 is the more sophisticated option. The Petit Danois is 'lively, but not too expensive', and there is an Internet café called Powder Monkey.

The nightlife in Tignes is limited by comparison. Harry's Bar boasts a strong following, while Grizzly's Bar in Val Claret is warmly recommended ('one of the few drinking joints with character') along with Le Café de la Poste and La Grotte de Yéti. The Fish Tank, Crowded House and The Wobbly Rabbit all have a strong following, and the Caves du Lac in Tignes-le-Lac has a small dance floor and is much praised ('best nightclub in town'). Other discos are Jack's Club in Le Lac, Sub Zero and Blue Girl in Val Claret.

Childcare

The construction of a long-overdue children's village has greatly improved Val's attraction as a base for families. It caters for children aged three to 13 from 8.30am to 6.30pm daily, with ski lessons for older children. Le Petit Poucet kindergarten collects and delivers little ones aged three and over from your chalet or hotel.

ESF, Snow Fun and Evolution 2 all cater for young beginners from three to four years old. Hors-Limites give snowboard lessons from six years of age, and Billabong Snowboard School from seven years. Snow Fun received mixed reports: 'instruction generally good but the teacher took his class of five- and six-year-olds to a café for a hot chocolate break mid-morning. They were asked to bring 10FF with them for the drink but couldn't go to the loo afterwards because that required another 2FF. This happened every day'.

Skiing facts: Tignes

TOURIST INFORMATION
BP 51, F–73321 Tignes, Savoie
Tel 33 479 40 04 40
Fax 33 479 40 03 15
Email information@tignes.net
Web site www.tignes.net

THE RESORT
By road Calais 1,001km
By rail Bourg-St-Maurice 26km
Airport transfer Chambéry 2hrs, Geneva 2½hrs , Lyon 2½hrs
Visitor beds 28,000
Transport free ski bus

THE SKIING
Linked or nearby resorts Val d'Isère (l), Sainte-Foy (n)
Number of lifts 97 in L'Espace Killy
Total of trails/pistes 300km in L'Espace Killy (15% easy, 46% intermediate, 28% difficult, 11% very difficult)
Beginners 5 free lifts
Summer skiing 7 pistes and 14 lifts on Grande Motte Glacier

LIFT PASSES
Area pass L'Espace Killy 915–1,070FF for 6 days
Pensioners 60–69yrs 899–971FF for 6 days, 70–74yrs 537–609FF, free for 75yrs and over
Credit cards yes

TUITION
Skiing ESF (☎ 479 06 30 28),
ESI (☎ 479 06 36 15),
Evolution 2 (☎ 479 06 43 78),
Snow Fun (☎ 479 06 46 10)
Snowboarding as ski schools, and Snocool (☎ 615 34 54 63),
Surf Feeling (☎ 479 06 53 63),
Kébra Surfing (☎ 479 06 43 37)
Other courses cross-country, extreme skiing/boarding, heli-skiing/boarding, race-training, skiing for the disabled, snowblading, teen skiing, telemark
Guiding through ski schools, and Bureau des Guides (☎ 479 06 42 76)

CHILDREN
Lift pass 5–12yrs 746–915FF for 6 days
Ski & board school ESF, ESI, Evolution 2, Snow Fun
Kindergarten (ski/non-ski) Les Marmottons (☎ 479 06 51 67)

OTHER SPORTS
Dog-sledding, hang-gliding, ice-climbing, ice-diving, night-skiing, parapente, skating, ski-jöring, squash, snowshoeing, indoor tennis

FOOD AND DRINK
Coffee 10–15FF, glass of wine 12–16FF, small beer 15–25FF, soft drink 16–24FF, dish of the day 90–110FF

In Tignes, Les Marmottons is for children from two years old. The ESF offers all-day ski lessons with lunch from four years of age, and the International Ski School (ESI) from five.

Linked or nearby resorts

Sainte-Foy
top 2,620m (8,596ft) bottom 1,550m (5,084ft)

Sainte-Foy is an unremarkable old hamlet that you drive through on the road up from **Bourg-St-Maurice** to Tignes and Val d'Isère. But just above it, reached by a side road, is a raw and exciting ski resort of the same name. We continue to receive unfavourable comments about the Zigzags Snow-shop, the sole rental outlet ('they gave me one boot to try on and whinged like hell when I wanted to try on the other. I ended up having to get a pisteur to adjust my bindings because one ski kept falling off'. Another reporter commented: 'after a wasted morning in the shop we gave up and went down to Bourg-St-Maurice where staff were friendly and helpful'.

The locals come to Sainte-Foy to enjoy untracked powder and to get away from the crowds at peak times. The resort is also an excellent location for freeriders looking for natural drops and walls. One reporter remarked: 'the piste map is a complete smokescreen: it gives no indication of the hugeness of the off-piste terrain'. A guide is essential for enjoying the full off-piste potential. Two outstanding itineraries are the Face Nord de Foliet and the Couloir Dudu, the latter an 800-m chute renowned for its spring powder. Both these runs go through the hamlet of **Le Crot** before ending at **Le Miroir** , with its rustic eatery Chez Marie ('a locals' fiercely guarded secret'). Sainte-Foy is popular with experienced riders. The Local ESF has a sound reputation, and Les P'tits Trappeurs crèche is situated at the base area.

Three chair-lifts take you up to the Col de l'Aiguille and the starting point for 600m vertical of challenging piste and some dramatic powder descents. There are a few simple but atmospheric mountain eating-places. Les Brevettes, at the top of the first chair, is praised for its omelettes, and neighbouring Chez Leon 'has to be booked'. Reporters continue to praise the British-owned Auberge sur la Montagne (☎ 479 06 95 83) in the neighbouring hamlet of **La Thuile**: 'this really is a gem of a place with heaps of mountain character. The food was gargantuan and utterly delicious'.

TOURIST INFORMATION
Tel 33 479 06 95 19
Fax 33 479 06 95 09
Email stefoy@wanadoo.fr
Web site www.sainte-foy-tarentaise.com

Valmorel

ALTITUDE 1,400m (4,592ft)

Beginners ✱✱✱ Intermediates ✱✱✱ Advanced ✱

Valmorel is an attractive family resort in the Tarentaise, which is reached by road from Moûtiers. It shares a network of 56 lifts and 152km of pistes with the popular French destinations of **St-François** and **Longchamp** in the Maurienne Valley and the beginner resort of **Doucy Combelouvière**. Together they market themselves as Le Grand Domaine and offer a wide range of skiing, mainly below advanced level. Unlike its purpose-built forerunners, the village is architecturally pleasing and fits so snugly into its mountain environment that it is hard to believe that it was constructed only in 1976. Central Valmorel is often referred to as Bourg-Morel to distinguish it from the satellite residential areas, called *hameaux*, which lie some distance outside the small but charming car-free centre.

> ✔ Protected learning areas
> ✔ Sympathetic architecture
> ✔ Family atmosphere
> ✔ Central pedestrian area
> ✔ Value for money
> ✘ Few non-skiing activities
> ✘ No shuttle bus around residential satellites

It is important to note that the colour-coding on the local lift map flies in the face of all accepted procedure in Europe for reasons that are not at all clear. Green is listed as easy, blue as intermediate, red as difficult, and black as very difficult.

On the snow
top 2,550m (8,364ft) bottom 1,250m (4,100ft)

Valmorel is a planned family resort with exceptional nursery slopes (for adults and children), which are closed off to passing skiers and snowboarders. Its terrain is also sufficiently testing to keep competent skiers and snowboarders interested for a week. Mountain access is from various satellite hamlets at different altitudes. The Télébourg gondola runs from Bourg-Morel in two stages up to the hamlets of Crève-Coeur and Mottet, but is designed more as a people-carrier than a ski lift.

Le Grand Domaine network is divided into the bowl above Valmorel and a straight up-and-down system of lifts between Longchamp and St-François across the Col de la Madeleine. All three sectors are accessible by blue (easy) pistes.

Beginners

Valmorel is one of the best resorts in the Alps for beginners – both adults and children. The latter have a protected nursery area with a rope-tow at the Saperlipopette kindergarten down by the Télébourg tower, as well as a totally enclosed area with toys and a lift up the mountain in the Pierrafort area. A similarly enclosed adult training area can be found by the Bois de la Croix drag-lift. The linked resort of Doucy Combelouvière provides a network of the easiest of green (beginner) runs.

Intermediates

This is a resort where you always feel you are going somewhere, rather than skiing the same runs or similar pistes in the same bowl over and over again. The long runs down into the Celliers Valley and the exciting descents off the Col de Gollet provide classic skiing. Bump bashers will want to hit the two red (intermediate) runs under the Madeleine chair, where the snow keeps cool and crisp. Reverdy off the Lauzière chair is a steeper option.

WHAT'S NEW

The Roset chair-lift in the Madeleine area opens up a new red run
Prariond drag-lift at Pierrafort

Advanced

There are not many black (difficult) runs, nor are they especially ferocious, although the monster bumps under the Gollet chair have been used in championship competitions. The Mottet chair also leads to some testing moguls and is the setting-off point for the longest and most interesting black, called the Noire du Mottet.

Off-piste

The beauty of Valmorel's off-piste is that even during the high-season weeks you can usually find whole stretches of untracked powder long after a snowfall. With its family image, the resort does not normally attract advanced skiers and snowboarders. Excellent powder-skiing after a snowfall can be found down the ridge between Mottet and Gollet.

Snowboarding

Valmorel has never been a great place for riders: too many skier families and a dearth of cool bars in which to hang out in the evenings. However, the easy pistes will suit first-timers and the more experienced can try the terrain park with its boardercross course and half-pipe. The Biollene piste is ideal for novice riders.

Tuition and guiding

Classes meet at the French Ski School (ESF) headquarters at the top of the Télébourg people-mover. Lessons given in English are held in the afternoons from Sunday to Friday; and in French in the mornings, from Monday to Saturday. One reporter described organisation during half-term as 'absolute chaos'.

Mountain restaurants

These are mostly self-service and offer value for money rather than haute cuisine. The Alpage at the top of the Altispace chair-lift is recom-

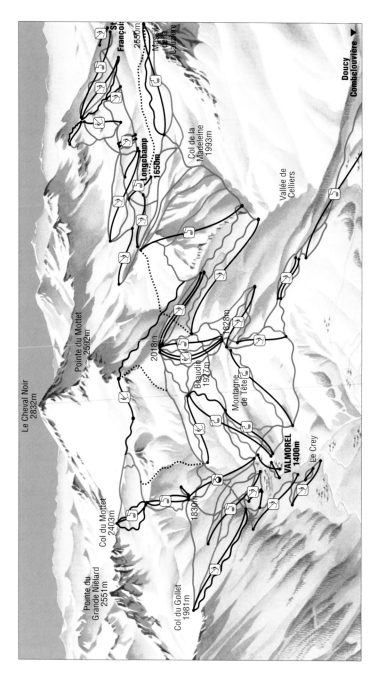

mended: 'a basic cafeteria with ample space and inspiring views'. Altipiano on Pierrafort is smarter, while the Banquoise 2000 refuge on Col de la Madeleine is self-service yet characterful, with rustic tables and a log fire. Les 2 Mazots has the best *croûte au fromage*, and Le Grenier, next to the ski school, is extremely popular.

Accommodation

The resort boasts three hotels that are all currently being modernised. The only three-star is the Planchamp (☎ 479 09 97 00) above the main village. The two-star Hotel du Bourg (☎ 479 09 06 66) is situated in the village centre, and Hotel la Fontaine (☎ 479 09 87 77) has bigger, better rooms. Self-catered apartments are generally larger and better-designed than their counterparts in other French purpose-built resorts, and most provide easy access to the pistes. There is no shuttle bus around the hamlets, and the Télébourg people-mover delivers residents either too high or too low for convenience.

Eating in and out

This is not a resort renowned for fine dining, although reporters noted La Grange has the ubiquitous range of Savoie specialities. Planchamp is 'cosy with a great atmosphere'. L'Aigle Blanche, just outside the village, is worth the visit. Ski-Roc is best for rabbit filet with garlic. Jumbo Lolo serves Tex-Mex, and La Marmite is recommended for steak frites, while Chez Albert champions pizza. Two new eateries are La Ferme du Soleil for local specialities, and Le Champ de Lune, which is said to offer 'farm and gourmet cuisine'.

Après-ski

Jean's Club under the Télébourg tower is the only disco. Loud Top-20-type music is played in the Perce Neige, Café de la Gare and at La Cordée. The Shaker Bar in the Hotel la Fontaine provides comfortable sofas and karaoke evenings. The resort organises a free weekly concert of music ranging from rock to jazz. Other activities include dog-sledding, hang-gliding, microlight, parapente, sleigh rides, snowshoeing and a weekly children's show during the French school holidays.

Childcare

Valmorel's childminding service is the Saperlipopette nursery. The school has bedrooms and playrooms for infants from six months of age. Reservations should be made well in advance, as the school keeps to a strict ratio of five children per nanny. 'Good English, good care and exceptionally well-organised' was one of a number of positive comments about the nursery. Saperlipopette also has a ski kindergarten.

TOURIST INFORMATION
Tel 33 479 09 85 55
Fax 33 479 09 85 29
Email info@valmorel.com
Web site www.valmorel.com

Round-up

RESORTS COVERED Barèges and La Mongie, Cauterets, Chamrousse, La
Clusaz, Font-Romeu, Isola 2000, Pra-Loup, Puy-St-Vincent, St-Lary, Valloire

Barèges and La Mongie
top 2,350m (7,708ft) bottom 1,250m (4,100ft)

Barèges was one of the original ski resorts of the Pyrenees. At first sight,
the little spa village is down-at-heel and grey in its position near the
head of a narrow valley. However, its lack of size engenders a friendly
atmosphere. Prices are low by French standards but there is little to do
after skiing except soak up the sulphur waters of the thermal spa. The
village consists of not much more than a single street climbing steeply
beside a river, surrounded by tree-studded mountainside. This is not a
natural site for a village, and none would have appeared had it not been
for the sulphur springs that gained notoriety in the seventeenth century.
Over the Col du Tourmalet, linked by both bus and lifts, is the more
modern, and considerably less charming, resort of La Mongie. The lift
links sometimes close in bad weather.

Snowfall in the Pyrenees is a subject that always causes disagree-
ment. There is little to support the belief that the mountains receive less
precipitation in winter than the Alps; the trouble is that it does not
always fall as snow. Because the Pyrenees are further west and closer to
the warm Atlantic, the winter is shorter, but the advantage is the high
number of sunny days.

Barèges and La Mongie form the largest ski area in the Pyrenees,
sharing 120km of wide, mainly easy-to-intermediate pistes served by 47
lifts. The area's upper slopes are open and sunny, while the lower ones
above Barèges offer sheltered tree-level skiing. The slopes are reached
from Barèges by two mountain access lifts. Queues can be a serious
problem at weekends; as Barèges cannot cope with many cars, the lifts
from the top of the village and from **Tournaboup** (just outside Barèges)
become crowded, and the Col du Tourmalet can turn into a bottleneck
in both directions.

Of the two resorts, La Mongie is the better base for complete beginners, with easy slopes that keep their snow relatively well immediately
around the resort. The main nursery area is at the top of La Laquette
gondola; Tournaboup has a small nursery slope, and there is also a
baby-lift at **La Mongie-Tourmalet**.

D'Ayré, at 2,020m, provides some of the area's steepest skiing, and
there is no easy way down from the top of the funicular. Some fairly
sheer slopes lie below the Col du Tourmalet. The most challenging run
around La Mongie is the black under the Prade Berde chair-lift. La
Mongie has a boardercross course and three other dedicated snowboard spots at different points around the ski area.

French Pyrenean resorts have made considerable efforts to improve ski school standards in recent years, and the number of fluent English-speaking instructors has risen. Ecoloski and the French Ski School (ESF) provide tuition in Barèges. La Mongie and La Mongie-Tourmalet also have their own ski schools. The ESF and Ecoloski in Barèges both have a ski kindergarten for children from four years of age. The two non-ski kindergartens take children from two to six years old. Hélios is an activity centre for three- to 12-year olds. La Mongie has a ski and non-ski kindergarten.

The few mountain eating-places are inexpensive in comparison with those in the Alps. Chez Louisette is popular and Le Bastan is 'cheerful and cheap'. Le Yeti in La Mongie is recommended, too. Those in search of luxury will be disappointed, as Barèges has nothing more superior than its ten simple one- and two-star hotels. Of these, the family-run Richelieu (☎ 562 92 68 11) is 'clean and friendly' and is located just below the funicular station, and Hotel Igloo (☎ 562 92 68 10) is close to La Laquette gondola. La Mongie has one three-star hotel Le Pourteilh (☎ 562 91 93 33), plus a handful of two-stars.

These are quiet resorts, with nightlife centring on a few bars and a handful of restaurants. However, Le Jonathan disco in Barèges is lively in high season, and Le Pitchounet in Barèges serves a good brasserade. La Rozell crèperie in Barèges is warmly praised, while Le Nem is Chinese. Many visitors come to Barèges for the spa. La Mongie has 20 restaurants, a dozen shops, a few bars and a cinema.

TOURIST INFORMATION
Tel (Barèges) 33 562 92 16 00/(La Mongie) 33 562 91 94 15
Fax (Barèges) 33 562 92 69 13/(La Mongie) 33 562 95 33 13
Email station.bareges@wanadoo.fr
Web site www.bareges.com

Cauterets
top 2,350m (7,710ft) bottom 1,000m (3,280ft)

This attractive thermal spa became a ski station in 1962 and today it has more than 22,000 visitor beds in a large selection of hotels. The nearest airport is Lourdes, which is 40km away. The skiing is in the exposed Cirque du Lys bowl, accessed by a two-stage cable-car, which also brings skiers back to the resort at the end of the day. The terrain is best suited to beginners and intermediates. The 35 pistes include two blacks, with the rest equally divided between red, blue and green. These are served by 12 lifts. Another small but developing ski area is nearby at **Pont d'Espagne**, which is renowned for its 37km of cross-country trails; it now has a gondola, a chair-lift and two drag-lifts. The two ski schools at Cauterets are the ESF and Snow Fun. Garderie Les Marmottes accepts children from two months and the Mini-Club takes three- to seven-year-olds.

The extensive choice of accommodation includes gîtes, chalets and hotels, some of which date from the Belle Epoque. Hotel Bordeaux

(☎ 562 92 52 50) is a comfortable three-star, and the three-star Hotel-Résidence Aladin (☎ 562 92 60 00) offers a spa, a swimming-pool, squash courts and sauna. Restaurants include La Flambée pizzeria, La Raclette and Aladin. Après-ski is centred on the spa, a handful of bars, a casino, a couple of discos and ice-skating.

TOURIST INFORMATION
Tel 33 562 92 50 27
Fax 33 562 92 59 12
Email espaces.cauterets@cauterets.com
Web site www.cauterets.com

Chamrousse
top 2,255m (7,398ft) bottom 1,700m (5,577ft)

Chamrousse offers some of the closest skiing to Grenoble – being 30 minutes from the city – and was the scene of Jean-Claude Killy's epic victories in the 1968 Grenoble Winter Olympics.

The resort comprises an unattractive, albeit reasonably convenient, collection of buildings on two levels – 1650 and 1750 – and the ski area offers 77km of piste served by 26 lifts. There is a boardercross slope and half-pipe. The ESF teaches skiing and snowboarding to adults, and children from three years old, while Les Marmots ski kindergarten gives lessons to children aged three to 12 years and also caters for non-skiers aged three months to 12 years Chamrousse's facilities include three hotels, 25 restaurants, shops and bars, an ice-rink and an indoor heated swimming-pool.

TOURIST INFORMATION
Tel 33 476 89 92 65
Fax 33 476 89 98 06
Email infos@chamrousse.com
Web site www.chamrousse.com

La Clusaz
top 2,600m (8,528ft) bottom 1,100m (3,608ft)

La Clusaz is a large, spread-out resort off the Autoroute Blanche on the way to Chamonix, less than two hours' drive from Geneva Airport. Reporters remarked on its value for money ('remarkably cheap') and applauded it as 'a very French resort, and ideal place to get away from fellow Brits. All the people are very friendly and easy-going; a charming village'. However, one drawback is its lack of altitude. The village itself lies at 1,100m, which is extremely low by Haute Savoie standards, and the ski area, with its 38 lifts, goes up to only 2,600m. The 40 lifts of nearby **Le Grand-Bornand** are included in the regional Aravis lift pass.

La Clusaz has five ski areas spread around the sides of a number of neighbouring valleys. Mountain access to Beauregard and L'Aiguille is by lifts from the resort centre. The other three areas (Balme, L'Etale and Croix-Fry/Merdassier) are reached from various points along the valleys via a satisfactory ski-bus network. Despite roads and rivers all five are linked by lift or piste.

The best novice slopes are at Crêt du Merle in L'Aiguille sector and on the plateau top of Beauregard. The skiing is best suited to intermediates, and the pistes are of limited appeal to advanced skiers. The resort has two ski schools: the ESF ('the instruction was excellent and very hard work') and Sno Académie. Both schools teach boarding, and there is a terrain park in the Etale sector. La Clusaz is rated as one of the best-equipped French resorts for children. Le Club des Mouflets non-ski kindergarten cares for children aged eight months to four-and-a-half years, while Le Club des Champions provides daycare with optional ski lessons for children from three-and-a-half to six years old.

The village is built around a large church, with a stylish shopping precinct beside it and a fast-flowing stream below. Non-skiing activities include parapente, skating, sleigh rides, snowmobiling, snowshoeing and swimming. Accommodation is divided between tour-operator chalets and a selection of seven three-star and thirteen two-star hotels. We have glowing reports of the three-star Hotel Beauregard (☎ 450 32 69 00) ('extremely well-fitted, modern pine interior, the food is excellent and it really deserves a four-star rating'). The other three-stars include Les Chalets de la Serraz (☎ 450 02 48 29), Le Vieux Chalet (☎ 450 02 41 53) and Hotel Alpen'roc (☎ 450 02 58 96). The two-stars that receive favourable reports are hotels Christiania (☎ 450 02 60 60) and Floralp (☎ 450 02 41 46). The skiing convenience here is low, and location of accommodation is crucial.

La Clusaz has a much wider choice of restaurants than you would expect in a resort of this size. Le Foly is an attractive and expensive log-cabin in the Confins Valley serving regional specialities. The gastronomic Symphonie in the Hotel Beauregard offers 'excellent cuisine with cheerful service in a warm atmosphere'. Le Coin du Feu is recommended for its 'delicious *crêpe sucré*'. La P'tite Table de Pervenche has 'great *galettes*', and St Joseph was said to be 'top class'.

Après-ski centres on a few bars. Le Pressoir is the 'in' place for snowboarders, while resort workers meet in the Lion d'Or. Les Caves du Paccaly and Le Grenier are both popular meeting places. L'Ecluse is said to be the best of the discos, with a glass dance-floor over the river, while Le Club 18 has live bands and attracts the locals and an older clientèle. Nightlife is quiet during the week, some would say too quiet, but can become extremely lively during weekends.

TOURIST INFORMATION
Tel 33 450 32 65 00
Fax 33 450 32 65 01
Email infos@laclusaz.com
Web site www.laclusaz.com

Font-Romeu
top 2,204m (7,229ft) bottom 1,800m (5,906ft)

The resort, 19km from Perpignan and 200km from Toulouse, is set on a sunny plateau known for its mild climate, making it unreliable for snow at the beginning and end of the season. The skiing is 4km from the village and is linked by a bus service. The 52km of piste and 28 lifts suit beginners to intermediates and families. Weekend queues are a problem as the resort is popular with both French and Spanish skiers. Fifty per cent of the total skiing terrain is covered by snow-cannon. The ESF and ESI are the two ski and snowboard schools.

There are two dozen hotels and pensions including four three-stars: Hotel Carlit (☎ 468 30 80 30), Le Grand Tetras (☎ 468 30 01 20), La Montagne (☎ 468 30 36 44) and Sun Valley (☎ 468 30 21 21). The resort also boasts three children's holiday centres where those as young as four years old can stay during their school holidays; at Le Poussinet Centre de Vacances children from six to 18 can combine academic work with a variety of winter sports. The resort's après-ski activities include a wide choice of shops and restaurants, a casino, cinemas, a choice of discos and bars, and an ice-hockey stadium. Font-Romeu is a training centre for dogs and dog-handlers for the sport of dog-sledding. Cross-country skiing is prominent here, with two specialist schools. The resort also has a terrain park.

TOURIST INFORMATION
Tel 33 468 30 68 30
Fax 33 468 30 29 70
Email office@font-romeu-station.com
Web site www.font-romeu-station.com

Isola 2000
top 2,610m (8,561ft) bottom 1,800m (5,904ft)

Isola is a purpose-built resort and the most southerly ski area in France. In reasonable weather conditions it is a 90-minute drive north of Nice along the dramatic road beside the Tinée Ravines. The resort, which offers 120km of piste served by 23 lifts and boasts a respectable vertical drop of 860m, was built by a British property company in the 1960s. Created with families in mind, it has a convenient complex of shops, bars, economically designed apartments and hotels, and a large, sunny nursery area. Isola is not accessible from the north, which in part accounts for why so few tour operators offer it in their brochures. However, British skiers make up a big slice of the winter business, and many of them own apartments in the resort.

Isola's original building, the ugly and soulless Front de Neige Centre, is right on the slopes. The more attractive wood-clad additions behind it improve the resort's aesthetic appeal. Hotel Le Chastillon (☎ 493 23 26 00) and Hotel Diva (☎ 493 23 17 71) are the only four-stars, and Hotel Pas du Loup (☎ 493 23 27 00) and Hotel de France (☎ 493 02 17 04) are also recommended. Restaurants include La Dolce Vita,

La Buissonnière, L'Edelweiss and La Raclette. Nightlife largely revolves around a dozen bars and the two discos, La Cuba Loca and La Tanière.

The ski area is limited, but varied enough for beginners, families with small children and intermediates. The ESF is the only ski school here. The non-ski Miniclub kindergarten takes children from two to five years old, and the ski kindergarten, Le Caribou, caters for little ones from four years of age. The resorts of **Auron** and **Valberg** are both within easy reach for a day's skiing.

TOURIST INFORMATION
Tel 33 493 23 15 15
Fax 33 493 23 14 25
Email isola@cote-dazur.com
Web site www.isola-2000.com

Pra-Loup
top 2,500m (8,202ft) bottom 1,600m (5,249ft)

This small resort in the Alpes de Haute Provence was named after the wolves that once frequented these pine forests. It has a surprisingly extensive range of beginner and intermediate trails, yet few advanced. The 167km of piste is shared with neighbouring **La Foux d'Allos**. The skiing takes place on two main mountains, accessible by cable-car from the top of the village at 1600. Intermediates will find open-bowl skiing and good tree-line runs with spectacular scenery. The off-piste is extensive (you will need a guide), but there are only five black (difficult) runs. Weekend queues are said to be 'fearsome'. The ESF and ESI ski schools are rated as 'excellent', and heli-skiing is also available through the ESI. Les P'tits Loups day nursery caters for children from six months to six years.

The resort is split into the two villages of 1500 and 1600, which are linked by a chair-lift and consist of a collection of hotels and apartments built in the 1960s, along with some older chalets. Reporters recommended either staying close to the lifts at Pra-Loup 1500 or at the top of 1600. Prices at the restaurants and bars are lower than in better-known French resorts. On the mountain, La Costebelle is said to be 'busy', while Dalle en Pente is 'much nicer, more laid back and slightly cheaper'. Hotel Club Les Bergers (☎ 492 84 14 54) is recommended ('the nicest of hotels'), while Hotel Le Prieuré (☎ 492 84 11 43) is 'very welcoming, warm and comfortable'. Le Loup Garou and Le Sham'rock are the hottest nightspots – other après-ski activities on offer here being indoor tennis, snowscooting, swimming and night-skiing.

TOURIST INFORMATION
Tel 33 492 84 10 04
Fax 33 492 84 02 93
Email info@praloup.com
Web site www.praloup.com

Puy-St-Vincent
top 2,750m (9,022ft) bottom 1,350m (4,429ft)

Puy-St-Vincent is an established resort that was extremely popular with British families in the 1970s. It is 20km from **Briançon**, three hours' drive from Grenoble or Turin and on the edge of the Ecrins National Park. Its microclimate usually ensures secure late-season snow cover along with 300 days of sunshine per year.

Puy-St-Vincent 1400 is an unspoilt mountain village with one three-star and three two-star hotels. It is connected by a double chair-lift and a drag-lift to the higher *station de ski* of Puy-St-Vincent 1600, which is dominated by a central apartment block that has seen better days. Newer *résidences* have been built on the edge of the piste. The ski area is small but challenging, with enough variety to suit all standards of skier. Queues are a rarity. The ski area boasts five chair-lifts, including two that give easy access to the main skiing, which goes up to 2,750m. The ESF and the ESI both offer group lessons and a range of courses. The ESI runs classes for British children during the peak holiday weeks. Les P'tits Loups kindergarten at 1600 takes children from 18 months.

Accommodation is mainly in apartments, with just three hotels of which the Saint Roche (☎ 492 23 32 79) is the only three-star. The St-Vincent and Cadran Solaire restaurants are both recommended. There is a karaoke bar, a disco and night-skiing. As one reporter put it: 'Puy is a resort which visitors either love or hate. To some it is too small, with not enough to occupy avid skiers by day or après-skiers by night. To others it has great charm, character and intimacy'.

TOURIST INFORMATION
Tel 33 492 23 35 80
Fax 33 492 23 45 23
Email courrier@puysaintvincent.net
Web site www.puysaintvincent.com

St-Lary Soulan
top 2,450m (8,038ft) bottom 830m (2,723ft)

St-Lary Soulan, 80km from Lourdes, is a typically Pyrenean village of stone-built houses and one main, rather narrow street. The skiing is suitable for beginners to intermediates and it begins a four-minute walk from the village centre at the cable-car to **St-Lary Pla d'Adet** (1,700m) a small but dull modern ski station with some accommodation. It is linked by road and by lift to an alternative base at **St-Lary La Cabane** (1,600m). The fourth base area of **St-Lary Espiaube** (1,600m) is also reached by road, or on skis from **Soum de Matte**. The ski area is served by 47 lifts but is mainly treeless and lacks variety. The terrain park is in the Vallon du Portet sector.

There are six nursery slopes, and two ski schools take children from four years old as well as adults. Three mountain guiding companies arrange popular ski-tours, and three crèches care for non-skiing children. Grand Hotel Mir (☎ 562 39 40 03) is recommended, as well as the Mercure Coralia (☎ 562 99 50 00), Hotel La Terrasse Fleurie (☎ 562 40 76 00) and Les Arches (☎ 562 49 10 10). At Espiaube, Hotel La Sapinière (☎ 562 98 44 04) provides reasonable accommodation. The resort boasts more than 30 restaurants and a range of shops.

TOURIST INFORMATION
Tel 33 562 39 50 81
Fax 33 562 39 50 06
Email st-lary@wanadoo.fr
Web site www.saintlary.com

Valloire
top 2,600m (8,528ft) bottom 1,430m (4,690ft)

Valloire is an attractive, reasonably large village set in an isolated bowl above the Maurienne Valley. It is still very much a traditional French farming community, and the odd whiff of manure mingling with the aroma of freshly baked bread is all part of the atmosphere.

This friendly, medium-priced resort is uncrowded except in high season, when its proximity to the Italian border means that it can be busy and very noisy. The 150km of skiing is served by 36 lifts and is divided between three areas – La Sétaz, Le Crey du Quart and **Valmeinier** – on adjacent mountains reached by lifts that start a few minutes' walk away from the village centre and rise to 2,600m. The terrain is varied, and some of the runs are as long as 1,000 vertical metres. The skiing is not difficult.

Mountain access to La Sétaz is by a six-person gondola from the village up to Thimel, followed by a chair- and drag-lift to the summit. Served by artificial snow-cannon and groomed to a high standard, the area provides a good choice of runs from wide reds to gently meandering blue (easy) runs. Access to Le Crey du Quart is either by the Montissot and Colerieux chair-lifts, or directly from Valloire by an eight-person gondola. The skiing at Le Crey du Quart is mainly of the red motorway variety, with gentler slopes going down towards Valloire. Runs off the back of Le Crey du Quart lead down into the Valmeinier ski area, which spans both sides of the adjacent valley.

The ski schools are the ESF and ESI, both of which offer alpine skiing, snowboarding, cross-country and children's tuition. The resort has its own Bureau des Guides for off-piste skiing. Accommodation includes Le Sétaz (☎ 479 59 01 03), Grand Hotel de Valloire et du Galibier (☎ 479 59 00 95), and a range of apartments and chalets. A choice of 20 restaurants is available. Valloire boasts a dozen bars, a skating rink and a fitness centre.

TOURIST INFORMATION
Tel 33 479 59 03 96
Fax 33 479 59 09 66
Email info@valloire.net
Web site www.valloire.net

Italy

Italy seems destined to be side-lined as a major European destination for British skiers. After a period of popularity in the 1990s that was fuelled more by favourable exchange rates than by its reputation as a ski country, Italy has again lost its edge. Those holiday-makers who switched from the more expensive France, Switzerland and Austria have either returned to their regular skiing grounds or migrated across the Atlantic in search of fresh pastures. For a while back there, it looked as if the country that gave us Alberto Tomba – possibly the finest technical skier of all time – would join its Alpine neighbours as an equal rival for top piste billing.

Those travel companies who have moved their operations elsewhere mumble about unpredictable weather, shortage of beds and the difficulties of dealing with Italian businesses. Certainly Italy suffered badly in both the 1998–9 and 1999–2000 seasons from insufficient snowfalls compared to the rest of Europe. But in the 2000–1 season snow cover was better, and the Milky Way revelled in exceptional conditions from December until the lifts closed in April. Exchange rates continue to be extremely favourable, the economy has enjoyed a period of stability, and the vociferous welcome is far warmer than you will find anywhere else in Europe. But for the present the number of British visitors remains depressingly low.

At first glance, it is hard to explain why Italy should lag so far behind its neighbours. However, skiers and snowboarders are a discerning lot. They are aware that despite its recent spell of popularity, the fragile fabric of Italian skiing remains largely unchanged. Lift systems have been improved, but enormous investment is needed to bring the main ski areas into line with the Trois Vallées, the SkiWelt and their other European rivals. Heavy spending on artificial snowmaking can never compensate for the unreliability of the natural product.

This said, Italy has considerable compensations. First-time visitors will be delighted by the Italian zest for enjoyment, both on and off the slopes, and as a nation it has raised the pastime of eating on the mountain to an art form. The Italian penchant for partying can be experienced in its nightlife, which starts early in the afternoon and carries on well into the small hours. For families with young children, however, there are resorts that are more child-friendly in other European countries. Although the Italians are well-known for their love of children, the major Italian resorts are mysteriously lacking in childcare facilities. This is possibly due to the fact that Italian families often travel as a whole – complete with granny to look after the *bambini*.

Side-lined it may be, but with the advent of low-cost airlines and Internet hotel bookings, you can always make your own way to Italy. Few ski destinations provide greater overall enjoyment.

Bormio

ALTITUDE 1,225m (4,018ft)

Beginners ✱✱✱ Intermediates ✱✱✱ Advanced ✱

Bormio is one of Italy's most important ski towns, although the amount of skiing is limited in comparison with the larger and better-known circuits. A high top-lift altitude and a neighbouring glacier allow the season to last well into April. The resort shares a lift pass, but not a lift link, with the neighbouring village of **Santa Caterina** and with the small **San Colombano** ski area above the village of **Oga** on the opposite side of the valley. The lift pass is also valid for **Livigno**, which is an hour's drive over a pass to the west. **St Moritz**, across the Swiss border, is another option for a day's excursion.

✔ Lack of crowds on the slopes
✔ Late-season skiing
✔ Attractive medieval town centre
✔ High standard of restaurants
✔ Range of activities for non-skiers
✘ Long airport transfer
✘ Unattractive suburbs
✘ Lack of childcare facilities

Bormio's location at a crossroads in the Valtellina region in the mountains of Lombardy made it a natural staging post for trans-Alpine traffic. Attracted by hot springs and spectacular views over what is now the Stelvio National Park, the Romans built a town and thermal bath complex at the foot of the pass. The town prospered during the Middle Ages, and its ancient cobbled streets date from that time. In subsequent centuries it was sidelined by history, but the post-World War II tourist boom has restored some of its former vitality. Today its rather ugly suburbs, with their modern hotels and high-rise apartment blocks, spread over the broad valley floor but do not tarnish the charm of the pedestrianised centre. As one reporter summed it up: 'Bormio is much nicer than the brochures suggest. It is upmarket, yet cheaper than the UK. It is authentically Italian and ideal for families and couples but not suitable for those looking for a rowdy nightlife'.

Bormio's nearest airports are Bergamo and Milan, both officially three-and-a-half hours away, although reporters have experienced transfer times of up to six-and-a-half hours from Bergamo. The drive from Milan includes a breathtakingly beautiful section along the shore of Lake Como.

On the snow
top 3,012m (9,879ft) bottom 1,225m (4,018ft)

Bormio's first lifts opened in the 1960s, but the resort came of age in 1985 when it hosted the Alpine Skiing World Championships. In

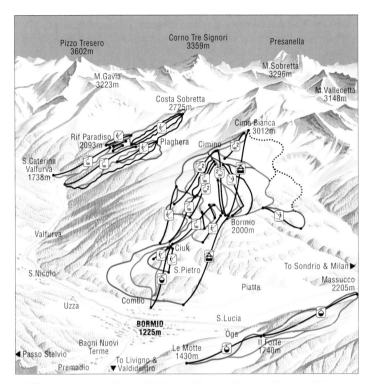

2005 it will be the venue once again. It currently boasts 17 lifts and 50km of pistes, of which 68 per cent are graded intermediate. The slopes rise steeply on a single broad mountain served by two base-stations, both within a few minutes' walk of the town centre. The main one is the starting point for the two-stage cable-car to the Cima Bianca via Bormio 2000, a substantial mid-station with a large family hotel and a small shopping mall. This can also be reached by car in most conditions. The alternative is the six-seater gondola to **Ciuk**, a lower mid-station, which also has accommodation and restaurants. The top third of the mountain is above the tree-line, with a network of chair-lifts providing a variety of choices. Lower down, the skiing takes place in glades cut from the forest, ensuring good visibility when the weather closes in. It is possible to make day-trips to the nearby resorts of Livigno, Santa Caterina and San Colombano. Between May and November, there is 20km of summer skiing on the Stelvio Glacier.

Beginners
The only nursery slopes are at Bormio 2000; this is a mixed blessing as it means that everyone has to buy a lift pass from day one. On the positive side, the result is that everyone learns halfway up the mountain,

which gives a better feeling of what skiing is all about. After a few days of mastering the basic manoeuvres, beginners will find plenty of easy pistes in the wooded area down to Ciuk. By the end of the week, many will be skiing the blue (easy) runs from the top of the cable-car.

Intermediates

For the two-week-plus brigade, Bormio's slopes are blissful – there are no particularly steep sections and lots of high-speed cruising. The 14-km descent from the Cima Bianca to the town is just one of many exhilarating options. The bottom section of the Bosco Basso piste below Ciuk has been widened to provide an easy alternative route back to the gondola station.

Advanced

Strong piste-skiers may be frustrated by the lack of challenge on Bormio's slopes, as the two short runs that are graded black (difficult) might well be listed as red (intermediate) in a steeper resort. The Stelvio FIS course, which runs from just above La Rocca past Ciuk to the bottom of the gondola, is a regular choice for the World Cup circuit.

Off-piste

The powder opportunities off the Cima Bianca more than compensate for the shortage of black bump runs. To the west of the main piste a steep, open bowl leads down to some shallow-gradient, tree-level skiing. Those who plan to go below the right-hand turn-off to Bormio 2000 should check first that the Ornella drag-lift is running. To the east of the pistes, a wider choice of terrain gives access to a more heavily wooded area. A long trail leads back to the Praimont chair. Those who are prepared to hire a guide (Bormio has a choice of two mountain guiding companies) and climb on skins will find magnificent terrain in both winter and summer on the **Stelvio Glacier**.

Snowboarding

Although freeriders can have some fun in the powder and in the trees when conditions are good, snowboarders are otherwise completely ignored here. There is no pipe or terrain park; the nearest is on the Stelvio Pass, 19km away.

Tuition and guiding

Of the six ski schools in Bormio, the Alta Valtellina, based near the nursery slopes at Bormio 2000, is highly recommended for its young, friendly, English-speaking instructors. The more traditional options include the Nazionale and Bormio 2000. The Anzi School is for hotel guests only. The Sertorelli and the Capitani organisations specialise in summer ski-touring, retaining only a skeleton winter staff for their valued clients. Ortler Cevedale Alpine Guides and Associazione Guide Alpine Alta Valtellina are the off-piste mountain guiding companies.

Mountain restaurants

The favoured stopping-off point for lunch or refreshments is La Rocca, an old-fashioned hut on the main trail from the top of the mountain to Bormio 2000. It has two rooms, each with a wood-burning stove and friendly service. It, too, hosts dinner followed by a torchlit descent whenever there is sufficient demand. The Rhondendri near the top of La Rocca chair is also recommended ('quiet, small and pleasant, with a splendid viewing position at the top of a black mogul run'). The Girasole Hotel and the self-service cafeteria at Bormio 2000 are also convenient, though less traditional.

Accommodation

The modernised four-star Hotel Posta (☎ 0342 904753), on a pedestrianised street in the old town, offers luxurious accommodation, a swimming-pool and fitness centre. The other four-star recommendations include the Rezia (☎ 0342 904721) and the Palace (☎ 0342 903131). Those who prefer to be near the lifts should consider one of the modern three-star options: the Derby (☎ 0342 904433), the Nevada (☎ 0342 910888), the Funivia (☎ 0342 903242) or the Gufo (☎ 0342 904727). In the two-star category, the family-run Dante (☎ 0342 901329) and the Bormio (☎ 0342 905092) offer exceptional value in central locations. Hotel Aurora (☎ 0342 910052) is praised by reporters: 'the hotel was very clean and warm, the staff friendly and helpful, and the food excellent'.

As the town of Bormio is only ski-in ski-out when snow conditions are good in January and February, there is a strong case to be made for staying in the three-star Girasole (☎ 0342 904652) at Bormio 2000. This is especially true for holidays over the Easter period when the main resort begins to wind down. The hotel is run by the hospitable Alfredo Cantoni and his English wife, Elizabeth, with a strong emphasis on family entertainment.

Eating in and out

Although *pizzocheri*, a rather gritty indigenous pasta, is something of an acquired taste, the Valtellina also has an interesting range of specialities including charcuterie, mushrooms and locally produced wines. The best places to try them are the Rasiga ('a beautifully converted saw mill'), the Vecchia Combo, the Taulà and Osteria dei Magri. All four restaurants will prepare multi-course gourmet feasts at modest all-inclusive rates, provided they are booked in advance. Bormio also has five pizzerias and a spaghetteria. Self-catering is not the norm in a resort with a wide choice of cheap eating-places, but the specialist grocery shops on the Via Roma stock all the necessary ingredients for home cooking on a magnificent scale.

Après-ski

Bormio is the most Italian of resorts, with a strong sense of style in its immaculate shops and restaurants. In the early evening, chattering crowds stroll down the narrow cobbled streets and fill the bars and cafés on the historic Via Roma, the centre of activity in the old town. The Bagni Vecchi, a few miles out of town in a cave in the hillside, comprises a natural sauna and curative hot baths. It includes an atmospheric turn-of-the-century spa complex offering a range of treatments for weary skiers. In town, the naturally heated water has been put to good use in the large public swimming-pool.

The Gorky on the Via Roma and the Vagabond in the church square are the pubs of choice, both after skiing and after dinner. Late nightlife focuses on the King's Club disco, which is open until 3am, with the piano bar at the Aurora Hotel a less frenetic option.

Childcare
The ski schools will take children from four years of age, provided there are other children with whom to make up a class. Older children have to fit in with the adult classes. There is no formal crèche service, but the Girasole Hotel can arrange local babysitters to care for children during the day and in the evening.

Linked or nearby resorts

Santa Caterina
top 2,725m (8,940ft) bottom 1,738m (5,702ft)
Santa Caterina (or 'San Cat', as it is known) is a quiet, attractive village with eight lifts and 40km of its own skiing. It is situated 30 minutes by bus from Bormio, up a mountain road that is a dead-end in winter when the Gavia Pass is closed. It shares a lift pass with its larger neighbour, Bormio, and it usually has better snow. Local skiing is on the northeast-facing slopes of the Sobretta. The higher slopes are fairly steep and graded black; some intermediate trails wind down between the trees.

The Santa Caterina Ski School receives mixed but generally favourable reviews. The Bimbi Sulla Neve kindergarten cares for children from 10am to 1pm. Of the two cross-country trails, the 10-km Pista Valtellina is challenging, while the 8-km Pista La Fonte is classified as easy. There is also skating on a natural rink.

The San Matteo Hotel (☎ 0342 925121) is recommended for comfort and food. Nightlife is limited, with one fairly large disco and a number of cosy bars that remain open until after midnight.

TOURIST INFORMATION

Bormio
Tel 39 0342 903300
Fax 39 0342 904696
Email apt.bormio@provincia.so.it
Web site www.valtellinaonline.com

Santa Caterina
Tel 39 0342 935598
Fax 39 0342 925549
Email apt.santa.caterina@provincia.so.it
Web site www.santacaterina.it

Cervinia

ALTITUDE 2,050m (6,726ft)

Beginners ✳✳✳ Intermediates ✳✳✳ Snowboarders ✳

Cervinia is Italy's most snow-sure resort, set at 2,050m in the Aosta Valley within easy reach of Turin. It is dominated by Il Cervino, which is considerably better known under its Swiss name of the Matterhorn. The substantial ski area is linked with **Zermatt**, and in recent seasons the adjacent resorts have operated a joint lift pass covering all of Cervinia and the Klein Matterhorn sector of Zermatt, as well as their own separate lift passes. Cervinia has a reputation as a resort best suited to beginners and intermediates, so the real advantage of this arrangement is that accomplished snow-users can enjoy some of the challenges offered on the Zermatt side of the mountain. However, the frequent closure of the link because of weather conditions means that visits are best arranged on a daily basis.

✔ Excellent snow record
✔ Value for money
✔ Alpine scenery
✔ Sunny slopes
✔ Extensive skiing season
✔ Long runs
✘ Heavy traffic
✘ Inconvenient lift access
✘ Lift queues
✘ Unattractive village

Cervinia's skiing is linked to the nearby village of **Valtournenche** (1,524m), and the 12-person gondola greatly enhances this end of the ski area.

Mussolini, who was instrumental in the resort's construction in the 1930s, decreed the name should change from Breuil to the more Italian-sounding Cervinia. A nucleus of original buildings reflects the austere imperial style of the time. Post-war concrete edifices, thrown up without regard for the extraordinarily beautiful mountain environment, resemble 1960s' council flats. More recent additions have façades of wood and natural stone but, despite some tarting up, the buildings have little mountain charm. Nevertheless, Cervinia's large number of annual visitors has earned it the unassailable title of the most popular resort in Italy with the British; from December to April, about 1,000 British snow-users a week holiday here and not all of them can be wrong. The ambience remains overwhelmingly Italian, making weekends and school holiday periods hectic and prone to queues, though these are cheerful and unaggressive.

Parking at weekends is chaotic, since the influx from Milan and Turin insists on parking in the street instead of in the five free and one fee-paying parking areas. There is no free ski bus, but a municipal bus makes circuits every 20 minutes as far as **Cieloalto** until 8pm.

Cervinia is more expensive than the Italian resorts that are farther from Switzerland and is not as chic as **Cortina d'Ampezzo** or even **Courmayeur**. However, it has a vibrant atmosphere.

On the snow
top 3,883m (12,740ft) bottom 2,050m (6,726ft)

For years Italy's highest resort has been unfairly dismissed by competent snow-users as a playground for beginners and lower intermediates – no match for its swanky Swiss neighbour. Certainly it is true that, despite warnings of *solo per esperti* (only for experts), most of the handful of black (difficult) runs would be graded red (intermediate) on the Swiss side of the mountain.

Snow-users now have a choice of three lift passes. The first covers just Cervinia and Valtournenche, the second includes the Swiss Klein Matterhorn lifts, and the third includes all the Zermatt sectors. In practice, it is extremely difficult for anyone to explore the whole of Zermatt at leisure and return to the top of Klein Matterhorn for the long run home in one day.

The majority of snow-users will be perfectly content with the wide, open motorway cruising that Cervinia has to offer. The length and quantity of Cervinia's flattering red and blue (easy) runs provide hours of effortless cruising, but reporters criticised the lack of variety.

Mountain access is most direct from the queue-prone gondola and cable-car, which are an irritating hike uphill from the village. Access is also possible from drag-lifts in the nursery area to the left of the village, or from the satellite areas of Cieloalto and Valtournenche. Plan Maison is the mid-mountain station from which the main lifts fan out, with cable-cars rising to Plateau Rosa and the Swiss border.

When the resort opened in 1936 the lift system was considered state-of-the-art but it has since been updated only in parts, and considerable investment is now needed. Today some 76,000 snow-users per hour can be transported uphill, although not without annoying queues at weekends and during peak periods for some of the most essential links.

Beginners

If you learn to ski in this resort you will wonder what all the fuss is about. Beginners tend to spend no more than two days on the conveniently accessed nursery slopes at the village edge. Cervinia's excellent snow record means that novices have good conditions on the nursery slopes, before moving up to the network of green (beginner) and blue pistes at Plan Maison. There are few resorts where beginners can graduate so quickly and are able to ski runs as high as the top-to-bottom, wide and well-groomed blue piste from Plateau Rosa down to the village, which is a drop of nearly 1,500 vertical metres.

Intermediates

The 8-km Ventina (no.7 on the resort's piste map) from Plateau Rosa down to the resort is a classic alpine run. The series of runs from the

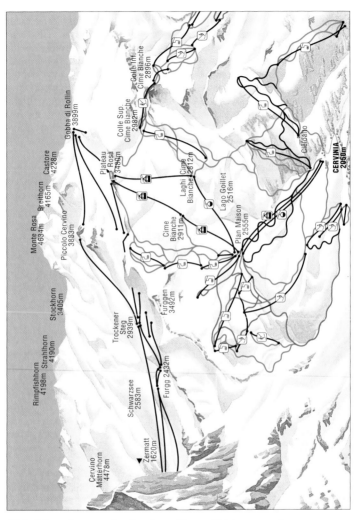

Klein Matterhorn to the farming village of Valtournenche measures a total 22km and is long enough to transform even the toughest skier's knees to noodles. Many red runs in Cervinia would be graded blue in Switzerland. In fact, snow-users used to the intimidating steep slopes in **Chamonix** or **Val d'Isère** will find the gradual pitch of Cervinia's pistes both ego-boosting and useful for advancing technical skills.

Advanced

'Not even a hint of challenge,' commented one reporter, 'even the blacks in Cieloalto are groomed flat'. The one true pisted challenge used to be the run down from Furggen, on the shoulder of the Matterhorn, from where you could see both resorts simultaneously. This was reached by an ancient cable-car and began from a cliff face after a walk down an internal staircase of nearly 300 steps. However, the piste became inaccessible when the cable-car was closed some years ago after failing a safety test. It now looks as if the closure is permanent. The marked black runs on Cieloalto and down from Plan Maison will not increase anyone's insurance premium. Zermatt's skiing is considerably more challenging.

Off-piste

On powder days, especially when the wind closes upper lifts, the skiing among the trees on the shoulder above Cieloalto is a good off-piste option. More ambitious routes require guides and mountaineering gear. Heli-skiing and heli-boarding are available on the Italian side of the mountain and, in addition to ski-touring, provides access to a wealth of glacier runs.

Snowboarding

The Carosello area has now become a terrain park, with a half-pipe, boardercross course and music played over loudspeakers to complete the atmosphere.

Tuition and guiding

We continue to receive mixed reports on both the main Cervino School and the smaller Cieloalto. One reporter commented: 'the Cervino seems prone to the follow-my-leader school of instruction'. Another said that his private lesson lesson with Cervino was 'money well spent'. One family 'thoroughly enjoyed our week (with Cieloalto), although I am not sure how much our technique improved'. We have no reports of the Breuil ski school. Valtournenche has its own ski school. Mountain guides from the local bureau in Cervinia charge considerably less than their Swiss counterparts but have equal expertise on the border peaks.

Mountain restaurants

The piste map shows where to stop for lunch. Cervinia's mountain meals are not cheap by Italian standards but are still much better value than on the other side of the Matterhorn. Bar Ventina on the eponymous run down from Plateau Rosa, Bar Bontadini on the slope of the same name and Chalet Etoile near the Rocce Nere chair-lift are among the best for polenta and fondue. Bar Le Pousset, just below Laghi Cime Bianche, is also recommended. Baita Cretaz da Mario on the nursery slopes receives outstanding reviews for its cuisine, relaxed and attentive service and 'lovely linen tablecloths'. The Igloo – run by Pauline, an English exile – at the top of the Bardoney chair is praised for its tasty food and large portions. La Motta da Felice at the top of the Motta drag-lift is not to be missed, either.

Skiing facts: Cervinia

TOURIST INFORMATION
Via Carrel 29, I–11021 Breuil-Cervinia, AO
Tel 39 01661 949136
Fax 39 01661 949731
Email breuil-cervinia@netvallee.it
Web site www.montecervino.it

THE RESORT
By road Calais 1,000km
By rail Châtillon 27km,
regular buses to resort
Airport transfer Turin or Geneva 2hrs
Visitor beds 2,800
Transport no free bus service

THE SKIING
Linked or nearby resorts Zermatt (I),
Valtournenche (I)
Number of lifts 23 (69 including
Valtournenche and Zermatt)
Total of trails/pistes 200km in Cervinia
(30% easy, 60% intermediate,
10% difficult), 350km with Zermatt
Beginners 2 lifts, points tickets available
Summer skiing on Plateau Rosa, 8 lifts

LIFT PASSES
Area pass (covers Cervinia and Swiss
Klein Matterhorn lifts)
L280–338,000 for 6 days
Pensioners 65yrs and over,
20% reduction
Credit cards yes

TUITION
Skiing Breuil (☎ 01661 940960),
Cervino (☎ 01661 949034),
Cieloalto (☎ 01661 948451)
Snowboarding as ski schools
Other courses cross-country, extreme
skiing/boarding, heli-skiing/boarding,
skiing for the disabled, snowblading,
telemark
Guiding Guide del Cervino
(☎ 01661 948169),
Heliski Cervinia (☎ 01661 949267)

CHILDREN
Lift pass 8–11yrs L210,000, free for
under 8yrs with parent
Ski & board school as adults
Kindergarten (non-ski) Kid Zone
(☎ 00339 1599155)

OTHER SPORTS
Climbing wall, free-flying, horse-riding,
ice-climbing, parapente, skating,
swimming

FOOD AND DRINK
Coffee L1,600, glass of wine L2,500,
small beer L3,500–4,000,
soft drink L3,500,
dish of the day L25,000

Accommodation
Cervinia has virtually no chalet or self-catering accommodation. Many of its 40 hotels date from the 1930s and are not always convenient for the lifts. The Hermitage (☎ 01661 948998) is a four-star hotel with the highest standards of service, cuisine and price. Another four-star, the Punta Maquignaz (☎ 01661 949145), is an attractive wood-clad hotel close to the drag-lifts. You can ski back to the Petit Palais (☎ 01661 949298), which is close to the cable-car and a five-minute walk from

the village centre. The Cristallo (☎ 01661 943411) is the oldest hotel, an ugly arc of white concrete, though agreeably decorated inside and with a swimming-pool. The Jumeaux (☎ 01661 949044) is 'pleasant, quiet and well run', while Da Compagnoni (☎ 01661 949068) on the main street is 'simple, convenient and welcoming'. Reporters staying at Hotel President (☎ 01661 949476) found it to be 'rather formal but very good buffet breakfast and dinners', and Hotel Breuil (☎ 01661 949537) is 'clean, spacious and very acceptable'.

Eating in and out

The resort has a reasonable range of restaurants, which are priced rather highly compared with tourist expectations of Italy, but are mostly good value. The Hermitage has 'truly outstanding cuisine', and Le Bistrot de l'Abbé is a close contender. Le Nicchia is similarly rich for pocket and paunch, while La Tana is recommended for wild boar, venison and everything with porcini mushrooms. The Copa Pan is a long-standing favourite: 'beautiful beamed room with a small bar centred around an open fire was the setting for probably the best meal I have had in my whole life'. La Maison de Saussure is the place to try the typical Valdostana specialities, and it is hard to beat the pizzas at Al Solito Posto and the Matterhorn Pizzeria. Chalet Etoile received praise, too.

Après-ski

Lino's Bar beside the ice-rink is busy when the lifts close and just as popular later in the evening. Skating is a passionate pastime here, but reporters complained that the nightlife lacks lustre. 'Like the skiing,' said one reporter, 'it is all intermediate' – although another claimed it is 'friendly and lively'. Ymeletrob cocktail bar is the liveliest, thanks to its animated patron, Renzo. The Copa Pan Irish bar is popular and serves Murphy's beer, while The Garage is the hippest disco ('loud and popular, it is still going strong well into the small hours'). The Dragon bar remains as popular as ever.

Childcare

Italians appear to bring their grandmothers or nannies with them, as Cervinia still does not have a daycare centre for those too young for regular ski lessons. Kid Zone is now the only non-ski kindergarten. The tourist information office has a list of officially sanctioned babysitters but admits that few speak English.

Cortina d'Ampezzo

ALTITUDE 1,224m (4,015ft)

Beginners ✱✱✱ Intermediates ✱✱✱ Advanced ✱✱✱ Snowboarding ✱✱

If we had to single out one ski resort in the world for the sheer beauty of its setting, combined with an attractive town and a truly all-round winter-sports resort, it would be Cortina d'Ampezzo in the craggy Dolomite mountains. Cortina sits in isolated splendour in the Ampezzo Valley, less than two hours' journey by road from Venice. Unlike its neighbours in the German-speaking Sud Tirol, Cortina is Italian to its voluptuous core and largely devoid of German and Austrian tourists. Some 70 per cent of its winter visitors are Italian.

✔ Extensive nursery slopes
✔ Variety of restaurants
✔ Long runs
✔ Activities for non-skiers
✔ Beautiful scenery
✔ Extensive cross-country
✔ Tree-level skiing
✔ Lively nightlife
✔ Resort ambience
✘ Spread-out ski areas
✘ Heavy traffic outside pedestrian area
✘ Oversubscribed ski bus system

The large, attractive town is centred on the main shopping street of Corso Italia and the Piazza Venezia with its green-and-white bell tower ('a lovely, lovely town, with loads of ambience'). The large, frescoed buildings have an air of faded grandeur, and the views of the pink rock-faces of Monte Cristallo are sensational. More recent architectural additions display a sympathetic Italian alpine style in keeping with the town's dramatic surroundings.

The centre is mercifully traffic-free, with cars confined to a busy one-way perimeter road. Parking is a problem in the centre, and reporters warned: 'if your hotel provides a private parking space at extra cost, pay up and don't complain'. Drivers should aim to avoid the huge Friday night/Saturday morning exodus, with queues that tail back all the way to the motorway exit.

However, Cortina's upmarket reputation can deter those skiers who see Italy as the destination for cheap and cheerful holidays, although by international standards it is not an exclusive or overtly expensive resort. There are plenty of charming, family-run hotels with reasonable prices as well as simple, welcoming bars. Cortina has some of the best nursery slopes anywhere, as well as long, challenging runs for intermediate to accomplished skiers and snowboarders.

On the snow
top 3,243m (10,640ft) bottom 1,224m (4,015ft)

The skiing is divided between the main Tofana-Socrepes area to the west of town, which is reached via the Freccia nel Cielo (arrow in the sky) cable-car, and Staunies-Faloria on the other side of town, which consists of two sectors separated by a minor road. A scattering of smaller ski areas along the Passo Falzarego road still belong to individual farmers. One of these areas, Cinque Torri, reached by an isolated two-stage chair-lift, is small and uncrowded with reliable snow (it is north-facing), long runs and breathtaking scenery.

Passo Falzarego, further down the road and a 20-minute bus ride from the town centre, links in one direction only into the **Sella Ronda** circuit and shares the Dolomiti Superski lift pass. You need to start early in the day in order to achieve any distance on skis. At Passo Falzarego the dramatic cable-car soars 640 vertical metres up a cliff-face to Lagazuoi, followed by a beautiful 11-km red (intermediate) run past a shimmering turquoise ice-fall and several welcoming huts before reaching **Armentarola** and **San Cassiano** beyond. However, the whole day is a rush and can be stressful. To return to Cortina you take either a bus from Armentarola to Falzarego or one of the waiting taxis at Armentarola to Lagazuoi.

WHAT'S NEW
Terrain parks at Faloria and Tofana
Increased snowmaking
Hotel Cristallo reopens after ten years

The buses linking the town with the various fragmented ski areas are both infrequent and hopelessly oversubscribed at peak hours. To enjoy the skiing to its full, you need your own car and a driver mentally equipped to cope with the stress of securing rare and much sought-after parking spaces against fearless Roman opposition in supercharged Alfa Romeos.

Both Tofana and Faloria can be reached on foot from most of the accommodation if you are prepared for a hearty hike in ski boots. Morning queues for the Tofana cable-car are not a problem owing to the late rising-time of the average Cortina visitor – the morning rush-hour never starts before 10.30am. The top section of Tofana is designated for sunbathers and sightseers only.

Beginners

A long serpentine blue (easy) piste takes you down from Tofana's mid-station to link with Socrepes, one of the best nursery slopes in Europe. Socrepes looks like a kind of sloping Kensington Gardens interspersed with easily negotiable lifts, including a chair-lift. The more isolated Pierosà-Miétres is an equally gentle sector.

Intermediates

The majority of Cortina's skiing is of intermediate standard, with long runs in both the main ski areas. Between the resort and Col Drusciè the

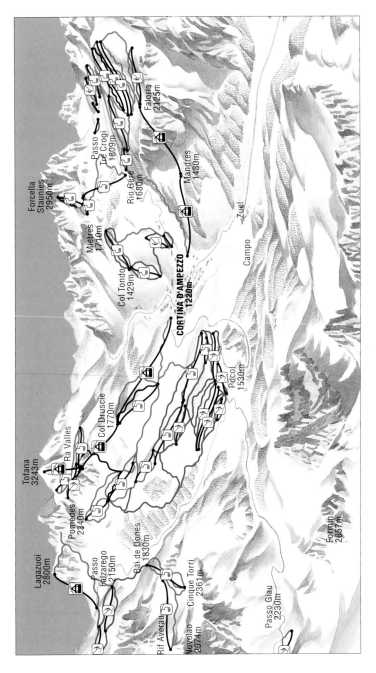

Tofana cable-car travels over gentle, tree-lined terrain and open fields with wide and easy trails, which cross rough roads without much warning to either skiers or drivers. Poor snow conditions often make these runs testing, which gives them their red and black (difficult) gradings. However, snowmaking is increasing and can now cover up to 95 per cent of the terrain. The second stage of the cable-car climbs the sheer, rocky mountainside to Ra Valles, in the middle of a pleasant bowl.

A day-trip into the Sella Ronda ski area should not be missed for anyone of intermediate standard and upwards. The good-value Dolomiti Superski lift pass covers both Cortina and the Sella Ronda.

Advanced

Higher up at Tofana, the Ra Valles sector at 2,700m offers the best snow in the resort. Near the bottom of the Tofana bowl, a gap in the rock gives access to an exhilarating black trail, which has a fairly steep south-facing stretch in the middle. The run ends up at the Pomedes chair-lifts, an area that itself offers some excellent runs including a couple of good blacks and the spectacular Canelone downhill racecourse.

The most dramatic skiing is found between Cristallo and Cresta Bianche, two soaring cathedrals of granite that dominate the landscape. From the foot of Monte Cristallo a four-stage chair climbs to Forcella Staunies, which starts with a steep black mogul field so sandwiched between the rock walls that it creates an illusion of narrowness. Halfway down, the bumps flatten out into a wide red race track.

Off-piste

After a fresh snowfall Forcella Staunies becomes an appealing off-piste area, as do the higher reaches of Tofana. Gruppo Guide Alpine Cortina, the resort's ski guiding organisation, arranges day ski-tours.

Snowboarding

The Tofana area is the most popular riders' area here, with plenty of powder opportunities and drop-offs. Cortina now has a small terrain park at Faloria and an additional terrain park is planned for Tofana during the 2001–2 season. The terrain is well-suited to riders.

Cross-country

This is a popular sport in the Cortina area, with the Centro Fondo Cortina offering private lessons. Six trails in the valley north and east of the resort give a total 58km of loipe.

Tuition and guiding

The main Scuola Sci Cortina has meeting places at Socrepes, Pocol, Rio Gere and Pierosà-Miétres. The standards appear to be mixed, depending mainly on the level of English spoken by the instructor. Scuola Sci Azzurra and Scuola Sci Cristallo-Cortina are smaller alternatives. Snowboarding lessons are available through the Scuola Sci Cortina and Scuola Sci Cristallo-Cortina.

Skiing facts: Cortina d'Ampezzo

TOURIST INFORMATION
Piazzetta San Francesco 8, I-32043
Cortina d'Ampezzo, BL
Tel 39 0436 3231
Fax 39 0436 3235
Email infocortina@apt-dolomiti-cortina.it
Web site www.apt-dolomiti-cortina.it

THE RESORT
By road Calais 1,200km
By rail Calalzo–Pieve di Cadore 35km
Airport transfer Venice 2hrs
Visitor beds 23,000
Transport free bus connects town centre with main lifts

THE SKIING
Linked or nearby resorts Armentarola (I), San Cassiano (I), San Vito di Cadore (n), Kronplatz (n)
Number of lifts 37 in Cortina, 48 in area
Total of trails/pistes 140km in area (44% easy, 49% intermediate, 7% difficult)
Beginners 5 runs, 2 lifts, points tickets available

LIFT PASSES
Area pass Dolomiti Superski (covers 460 lifts)
L275,000–313,000, Skipass Cortina
L251,000–286,000. Both for 6 days
Pensioners 15% reduction for over 60yrs
Credit cards yes

TUITION
Skiing Scuola Sci Cortina
(☎ 0436 2911), Azzurra (☎ 0436 2694), Cristallo-Cortina (☎ 0436 870 073)
Snowboarding Scuola Sci Cortina
Other courses cross-country, extreme skiing/boarding, race-training, skiing for the disabled, ski-touring, telemark
Guiding Guide Alpine (☎ 0436 868 505)

CHILDREN
Lift pass Dolomiti Superski
L193,000–219,000, free for 7yrs and under, Skipass Cortina
L176,000–200,000. Both for 6 days
Ski & board school as adults
Kindergarten Miniclub
(☎ 335 707 0957)

OTHER SPORTS
Bobsleigh, bob-rafting, curling, dog-sledding, hang-gliding, horse-riding, ice-hockey, ice-polo, indoor tennis, parapente, skating, ski-jöring, ski jumping, snowmobiling, snow-rafting, snowshoeing, swimming, taxi bob

FOOD AND DRINK
Coffee L1,800, glass of wine L1,800–2,500, small beer L3,000,
soft drink L3,000,
dish of the day L13,000–25,000

Mountain restaurants

Eating is a memorable experience in Cortina, and the choice of restaurants is extensive in the main ski areas, as well as being good value for money. Rifugio Duca d'Aosta is recommended with its wood-panelled walls and heart-warming local dishes. Simple mountain fare can be eaten at Rifugio Son Forca, which is reached by a modern chair-lift from Rio Gere on the road separating the Cristallo and Faloria ski areas.

Rifugio Pomedes is a summer climbing hut with hand-carved furniture and a varied menu. Reporters praised El Faral at the foot of Socrepes, and Col Taron in the same area, which serves delicious pasta.

The next stage down the mountain from the Duca d'Aosta is Baità Pie Tofana, a relaxed eating place with a sun terrace and attractive interior. Rifugio Averau at Cinque Torri, reached by a rope tow, has stunning views and some of the best mountain food in the resort. Rifugio Lagazuoi is situated a steep but worthwhile walk from the top of the Falzarego cable-car. Other recommended eating places are the Tondi restaurant, and Rifugio Scotoni on the long run down to **Armentarola** in the Sella Ronda.

Accommodation

Hotels range from the large international variety to simple, family-run establishments. A large number of private apartments and chalets are also available. The five-star Miramonti Majestic Grand Hotel (☎ 0436 4201) is 2km out of town and badly in need of a face-lift. It is to be hoped that the new owners will update the decoration in the near future. The five-star Hotel Cristallo reopens for the 2001–2 season after ten years of being closed. The four-stars include the attractive Hotel de la Poste (☎ 0436 4271), an old coaching inn run for generations by the Manaigo family, which is 'comfortable, with huge bathrooms. Its position on the high street is convenient if rather noisy'. Also well-located is the Hotel Ancora (☎ 0436 3261) on the Corso Italia, run by the indomitable Flavia Sartor, who uses the hotel to house her enormous collection of antiques and paintings. The Parc Victoria (☎ 0436 3246) is advantageously placed and comfortably furnished by the Angeli family, who own the hotel. The three-star, family-run Aquila (☎ 0436 2618) is highly recommended. The Italia is a popular two-star with wholesome food and a loyal following. Two-star Hotel Montana (☎ 0436 860498) is highly recommended ('centrally located, cosy, comfortable and friendly'). The Olimpia (☎ 0436 3256) is one of the cheapest and most central B&Bs and is said to be comfortable with large rooms.

Eating in and out

Dining is taken seriously in Cortina. More than 80 restaurants cater for all tastes, from simple pizzas to gourmet dining. Michelin-starred Tivoli on the edge of town has a warm ambience with delicious and often unusual cooking. Toulà is a converted barn with a rustic atmosphere and first-rate food. The Croda Caffé, Il Ponte and the Cinque Torri are all good for pizzas. Leone e Anna specialises in Sardinian cuisine, while El Zoco has grilled meats. For self-caterers or those trying to save money, the Cooperativa department store has 'an outstanding wine selection at very reasonable prices'.

Après-ski

'In one week you can only scratch the surface of Cortina's après-ski,' commented one reporter. At about 5pm the early evening *passeggiata* along the pedestrianised Corso Italia heralds the start of the off-slope festivities. The street becomes alive with promenading, fur-clad Italians: 'Like a fashion show with mobile phones'. Cortina's shopping is absorbing and varied and includes antique and jewellery shops, sportswear and designer boutiques, interesting delicatessens and the six-storey Cooperativa department store, an Aladdin's Cave that seems to sell everything, with reasonable prices to match. As one reporter commented: 'it's the only town we know where the Co-op has marble floors and sells designer clothes'.

Before dinner the action starts at the Enoteca wine bar, a serious drinking spot with a magnificent cellar, which closes at 9pm. Jerry's Wine Bar is another popular meeting place. Later on, the Hyppo, Area and VIP discos are extremely lively. The entrance fee for the nightclubs does not subsidise the drink prices, as in some comparably smart resorts; partying is consequently an expensive occupation here.

Childcare
Cortina has some of the most extensive nursery slopes we have encountered in Europe, and for winter 2000–1 a ski and non-ski kindergarten, Miniclub, for three- to 11-year-olds was reintroduced. The adult ski schools all offer children's tuition.

Linked or nearby resorts

Kronplatz
top 2,275m (7,464ft) bottom 900m (2,953ft)

This interesting ski area on the Italian–Austrian border is also known as **Plan de Corones** and is covered by the Dolomiti Superski lift pass. The region is little-known outside Italy and Germany, yet is an easy 60-km day-trip from Cortina. Eighty-five kilometres of piste are serviced by 33 lifts, of which an astonishing 12 are gondolas. The resort has a half-pipe served by a six-person chair-lift. The ski area can be reached from five different bases including **Bruneck** and **St Vigil**. Most of these bases have car parks and they have 22,000 beds between them. Kronplatz has six ski schools, one guiding company (Alpine School Pustertal), four kindergarten, five cross-country tracks and a half-pipe. Reporters commented on its superb lifts including a new eight-seater gondola, wide variety of intermediate runs and excellent snowmaking.

TOURIST INFORMATION
Tel 39 0474 555 447
Fax 39 0474 530 018
Email info@kronplatz.com
Web site www.kronplatz.com

Courmayeur

ALTITUDE 1,224m (4,016ft)

Beginners ✻ Intermediates ✻✻✻ Advanced ✻✻ Snowboarders ✻✻

Courmayeur is a delightful old village, which established its reputation first as a climbing base for the forbidding granite peaks of Mont Blanc, Western Europe's highest massif, and second as a popular nineteenth-century spa with its curative, pungent-smelling waters. Its role as an internationally acclaimed ski resort came about only with the opening of the Mont Blanc tunnel in 1965. At 11.31am on 14 August a delighted Italian miner thrust his fist through a hole in the rock-face 5km beneath Mont Blanc and swapped a bottle of Asti Spumante for a bottle of Veuve Clicquot with his French counterpart. The tunnel, then the longest underground road route in the world at 11.6km, ended Courmayeur's international isolation and linked it with **Chamonix**. Suddenly, Geneva Airport was only a 90-minute drive away. However, throughout the past two seasons Courmayeur has become once again a delightful backwater since the tunnel was closed after the tragic fire of March 1999.

- ✔ Beautiful scenery
- ✔ Village atmosphere
- ✔ Easy resort access
- ✔ Superb restaurants
- ✔ Lively nightlife
- ✔ Varied off-piste
- ✔ Long vertical drop
- ✔ Tree-level skiing
- ✔ Comprehensive snowmaking
- ✔ Extensive cross-country skiing
- ✘ Lack of skiing convenience
- ✘ Peak period queues

No longer could visitors from Chamonix or **Megève** pop over for lunch. Skiers from Britain had either to fly to Turin or to take the longer two-and-a-half hour transfer from Geneva through the Grand St Bernard tunnel. The Mont Blanc tunnel has now been rebuilt and is due to open in autumn 2001. However, considerable controversy still surrounds it and whether it will be open for skiers this season remains to be seen.

An advantage of the closure has been the almost complete absence of traffic on the main road that separates the village from the ski area, and the resulting purer air in the village. A joint lift pass with other resorts in the Aosta valley went a long way towards compensating for the loss of access to Chamonix and makes Courmayeur a good base from which to explore the substantial amount of skiing available in this corner of Italy.

The heart of the old village is a charming maze of cobbled alleys. It is largely traffic-free and lined with fashion boutiques, delicatessens and

antique shops. There are more bars, cafés and restaurants than could ever seem necessary, with a lively clientèle. The atmosphere is, as one reader put it, 'completely compelling – this is real Italy, garnished with real skiing'. These days the suburbs stretch endlessly outwards, and, for anyone interested in observing and therefore contributing to the prolonged après-ski *passeggiata* along Via Roma, it is important to find accommodation within easy walking distance of the pedestrian precinct. Courmayeur is the favourite resort of the Milanese, a clientèle for whom lunch is frequently a greater priority than skiing, and as a result it proudly boasts some of the finest mountain restaurants in the Alps. Reporters consistently remarked on the friendliness of the locals, in startling contrast to the dour Gallic attitude of those on the other side of the mountain.

On the snow
top 2,624m (8,609ft) bottom 1,700m (5,577ft)

The main mountain access is by a cable-car across the river gorge. This takes you up to Plan Chécrouit, a sunny plateau from where, annoyingly, you have to plod a further 75m to the foot of the lifts. At the end of the day you can take the cable-car back down, with skis and boots left in lockers at Plan Chécrouit. The alternative is to ski down to **Dolonne** and take a ski bus back across the river to Courmayeur.

A new gondola is planned from Dolonne to the existing gondola station at Plan Chécrouit, and this will ease the cable-car congestion at peak times and eliminate the mountain walk. However, the locals are divided on what they consider to be the best type of lift, and discussions continue. The mountain can also be reached by cable-car from the hamlet of **Val Veny**.

Extensive investment in snow-cannon has done much to improve skiing on the lower slopes down to Plan Chécrouit, Dolonne and to Val Veny. However, the skiing is not satisfactory for everyone; the pisted runs are mainly short and lack challenge. Advanced skiers will be more interested in the separate off-piste ski area shared with Chamonix, reached by the three-stage Mont Blanc cable-car at **La Palud**, near the village of **Entrèves** on the tunnel side of Courmayeur. You are strongly advised to hire the services of a mountain guide.

Opportunities for cross-country skiing are enormous here, with a major nordic centre at **Val Ferret**, a 15-minute drive away at the foot of the Grandes Jorasses. The centre offers four loipes totalling 30km, which wind through spectacular scenery. Cross-country tours can be arranged in the spring through the ski schools.

Beginners
The easiest slopes are somewhat hazardous, with those at Plan Chécrouit cramped by buildings and crowds of skiers descending from the main pistes. The main nursery slope is situated at the top of the Maison Vieille chair-lift. The baby slopes at the top of Val Veny and Dolonne are quieter.

Intermediates

The east-facing Chécrouit bowl has many short intermediate runs served by a variety of lifts including a six-seater gondola. The pistes are often crowded, especially at the bottom where they merge. There are some surprisingly steep and narrow passages, even on some of the blue (easy) runs. The wooded, north-facing Val Veny side of the mountain is linked in a couple of places with the Chécrouit Bowl; the Val Veny side has longer and more varied pistes with two red (intermediate) runs and a black (difficult) trail following the fall-line through the trees. Queuing for the Plan Chécrouit and Mont Blanc areas is much worse at week-ends, when the crowds arrive from Turin and Milan. Quad-chairs at La Gabba, Aretu and Zerotta have eased some of the other bottlenecks on the mountain, but the Youla cable-car can still be a problem.

Advanced

The pistes served by the Gabba quad-chair at the top of the ski area and to the west of Lago Chécrouit keep their snow well. The off-piste run underneath them is testing. The Youla cable-car above Lago Chécrouit provides access into a deep and sheltered bowl, which serves a single, uncomplicated red run with plenty of space for short off-piste excursions when snow conditions are good.

Off-piste

The top of the two-stage cable-car at Cresta d'Arp is the starting point at 2,755m for some serious powder runs. The long itinerary routes down into Val Veny or Dolonne provide considerable challenge. Avalanche safety has been improved and the service of a guide is no longer mandatory, but still advised. One takes you down 1,500m vertical to the satellite village of Dolonne or to the river bank near **Pré-St-Didier**; the other brings you through the beautiful Vallon de Youla to **La Balme**, a few kilometres from **La Thuile**.

From the nearby hamlet of La Palud, the Mont Blanc cable-car rises over 3,000m to Punta Helbronner, giving easy access to the Vallée Blanche by avoiding the dreaded ice steps. For the past two seasons there has been no easy way home from Chamonix, but it is hoped that this situation will change in time for winter 2001–2. Alternatively, you can cruise the 10km back down the Toula Glacier to La Palud; it is steep at the top and involves a clamber along a fixed rope and the hair-raising negotiation of an exposed and awkward staircase – again, you are strongly advised to take a guide. Heli-skiing on the **Ruitor Glacier** is still possible, although the future of the sport in Italy is now under serious debate on ecological grounds.

Snowboarding

Beginner snowboarders should head for Val Veny. Plan Chécrouit has plenty of intermediate runs around the main ski area for riders. Courmayeur has neither terrain park nor half-pipe, but the off-piste at Cresta d'Arp makes for some excellent freeriding.

Tuition and guiding

We continue to receive mixed reports of the Scuola di Sci Monte
Bianco. The standard of spoken English has improved greatly in recent
years, and the general verdict is that private instructors and guides are
excellent value but that group instructors are often jaded: 'our instructor gave the impression that he wasn't interested in our skiing at all. He
was never enthusiastic or encouraging'.

However, the strong presence of Interski (see *Which tour
operator?*), a British tour operator that has been allowed to establish its
own private British Association of Snowsport Instructors (BASI)
ski school for a mixed clientèle of adults and schoolchildren, has served
to raise standards.

Mountain restaurants

Food in Courmayeur is taken just as seriously as skiing. In our experience there is nowhere you can eat better for less money in a greater variety of mountain restaurants than in Courmayeur. The prices are actually
lower than in the resort itself. One reporter commented: 'it is hard to ski
when you could be eating. The atmosphere in the huts scattered around
the mountain is an integral part of our annual visit here'.

The Christiania at Plan Chécrouit is singled out for special praise:
'good meeting point for families, great pizzas' and 'the freshest seafood
I have ever tasted; the owner comes from Elba and obviously pines for
home'. The Chiecco, situated just above Plan Chécrouit, serves full
meals and 'heavenly desserts'. La Grolla at Peindeint on the Val Veny
side merits a visit ('expensive, but worth it and difficult to find – thank
goodness'). On the Mont Blanc side there are bars at each lift stage. The
Rifugio Pavillon at the top of the first stage of the cable-car is reportedly
excellent and has a sun terrace. Rifugio Torino, at the next stage, is also
said to be good. Rifugio Maison Vieille at Col Chécrouit has a large
wood-burning stove, serves pasta, polenta and sausages and has an
extensive wine list.

Accommodation

The resort has six four-star hotels including the Gallia Gran Baita
(☎ 0165 844040), which is described as 'worthy of its rating, but too
far out of town unless you have a car'. Few of the hotels, apartments
and chalets are well-situated for the main cable-car. However, the comfortable and expensive Hotel Pavillon (☎ 0165 846120) ('the service
was impressive') is well placed 150m from the cable-car and boasts a
swimming-pool and sauna. Three-star Hotel Courmayeur (☎ 0165
846732) is 'friendly, with a roaring log fire in the sitting area'. The family-run Bouton d'Or (☎ 0165 846729) is 'conveniently located, quiet,
comfortable and has its own parking'. Auberge de la Maison (☎ 0165
869811) in the quiet little hamlet of Entrèves ('an outstandingly stylish
three-star') has friendly owners and comfortable rooms.

Skiing facts: Courmayeur

TOURIST INFORMATION
Piazzale Monte Bianco 13, I-11013
Courmayeur (AO)
Tel 39 0165 842060
Fax 39 0165 842072
Email apt.montebianco@psw.it
Web site www.courmayeur.net

THE RESORT
By road Calais 968km
By rail Pré-St-Didier 5km, regular buses from station
Airport transfer Turin 3hrs (Geneva 2½hrs through Grand St Bernard tunnel)
Visitor beds 6,096
Transport ski bus not included in lift pass

THE SKIING
Linked or nearby resorts Cervinia (n), Chamonix (n), Champoluc (n), Gressoney-la-Trinité (n), Pila (n), La Thuile (n)
Number of lifts 25
Total of trails/pistes 100km (20% easy, 70% intermediate, 10% difficult)
Beginners 9 lifts, 3 of them are free

LIFT PASSES
Area pass (Aosta Valley Skipass) L300,000 for 6 days
Pensioners no reductions
Credit cards yes

TUITION
Skiing Scuola di Sci Monte Bianco (☎ 0165 842477)
Snowboarding as ski school
Other courses cross-country, telemark
Guiding Air Vallée (☎ 0165 869814), Società delle Guide Alpine di Courmayeur (☎ 0165 842064)

CHILDREN
Lift pass 9–12yrs, Aosta Valley Skipass L203,000–228,000 for 6 days, 8yrs and under included on parent's lift pass
Ski & board school as adults, Interski (☎ 01623 456333 UK)
Kindergarten (ski) Kinderheim at Plan Chécrouit (☎ 0165 842477), (non-ski) Kinderheim at Sports Centre Crèche (☎ 0165 844096)

OTHER SPORTS
Curling, dog sledding, horse-riding, ice-climbing, indoor climbing wall, indoor golf, indoor tennis and squash, parapente, skating, sleigh-rides, snowbiking, snowshoeing, swimming

FOOD AND DRINK
Coffee L1,500–1,800, glass of wine L2,000–3,000, small beer L3,000–4,000, soft drink L2,600–3,500, dish of the day L25,000–30,000

Eating in and out
Restaurants are varied, plentiful and lively. Pierre Alexis rates as one of the best in town ('an extraordinary wine list to complement great food'). Courmayeur also has plenty of pizzerias including Mont Fréty ('wonderful for families'). Cadran Solaire is praised for both cuisine and ambience. La Maison de Filippo at Entrèves is an exercise in unparalleled gluttony; it offers a fixed-price menu of more than 30 courses.

Après-ski

The evening begins with cocktails in the American Bar and evolves into a hanging-out situation, with certain times for certain bars, and often more than one in a night or a return visit after dinner. The Bar Roma, with its comfortable sofas and armchairs, fills up early. Ziggi's is a cyber-café, the Red Lion is frequented by snowboarders, and Cadran Solaire is where the sophisticated Milanese go. Bar Posta and Bar delle Guide both have a good atmosphere, and there are also two discos.

The swimming-pool is 5km away at Pré-St-Didier, and the floodlit skating-rink with disco music is open every evening until midnight.

Childcare

The Kinderheim up at Plan Chécrouit looks after children from six months old. Staff pick up children from the bottom of the cable-car in the village and return at the end of the day. A new Kinderheim at the sports centre now cares for children from nine months old and is particularly useful for parents wanting to ski on the Mont Blanc side. The Scuola di Sci Monte Bianco offers lessons, with lunch included.

Livigno

ALTITUDE 1,820m (5,970ft)

Beginners ✱✱✱ Intermediates ✱✱ Snowboarders ✱

Livigno – the cheapest of all Alpine resorts – is a duty-free village in one of the highest and remotest corners of Italy. It is user-friendly for skiers and revellers alike, but you have to suffer a three- to five-hour transfer from Bergamo, Milan or Zurich airports. What you get during your stay is a large, exposed ski area with a fine snow record, which is best suited to beginners and intermediate snow-users. The resort's main problem has always been access. The community developed near the Roman road from Milan to Innsbruck, a route that crossed the neighbouring Passo di San Giacomo. As frontiers moved back and forth, the Spol Valley became a distant border outpost of first Switzerland, then Italy and lastly the Austro-Hungarian Empire. Today, it has slow road links with **Bormio** to the east, **St Moritz** to the west, and with **Davos** via the Klosters–Engadine tunnel under the Flüela Pass.

- ✔ Ski-in ski-out convenience
- ✔ Reliable snow cover
- ✔ Low prices and duty-free
- ✔ Choice of restaurants
- ✔ Recommended for telemark
- ✘ Long airport transfer
- ✘ Poor road links
- ✘ Bleak location
- ✘ No real resort centre
- ✘ Heavy traffic

Livigno's *raison d'être* is shopping, with stores dedicated to cheap alcohol, clothing and consumer durables ('Armani clothing a third of the price it is in the UK'). It competes on price with Andorra. Livigno's fiscal privileges date from 1600 and were confirmed in 1805 when Napoleon, then the ruler of the Kingdom of Italy, granted 'customs benefits' that were validated by the Austro-Hungarian Empire in 1818, and by the European Community in 1960.

Although many of the individual buildings are attractive, Livigno's lack of town planning makes it unsympathetic overall. Its high, bleak location has earned it the nickname 'Piccolo Tibet' (Little Tibet), a description that is particularly apt in bad weather. An efficient, free bus service links the four hamlets of **Santa Maria**, **San Antonio**, **San Rocco** and **Trepalle**, which, stretched over 12km, make up the resort. A pedestrianised zone has been achieved by blocking off the centre section of the main road through San Antonio. It provides a rather tacky focus, crammed full of hotels, restaurants and noisy bars. Santa Maria is more distinguished architecturally but its charm is diluted by heavy traffic in its narrow streets.

On the snow
top 2,797m (9,177ft) bottom 1,820m (5,970ft)

International visitors began skiing in Livigno in 1964, when the Munt La Schera tunnel opened the resort up to northern Europe. In those days it had one lift; today there are 30, serving 115km of predominantly gentle slopes on both sides of the valley. The core of the skiing is on the ski-in ski-out, south-east-facing Carosello, which catches the morning sun. The two-stage Carosello 3000 gondola provides rapid access from the town to the highest point. The Carosello links with two supplementary areas, one served by the Federia drag-lift on the back side of the mountain, where the snow is better protected from the sun, and the other on Costaccia, where the high-speed Vetta quad-chair along the ridge gives various options.

The skiing is generally steeper on the west-facing side of the valley, where the setting sun attracts skiers late into the afternoon. The gondola station for Mottolino is at the suburb of **Teola**, a long walk or a short bus ride from the town centre. There are notoriously chilly chair-lift connections with Monte della Neve, the departure point for the best skiing in the resort, and Trepalle, a windswept outpost on the road to Bormio.

Livigno has become the self-appointed telemark capital of the Alps, thanks to the annual Skieda International Festival.

Beginners

Livigno is justly proud of a lift system that provides blanket coverage of sun-soaked, resort-level nursery slopes within a stone's throw of the main street. The runs straggle along the flank of the mountain on the Carosello side, leaving beginners with no excuses for not practising when classes are over. The best graduation slopes for progressive novices are from Monte della Neve and Mottolino to Trepalle.

Intermediates

The heart of the skiing is Carosello at 2,797m and the linked area of Blesaccia, which together offer the widest choice of long descents. The toughest intermediate options in a generally flattering environment are on the slopes above Val Federia. On the other side of the valley, the rolling red (intermediate) runs from Mottolino, Monte Sponda and Monte della Neve back to Teola are rewarding, but those to Trepalle are rather short.

Advanced

The creators of the piste map have taken pains to include some statutory black (difficult) runs, but the grading is strictly complimentary. This is not a resort for advanced snow-users. Livigno's two main mogul fields are at the extremes of the resort, below Costaccia and on the descent from Carosello. A longer and much better black run winds down from Monte della Neve to the bottom of the Monte Sponda chair.

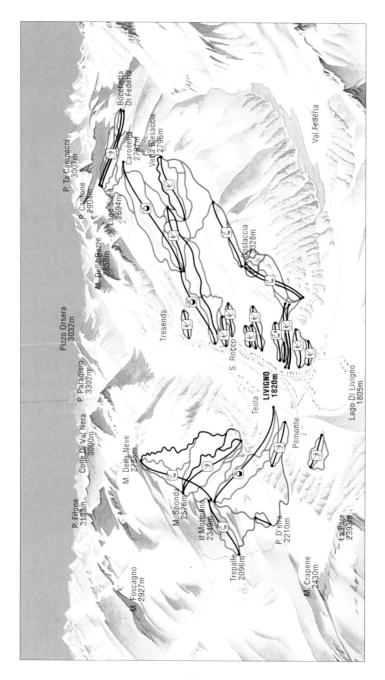

Off-piste

Very few visitors to Livigno have any intention of skiing off-piste, but extensive possibilities exist for those prepared to hire a guide and go exploring. The most accessible options are from Carosello 3000 and the ridge above Costaccia to Val Federia, or from Monte della Neve to Trepalle – but be prepared for long walk-outs.

Snowboarding

The wide pistes make Livigno a good place to learn, but that is where it ends. The half-pipe at Mottolino is unimpressive.

Tuition and guiding

Livigno has three ski schools. As far as British clients are concerned, Sci Livigno Galli Fedele is the major player. However, minority interests are better served by the Azzurra and Inverno-Estate schools, which offer telemark, ski-touring and snowboarding,

Mountain restaurants

The main self-service restaurants at the top of the Mottolino and Carosello gondolas offer consistency at competitive prices, while the restaurant La Costaccia is known for its outdoor barbecue. More atmospheric mountain lunches can be found in the Teas, the mountain huts once used by herdsmen working the summer pastures. The Tea Borch, below Carosello, and the Tea del Plan, below Costaccia, specialise in *pizzoccheri*, the local brown pasta that is traditionally prepared with cabbage and cheese. Tea Bourk is warmly recommended.

Accommodation

Livigno now boasts five four-stars. The Golf Parc Pare (☎ 0342 970263) and the Intermonti (☎ 0342 972100) are in Teola on the hillside overlooking the town – a suitable place to stay for the Mottolino lifts but not for the nightlife. The others comprise the Concordia (☎ 0342 990100), Flora (☎ 0342 996034) and the Posta (☎ 0342 996076). Convenient for both the nursery slopes and the après-ski are the Alpina (☎ 0342 996007), the Helvetia (☎ 0342 970066) and the Victoria (☎ 0342 970490). In Santa Maria, the Livigno (☎ 0342 996104) and the St Michael (☎ 0342 996392) are two quiet and expertly-run, family hotels. The Pedrana Rocco apartments (☎ 0342 997258) remain 'basic, but fairly big'.

Eating in and out

Livigno is not short of choice with the emphasis on quality local fare rather than haute cuisine. The Pesce d'Oro daringly advertises 'fresh fish every week' but still enjoys a sound reputation. The Camana Veglia employs a notably good chef, while the Bellavista wins many friends with its pizzas. Reporters recommended Mario's as 'the best restaurant, both in quality and value'.

Skiing facts: Livigno

TOURIST INFORMATION
Via dala Gesa 65, I–23030 Livigno (SO)
Tel 39 0342 996379
Fax 39 0342 996881
Email info@aptlivigno.it
Web site www.aptlivigno.it

THE RESORT
By road Calais 1,072km
By rail Tirano 2½hrs
Airport transfer Milan 3–5hrs,
Zurich 3–5hrs, Bergamo 4hrs
Visitor beds 8,500
Transport free ski bus

THE SKIING
Linked or nearby resorts Bormio (n),
Santa Caterina (n), St Moritz (n),
Valdidentro (n), Valdisotto (n)
Number of lifts 30
Total of trails/pistes 115km (40% easy,
45% intermediate, 15% difficult)
Beginners 12 lifts, 5km of runs
Summer skiing Stelvio Pass

LIFT PASSES
Area pass (covers Bormio, Santa
Caterina, Valdidentro, Valdisotto and 1
day in St Moritz) L225,000–265,000 for
6 days
Pensioners 65yrs and over, as children
Credit cards yes

TUITION
Skiing Scuola Sci Azzurra
(☎ 0342 997683), Inverno-Estate
(☎ 0342 996276),
Sci Livigno Galli Fedele (☎ 0342
970300)
Snowboarding as ski schools
Other courses cross-country, extreme
skiing/boarding, monoski, race-training,
seniors, skiing for the disabled,
ski-touring, telemark
Guiding Matteo Galli (☎ 0342 970618),
Lodovico Sport (☎ 0342 996107),
Mario Mottini (☎ 0335 432057)

CHILDREN
Lift pass 14yrs and under
L158,000–185,000 for 6 days
Ski & board school as adults
Kindergarten (ski) Inverno-Estate, (non-
ski) Ali-Baba at Inverno-Estate

OTHER SPORTS
Climbing wall, horse-riding, ice-climbing,
ice-driving, night-skiing, parapente,
skating, sleigh rides, snowmobiling,
snowshoeing, swimming

FOOD AND DRINK
Coffee L1,500, glass of wine L2,000,
small beer L3,000, soft drink L3,000,
dish of the day L18,000–20,000

Après-ski
The après is cheap and cheerful, with lots of duty-free alcohol. Tea del Vidal is a cheerful pit-stop on the Mottolino side. In town, the most popular watering-hole is Foxi's Pub, with a slide for an entrance. Noisy alternatives include the Underground and Galli's bar in San Antonio. Il Cielo is rated as the smartest disco by the Italians, yet the Kokodi is preferred by British visitors.

Childcare
Skiing tuition is available at Livigno's four ski schools, while Ski School Inverno-Estate operates both a ski- and a non-ski kindergarten.

Madonna di Campiglio

ALTITUDE 1,550m (5,085ft)

Beginners ✱✱✱ Intermediates ✱✱✱ Advanced ✱ Snowboarding ✱✱✱

Madonna di Campiglio is one of Italy's two smartest resorts. Though pocket-sized in comparison with the equally expensive but more sophisticated **Cortina d'Ampezzo**, it is a definite rival in terms of social prestige. The town of Madonna stands on the site of a mountain hospice dating back 800 years, and its first cable-car was built in 1935. Today, it is compact and congenial with a predominantly modern architectural style and a high standard of hotel accommodation.

✔ Beautiful scenery
✔ Extensive snowmaking
✔ Intensive piste-grooming
✔ Excellent nursery slopes
✔ Attractive cross-country
✗ High prices
✗ Skiing lacks challenge

Situated in a narrow valley in the Brenta Dolomites, Madonna is reached by a 75-km climb through galleried tunnels past spectacular drops from the *autostrada* and the valley town of Trento. The nearest airport is two-and-a-half hours' drive away at Verona.

The ski area is officially rated as Italy's premier for piste-grooming, and regularly hosts international winter sports events, including World Cup ski races and snowboarding championships. Long stays are the rule, with the better hotels booked out for the whole season. Eighty per cent of the resort's clientèle is Italian.

The village runs north–south, with the slopes coming right down to the town on either side. In the past the resort has been blighted by heavy traffic in high season and near-impossible parking. However, the long-awaited 1.8-km-long road bypass tunnel opened in December 1999 and has considerably reduced traffic. Four new underground car parks were built during the 2000–1 season and there are plans to pedestrianise the village. A free ski bus covers the region well.

On the snow
top 2,505m (8,219ft) bottom 1,520m (4,987ft)

Although there are now some ultra-modern covered chair-lifts and swift gondolas, with more being upgraded every year, part of the lift system still dates from the 1950s. Today a modest 25 lifts cover 90km of pistes in the Madonna core area, although an additional 25 lifts and 60km of pistes can be accessed with the Superskirama lift pass, including the separate but linked resorts of **Folgarida** and **Marilleva**.

Madonna is a resort with flattering skiing and excellent nursery slopes, as well as a good range of far-flung intermediate terrain.

However, it has little to offer the expert or off-piste snow-user. What initially appear to be three entirely separate zones are cunningly inter-linked at valley level by a snow-cannon-maintained piste that winds beneath a series of road bridges.

An ancient cable-car climbs slowly up to the first area, 5-Laghi, from the centre of town. The second is reached by a fast jumbo gondola north of the town centre, whisking you up to Pradalago at 2,100m, which is linked to Marilleva and Folgarida. The third area, Monte Spinale/Grosté, is dramatically positioned beneath the towering granite cliff faces of Petra Grande and is reached by high-speed gondola from the east of town.

The resort has accommodation for more than 27,000 visitors, who in theory can be carried uphill in less than an hour. January and March are the best months in which to visit – you have the slopes largely to yourself. Overcrowding is the norm at Christmas and New Year, as well as during the February school holidays, particularly at the budget resorts of Marilleva and Folgarida.

> **WHAT'S NEW**
>
> Ski bus service is now free

When viewed from the village, the mountains appear steep; from above, they open into a civilised network of wide trails. Only the Grosté sector is entirely above the tree-line and is not covered by the exhaustive system of about 500 snow-cannon. Proficient skiers need to invest in the slightly more expensive regional Superskirama lift pass that covers Folgarida and Marilleva. You can now buy a keycard, which provides a convenient hands-free entrance to all the lifts. A separate ticket is some-what redundantly issued as soon as you cross into the territory of the neighbouring resorts.

Beginners

Novices taking tuition should not buy a lift pass, as they will be taken by bus to the private Campo Carlo Magno nursery area five minutes' drive away. Beginners who are not enrolled at the ski or snowboard school pay a small fee for the use of the nursery lifts. This is a superb learning area, serviced by its own drag-lifts and snowmaking. Another private nursery area called Bambi is run by Des Alpes Ski School on the east side of Madonna.

All of Madonna's terrain is accessible to inexperienced snow-users, and blue (easy) runs make up more than half the slopes in the main Madonna area. The Zeledria blue continues for more than 3km all the way down to town from Pradalago, as does the Pozza Vecia on the other side of the mountain; this run can be combined with the Boch blue, pro-viding a non-stop beginner cruise of 5km.

Intermediates

Madonna's ski area is ideal for intermediate skiers and boarders, with lots of long cruises on attractive tree-lined trails. Folgarida and

Marilleva also provide a supply of flattering cruising pistes, including the long red (intermediate) Genziana. The two highest runs in the resort, reached by the Grosté chairs, are suitable for anyone who can ski parallel. The granite cliffs are truly spectacular. However, this is the most popular area of the resort with Italian visitors and should be avoided at peak holiday times. At the top of the Boch chair you can ski or ride Spinale Diretta, the resort's trickiest red piste.

Advanced

There is little challenge for mogul skiers in a resort where every bump is flattened nightly by a fleet of piste machines. None of the five runs listed as black (difficult) on the inadequate piste map is worthy of the grading. However, the Canelone Miramonti is a short, steep shock, and the FIS 3-Tre racecourse in the 5-Laghi area provides some challenge.

Off-piste

The ski schools seldom break away from the prepared pistes, although snowboarders do. Tempting lines run through the trees but do not always bring you back to the piste. Above Spinale and towards the Cima Brenta is a wide couloir that requires a mountain guide and ski-touring equipment.

Snowboarding

Madonna is rated as one of the two best snowboarding resorts in Italy (the other is **Selva**). The Grosté terrain park and boardercross course at 2,500m were used for the FIS snowboard world championships in January 2001. Madonna's terrain is well suited to beginner riders. An additional terrain park has been created on the 2,100-m peak of Doss del Sabion where the views are sensational, a few kilometres away above the nearby resort of **Pinzolo**.

Tuition and guiding

Confusingly, Madonna has six ski and snowboard schools, all affiliated to the national Scuola Italiana Sci, and each changes its uniform colour every season. English is indifferently spoken. Group lessons may have between eight and 12 pupils and run for two hours in two shifts during the mornings.

Mountain restaurants

'All furs and no food' is how one reporter, expecting a truffles-and-caviar experience, responded to the self-service inns that are all you get in Madonna. For a resort of this stature, cosy mountain restaurants are sadly absent. Most of the converted *malga* (old wooden barns that once served as summer shelters for farmers and cows) have been transformed into high-volume self-service establishments. One exception is Cascina Zeledria, tucked away in the woods, which offers *Delizie alle Piastra* – steaks that you cook yourself on a hot stone. A free snowcat tows you back up to the piste after lunch. Malga Boch has a pine

Skiing facts: Madonna di Campiglio

TOURIST INFORMATION
Via Pradolago 4, I-38084 Madonna di Campiglio (TN)
Tel 39 0465 442000
Fax 39 0465 440404
Email info@campiglio.net
Web site www.campiglio.net

THE RESORT
By road Calais 1,200km
By rail Trento 72km
Airport transfer Verona 2½hrs
Visitor beds 27,055
Transport free bus service

THE SKIING
Linked or nearby resorts Folgarida (l), Marilleva (l), Monte Bondonne (n), Pinzolo (n), Ponte di Legno-Tonale (n)
Number of lifts 26 in resort, 42 in linked area
Total of trails/pistes 90km in Madonna (44% easy, 40% intermediate, 16% difficult), 150km in linked area
Beginners 3 lifts, points tickets available

LIFT PASSES
Area pass Superskirama (covers Andalo, Folgarida, Marilleva, Monte Bondone, Pinzolo, Ponte di Legno-Tonale) L288,000–320,000 for 6 days
Pensioners 60yrs and over, as children
Credit cards yes

TUITION
Skiing Campo Carlo Magno (☎ 0465 443222), Des Alpes (☎ 0465 442850), 5-Laghi (☎ 0465 441650), Nazionale (☎ 0465 443243), Rainalter (☎ 0465 443300), Fondo Malghette (☎ 0465 441633)
Snowboarding as ski schools, Professional Snowboarding (☎ 0465 443251)
Other courses cross-country, telemark
Guiding Elicampiglio (☎ 0465 974044), Guide Alpine-Sci (☎ 0465 442634)

CHILDREN
Lift pass 8–13yrs L230,000–256,000 for 6 days. Free for 7yrs and under
Ski & board school as adults
Kindergarten (non-ski) Baby Parking (☎ 0465 442222)

OTHER SPORTS
Archery, curling, dog-sledding, horse-riding, ice-climbing, night-skiing, parapente, skating, slalom, snowshoeing, swimming

FOOD AND DRINK
Coffee L1,600–1,700, glass of wine L2,000–2,500, small beer L3,000–3,500, soft drink L3,000, dish of the day L15,000–18,000

interior and sometimes a DJ from the famous Zangola disco. La Grotte, in Albergo Fortini at the base of the Grosté gondola, is recommended by reporters. Agostini, on Pradalago, serves *picchiorosso*, a powerful secret-recipe grappa.

Accommodation
Most guests stay in the resort's 18 four-star and 37 three-star hotels, which are booked for most of the season. Relais Club des Alpes (☎ 0465 440000) carries the most cachet and is the most central. The

Savoia Palace (☎ 0465 441004) is well-positioned. Chalet Hermitage (☎ 0465 441558), completely renovated in 1999, is a 'bio-hotel' in an immense private park and boasts a health and beauty centre. The Lorenzetti (☎ 0465 441404) is also four-star, though more rustic in setting and décor, and has its own free shuttle bus. The Diana (☎ 0465 441011) is friendly, close to the lifts and furnished to a high standard. Arnica (☎ 0465 440377) is a conveniently central, modern B&B. Equally central is the old-style Villa Principe (☎ 0465 440011), which has some of the cheapest rooms in town. There are also chalet-apart-ments and self-catering establishments, which have swimming-pools and fitness centres.

Eating in and out

A must in Madonna is piling into heated snowcats and jolting up to the mountain restaurants of Malga Montagnoli, Cascina Zeledria or Malga Boch, where the service and food are better by night. In town, Antico Focolare is the in-place to eat, serving typical Trentino food in atmos-pheric surroundings with open fires. Artini has good cuisine but lacks atmosphere. Pappagallo has a generous set menu on Wednesdays. Cliffhanger serves fish platters. Lanterna d'Oro and Le Roi have the best pizzas. There are numerous supermarkets and delicatessens.

Après-ski

Immediately after skiing, the furs gather at Bar Suisse or the Franz-Josef Stube to flutter eyelashes behind dark glasses and make dates for later. Café Campiglio in the piazza is popular for coffee and cakes. However, although Madonna is often said to be lively, it doesn't really get into the groove until the early hours. The population then goes wild until 4am or sometimes even 8am in what has for 25 years been one of the most famous discos in the Italian Alps: the old cow barn, Zangola, 3km out of town but serviced by late-night buses. The disco features male strip-pers and dancing girls. Des Alpes has techno music as well as an upstairs piano bar. Not to be confused with the bar of the same name, Cantina del Suisse has a live band and is a warm-up nightspot for Zangola. Cliffhanger disco is open until the early hours and shows heli-skiing videos. La Stalla has karaoke and live music. The billiard bar and two garish video-game centres are extremely popular with Italian boys.

The many elegant boutiques in the resort include Martini for Trentino-Tyrolean clothing and carved wooden artefacts, and Chalet Ferrari for designer clothing.

Childcare

Most Italians leave the little ones at home or bring nanny or granny. Hotel Spinale has a children's club for its small residents, and the new non-ski kindergarten is Baby Parking. The ski schools accept children from four years old for mornings only in large classes of ten or more.

The Milky Way

ALTITUDE Montgenèvre 1,850m (6,068ft), Sauze d'Oulx 1,500m (4,920ft), Sestriere 2,035m (6,675ft)

Beginners ✱✱ Intermediates ✱✱✱ Advanced ✱✱

The Milky Way, or Via Lattea, straddles the border between France and Italy and is reached more easily from Turin than Grenoble. In recent years, snow cover has been unpredictable. However, after two seasons of minimal snow that seriously threatened commerce in the region, winter 2000–1 produced some of the best conditions in the whole of the northern hemisphere. The Milky Way is one of the great ski circuits of Europe, boasting 400km of groomed pistes served by 92 lifts. **Sestriere**, which successfully hosted the 1997 Alpine Skiing World Championships, follows **Salt Lake City** in Utah as the next venue for the Winter Olympics in 2006. We can now expect a major and much-needed investment in mountain facilities throughout the Milky Way over the next four years. Let us hope that there will be snow on the day.

✔ Large ski area
✔ Skiing convenience
✔ Extensive tree-line skiing
✔ Varied off-piste
✔ Value for money
✔ Lively après-ski (Sauze d'Oulx)
✗ Lack of non-skiing activities
✗ Limited mountain restaurants
✗ Poor trail-marking
✗ Lift queues

British skiers are more familiar with Sestriere's lively sister **Sauze d'Oulx** (pronounced Sow-Zee Doo) in the neighbouring valley, which is slowly but successfully shedding its reputation for lager-oriented nightlife rather than for the quality of its slopes. Annoyingly, the resort bus service is no longer free.

The third major resort (and the only French component) is **Montgenèvre**, an old stone village perched on the col separating France from Italy. It has been pleasantly developed for tourism and retains considerable charm. The first impression is of a higgledy-piggledy collection of bars, restaurants, shops and hotels lining an extremely busy main road where skiers joust with pantechnicons. The older part of the village is tucked away on the northern side and has plenty of atmosphere, despite the heavy traffic. Shopping facilities are limited, but the weekly open-air market adds colour and offers the occasional bargain. The Italian border is on the outskirts of town. In the past, both currencies have been in circulation here. The introduction of the euro provides visitors with welcome unification. The main part of **Sauze d'Oulx**, adjacent to the slopes, is a largely uninspiring collection of modern edifices constructed with budget rather than beauty in mind. In its past, raucous revellers, still in their ski boots and awash with cheap lager, would stagger homewards from the infamous Andy Capp Bar at 3am to a collection of shabby two-star hotels for a few hours of further recreation before hitting the slopes again. To the young British skiers who flocked to this corner of Piedmont each winter in search of dissolute pleasures, it was known as 'Suzy does it'. However, Suzy, it seems, has matured beyond the excesses of her youth and is trying to cultivate a more sober image. Significantly, the Andy Capp is no more.

WHAT'S NEW

Quad chair-lift from Valle Gimont to Col Saurel with new red piste

Sestriere, once one of the most fashionable wintering holes in Europe, was purpose-built in 1930 by Giovanni Agnelli, the founder of Fiat, who was frustrated by the fact that members of his family spent so much of their winter skiing abroad. Its location on a high, cold and barren pass is not enchanting, but the snow here is usually the best in the region. The skyline is dominated by the twin towers of the Albergo Duchi d'Aosta, once one of the smartest hotels in Europe but now a Club Med. The village is compact, but, despite being essentially Italian, appears to lack soul. As one reporter put it: 'there is no continuity, resulting in a confusion of styles, which seem to compete rather than harmonise'. Buses run to and from the satellites of **Borgata** and **Grangesises**.

The more shrewd Italians have now abandoned Sestriere for nearby **Sansicario**, which is a smaller, more sophisticated and modern development with its own ski area. It is linked to Sestriere and Sauze d'Oulx on one side and **Cesana Torinese** on the other.

On the snow
top 2,823m (9,262ft) bottom 1,350m (4,428ft)

The Milky Way now has an electronic, hands-free lift pass. Montgenèvre's slopes are on both sides of the Col de Montgenèvre. The south-facing side, Chalvet, is slightly higher, with runs going up to 2,600m, and is usually less crowded than the north-facing pistes, which create the main link with the Italian resorts. Mountain access on the other side of the pass is by gondola from the **Briançon** end of the village, as well as by drag-lifts and a chair from the centre. These serve easy runs through woods, opening into wide nursery slopes above the road. From the top of the gondola there is a choice of three small ski areas. The wide, sheltered bowl of Le Querelay/Les Anges features ruined fortress buildings around the crest with some red (intermediate) and black (difficult) runs beneath them, but no challenging skiing.

The Milky Way link from Montgenèvre starts with a poorly signposted traverse around the mountain, which is easy to miss in bad light. Otherwise it is not difficult, and leads to a long run that starts as red and becomes blue (easy), past the Gimont drag-lifts and down to **Clavière**. The north-facing slopes of Monti della Luna above Clavière

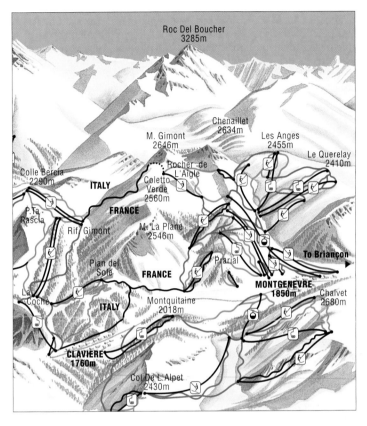

and Cesana Torinese offer plenty of challenge, including some vast trails through the woods and satisfying off-piste.

Reporters were unanimous in their opinion that the best skiing in the Milky Way is above Sestriere ('Sauze' lifts are, to say the least, anti-quated and slow.') The Sestriere end of the lift system was upgraded for the 1997 Alpine World Championships and further improvements are now scheduled for the 2006 Olympics. The bulk of the skiing is on Sises and Banchetta mountains, which are separated by a deep valley.

The Sauze d'Oulx slopes face west and north, and the majority of them are below the tree-line. A quad-chair takes you up to the centre of the skiing at **Sportinia**, a sunny woodland clearing with a few hotels, a small busy nursery area and a variety of restaurants. Above it is some wide, open intermediate skiing served by several chair- and drag-lifts. Below Sportinia are wide runs back through the woods, graded red and black; these are quite steep in places, although never really demanding. There are also blue and black runs down to the hamlet of **Jouvenceaux**.

Queues in Montgenèvre are bad only at weekends. The main queue problems at the Italian end of the Milky Way are on the Sauze side of the mountain, described as 'horrendous' by a reporter who was there during an Italian bank holiday. The local lift map has improved, but it is still sometimes difficult to work out exactly where on the mountain you are. Reporters described trail-marking as virtually non-existent to the point of being dangerous, which adds to the problems of orientation.

Beginners

A dozen nursery slopes are scattered around the different resorts of the Milky Way on both sides of the border, and the area is ideal learner territory. The main nursery slope for Sauze is at Sportinia; it is open and sunny but often very crowded. Nursery slopes are also available at Belvédère on the Genevris side, as well as in the village when there is snow. The Montgenèvre end of the circuit has the best blue runs.

Intermediates

The long No. 21 down to Sansicario from Monte Fraiteve is satisfyingly varied and one of the best on the circuit. No. 11 from Col Basset to Clotes, and No. 12 to Jouvenceaux are both favourites among reporters. Old hands say that high-season crowds are a problem throughout the Milky Way but particularly around Sestriere. One tip is to ski the remote Genevris/Moncrons/Bourget sector on Saturdays and Sundays ('a pleasure to ski and no queues at all').

Advanced

An assortment of black runs are scattered throughout the Milky Way, but reporters complained that they are overgraded and lack the challenge you would expect to find on a comparable run in the French Alps. The Sauze sector quite wrongly has a novice label attached to it because of the predominance of beginner and early-intermediate skiers that it attracts. In fact, some of the reds here could easily be graded black, and a few of the blacks (notably No. 33 and No. 21) are seriously challenging in difficult snow conditions. The best of the skiing is found above Sansicario and Sestriere, although this may not be apparent from the local piste map.

The steep Motta drag- and chair-lifts serve the toughest of Sestriere's skiing and climb to the top point of the Milky Way. Here the mogulled slopes beside the drag can have gradients of up to 30 degrees.

Off-piste

Monte Fraiteve is an exposed crest with impressive views of the French mountains, where the ski areas of Sauze d'Oulx, Sestriere and Sansicario meet. It is also the start of the famous Rio Nero off-piste run, which is a long descent that follows a river gully down to the Oulx–Cesana road, 1,600m below. An infrequent bus service takes you back to the lifts at Cesana. Heli-skiing drops on the top of Valle

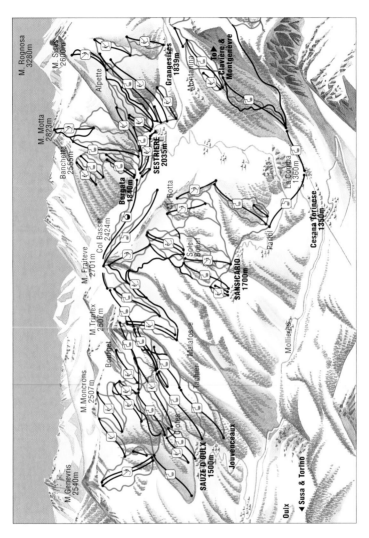

d'Argentera and Val Thuras can now be arranged from all the resorts through either Guide Alpine Valsusa or Elisusa Heli-skiing.

Snowboarding

First-timers are not particularly well served here and the dominance of drag-lifts is off-putting. Freeriders, however, can have some fun on the long Rio Nero off-piste route. Sestriere now has a terrain park with boardercross obstacles and a half-pipe adjoining the Giovanni Alberto Agnelli race course.

281

Tuition and guiding

The French Ski School (ESF) at Montgenèvre receives sound reports ('first class – patient instructors all with good spoken English') for all grades of skier and for private lessons. Reports of the Sauze d'Oulx Ski School are much improved ('after Zermatt, the attitude of the instructors was like a breath of fresh air. Lessons were made to be fun'). The school has two rivals, Sauze Project and Sauze Sportinia. Sportinia achieves a high standard of teaching, though one reader complained that his instructor had only a few English phrases. Reports of the Sestriere ski school, which has in the past been the subject of criticism, are encouraging: 'our instructor spoke excellent English and tuition was friendly and competent'. We have no reports of the Olimpionica ski school at Sestriere nor of the Borgata school.

Mountain restaurants

'You can eat out in the mountain restaurants on the Italian side for the cost of a drink in Courchevel,' enthused one reporter. Montgenèvre is seriously short of mountain restaurants, with just the Altitude 2000 and Gondrands. The first-rate and inexpensive bars and restaurants above Clavière (particularly La Coche) help make up for this shortfall.

The five busy restaurants at Sportinia maintain a high standard ('but eating in Piccadilly Circus is not my idea of a fun holiday'). Chalet Genevris in the area of the same name is renowned for its lunchtime fixed-price barbecue, and Ciao Pais is 'old fashioned and best saved for a day when a long lunch is called for'.

Sestriere's Bar Chisonetto, halfway down Red No. 8 on Banchetta, is recommended for its hamburgers. Bar Conchinetto is a traditional wood-and-stone restaurant noted for its polenta, while atmospheric La Gargote is more expensive and Alpette is praised for its pasta. One reporter warned that the mountain WCs are 'mostly of the shower-tray variety – these can prove more challenging than the average off-piste itinerary for anyone in a one-piece suit'.

Accommodation

Montgenèvre's accommodation is mostly in apartments scattered along the road, in the old village, and on the lower south-facing slopes; there are also a few catered chalets. Access to the skiing is easy from most places, but the Italian end of the village is more convenient. The pick of Montgenèvre's half a dozen less-than-luxurious hotels are the Napoléon (☎ 492 21 92 04) and the more attractive Valérie (☎ 492 21 90 02), near the church.

Accommodation in Sauze is mainly in hotels of variable quality. The Hermitage (☎ 0122 850385) is recommended along with the Biancaneve (☎ 0122 850160) 'clean and comfortable' and Stella Alpina (☎ 0122 858731) 'pleasant staff and perfectly adequate'. The Sauze (☎ 0122 850285) is 'clean and spacious', while the Gran Baita (☎ 0122 850183) is praised as 'excellent – very clean, the staff are pleasant'. San Giorgio (☎ 0122 850162) is 'friendly and inexpensive', the Chaberton

(☎ 0122 858173) is a basic B&B and the Savoia Debili (☎ 0122 850184) lies close to the lifts. La Torre (☎ 0122 850020) and Il Capricorno (☎ 0122 850273) are the only four-stars. You can be first on the nursery slopes by staying at the Monte Triplex (☎ 0122 850226).

Sestriere's accommodation is in hotels, modern apartments and at Club Med. The restored Principi de Piemonte Grand Hotel (☎ 0122 7941) is situated a couple of kilometres out of town but has its own access lift to the Sises ski area.

Il Fraitevino (☎ 0122 76022) is 'very simple for a four-star, but convenient'. The Belvedere (☎ 0122 77091) and Banchetta (☎ 0122 70307) are also recommended. The Biancaneve (☎ 0122 755176), which stands just outside the town, provides its own minibus service to the slopes.

Eating in and out

Montgenèvre boasts more than a dozen eating-places, including the Ca del Sol for pizzas, Les Chalmettes, L'Estable ('home-cooked cuisine'), Pizzeria Le Transalpin, Le Refuge and smart Le Jamy.

In Sauze, Del Falco is praised ('atmosphere, food and wine all excellent') along with Old Inn, Giorgio's and Bruscetta. Del Borgo exudes 'a pleasant buzz' and is famed for its tiramisù.

Eating-places in Sestriere range from pizzerias to smart, international restaurants. Ristorante du Grandpère in the nearby hamlet of Champlas Janvier is praised for its wild boar stew and polenta. Antica Spelonca offers 'a wonderful atmosphere and fine food', while Antica Osteria is an ancient chalet with considerable charm, and L'Teit serves 'the best pizzas we have ever eaten'. Jolly supermarket is said to be reasonably priced.

Après-ski

Off-slopes activity in Montgenèvre is limited, although a good choice of inexpensive bar-restaurants is on offer; three have nightclubs attached. The Ca del Sol and Le Graal are both popular bars, and the Blue Night is the disco. The village provides a good skating-rink.

In Sauze, the New Scotch Bar (near the bottom of the home run) catches the early evening crowd and is awash with pints of Tartan long before dark. Later on, the action moves to the Cotton Club, Hotel Derby Bar and the Vagabondia. Max's Bar shows British sport on satellite TV. The Village Café and La Taverna both host live music six nights a week, while the Bandito, Schuss and Rimini Nord discos 'keep you dancing as long as you want'. Entry to all clubs is free, which is in pleasant contrast to France.

Sestriere's nightlife is fairly lively and stylish when the Italians are in residence at weekends and in holiday periods, though at other times it is quiet. The Black Sun and Tabata discos are popular at weekends. Brahms Pub is Irish and serves Guinness. Anno Zero, Pinky Bar, Maialetto and People Pub are all popular, too.

Skiing facts: Montegenèvre

TOURIST INFORMATION
F–05100 Montgenèvre, Hautes-Alpes
Tel 33 492 21 52 52
Fax 33 492 21 92 45
Email
office.tourisme.montgenevre@wanadoo.fr
Web site www.montgenevre.com

THE RESORT
By road Calais 978km
By rail TGV direct to Oulx 20km,
Briançon 10km
Airport transfer Turin 1hr 20mins,
Grenoble 3hrs
Visitor beds 8,000
Transport free bus service

THE SKIING
Linked or nearby resorts Bardonecchia
(n), Borgata (I), Cesana Torinese (I),
Clavière (I), Grangesises (I), Jouvenceaux
(I), Sansicario (I), Sauze d'Oulx (I),
Sestriere (I), Sportinia (I)
Number of lifts 39 in
Montgenèvre–Monti della Luna, 92 in
Milky Way
Total of trails/pistes 100km in
Montgenèvre–Monti della Luna
(37% easy, 43% intermediate,
20% difficult), 400km in Milky Way
Beginners 1 free lift

LIFT PASSES
Area pass Milky Way 770FF for 6 days
Pensioners 60–69yrs Milky Way 578FF,
free for 70yrs and over
Credit cards yes

TUITION
Skiing ESF (☎ 492 21 90 46)
Snowboarding as ski school
Other courses cross-country, freestyle,
race-training
Guiding through ski school,
Guide Alpine Valsusa (☎ 0335 398984),
Elisusa Heli-skiing (☎ 0122 62 31 62)

CHILDREN
Lift pass 6–12yrs Milky Way 616FF for
6 days. Beginners pass (covers 7 lifts)
70FF per day
Ski & board school as adults
Kindergarten (ski) ESF Jardin d'Enfants
(☎ 492 21 90 46), (non-ski) Garderie
(☎ 492 21 52 50)

OTHER SPORTS
Heli-skiing/boarding, horse-
riding, parapente, skating, snowmobiling,
snowshoeing

FOOD AND DRINK
Coffee 12FF, glass of wine 10FF,
small beer 15FF, soft drink 15FF,
dish of the day 70FF

Childcare
Montgenèvre's Garderie cares for children from one to four years old, and the ESF takes three- to five-year-olds in its ski kindergarten. Although Italy is not renowned for its childcare facilities, the Milky Way is a notable exception. Sauze has Dumbo, which caters for non-skiing children all day – parents must provide their children's lunch, which staff will heat up. The ski schools take children from four years old. Sestriere now provides the Kinderheim for daycare for those from two to six years old. Club Med looks after its smallest members from four years old, as does the ski school, and there is a mini-club at nearby Grangesises.

Linked or nearby resorts

Bardonecchia
top 2,750m (9,022ft) bottom 1,312m (4,303ft)

This is a large and traditional market town set in a sunny valley and surrounded by beautiful scenery. Although not part of the Milky Way circuit, it lies close to both Montgenèvre and Sestriere. The resort is popular with Italians, who flood in from Turin at weekends and on public holidays. The ski area is spread over three sectors, and these are linked by a free ski bus ('queues are rare – even during the Italian holiday periods'). The area boasts a total of 140km of piste, served by 24 lifts, and offers a surprising degree of challenge. We have favourable reports of Ski School Bardonecchia ('the instructors were competent and their English was of a high standard.') The ski school puts on mixed classes for adults and children. Facilities for small children are non-existent. Restaurants El Gaucho and Il Caminetto are both recommended.

The nightlife is limited to a dozen rather dull bars ('not enough après-ski'). Hotels are quite spread out and include Des Geneys Splendid (☎ 0122 99001), Asplenia (☎ 0122 999870), La Nigritella (☎ 0122 980477) and Park Hotel Rosa (☎ 0122 902087).

TOURIST INFORMATION
Tel 39 0122 99032
Fax 39 0122 980612
Email bardonecchia@montagnedoc.it
Web site www.montagnedoc.it

Borgata
top 2,823m (9,262ft) bottom 1,840m (6,035ft)

This is a small resort five minutes by road from Sestriere, with an infrequent bus service between the two. Hotel Hermitage (☎ 0122 70346)) is recommended ('nice rooms, but the food was not up to much'). Reporters who stayed in the Nube d'Argenta self-catering apartments (☎ 0122 70263) all praised them as 'clean, modern and convenient for the lifts'.

There were complaints about the ski school ('very poor, with limited spoken English, but the teachers were pleasant enough'). Shopping is almost non-existent ('a poor selection of postcards and no stamps'). The nightlife is quiet ('a couple of sleepy bars'). As one reporter put it: 'when the sun goes down, it is time to eat and go to bed'.

TOURIST INFORMATION
Tel 39 0122 755449
Fax 39 0122 755171
Email borgata@montagnedoc.it
Web site www.montagnedoc.it

Skiing facts: Sauze d'Oulx

TOURIST INFORMATION
Piazza Assietta 18, I–0050 Sauze d'Oulx, Piedmont
Tel 39 0122 858009
Fax 39 0122 850700
Email sauze@montagnedoc.it
Web site www.montagnedoc.it

THE RESORT
By road Calais 998km
By rail Oulx 5km, frequent buses to resort
Airport transfer Turin 1hr
Visitor beds 2,009
Transport ski bus, L9,000 for 6 days

THE SKIING
Linked or nearby resorts Bardonecchia (n), Borgata (l), Cesana Torinese (l), Clavière (l), Grangesises (l), Jouvenceaux (l), Montgenèvre (l), Sansicario (l), Sestriere (l), Sportinia (l)
Number of lifts 35 in Sauze d'Oulx, 92 in Milky Way
Total of trails/pistes 120km in Sauze d'Oulx (27% easy, 61% intermediate, 12% difficult), 400km in Milky Way
Beginners 2 lifts in Sauze d'Oulx, points tickets available

LIFT PASSES
Area pass Milky Way L220,000–280,000 for 6 days
Pensioners 60yrs and over Milky Way L202,000–258,000 for 6 days
Credit cards yes

TUITION
Skiing Sauze d'Oulx Ski School (☎ 0122 858084),
Sauze Project (☎ 0122 858942),
Sauze Sportinia (☎ 0122 850218)
Snowboarding as ski schools
Other courses cross-country
Guiding through ski schools, Guide Alpine Valsusa (☎ 0335 398984), Elisusa Heli-skiing (☎ 0122 623162)

CHILDREN
Lift pass 8–12yrs Milky Way L202,000–258,000 for 6 days
Ski & board school as adults
Kindergarten (ski) none, (non-ski) Dumbo (☎ 0347 6913531)

FOOD AND DRINK
Coffee L1,600, glass of wine L2,000, small beer L3,000, soft drink L3,500, dish of the day L25,000–30,000

Cesana Torinese
top 2,823m (9,262ft) bottom 1,350m (4,428ft)

This attractively shabby old village dates from the twelfth century and is set on a busy road junction at the foot of the Italian approach to the Montgenèvre Pass. It is rather confined and shaded, and accommodation is mainly in apartments and a few hotels. The chair-lifts up to the skiing above Clavière and Sansicario are a long walk from the centre, and the place can be safely recommended only to those with a car. The Chaberton (☎ 0122 89147) is a three-star hotel and there are half a dozen small one-stars. Restaurant La Selvaggia specialises in regional dishes, La Noblerot is for French cuisine and the smart Fraiteve serves truffles. Brusachoeur is a popular pizzeria. Nightspots include the Pussy-Cat pub and the Cremeria Rinaldo e Luciana bar.

TOURIST INFORMATION
Tel/Fax 39 0122 89202
Email cesana@montagnadoc.it
Web site www.montagnadoc.it

Clavière
top 2,823m (9,262ft) bottom 1,760m (5,773ft)

Clavière is a small village on the Franco-Italian border, which during the eighteenth century was part of Montgenèvre. The village consists of ten hotels and a row of shops on the Italian side, specialising in food and cheap local alcohol. Reporters commented that Clavière has a pleasant, relaxed atmosphere; it is tightly enclosed by wooded slopes, and the nursery area is small and steep. Lifts give access to the skiing above Montgenèvre and Cesana, with easy runs back from both. Queuing is not a problem, although the resort does tend to become busier at weekends.

There is a 15-km cross-country trail up to Montgenèvre and back, as well as a floodlit skating-rink. The ski school has some English-speaking instructors and, outside high season, mainly English-speaking pupils. At weekends the village suffers from heavy through-traffic.

Along the road are nine hotels: the two-star Hotel Roma (☎ 0122 878812), close to the main chair-lift, is praised ('good value, plenty of food and comfortable rooms'). Others include the Grand Albergo Clavière (☎ 0122 878787), Passero Pellegrino (☎ 0122 878914), Pian del Sole (☎ 0122 878085) and the Savoia (☎ 0122 878803). Recommended restaurants include L'Gran Bouc, Gallo Cedrone, Pizzeria Kilt and La Montanina. Clavière boasts 14 bars but is 'not a place for those interested in a hectic après-ski'.

TOURIST INFORMATION
Tel 39 0122 878856
Fax 39 0122 878888
Email claviere@montagnedoc.it
Web site www.montagnedoc.it

Sansicario
top 2,823m (9,262ft) bottom 1,710m (5,609ft)

The village is in a sunny position halfway up the west-facing mountain-side and is well placed for exploring the Milky Way. It is purpose-built, consisting mainly of apartment buildings linked to a neat commercial precinct by shuttle lift. Facilities for beginners, especially children, are good. A ski- and non-ski kindergarten provides daycare for three- to 11-year-olds, and it has its own ski school. The choice of après-ski facilities is limited.

Skiing facts: Sestriere

TOURIST INFORMATION
Piazza Agnelli, I–10058 Sestriere,
Piedmont
Tel 39 0122 755444
Fax 39 0122 755171
Email sestriere@montagnedoc.it
Web site www.montagnedoc.it

THE RESORT
By road Calais 1,020km
By rail Oulx 22km, buses to resort
Airport transfer Turin 1½hrs
Visitor beds 4,200
Transport ski bus L3,000 per day

THE SKIING
Linked or nearby resorts Bardonecchia
(n), Borgata (l), Cesana Torinese (l),
Clavière (l), Grangesises (l), Jouvenceaux
(l), Montgenèvre (l), Sansicario (l), Sauze
d'Oulx (l), Sportinia (l)
Number of lifts 32 in Sestriere,
92 in Milky Way
Total of trails/pistes 120km in Sestriere
(39% easy, 42% intermediate,
19% difficult), 400km in Milky Way
Beginners 11 nursery slopes in area,
points tickets available

LIFT PASSES
Area pass Milky Way L220,000–280,000
for 6 days

Pensioners 60yrs and over Milky Way
L202,000–258,000 for 6 days
Credit cards yes

TUITION
Skiing Borgata (☎ 0122 77497),
Olimpionica (☎ 0122 77116),
Sestriere Ski School (☎ 0122 77060)
Snowboarding as ski schools
Other courses cross-country, heli-skiing/
boarding
Guiding through ski schools, Guide
Alpine Valsusa (☎ 0335 398984),
Elisusa Heli-skiing (☎ 0122 623162)

CHILDREN
Lift pass 8–12yrs Milky Way
L202,000–258,000 for 6 days
Ski & board school as adults
Kindergarten Kinderheim
(☎ 0122 755444)

OTHER SPORTS
Sauze d'Oulx/Sestriere: Dog-sledding,
night-skiing/boarding, parapente,
snowmobiling

FOOD AND DRINK
Coffee L1,500, glass of wine L3,000,
small beer L3,500, soft drink L3,500,
dish of the day L20,000–30,000

Accommodation is of a generally high standard, mostly in apartments but with a few comfortable and expensive hotels. The most attractive is the Rio Envers (☎ 0122 811333), a short walk from the centre. The Sansicario (☎ 0122 811222) is simpler.

TOURIST INFORMATION
Tel/Fax 39 0122 89202
Email cesana@montagnadoc.it
Web site www.montagnedoc.it

Monterosa Ski

ALTITUDE Champoluc 1,568m (5,144ft), Gressoney-la-Trinité 1,624m
(5,327ft), Alagna 1,200m (3,936ft)

Beginners **✶✶** Intermediates **✶✶✶** Advanced **✶** Snowboarders **✶**

The introduction of a single ski pass covering the whole of the Aosta Valley has encouraged British skiers and riders based in **Courmayeur** to sample Monterosa Ski. The area comprises the resorts of **Champoluc, Gressoney-La-Trinité** and **Alagna** on the southern side of the border with Switzerland. The re-opening of the Mont Blanc tunnel – it is hoped in time for the 2001–2 season – and the construction of major new lifts in Alagna will help to reinforce this region as one of Italy's more important ski areas. Although the three villages are close as the crow flies and well connected by the lift system (at least in the case of Champoluc and Gressoney), it takes two to three hours to drive between any two of them.

Champoluc, at the top of the Ayas Valley, is reached by a long and winding road up from the Turin–Aosta *autostrada* and is set around a church and a fast-running mountain river. The old quarter was built in the fifteenth century, but the village has expanded in recent years to accommodate the requirements of a small ski resort. Gressoney-La-Trinité is on a similar scale, with a network of cobbled streets and wooden chalets surrounded by contemporary buildings. **Gressoney-St-Jean**, 5km down the valley, is larger and more attractive, while the outpost of **Stafal**, a modern hamlet above Gressoney-la-Trinité, tries to make up in convenience what it lacks in soul.

- ✔ Excellent off-piste (Alagna)
- ✔ Strong regional identity
- ✔ Rustic charm
- ✔ High-quality local cuisine
- ✔ No crowds or queues
- ✔ Low prices
- ✗ Shortage of non-skiing activities
- ✗ Limited nightlife
- ✗ Shortage of English-speaking ski school instructors

Given its remote location, Alagna is built on a puzzlingly large scale, with decaying buildings surrounding a church where bell-ringing rules. This is a genuine oddball of a place, which has unique wooden houses with built-in hay frames, and a charm all of its own. However, to the chagrin of powder purists who saw it as one of the last secret playgrounds of the Alps, Alagna has been transformed by major new lifts that give it a far wider appeal. A smart, new, two-stage cable-car now takes you up to Punta Indren at 3,260m and the start of a new summer ski area. Initially it will be open during June and July. This period may be extended, although much depends on demand and snow conditions. The hopeless regional piste map resembles 'the footwork of a drunken spider'. On-piste signposts are plentiful and accurate.

On the snow
top 3,370m (11,056ft) bottom 1,200m (3,936ft)

The collection of slow chairs and ancient cable-cars is slowly being updated into a modern lift system, but main access lifts from Champoluc and the Gressoney valley are susceptible to wind closure. All pistes eventually lead to Stafal, which is the central link in the chain of 42 lifts. Head up in the cable-car and chair-lift to the west and you reach the Colle Bettaforca, the departure point for the descents to Champoluc. Take the two-stage gondola to the east and you come to the Passo del Salati, the start of the Alagna connection. Until now skiers have had to venture off-piste to reach Alagna, but work on a new red (intermediate) run started in summer 2001. With slopes on both sides of the valley, Gressoney has the lion's share of the skiing in an area that totals 180km of pistes.

There are two points of departure from Champoluc, one on the outskirts of the village and the other up the hill in **Frachey**, which provides much quicker access to the main area. Three small satellite areas – **Antagnod**, **Brusson** and Gressoney-St-Jean – are not connected to the central system.

WHAT'S NEW

Major new lifts in Alagna
Summer skiing
Piste from Passo del Salati to Alagna ski area
Baby Snowpark in Gressoney-La-Trinité

Beginners
The best place to learn is the sunny nursery slope at Crest, at the top of the first stage of the Champoluc gondola. In Gressoney, beginners congregate around the Punta Jolanda lift, then progress via the 70-person cable-car to the wide plateau above Stafal on the Bettaforca side. Champoluc boasts its own sunny beginner area reached by gondola from the village centre.

Intermediates
Both Gressoney and Champoluc offer plenty of interlinked intermediate cruising, rather more in fact than the piste map suggests; it is so badly printed that most of the blue (easy) runs appear to be black (difficult). Stadio dello Slalom above Champoluc is a challenging red used for local races. One reporter described the home run to Champoluc as 'one of the best-maintained runs I have ever seen'.

Advanced
The best black piste in the area is the 7-km descent from the top of the Punta Indren in Alagna, but even this would not be so severely rated in other resorts. The same could be said of the only mogul field, which is at Sarezza in Champoluc. Diretta Stafal is an exhilarating black run in the Gressoney valley.

Off-piste

In the right conditions, all three resorts present challenges that are made all the more testing by bumpy terrain and narrow defiles between rock walls. The Mos and the Bettolina in Gressoney are excellent examples of this and they should not be attempted without a guide. The same is true of most of the skiing in Alagna, where the new cable-car should provide speedy access to huge snowfields that – inevitably in a predominantly south- and west-facing resort – are prone to avalanche.

The north-facing slopes in the Alta Valsesia National Park give a sense of extreme adventure, especially when accessed by the couloir at the top of the Malfatta. Alternatively, there is extensive heli-skiing, with glacier drops at over 4,000m in the Monterosa range.

Snowboarding

Monterosa Ski provide no special facilities for snowboarders, although the absence of drag-lifts is a bonus point. The off-piste challenge of the Alagna sector makes it extremely popular among the international hardcore of committed freeriders who might otherwise be found on the Grands Montets in **Chamonix**.

Tuition and guiding

In Gressoney, only five out of 30 ski instructors speak English, so you should request one of them when booking lessons in advance. The situation in Champoluc is similar ('delightful chap, enjoyed myself a lot, but didn't learn much because of his limited English'). Qualified alpine guides are available through the respective tourist information offices, but again language can be a problem. Champoluc, Gressoney and Alagna all have mountain guiding associations.

Mountain restaurants

One reporter complained that 'some of the larger places were very functional and the service very slow indeed'. Bedemie, on the route down to Gressoney from Gabiet, has 'a beautiful terrace and nourishing soup', while Albergho del Ponte above Gabiet is praised for its cheap and superlative spaghetti carbonara. Rifugio Guglielmina, reached by a short off-piste route from Passo del Salati, is recommended for both its food and the view, and Bettaforca has 'the biggest and best mixed grill in the business'. La Baita Refuge offers superb mushroom pasta and friendly service.

Accommodation

In Champoluc the Hotel Castor (☎ 0125 307117) is described by one reporter as 'an absolute gem, Italian-owned but managed by an Englishman who has married into the family'. The three-star Ayas (☎ 0125 308128) and Hotel de Champoluc (☎ 0125 308088) are also recommended. The two-star Favre (☎ 0125 307131) is small, well-managed and friendly, while the four-star Monboso (☎ 0125 366302) at Stafal is under new management and 'of an excellent standard'. Hotel Lo Scoiàttolo (☎ 0125 366313) in Gressoney-La-Trinité is equally comfortable but with a better ambience. In the same resort, Hotel Residence (☎ 0125 366148) remains popular with reporters: 'the rooms were comfortable, the food good, the staff helpful and the wine was reasonably priced'. In Gressoney-St-Jean, Hotel Stadel (☎ 0125 355264) is 'very friendly, but English hardly spoken', while in Alagna the Hotel Mirella (☎ 0163 922965), a B&B with rooms over a cake shop, is 'a must if you can get in'; if not, try the Genzianella (☎ 0165 922915) or the much smarter Cristallo (☎ 0163 91285).

Eating in and out
Le Sapin in Champoluc looks unpromising but serves 'acceptable food at reasonable prices'. Lo Bistrot is 'very friendly and welcoming', and the Favre remains consistently good, with a bias towards gargantuan feasts of local game. Cuisine at the Villa Anna Maria was described as 'variable, but the restaurant has an honest wine list', while Le Petit Coq and La Grange at Frachey are recommended, too. Capanna Carla in Gressoney-La-Trinité provides typical local cuisine at reasonable prices. In Alagna, Fum Diss offers 'superb game and polenta', and Ristorante Unione Alagnese is 'not to be missed'.

Après-ski
This is the kind of area where the nightlife is described by tour operators as 'informal and relaxed' – often a euphemism for dead in the winter. What there is takes place in the bars of family hotels, where locals and tourists drink and play cards. The Champoluc disco scene centres on the Gram Parsons in Frachey, while Gressoney-St-Jean offers Il Futuro. Gamblers with their own transport can visit the casino in St-Vincent (25km from Champoluc, 70km from Gressoney). The relaxed nightlife in Gressoney-La-Trinité consists of cafés such as the Hirsch Stube and the Petit Bar. The Wanderbar in Stafal catches the crowds as they leave the slopes. Other activities include squash and skating.

Childcare
Daycare in the area is extremely limited, with no crèche or kindergarten facilities in Champoluc apart from the Hotel Castor, while the ski school at Champoluc takes children from five years old. Hotel Monboso, above Gressoney at Stafal, offers a mini-club for residents' children aged four to eight years. In Gressoney, those over six years old must join the adult classes, yet children under eight years ski free. Antagnod has its Baby Snowpark with a magic carpet and Gressoney-La-Trinité plans a similar one for 2001–2.

TOURIST INFORMATION
Tel 39 0125 303111
Fax 39 0125 303145
Email kikesly@tin.it
Web site www.monterosa-ski.com

Sella Ronda

ALTITUDE 1,440–1,563m (4,724–5,128ft)

Beginners ✱✱✱ Intermediates ✱✱✱ Advanced ✱✱ Snowboarders ✱✱

The Dolomites are home to the largest and most beautiful ski area in the world – 200km of pistes served by 460 lifts in one region. Others try to compete but nowhere else actually succeeds. Similarly, the backdrop of craggy peaks and dramatic cliff faces, which take on a distinctive and glorious shade of rose-pink in the light of the setting sun, is without parallel. By no means all the area's runs and resorts are linked by lift, yet all are included in the Dolomiti Superski lift pass, which at around £100 represents the best-value lift pass in the northern hemisphere. The pass is now hands-free throughout the region. At the core of this region lies the Sella Ronda, a celebrated circuit of four valleys involving 90 minutes of lifts, 120 minutes of downhill skiing and an always undetermined joker factor of queuing time. It can be skied in both directions, but clockwise involves less poling and skating. Miss the crucial lift home because of deteriorating weather or volume of people and you are in for an expensive taxi ride. Reporters praised the piste marking: 'signposting was excellent, easy to follow – even in the more populated areas'.

✔ Outstanding scenery
✔ Range of mountain restaurants
✔ Extensive ski-touring
✔ Good children's facilities (Selva)
✔ Excellent-value lift pass
✘ Unreliable snow record
✘ Lack of skiing convenience
✘ High-season lift queues
✘ Heavy traffic (Canazei)

Much has been done in recent years to improve the antiquated lifts that once blighted the Sella Ronda, but, despite continuing innovations, queues can still become chronic at high-season weekends and during the Italian school holidays ('it was the first time we have ever seen staff specifically employed to pack people into gondolas – we thought only the Tokyo underground needed these'). Skiers and snowboarders are strongly advised to stray from the actual circuit, which anyway is less than enchanting, and explore and enjoy individual valleys for their own merits.

The best-known, but by no means the most important, of these valleys is **Val Gardena**. **Selva Gardena**, or **Wolkenstein** as it is also known in this bilingual border area of Italy, is the actual name of the resort. It is an unassuming village, which sprawls in suburban style up the Val Gardena. The village maintains a quiet, unsophisticated charm, which makes it popular with families. Examples of the local woodcarving industry colourfully adorn houses and even lamp-posts.

The second most popular resort is **Canazei**, a large, attractive and lively village on a busy main road in the Italian-speaking Val di Fassa. It is the best place to stay for those in search of non-skiing activities and a lively nightlife. The village itself is a tangle of narrow streets with a mixture of old farm buildings, new hotels and some delightful shops. Such is the scramble for beds in the Val di Fassa that tour operators offer hotels in outlying villages as far away as **Pera**, **Pozza di Fassa**, **Vigo di Fassa** and even distant **Moena**.

On the periphery of the Sella Ronda circuit lies a whole range of resorts, from established international ski towns such as chic **Cortina d'Ampezzo** to sleepy and essentially Italian villages such as **San Martino di Castrozza**. You cannot hope to ski the whole area in a week, or even in a season.

Vastly improved services to the upgraded airports at Venice and Verona, coupled with two-and-a-half-hour motorway transfers to most Dolomite resorts, have re-opened this unspoilt corner of the European ski map. The layout of the Sella Ronda and the whole Dolomiti Superski region is not as confusing as it sounds, and you will soon get your bearings. The lift map has been greatly improved, although annoyingly you need to obtain separate detailed maps for each sector. You can also invest in the Ordnance Survey-style map of the region, called *Sellaronda e Valli Ladine Carta Sciistica*, which can be bought at any newsagent in the resorts. It shows all the lifts and gives fairly accurate colour gradings.

On the snow
top 2,950m (9,676ft) bottom 1,225m (4,018ft)

With its mainly blue (easy) and unproblematic red (intermediate) runs, the Sella Ronda is better for seeing some wonderful scenery than for really challenging skiing or snowboarding. Although the peaks of these mountains are high, virtually all the skiing takes place lower down; this is the main cause of the Dolomites' variable snow records. Cover in recent seasons has been particularly erratic at these low altitudes, with links on south-facing slopes liable to closure even in February. This climatic handicap has been partially offset by heavy investment in modern snowmaking techniques. However, you can't make snow without low temperatures. One reporter recounted having to remove her skis and walk certain sections of the circuit during a mild spell, and indeed short walks between lifts are not uncommon, even when conditions are good.

The Sella Ronda can be skied with all kinds of variations. Clockwise mountain access from Selva Gardena is via the Dantercëpies gondola to the start of a long and mainly red cruise through 730m vertical all the way to **Colfosco**. From here a chair-lift takes you to **Corvara**, and a 12-person gondola brings you to Boè and the Crep de Munt for a short red run down to **Campolongo**. You can take a drag-lift up to the Rifugio Bec de Roces, which is the start of a pleasant red and blue run with dramatic backdrops down into **Arabba**. New lifts here have greatly reduced queues. The cable-car to Belvedere involves more skiing and a

much more challenging piste that allows you to rejoin the blue route before Pont de Vauz. Two more chairs brings you up to Sas Becè and the red run down to Lupo Bianco. Take a short red off the circuit into Canazei or continue via a gondola up to Col Salei. From here, a short red and a long blue cruise through 700m vertical return skiers and riders to Selva Gardena.

Beginners
The best of the novice skiing is found in the Alta Badia sector, bordered by **Armentarola** in the east, Corvara in the west and **La Villa** in the north. The wooded meadows here are reminiscent of the Austrian Tyrol. At the other end of the circuit, try the long blue that starts above the Passo Sella at 2,400m and takes you gently all the way down to Selva at 1,563m.

Intermediates
The whole of the Sella Ronda is ideally suited to cruisers who really want to put some mileage beneath their skis each day in this outstanding setting. Where to base yourself is a matter of personal choice. The Selva Gardena–Canazei end of the circuit has some of the better long runs, though fans of Corvara and Colfosco would strongly disagree. The favourite run among reporters is the Armentarola piste from Lagazuoi. Another enjoyable area is Mont de Seura: 'tricky but interesting red runs across the top of the mountain with lovely views'. One experienced reporter commented that the red run from Seceda to Cucxa Cucastel 'is not recommended for anyone with vertigo due to the massive cliff over the barrier'.

Advanced
Arabba is the Argentière of Italy and the place in which to base yourself for the toughest skiing in the area. Anyone who imagines that the Dolomites consist solely of scenic blue cruising runs is in for a wicked shock. From the edge of the village a two-stage jumbo gondola and a cable-car take you up nearly 900m over the granite cliffs off the Soura Sass to the start of what is, by any standard, some serious advanced skiing. The black (difficult) runs down the steep front face are testing in the extreme.

Alternatively, from the halfway stage of the gondola you can ski off the Sella Ronda on a wonderful 20-km journey down usually deserted pistes to the town of **Malga Ciapela**. From here you pay a daily L50,000 or six-day L200,000 supplement to your lift pass for the three cable-cars ('clearly ancient and one wonders about safety') to near the top of the 3,342-m Marmolada revered by mountaineers in the same breath as the Matterhorn, the Eiger and Mont Blanc; the lifts open only in February. At the top of the second lift, the World War I museum depicting the deeds of the Alpine Brigade is worth a visit. From the summit, a long red run takes you to within a couple of slow lifts of the home run back down to Arabba.

Off-piste
Passo Pordoi, between Arabba and Canazei, is the base-station of the Sass Pordoi cable-car, which takes you up to the Rifugio Maria at 2,950m. Piste-grooming machines have never made it up here, and all the skiing is as nature intended. The long run down the Val de Mezdi is one of the most taxing in the Dolomites and should not be attempted without the services of a guide. The front face of Sass Pordoi is a shorter, difficult challenge, with a steep and usually icy entrance guaranteed to get anyone's adrenaline pumping; falling is not advised. Powderhounds can also enjoy moderately priced heli-skiing off the Marmolada peak.

Snowboarding
Riders of all standards from beginner to expert are well catered for here, with gentle runs as well as half-pipes in the Colfosco, Plan de Gralba-Piz Sella, Belvedere, Pordoi and Seceda areas. Passo Pordoi has the best freeriding terrain in the area and a terrain park (not open early season). However, the number of difficult drag-lifts and long, flat pistes, such as the blue run from Passo Pordoi towards Arabba, may deter some riders.

Cross-country
For cross-country enthusiasts, the Dolomiti Superski area claims a mighty 1,033km of prepared loipe scattered throughout the region; some of the most scenic (98km) trails are situated in Selva Gardena. However, one reporter suggested: 'the only places to base yourself are Selva and Corvara, and a car is essential'.

Tuition and guiding
The Selva Gardena Ski School continues to generate first-rate reports, and tuition appears to be of a high standard: 'good teaching and no silly end-of-week races'. Reporters noted that the standard of English spoken by instructors throughout the Sella Ronda appears to have improved dramatically in recent years. The other ski schools in Val Gardena are Ski School 2000, Dolomiti Ski Eagles, Saslong and the two Italian ski schools at **Santa Cristina** and **Ortisei**. The Canazei Marmolada Ski School offers tuition in alpine skiing, cross-country, extreme skiing/boarding, race-training, skiing for the disabled, snow-boarding, and telemark. Its ski classes now receive more favourable reports, although 'organisation during the main holiday weeks seems to be somewhat chaotic'.

Mountain restaurants
The Dolomites abound with mountain eateries, with much the best to be found in the Italian- rather than the German-speaking sectors. Rifugio Lagazuoi is singled out as 'spectacular value with amazing views', and Rifugio Pralongia is praised for 'well-prepared meals at nice prices'. Rifugio Porta Vescovo is 'modern, clean, bright and has

excellent food', while Villa Frainela at Dantercëpies serves 'home-made *strudel* and traditional cakes that are to die for'.

Pizzeria El Table in Arabba comes strongly recommended, while Rifugio Bec de Roces, reached by a chair-lift from Arabba, offers a self-service downstairs and a waiter-service restaurant upstairs ('fantastic views and the most amazing lunch'). Plan Boè above the village is popular for traditional Austro-Italian fare, and Trapper's Bar, on the Passo Campolongo between Corvara and Arabba, has a sun terrace and live music. Forcelles above Colfosco is warmly praised. Rifugio Crep de Munt, above Corvara, also has a terrace and a warm welcome. Try Mesules – its position on the edge of the road and the piste between Selva and Colfosco means it can be reached by skiers and non-skiers alike. Panorama (on the Selva side of the Dantercëpies piste) is 'a real sun-trap with good food'.

Rifugio Scotoni is a welcome wayside warming hut on the run down from Lagazuoi if you are unable to make it to the even cosier Alpina, 2km further on. Either way, you may need some refreshment before the next lift, which is one of the quaintest in the region – a horse-drawn tow (L3,000 supplement).

A more gastronomic lunch can be found at the Hotel Grand Angel on the edge of the Armentarola cross-country track. Baita del Gigio, on the nursery slopes above Malga Ciapela, is worth the long run down and is exceptionally good value. Chez Anna, on the run from Seceda to Ortisei, is said to be worth a visit for spectacular ham-and-eggs, while Baita Fredarola, near Belvedere, is recommended for its pizzas. Way off the beaten track is the Ospizio di Santa Croce, reached by a ski bus from La Villa to **Pedraces** and two lifts up to the Abbey of the Holy Cross. Ristorante Lé, at the top of the chair, is renowned for the best *Gulaschsuppe* in the Sud Tyrol.

Accommodation

In Selva Gardena, Sporthotel Gran Baita (☎ 0471 795210) is the pick of a dozen four-stars, together with the Aaritz (☎ 0471 795011) and the Alpenroyal (☎ 0471 795178). The centrally situated Hotel Antares (☎ 0471 795400) is also praised. The three-star Hotel Laurin (☎ 0471 795105) is a favourite among visitors and renowned for its food. We have good reports, too, of the Hotel Solaia (☎ 0471 795104). The Rodella (☎ 0471 794553) is 'family-run and beautifully clean with a lovely atmosphere', while the Stella (☎ 0471 795162) is 'simple, inexpensive and thoroughly recommended'. The more spacious Savoy (☎ 0471 795343) is praised for its restaurant. Hotel Continental (☎ 0471 795411) is well located for skiers beneath the Dantercëpies gondola, but 'non-skiers should note that the ten-minute walk into town can be steep and icy'.

In Canazei, the four-star Astoria (☎ 0462 601302) and La Perla (☎ 0462 602453) are the most luxurious hotels in town. The Croce Bianca (☎ 0462 601111), with hand-painted pine furniture in abundance, is also warmly recommended. The Dolomiti (☎ 0462 601106) is built in grand hotel style, while Hotel Bellevue (☎ 0462 601104) is well placed for the skiing, which is inconvenient from many of the village hotels. One reporter lauded the Stella Alpina (☎ 0462 601127) ('good value B&B with friendly service').

Eating in and out

In Selva Gardena, reporters said one of the best restaurants is Pizzeria Rino, while the Laurinkeller remains famed for its steaks and spareribs. Pizzeria Miravalle is praised for 'its high standard of cuisine with an excellent, varied menu'. Other eateries include Armin's Grillstube, Scoiàttolo, Frëina and the restaurant in the Sporthotel Gran Baita. In Santa Cristina, Plaza and Iman are recommended along with Uridl for authentic local dishes.

Canazei boasts many modestly priced restaurants: Rosticceria Meleser is particularly singled out for praise ('you must book at weekends'), as is La Stua dei Ladinos. Rosengarten provides 'simple décor, but good food'. The Italia is popular with the locals and puts on live music. Try Al Vecchio Mulino for local Italian dishes, while the Dolomiti is said to be 'pretentious and overpriced'.

Après-ski

At first sight, Selva Gardena does not appear to have much of a nightlife. Half-a-dozen cafés serve home-made cakes and pastries, but the resort is quiet in the evening, with few lights, seemingly little activity and none of the buzz of a serious party resort. In fact, behind the shutters is a thriving après-ski scene and a wide choice of nightspots, but light sleepers are unlikely to have their slumber disturbed. The Luislkeller is the most popular haunt, along with Goalie's Pub, the Laurinkeller and La Bula. Bar La Stua has twice-weekly folk-music evenings, and the Speckkeller can also be lively, as can Bar 200, Crazy Pub and Tubla in Santa Cristina. Principal discos are the Dali and the Heustadl in Selva.

In Canazei, The Montanara Bar is the place to meet for après-ski, as is the Frog's Pub, a few kilometres up the valley road in Alba. Peter's Bar by the Belvedere gondola is busy immediately after skiing, while popular nightspots include the Husky Pub, La Teneta and El Binocol.

Childcare

A major plus point of the region is that children aged seven years and under ski free. The Selva nursery slopes are based below the Dantercëpies gondola at the northern edge of the village. In the kindergarten at the bottom of the Biancaneve drag-lift, toddlers and small children are taught the rudiments of skiing among cartoon characters. Instructors are plentiful and patient, and there seems to be none of the 'here is an entire generation to be put off skiing' attitude that you encounter in some French resorts. The surrounding area is ideal for older children to learn or improve their skiing or snowboarding.

In Canazei, the Kinderland crèche and kindergarten, run by the Canazei Marmolada ski school, caters for children all day with a mixture of daycare and lessons for older children.

TOURIST INFORMATION
Canazei
Tel 39 0462 602466
Fax 39 0462 602278
Email info@fassa.com
Web site www.fassa.com

Linked or nearby resorts

Arabba
top 2,950m (9,676ft) bottom 1,600m (3,808ft)

This small, unspoilt village with only 2,000 beds is tucked away in a fold of the landscape and is surrounded by the most challenging skiing in the area. The village itself is hopeless for non-skiers. We have received positive reports of the ski school: 'expert, informative tuition delivered in good English with a smile and a true sense of fun'. However, the nursery slope suffers from through-traffic, and the resort is not recommended for complete beginners. The crèche and ski kindergarten look after children aged two years and over on weekdays from 9am to 4.30pm. The principal language here is Italian, although Arabba is only a couple of kilometres south of the Sud-Tyrol border.

The Grifone (☎ 0436 780034) is a modern five-star hotel with an first-rate reputation but it is outside the village in an isolated position up a steep road. The Sporthotel Arabba (☎ 0436 79321) is another smart hotel, yet the three-star Portavescovo (☎ 0436 79139), which has a pool and fitness centre ('lovely hotel – highly recommended'), is more lively and houses the Stübe Bar. Restaurant El Table 'has very tasty pizzas and pleasant atmosphere'. The nightlife is also centred on Peter's Bar ('try their lemon ice-cream') and the Sporthotel Bar. There is a disco, 'but this is not the place for those who like to party until dawn'. The Rue de Mans is an excellent restaurant just outside the village, which offers two supermarkets, a gift shop and a chemist. Public transport is limited to one daily bus to Corvara, and a hire car is strongly recommended for visiting nearby resorts.

TOURIST INFORMATION
Tel 39 0436 79130
Fax 39 0436 79300
Email infoarabba@apt-dolomiti-cortina.it
Web site www.apt-dolomiti-cortina.it

Campitello
top 2,950m (9,676ft) bottom 1,440m (4,723ft)

A small collection of old buildings make up this quiet village set beside a stream, well back from the main road. The Col Rodella cable-car (45-minute queues reported) goes up to the ski area, and there is no piste back down again. The village is ideal for complete beginners as some of the area's best nursery slopes are right on its doorstep. Hotels include the four-star Diamant Park (☎ 0462 750440) and Gran Chalet Soreghes (☎ 0462 750060). The Park Hotel Fedora (☎ 0462 750505) is next to the lift station, while the Medil (☎ 0462 750088) is a modern hotel built in traditional style with the addition of a fitness centre and bar with music. Hotel Sella Ronda (☎ 0462 750525) is an alpine-style hotel owned by a priest, and Hotel Rubino Executive (☎ 0462 750225) offers a swimming-pool and piano bar among its many facilities.

TOURIST INFORMATION
Tel 39 0462 750500
Fax 39 0462 750219

Colfosco
top 2,950m (9,676ft) bottom 1,650m (5,412ft)

Colfosco has easy access to both Selva Gardena and Corvara's skiing, although the village also has a small ski area of its own with good nursery slopes. Recommended hotels are the Capella (☎ 0471 836183), Alta Badia (☎ 0471 836616) and the Kolfuschgerhof (☎ 0471 636188). Speckstube Peter, Mesoles, La Stria, Matthiaskeller and Tabladel are the most popular eating-places.

TOURIST INFORMATION
as Selva Gardena

Corvara
top 2,950m (9,676ft) bottom 1,550m (5,085ft)

This pleasant Sella Ronda resort fails to attract any British tour operators, yet it is strategically placed for some of the best skiing in the region. Planac Parkhotel (☎ 0471 836210) is a smart four-star, while Hotel Posta Zirm (☎ 0471 836175), the old post house at the bottom of the Col Alto chair-lift, boasts a strong international following. The building dates from 1808 and has been carefully renovated; the hotel also keeps alive the tradition of the tea-dance ('it's good fun – when did you last see a man in a purple and silver one-piece suit with the zip pulled halfway down to reveal a giant gold medallion as he grooved away to hits from the 1970s?'). Corvara provides plenty of easy runs for beginners, cross-country skiing and an outdoor skating-rink. The ski school includes a kindergarten for children from three years of age, but English is not widely spoken. One reporter warmly recommended the Raetia Café, on the main street, for its wide selection of teas.

Skiing facts: Selva Gardena

TOURIST INFORMATION
Str. Dursan 78/bis, I–39047 S. Cristina
Tel 39 0471 792277
Fax 39 0471 792235
Email info@val-gardena.com
Web site www.val-gardena.com

THE RESORT
By road Calais 1,226km
By rail bus service from Bressanone
35km, Bolzano 40km, Chiusa 27km
Airport transfer Munich and Milan
3–4hrs, Verona 2–3hrs,
Innsbruck 1½hrs
Visitor beds 18,000 in Val Gardena
Transport free ski bus between Ortisei
and Selva Gardena

THE SKIING
Linked or nearby resorts Arabba (I),
Armentarola (I), Campitello (I), Canazei
(I), Colfosco (I), Cortina d'Ampezzo (I),
Corvara (I), La Villa (I), Ortisei (I),
Pedraces (I), San Cassiano (I), Santa
Cristina (I)
Number of lifts 81 in Val Gardena, 460
in region
Total of trails/pistes 175km in Val
Gardena/Alpe di Siusi, 1,200km in region
(30% easy, 60% intermediate,
10% difficult)
Beginners 15 lifts, points tickets
available

LIFT PASSES
Area pass Dolomiti Superski (covers 460
lifts) L289,000–327,000 for 6 days
Pensioners 15% discount for

60yrs and over
Credit cards yes

TUITION
Skiing Selva Gardena Ski School
(☎ 0471 795156), Snowboard and Ski
School 2000 (☎ 0471 773125), Dolomiti
Ski Eagles (Ski Academy) (☎ 0471
773182), Santa Cristina (☎ 0471
792045), Ortisei (☎ 0471 796153),
Saslong (☎ 0471 786248)
Snowboarding as ski schools
Other courses cross-country, extreme
skiing/boarding, race-training, telemark
Guiding Val Gardena Guides (☎ 0471
794133), Catores Alpine School
(☎ 0471 798223)

CHILDREN
Lift pass Val Gardena only
L201,000–229,000, Dolomiti Superski
free for 7yrs and under
Ski & board school as adults
Kindergarten (ski/non-ski)
Selva Gardena (☎ 0471 795156),
S. Cristina (☎ 0471 792045),
Ortisei (☎ 0471 796153)

OTHER SPORTS
Ice-climbing, indoor climbing wall, indoor
tennis, parapente, skating, squash,
swimming, tobogganing

FOOD AND DRINK
Coffee L1,800-3,000, glass of wine
L3,000–4,000, small beer L3,500,
soft drink L3,500,
dish of the day L18,000–30,000

TOURIST INFORMATION
as Selva Gardena

San Cassiano
top 2,950m (9,676ft) bottom 1,537m (5,041ft)

A small, roadside village with mainly new Dolomite-style buildings, San Cassiano has some good skiing and snowboarding for beginners and early intermediates who want to avoid challenges. Long, easy runs go down to the village from Pralongia and Piz Sorega. Reporters mentioned the lack of spoken English in the resort, which attracts mainly wealthy Italians. The downside of this is being the sole English speaker in a ski class where lessons become 'laborious, with everything spoken in German and Italian'.

The Rosa Alpina (☎ 0471 849500) is a large and comfortable hotel in the village centre and, with a live band, is also the focal point for nightlife. The Ski Bar is recommended for tasty, cheap pizzas, and the Capanna Alpina, Saré and Tirol are all busy restaurants. La Siriola, Rosa Alpina, Fanes and the restaurant in Hotel Diamant are more expensive. There is bowling at the Diamant, but otherwise the village tends to be on the quiet side. **Armentarola**, with its own hotels and restaurants, is a kilometre away.

TOURIST INFORMATION
as Selva Gardena

La Thuile and La Rosière

ALTITUDE La Thuile 1,441m (4,728ft), La Rosière 1,850m (6,070ft)

Beginners ✳✳✳ Intermediates ✳✳✳ Advanced ✳ Snowboarders ✳

The overriding attraction of this extensive but gentle ski area, which stretches in an uneasy *entente cordiale* across the Italian–French border on both sides of the Petit-St-Bernard, is the lack of crowds on its pistes – even at New Year. In winter 2000–1 the Italian side was blessed with more snow than almost any other ski resort in Europe ('quite extraordinarily deep – in sharp contrast to conditions in resorts just a few miles away as the crow flies'). On the French side skiers tend to drive on up the Tarentaise past the turn-off at **Bourg-St-Maurice** to the more sophisticated charms of L'Espace Killy (**Val d'Isère** and **Tignes**), while remote road access in the Aosta Valley keeps the Italians in **Courmayeur**.

La Thuile is an old mining town clawing its way back to tourist-led prosperity, while La Rosière is a third-generation purpose-built resort content to rely on the rustic charm of its 1970s' chalet-style architecture and the popularity of its low prices. Development at La Rosière on the French side in recent years has been restricted to a single high-speed quad and one large block of apartments; this is a source of much irritation to its go-ahead Italian neighbour.

> **LA THUILE**
> ✔ Lack of crowds
> ✔ Off-piste opportunities
> ✔ Choice of restaurants
> ✘ Little resort atmosphere
> ✘ Limited nightlife
> ✘ Few mountain restaurants
> ✘ Lack of childcare facilities

In summer the resorts are joined by road over the Col du Petit-St-Bernard Pass; in winter the car journey from Geneva via either the Mont Blanc Tunnel (which will we hope be open for the 2001–2 season) or from Turin takes less than two hours. The alternative is to drive from Geneva via the Grand-St-Bernard Tunnel, which doubles the journey time. It is widely held that Hannibal led 30,000 men, 8,000 horses and his 30 elephants over the pass in the course of his epic journey from Spain to Rome in 218BC. Under continuous attack from a murderous army of local Celts, who rained down rocks upon his column from every vantage point, it took him 15 days to cross from Bourg-St-Maurice.

The heart of La Thuile is the Planibel, an integrated tourist unit with a hotel, apartments, a sports complex and a selection of shops and bars. The shops major on ski clothing and equipment, with no thought for the chic boutique factor that dominates in neighbouring Courmayeur. The efficient, but discouragingly clinical, complex contrasts sharply with the rest of the resort, which sprawls haphazardly through the surrounding pine forests.

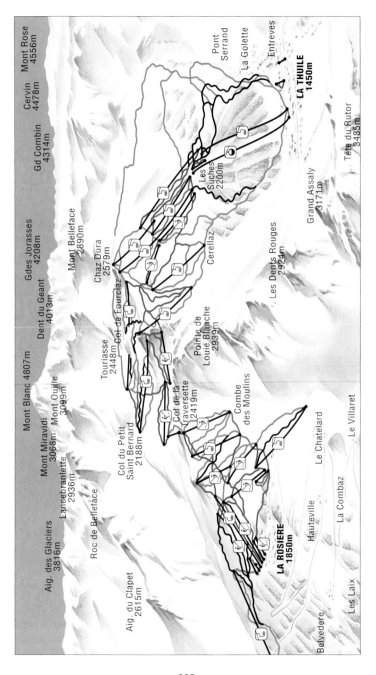

La Rosière is situated at 1,850m on the French side of the col named after St Bernard of Clairvaux, patron saint of the Alps. The original hamlet was the home of Jean Arpin, one of France's first ski instructors, who earned his bronze badge in 1939 at the age of 18 shortly before he and the other inhabitants of the hamlet were forced to evacuate their houses at an hour's notice as Mussolini invaded over the pass.

> **LA ROSIÈRE**
> ✔ Ski-in ski-out convenience
> ✔ Facilities for children
> ✗ Unsuitable for non-skiers
> ✗ Limited nightlife
> ✗ Disappointing mountain restaurants

After World War II Arpin set about developing La Rosière as a ski resort, but the first drag-lifts were not built until 1961. The ski area was linked to that of La Thuile on the far side of the *col* in 1984. The village has slowly developed along the bends of the mountain road from Seez to the Petit-St-Bernard Pass. The result is an attractive, neo-Savoyard tiered village with low-rise accommodation built from wood and local, roughly hewn stone. In winter, the road ends in a bank of snow outside the Relais du Petit-St-Bernard hotel. Just beyond the hotel lie the kennels of the St Bernard dogs, which on and off have maintained a presence here as rescuers of snowbound travellers since the seventeenth century. The brandy-bearers are always willing to pose for snaps in exchange for scraps.

The lift pass includes a day-out in **Les Arcs**, easily reached by funicular from Bourg-St-Maurice, and in **Sainte-Foy**, the best-kept secret of the Tarentaise, as well as in **Pila** and Courmayeur in the Aosta Valley.

On the snow
top 2,641m (8,665ft) bottom 1,176m (3,858ft)

Both La Thuile and La Rosière have wide open slopes well suited to beginners and intermediates. In La Thuile these are supplemented by much tougher runs through the steeply wooded area just above the resort. In La Rosière, because of the greater height of the base, the slopes are predominantly above the tree-line. The highest point in the linked area is Bélvèdere, where lifts are often closed due to high winds.

La Thuile's main slopes face east, with a steeper north-facing area going down to the Petit-St-Bernard Pass. By taking the long, loopy alternative routes, it is possible for novices to cover the whole area. Most of the skiing in La Rosière faces south; these slopes are generally easier, with gentle blue (easy) pistes above the resort giving way to red (intermediate) ones on the higher part of the Col de la Traversette. As a result of being on different sides of an alpine divide, each resort has its own micro-climate; this often means that one is shrouded in cloud while the other is bathed in sunshine. By checking at the respective base-stations before deciding where to go, it may be possible to turn an unpromising day into a brilliant one. However, the infamous *Vent du St Bernard*, a wind which cuts through even the most technical ski clothing –

especially on the long slow Belvédère lift on the Italian side – must be endured throughout the winter.

Beginners

Although there is a small nursery slope at resort level, the steepness of the lower mountain at La Thuile means that beginners soon take Les Suches gondola to the green (beginner) pistes served by La Combe lift. In La Rosière, there are several short nursery slopes near the resort, with more at the altiport nearby. Two of the beginner lifts are free. Adventurous learners will soon move up the mountain to Les Eucherts, La Poletta and Roches Noires lifts, which serve a network of blue runs.

Intermediates

The linked area's 140km of undulating blue and red pistes provide plenty of scope for the average motorway cruiser. La Thuile offers a long run around the edges of the ski area from Chaz Dura and Belvédère, augmented by more aggressive terrain towards the road of the Petit-St-Bernard (a piste in winter), which usually holds the best snow. The main link with La Rosière has a tricky start, but the runs below the Col de la Traversette are mainly short reds with plenty of blue alternatives on the way down to lunch.

Advanced

The most testing black (difficult) runs are in the Touriasse sector from Belvédère or Chaz Dura to the Petit-St-Bernard Pass, between the San Bernardo and Fourclaz chair-lifts. In bad light, the Europa World Cup track through the woods from Les Suches to Golette is more user-friendly. The Ecureuil and Eterlou runs down to Les Ecudets below La Rosière's five black runs do not deserve their gradings, although their severity is frequently increased by indifferent snow conditions.

Off-piste

First-time visitors to the resort will be surprised by the variety and quality of La Thuile's off-piste possibilities. Wannabee powderhounds will find the regular pitch they need to gain confidence on the ungroomed sections under the chairs, while experts will enjoy the chal-lenge of wooded, north-facing slopes between the pistes on the Touriasse. Better still is the heli-skiing, which begins at the top of the Ruitor Glacier (3,486m) on the Italian side, progresses through the glacial terrain, before ending in the village of **Miroir** (1,220m) over the border in France.

The 20-km run from the Ruitor Glacier to La Rosière is suitable for intermediates and upwards, but the descent to La Thuile is a real adven-ture, complete with a short rope section across an ice gully and a long walk at the bottom. Further extensive heli-skiing and heli-boarding options are available in **Valgrisenche**.

Snowboarding

La Rosière has a 500-m-long terrain park, while La Thuile boasts a terrain park and a good half-pipe, as well as the best slopes for freeriders. La Combe, an encouragingly wide, flat area above Les Suches, is ideal learner riding territory. The transition to blue runs is best made in the catchment area of the Chalet Express, a chair-lift that is particularly easy to get on and off; board cred requires regular visits to the lively La Clotze Bar at the bottom of it. The Shop Snow School is a new snowboard school in La Rosière.

Tuition and guiding

The choice lies between La Thuile Ski School, the French Ski School (ESF) in La Rosière and Evolution 2. The last receives favourable reports: 'a good mixture of encouragement and pushing'. We have conflicting reports of La Thuile's ski school: 'the instructor's English was excellent and the standard of tuition high' and 'our instructor's English was so limited she had problems understanding our questions'.

Mountain restaurants

La Thuile is the exception to the rule that skiers invariably eat well on Italian mountain tops. This is not so much a question of quality as of availability. Les Suches self-service is undeniably soulless ('a motorway-style cafeteria, but the food was not bad'), while Le Foyer, higher up on the same hill, offers substantial but unsophisticated fare; both restaurants are criticised by reporters for their 'hole-in-the-ground style loos; it is not easy to balance in ski boots'.

There are two fashionable Blues bars: the Roxi at the bottom of the Fourclaz chair and nautical Off Shore by the Belvédère chair. Both serve sandwiches and drinks to an aggressive backing track. The Bar du Lac at the bottom of the San Bernardo chair serves a simple selection of Italian dishes at lunch-time.

The on-mountain options in La Rosière are Plan Repos, an adequate but crowded self-service restaurant with a large and sunny terrace, La Traversette at the bottom of the Fort chair and L'Ancolie, a pleasant inn with home-made food above the cross-country track at the outlying hamlet of **Les Eucherts** (linked to La Rosière by a free bus service while the lifts are open).

Accommodation

The four-star Planibel Hotel (☎ 0165 884541) in La Thuile is the most convenient and luxurious place to stay. Reports are now more favourable: 'I disagree about the reception staff lacking warmth. The rooms are well appointed but I would suggest the corridors would benefit from redecorating'. At Chalet Alpina (☎ 0165 884187), a 500-m walk away across a stream, Eddy Nico (South African-born but of Italian descent) and his British wife, Debbie, extend a warm welcome to their clients, who return year after year.

Skiing facts: La Thuile

TOURIST INFORMATION
I–11016 La Thuile, Aosta
Tel 39 0165 885179
Fax 39 0165 885196
Email iat.lathuile@psw.it
Web site www.lathuile.net

THE RESORT
By road Calais 938km
By rail Pré-Saint-Didier 10km
Airport transfer Turin 3hrs
Visitor beds 2,400
Transport free bus service in the village

THE SKIING
Linked or nearby resorts La Rosière (I),
Courmayeur (n)
Number of lifts 16 in La Thuile, 35 in
linked area
Total of trails/pistes 100km La Thuile,
140km in linked area (44% easy,
36% intermediate, 20% difficult)
Beginners 2 lifts, one of them is free

LIFT PASSES
Area pass La Thuile/La Rosière
L234,000–260,000 for 6 days
Pensioners 65yrs and over

L180,000–202,000 for 6 days
Credit cards yes

TUITION
Skiing La Thuile Ski School
(☎ 0165 884123)
Snowboarding as ski school
Other courses cross-country,
heli-skiing/boarding, race-training,
telemark
Guiding Guide Alpine Ruitor La Thuile
(☎ as ski school)

CHILDREN
Lift pass L180,000–202,000 for six
days, free for 8yrs and under
Ski & board school as adults
Kindergarten (non-ski) Il Grande Albero
(☎ 0165 884986),
Miniclub La Thuile (☎ 0165 884541)

OTHER SPORTS
Horse-riding, squash, swimming

FOOD AND DRINK
Coffee L1,800, glass of wine L1,800,
small beer L3,500, soft drink L3,500,
dish of the day L25,000–40,000

The Entrèves (☎ 0165 884134) creates a cheerful family atmosphere, while the Planibel Apartments (☎ 0165 884541) enjoy the advantages of the hotel with none of the disadvantages.

In La Rosière, the emphasis is on self-catering apartments. Hotel accommodation is limited, but the Relais du Petit-St-Bernard (☎ 479 06 80 48) is ideally situated at the foot of the pistes. The family-run Hotel Le Solaret (☎ 479 06 80 47) is also recommended.

Eating in and out
Valdostana cuisine, with its emphasis on game, polenta and mushrooms, is well represented in La Thuile. Le Rascard specialises in guinea-fowl stuffed with green peppers and spinach, while the long-running La Bricole, a converted barn, is known for its chamois, polenta and extensive wine list.

Fish lovers can enjoy lake perch at La Fordze. La Spaghetteria serves food that is 'cheap and tasty', while Pizza al Taglio 'is great for take-aways'. For ice-cream lovers the Cremeria in the Planibel complex is 'unmissable'. In the old village, La Grotta features pizza.

Although La Rosière's has a total of eight eateries, off-slope life tends to focus around two restaurants: Le P'tit Relais, the most popular pizzeria-bar in town, and the one at the Relais du Petit-St-Bernard, which serves local specialities, pizza and crêpes. Favoured alternatives include La Pitchounette, L'Ancolie and Le Plein Soleil. However, gourmets should make the 7-km trek to La Chaumière, a converted Savoyard farmhouse, which is full of atmosphere, in the small village of **Mousselard**.

Après-ski

Given their attraction for families, it is hardly surprising that neither La Thuile nor La Rosière is known for its riotous nightlife. In La Thuile, Planibel's Rendez-vous bar is 'decidedly laddish, especially late at night when the karaoke gets going'. Le Rascard is where riders hang out. Bar La Buvette near the gondola station attracts the later afternoon crowds. La Bricole video-disco has a genuine pub atmosphere, which appeals to British visitors, as well as live music at weekends. Night owls go to the Fantasia disco. The piano bar in the Planibel attracts an older and more sedate crowd.

La Rosière's entertainment starts at Le P'tit Relais when the lifts close and continues at Arpin's Bar, which has karaoke, and La Terrasse du Yéti. The resort has one disco.

Childcare

Il Grande Albero is the crèche for small children up to three years old, and Miniclub La Thuile is a free non-skiing kindergarten for children from four years old. In La Rosière, Les Galopines nursery takes care of children from 12 months to three years old. The programme includes skiing, organised games and lunch. Club Loisirs is for non-skiers aged three to 12 years. The nursery prides itself on having English-, German- and Danish-speaking staff. The new Evolution 2 ski school at La Rosière receives praise: 'for the first time our children really enjoyed their lessons with an English-speaking instructor'. La Thuile has a free lift pass for children up to eight years old.

TOURIST INFORMATION
La Rosière
Tel 33 479 06 80 51
Fax 33 479 06 83 20
Email info@larosiere.net
Web site www.larosiere.net

Round-up

RESODS COVERED Cavalese, Macugnaga, Madesimo, Passo Tonale, Pila, San Martino di Castrozza, Val di Fassa

Cavalese
top 2,230m (7,316ft) bottom 980m (3,215ft)

Cavalese is the best-known resort of the **Val di Fiemme**, the collective name given to the 11 small towns and villages in the Trentino region in northern Italy to the south of the **Val di Fassa**. The other significant ski areas in the valley are **Latemar**, above the villages of **Pampeago** and **Predazzo**, and Bellamonte-Alpe Lusia above the village of **Bellamonte**. **Passo Rolle** and **Passo Lavazè** are two other small resorts farther along the valley. A sixth small area, **Ziano di Fiemme**, has night-skiing. The Fiemme-Obereggen area lift pass gives access to a total of 51 ski lifts serving 140km of groomed pistes. All the areas are linked by free shuttle bus.

As well as being the Val di Fiemme's principal town, Cavalese is also the resort base for **Alpe Cermis**, the area's main ski centre. This boasts 37 lifts of its own and is reached from the town by a cable-car giving magnificent views across the valley, with pistes for all standards of skier. The area has a total of seven ski and snowboard schools and two off-piste guiding companies. Courses include ski-jumping and race-training. Alpe Cermis, Bellamonte and Predazzo all have kindergartens.

Cavalese is the headquarters of Italian cross-country skiing and boasts 150km of trails. The Marcialonga di Fiemme e Fassa is a 75-km international cross-country marathon held every January. The race attracts more than 6,000 athletes and starts at **Moena** in the Val di Fassa and finishes at Cavalese.

Hotels in Cavalese include the Park Hotel Azalea (☎ 0462 340109) and the Bellavista (☎ 0462 340205), and there are restaurants to suit every budget. The region offers six ski schools and four kindergarten. Other activities available in the valley include dog-sledding, indoor tennis and ski-orienteering.

TOURIST INFORMATION
Tel 39 0462 241111
Fax 39 0462 241199
Email fiemme@dolomitisuperski.com
Web site www.dolomitisuperski.com

Macugnaga
top 2,984m (9,790ft) bottom 1,327m (4,353ft)

Macugnaga is made up of five villages: **Staffa**, **Pecetto**, **Isella**, **Borca** and **Pestarena**. They lie at the foot of the spectacular east face of the Monte Rosa, close to the Swiss border and two hours' drive from Turin.

Macugnaga's proximity to the border has resulted in a style of architecture more in keeping with Switzerland than with Italy.

Staffa and Pecetto have their own small ski areas, which are linked by ski bus. One reporter summed up the area as 'a marvellous introduction to skiing'. Reporters praised the 'short queues, if any at all; often you can finish your run and ski right back on to an empty chairlift'. Staffa provides better skiing for beginners ('only ten people on the nursery slopes at the very busiest'), a cable-car rising to the summit and a number of longer runs. We have encouraging reports of Scuola Sci Macugnaga: 'excellent value for money'. Off-piste enthusiasts can hire a local mountain guide to ski over the back of Monte Moro to **Saas-Fee** in Switzerland or book heli-skiing trips through Giana Helicopter.

The villages between them have 15 hotels, including Hotel Dufour (☎ 0324 65529) in Staffa's main square, which was said to be 'clean and friendly, with plentiful and delicious food'. Hotel Zumstein (☎ 0324 65490) is close to the resort centre and the cable-car. Also recommended is Hotel Girasole (☎ 0324 65052). Hotel Chez Felice (☎ 0324 65490) is an unassuming two-star. Restaurants include the Miramonti ('good lunchtime pizzas and great fondue nights') in Pecetto, the Glacier ('you must book at weekends') and Ghiacci del Rosa at the Mt Belvedere base. There are various other bars and restaurants and a few small shops, but on the whole the nightlife is limited. The Big Ben disco 'appears to be in a 1960s' time warp'. Skating and night-skiing are two of the other activities on offer, as well as a visit to the gold mines.

TOURIST INFORMATION
Tel 39 0324 65119
Fax 39 0324 65775
Email sviva@libero.it
Web site www.macugnaga-online.it

Madesimo
top 2,984m (9,790ft) bottom 1,530m (5,018ft)

This small, attractive resort, centred on an old church, is situated a two-hour drive north of Bergamo. It is right on the Swiss border and close enough for a shopping spree in **St Moritz**. The old village has narrow streets with a few shops and some old converted farmhouses, as well as some less pleasing concrete buildings.

The skiing is mostly intermediate and is concentrated on the usually uncrowded slopes of the 2,984-m Pizzo Groppera, with long runs leading down into the neighbouring Valle di Lei. The high altitude normally ensures reasonable snow conditions. Sixteen lifts serve 50km of mostly red (intermediate) pistes and some challenging black (difficult) trails, including the famous Canalone run. There are two terrain parks and a half-pipe. The nursery slopes are pleasant and served by a quad chairlift, and the Madesimo Ski School has a reputation for small classes ('excellent, with plenty of English-speaking instructors').

Hotels include the four-star Emet (☎ 0343 53395) and the family-run Andossi (☎ 0343 57000), which provides a fitness room and a lively bar. The Harlequin (☎ 0343 53005) has 'small rooms, but a brilliant location and delicious hot chocolate in the hotel bar'. Hotel Cascata e Crystal (☎ 0343 53108) offers excellent facilities including a swimming-pool, piano bar and a mini-club for four- to 12-year-olds. You can ski back to most of the accommodation.

TOURIST INFORMATION
Tel 39 0343 53015
Fax 39 0343 53782
Email infomad@madesimo.com
Web site www.madesimo.com

Passo Tonale
top 3,069m (10,069ft) bottom 1,883m (6,178ft)

Passo Tonale is one of a group of Italian resorts which, with the lure of good snow and low prices, are dramatically increasing in popularity. The resort is situated 100km from Bolzano and shares its skiing with the charming village of **Ponte di Legno**, 600m along the pass to the west. Together they offer 28 lifts and 70km of pistes.

Hotels hug the single roadway, but fortunately there is little through-traffic by night. You can walk across the village in ten minutes. The only bus runs seven times daily to Ponte di Legno. The clientèle is a combination of families, ski clubs and school groups, who all appreciate the easy, affordable skiing.

Passo Tonale is a resort with exceptional snow quality, ideal beginner and easy intermediate terrain, as well as extensive ski-touring and off-piste. As one reporter commented: 'of all the resorts we have visited this is probably one of the best for beginners, although high-altitude and exposed pistes can make it very cold'.

Mountain access is on either side of the main road, with most of the chair- and drag-lifts starting from the south-facing snowfields. The only cable-car is a 1-km walk west from the village; at the top is a chair-lift that leads to two drags on the Presena Glacier, which has summer skiing. Ponte di Legno is a separate sector, normally accessible on skis or by bus, with a handful of lifts starting at the edge of the forest. The Contrabbandieri and Valbiolo chair-lifts together serve a 4.5-km red run and access an ungroomed area. Night-skiing is now available.

Passo Tonale provides a choice of four schools. Instructors at both Tonale–Presena and Ponte di Legno–Tonale are described as 'unspoilt, simple and sympathetic'. We have also received a favourable report for the third school, Il Castellaccio. G & G is the specialist snowboard school. The Miniclub in the Hotel Miramonti cares for small non-skiers, while Fantaski is the ski kindergarten.

Negritella, up the mountain, serves 'very good local dishes in a friendly and efficient environment'. Passo Tonale boasts ten hotels including the attractive Orchidea (☎ 0364 903935), Hotel Redivalle

(☎ 0364 903814) and the historic Mirandola Hospice (☎ 0364 903933), where resident guests must rely on snowmobile transport, which is available until 2am. For fine dining, the snowmobile ride up to the hospice is mandatory. The two-star Biancaneve (☎ 0364 903997) serves good food. Sporthotel Vittoria (☎ 0364 91348) includes a pub with live music and is often used by school parties.

In town, intimate décor and delicious gorgonzola *Spätzle* are found at Il Focolare, while La Torretta is praised for 'the best thin, crispy-base pizza'. Palla di Neve and Antares are recommended for pasta. Bar Cady, Nico's and the UFO are popular bars, along with Pub Miramonti and Crazy Horse. El Bait is quiet and cosy, Antares features live music and Heaven is equally busy. Other sports include dog-sledding at the Tonale Pass.

TOURIST INFORMATION
Tel 39 0364 903838
Fax 39 0364 903896
Email tonale@valdisole.net
Web site www.valdisole.net

Pila
top 2,750m (9,022ft) bottom 1,750m (5,741ft)

Pila has undergone tremendous expansion in recent years and is now linked to the regional capital, **Aosta**, by an 18-minute gondola ride. It offers 70km of mainly intermediate trails served by 12 lifts, and five mountain restaurants are dotted around the slopes. Pila Ski and Snowboard School organises all-day tuition for adults and children, Nazca Snowboard Camp is the specialist boarders' school and heli-skiing is available through Coop Interguides. The area has a terrain park with a half-pipe. Biancaneve is the kindergarten for children from 18 months up to 12 years old, and the Wild Surf Pila ski kindergarten accepts children from three years of age. Hotels include the ski-in ski-out Etoile de Neige (☎ 0165 521541) and the Printemps (☎ 0165 521246), which runs a disco. Pila boasts ten restaurants as well as shops and cafés. Other activities include shopping trips to the ancient Roman town of Aosta.

TOURIST INFORMATION
Tel 39 0165 521148
Fax 39 0165 521437
Email info@pila.it
Web site www.pila.it

San Martino di Castrozza
top 2,385m (7,825ft) bottom 1,450m (4,757ft)

San Martino is on the eastern edge of the Trentino Dolomites, surrounded by wild forest with pink mountain peaks above. In 1700, the violin-maker Stradivari used to go into the same woods to select the spruce for his violins. Skiing started at San Martino di Castrozza in the early 1930s, and it has developed into three separate areas (two of which are linked) with 60km of piste and 26 lifts.

Nuova Scuola Nazionale di Sci accepts adults and children from five years old. Gruppo Guide Alpine and Aquile de San Martino will supply guides for the long off-piste descents of the Pale Highlands, and the Rosetta cable-car is open in February and March for ski-touring and snowshoeing expeditions. Accommodation includes four-star Hotel Savoia (☎ 0439 68094) and the three-star Hotel-Residence Colfosco (☎ 0439 68224).

TOURIST INFORMATION
Tel 39 0439 768867
Fax 39 0439 768814
Email info@sanmartino.com
Web site www.sanmartino.com

Val di Fassa
top 2,949m (9,676ft) bottom 1,320m (4,330ft)
The main resorts in the valley for tourism are **Canazei** and **Campitello**, which act as gateways to the giant **Sella Ronda** ski area (see separate chapter). These, together with the villages of **Vigo di Fassa**, Moena, **Pozza di Fassa**, **Soraga** and **Mazzin**, are all connected by a free ski bus. Each of these little Italian communities has its own tiny ski area. Altogether the Val di Fassa offers around 200km of pistes. The Val di Fassa and Carezza ski pass covers the separate ski areas in **Alba**, Canazei, Campitello, Pozza di Fassa, **Pera**, Vigo di Fassa and **Carezza**. Alba has a half-pipe. Park Bimbo Neve in Pozza di Fassa, Mini Club Tananai in Vigo di Fassa and Babylandia in Moena all offer care for skiing and non-skiing children.

Traditional Moena is the principal town of the valley, which includes the Hotel Alle Alpi (☎ 0462 573122) and two renowned restaurants: the Malga Panna and Fuchiade (on the Pellegrino Pass). Other accommodation is available in the neighbouring hamlets of Alba, **Penia** and **Passo San Pellegrino**. Vigo di Fassa boasts 40 tourist hotels including the comfortable Park Hotel Corona (☎ 0462 764211), where the former Olympic champion Alberto Tomba is often a guest. Pozza di Fassa has a further 55 hotels.

Moena is the starting point every January for an annual cross-country marathon. Floodlit cross-country skiing is available at Pozza di Fassa; altogether the area boasts 70km of loipe.

TOURIST INFORMATION
Tel 39 0462 602466
Fax 39 0462 602278
Email info@fassa.com
Web site www.fassa.com

Switzerland

Switzerland is an increasingly popular destination for discerning skiers and snowboarders in search of authentic Alpine atmosphere and challenging, still-unspoilt mountainsides. While it is certainly not true that British holidaymakers introduced the sport here, they did help to promote it in the Parsenn, the Bernese Oberland and the Engadine during the early twentieth century. Their enduring love affair with the 'land of Heidi' has happily resumed after a glitch in the 1990s when high domestic prices and an unfavourable rate of exchange seriously affected Swiss tourism. During these troubled years all but the most ardent and well-heeled winter-sports visitors had little option but to desert some of the most beautiful skiing grounds in the world and turn to more affordable pastures. Today the visitors are back. Prices remain high, although value for money here generally surpasses that of the French Alps. Consequently, most of the mass-market tour operators are happy to leave the business of bringing tourists to Swiss resorts – other than **Verbier** and **Zermatt** – to a handful of small, independent operators with local expertise (see *Who goes where?*).

One reason for Switzerland's continuing charm is that environmental pressure has largely prevented the overdevelopment of Swiss ski villages. The concept of the giant, linked ski area, so popular in the 1960s and 1970s, was never fully realised here; even the **Portes du Soleil** only just brushes into Switzerland. New investment in uphill transport has transformed the skiing opportunities in major resorts such as **St Moritz**, Verbier and Zermatt.

Almost all Swiss resorts can be reached by train from Geneva and Zurich airports. Crossair Saturday flights to Sion in the Rhône Valley give speedy access to **Crans Montana**, Verbier and Zermatt. Two types of rail pass operate in Switzerland, both of which are available from the Switzerland Travel Centre in London (see *Skiing by numbers*). These passes allow either airport transfers to and from your resort, or 'rover' facilities for the duration of your stay. As might be expected, trains run on time in Switzerland. However, the Swiss themselves rarely travel with more than hand luggage; trolleys are consequently scarce, and there is little provision for suitcases on trains. You are therefore strongly advised to send your luggage separately. You can do this from your departure airport and it should arrive at your destination on the same day.

Crans Montana

ALTITUDE 1,500m (4,920ft)

Beginners ✳✳ Intermediates ✳✳✳ Advanced ✳ Snowboarders ✳✳✳

In the 1890s the town of Crans was a centre for tuberculosis clinics, and the emphasis on health remains today. Together with the adjoining resorts of **Montana** and **Aminona**, Crans has a host of hotels that contain wellness centres, enabling their elite, older patrons to enjoy a combination of skiing and health treatments. The chic shopping at Crans is advertised as the finest in the Alps, with Gucci, Chanel and Valentino just a few of the designer boutiques here. This well-heeled health-seeking clientèle mixes incongruously with a huge snowboarding crowd, which comes here for some of the best facilities in the Alps.

Crans Montana sits on a sunny plateau, dotted with larches and lakes, and the view across the Rhône Valley of 160km of the Alps is the most spectacular of all Alpine panoramas. However, it is sometimes hard to

✔ Short airport transfer
✔ Exceptional sunshine record
✔ High standard of hotels
✔ Ample non-skiing activities
✔ Superb mountain views
✔ Lack of queues
✔ Glacier skiing
✔ Facilities for children
✘ Heavy traffic during high season
✘ Spread-out resort

believe that the three towns owe their existence to the once pure mountain air. The urban conglomeration sprawls untidily for more than two kilometres along a busy main road. A funicular takes only 12 minutes to carry snow-users up to Montana from the valley town of Sierre, thus encouraging visitors to leave their cars down below. Crossair runs a weekly direct service on winter Saturdays between Heathrow and Sion, which is only 30 minutes from the resort.

On the snow
top 3,000m (9,840ft) bottom 1,500m (4,920ft)

Crans Montana is an intermediate's resort with good beginner terrain. All the pistes are easier than their ratings suggest. 'The lack of lift queues and well-groomed wide pistes made it a very civilised holiday,' said one reporter. Mountain access is a five-minute uphill walk from the town centres, and there is underground parking at the lift stations. More than half the uphill transport is by antiquated drag-lift.

A smart 30-person Funitel gondola gives direct access to the top of the ski area at Plaine-Morte. A six-person gondola from Montana and the eight-person Cry d'Err gondola at Crans lead up through the woods to Cry d'Err, where a cable-car and chair-lift continue to the 2,600-m summit of that sector. According to reporters, the red (intermediate) piste from Cry d'Err towards Pas du Loup is busy in the morning, when everybody uses it as a warm-up run.

Between Montana and Aminona, the glacier skiing at 3,000m on Plaine-Morte is reached by the Funitel continuing upwards from the Violettes gondolas, which start from the outskirts of Montana at Barzettes. The resort's longest run is the 1,500-vertical-metre drop from the glacier to town-level. From Crans Montana a bus takes skiers to Aminona, where a gondola rises to Petit Bonvin at 2,400m.

Piste maintenance has received some criticism: 'the list showing which runs were open and which were closed was never up-to-date' and 'pistes were groomed, however piste markers were not always where they should be'. The resort has a convenient hands-free lift pass.

The 50km of langlauf tracks include a 10-km loipe, set unusually at an altitude of 3,000m, on the Plaine-Morte Glacier.

Beginners

Starting at the top, beginners have three short but easy runs on the Plaine-Morte Glacier, where good snow is guaranteed. The nursery slopes down by the golf course in Crans are even easier, but susceptible to sun. Cry d'Err has the most blue (easy) runs, of which a handful are accessible by eight lifts providing skiing all the way down into Crans or Montana. However, it is not possible to ski back to Aminona entirely on blue pistes. The village of **Bluche**, five minutes' drive away, has a free nursery slope lift.

Intermediates

The standard of piste-grooming everywhere is high, but dramatic passages between rock walls, such as on the long red (intermediate) run from Plaine-Morte, provide an additional thrill. The largest conflux of intermediate pistes is in the Violettes sector, with winding trails through the woods. The Toula chair- and drag-lifts lead to steeper reds. Most exciting are the Nationale World Cup piste and Chetseron, which are well-groomed but have the occasional banked drop-off designed to make the stomach flip when taken at high speed.

Advanced

The only officially graded black (difficult) run in the entire resort is a bumpy fall-line pitch on the ridge under the Toula chair-lift ('no more than a red really'), which is often impeccably groomed on the lower section. The Plaine-Morte run is said to be avalanche-prone and, although perfectly safe when officially open, its gunbarrel passages and changes in direction require a high level of concentration.

Off-piste

There are no death-defying couloirs in Crans Montana, but three unmarked itineraries do require guides. From the Plaine-Morte Glacier it is possible to ski across open slopes and through three bands of rock down to the lake at **Zeuzier**. By walking through tunnels (torches required) and skiing a summer roadway you reach the ski lifts in the neighbouring resort of **Anzère**. Another route from the glacier guarantees fresh powder (or spring snow later in the season) to the Vallon d'Ertenze. The only way out at the bottom is by helicopter. A third route from the east side of the glacier goes to Amonina via Les Faverges trail.

Snowboarding

Crans Montana is a very active snowboarding centre ('the pistes are so wide here that skiers and boarders get along well'), with some first-rate facilities for freestylers and some of the best snowboarding tuition in the Alps at a choice of three schools. The terrain park is in Aminona and there is a half-pipe at Cry d'Err. The nearby resort of Anzère is highly recommended for advanced freeriding.

Tuition and guiding

There are two branches of the Swiss Snowsports School (ESS) in Crans and in Montana. Teaching in Montana received mixed reports: 'the instructor spoke good English, was cheerful and friendly, but there was very little individual tuition or correction'. Reporters also warned that 'if you book classes through a tour operator you need to check whether you are with the Crans or Montana ski school, as they both meet at similar places but are different organisations and won't take each other's vouchers'. Ski & Sky organises group and private lessons. Surf Evasion, affiliated with the Montana Ski School, and Stoked are the specialist snowboard schools. The Swiss Snowboard School in Crans, part of the ESS, is highly respected.

Mountain restaurants

The Café de la Cure alongside the blue run down to Aminona has character, but the best inns with sunny terraces are Merbé ('Great food but a little expensive') and Plumachit ('good atmosphere and food at an OK price'). The Cabane des Violettes is an authentic alpine club touring hut with simple meals. Lift-station eateries at Petit Bonvin, Plaine-Morte and Cry d'Err ('the bread was not very fresh and the soup of the day seemed to be leek every day') are adequate. Amadeus is a boarders' hang-out ('excellent for cheap snacks').

Accommodation

The resort that sprawls across its three communities has few pretensions to charm. Traditionally Crans was the smartest of the three towns, followed by mass-market Montana and sleepy Aminona. Today the social divisions have come down as the concrete has gone up, and Crans and Montana have equally impressive four- and five-star establishments as well as more reasonably priced hotels, while accommodation in Aminona is confined to large apartment blocks.

The Hostellerie Pas de l'Ours (☎ 27 485 9334) in Crans is a small chalet-style establishment decorated in a bear theme, in keeping with its name. Its enormous suites all have spa baths and unusual log fireplaces. This, together with the Crans-Ambassador (☎ 27 481 4811) in Montana, and the Hotel Royal (☎ 27 481 3931) and Grand Hotel du Golf (☎ 27 481 4242), both in Crans, head the luxury cast. The Crans-Ambassador contains an impressive health centre, while Hotel Royal is building its own Wellness Centre ready for the summer of 2002.

The three-star Mont Blanc (☎ 27 481 3143), on a hill above Crans, has 'the biggest terrace and best views'. In Montana, Hotel St George (☎ 27 481 2414) is 'conveniently placed with good food and service. However, the rooms are shamefully pokey for a four-star'. La Prairie (☎ 27 481 4421) is said to be 'the best three-star in town'.

Eating in and out

The resort has an impressive 80 restaurants. The most celebrated non-hotel gourmet dining is at the Cervin, the Nouvelle Rôtisserie and La Poste. The Hostellerie de la Pas de l'Ours has splendid cuisine in an attractive dining room. The Mont Blanc, in the woods above Crans, has a marmot zoo and serves tasty sea bass. The modestly priced Diligence in Montana specialises in Middle Eastern cuisine ('the locals eat here as well as regular weekenders, so booking is essential'). Valais-style raclette and fondue are on offer at the Bergerie du Cervin, Le Chalet, Le Gréni in Montana ('expensive but excellent – Roger Moore's third home') and La Dent-Blanc. Michelangelo's in Montana serves 'superb Italian food'. Zapata is a Mexican restaurant, and snowboarders congregate at the pub-style San Nick's.

Après-ski

The Absolut Disco in Crans heads the list of late-night entertainment spots, which includes seven discos, although younger visitors feel that there is room for improvement ('with a few more cafés, bars and a decent nightclub, this resort could seriously be going places'). The most popular bars are Amadeus in Montana ('cheap beer and wine and good music') and Constellation in Crans. The Indiana Café and New Pub both attract a young crowd. Teenagers flock to Montana's Number Two's for late drinking. In Crans, The Barocke has mostly techno music and the Memphis is a comfortable jazz bar. The older set can be found at Miedzor, Aida Castel and the Crans-Ambassador bar. Other popular bars include Punch (a Cuban bar) and Le Postillon.

Childcare

Infants from three months old can attend the Fleurs des Champs kindergarten, next to Hotel Eldorado in Montana ('excellent facilities although not all the staff speak English'). Garderie Zig-Zag, also in Montana, takes children of between two and six years of age. We have good reports about the Montana Ski School's Jardin des Neiges up on the Grand Signal mid-station. The Swiss Snowsports School also has a kindergarten.

Skiing facts: Crans Montana

TOURIST INFORMATION
CP 372, CH-3962 Crans Montana
Tel 41 27 485 0404
Fax 41 27 485 0460
Email information@crans-montana.ch
Web site www.crans-montana.ch

THE RESORT
By road Calais 901km
By rail Sierre 18km, bus to resort
Airport transfer Geneva 1½hrs,
Sion ½hr
Visitor beds 40,000
Transport free bus service

THE SKIING
Linked or nearby resorts Aminona (l),
Anzère (n), Bluche (n)
Number of lifts 35
Total of trails/pistes 160km (38% easy,
50% intermediate, 12% difficult)
Beginners 7 lifts, 1 free lift at Bluche
(2km away)
Summer skiing July–Aug, 2 lifts on
Plaine-Morte Glacier

LIFT PASSES
Area pass SF239 for 6 days
Pensioners women 62yrs and over, men
65yrs and over SF203 for 6 days
Credit cards yes

TUITION
Skiing ESS Crans (☎ 27 485 9370),
ESS Montana (☎ 27 481 1480),
Ski & Sky (☎ 27 485 4250)

Snowboarding Stoked (☎ 27 480 2421),
Surf Evasion (ESS Montana), Swiss
Snowboard School (ESS Crans)
Other courses Big Foot, cross-country,
extreme skiing/boarding, heli-skiing/
boarding, moguls, race-training, seniors,
skiing for the disabled, snowblading, ski-
touring, skwal, teen skiing, telemark
Guiding ESS Crans and Montana

CHILDREN
Lift pass 6–15yrs SF143,
students 15% reduction
Ski & board school as adults
Kindergarten (ski/non-ski) ESS Crans
and Montana, Fleurs des Champs
(☎ 27 481 2367), Jardin des Neiges
(☎ 27 481 1480), Zig-Zag (☎ 27 481
2205)

OTHER SPORTS
Alpine flights, curling, dog-sledding on
the frozen lake, horse-riding, hot-air
ballooning, indoor climbing wall, indoor
golf, tennis and squash, luge-ing,
night-skiing, night-snowshoeing,
parapente, skating, sleigh rides,
snowbiking, tobogganing

FOOD AND DRINK
Coffee SF2.80–4, glass of wine SF3–4,
small beer SF3.50–5, soft drink SF5,
dish of the day SF18

Davos and Klosters

ALTITUDE Davos 1,560m (5,117ft), Klosters 1,192m (3,911ft)

Beginners ✱ Intermediates ✱✱✱ Advanced ✱✱✱ Snowboarders ✱✱✱

Davos is the European birthplace of downhill skiing. The first pair of skis was brought here from Norway in 1882 by a former patient at the tuberculosis clinic run by Dr Alexander Spengler. Some 20 years earlier the German-born doctor had recognised the beneficial affects of the mountain climate in this corner of Switzerland and begun the trans-formation of Davos from remote mountain community to international resort. His son Carl tried out the giant Lapp hunting skis, and his abortive flounderings on the slopes above the town created local interest. The fol-lowing year Robert Paulcke, who owned the Davos pharmacy, gave his teenage son Wilhelm a pair for Christmas. It so happened that one of his teachers, Agnes Duborgh, came from Norway and had a vague idea of what you were meant to do with them. Within weeks, this new 'skiing' was the rage of Davos secondary school.

- ✔ Long runs
- ✔ Large linked ski area
- ✔ Good restaurants at all levels
- ✔ Off-piste for all standards
- ✔ Impressive slope grooming
- ✔ Ski-touring opportunities
- ✔ Tree-level skiing
- ✔ Good-value lift pass
- ✔ Village atmosphere (Klosters)
- ✗ Straggling town (Davos)
- ✗ Lack of skiing convenience

Saddle-maker Tobias Branger and his brother Johann had the fore-sight to realise that this skiing business could be as big as cheese, choc-olate and watches. They imported skis from Norway and improved the leather-and-metal bindings. But in order to become the first Swiss ski instructors, they first had to learn to ski. To avoid embarrassment they did this by night. In 1894, accompanied by Dr Arthur Conan Doyle, they crossed the Maienfeld Furka Pass to **Arosa** on skis.

The slopes of the Parsenn, which Davos shares with **Klosters**, its much more attractive neighbour, developed gradually with the intro-duction of the annual Parsenn Derby race in 1924, the opening of the funicular railway in 1931 and the installation of the first drag-lift in 1934 (said to be the first in the world). In recent years Davos has estab-lished itself as one of Europe's best-known conference centres, hosting the annual World Economic Forum.

The town – it claims to be the highest in Europe – straggles incon-veniently for four miles from the railway station of Davos Dorf to Davos Platz. It consists largely of giant hotels, built in practical style, interspersed with expensive boutiques and a good range of other shops. The efficient bus service is included in the lift pass and runs in a loop around the one-way system. Nevertheless, where to stay deserves serious consideration. Davos Dorf is quiet and stately with handsome old hotels, while Davos Platz is the bustling commercial heart. Dorf gives the most direct access to the main Parsenn ski area, but Platz has the lion's share of the nightlife. Enthusiasts will enjoy the renovated Wintersport Museum at Platz, which traces the development of equipment and clothing through the years.

Klosters, by contrast, is a small, rural farming community. It welcomed its first winter-sports enthusiasts in 1904, and has prospered from its connection with the British royal family, in particular Prince Charles.

WHAT'S NEW
Parsennbahn funicular rebuilt as a high-speed cable railway

Despite its high 'by Royal Appointment' profile, it remains essentially a small and discreet Swiss village.

Again, the resort is divided into two bed bases. Klosters Platz is the main community clustered around the railway station and the Gotschna cable-car. Klosters Dorf is a sleepy outpost at the bottom of the Madrisa lift system. The two are connected by a regular bus service, but only those of a reclusive disposition should consider staying in Dorf. Platz is conveniently compact, with a range of hotels in each category. A new bypass road tunnel (not due to be finished until 2005) will enable Klosters to be pedestrianised and should solve the valley's unsightly traffic problem. This tunnel will link to a second and much more ambitious 21-km Chunnel-style rail/road tunnel that will provide a direct link to the Engadine Valley, allowing skiers from **St Moritz** to reach Klosters and Davos in 45 minutes.

On the snow
top 2,844m (9,328ft) bottom 813m (2,667ft)

Much has changed since the Davos English Ski Club built its first mountain refuge on the Parsenn in 1906, only to have it destroyed almost immediately in a fatal avalanche. Where there were once no lifts, a sophisticated network of 54 now covers five separate areas. The largest of these, which Davos shares with Klosters, is the Parsenn.

It is dominated by the 2,844-m Weissfluhgipfel, the highest point on the piste map. The Weissfluhjoch, 180m beneath the summit, is the starting point for a web of wide, sweeping runs that flatter your skiing technique. However, the steeper slopes at the Klosters end of the circuit are sufficiently long and demanding to deter all but truly accomplished skiers. In mid-season snow conditions it is possible to ski 12km through a full 2,000 vertical metres down to **Küblis** and **Serneus**.

Three of the different lift companies that manage the skiing in the region have now amalgamated, with the result that the slopes are well looked after and access is greatly enhanced by a hands-free electronic lift pass system.

The Parsenn is accessed most directly by the Parsennbahn funicular from Davos Dorf, but it is also reached from Davos Platz via the

Schatzalp/Strela lift system. In 2000–1 a new six-person chair-lift was installed from the mid-station of the Parsennbahn up to the Weissfluhjoch. Work started in summer 2001 on rebuilding the entire railway as a two-train cable system on the existing track. This was scheduled to be completed in time for the 2001–2 season and should transform mountain access. The two-stage Gotschna cable-car provides the only access to the slopes from Klosters, with the second stage carrying fewer people than the first, resulting in a scrum. Plans to rectify this situation appear to have been postponed indefinitely. Once up the mountain, however, the crowds thin out and the Parsenn provides a pleasing combination of intermediate and steeper terrain.

This skiing heartland is supplemented by four further ski areas, three of them on the other side of the Davos Valley, and the fourth beyond Klosters. In the Davos catchment area, the three peaks are Pischa, Jakobshorn and Rinerhorn. They are accessed by bus from Dorf, directly from Platz, and by bus or train from **Glaris**, the next stop on the line down to Chur ('buses and trains on time and comfortable'). Beyond Klosters, the alternative to the Parsenn is the Madrisa, where the slopes stretch up to the Swiss–Austrian border.

In contrast to the Parsenn, these outlying areas are often enticingly empty. The easiest to reach from the Parsenn is Strela, a remote ski area linked by rickety cable-car across the Hauptertälli from the Weissfluhjoch. Here the slopes are sunny and uncrowded.

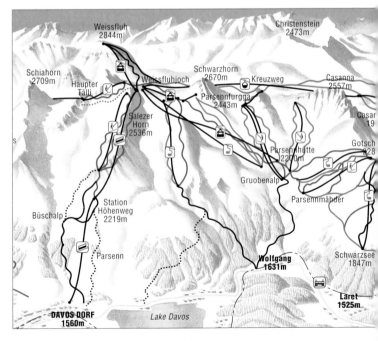

Beginners

Like many large, non-purpose-built resorts, Davos is not the place to learn to ski from scratch. If you must, the wide Bolgen nursery slope at the bottom of the Jakobshorn, a short walk from Platz, is the best starting point. In Dorf the equivalent is Bünda, which has a longer but steeper pitch. In Klosters, the sunny, user-friendly nursery slopes are up the mountain on the Madrisa, which means buying a full lift pass and returning by gondola at the end of the day. Once the basics of skiing or snowboarding are mastered, there is no shortage of blue (easy) runs.

Intermediates

Those who profit most from the Davos/Klosters area are intermediates with the energy to ski all the hours the lift company allows. Nearly all the marked runs are blue or red (intermediate), most are invitingly wide, and several are more than 10km long. The ones from the top of the Weissfluh to the valley villages of Küblis, **Saas** and Serneus start high above the tree-line, then track down through the woods to the railway line, providing a degree of excitement that is definitely not attainable in more crowded places. Another unmissable cruiser starts at the top of the Madrisa lift system and descends to Klosters Dorf via the Schlappin Valley. All five ski areas offer plenty of easy terrain, so there is no excuse for not ranging far and wide.

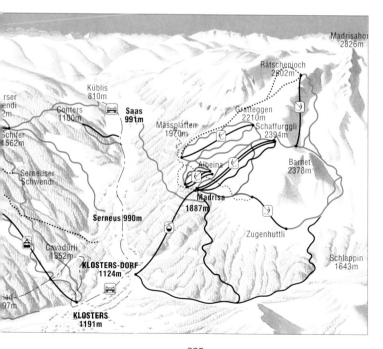

Advanced

Since the mountains in the area become steeper near the bottom, the black (difficult) runs are mostly confined to the lower sections, which means that they can be icy in all but the most favourable snow conditions. The advantage is that they are generally among trees, and therefore the visibility is always good. The best conditions are usually on the north-facing Klosters side; the Gotschnawang, which is no longer marked as a piste and is in any case rarely open, and the Drostobel provide serious challenges. Turn right from the Gotschnagrat and you come to a prime mogul-basher under the Schwarzeealp chair. Further gruelling bump runs on the Standard Ersatz and the Unterer Standard immediately above Davos Dorf offer considerable challenge. The most highly recommended black run starts on the Meierhofer Tälli at the top of the Parsenn and goes down to the hamlet of Wolfgang.

Off-piste

Those who are prepared to don skins and climb a bit can explore the huge potential for deep-snow adventure in one of Switzerland's most extensive ski areas. The longest, but by no means the most exciting, of the runs are the 18-km descents to Fideris and Jenaz, each with short climbing sections along the way. The Madrisa provides excellent opportunities for learning powder technique and is also the starting point for the trans-border loop to the hamlet of **Gargellen** at the head of the Montafon Valley. The best part of the tour is down to the attractive village of **St Antönien**.

Skiing to Arosa in the tracks of Conan Doyle is a more serious business, with a three- to four-hour climb to the Maienfeld Furka Pass above **Frauenkirch**, followed by a gentle descent through woods to the bottom of the valley and then a 40-minute plod up through the town to the railway station for the three-hour return to Davos.

Snowboarding

Throwing tradition out of the window, the area has embraced snowboarding with enthusiasm and admirable commercial acumen. It is ideal for riders, with lots of trees, a boardercross circuit and night-riding. Snowboarders who used to range all over the mountain in large numbers now congregate at the Parsenn terrain park, with its two half-pipes, and on the Jakobshorn. They are joined by carving skiers, who can try the dedicated courses beneath the Totalp chair-lift.

Cross-country

Davos offers 75km of prepared cross-country trails on the valley floor and in the Sertigtal and Dischmatal areas. Evening expeditions can be made on the 2.5-km floodlit section, and dogs are allowed on some of the trails. The highlights of the cross-country year are the Davos Nordic World Cup and the 20-km Volks Langlauf.

Tuition and guiding

The Swiss Snowsports School Davos (SSSD) offers ski and snowboard classes for adults and teenagers. Half-day safety classes for off-piste beginners (with a maximum of six per group) are available, covering the use of ABS-rucksacks and avalanche transceivers. Daily or weekly guided ski-tours can be arranged between January and Easter. We have no reports on either the New Trend Ski School in Davos or the Swiss Snowsports School Klosters (SSSK). Bananas is the specialist snow-boarding school in both resorts ('more flexible in their arrangements and very helpful'), while Top Secret Snowboarding School in Davos Platz is highly recommended for first-timers.

The Saas Ski and Snowboard School (Saas S&S-S) in Klosters, which in the past has received complimentary reports ('friendly instructors with good English'), no longer seems as competitive.

Mountain restaurants

'Go low' is the recommendation in an area where skiing to lunch should be an integral part of a long adventure run. Intelligent use of the piste map makes it possible to locate the many small establishments in the woods on the way down to the outlying villages. The restaurant at the Teufi on the off-piste descent from the Jakobshorn is recommended, as is the Hotel Kulm (also known as Jakob's) in Wolfgang. Another winner is the pizzeria at the end of the Schlappin run in Klosters Dorf. The Erika on Madrisa is recommended. The Alte Conterser Schwendi is renowned for its rösti and other local specialities, as is the Serneuser Schwendi ('popular, but a bit noisy and smoky'). The Gotschna at Serneus serves delicious cheese dishes. The Strela Alp restaurant is frequented by as many walkers as skiers. Berghaus Schifer is praised for staff who were unfailingly friendly, and reasonably priced food.

Accommodation

Davos has two five-star hotels: the Steigenberger Belvédère (☎ 81 415 6000), up on the hillside above Platz, and the Flüela (☎ 81 410 1717), opposite the railway station in Dorf. Both offer old-fashioned comfort in the stolid Swiss manner, a style emulated by many of their competitors in the four- and three-star brackets. The four-star Victoria Turmhotel (☎ 81 417 53 00) at Dorf is warmly recommended: 'excellent health centre and splendid food'. In Platz, the Waldhotel Bellevue (☎ 81 415 3747) is rich in tradition. The same can be said of the Berghotel Schatzalp (☎ 81 413 8381).

In Klosters, the four-stars are headed by the Walserhof (☎ 81 422 1340), which has a top reputation. The Chesa Grischuna (☎ 81 422 2222) is rustic and has a popular bar. The modern Hotel Alpina (☎ 81 410 2424) is opposite the railway station ('extremely convenient with a wonderful swimming-pool. Our good-sized bedroom was immaculately clean and comfortable. On the downside, some bedrooms were too close to the busy station for comfort'). The 30-room Wynegg (☎ 81 422 1340) is a resort institution, run much like a large chalet for

Skiing facts: Davos

TOURIST INFORMATION
Promenade 67, CH-7270 Davos
Tel 41 81 415 2121
Fax 41 81 415 2100
Email davos@davos.ch
Web site www.davos.ch

THE RESORT
By road Calais 1,010km
By rail Davos Dorf and Davos Platz
stations in resort
Airport transfer Zurich 2½hrs
Visitor beds 24,251
Transport free ski bus with lift pass,
free ski train with Rega Pass

THE SKIING
Linked or nearby resorts Arosa (n),
Gargellen (n), Glaris (l), Klosters (l),
Küblis (l), Saas (l), Serneus (l),
St Moritz (n), Wolfgang (l)
Number of lifts 55 in Davos/Klosters
area
Total of trails/pistes 320km in
Davos/Klosters area (30% easy,
40% intermediate, 30% difficult)
Beginners 2 lifts

LIFT PASSES
Area pass Rega Pass (covers all Davos
and Klosters lifts, buses and railway)
SF279 for 6 days

Pensioners 10% reduction for women
62yrs and over, men 65yrs and over
Credit cards yes

TUITION
Skiing New Trend (☎ 81 413 20 40),
SSD (☎ 81 416 2454)
Snowboarding Bananas Davos
(☎ 81 410 1014), SSSD, Top Secret
(☎ 81 413 20 40)
Other courses cross-country, extreme
skiing/boarding, moguls, powder clinics,
race-training, seniors, snowblading, teen
skiing, telemark
Guiding SSSD

CHILDREN
Lift pass 6–16yrs, Rega Pass SF168
for 6 days
Ski & board school as adults
Kindergarten (ski/non-ski)
SSSD (☎ 81 416 2454)

FOOD AND DRINK
Coffee SF3.80, glass of wine SF8–10,
small beer SF4.50–5, soft drink SF4,
dish of the day SF16–25

its mainly British guests. The overspill can find a quieter refuge in the Bundnerhof (☎ 81 422 1450) next door. Four-star Hotel Pardenn (☎ 81 422 1141) now receives more favourable reports than in previous years: 'Generally the hotel was pleasant and clean. The service in the restaurant was friendly and prompt and the food was very good'. The Silvretta Parkhotel (☎ 81 423 3435) had 'good-sized rooms but the rest of the hotel was a little spartan and lacking atmosphere'. The Vereina (☎ 81 410 2727) has been demolished and rebuilt as a modern four-star.

Eating in and out

In Davos, as elsewhere in Switzerland, those who stray outside half-board deals must pay highly for the privilege. Money is well spent in Hubli's Landhaus, the Magic Mountain restaurant in the Waldhotel Bellevue, and the Stübli in the Flüela hotel. Try the Zauberberg restaurant in the Hotel Europe or the Goldener Drachen in the Hotel Bahnhof Terminus for Far Eastern cuisine. Local dining, at correspondingly lower prices, can be found in the outlying villages of Frauenkirch, Wolfgang and **Laret**.

In Klosters, the Chesa Grischuna must be booked three days in advance, and tables at rival establishments require at least one day's notice. This is certainly true of the Wynegg, which capitalises on its royal connections to serve meals that are more rustic than gastronomic. Hotel Walserhof ('the food is excellent, more French in style than pure Swiss') has a Michelin-rated restaurant presided over by the renowned Swiss chef, Beat Bolliger. Other favourable eateries are in the hotels Alte Post, Alpina, Vereina, Kurhaus and Rustico.

Après-ski

In the late afternoons, the high-lifers at Davos congregate in the Café Schneider in Platz and the Café Weber in Dorf, both specialists in temptation cakes. The most favoured bar is the rustic Chämi, which is full to bursting with revellers of all ages until closing time. As the resort attracts a lot of non-skiers, the entertainment on offer is extensive. In the pre-dinner hours, major league ice-hockey matches take place in the handsome Sports Centre; other activities include skating on the largest natural ice-rink in Europe.

The area's pulsating nightlife can be found in Davos Platz, and especially in the Ex-Bar. The laser show at the Cabanna Club disco in Hotel Europe attracts a young crowd, while the Carigiet bar in the Hotel Steigenberger and the Piano Bar Tonic in the Hotel Europe cater for an older clientèle. The Cava Grischa has modern techno and disco. Casino Davos houses 130 slot machines, and the Scala restaurant in the same building stays open until 1.30am. Riders hang out in the Bolgenschanze bar and disco.

After-skiing activities in Klosters start with a drink at Gaudi's at the foot of the slopes. The Steinbock Bar attracts locals as well as tourists. Alternative watering holes include the Chesa Grischuna, the Fellini Bar, and the Piano Bar in the Silvretta Parkhotel. For late-night dancing try the Casa Antica, the Kir Royal, or Don Alberto and the Mountain Pub in Klosters Dorf.

Childcare

The Swiss Snowsports School Davos offers children's classes for three-year-olds and upwards on Bünda or Bolgen, with supervised lunch and lifts included in the price, and a Bobo Wonderland playground, complete with cartoon characters, in each area. In Klosters the Toby kindergarten, based in the Saaseralp mountain-top restaurant at Madrisa, is

Skiing facts: Klosters

TOURIST INFORMATION
Alte Bahnhofstrasse
CH-7250 Klosters
Tel 41 81 410 2020
Fax 41 81 410 2010
Email info@klosters.ch
Web site www.klosters.ch

THE RESORT
By road Calais 1,000km
By rail Klosters Dorf and Klosters Platz
stations in resort
Airport transfer Zurich 2½hrs
Visitor beds 8,800
Transport free ski bus with lift pass,
free ski train with Rega Pass

THE SKIING
Linked or nearby resorts Arosa (n),
Davos (l), Gargellen (n), Glaris (l)
Küblis (l), Saas (l), Serneus (l),
St Moritz (n), Wolfgang (l)
Number of lifts 55 in Davos/Klosters
area
Total of trails/pistes 320km in
Davos/Klosters area (30% easy,
40% intermediate, 30% difficult)
Beginners 4 lifts, 1 of them is free

LIFT PASSES
Area pass Rega Pass (covers all Davos
and Klosters lifts, buses and railway),
SF279 for 6 days
Pensioners 10% reduction for women
62yrs and over, men 65yrs and over
Credit cards yes

TUITION
Skiing SSSK (☎ 81 410 2028),
Saas S&S-S (☎ 81 420 2233)
Snowboarding as ski schools,
Bananas Klosters (☎ 81 422 6660)
Other courses cross-country, extreme
skiing/boarding, moguls, powder clinics,
race-training, seniors, snowblading,
teen skiing, telemark
Guiding through ski schools

CHILDREN
Lift pass 6–16yrs, Rega Pass SF168 for
6 days
Ski & board school as adults
Kindergarten (ski) Snow Garden
(☎ 81 410 2028), (non-ski) Haus Fliana
(☎ 81 410 2020), Toby Kindergarten
(☎ 81 410 2028)

OTHER SPORTS
Davos/Klosters: climbing wall, curling,
dog-sledding, hang-gliding, horse-riding,
ice-climbing, ice speed-skating, indoor
badminton, golf, squash and tennis,
night-skiing/boarding, parapente,
skating, ski-jöring, sleigh rides,
SnowCarting (Davos), snowshoeing,
swimming

FOOD AND DRINK
Coffee SF3.50, glass of wine SF8–10,
small beer SF5, soft drink SF4,
dish of the day SF16–25

for non-skiers over two years old, and the Snow Garden is for skiers
over four. The area is inconvenient to reach for parents who choose to
ski on the Parsenn. Haus Fliana contains a kindergarten for two- to six-
year-olds and is in town.

Jungfrau

ALTITUDE Wengen 1,274m (4,180ft), Grindelwald 1,034m (3,393ft), Mürren 1,650m (5,412ft)

Beginners (except Mürren) ✳✳✳ Intermediates ✳✳✳ Advanced ✳✳
Snowboarders ✳✳

The Jungfrau region is one of the most popular in Switzerland with British skiers. It is recognised as the nursery of modern skiing and has always had an edge on quality that it has maintained over the years, despite variable snow cover. Trains are a crucial part of any holiday to the region's principal resorts of Wengen, Grindelwald and Mürren; the mountain railway, which dates from the 1880s, is still the backbone of the lift system today, making both Wengen and Grindelwald ideal bases for non-skiers. Wengen and Mürren remain traffic-free and remarkably unspoilt by the passage of a century. The three resorts share a ski pass that covers 42 lifts in the Jungfrau Top Ski region, offering 215km of wonderfully scenic skiing against the awesome backdrop of the Eiger, Mönch and Jungfrau mountains.

> ✔ Beautiful scenery
> ✔ Variety of slopes
> ✔ Car-free villages
>   (Wengen/Mürren)
> ✔ Facilities for non-skiers
> ✗ Poorly linked ski areas
> ✗ Uncertain snow cover

Henry Lunn, a non-skiing Methodist minister and one-time lawn tennis equipment salesman, is credited with introducing the first-ever ski package holidays here in the winter of 1910–11. To encourage the class-conscious British to come on his tours he founded the Public Schools Alpine Sports Club, and also managed to persuade the Swiss to continue to operate their mountain railways during the winter. His more distinguished son, Sir Arnold, went on to found the Kandahar Ski Club in Mürren, where slalom racing was first introduced in 1922.

Ski tourism started in Wengen with the Downhill Only Club, a pioneer band of British skiers formed in February 1925 to race against their Kandahar Club rivals in Mürren. The club name developed from its members' customary train ride up the mountain in order to ski down, a process considered distinctly unsporting by the standards of the day when people thought there should be no gain without pain. Both British ski clubs are alive and functioning in the resorts today.

Wengen, Grindelwald and Mürren are all reached by rail from Interlaken. The track divides at Zweilütschinen, with the left-hand fork veering towards Grindelwald. The right-hand fork goes to Lauterbrunnen, which is more of a railway halt than a resort, although it does have a number of hotels, and some reporters consider it a convenient and much cheaper base from which to ski the area.

Trains from Lauterbrunnen run steeply up to Mürren on one side of the valley and up to Wengen on the other. The railway climbs up to the main ski area at Kleine Scheidegg, above Wengen, before descending into Grindelwald. Trains stop at wayside halts throughout the area to pick up and set down skiers, and run as accurately as a Swiss watch to a timetable printed on the back of the piste map. However, this form of transport is painfully slow, and the trains can be as crowded as the London Underground at rush hour, although the network has been augmented by conventional cableways and chairs.

Wengen remains much as it was – a single pedestrian street of unremarkable shops and a cluster of chalets around one of the best nursery slopes in the Alps. There is also a magnificent skating-rink.

Grindelwald is the oldest of the three villages – a large and busy year-round resort spread along the valley floor between the soaring peaks of the Wetterhorn and the Eiger on the one side, and the gentler wooded slopes of its own First ski area on the other. There are few more cosmopolitan resorts to be found in the world, with myriad nationalities listed among the guests here; not least the Japanese, who arrive in numbers to visit the Eiger and the Jungfraujoch, which at 3,454m is the highest station in Europe.

Mürren, as one reader elegantly described it, 'is like a coveted biscuit jar hidden above the kitchen cabinet. It is high up, difficult to reach, but full of delights once within your grasp'. Certainly, it has few rivals as the prettiest and most unspoilt ski village in Switzerland. Old chalets and hotels line the paths between the railway station at one end and the cable-car at the other. This car-free village is on a sunny shelf perched on top of a 500-m rock-face above Lauterbrunnen. The same British families, nearly all of them members of the Kandahar Club, have been returning here for generations and have forged firm links with the local villagers.

On the snow
top 2,970m (9,724ft) bottom 796m (2,611ft)
A circuit of lifts around the Lauberhorn and Tschuggen peaks links the ski areas of Wengen and Grindelwald through the Männlichen and Kleine Scheidegg. Skiers have a choice of taking the train up to Kleine Scheidegg and Eigergletscher or climbing the Männlichen ridge by cable-car from Wengen. The bottom station, destroyed in an avalanche in 1999, has now been rebuilt in a safer position.

From Grindelwald a gondola rises to the Männlichen, while the train also carries on up to Kleine Scheidegg. On the other side of Grindelwald, the First area is easily accessible, even for Wengen-based skiers. The areas complement each other well, and one of the pleasures of visiting any of them is to spend days exploring the others.

Mürren, separated from the other two resorts by the Lauterbrunnen Valley, sits on an east-facing shelf. Its skiing is spread across three parallel ridges – the Schiltgrat, the Allmendhubel and the Maulerhubel – which run roughly north and south above the village. Lift queues are not a problem in Mürren ('there were simply not enough people').

Beginners

Wengen has an excellent nursery area in the middle of the village, with a baby lift, a magic carpet and an unusual three-person drag-lift, which is surprisingly easy for snowboarders to use. There are also enjoyably long blue (easy) runs on which even those with little technique can stretch their legs. From Kleine Scheidegg, a broad tree-lined road leads to Brandegg and on to Grindelwald.

Grindelwald also has nursery slopes right by the village and others up on the Hohwald and Bargelegg lifts, although beginners will want to return to base via the First gondola.

Mürren is not an ideal resort for beginners. The small nursery slope is on the upper road behind the Jungfrau Hotel; this is where the world's first modern slalom was set. Another beginners' area lies at the top of the Allmendhubel lift and is served by a small tow.

Intermediates

Wengen and Grindelwald owe much of their popularity with families to their long, gentle, cruising runs. You can take the Männlichen cable-car and explore the route under the gondola right down to **Grund**. From there the train goes up to Kleine Scheidegg, which has a similarly well-networked area, improved by the installation of a detachable quad on the Lauberhorn. The famous World Cup racecourse – at two-and-a-half kilometres the longest in the world – forms a fairly testing descent. The Standard run offers an easier way down.

From Grindelwald, the First gondola leads to the Stepfi, a satisfying red (intermediate) run from Oberlager down to the Hotel Wetterhorn. This is a pleasant stop-off before returning by bus to Grindelwald.

At Mürren, some very pretty intermediate skiing can be reached by taking the Allmendhubel railway and then a small T-bar to the Hogs Back area; turn right towards the Maulerhubel T-bar, at the top of which is a wide area of open slopes leading either back to the bottom of Maulerhubel or off to the mid-station on the main railway. You can return to the village from the bottom of the Maulerhubel on the wide Palace Run.

Advanced

From Wengen, the train up to Eigergletscher leads to the black (difficult) runs of Blackrock and Oh God. In sunny weather these are best left until late morning, as they can be hard and icy before the sun reaches them. The Aspen run is the steepest way down from the Männlichen towards Grund. Grindelwald's First area has a challenging black piste under the gondola. At Mürren, the extremely steep run from the top of the Schilthorn can be followed by another steep pitch alongside the Muttleren chair-lift, and then the Kanonenrohr, to give an almost continuous black run with plenty of challenge.

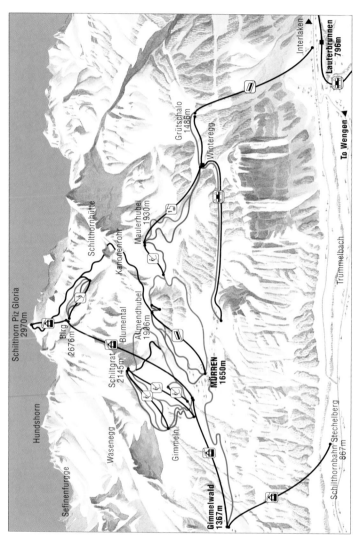

Off-piste

All three resorts have a great deal of easily accessible off-piste skiing between the trails. In Mürren, the Blumental is famous for its powder, Tschingelchrachen off the Schilthornbahn should be treated with care as it is very steep and often closed, and Hidden Valley from the summit of the Maulerhubel to Grutsch is a delight. The White Hare, which starts from the foot of the Eigerwand, is a dramatic and exciting powder run; it can be accessed from both Wengen and Grindelwald.

Local mountain guides are essential here, and Grindelwald's Bergsteigerzentrum is one of the most famous guiding establishments in the world; both ski-touring and heli-skiing can be organised through the centre. Day tours over to the **Lötschental** can be arranged.

Snowboarding

Wengen, which is the best spot for beginners, has a new terrain park with a boardercross course, served by the Bumps lift. Grindelwald has a large terrain park at Oberjoch with a half-pipe and a boardercross course. At Mürren there is a half-pipe and some challenging freeriding. Mad House is Grindelwald's specialist board school.

Tuition and guiding

The Swiss Snowsports School (SSS) operates in each village. Group lessons are given mornings-only from Sunday to Friday. Most, but by no means all, instructors speak more than adequate English. The SSS in Wengen received favourable reports: 'our very able and understanding instructor got half a dozen novices from side-stepping to parallel turns on red (intermediate) runs in 18 hours of lessons over six days'. We have no reports on Privat Ski and Snowboard School in Wengen.

Mountain restaurants

The Hotel Jungfrau at Wengernalp has beautiful views, a friendly atmosphere and the best rösti ('avoid the gorgonzola. It will blow your socks off'). At Grindelwald the Brandegg restaurant is famed for its apple fritters ('remember to ask for the sauce'). The Kleine Scheidegg station buffet 'has got to be the best station buffet in the world'. The Jägerstübli is a farmhouse below Männlichen, with a 'cosy ambience'.

The Aspen above Grund has a loyal clientèle. Mary's Café, just above Wengen, is recommended. The restaurant at Bort above Grindelwald is 'pleasant and reasonably priced, but the food is not exceptional'. The big self-service at First boasts 'a glorious hamburger'. Hotel Wetterhorn on the way down to Grindelwald has a 'convivial atmosphere and delicious food'.

Above Mürren, the Schilthorn Tavern has 'copious portions and reasonable prices'. Pension Sonnenburg is praised for its rösti. Restaurant Birg is 'worth a visit, if only for the view from the terrace'. Gimmeln has 'tasty raclette and *Apfelküchen*'. We continue to receive complimentary reports of the revolving Piz Gloria on the summit of the Schilthorn ('excellent value and views'). One reporter had 'an imaginative salad – it took a full revolution to demolish it'. The Schilthornhütte, on the descent from here, is a mountain refuge serving simple dishes (a 'fun atmosphere and wonderful views').

Accommodation

In Wengen the accommodation is split between hotels, apartments and chalets. The attractive resort is quite spread out and distinctly steep. ParkHotel Beausite (☎ 33 856 5161) is warmly recommended ('superb, with excellent and plentiful food. No extra charge for children's high tea'). The Bernerhof (☎ 33 855 2721) is 'friendly and comfortable'. The Hotel Eiger (☎ 33 855 1131) is central and has long been a favourite among the British. The Falken (☎ 33 856 5121) is variously described as 'delightfully old-fashioned', 'ramshackle' and 'very comfortable'. The ski-in ski-out Hotel Brunner (☎ 33 855 2494), on the piste, a ten-minute walk above the village centre, is described as 'one of those Alpine secrets that visitors – many of them with children – like to keep to themselves'. Hotel Regina (☎ 33 855 1512) is 'big, old, well-kept, with excellent service' and unusual food.

The three-star Hotel Belvédère (☎ 33 855 2412) is a seven-minute uphill walk from the station and has 'grand art-deco public rooms'. The four-star Hotel Sunstar (☎ 33 856 5111) has family 'maisonettes', a swimming-pool, and is one of the most conveniently placed hotels in town. Club Med here has a fine reputation, although the presence of large, noisy classes of French skiers on crowded pistes can lead to Agincourt-style confrontations with the more conservative Brits.

Grindelwald has the five-star Grand Hotel Regina (☎ 33 854 8601), which is partly decorated with eighteenth-century antiques and is famous for the ice sculptures in its grounds. A host of four-star hotels include the 'excellent' Hotel Spinne (☎ 33 854 8888). The Hotel Alpenhof (☎ 33 853 5270), a few minutes' walk from the village, has a sound reputation. Hotel Derby (☎ 33 854 5461) and Hotel Hirschen (☎ 33 854 8484) are both recommended. Hotel Bodmi (☎ 33 853 1220) on the nursery slopes is convenient for families, and Parkhotel Schoenegg (☎ 33 853 1853) is warmly acclaimed. Hotel Bernerhof (☎ 33 853 1021) is centrally located close to the station and has 'friendly and attentive service'. Hotel Kreuz & Post (☎ 33 854 5492) has, according to one reporter, 'the best food we have ever experienced in a package-deal hotel'.

In Mürren the Hotel Eiger (☎ 33 855 1331), across the road from the railway station, boasts some luxurious suites as well as standard hotel rooms and apartments. Hotel Jungfrau (☎ 33 855 4545), which has been criticised in the past, has changed owners and 'is now enormously improved'. The Alpenruh (☎ 33 855 1055) at the Schilthornbahn end of the village has 'an excellent restaurant'. The popular Edelweiss (☎ 33 855 1312) is 'convenient, clean and friendly', and the Blumental (☎ 33 855 1826) is also recommended, together with the simpler Belmont (☎ 33 855 3535).

The village of Lauterbrunnen in the valley below is well placed for less expensive accommodation and the chance to try a different area each day, but it suffers from being hemmed in by sheer mountains.

Eating in and out

Most restaurants in Wengen are in hotels, but Sina's Italian is warmly recommended ('good value for money in a warm and friendly ambience'). Mary's Café offers cheese fondue accompanied by alpenhorn-blowing contests on Tuesdays. Restaurant Wengen in the Hotel

Hirschen specialises in fondue *chinoise*. The Berghaus is known for its fresh fish and the Bernerhof for fondue and raclette. On sunny days, the Hotel Eiger has outdoor tables next to the railway station.

In Grindelwald, the à la carte Derby Restaurant is one of the best places to dine. Reporters also speak warmly of the Schweizerhof. The restaurant in the Hotel Alte Post is popular with the locals. The Alpina is good for fondue, and the Cava restaurant in the Hotel Derby has 'the best fondue and pasta in town'.

In Mürren, the Hotel Eiger's stübli has an excellent, if somewhat expensive, menu. At the other end of the village, the Alpenruh comes well recommended, and the Belmont offers 'excellent value'. The Edelweiss and Stägerstübli are both recommended. The supermarket is said to be adequate and there is also a butcher's shop.

Après-ski

Wengen's nightlife remains muted in comparison with other Alpine resorts. The last ski trains of the day are full of families with toboggans going up to Wengernalp for the 4-km descent back to the village. This acquires an added dimension when ski racers are in the town for the Lauberhorn Downhill: 'being passed by the entire Austrian national team was an interesting experience. They don't slow down just because they are not on skis'. The TeePee Après Ski Bar at Kleine Scheidegg is busier during the skiing day. Crowds gather in Mary's Café, and the ice-bar outside the Hotel Brunner is lively. The Eiger Bar is 'very sedate, with serious pipe-smokers', and the Red Hot Chilli Bar has 'big mugs of glühwein'.

In the village itself the twin skating-rinks at times offer ice-hockey matches on one and curling on the other. In the afternoons it seems that there are almost as many people skating as there are skiing. Reporters complain that Wengen has no real tea-and-cakes places apart from Café Grübi, which is full of atmosphere but rather cramped. The Tanne, Sina's Pub and Hot Chilli are the most popular bars, while the disco is to be found in Tiffany's in the Silberhorn.

In Grindelwald the Espresso bar draws a young crowd straight after skiing, while the Gepsi attracts a slightly older clientèle. Later on the Chälli bar in the Hotel Kreuz and Post, the Cava in the Derby, and Herby's in the Regina are the most popular. The Plaza Club and the Mescalero rock on into the small hours. SnowCarting and daily llama treks around the First ski area are added attractions.

For such a small village, Mürren is surprisingly lively after skiing, although only during high season. The Ballon bar in the Palace Hotel ('prices can be a bit rich on the budget'), together with the Grübi in the Jungfrau and the Pub in the Belmont, are all popular. The Tächi bar in the Hotel Eiger is one of the main meeting places. The Bliemlichäller disco in the Blumental and the Inferno disco in the Palace Hotel buzz at weekends and in high season. The village boasts an excellent sports centre.

Skiing facts: Wengen

TOURIST INFORMATION
CH-3823 Wengen, Bernese Oberland
Tel 41 33 855 1414
Fax 41 33 855 3060
Email information@wengen.com
Web site www.wengen-muerren.ch

THE RESORT
By road Calais 835km
By rail station in resort
Airport transfer Zurich 3hrs, Geneva 4hrs
Visitor beds 2,500
Transport taxis, otherwise traffic-free resort

THE SKIING
Linked or nearby resorts Grindelwald (l), Grund (l), Lauterbrunnen (n), Mürren (n)
Number of lifts 42 in Jungfrau Top Ski region
Total of trails/pistes 215km in Jungfrau Top Ski region (28% easy, 57% intermediate, 15% difficult)
Beginners 3 lifts, points tickets available
Summer skiing 1 lift at Jungfraujoch

LIFT PASSES
Area pass Jungfrau (covers Wengen, Grindelwald and Mürren) SF254 for 6 days
Pensioners SF229 from 62yrs
Credit cards yes

TUITION
Skiing Privat Ski and Snowboard School (☎ 33 855 5005), SSS (☎ 33 856 2022)
Snowboarding as ski schools
Other courses heli-skiing/boarding, race training, telemark
Guiding through ski schools

CHILDREN
Lift pass under 6yrs SF22 (or free if with parent), 6–15yrs SF127, 16–19yrs SF203, all for 6 days
Ski & board school as adults
Kindergarten (non-ski) Sylvie's Playhouse (☎ 33 855 3681)

OTHER SPORTS
Curling, hang-gliding, ice-hockey, para-pente, skating, sleigh rides, snowshoe-ing, tobogganing

FOOD AND DRINK
Coffee SF3.50, glass of wine SF5, small beer SF3.50–5, soft drink SF3.80, dish of the day SF15–25

Childcare

We have pleasing reports of high standards of tuition in all three resorts. One reporter said that he 'would recommend the SSS in Wengen to anyone with small children. Our son's teacher was great. She spoke good English and had endless patience, hugs, and cuddles for her little group'. However, the decision by all three branches of the SSS to run group lessons only in the mornings seriously detracts from Jungfrau's erstwhile reputation as an ideal area for families with young children ('some unhappy parents found their skiing day curtailed at lunch-time'). The non-ski Sylvie's Playhouse in Wengen accepts children from two to seven years old and has a sound reputation ('we can't praise it highly enough. It is very, very good, with friendly,

Skiing facts: Grindelwald

TOURIST INFORMATION
CH-3818 Grindelwald, Bernese Oberland
Tel 41 33 854 1212
Fax 41 33 854 1210
Email touristcenter@grindelwald.ch
Web site www.grindelwald.ch

THE RESORT
By road Calais 835km
By rail station in resort
Airport transfer Zurich 2hrs, Geneva 3hrs
Visitor beds 11,700
Transport ski bus free with lift pass

THE SKIING
Linked or nearby resorts Grund (n), Lauterbrunnen (n), Mürren (n), Wengen (l)
Number of lifts 42 in Jungfrau Top Ski Region
Total of trails/pistes 215km in Jungfrau Top Ski Region (28% easy, 57% intermediate, 15% difficult)
Beginners 5 lifts, points tickets available

LIFT PASSES
Area pass Jungfrau (covers Wengen, Grindelwald and Mürren) SF254 for 6 days
Pensioners SF229 62yrs
Credit cards yes

TUITION
Skiing (SSS ☎ 33 853 5200)
Snowboarding Mad House SSS, (☎ 33 853 5969)
Other courses cross-country, heli-skiing/boarding, race-training, telemark
Guiding Bergsteigerzentrum Grindelwald (☎ 33 853 1200)

CHILDREN
Lift pass 6yrs and under SF22 (or free if with parent), 6–15yrs SF127, 16–19yrs SF203, all for 6 days
Ski & board school as adults
Kindergarten (non-ski) Kinderhart-Crèche Sunshine (☎ 33 853 3004), (ski/non-ski) Kinderclub Bodmi (☎ 33 853 5200)

OTHER SPORTS
Curling, llama treks, parapente, skating, SnowCarting, snowshoeing

FOOD AND DRINK
Coffee SF3.50, glass of wine SF5, small beer SF3.50–4, soft drink SF3.80, dish of the day SF15–20

helpful and caring staff'). Children are taken to and from ski school, but unfortunately it is closed on Saturday. In Grindelwald, Kinderclub Bodmi caters for pre-ski children in its play area on the nursery slopes. Kinderhart-Crèche Sunshine takes children from one month. Simi's Childcare in Mürren looks after small non-skiers, but the resort has limited easy skiing.

Skiing facts: Mürren

TOURIST INFORMATION
CH-3825 Mürren, Bernese Oberland
Tel 41 33 856 8686
Fax 41 33 856 8696
Email info@muerren.ch
Web site www.wengen-muerren.ch

THE RESORT
By road Calais 835km
By rail station in resort
Airport transfer Zurich 3hrs,
Geneva 4hrs
Visitor beds 2,000
Transport traffic-free resort

THE SKIING
Linked or nearby resorts Grindelwald
(n), Grund (n), Lauterbrunnen (n),
Wengen (n)
Number of lifts 12 in Mürren, 42 in
Jungfrau Top Ski region
Total of trails/pistes 215km in Jungfrau
Top Ski region (28% easy,
57% intermediate, 15% difficult)
Beginners 1 free lift, points tickets
available

LIFT PASSES
Area pass Jungfrau (covers Wengen,
Grindelwald and Mürren) SF254 for
6 days
Pensioners SF229 from 62yrs
Credit cards yes

TUITION
Skiing SSS (☎ 33 855 1247)
Snowboarding as ski school
Other courses cross-country,
heli-skiing/boarding, snowblading,
telemark
Guiding through ski school

CHILDREN
Lift pass under 6yrs SF22 (or free if with
parent), 6–15yrs SF127, 16–19yrs
SF203, all for 6 days
Ski & board school as adults
Kindergarten (non-ski) Simi's Childcare
(☎ 33 856 8686)

OTHER SPORTS
Curling, hang-gliding, ice-hockey,
climbing wall, indoor tennis and squash,
parapente, skating, snowmobiling,
swimming

FOOD AND DRINK
Coffee SF3.40, glass of wine SF5,
small beer SF3.50–4, soft drink SF3.80,
dish of the day SF17–20

St Moritz

ALTITUDE 1,800m (5,904ft)

Beginners ✶ Intermediates ✶✶ Advanced ✶✶ Snowboarders ✶

St Moritz is an all-round winter sports resort located on two levels, above and along the shores of a fir-lined lake in the scenic Engadine valley, three to four hours by road from Zurich. Winter Alpine holidays were invented here in 1864 by the British, and while other resorts have long since emulated its seasonal formula of snow fun, few have eclipsed its hedonistic allure. However, the urban architecture is bland; the beauty of St Moritz lies not in the views of the resort itself, but in the views from it.

✔ Wealth of luxury hotels
✔ Fine dining opportunities
✔ Good snow record
✔ Facilities for cross-country skiing
✔ Choice of winter sports
✘ Lift queues at peak times
✘ Widely dispersed ski sectors
✘ High prices
✘ Long airport transfer
✘ Lack of architectural charm

The resort sets the world standard for luxury and indulgence. Skating, curling, golf, cricket, polo and a number of exotic horse-racing events take place throughout the winter on the frozen lake. The Cresta run, the origin of the new Olympic sport of skeleton tobogganing, has been the ultimate demonstration of machismo for more than 100 years. The Cresta still maintains a sexist men-only stance. Novices aged over 18, with an introduction to the private St Moritz Tobogganing Club, can try their luck four mornings a week from Christmas to the end of February. Speeds of up to 100kph can be achieved by riders sledging head-first on the ice. The bob-sleigh also made its debut here. St Moritz has twice been the venue for the Winter Olympics, and in 2003 the resort will play host to the Alpine Ski World Championships for the fourth time in its history.

The Upper Engadine regional ski pass covers 57 lifts and 350km of pistes from one end of the valley to the other. **Celerina**, **Pontresina**, **Silvaplana** and **Sils Maria** are outlying villages with ski lifts. **Dorf** is the name used for St Moritz proper, and **Bad** is down on the lake below.

On the snow
top 3,303m (10,834ft) bottom 1,720m (5,642ft)

The region divides into the sectors of Corviglia, Corvatsch and Diavolezza–Lagalb. The home mountain of St Moritz is Corviglia. The ski area can be reached by funicular from Dorf, by cable-car from Bad, by chair-lift from Suvretta and by gondola from Celerina. The ski area continues up to 3,057m at Piz Nair. Summer skiing is no longer available on the Diavolezza Glacier. Corvatsch, on the other side of the

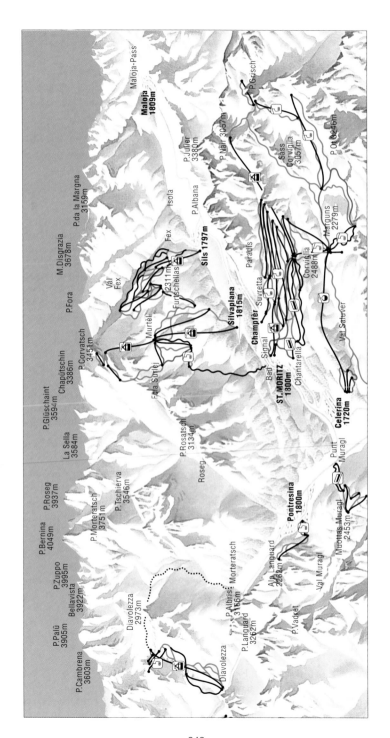

Maloja-Pass

Maloja
1809m

P.Grysch

P.Nair 3057m

P.Julier 3380m

Sass Corviglia 3057m

P.Ot 6246m

P.da la Margna 3159m

M.Disgrazia 3678m

P.Fora

P.Albana

Isola

Marguns 2279m

Val Fex

Fex

Sils 1797m

2311m

Furtschellas

Paradis

Corviglia 2488m

Val Sattviér

Murtèl

Silvaplana 1815m

Suvretta

Champfèr

Signal

P.Corvatsch 3451m

Fda Surlej

Chantarella

Bad

ST.MORITZ 1800m

Celerina 1720m

Chapütschin 3386m

P.Glüschaint 3594m

La Sella 3584m

P.Rosatsch 3134m

Roseg.

Punt Muragl

P.Roseg 3937m

P.Tschierva 3546m

P.Morteratsch 375m

Pontresina 1800m

Murtèl Muragl 2453m

P.Bernina 4049m

P.Zuppo 3995m

Bellavista 3922m

Morteratsch

Alp Languard 2262m

Val Muragl

P.Palü 3905m

P.Cambrena 3603m

Diavolezza 2973m

P.Albris: 3166m

P.Vadret

P.Languard 3262m

Diavolezza

343

valley, has more advanced terrain and is accessed from Sils Maria and **Surlej**. Diavolezza and Lagalb, both at nearly 3,000m, are reached by train or bus.

The frozen lakes of the Engadine and the forest trails make St Moritz one of the most interesting and beautiful cross-country areas in the Alps, with loipe of every standard. Bad is the more convenient base for serious langlaufers. The 42-km Engadine Marathon is held here each season and attracts thousands of entrants.

Beginners

There are nursery slopes at Corviglia, and guests at the Suvretta House even have their own beginner lift. However, because of the spread-out nature of St Moritz and its high prices, this is not the ideal resort in which to learn. A long, gentle blue (easy) run goes down from the Marmite restaurant on Corviglia, through the woods back into St Moritz, or all the way across to the cable-car at Bad. Every sector has some blue runs. The Furtschellas drag-lifts go up to blue runs at 2,800m above Sils Maria, but beginners will have to ride the cable-car down.

Intermediates

The highest skiing is found at Corvatsch, which links with red (intermediate) runs on Furtschellas. South-facing Corviglia has a number of flattering reds, and the run under the Piz Grisch chair always has excellent snow. The least crowded skiing, however, is out of St Moritz in the Lagalb sector at nearly 3,000m. The Giandas red under the cable-car boasts the longest and most direct fall-line skiing in the Engadine.

Advanced

The black (difficult) Hahnensee run from the top of Corvatsch winds over open snowfields and on into the woods at the edge of Bad, providing around 8km of non-stop skiing for 1,600 vertical metres. At Diavolezza, the Schwarzer Hang black piste drops through bands of rock for some first-rate steep skiing down the Bernina black run all the way to the bottom. The Diavolezza itinerary is long, steep and scenic.

Off-piste

The steep face of Piz Nair provides incredible thrills when enough powder snow covers the sheer rock. The long glacier itinerary from the top of Diavolezza, around and over crevasses to Morteratsch, is one of the classic off-piste routes in the Alps. Although off-piste guiding is not widely in demand, it is available through the St Moritz SSS, All Activities Agency (AAA) and The St Moritz Experience. Heli Bernina and Heliswiss offer heli-skiing.

Snowboarding

Although much of the terrain is suitable for riders, the resort's high prices for accommodation and nightlife are off-putting. The Diavolezza area is particularly recommended for freeriding, while the terrain park at Corviglia, reached by the Munt da San Murezzan chair-lift, contains a half-pipe and obstacle course.

Tuition and guiding

In 1929 the St Moritz and Suvretta were Switzerland's first ski schools, and today are both branches of the Swiss Snowsports School (SSS). Together they employ 300 instructors. The Palace Hotel has its own school. Snowboard School St Moritz and The Wave Snowboard School are part of the St Moritz/Suvretta SSS.

Mountain restaurants

Renowned among snow-users and gourmets alike, the Marmite, on Corviglia, is an essential lunch stop. Reservations are always necessary. The owner, Reto Mathis, whose father, Hartly, was the first man to bring haute cuisine to the high mountains, counts caviar and truffles by the kilo. Also on Corviglia, the Skihütte Alpina is great for pasta and rustic charm. Cheese specialities are best at the Piz Nair. The Suvretta owns three mountain eateries – the intimate Chassellas, the Chamanna, which is frequented by snowboarders, and Trutz Lodge, which boasts self-service and à la carte restaurants.

Accommodation

Badrutt's Palace Hotel (☎ 81 837 1000), with its grotesque tower, is the most famous of the five-stars and has its own ski school. The pastel blocks of the Kulm (☎ 81 836 8000) are preferred by Cresta members. The Suvretta House (☎ 81 836 3636) is a mini resort within a resort, with its own spa, skating-rink, nursery slope and ski ift. The Carlton (☎ 81 836 7000) has a country-house atmosphere. The four-star Schweizerhof (☎ 81 837 0707) and Steffani (☎ 81 832 2101) hotels, both with active nightlife, are downtown and affordable. The Park Hotel Kurhaus (☎ 81 832 2111) is next to the cross-country track in Bad. Three-star Hotel Waldhaus am See (☎ 81 833 7676) is pleasant, albeit a brisk walk from the town centre.

Eating in and out

Hanselmann's in the town centre has been around for more than 100 years and serves coffee, pastries and delectable ice-cream. Lunch at the Chesa Veglia, an architectural museum-piece owned by the Palace Hotel, is not expensive compared with dinner. The Suvretta's Trutz Lodge, reached by a chair-lift that runs at night, is open for evening fondue parties. In Celerina, the Stuvetta Veglia is recommended.

Après-ski

The Palace Hotel's Kings Club is still the place to go. The stübli at the Schweizerhof has late-night dancing on tables, and after 10pm is so crowded that you could not possibly fall off. The Vivai disco is popular and the Muli Bar hosts country-and-western music. Bobby's Bar is for the under-20s and the Prince disco is opposite the Kulm Hotel. The

Cascade Bar and the Cava Bar in the Hotel Steffani are both praised. The Devil's Place bar at Hotel Waldhaus am See claims the world's biggest range of malt whisky.

Childcare

The kindergarten in the Schweizerhof and Park Hotel Kurhaus both accept children over three years old on a daily basis, with lunch included. The Suvretta's Teddy Bear Club has a kindergarten for children from 12 months old, and a dedicated children's restaurant; both are for residents. The ski schools accept children over four years old.

Linked or nearby resorts

Celerina
top 3,057m (10,030ft) bottom 1,720m (5,643ft)

A village atmosphere, old stone houses painted with the local graffito designs, and ski access to Corviglia make Celerina an attractive and quiet alternative to St Moritz. The village has just 1,850 visitor beds and its own ski and snowboard school. Tobyland is the ski kindergarten for children from three-and-a-half years old and the four-star Hotel Cresta Palace (☎ 81 836 5656) offers daycare. The Cresta Kulm (☎ 81 836 8080) is the other four-star. Chesa Rosatsch (☎ 81 837 0101) is a 350-year-old inn.

TOURIST INFORMATION
Tel 41 81 830 0011
Fax 41 81 830 0019
Email info@celerina.ch
Web site www.celerina.ch

Pontresina
top 2,978m (9,770ft) bottom 1,800m (5,904ft)

With no big lifts of its own, Pontresina is about midway between the outlying Diavolezza sector and Corviglia. It has good indoor sports facilities. Grand Hotel Kronenhof (☎ 81 842 0111) is the only five-star in the resort. Kochendorfer's Albris (☎ 81 838 8040) is an inexpensive hotel. The Steinbock (☎ 81 842 6371) is comfortable and traditional. The four-star Saratz Hotel (☎ 81 839 4000) is highly praised, with a renowned restaurant and a kindergarten for children from three years old. Allegra Garni (☎ 81 838 9900) is the resort's newest hotel.

TOURIST INFORMATION
Tel 41 81 838 8300
Fax 41 81 838 8310
Email info@pontresina.com
Web site www.pontresina.com

Skiing facts: St Moritz

TOURIST INFORMATION
Via Maistra 12,
CH-7500 St Moritz, Graubunden
Tel 41 81 837 3333
Fax 41 81 837 3377
Email information@stmoritz.ch
Web site www.stmoritz.ch

THE RESORT
By road Calais 1,047km
By rail station in resort
Airport transfer Zurich 3–4hrs
Visitor beds 13,089
Transport bus free with ski pass

THE SKIING
Linked or nearby resorts Celerina (l),
Champfèr (n), Livigno (n), Pontresina (n),
Samedan (n), Sils Maria (l), Silvaplana (l),
Surlej (l), Zuoz (n)
Number of lifts 57 in linked area
Total of trails/pistes 350km in linked
area (35% easy, 25% intermediate,
40% difficult)
Beginners 5 lifts

LIFT PASSES
Area pass Upper Engadine (covers St
Moritz, Celerina, Silvaplana, Pontresina,
Sils), SF254–282 for 6 days including
one day's skiing in Livigno
Credit cards yes
Pensioners no reductions

TUITION
Skiing St Moritz SSS (☎ 81 830 0101),
Suvretta SSS (☎ 81 836 3600)
Snowboarding as ski schools
Other courses cross-country, heli-
skiing/boarding, race-training, slalom,
snowblading, telemark
Guiding Heli Bernina (☎ 81 852 4677),
Heliswiss (☎ 81 852 3535), The St
Moritz Experience (☎ 81 833 7714),
St Moritz SSS, AAA (☎ 81 832 2233)

CHILDREN
Lift pass SF141 for 6–16yrs
Ski & board school as adults
Kindergarten (ski) St Moritz SSS, (non-
ski) Park Hotel Kurhaus (☎ 81 832 2111),
Hotel Schweizerhof (☎ 81 837 0707)

OTHER SPORTS
Climbing wall, the Cresta, cricket, curling,
dog-sledding, golf and cricket on the
frozen lake, hang-gliding, horse-racing,
horse-riding, hot-air ballooning,
ice-driving, indoor tennis and squash,
night-skiing, Olympic bob-run, parapente, polo, skating, ski-jöring, ski-jumping, sleigh rides, snowbiking,
snowshoeing, speed skiing, swimming

FOOD AND DRINK
Coffee SF3.80–4.50, glass of wine
SF6–7, small beer SF4.50–5,
soft drink SF4, dish of the day SF16–25

Verbier

ALTITUDE 1,500m (4,920ft)

Intermediates **✱✱** Advanced **✱✱✱** Snowboarders **✱✱✱**

Verbier ranks alongside **St Anton, Val d'Isère, Chamonix, Zermatt** and **Whistler** in the international skiing hall of fame. Not only does it have an enormous range and variety of challenging pistes, but it is also home to some of Europe's most exciting lift-served, off-piste skiing. Nowhere is there a more extensive and diverse menu of glaciers, couloirs and deep powder bowls to tickle the palates of advanced skiers. The Savolèyres and Lac des Vaux sectors provide a much more limited playground for intermediates, while beginners here are best described as 'aspiring experts'.

✔ Easy rail and road access
✔ Wealth of off-piste
✔ Excellent sunshine record
✘ Expensive nightlife
✘ Large, spread-out village
✘ Inadequate mountain restaurants
✘ Traffic and difficult parking

Unlike its pedigree Swiss rivals in the Parsenn and the Bernese Oberland, Verbier does not have a historic skiing tradition. The first lift – a curious petrol-driven cable that pulled a 12-person sledge up 200m – was not built until 1946, and serious skiing here started to take off only 11 years later with the construction of Les Attelas cable-car. International skiers were immediately attracted to the demanding terrain that this opened up, and during the boom years of the 1960s and 1970s Verbier gradually developed into one of the most famous ski resorts in Europe.

However, the mountain path to its present status has been marked by a series of pitfalls. Lack of investment in mountain facilities coupled with an abysmal rate of exchange in the late 1980s saw Verbier plunge in popularity. The number of British visitors fell to seven per cent. But in recent years the lift company Téléverbier (partly owned by France's Compagnie des Alpes) has revamped the lift system, and Verbier has climbed back out of the crevasse and reinvented itself as a resort with a huge international following among serious skiers and snowboarders.

Anyone expecting a chocolate-box village of Heidi-style chalets is in for a disappointment. The resort comprises concrete apartment blocks and some less severe wooden buildings. Only 1,500 of the 15,000 beds are in hotels, and none of these has doorstep skiing. The straggling village is dominated by a church with a 20-m spire, built in 1962. This, depending on your viewpoint, is seen as a monstrous intrusion on the mountainside or an outstanding example of period architecture. But

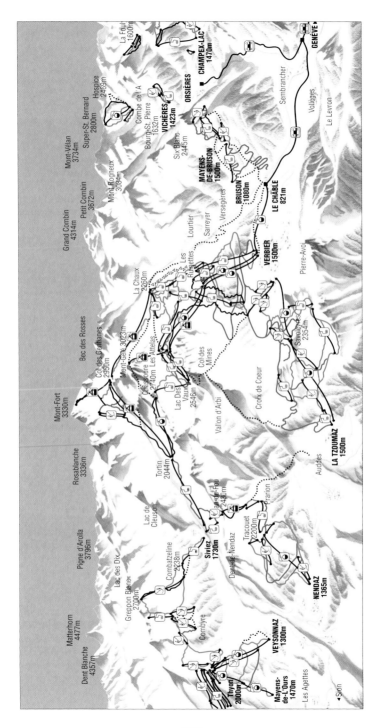

349

Verbier's plus points include less than two hours' motorway access from Geneva and more than 300 days of sunshine per year.

An essential part of Verbier's appeal is that it links to the so-called Four Valleys, the ski area it shares with its neighbours, comprising 410km of piste served by 96 lifts. Since the introduction of a hands-free, computerised lift ticket, **Thyon**, **Nendaz** and **Veysonnaz** have been arguing bitterly about revenue sharing. However, the current agreement secures the links for a further five seasons. Computerised pass-readers are now being installed on every lift to analyse which sectors attract the most skiers and consequently where future investment should be made. Verbier's skiing also includes the separate family resorts of **Bruson**, **Fouly** and **Vichères**.

On the snow
top 3,330m (10,925ft) bottom 1,500m (4,920ft)

The main reason for Verbier's comeback is its renovated lift system. This began with the introduction in 1994 of the Funispace 30-person giant gondola, linking Les Ruinettes to Les Attelas, followed by the eight-person gondola at Tortin in 1998, giving easy access to one of Verbier's most notoriously steep slopes. A new gondola, from Le Châble to Verbier and Les Ruinettes, will be open for the 2001–2 season, which will increase uphill capacity from 700 to 1,200 people an hour. The idea is to encourage day visitors to leave their cars in Le Châble, where the parking area has been doubled in size. It should also put an end to queues at Verbier's Medran lift station, even at peak hours. Piste-grooming has improved enormously in recent years.

> **WHAT'S NEW**
>
> Five-star Hotel Le Chalet d'Adrien opens in December 2001
> Le Châble–Ruinettes gondola opens for 2001–2 season

Verbier's best skiing is not visible from the resort and almost impossible to decipher from the cramped piste map, which receives universal criticism from readers: 'runs on the map are missing from the mountain'. 'The piste map is useless to anyone who doesn't know the resort.' Lifts passes here are extremely complicated and therefore we have listed only the Four Valleys and Family Pass in the *Skiing Facts* box towards the end of this entry. You are advised to assess the area you want to cover before parting with any money.

Main mountain access is by the two gondolas from the Medran base area. From Les Ruinettes mid-station, the Funitel gondola zips up to Attelas at 2,740m. From here skiers can ride a cable-car up to Mont Gelé (3,023m), ski down into the intermediate Lac des Vaux sector for chair-lift access to Tortin and further cable-cars to Mont-Fort (3,330m), or ski over to the south-facing intermediate runs of La Chaux, where the 150-person Jumbo cable-car rises to the glacial slopes of Gentianes and Mont-Fort.

Savolèyres is a separate intermediate mountain, accessed by an old (1970) gondola, with sunny south-facing slopes towards Verbier and longer, better runs down its back side to **Tzoumaz**. The glacier is no longer open for summer skiing.

Beginners
Novices should 'go somewhere else, unless your main aim is après-ski', according to one reporter. There is one short nursery slope mid-town on the Moulins golf course, and another crowded area on Esserts. Those certain of their snowploughing technique can ski blue (easy) runs higher up the mountain on the usually excellent snow at Lac des Vaux.

Intermediates
Savolèyres and its north side down to Tzoumaz, along with La Chaux and Lac des Vaux, are the best areas for intermediate skiing. It is impossible to ski all the way down to Les Savolèyres base-station on piste, which is a cause of much complaint as skiers are diverted sideways across the mountain to a dead-end bus stop. Verbier's main arterial highway, the pistes from Attelas to Les Ruinettes, and the inescapable roadway to the main lift station at Medran, are unreasonably overcrowded. The bottom road is made even more dangerous by a profusion of pedestrians, children on sledges, and dogs. However, a new slope has been built, which starts under Les Ruinettes and passes through the Clambin area, providing a good alternative route.

Advanced
Except for the one run down Mont-Fort, all of Verbier's black (difficult) pistes have been reclassified as 'ski itineraries' to avoid legal responsibility in case of accident. Skied by so many on a daily basis, such itineraries are essentially pistes, albeit not groomed. Most notorious is Tortin, a steep, wide slope usually pounded into bumps and often dangerous to access because of exposed rocks at the top. Gentianes, the run under the eponymous cable-car, offers a huge scope of bumps and ravines. Col des Mines (an open, south-facing slope returning to Verbier) and Vallon d'Arbi (a scenic, steep-sided valley leading to Tzoumaz) are both accessed by a traverse beginning in Lac des Vaux. It is important to respect warning signs if this traverse is closed. Marked itineraries down to Le Châble (800m) from Verbier are seldom skiable owing to poor snow cover.

Off-piste
We could devote an entire book to describing Verbier's off-piste. Only a decade ago Creblet, the front face of Mont Gelé, and the back of Mont-Fort down to Cleuson were considered radical descents. These days, like Stairway to Heaven and Hidden Valley, they are skied-out within an hour of a fresh snowfall. Reporters remarked on 'very good tree skiing at Bruson'. Bec des Rosses (3,220m) is now the venue for extreme snowboarding contests, and skiing off the back down into Fionnay wins jealous admiration. The 'North Face' of Mont-Fort, with its B52 and Poubelle variants, is routinely skied, despite its 'if-you-fall-

you-die' start. The Grand Banana and Paradise are examples of off-piste sectors that are not so much difficult to ski as dangerous to access. Reporters warned that skiers should be aware of the dangers all around them: 'we were skiing Creblet after things had opened up following a fresh snowfall. A couple of snowboarders in one of the couloirs off Attelas triggered a large avalanche that swept down well into the left-hand side of the bowl. Fortunately there wasn't anyone in the way'.

Snowboarding

Boarders are welcomed in Verbier, with its awesome freeriding from Mont Gelé. Thanks to new, cheaper accommodation at The Bunker they now make up an increasing proportion of Verbier's population. The terrain park at La Chaux offers three runs for boarders and freestylers, with music and a bar at the base. Both Mont-Fort and Les Ruinettes have terrain parks with half-pipes and obstacles.

Tuition and guiding

We have mixed reports of the Swiss Snowsports School (ESS), which has expanded in recent years. All children and beginner adults gather in the Medran parking lot; other adults meet at Les Ruinettes. La Fantastique and Adrénaline ('great fun') provide healthy competition. No Limits offers extreme skiing and boarding. Bureau des Guides is the official mountain guiding operation. Off-piste skiers should beware of local ski bums in Pub Mont-Fort offering illegal and uninsured guiding.

Mountain restaurants

Nowhere in the Four Valleys is there a gourmet mountain restaurant to compare with those in Zermatt or St Moritz, except in price. The best are Cabane Mont-Fort, a newly renovated Haute Route touring hut with an olde-worlde atmosphere, which serves fondue and other typically Swiss fare, and Chez Odette at Siviez ('a friendly welcome complete with aperitif and good food'). Chez Dany ('still worth a visit') at Clambin is perennially overcrowded and serves cheese dishes. There are fast-food terraces at La Chaux ('an outdoor sun-trap') and Les Attelas.

On Savolèyres, the primitive Buvette de la Marlenaz is far off-piste. The station café at Le Châble is warmly recommended by one reporter: 'don't tell anybody, as the seating is limited'. Chez Simon is recommended for its *vin chaud*. Les Ruinettes, Tortin and Gentianes self-services were all described as 'uninspired and busy'.

Accommodation

In December 2001 Le Chalet d'Adrien (☎ 27 771 6200) opens as Verbier's first five-star hotel. Until now the most comfortable, albeit not very central, hotel was the modern and elegant Rois Mages (☎ 27 771 6364). The four-star Rosalp (☎ 27 771 6323) suffers from cramped rooms. The modest Hotel Verbier (☎ 27 771 6688) in the village square is friendly, as is Serge Tacchini's Mazot (☎ 27 775 3550). Around the corner Hotel Vanessa (☎ 27 775 2800) is 'wonderfully convenient with good food'. The four-star Montpelier (☎ 27 771 6131) receives praise. Hotel Bristol (☎ 27 771 6577) is said to be extremely convenient and has the advantage of a small, free parking area, which is a rarity in the resort. However, 'the hotel houses a disco on the first floor, which can provide some noise late into the night'. Les Touristes (☎ 27 771 2147) is reported to be good value.

Some 90 per cent of visitors stay in tour-operator-run chalets or in the wealth of self-catering apartments. A cheaper option is The Bunker (☎ 27 771 6602), next to the snowboard centre, which was once a nuclear bunker but has now been turned into simple dormitory accommodation at 25SF per night with breakfast.

Eating in and out

The Rosalp remains a true gourmet treat and one of the best restaurants in Switzerland. Of the cheeseries, the best are the unpretentious and homey Les Touristes and Au Vieux-Verbier. Borsalino ('the best'), Chez Martin and Al Capone all serve pizzas. Harold's in the square is famous for burgers. Grotte à Max has an interesting range of rösti dishes, with kangaroo and ostrich. The Hacienda Café ('the worst') features Tex-Mex, with indifferent success. Le Bouchon Gourmand wins good reviews for its south-western French dishes. The Relais des Neiges is recommended for simple home cooking at modest prices, while Verbier Beach is also good value. Hotel Montpelier's restaurant offers outstanding cuisine and is second to the Rosalp as the best eatery in the resort.

Après-ski

Hotel Farinet, in the central square, is a major resort rendezvous. Fer à Cheval, sometimes serving free pizza, is packed out as soon as the lifts close. Harold's Snack is a cybercafé. The most original hang-out remains the Offshore, famed for its pink VW. Chalet girls and ski bums flock to the Pub Mont-Fort ('a local favourite, but I still have to work out why'). The Farm Club is as expensive as ever, with vodka at around £100 a bottle, and 'the biggest downside is the ridiculous queues to get in'. Ravers prefer the Scotch ('very basic') or Marshall's ('techno'). Crok No Name is Verbier's most sophisticated bar ('a nice place to drink, especially if you get one of the comfy seats'), although the over-50s will find Jacky's piano bar more to their taste. Sub-teens will enjoy the video games and pool tables at the Big Ben. The Nelson is 'crowded and with the décor and atmosphere of a Birmingham pub'. Garbo & Murphy's bar is recommended by several reporters.

Childcare

Chez les Schtroumpfs has an excellent reputation for day-long indoor childminding (for ages five months to seven years). The Kids Club skiing programme for children over three years is run by the ESS at its Moulins nursery site, which has its own lift and restaurant.

Linked or nearby resorts

Bruson
top 2,445m (8,022ft) **bottom** 1,100m (3,543ft)

Verbier's lift company has future plans for a direct gondola from the valley train station in Le Châble to the top of Bruson. But for the moment Bruson remains uncrowded and boasts some of the best steep powder skiing available on the Four Valleys ski pass, especially in its larch forests.

Two chair-lifts and two T-bars make up the lift system, serving only 30km of groomed pistes. With some hiking, however, long excursions down to **Sembrancher** and **Orsières** over snow-filled pastures, then a free train-ride back to Le Châble, are possible. Access is by free bus from Le Châble, itself connected to Verbier by gondola or another free bus. Bruson has two hotels, apartments midway up the mountain, and a restaurant.

TOURIST INFORMATION
Tel 41 27 776 1682
Fax 41 27 776 1541

Champex-Lac
top 2,188m (7,178ft) **bottom** 1,470m (4,823ft)

The narrow hairpin road up to Champex guarantees that this delightfully forested family resort, with its scenic frozen lake and 3,000 beds, never sees a queue. Unfortunately for Verbier-based skiers, the resort has opted out of the Four Valleys lift pass and you must buy a separate ticket. Skiing is limited: four lifts (two of them for beginners) access no more than 25km of pistes, which are very steep if taken off-piste directly under the main chair. Powder on the north face remains good for weeks, and the resort's clientèle rarely ventures into the untracked snow among the trees.

The Belvédère (☎ 27 783 1114) is outstandingly characterful and one of the more unusual hotels in the Alps. Its few bedrooms are panelled in broad Arolla pine and furnished with hand-painted furniture. The food is of a high standard and modestly priced. Champex has a small branch of the Swiss Snowsports School. The kindergarten has now closed down.

TOURIST INFORMATION
Tel 41 27 783 1227
Fax 41 27 783 3527
Email info@saint-bernard.ch
Web site www.saint-bernard.ch

Skiing facts: Verbier

TOURIST INFORMATION
CH-1936 Verbier, Val de Bagnes
Tel 41 27 775 3888
Fax 41 27 775 3889
Email verbiertourism@verbier.ch
Web site www.verbier.ch

THE RESORT
By road Calais 998km
By rail Le Châble 15mins
Airport transfer Geneva 2hrs
Visitor beds 15,000
Transport free ski bus

THE SKIING
Linked or nearby resorts Bruson (n),
Champex-Lac (n), La Fouly (n), Nendaz
(l), Super-St-Bernard (n), La Tzoumaz (l),
Thyon (l), Veysonnaz (l), Vichères (n)
Number of lifts 39 in Verbier, 95 in area
Total of trails/pistes 150km in Verbier,
410km in area (33% easy,
42% intermediate, 6% difficult,
19% very difficult)
Beginners 4 nursery slopes

LIFT PASSES
Area pass Four Valleys SF303 for 6 days.
Family Pass (covers whole area) SF303
for 1st adult, 30% reduction for 2nd,
30% reduction for 16–20yrs, 15%
reduction for 17–20yrs (without parent)
Pensioners 40% reduction for 6 days for
65yrs and over
Credit cards yes

TUITION
Skiing Adrénaline (☎ 27 771 7459),
ESS (☎ 27 775 3363) La Fantastique
(☎ 27 771 4141)
Snowboarding as ski schools,
and No Limits (☎ 27 771 5556)
Other courses extreme skiing/boarding,
heli-skiing/boarding, moguls,
race-training, telemark
Guiding Air Glaciers (heli-ski) (☎ 27
329 1415), Bureau des Guides (☎ 27
775 3363), No Limits (☎ 27 771 7250)

CHILDREN
Lift pass 7–15yrs 60% reduction on
adult price
Ski & board school as adults
Kindergarten (ski) ESS Kids Club
(☎ 27 771 4469), (non-ski) Les
Schtroumpfs (☎ 27 771 6585)

OTHER SPORTS
Climbing wall, curling, hang-gliding,
horse-riding (Le Châble), ice-climbing,
indoor golf, parapente, skating,
ski-touring, snowbiking, SnowCarting,
snowshoeing, squash, swimming, tubing

FOOD AND DRINK
Coffee SF3, glass of wine SF3,
small beer SF3.50–4, soft drink SF3.80,
dish of the day SF15–20

Nendaz
top 3,330m (10,925ft) bottom 1,365m (4,478ft)

Nendaz offers cheaper accommodation than Verbier but complicated
and inefficient access to the best of the Four Valleys skiing, although a
free bus does run from Nendaz to **Siviez**. The ESS, Neige Aventure and
Arc-en-Ciel are the ski schools, while Le Petit Bec is a kindergarten for
children aged 16 months to seven years.

TOURIST INFORMATION
Tel 41 27 289 55 89
Fax 41 27 289 55 83
Email info@nendaz.ch
Web site www.nendaz.ch

Siviez
top 3,330m (10,925ft) bottom 1,730m (5,676ft)

Skiers desperate to save money and determined to be first up Mont-Fort might consider Siviez. It is sunny and at the hub of the Four Valleys, with a high-speed chair link to the Gentianes–Mont-Fort cable-cars. Accommodation is limited to one hotel, a concrete apartment block and a youth hostel.

TOURIST INFORMATION
Tel 41 27 289 55 89
Fax 41 27 289 55 83

Veysonnaz
top 3,330m (10,925ft) bottom 1,400m (4,593ft)

This is a useful back door into the Four Valleys, reached by a winding 14-km mountain road from Sion. Gondolas take you up into its own considerable ski area from the little village and, more conveniently, from a second base area 3km away at **Mayen-de-L'Ours**. A bus service connects the two. The red (intermediate) piste de l'Ours, the main fall-line run, is a natural racecourse that is regularly used by the Swiss national team. Thyon, an unexpected piste-side community situated at the top of the Mayen-de-l'Ours gondola, is little more than a collection of apartment blocks and a hotel. From here a series of blue (easy) runs take you down to the sunny hamlet of Les Collons, or alternatively a red run connects with Siviez and Verbier. Hotel Magrappé (☎ 27 207 1817) is 'warm, comfortable and friendly'.

TOURIST INFORMATION
Tel 41 27 207 1053
Fax 41 27 207 1409
Email tourism@veysonnaz.ch
Web site www.veysonnaz.ch

Zermatt

ALTITUDE 1,620m (5,314ft)

Beginners ✳ Intermediates ✳✳✳ Advanced ✳✳✳ Snowboarders ✳✳

'If you were to visit only one resort in the world, this would be it,' said one reporter. Certainly, if you take your skiing with sugar and cream, then Zermatt is the resort in which to stay – provided, of course, you have both the wherewithal and the luck to find a vacant room in a tourist centre that has no low season at all. Arriving by train from the end-of-the-road hamlet of Täsch is a breathtaking experience – you are greeted by stunning mountain scenery, dominated by the Matterhorn. At the station, backpackers mingle with fur-clad socialites surrounded by mounds of Louis Vuitton luggage; all are equally awestruck by the Alpine setting. Zermatt is one of the most scenically beautiful ski resorts in the world. It is Switzerland's southernmost skiing terrain, with 29 summits of over 4,000m. A dynamic new learning academy called Stoked The Ski School (a stablemate to Stoked The Snowboarding School) was introduced here for the 2000–1 season to rival the much-criticised branch of the Swiss Snowsports School (SSS).

✔ Superlative scenery
✔ Excellent mountain restaurants
✔ High standard of accommodation
✔ Alpine charm
✔ Lively après-ski
✔ Activities for non-skiers
✔ Extensive ski area
✔ Car-free resort
✔ Glacier skiing
✔ High prices
✘ Spread-out resort
✘ Long airport transfer

Zermatt was a settlement from the early Middle Ages and inaugurated its first three tourist beds in 1838. Development has since been constrained by steep valley walls, leaving nothing between the Matterhorn and the village edge but open pasture dotted with wooden barns. In Zermatt's narrow lanes, sheep are still shorn outside centuries-old wooden *mazots* (ramshackle barns on stilts fitted with stone discs to keep the rats at bay), but the conflux of electric taxis ('efficient and exhilarating, if grossly expensive') and horse-drawn carriages on the main thoroughfare provide a fresh interpretation of 'traffic free'. Complimentary but 'hopelessly inadequate' ski buses link the separate ski areas, but any visitor to Zermatt must be prepared for a considerable amount of walking in ski boots.

The lift system dates from the construction of the Gornergrat cog railway in 1898. The lift attendants were described as unsmiling: 'many sat there with a face as expressionless as a smoked herring'. A combined lift pass with **Cervinia**, which is linked off the back of the Klein Matterhorn, is available, but is one of the two most expensive in Europe. It is more sensible to pay the daily supplement for the occasional foray across the border for a lazy lunch on Italian territory. Cervinia's skiing is bland by comparison, but on a sunny day in good snow conditions the run down to the town or to the linked resort of **Valtournenche** can be sensational and a welcome contrast to Zermatt's more demanding slopes. Skiing used to continue all year here on the glacier, but Zermatt has followed the lead of **Tignes** and other major glacial resorts by closing its high-altitude lifts for part of the summer. In 2001 Zermatt was not open for skiing from May 5 to July 7.

On the snow
top 3,899m (12,788ft) bottom 1,620m (5,314ft)
Zermatt is a resort for the adept skier with deep pockets and a taste for good living. No competent skier will find him- or herself outclassed by any groomed slope in Zermatt. Queuing at high season can be a serious problem, particularly for the gondola and cable–car that lead from the top of the town to Furi, and onwards to the Klein Matterhorn and Schwarzsee. Queues for the Gornergrat cog railway can be even worse. There is a convenient hands-free lift pass. ▮

The three once-separate ski areas are now linked – albeit tenuously – and mountain access has been transformed by the addition of the cable-car from Gant to Hohtälli. This effectively links the Sunnegga and Gornergrat areas and dispenses with the necessity of taking the long, slow, but beautiful train journey up the Gornergrat.

An underground funicular runs up to the Sunnegga sector, with sunny slopes continuing up to Blauherd and Rothorn, which are connected by an efficient 150-person cable-car. From here you can either return towards the resort or take the long run down to Gant and the cable-car to the Hohtälli–Stockhorn–Gornergrat sector.

Zermatt's other ski area, the Trockener Steg/Klein Matterhorn, stretches up to the Italian frontier. It can be reached from Gornergrat but is more easily accessed from the resort by gondola or cable-car to Furi. From there, lifts branch left for the Trockener Steg and Klein Matterhorn sectors and right for the Schwarzsee area, with Furgg straight up the middle. Zermatt retains 16 antiquated drag-lifts among its portfolio of more modern lifts. Reporters complain of inconsistent piste-grading: 'some blue (easy) runs seemed more like red (intermediate) ones and yet the reds were very straightforward, especially on Trockener Steg'.

Beginners
Zermatt is not highly recommended for novices, but beginners do have the rare chance to ski at exceptionally high altitude on the Theodul Glacier (Klein Matterhorn sector). Normally, the SSS takes beginners to the nursery slope just below Sunnegga. From here they progress by gondola to Blauherd for the blue run back down to Sunnegga and

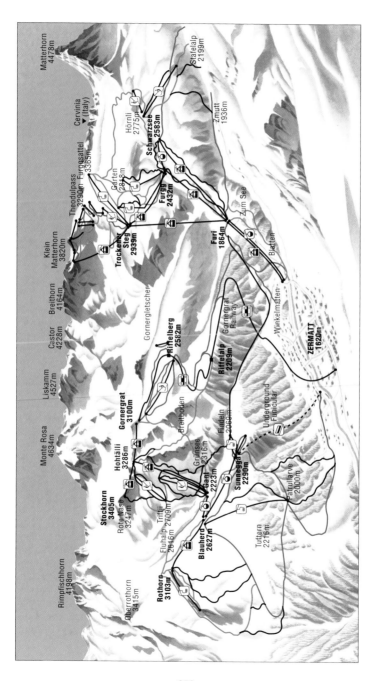

Patrullarve. Stoked The Ski School takes beginners to Trockener Steg where the slope is wide and open. Gornergrat offers more beginner terrain, but it is important to get off the train at Rotenboden, one stop earlier, to avoid a 'nasty bit' at the top.

Intermediates

Zermatt's red runs often become more than ordinarily testing owing to icy conditions and extreme overcrowding on the narrow sections down to the village. The highest and easiest intermediate skiing is in the Klein Matterhorn and Trockener Steg sectors. From the Klein Matterhorn, the long KL red flows alongside blue-ice crevasses down past the Plateau Rosa T-bars and over to the Testa T-bar.

Adventurous intermediates will be thrilled by the Kelle run from Gornergrat, passing over a ridge to link up at Breitboden with the classic White Hare red, which begins with a narrow, challenging passage up at Hohtälli. Intermediate skiing on the Sunnegga–Blauherd sector is sunnier and smoother, making ideal 'ski to lunch' terrain.

Advanced

Triftji is one of the most famous black (difficult) runs in the Alps. Unfortunately, this and the other black trails down under the Hohtälli–Rote Nase sector do not receive sufficient snow early on, so they are often closed until mid-January. Together, the Stockhorn and Grieschumme blacks make an almost perfect fall-line descent from Rote Nase down to Gant, a bone-jarring bump bonanza that only the most rubber-legged will achieve without stopping.

Further afield, and invisible to spectators, is Zermatt's least crowded, best black-run skiing. Sloping sharply down from the Stafel–Hörnli drag-lift into the tree-line, Tiefbach and Momatt are steep runs that dive towards Zmutt and the borders of the resort. Notorious as an accident black-spot as well as an expert run, the Furgg–Furi stretch is described by one reporter as being 'like the M25' in late afternoon, when it is the main homeward-bound route. But early in the morning, when Furgg–Furi has yet to be scraped clean of snow, it makes an excellent downhill course for more advanced skiers.

Off-piste

The Schwarzsee sector is cold and uncrowded. The Aroleid trail under the cable-car is normally a bump run all the way to Furi. Less skied are the Garten gullies. From the top of the Furgg–Garten drag, and to the left of the Garten red run, the two Garten couloirs offer a choice of narrow chutes, which are very steep for the first 40m but not life-threatening should you fall. At the bottom a favourite 'sky ramp' jump of about 20m has the attractions of a perfect landing and good views for spectators from the Garten lift. Down from Rothorn on the sunny side of the mountain, three itineraries (Chamois, Marmotte and Arbzug) become wide-open powder routes after a good storm.

A day's heli-skiing excursion to the Monte Rosa or the Alphubeljoch above Zermatt is a popular way to escape the pistes ('the most amazing experience – we were flown past the Matterhorn and dropped on to a tiny ledge in what seemed the middle of nowhere').

Snowboarding

Zermatt is a serious destination for snowboarders with stupendous possibilities for freeriding. Stoked The Snowboarding School is acknowledged as one of the best in the Alps. The terrain park at Blauherd has a special area for beginners. The terrain park at Rotenboden, beneath the Gornergrat and accessed by the Riffelberg-Gifthittli chair, has jumps and a half-pipe. The Trockener Steg Park contains slides and tubes.

Tuition and guiding

Zermatt now has a welcome new ski school called (appropriately, but perhaps confusingly) The Ski School and is also known as Stoked. Its young, international team – it was founded by two directors of The Stoked Snowboarding School – now provides the competition that the old and staid SSS sorely lacked. In winter 2000–1 the school was booked continuously from December and plans to increase the number of instructors for this year. It has established an office at the bottom of the new passenger elevator that gives access to the Furi lifts at the foot of the Klein Matterhorn sector. In 2000–1 all the full-time instructors were aged between 18 and 31, and half of them were women.

One consistent complaint levelled against the SSS has been that it employs a disproportionate number of instructors aged over 65. Readers have accused us of ageism, but over the past five years ski technique has undergone the most fundamental changes in all of its 3,000-year history. There are those who choose to ski with more mature instructors, but personally we would rather seek to absorb the fresh skills of a younger generation.

Of course, the SSS has some excellent instructors among its number who are regularly booked through the concierges of major hotels and remain busy all season. However, reporters complain that the stranger in town who presents him- or herself at the SSS office must take pot luck, with an apparently large number of booby prizes in the bran tub. In direct contrast to this criticism, however, one reporter wrote: 'the Swiss Ski School was excellent – as good as, if not better, than most of the others I have experienced in Europe and Canada. Your comments in *The Guide* are grossly unfair'.

Mountain restaurants

'Eating well here is of the utmost importance and not indulging in a sit-down meal borders on the criminal,' said one reporter. 'Standards of food are extremely high and dishes rarely fail to dazzle'. This is no place to pack a picnic – not when old wooden barns such as Chez Vrony, in Findeln, provide crystal glasses, starched napkins, sofas on the terrace and intimate nooks and crannies for serious dining. 'Visitors keep this place busy all year, but they haven't lowered the standards of cooking or ruined the atmosphere'. Also in Findeln, Paradies and the Findlerhof, run by mountain guide Franz Schwery, are warmly recommended. The centuries-old hamlet of Zum See houses an inn of the same name, which is run by Max and Greti and has an established reputation as one of Zermatt's best – it is worth trying the curried noodles and king prawns here. Higher up in the Furi sector, Simi is the rösti head-quarters but also serves delicious salads at reasonable prices. Tony's Grotta at Riffelalp has delectable pasta. Fluhalp, at the top of Rothorn, has some of the finest food and certainly the best panorama of the Matterhorn ('the salad of rare sliced lamb loin was quite delectable'). Stafelalp is 'charmingly situated with unusual views of the Matterhorn'.

Accommodation

Hotel-keepers rule in Zermatt and chalet accommodation is minimal. The five-star experience of the venerable Zermatterhof (☎ 27 966 6600) is as smooth as ever. The rival Mont Cervin (☎ 27 966 8888) has fewer balconies but sumptuous apartments in its annex.

The four-star Monte Rosa (☎ 27 966 0333), a favourite of Sir Winston Churchill and the base from which Edward Whymper, the Victorian mountaineer, set off to conquer the Matterhorn, exudes understated opulence ('the service and food were faultless'). The four-star Alex (☎ 27 966 7070) is a large hotel with a nightclub and swimming-pool. Reporters comment that 'some of the rooms are a bit small, but the location is ideal and there is an amazing range of facilities'. Its sister hotel, the Alex Schlosshotel Tenne (☎ 27 967 1801) is an Alpine–Byzantine architectural mélange ('what a superb antidote to sterile, corporate, overdone hotel chains. Friendly attentive service, an owner who seemed to take a genuine interest in his guests, plus a ski-room that doubled as a nuclear shelter'). The Relais & Chateau Schönegg (☎ 27 966 3434) is a chalet-style establishment close to the river and the Sunnegga lift station. Hotel Alpenhof (☎ 27 967 4333) contains an exquisite spa that offers a comprehensive range of health and beauty treatments.

Of the other four-stars, the Albana Real (☎ 27 966 6161) is 'mod-ern and comfortable'. Hotel Allalin (☎ 27 966 8266) had 'bathrooms so spic and span they could have been used in a Mr Clean advertise-ment. The nearby church bell that rings at 7am could, however, wake the dead'. Parkhotel Beau-Site (☎ 27 967 4141) receives praise: 'superb, with good-sized rooms, excellent food and service, but the wine was overpriced'. Hotel Nicoletta (☎ 27 966 0777) and Hotel La Ginabelle (☎ 27 966 5000) are both recommended for families with small children, as they have kindergartens.

The three-stars include Hotel Holiday (☎ 27 967 1203), a family-run establishment with good food, close to the Sunnegga Express. Nearby Hotel Parnass (☎ 27 967 1179) is said to have 'a quiet and relaxed atmosphere – not wildly luxurious, but good value for money'. Hotel Bijou (☎ 27 966 5151), two minutes' walk from the Klein Matterhorn

Skiing facts: Zermatt

TOURIST INFORMATION
Bahnhofplatz,
CH-3920 Zermatt
Tel 41 27 967 0181
Fax 41 27 967 0185
Email zermatt@wallis.ch
Web site www.zermatt.ch

THE RESORT
By road Calais 1,076km
By rail station in resort, or Visp 36km
Airport transfer Geneva 4hrs,
Milan 3hrs, Sion 1½ hours, Zurich 5hrs
Visitor beds 13,200
Transport free ski bus with ski pass

THE SKIING
Linked or nearby resorts Cervinia (I),
Crans Montana (n), Grächen (n),
Riederalp (n), Saas-Fee (n)
Number of lifts 39; 70 with Cervinia
Total of trails/pistes 150km in Zermatt,
245km including Cervinia (29% easy,
42% intermediate, 29% difficult)
Beginners 3 runs
Summer skiing 21km of trails and 6 lifts
on Klein Matterhorn Glacier during part of
summer

LIFT PASSES
Area pass SF306 for 6 days
Pensioners 25% reduction for men
65yrs and over, women 62yrs and over
Credit cards yes

TUITION
Skiing SSS (☎ 27 966 2466),
Stoked The Ski School (☎ 27 967 8788)
Snowboarding SSS, Stoked The
Snowboarding School (☎ 27 967 8788)
Other courses cross-country, heli-skiing/
boarding, teen snowboarding, telemark
Guiding Alpin Center (☎ 27 966 2460),
Air Zermatt (☎ 27 966 8686)

CHILDREN
Lift pass free for under 9 yrs,
50% reduction for 9–16yrs
Ski & board school as adults
Kindergarten (ski) SSS, (non-ski)
Kinderclub Pumuckel at Hotel La
Ginabelle (☎ 27 966 5000),
Kinderparadies (☎ 27 967 7252), Hotel
Nicoletta kindergarten (☎ 27 967 0151),
SSS Pingu-Club (☎ 27 966 2466)

OTHER SPORTS
Curling, dog-sledding, gorge-climbing,
helicopter rides, ice-climbing, indoor
tennis and squash, parapente,
rock-climbing, skating, sleigh rides,
snowshoeing

FOOD AND DRINK
Coffee SF3.30, glass of wine SF3–3.50,
small beer SF4.30, soft drink SF4,
dish of the day SF20–28

lift, is praised by several reporters as 'small and friendly with rooms even better than a four-star; the food was a culinary delight each evening'. The Excelsior (☎ 27 966 3500) is 'central, next to a bus stop, and caters for vegetarians'. Le Petit Hotel (☎ 27 966 4266) receives glowing reports ('I can't speak highly enough about this modest but extremely comfortable hotel. Only one tiny problem that it is 100m up a slightly icy road from the church, which can make things slippery in ski boots, but this is a tiny price to pay for such a lovely little hotel'). We also have good reports of the Darioli (☎ 27 967 2748). The chalet-style Malteserhaus (☎ 27 455 1838) has generously sized apartments.

Eating in and out

Zermatt's restaurants (there are more than a hundred) have a deserved reputation for high quality and price. Le Gitan was well-praised ('my lamb with garlic was nothing short of phenomenal'), and Le Cervin brasserie in the Mont Cervin is highly recommended. American-style steaks are grilled at the Viktoria-Centre. Lamb from the owner's own flock (watch out for the sheepdog in the foyer) is succulent at the Schäferstübli. Portofino, upstairs at the Post, is good for fresh fish. The Walliserkanne received a mixed report: 'the food is good but dealing with the staff is like being with your least favourite relative'. The Whymperstube in the Hotel Monte Rosa serves traditional fondues in an Edwardian ambience. Far Eastern cuisine is becoming increasingly popular in the resort, with Chinese, Japanese and Thai restaurants to choose from. China Garden, behind the Derby Hotel, serves 'Chinese food as authentic as you'll get in Switzerland'. Hotel Albana houses a Thai restaurant ('one of the best I have encountered anywhere in the world'). Myoko is a new sushi restaurant ('quite superb, with chefs from Tokyo and Kyoto who are supreme masters of their art, but I don't want to mention the cost'). The Pipe serves American-style snacks. Chez Gaby, the Spaghetti Factory and the Cheminée steak house are, according to one reporter, 'not so good any more'. Zermatt has about 15 grocery shops.

Après-ski

Après-ski starts with cakes and hot chocolate at Zellners: 'the air is thick with the scent of chocolate. They also serve delicious ice-cream and opulent cakes'. Later on, Elsie's Place, by the church, is expensive and crowded, but irresistible for champagne and oysters or snails. The Post Hotel complex caters for everybody; the Pink Elephant has a high standard of live jazz; Le Village is for house music, and Le Broken is a traditional disco that incites dancing on huge beer barrels until 3am. The Post's Boathouse bar, not to be confused with the Zermatt Yacht, Golf and Country Club, is decorated like the inside of a sloop. Hotel Pollux has a T-Bar. The Alex Hotel's nightclub is sedate but it is the only place where 30-somethings and upwards can dance to music that allows conversation. Grampi's Pub ('good service and a friendly atmosphere') is a glass-fronted haunt. Murphy's Pub is said to have 'excellent live music in a busy atmosphere'. Z'Alt Hischi is a small, atmospheric 'rusty little nook' in the old part of town, with an extensive collection of Rolling Stones CDs. The North Wall and the Brown Cow are where you find the resort workers. The Pipe is the favourite among riders and freeride skiers ('great atmosphere, outrageous drinking games and friendly staff'). Vernissage is good, but reporters rated the Papperla ('decibel levels rise quickly as it gets rowdy and jam-packed') the coolest après-ski spot in town.

There are a number of expensive jewellery shops and some good sports shops, but few of the chic boutiques one finds in **Crans Montana** or **St Moritz**. Glacier Sports ('admitted they couldn't find me new ski boots, rather than pushing something unsuitable') and Julen Sport are both recommended ski shops.

Childcare

Zermatt's facilities for families with small children have greatly improved in recent years, and the resort now offers a good choice of daycare. A bonus is the free lift pass for all children up to nine years old. The SSS Pingu-Club ('where kids can jump around on the snow with a huge cuddly penguin') cares for four- to six-year-olds all day at its kindergarten up the mountain at Riffelberg. Children meet outside the tourist information office then travel up (and down) by special train. Care includes indoor and outdoor games and ski lessons. 'Well organised and absolutely excellent,' said one reporter. The SSS also accepts children from six to 12 years with supervised lunch at Blauherd or Riffelberg. Stoked The Ski School runs group lessons and plans to open a ski kindergarten at Trockener Steg for 2001–2. It also runs snowboarding classes for children and teenagers. Packages are available for six- to nine-year-olds, including lunch, board and boots, knee protectors and safety helmet.

At Hotel Nicoletta, Seiler's Children's Paradise takes kids from two years old. Childminding, with optional ski lessons (from six years old) on a baby slope by the river, is available at Hotel La Ginabelle's Kinderclub Pumuckel for children from two-and-a-half years old. Kinderparadies cares for children from two years and is also open as a babysitting service in the evenings until 10pm.

Round-up

Adelboden and Lenk
top 2,357m (7,733ft) bottom 1,068m (3,503ft)

Adelboden is an unspoilt village of wooden chalets located on a sunny terrace at the bottom of the Wildstrubelmassiv. It has the advantage of no through-traffic. **Lenk** is a traditional spa village with its own sulphur spring, situated at the end of the wide Simmen Valley. The two villages share a 170-km ski area served by 55 lifts. Reporters described the ski area as having 'no challenge on piste, but quite a lot of scope off-piste and not many people sharing it with you'. The new six-seater gondola enhances the lift links between the resorts. Lift passes for more than four days give you one day's free skiing in **Gstaad**.

Adelboden and Lenk ski schools both organise tuition for adults and children from four years old. Lenk also caters for disabled skiers. Crazy Sports and Timeless Snowboarding are Adelboden's specialist snow-boarding schools, while Adrenaline is the equivalent in Lenk. Alpine School Adelboden and Hansrüdi Rösli in Lenk provide off-piste guides. The Gastekindergarten in Adelboden cares for three- to six-year-olds, and the crèche in Lenk's Hotel Krone (☎ 41 736 3344) takes non-skiers of all ages. Adlis Winterspielgarten is the ski kindergarten in Adelboden, while the SSS Lenk accepts skiers from three years old.

Adelboden's recommended hotels include the Beau Site (☎ 33 673 2222), the attractively located Parkhotel Bellevue (☎ 33 673 8000) and Arena Hotel Steinmattli (☎ 33 673 3939). Hotel Huldi Waldhaus (☎ 33 673 1531) was described as 'very welcoming'. Hotel Krone in Lenk is recommended for families. Adelboden has 23 restaurants in and around town. Other sports available in both resorts include cross-country, curling, dog-sledding and night-skiing. Lenk offers the unusual sports of ski-jöring and board-jöring.

TOURIST INFORMATION
Tel (Adelboden) 41 33 673 8080/(Lenk) 41 33 733 3131
Fax (Adelboden) 41 33 673 8092/(Lenk) 41 33 733 2027
Email info@adelboden.ch / info@lenk.ch
Web site www.adelboden.ch / www.lenk.ch

Andermatt
top 2,965m (9,725ft) bottom 1,445m (4,740ft)

Andermatt is a retreat for a dedicated skiing minority. It boasts enor-mous off-piste opportunities and a reputation for generous dumps of snow, but is in fact one of Switzerland's lesser-known little gems. The resort is situated at a major Alpine crossroads on the route to the St

Gotthard Pass into Italy and was once one of the busiest of Swiss resorts. Now the high Urseren Valley, of which Andermatt is the main village, is underpassed by the Gotthard road and rail tunnels, making it a virtual dead-end in winter.

Four ski areas, with a total of 13 lifts and 56km of piste, run along the sides of the Urseren Valley, between the Furka and Oberalp passes. The two main areas lie at either end of Andermatt; the two smaller and less popular ones lie to the south-west, above the villages of **Hospental** and **Realp**. Descents down the shaded face of Gemsstock, which has 800m of severe vertical and treacherous off-piste skiing in the bowl, should not be tackled without a guide; nor should some of the long off-piste alternatives in other directions from the top-station. Beginners tend to ski in the Grossboden area. Andermatt is part of the Gottard–Oberalp area, which links the resort with three further villages of **Disentis**, **Oberalp** and **Sedrun**, making a total ski area of 34 lifts and 166km of piste. Andermatt has a convenient hands-free lift pass.

Andermatt has an SSS for adults and children from four-and-a-half years old. The off-piste guiding companies are Alpine Sport-school, Bergschool Uri and Montanara.

Andermatt itself has cobbled streets and a traditional character. However, it is one of Switzerland's major centres for the training of alpine troops, and severe barrack buildings are a feature of the architecture. The heart of the old village receives little sun as it is hemmed in by mountains. There is not much traffic and no public transport. Accommodation is in a mixture of hotels and appealing old chalets. Drei Könige & Post (☎ 41 887 0001) is a recommended three-star. Hotel Schweizerhof (☎ 41 887 1189) is a two-star, described as 'a bit old but quite central – the food was satisfactory'. Pension Sternen (☎ 41 887 1130) is reported to have a cosy atmosphere with 'excellent Rösti for lunch'.

TOURIST INFORMATION
Tel 41 41 887 1454
Fax 41 41 887 0185
Email info@andermatt.ch
Web site www.andermatt.ch

Arosa
top 2,653m (8,702ft) bottom 1,800m (5,904ft)

In 1883, ski-tourer Dr Otto Herwig-Hold stumbled across the tiny village of Inner Arosa high in the Swiss Graubunden. He climbed to the top of the 2,512-m Hörnli, looked down at the village and realised that it was the perfect site on which to build his new tuberculosis sanatorium. With its wide range of international patients, the hospital soon put Arosa on the Alpine map.

Today the resort is one of the truly all-round ski resorts of the Alps. Arosa's skiers are not here to bash the pistes from dawn until dusk; instead they are in search of the complete winter-sports experience. The ski area consists of wide, sunny slopes, mostly above the tree-line, and covering the three peaks of Hörnli, Weisshorn and Bruggerhorn. It is well linked and, though small with only 15 lifts, boasts a total of 70km of piste. Much of this is made up of blue (easy) and red (intermediate) runs over hilly rather than mountainous terrain. One of the only hazards of Arosa's skiing is the number of pedestrians and tobogganers on the piste; non-skiers can buy hiking passes that allow them to use gondolas and some chair-lifts. The free buses circulate frequently.

The top of the Hörnli is the starting point for a variety of ski-tours, involving skins (artificial seal skins that allow you to travel uphill on skis) and public transport, to neighbouring resorts. Arosa has a dramatic half-pipe and is keen to promote snowboarding. The SSS and the ABC Snowsportschool both offer courses in cross-country, skiing for the disabled, snowblading and telemark.

Arosa Kulm (☎ 81 378 8888) and the Tschuggen Grand Hotel (☎ 81 378 9999) are the two five-stars, while Waldhotel National (☎ 81 378 5555) is 'convenient, comfortable, but lacking in style'. Each bedroom at Hotel Eden (☎ 81 377 0261) is decorated in an individual style. Hotel Cristallo (☎ 81 378 6868) was described by reporters as 'a good place with very smart bathrooms and four-posters'. Hotel Alpensonne (☎ 81 377 1547) offers 'friendly service and a pleasant atmosphere'.

Carmennahütte is the best of half-a-dozen mountain restaurants, all of which are reachable on foot. The choice of resort restaurants is limited. Kitchen (in Hotel Eden), Crazy, Halligalli and Nuts are the nightclubs. Access to the village is tricky, with 244 bends in the scenic 32-km road from the busy, medieval valley town of Chur. Taking the train through stunning scenery is the better option. Once in the village, a toboggan is the essential form of transport.

TOURIST INFORMATION
Tel 41 81 378 7020
Fax 41 81 378 7021
Email arosa@arosa.ch
Web site www.arosa.ch

Brienz–Meiringen–Hasliberg
top 2,433m (7,982ft) bottom 1,061m (3,481ft)

Meiringen–Hasliberg is situated in the Bernese Oberland, halfway between Lucerne and Interlaken. The resorts have joined forces with **Brienz–Axalp**, to form the Alpen Region Brienz–Meiringen–Hasliberg. Meiringen is best known for the Reichenbach Fall where Sir Arthur Conan Doyle's character of Sherlock Holmes fell to his untimely death during his final struggle with arch-villain Moriarty. The sweet-toothed might also be interested to hear that meringues were originally created in Meiringen.

The Meiringen–Hasliberg area has 16 lifts and 60km of slopes, 40 per cent of which are rated intermediate. Mountain access is by cable-car from Meiringen via Hasliberg Reuti and on to the main ski area, or by gondola from Hasliberg Wasserwendi at 1,160m. The terrain here is ideal for snowboarders, with a half-pipe and natural obstacles that form Switzerland's first 'natural snowboard park'. Brienz–Axalp, which is not linked into the main area, has four of its own lifts and 20km of runs.

The resorts do not have a crèche, but the SSS has a ski kindergarten and is praised as 'excellent, and I find it hard to imagine better facilities for teaching children'. SSS is the main school, with Team Spirit the alternative. Alpine skiing, snowboarding, cross-country and telemark are among the courses on offer. Off-piste guiding is available with the SSS, Bergsteigerschule Castor or Team Spirit.

There are five mountain restaurants in the ski area, including a new one with a scenic lookout tower called the Alpen Tower. Meiringen has 15 hotels, among which are the Alpin Sherpa Hotel (☎ 33 972 5252), Parkhotel du Sauvage (☎ 33 971 4141) and three-star Sporthotel Sherlock Holmes (☎ 33 972 9889). Hasliberg's 16 hotels include the Bären (☎ 33 971 6022) and the Bellevue (☎ 33 971 2341). Hotel Brienz (☎ 33 951 3551) and Grandhotel Giessbach (☎ 33 952 2525) are both in Brienz. Other activities available in the resorts include horse-riding, ice-climbing and indoor tennis. The Sherlock Holmes museum hosts mystery nights and mystery weekends.

TOURIST INFORMATION
Tel 41 33 972 5050
Fax 41 33 972 5055
Email info@alpenregion.ch
Web site www.alpenregion.ch

Flims and Laax
top 3,018m (9,902ft) bottom 1,100m (3,609ft)

Flims is a year-round destination that lies in the heart of the Graubunden on the route of the famous Glacier Express train. Together with its neighbours, **Laax** and **Falera**, it serves the wide south-facing ski area known as the Alpine Arena. **Flims Dorf** is the livelier and more convenient part of the village in which to stay. The hotels in **Flims Waldhaus** are not within easy walking distance of the lifts, but the larger ones have a courtesy minibus service to the base-station in Flims.

The pleasant old village of Laax is 5km to the west, with a modern satellite base-station at **Laax-Murscheg**, and low-cost, on-mountain accommodation called Crap Mountain Hostel (☎ 81 927 7373). In recent years Laax has become a popular snowboarding base. The farming hamlet of Falera offers a rustic alternative.

There are 'theme park' nursery areas for children, called Dreamlands, in Flims, Laax and Falera, and higher up the mountain some gentle practice slopes are inviting for beginners. A total of 28 lifts and 220km of mainly motorway-style piste give the intermediate snow-user the run of the mountain. The longest run is the Weisser Schuss from La Siala to Flims (14km). The off-piste potential is surprisingly high, with tree-level runs above Laax.

Snowboard Fahrschule and the SSS offer lessons at all three bases. The Crap Sogn Gion and the Vorab Glacier areas each boast two well-maintained half-pipes and terrain parks. The two off-piste guiding companies are called Alpine Action Unlimited and Swiss Mountaineer School Mountain Fantasy. Cross-country trails along the valley floor are available at Flims, and the neighbouring villages of **Trin** and **Sagogn**. Snowboard Fahrschule and the SSS offer classes for children from four years old, and reports of the ski kindergarten are favourable. Both the Park Hotels Waldhaus (☎ 81 928 4848) and the Hotel Adula (☎ 81 928 2828) have crèches. Other sports available in the resorts include indoor tennis, skating, sleigh rides, SnowCarting and children's snowmobiling.

The best mountain eateries are at the lower levels and not on the skiing trails, although the Runca hut below Startgels and the Tegia Larnags are both worth the detour. Among the higher altitude options, the Segnes-Hütte is welcoming, the Foppa is an old wooden chalet with a sun terrace, and the popular Elephant restaurant at Crap Masegn and Capalari on the Crap Sogn Gion have delicious food.

The choice of accommodation ranges from the five-star Park Hotels Waldhaus, which comprises five buildings with opulent rooms, to the well-run three-star Hotel La Siala (☎ 81 927 2222) in Falera. Hotel Adula is praised for its children's facilities. Hotel Sunstar Surselva (☎ 81 928 4848) is said to be 'excellent and central', with a swimming-pool and health centre. The top choice in Laax is the Posta Veglia (☎ 81 921 4466). Laax is the more 'happening' base for snowboarders.

Recommended restaurants include Pizzeria Pomodoro, the Barga in Hotel Adula, La Cena in the Park Hotels Waldhaus and the Posta Veglia. Later on the action focuses on the Angel Flims at the base-station, the Crap Bar and the Casa Veglia at the Laax base-station, the Red Cat in Laax or the quieter Segnes Bar in Flims.

TOURIST INFORMATION
Tel 41 81 920 9200
Fax 41 81 920 9201
Email tourismus@alpenarena.ch
Web site www.alpenarena.ch

Gstaad
top 2,979m (9,744ft) bottom 1,000m (3,280ft)
Skiing is only a decorative accessory to the charm of this low-lying resort. The village stands at 1,050m, with none of the local skiing above 2,200m, which means that snow cover can be unreliable. The redeeming factor is the proximity of Les Diablerets Glacier, where the lifts go up to 2,979m. Regulars argue that the sheer extent of the skiing included in the Ski Gstaad lift pass – 67 lifts covering 250km of piste (nearly half of it rated as easy) and ten villages – makes up for the lack of challenge.

The local skiing is inconveniently divided into three separate areas. Regular ski buses to the surrounding villages of **Rougemont**, **Saanenmöser** and **Schönried** give access to slopes offering more scope. Schönried now has a pedestrianised centre. The other villages covered on the lift pass are **St Stephan**, **Zweisimmen**, **Lauenen**, **Gsteig**, **Saanen** and **Château d'Oex**.

Gstaad has terrain parks at Hornberg above Saanenmöser, at Rinderberg above Zweisimmen, and a new one on the Eggli. Heli-skiing and ski-touring are available, ice-climbing, tubing and snowshoeing are some of the alternative sports on offer and there are 140km of cross-country loipe. The area's four ski and snowboard schools take children from four years old. Recommended mountain restaurants include Chemihütte ('by far the best') above St Stephan, and Cabane de la Sarouche at Château d'Oex. Ruble-Rougemont at the bottom of the Gouilles chair-lift is 'half the price of anywhere else'.

Gstaad is filled with top-quality hotels and a cluster of well-preserved wooden buildings in the traffic-free village centre. The best-known hotel is the Palace (☎ 33 748 5000), which has fairytale turrets and sits on the hill like a feudal castle dominating the village and its daily life. It has, however, received criticism: 'apart from being vulgar, it managed to charge us the same for a couple of whiskies as we had earlier paid for our dinner in the town below'. The Grand Hotel Park (☎ 33 748 9800) is opulent. The four-star Bernerhof (☎ 33 748 8844)) is conveniently close to the railway station, and the Christiania (☎ 33 744 5121) has individually designed bedrooms. The four-star Olden (☎ 33 744 3444) is family-run and cosy, as is the Posthotel Rössli (☎ 33 748 4242). Sporthotel Rütti (☎ 33 744 2921) is 'fairly basic' but has a high standard of food and is said to be good value. Most of the cheaper hotels are in the surrounding villages of Schönried, Saanenmöser, Saanen and Gsteig. Hotels can arrange babysitting and the Palace Hotel has a nursery.

Recommended restaurants include the Sonnenhof, La Cave in the Hotel Olden and the sixteenth-century Chlösterli. The Bären at Gsteig offers traditional Swiss fare. Café du Cerf in Rougemont is a typical Swiss restaurant with live music at weekends. The Palace's Greengo nightclub is the main late-night venue for those who can afford it. The locals meet at Richi's. Other haunts include Pubbles in the Hotel Boo in Saanen, Club 95 at the Sporthotel Victoria and the Grotte in the Hotel Alpin Nova in Schönried. Down Town is a bar with live jazz in the Hotel Ermitage-Golf, also at Schönried. Château d'Oex is one of the major hot-air ballooning centres in the Alps. SnowCarting is another popular sport in the area.

TOURIST INFORMATION
Tel 41 33 748 8181
Fax 41 33 748 8184
Email gst@gstaad.ch
Web site www.gstaad.ch

Lenzerheide and Valbella
top 2,865m (9,397ft) bottom 1,500m (4,920ft)

Lenzerheide used to attract a fair number of British families, but in recent years it has decreased in popularity. The area has considerable charm, including magnificent cross-country skiing. The villages of Lenzerheide and **Valbella** lie at either end of a lake in a wide, wooded pass running from **Churwalden** to **Parpan**, **Lantsch** and **Lenz**, with high mountains on either side. Transport is based on an efficient system of buses.

The skiing is in two separate sectors, Rothorn and Danis-Stätzerhorn, on either side of the inconveniently wide pass. The skiing terrain in both is partly wooded and partly open. None of these pistes is particularly difficult, although the Rothorn cable-car opens up some off-piste skiing. A total of 33 lifts serve 155km of piste, with an additional four lifts and 27km of piste at nearby **Tschiertschen**. There are five branches of the SSS in the area, with three dedicated snowboard schools – Primus at Lenzerheide, Snowboard School Valbella and Exodus at Churwalden.

The main street of Lenzerheide has some attractive old buildings, and hotels include the four-star Sunstar (☎ 81 384 0121) and the Romantik Guarda Val (☎ 81 385 8585). Valbella has less character, being no more than a large community of hotels and concrete holiday homes crammed on to a hillside. Posthotel Valbella (☎ 81 384 1212) and the Valbella Inn (☎ 81 384 3636) are the only four-stars. As alternative bases to Lenzerheide, Churwalden is the ideal gateway to the skiing, Parpan is a typical Grison village, while Lantsch and Lenz are the starting points for cross-country skiing.

TOURIST INFORMATION
Tel 41 81 385 1120
Fax 41 81 385 1121
Email info@lenzerheide.ch
Web site www.lenzerheide.ch

Leysin
top 2,200m (7,218ft) bottom 1,200m (3,937ft)

The south-facing resort of Leysin, above the town of Aigle, is a successful and attractive mix of modern hotels and old chalets. The resort has long been associated with the diverse attractions of finishing schools, health clinics and cut-price holidays for students and schoolchildren. Today it is also one of the top resorts in Switzerland for snowboarders. The area boasts 60km of piste and 17 lifts. Most of the skiing and riding is in the popular Mayen/Berneuse area, reached by a choice of two cable-cars. There are nursery slopes at the Centre Sportif. Although most of the runs in the ski area are blue (easy), some good off-piste for skiers and freeriders can be found, particularly around Tour d'Ai.

Freestyle riders have a pro quarter-pipe and terrain park between Berneuse and Mayen. The SSS offers morning lessons for adults and all-day ones for children, while the Bureau des Guides organises off-piste excursions. Central Résidence is the local kindergarten, and takes children from two years old.

The all-glass revolving restaurant of Kuklos at Berneuse is said to be 'worth a visit, if only for the views of 29 peaks'. Free buses run regularly throughout the village, but the best-placed accommodation for the skiing is found in the four-star Hotel Classic-Terrasse (☎ 24 493 0606) ('large, comfortable rooms, which are a little overheated') and the simple Bel-Air (☎ 24 494 1339). La Fromagerie is a cheese restaurant as well as a museum. The town has two sports centres and a handful of bars and nightclubs, including the Top Pub. The resort has an indoor climbing wall, and other non-skiing activities include ski-jöring and go-karting on ice.

TOURIST INFORMATION
Tel 41 24 494 2244
Fax 41 24 494 1616
Email tourism@leysin.ch
Web site www.leysin.ch

Saas-Fee
top 3,600m (11,811ft) bottom 1,800m (5,904ft)

Saas-Fee is a delightfully unspoilt and picturesque resort set against one of the most dramatic glacial backdrops in the Alps. Its narrow streets are lined with some 56 hotels interspersed with ancient barns and chalets of blackened wood. Designer ski shops rub shoulders with working farmhouses where you can buy fresh milk by the pail, even in the centre of the village. In 2000–1 Saas-Fee broke new ground with the introduction of free weekly lift passes for all children under 16, provided both parents buy passes.

At this high altitude snow cover is virtually guaranteed, and the long vertical drop of 1,800m provides a total of 100km of runs. However, the groomed area is severely limited by the 'active' glaciers: 'not enough runs – some of the blues (easy) were in places worse than a black (difficult)'. The risk of falling down crevasses is extreme for anyone foolish enough to stray without a local guide. There are exceptional possibilities for ski-touring, and the local mountain guide association, Bergsteigerschule Saastal, has an impressive programme.

Saas-Fee has been a pioneer in the development of hi-tech ski lifts, and the main mountain access is by the Alpin Express cableway and the world's highest underground funicular system, the Metro Alpin. The area boasts 39 lifts, including those at the smaller, separate areas at the nearby villages of **Saas-Almagell**, **Saas-Balen** and **Saas-Grund**. Five drag-lifts at the bottom of the mountain are part of an excellent nursery-slope complex, which is flanked by a horseshoe of eight of the highest glaciers in Europe.

The SSS in Saas-Fee is run as a co-operative and suffers from poor organisation and overcrowding, especially during peak holiday periods. Inconveniently, only private lessons are available at weekends and in the afternoons ('a good private lesson, quite an elderly instructor but he did a lot of work on technique'). Snowboarding is big business here, and the SSS suffers fierce and healthy competition from the refreshingly radical Paradise Snowboard School. The two terrain parks include one beneath Mittelallalin, which has a boardercross course, half-pipe and various obstacles. Ice-climbing is a popular sport here.

The children's ski school hours are 'awkward, especially if you have more than one child'. Pulvo ski kindergarten takes children from three years old for one-and-a-half hours on weekday afternoons only, and SSS accepts children from five years old for weekday mornings only. The Bären-Club in the Hotel Garni Berghof offers all-day care for children from three to six years old.

Saas-Fee is traffic-free; on arrival you must leave your vehicle at the edge of the village in the pay car park. There are no buses, and electric taxis are not always available, making the position of your hotel of paramount importance.

Recommended hotels include the four-star Walliserhof (☎ 27 958 1900), the Metropol Grand (☎ 27 957 1001) ('extremely comfortable') and the Schweizerhof (☎ 27 957 5159). The four-star Saaserhof (☎ 27 957 3551) is conveniently situated. Hotel Gletschergarten (☎ 27 957 2175) is a chalet-style two-star, and the three-star Hotel Mistral (☎ 27 958 9210) 'deserves high praise'. The Allalin (☎ 27 957 1815) is 'very comfortable, with very good service and an excellent restaurant'. Hotel Europa (☎ 27 957 3191) is recommended ('a good standard of food and staff were helpful'). The Fletschhorn Waldhotel (☎ 27 957 2131) is a remarkable hotel set in the woods above Saas-Fee, housing an art gallery of modern paintings, sculptures and Persian carpets.

Recommended lunchtime restaurants include the rustic Berghaus Plattjen ('memorable home-made rösti') and the Gletschergrotte (beautiful location and excellent food – get there early'). The world's highest revolving restaurant at Mittelallalin receives criticism: 'the worst food at the highest prices'. The Maste 4 Mid-Station is said to be 'functional'. Zur Schaferstube, near the nursery slopes, is 'well worth seeking out, with beautifully presented salads and one of the cleanest, cosiest loos in the Alps'. Nearby is Boccolino ('friendly and efficient service').

Village eateries include the Hofsaal in the Schweizerhof and the Cheminée. The Fletschhorn Waldhotel has one of Switzerland's best restaurants. The Crazy Night is the hippest techno venue, with a Chevy on the dance floor. Rowdy drinking is frequent at Nesti's Ski Bar. Popcorn is 'lively, with good service and a comfortable mix of ages', while the Underground attracts a very young clientèle. Martin's Underground Bar is said to have 'live music and lots of atmosphere'.

TOURIST INFORMATION
Tel 41 27 958 1858
Fax 41 27 958 1860
Email to@saas-fee.ch
Web site www.saas-fee.ch

Villars and Les Diablerets
top 2,979m (9,744ft) bottom 1,128m (3,700ft)

Villars, situated on a sunny balcony above the Ollon Valley, is reached either by a winding road or a quaint Edwardian mountain railway. It has a strong international following as a family resort. The impressive intermediate skiing is linked directly by a quad-chair with the neighbouring resorts of **Gryon** and **Les Diablerets**. Together, the three areas provide 125km of piste, with four terrain parks, served by 47 lifts.

Les Diablerets Glacier, reached in 20 minutes by cable-car, provides high-altitude, snow-sure skiing, but can get crowded when conditions are poor in nearby Villars and **Gstaad**. The area is suitable for novices ('the blue runs won't prove intimidating to most beginners') and has mainly intermediate skiing. However, it is especially recommended for its extensive off-piste: 'plenty of easily accessible off-piste, including some good tree skiing'. It is important to hire the services of an experienced local guide.

The quickest access to the hub of the skiing in Villars is by gondola from the edge of town. A second gondola from the nearby village of **Barboleusaz** also feeds into the system. The nursery slope at Bretaye is gentle, and first-timers quickly graduate to a wide choice of blue runs. A drag-lift connects Bretaye with Roc d'Orsay. A separate ski area, Isenau, offers easy but limited skiing. The four-seater chair-lift between Bretaye and Les Chaux offers an easy link between Villars and Gryon. A new detachable six-seater chair-lift is being built from Les Rasses to Chaux-Ronde.

The two ski schools in Villars are SSS and the Villars Ski School. Riderschool is the snowboard specialist. Courses include women's ski clinics and teen skiing. The SSS has a school in Les Diablerets, and the New Devil School is for boarding. Bureau des Guides in Les Diablerets is the off-piste guiding company. Heli-skiing and heli-boarding are available from both resorts through a choice of three operations: Air Glaciers SA, Heli-Chablais in Leysin, and Flying Devil SA in Lausanne.

Villars SSS children's classes are praised by reporters, and the Pré Fleuri ski kindergarten is said to be 'quite excellent'. La Trotinette is a non-ski kindergarten for children from birth up to six years old. In Les Diablerets, Les Guignols offers daycare for babies and children up to 12 years old, and Diabloducus Park is the children's snow kindergarten for two- to eight-year-olds.

The Lac des Chavonnes is one of the great alpine restaurants, in a delightful lakeside setting above Villars; it is now only open by reservation outside the busiest weeks. The Col de Soud ('extremely good food') is an attractive chalet with superb views of Les Diablerets Glacier. La Crémaillère in Barboleusaz is a good-value option. Hotel du Lac at Bretaye has 'slow self-service. The table-service is a much better bet and no more expensive'. The self-service in Les Diablerets is rated 'poor – with smelly toilets'.

Hotel Bristol (☎ 24 496 3636), in Villars town centre, has a comfortable and modern interior. The three-star Hotel Elite (☎ 24 496 3900) is convenient for the gondola. The large Eurotel Victoria (☎ 24 495 3131) is an eyesore and is criticised for unfriendly staff, but contains 'spacious and clean apartments'. Four-star Hotel du Golf (☎ 24 495 2477), opposite the station, is praised by reporters. The Grand Hotel du Parc (☎ 24 496 2828) 'easily deserves its five stars'.

Les Diablerets is a sprawling village with mainly chalet accommodation. The few hotels seem out of place, but the overall atmosphere is relaxed. The Eurotel Victoria (☎ 24 492 3721), Hotel des Diablerets (☎ 24 492 0909) and the Mon Abri (☎ 24 492 3481) are recommended. Hotel Le Chamois (☎ 24 492 2653) has an in-house kindergarten. Dining in Villars takes place both in fine restaurants and informal stüblis. Le Mazarin restaurant in the Grand Hotel du Parc is the smartest in town. Vieux Villars and Café Carnotzet specialise in fondue and raclette. In Les Diablerets, Auberge de la Poste and Le Café des Diablerets are singled out for praise.

The nightlife in Les Diablerets and Villars is quiet and centres on a few bars and discos. Villars has the Fox and El Gringo discos; the latter was described by one reporter as 'the best club in the Alps'. Les Diablerets has the Pote Saloon and B'Bar discos.

TOURIST INFORMATION
Tel (Villars) 41 24 495 3232/ (Les Diablerets) 41 24 492 3358
Fax (Villars) 41 24 495 2794/ (Les Diablerets) 41 24 492 2348
Email information@villars.ch / info@diablerets.ch
Web site www.villars.ch / www.diablerets.ch

North America

Around 60,000 skiers and snowboarders from Britain make the transatlantic journey to North America each winter. What they find on arrival is a world in which everyone is intent upon having a good time. North American resorts tend to be owned and operated by a single large corporation. The result is a co-ordinated policy of keeping customers happy.

For 17 days in February 2002 the eyes of the world will be focused on the state of Utah, as what promises to be the most publicised Winter Olympics of all time unfolds in Park City, Deer Valley, Snowbasin, and other venues around Salt Lake City. We hope that some of the better aspects of American skiing will be noted and even emulated by lift companies in the French Alps. High on the list of cultural disparities is the lift queue. In North America a 'loading marshall' is on duty at major lift stations to organise civilised queuing in as speedy a fashion as possible. While polite entreaties from strangers of 'could we alternate with you?' may sound sugary to European ears, the American way is eminently preferable to the buffeting and barging that is the hallmark of the French lift queue.

North American prices remain reasonable, although the Canadian dollar is currently weaker against the pound than is the US dollar. It is possible to spend a fortnight staying in luxury accommodation in resorts such as Banff and Lake Louise for less than you would invest in a similar holiday in Zermatt or Courchevel 1850. However, we are frequently told by reporters that their reasons for returning to the United States or Canada each winter are by no means based on price alone. They point out that after a single visit to North America even the most famous Alpine resorts fail to measure up to their expectations.

Children's facilities are in another league to those in Europe. Ski instruction places its emphasis on fun, instead of the 'you are here to learn' attitude found particularly in French ski schools. Families tied to taking their skiing holiday during February half-term should seriously consider the transatlantic alternatives to Alpine resorts with their sky-high prices.

In general, the skiing is blander than in Europe. Apart from a few ranges such as the Tetons (Jackson Hole), the mountains lack the savage scenery and towering peaks of the Alps and the Dolomites. It is important to note that Americans operate a different colour-coding system from that in Europe: green is easy, blue is intermediate, black-diamond is difficult, and double-black-diamond is very difficult.

With the exception of the limited number of half-board chalet holidays available, most packages to North America are offered on a room-only basis, and the extra cost of food must be taken into consideration.

Aspen

ALTITUDE 7,945ft (2,422m)

Beginners ✴✴✴ Intermediates ✴✴✴ Advanced ✴✴✴ Snowboarders ✴✴

Aspen still suffers from its dated image as Hollywood-on-ice, being more of a winter playground for the rich, the famous and the wannabees than a ski resort for serious skiers. Certainly, it continues to attract a handful of big names in showbusiness and sport, some of whom, such as Jack Nicholson, Michael Douglas, Martina Navratilova and Chris Evert-Mill, have made their homes here. Others, such as Melanie Griffiths, Demi Moore and Kevin Costner, are regular visitors. What these celebrities have in common is that they are all fanatical skiers. Aspen enjoys some of the best skiing in North America for all standards, from complete beginner to advanced. The town's first claim to fame, however, was as a silver-mining centre. The brave and sometimes desperate miners defied vicious weather and marauding Ute native Americans to set up their first rickety camp in Colorado's Roaring Fork Valley in the late 1870s. During the boom years Aspen's population reached 12,000, and the town was served by two railways, six newspapers, three schools, ten churches and a notorious red-light district. But by 1893 it was all over; the silver market collapsed, and the town virtually died. It did not start to recover for almost 50 years.

- ✔ Excellent children's facilities
- ✔ Attractive Victorian town
- ✔ Wide choice of restaurants
- ✔ Ideal for non-skiers
- ✔ Lively nightlife
- ✔ Shopping opportunities
- ✘ Ski areas not linked
- ✘ High prices

The town of Aspen is situated at the foot of Aspen Mountain – now officially known as Ajax – and today boasts about 200 shops ('I'm sure even platinum card holders could find their credit limits here') and a large variety of restaurants. Planners have managed to conserve the low-rise appeal of the original Victorian mining town; the older buildings have been authentically refurbished, and recent additions are in sympathetic style.

Although considerably larger than most US ski resorts, the centre is relatively compact, and outlying hotels and the ski areas are served by a highly efficient bus service. Celebrity status attracts higher prices, and day-to-day living in Aspen is more expensive than in any of its Colorado counterparts. However, with a little care in your choice of restaurants and nightlife, it is still possible to have a moderately priced holiday. Last season (2000–1) Aspen finally bowed to commercial and guest pressure and opened up Ajax to snowboarders from April Fools Day. The only

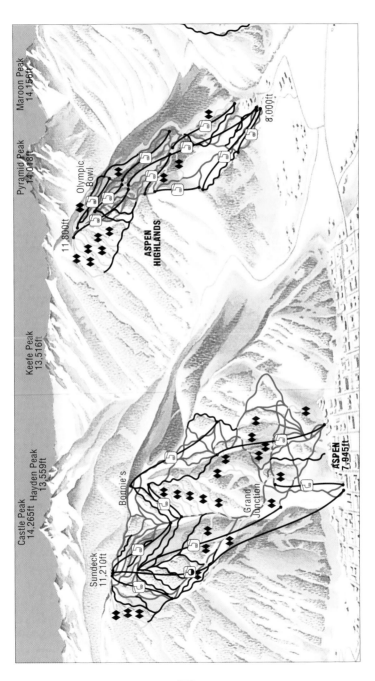

Castle Peak 14,265ft Hayden Peak 13,559ft

Keefe Peak 13,516ft

Pyramid Peak 14,018ft

Maroon Peak 14,156ft

Sundeck 11,210ft

Bonnie's

Grand Junction

ASPEN 7,945ft

Olympic Bowl

11,800ft

8,000ft

ASPEN HIGHLANDS

American resorts that still ban snowboarding are **Alta**, **Deer Valley**, **Taos** and **Mad River Glen**.

Snowmass is an alternative and cheaper accommodation base, but having come so far it seems a pity not to partake fully of Aspen's greater facilities. **Aspen Highlands** village opened in the 2000–1 season and is currently undergoing significant expansion, making it an important alternative base for those who want to enjoy more off-beat skiing and snowboarding.

Aspen has its own airport, served by flights from Denver, Minneapolis and Phoenix, which must at all times be booked in advance. Eagle County Airport (70 miles away) has direct flights from a number of hub cities.

On the snow
top 11,212ft (3,418m) bottom 7,870ft (2,399m)

Aspen covers four separate mountains: **Aspen Mountain**, Aspen Highlands, **Buttermilk** and Snowmass, 12 miles out of town. Aspen Mountain is strictly the reserve of good skiers and has no beginner slopes. Buttermilk is ideal beginners' and children's terrain, with no hidden surprises but plenty of variety for novices. Snowmass, which provides skiing for all levels, is the farthest of the separate ski areas from Aspen and is a resort in its own right under the same ownership. Aspen Highlands offers the toughest, most radical terrain and greatly adds to Aspen's appeal for advanced skiers.

WHAT'S NEW
Additional expert terrain in Highlands Bowl
Snowboarding permitted on Aspen Mountain

The four mountains are linked by free ski bus. A useful extra is the equipment transfer: at the end of the day you can have your skis or snowboard and boots taken from any of the ski areas to another for a nominal fee, and they will be waiting for you the next morning. As a welcome addition, free coffee, hot (non-alcoholic) cider and biscuits are served at all the information points on the mountain.

Beginners

Buttermilk is one of North America's best mountains for beginners, and Snowmass also contains excellent novice slopes. The area below Buttermilk's West Summit is packed with green (easy) runs, such as Westward Ho and Homestead Road, and more advanced beginners will thrive on a large network of long blue (intermediate) runs. The nursery slopes at Snowmass hug the lower slopes and most are accessed by the Fanny Hill high-speed quad. At Aspen Highlands the main nursery slopes, such as Apple Strudel, Riverside Drive and Nugget, are concentrated mid-mountain and are reached most quickly by the Exhibition quad-chair. The Skiwee lift at the base also serves a small beginner area.

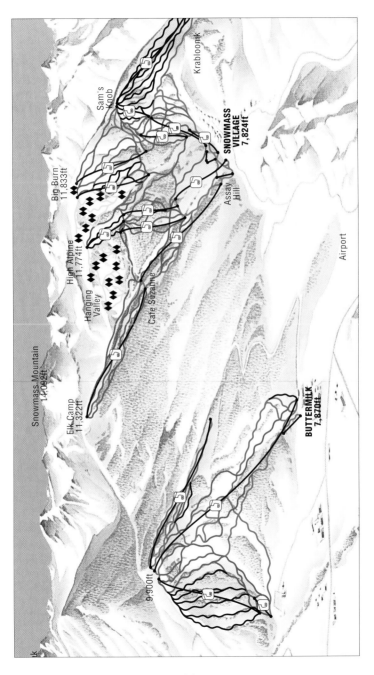

Intermediates

Among Aspen's four mountains, Snowmass has the largest intermediate appeal, with almost every run mid-mountain and below providing good cruising. Snowmass is famous for its Big Burn area, where a clutch of blue trails separated by a few trees provides almost unlimited scope for cruising. Although the runs have individual names (Whispering Jesse, Timberline, Wineskin, Mick's Gully, etc.), the Big Burn is one huge intermediate trail as much as a mile wide in places.

Plenty of strong intermediate skiing with top-to-bottom cruising is found on Aspen Mountain ('don't be put off by the tough rating. You don't have to ski the bumps'). Straying on to more difficult terrain by mistake is less likely here than at many resorts; most of the black-diamond (difficult) runs tend to be hidden away from the main slopes. The best area for middling skiers at Aspen Highlands is near the top of the mountain, where the Cloud Nine lift accesses runs such as Scarlett's, Grand Prix and Gunbarrel. Golden Horn and Thunderbowl offer enjoyable cruising.

Advanced

Ajax is riddled with short, sharp and quite steep double-black-diamond (very difficult) chutes, including the famous 'dump runs' such as Bear Paw, Short Snort and Zaugg Dump, which were created by miners throwing out spoil as they tunnelled their way into the mountain. One reporter warned: 'Watch out for Aztec – it might be groomed but it is pretty steep and can be very hard packed'. Walsh's is considered to be the most challenging trail. Bell Mountain, part of Ajax, provides first-rate opportunities for mogul skiers with its variety of individual faces, including Face of Bell, Shoulder of Bell and Back of Bell.

Much of the skiing at Aspen Highlands falls into the advanced category. The large and challenging gladed area to the left of the Exhibition quad-chair includes Bob's Glade, Upper Stein and Golden Horn Woods, which are all double-black-diamond trails. At Snowmass, real challenges are to be found in the largely gladed chutes in the Hanging Valley Wall and Hanging Valley Glades, and The Cirque has even steeper terrain mainly above the tree-line; access to all of these runs is on the Cirque lift.

Off-piste

Aspen Highlands offers some of the most exhilarating off-piste terrain in the valley, much of it accessed by the Loge Peak quad-chair at the top of the ski area. The chair follows a ridge with steep terrain on both sides. As you ride up, a dramatic area known as Steeplechase opens up on your left; this comprises about half-a-dozen steep chutes. On your right is even steeper terrain in Olympic Bowl, although the gradient is not always fully appreciable until you have progressed some way down the slopes. Deception is aptly named; it starts off at a fairly moderate pitch, but the farther down you ski, the steeper it becomes. During the past two years new steep areas (called the Y, B, G and O Zones) on Highlands Bowl have been opened, offering some of the most radical terrain of any resort in the USA.

Snowboarding

Snowboarders are now warmly welcomed on Ajax, and Buttermilk has ideal rolling terrain for riders, as well as a large terrain park and half-pipe. Snowmass boasts a competition-sized half-pipe, a beginner half-pipe and a terrain park, while superlative riding – and skiing – can be accessed by snowcat off the back of Aspen Mountain through Aspen Mountain Powder Tours.

Tuition and guiding

As well as traditional lessons, the Ski and Snowboard School of Aspen offers biathlon, race-training clinics, skiing for the disabled, women's ski seminars, off-piste tours at Aspen Highlands and Snowmass, and a variety of other courses. Ski Ambassadors are based on all four mountains to give free mountain tours at 10am and at 1.30pm. Aspen Adventures will organise off-piste tours.

Mountain restaurants

Only in Aspen could you find no less than three mountain restaurants – The Sundeck on Ajax, Bumps at Buttermilk, Gordon's High Alpine at Snowmass – where you can have a massage along with your lunch at $1 a minute. All of the restaurants are good for eating as well as relaxing. The fourth altitude restaurant at Ajax is Bonnie's ('an intimate place with superb strudel and hot apple dumplings'). Gwyn's, at the bottom of Ruthie's and Roch Run, provides table service, and, at the base of the Silver Queen gondola, the Ajax Tavern serves Mediterranean food.

Snowmass boasts six restaurants including Up 4 Pizza at the top of the Big Burn lift, which is warmly praised. Ullrhof, at the bottom of the same lift, puts on 'a hearty skier's breakfast, and has a wood-burning stove and sundeck'. Sam's Knob features a new upstairs dining-room called Finestra, complete with white linen tablecloths, which serves North Italian fare, while Café Suzanne, at the bottom of the Elk Camp lift, specialises in Mediterranean French food.

At Aspen Highlands, the Merry Go Round Restaurant at mid-mountain offers home-made soups, chilli and burgers. The Highlands Café is another breakfast and lunch spot, but at the base. Buttermilk boasts three mountain restaurants: the Café West near the bottom of Lift 3, which is designed in the style of a French café; Bump's, at the base, which includes a rôtisserie and grill; and the Cliffhouse, at the top of the Summit Express, which enjoys some of the best scenery on the mountain. Cloud Nine Café at Highlands serves Austrian specials and offers spectacular views of Pyramid peak.

Accommodation

In Aspen, skiers who can afford to live like celebrities should try the Little Nell (☎ 970 920 4600) and the St Regis Aspen (☎ 970 920 3300), although many people's favourite is Hotel Jerome (☎ 970 920 1000). Those on limited budgets can try one of the numerous modestly priced lodges such as the Limelite Lodge (☎ 970 925 3025). Hotel Durant (☎ 970 925 8500), St Moritz Lodge (☎ 970 925 3220) and the Innsbruck Inn (☎ 970 925 2980) are all recommended. The Aspen Mountain Lodge (☎ 970 925 7650) is a little more expensive but is also praised, and the Sardy House (☎ 970 920 2525) is a small Victorian hotel with a friendly atmosphere and first-rate cuisine. Top-of-the-range accommodation at Snowmass includes the Silvertree Hotel (☎ 970 923 3520), the Snowmass Club (☎ 970 923 5600), the Chamonix (☎ 970 923 3232) and Crestwood (☎ 970 923 2450). More reasonably priced are the Snowmass Mountain Chalet (☎ 970 923 3900) and the Stonebridge Inn (☎ 970 923 2420). For those counting their cents, the Pokolodi Lodge (☎ 970 923 4310) and the Snowmass Inn (☎ 970 923 4302) are both close to the slopes, as are the Aspenwood (☎ 970 923 2711) and Laurelwood (☎ 970 923 3110) condominiums.

Eating in and out

Aspen enjoys a huge variety of restaurants, with almost every type of cuisine. Bentley's is a Victorian-style pub and restaurant at the Wheeler Opera House, featuring American food and international beers.

The St Regis has three restaurants. Chart House on East Durant is well known for steaks and seafood, L'Hostaria is an authentic Italian restaurant, and Pacifica offers a fine selection of seafood and a caviar menu. Aspen features three gourmet Japanese restaurants – Kenichi, Takah Sushi and Matsuhisa – plus a Japanese take-away, while Sage, in the Snowmass Club, is a bistro serving contemporary Colorado cuisine. La Cocina, Little Annie's and The Steak Pit are lower priced.

Après-ski

Aspen has wall-to-wall après-ski in dozens of nightspots. The Jerome Bar (better known as the J-Bar), where miners once congregated, is always lively. The sundeck at the Ajax Tavern attracts the crowds when the lifts close, and Shooters is a Country-and-Western saloon with live bands. Mezzaluna offers inexpensive beers and pizzas. Aspen Billiards is casually elegant and smoke-free, while the Cigar Bar provides fine liqueurs. Club Chelsea attracts a sophisticated clientèle, whereas the glitterati congregate at the members-only Caribou Club or the 426. The health-conscious can try the Aspen Club's luxurious spa, where the comprehensive range of treatments include acupuncture, yoga, massage and 'body polish'.

Childcare

Aspen has an in-town nursery service (Kids Room) and a kindergarten at each mountain base. At Snowmass, Snow Cubs caters for children

Skiing facts: Aspen

TOURIST INFORMATION
Aspen Skiing Company, PO Box 1248, CO 81611
Tel 1 970 925 1220
Fax 1 970 920 0771
Email info@aspensnowmass.com
Web site www.aspensnowmass.com

THE RESORT
Airport transfer Eagle County Airport 1½hrs, Aspen Airport 10mins
Visitor beds 12,000 in area
Transport free shuttle bus between all 4 mountains

THE SKIING
Linked or nearby resorts none
Number of lifts 39 in resort
Total of trails/pistes 4,730 acres (16% easy, 40% intermediate, 24% difficult, 20% very difficult on 4 mountains
Beginners 3 slopes and 2 beginner lifts. Free lifts on first day with ski school

LIFT PASSES
Area pass (covers all 4 mountains) $330 for 6 days, $234 for advance bookings
Pensioners 65–74yrs 20% reduction, Silver Pass for 75yrs and over $149 for unlimited skiing all season
Credit cards yes

TUITION
Skiing Ski and Snowboard School of Aspen (☎ 970 925 1227)
Snowboarding as regular ski school
Other courses biathlon, cross-country, moguls, powder clinics, race-training, seniors, skiing for the disabled, snow-blading, snowcat skiing/boarding, teen skiing, telemark, women's ski clinics
Guiding through ski school, Aspen Adventures (☎ 970 925 7625)

CHILDREN
Lift pass 7–12yrs $198, 13–17yrs $234, both for 6 days. Free for 6yrs and under
Ski and board school as adults, and Too Cool For School (☎ 970 925 1220)
Kindergarten (ski) through ski school, one at each base area (☎ 970 925 1227), (non-ski) Kids Room (☎ 701 456 7888), Snow Cubs at Snowmass (☎ 970 923 1227)

OTHER SPORTS
Climbing wall, curling, dog-sledding, hang-gliding, helicopter rides, hot-air ballooning, ice-climbing, indoor tennis and squash, parapente, skating, sleigh rides, snowmobiling, snowshoeing, tubing, swimming

FOOD AND DRINK
Coffee $2 (free at mountain bases), glass of wine $5, small beer $3.50, soft drink $2, dish of the day $8–15

aged between six weeks and three years. Older children can join the Big Burn Bears from three-and-a-half or the Grizzlies from five years. The Powder Pandas Ski School at Buttermilk is for kids aged between three and six.

Banff and Lake Louise

ALTITUDE 5,350ft (1,631m)

Beginners ✶✶ Intermediates ✶✶✶ Advanced ✶✶ Snowboarders ✶✶

B anff and Lake Louise is the collective name given to three separate ski areas up to 35 miles apart, which are tucked away in the beautiful Banff National Park, between 90 minutes' and two hours' drive from Calgary Airport. Banff itself 'is an ordinary little tourist resort in mountainous country, with hills and a stream and snow-peaks beyond,' wrote the World War I poet Rupert Brooke a year before his death, 'but Lake Louise – Lake Louise is of another world'. Little has changed.

✔ Spectacular scenery
✔ Long skiing season
✔ Extensive children's facilities
✔ Few queues
✘ Distance between ski areas
✘ Extremely low temperatures
✘ Lack of slope-side lodging

Banff is a small, attractive community with a frontier-town atmosphere. Apart from the breathtaking scenery, the town is famous for its railway history and wildlife. It is quite common to glimpse elk grazing on vegetation protruding through the snow ('our children saw 120 elk in ten days'). It has its own small ski area at **Mount Norquay.**

After Canadian Pacific Railways started bringing tourists to Banff to marvel at the scenery, the company built the neo-Gothic Banff Springs Hotel in 1888 and promptly looked for a second site. It found it in a dramatic glacial setting at Lake Louise. The magnificent Chateau Lake Louise, Canada's most celebrated hotel, opened its doors in 1890. Lake Louise remains no more than a railway halt; the shopping mall barely constitutes a village.

The third ski area, **Sunshine Village**, has nominal accommodation up the mountain and nothing but a snack bar at the bottom.

The region remains the most popular destination in North America for British skiers, although **Whistler** and a clutch of up-and-coming resorts in both Alberta and British Columbia contest the title. Banff, which each summer plays host to four million tourists, provides the main bed base. Although small by European standards, the three ski areas do have sufficient terrain to keep most skiers and snowboarders happy for a week.

Charter flights from London and Manchester provide bargain-priced skiing amid spectacular scenery. However, the nine-hour flight, 90- to 120-minute transfer and seven-hour time difference have to be taken into consideration, and it really requires a visit of at least ten days to adjust and relax fully in such unfamiliar surroundings.

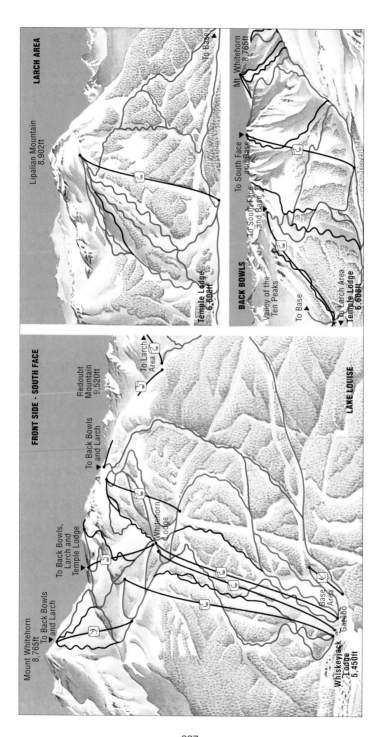

LARCH AREA

Lipalian Mountain 8,902ft

To Base

Temple Lodge 6,608ft

Mt Whitehorn 8,765ft

BACK BOWLS

To South Face and Base

To South Face and Base

Valley of the Ten Peaks

To Base

To Larch Area Temple Lodge 6,608ft

FRONT SIDE - SOUTH FACE

Mount Whitehorn 8,765ft
To Back Bowls and Larch

To Back Bowls, Larch and Temple Lodge

Whitehorn Lodge

To Back Bowls and Larch

Redoubt Mountain 9,520ft

To Larch Area

Base Area

Gazebo

Whiskeyjack Lodge 5,450ft

LAKE LOUISE

During the 2000–1 season, the region was blighted by unusually poor snow cover, although its record over the previous 15 years has been good. It is important to note that temperatures on the mountain can be extreme, falling to as low as -22°F (-30°C) for three or four weeks between December and mid-February. The daytime average in the valley at Banff is 19°F (-7°C) in January.

On the snow
top 8,650 ft (2,636 m) bottom 5,400ft (1,646m)

Lake Louise is the farthest ski area from Banff but is easily the largest and most varied. The skiing begins three miles from the tiny village of Lake Louise – its 11 lifts attracting the majority of daily skiers who make the bus journey from Banff. Importantly, Lake Louise boasts that every difficult run is matched by an easy one, allowing families and groups of mixed ability to ski together. From the Mount Whitehorn base at Whiskeyjack Lodge, the choice of three chair-lifts includes the Friendly Giant Express quad, which takes skiers to mid-mountain at Whitehorn Lodge. From here the Top of The World Express is another high-speed quad, providing the fastest way up and over to the Back Bowls or down to Mount Lipalian's Larch area.

Sunshine Village, ten miles from Banff, is the highest of the three resorts and has predominantly medium-length, moderately steep, intermediate terrain above the tree-line and virtually non-existent lift queues. Despite the name, sunshine is not guaranteed and it can be a bleak and cold place on a grey day. Goat's Eye Mountain almost doubles the size of the ski area and provides more advanced terrain. Mount Norquay is four miles from Banff and is the smallest, mainly beginner, area. However, the development of Mystic Ridge has increased its intermediate appeal and it also includes some steep pitches. A free bus service links Banff with the three resorts ('extremely efficient – one of the drivers provided a detailed description of the wildlife seen along the Trans-Canadian Highway, lucidly described all the mountains and told stories about tourist incidents with bear and big-horned sheep').The distances are such that it is difficult to ski more than one area in a day.

Reporters recommended taking time out to visit **Nakiska**, a small ski area situated an hour's drive from Banff. It was the site of the men's downhill at the Calgary Olympics in 1988: 'beautiful runs planned by computer, immaculately groomed and virtually deserted'. **Fortress Mountain**, a further 30 minutes by bus from Banff, shares a lift pass with Nakiska and is dramatically positioned at the foot of sheer, granite cliffs. The area is limited in size but has some excellent snowcat skiing.

Beginners

Because of Lake Louise's policy of ensuring an easy way down from each major lift, novices can share the pleasure of roaming the mountain almost at will. Although riding high-speed quads could seem daunting in other resorts, here you can board them confidently ('there were loaders to assist who were extremely helpful on the chair-lifts') and meander down the green (easy) Saddleback and Pika trails to the Larch chair. Alternatively, you can warm up on the Sunny T-bar and try skiing the long but gentle Wiwaxy trail, although one reporter warned this can be intimidating when very crowded. Cameron Way is less congested.

At Sunshine, the best choice of novice runs is served by the Wheeler double chair-lift from the Gondola mid-station. The Strawberry triple-chair and the Standish double-chair also give access to gentle terrain. A long, green trail starts from the top of Lookout Mountain, but in all cases beginners need to take care not to stray accidentally on to neighbouring black-diamond (difficult) runs. Beginners at Norquay are recommended to ski the runs off the Cascade quad-chair or the Sundance tow. Norquay has recently enhanced its beginner terrain.

Intermediates

At Lake Louise, intermediates can clock up huge mileage over all the terrain, with the possible exception of some of the steeper bowls. Skyline is a steepish blue from the high point of the ski area. Larch is a wide, fast-cruising blue. Stronger skiers will want to sample the black-diamond Ridge Run and Whitehorn No. 1 on the Back Bowls side. Most of the runs at Sunshine are within the grasp of intermediates. At Norquay, nearly all of Mystic Ridge trails were specifically created for skiers of medium experience.

Advanced

At Lake Louise, the Front Face offers challenging men's and women's downhill runs. Other tough black-diamond trails – Outer Limits, Sunset and the Flight Chutes – start higher up. Ptarmigan and Raven are testing glade runs on the Back Bowls side, and Exhibition has the additional challenge of exposing skiers to the gaze of people riding the Ptarmigan chair. Fall Line Glades, a 100-acre area between Exhibition and Ptarmigan provides some of the best tree-skiing in this part of Canada. Lone Pine, which is fiercely steep and mogulled, is the big challenge at Norquay. At Sunshine, runs such as Little Angel, Ecstasy and Big Angel offer steep chute skiing from the top of Lookout Mountain and 'stupendous views of the Rockies'. Goat's Eye Mountain has a number of long and tricky runs including Hell's Kitchen and Freefall ('a challenging mogul field through the trees').

Off-piste

Large areas of the Back Bowls at Lake Louise are permanently closed because of avalanche danger. However, Paradise Bowl and East Bowl normally provide challenging off-piste skiing. Serious powderhounds who do not mind a hike can join a daily three-hour guided trip into Purple Bowl. Seven gullies off the back of Mount Whitehorn provide heart-stopping gradients – the area being accessed by the Summit Platter lift.

At Sunshine, Goat's Eye Mountain boasts some excellent untracked terrain. Delirium Dive allows access to a steep bowl with more than 1,800ft of vertical with a gradient of up to 40 degrees. Here skiers and snowboarders are monitored through a check-in gate, where rules such as skiing or riding with a partner, carrying shovels and wearing avalanche transceivers must be adhered to. Helmets are also recommended.

Snowboarding

Riders are catered for with a large terrain park, which has a quarter-pipe, jumps and table-tops, reached from the Cascade chair-lift at Mount Norquay. Lake Louise has a terrain park with a big half-pipe, which is accessed by the Olympic chair off the Wiwaxy trail. Sunshine is a good freeriding mountain, with plenty of trees, as well as a terrain park and half-pipe. The Club Snowboard programme operates in all three areas. Lake Louise is an excellent place for first-time riders.

Tuition and guiding

All three resorts offer special packages for beginners, which include equipment rental, a beginner area lift ticket and a half-price pass, as well as a ski lesson. Instruction at Sunshine is said to be 'friendly and positive'. The Club Ski/Snowboard programme enables skiers to stay with one instructor for three hours a day, visiting all three areas. Banff's Caribou Snow School gives private and semi-private (small groups) tuition exclusively to guests staying in the Banff Caribou Lodge, the Banff Ptarmigan Inn, the Driftwood Inn and the Arrow Motel ('highly recommended one-to-one tuition'). All the resorts offer a free piste-guiding service, and RK Heli-ski Panorama organises guided trips.

Mountain restaurants

Reporters complained that the range and character of mountain eateries do not bear favourable comparison with those in the Alps. Lake Louise's Whiskeyjack Lodge looks 'better from the outside than the inside'. Another reporter summed up the mountain restaurants as 'utilitarian motorway service stations at worst, barn-like at best'. At Lake Louise, The Temple is singled out as the best 'with a nice outdoor terrace, a barbecue and wait-service upstairs – but the food is nothing special'. Another reporter recommended taking the free bus down to Chateau Lake Louise ('a longer lunch break but the deli is great value'). At Sunshine Village, Mad Trapper's Saloon serves 'Tex-Mex, good beer, good atmosphere and unlimited free peanuts', while Norquay's base lodge contains restaurants and an outside barbecue.

Accommodation

Unfortunately, not everyone has the budget to stay at Chateau Lake Louise (☎ 522 3511) or the Banff Springs Hotel (☎ 762 2211), both of which offer luxury rooms and suites, as well as restaurants, shops and health clubs. In November 2000 the hotels were rebranded for marketing reasons under the Fairmont banner, an American hotel chain owned by Canadian Pacific. Winter rates are considerably lower than those in summer, but these have inevitably increased because of the rise in resort's global popularity in recent years. However, there is plenty of choice elsewhere. In Lake Louise, the Post Hotel (☎ 522 3989) ('an award-winning wine list') and Deer Lodge (☎ 522 3747) are both recommended. In Banff, the Rimrock Resort Hotel (☎ 762 3356) is said to be 'luxurious in the extreme', and Mount Royal (☎ 762 3331) is conveniently located on Banff Avenue. The King Edward (☎ 762 2202), the town's original hotel, has been completely modernised.

The Banff Caribou Lodge (☎ 762 5887) is praised. The Inns of Banff (☎ 762 4581) ('not within easy walking distance of the town') has a small indoor swimming-pool and a large hot tub on the roof. Siding 29 Lodge (☎ 762 5575) is described as 'a no-frills hotel with large comfortable rooms and a heated underground car park', while the Red Carpet Inn (☎ 762 4184) is 'an extremely accommodating and friendly two-star'. Rundle Manor apartments (☎ 762 5544) are 'spacious, comfortable and cheap'. Norquay offers the Timberline Inn (☎ 762 2281) at the base of its access road, and the only on-mountain accommodation at Sunshine is the Sunshine Village Inn (☎ 760 5200).

Eating in and out
Banff enjoys a surprisingly wide range of restaurants, serving cuisine from at least a dozen countries. 'If you haven't been to Bumper's, you haven't been to Banff' is the motto of Bumper's Beef House. Joe Btfsplk's Diner looks like a misprint but serves 'meals like Mom used to make, including apple pie'. Silver Dragon is Chinese, while Sukiyaki House is one of six Japanese restaurants, and El Toro is a Greek restaurant despite its Spanish-sounding name. Guido's Spaghetti Factory is long established and offers 'good-value Italian food at reasonable prices, so don't be put off by the tatty entrance'. The Barbary Coast has 'plenty of atmosphere and a wide range of dishes including vegetarian options'. Melissa's serves 20oz steaks while Caboose Steak and Lobster at the railway depot is 'superb in every way'.

In Lake Louise The Post Hotel and Deer Lodge are warmly recommended for some of the best food in the region: 'pleasant décor and good service – Canadian fine dining at its finest'. In Lake Louise, The Station, which was used as a location for *Dr Zhivago*, is warmly praised: 'absolutely delightful, try to book into the old Victorian Canadian Pacific dining car'.

Après-ski
One reader described Banff's nightlife as 'refreshingly unsophisticated, plenty of cowboy bars and line dancing'. Wild Bill in Banff is a Western saloon, while Tommy's and The Rose & Crown are both British-style pubs. The Aurora is Banff's only over-21 nightclub and restaurant, with the added attraction of a 'Cigar, Martini and Scotch Room'. The nightlife at Lake Louise is largely confined to drinking in the Glacier Saloon at the Chateau, which provides a pool and live entertainment.

Skiing facts: Banff/Lake Louise

TOURIST INFORMATION
Ski Banff/Lake Louise/Sunshine,
PO Box 1085, Banff, AB
Tel 1 403 762 4561
Fax 1 403 762 8185
Email info@sblls.com
Web site www.sblls.com

THE RESORT
Airport transfer Calgary 90–120 mins
Visitor beds 14,846 in Banff/Lake Louise
Transport free ski buses

THE SKIING
Linked or nearby resorts Sunshine
Village (n), Mount Norquay (n)
Number of lifts 30 in area
Total of trails/pistes 62 miles at Lake
Louise, 52 miles at Sunshine Village,
10 miles at Mount Norquay (area: 25%
easy, 45% intermediate, 30% difficult)
Beginners 1 lift at Banff, 1 at Lake
Louise, 2 at Sunshine Village.
Tow passes available

LIFT PASSES
Area pass CDN$350 for 6 days
Pensioners 65yrs and over CDN$43
per day
Credit cards yes

TUITION
Skiing Banff Mt Norquay (☎ 403 762
4421), Caribou Snow School (☎ 762
5887), Club Ski/Snowboard (all
areas)(☎ 403 762 4561),
Lake Louise (☎ 403 522 1333),
Sunshine Village(☎ 403 762 6560)
Snowboarding as ski schools
Other courses cross-country, extreme
skiing/boarding, heli-skiing/boarding,
moguls, race-training, seniors, skiing for
the disabled, snowblading, telemark,
women's clinics
Guiding RK Heli-ski Panorama
(☎ 250 342 3889)

CHILDREN
Lift pass 6–12yrs CDN$128 for 6 days
Ski & board schools as adults
Kindergarten (ski/non-ski) as ski
schools

OTHER SPORTS
Broomball, dog-sledding, frozen waterfall
climbing, ice-fishing, skating, ski-jöring,
sleigh rides, snowmobiling, snowshoeing,
snow volleyball, swimming, tobogganing

FOOD AND DRINK
Coffee CDN$1.25, glass of wine CDN$4,
small beer CDN$3.75, soft drink
CDN$1.60–3, dish of the day CDN$9

Childcare
This is a great place for children who can stand the low temperatures.
At Lake Louise, the nursery takes babies from three weeks old. The
Kinderski programme is geared for three- to six-year-olds. There is also
a Club Ski JR programme, where children are guided around the mountain with instruction along the way ('class sizes excellent, the instructors were exceptionally friendly and the attitude was as much about
having fun as learning to ski'). At Sunshine Village and Mount
Norquay, daycare is for toddlers from 18 months.

Beaver Creek

ALTITUDE Beaver Creek 8,100ft (2,470m)

Beginners ✱✱✱ Intermediates ✱✱✱ Advanced ✱ Snowboarders ✱✱

Beaver Creek is an elegant family resort situated at the end of a private road, a 20-minute drive from its sister resort of **Vail**. The two are under the same giant corporate ownership and share a ski school and other mountain facilities, but there the similarity ends. While Vail is big and brash, Beaver Creek is more compact, with an intimate atmosphere and plenty of slope-side accommodation that enhances its appeal to families.

Like most other Colorado resorts, Beaver Creek first staked its claim to fame through gold, although it is far more successful now than it ever was as a mining village. James Lyon and Frederick Westlotom first struck pay-dirt here in 1881, but their Aurora mine never produced a decent strike,

- ✔ Favourable snow record
- ✔ Family-friendly resort
- ✔ Excellent ski school
- ✔ Easy introduction to off-piste
- ✘ Limited choice of mountain restaurants
- ✘ High prices

and the settlers who followed the miners fared little better in their attempts to farm the land. After its rebirth as a ski resort, Gerald Ford, the former USA president, made his home here and helped to put it on the world map. Today Beaver Creek exudes an air of sophistication and wealth, and the excellent childcare facilities consistently win it awards as one of America's top family resorts. The valley towns of Avon and Edwards house most of the workforce in the region and have a wider range of shops. Eagle Airport is a 45-minute drive away, with direct connections to hub cities, but it is liable to sudden closure in bad weather conditions.

Reporters praised Beaver Creek as 'very smart and friendly – we were offered cookies while waiting in the lift queue, and escalators carry you up from the bus stop to the base of the lifts'. Multi-day lift passes can be used at Vail, and also at **Arapahoe Basin**, **Breckenridge** and **Keystone**. A shuttle service operates between the resorts.

On the snow
top 11,440ft (3,488m) bottom 8,100ft (2,469m)

The substantial ski area of 146 tree-lined trails on undulating scenic terrain is served by a network of 13 lifts on four mountains. The skiing includes the linked villages of **Bachelor's Gulch** and **Arrowhead**, in the nearest approximation you will find in the United States to the ubiquitous European ski circuit. Main mountain access from Beaver Creek is by the high-speed Centennial Express chair, which takes you up to Spruce Saddle, the mid-mountain station. From here the Birds of Prey Express chair continues on to Summit Elevation, the highest point of the ski area. A number of green (easy) and double-black-diamond trails lead down to a choice of lifts as you progress farther into the ski area. The Strawberry Park Express and Elkhorn lifts also give access from Beaver Creek. You can also take the Bachelor's Gulch Express from Bachelor's Gulch or the Arrow Bahn Express from Arrowhead, and work your way along the adjoining mountains.

Beginners

The beginner areas are at the base of the Centennial Express lift, at the top of the Stump Park lift, and at Arrowhead. Once the basic techniques have been mastered, novices can ascend to Summit Elevation, from where green (easy) runs, including Red Buffalo, Jack Rabbit Alley and Booth Gardens, all lead gently down to the Drink of Water lift, providing the easiest introduction to linked-turn skiing amid delightful high mountain scenery. Flat Tops, Powell and Piney all lead on to Cinch, a green run that allows beginners to reach Spruce Saddle and the more low-altitude runs off the Haymeadow lift, before returning to the resort. One reporter recommended setting off from Arrowhead and concentrating turns on the lower half of Smooth Moose.

Intermediates

Long, cruising intermediate trails are the hallmark of Beaver Creek's skiing. The cross-mountain journeys to Bachelor's Gulch and Arrowhead enable you to feel you are going somewhere for the day rather than the more usual American experience of skiing variations of the same terrain over and over again. Grubstake and Gunders (off the Bachelor's Gulch Express) and Golden Bear, reached by the Arrow Bahn Express, are favourites with reporters. Stone Creek Meadows is a wide, fast trail that runs from Spruce Saddle to the bottom of the Rose Bowl and it is usually uncrowded. Harrier and Centennial are both enjoyable fall-line runs from Spruce Saddle to the resort, but reporters pointed out that both have black-diamond sections ('however, neither should pose a problem for anyone who can ski a European red run with even a modicum of confidence'). Raven Ridge on Grouse Mountain, served by the Grouse Mountain Express, is similarly graded on its lower section, 'but the less confident can always cut to the skier's right and join the easier lower half of Golden Eagle'. The Larkspur lift also accesses some pleasant intermediate runs. From the top you can cross to the trails served by the Strawberry Park Express.

Advanced

The most challenging terrain is found on Grouse Mountain. Screech Owl and Osprey are usually heavily mogulled. Royal Elk Glades is a steep double-black-diamond (very difficult) trail from the top of the mountain. Golden Eagle, from the top of the Birds of Prey Express, is the upper part of Beaver Creek's World Cup downhill course, which

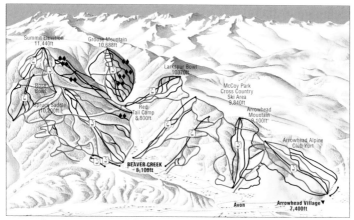

even when not prepared for racing can provide a demanding test of technical skills. One reporter said he spent 'almost my entire holiday' here and on the adjoining Peregrine and Goshawk double-black-diamonds. The Rose Bowl lift also serves a choice of black-diamond runs including Ripsaw, Spider and Cataract.

Off-piste

Early in the morning on big powder days, the local powderhounds head for Grouse Mountain, which provides some truly spectacular trails between the trees and along the edge of the ski area boundary. All runs lead down into the gulch, where a path brings you back to the bottom of the lift. Free mountain tours are run by the resort at weekends.

Tuition and guiding

The Beaver Creek Ski and Snowboard School is part of the impressive Vail/Beaver Creek Center. Here it is based at Village Hall and on the mountain at Spruce Saddle. We have continuing favourable reports: 'I learned much more in a week than I have ever done in Europe'. However, another reporter complained at the cost: '$95 a day seemed really excessive compared to what I paid in Italy, but I think it was prob-ably worth it'. The Center offers one of the largest skiing for the dis-abled programmes in North America.

Snowboarding

Beaver Creek is, according to one visiting rider, 'much too quiet and expensive'. Nevertheless, it does boast seven dedicated snowboard trails through chutes and gullies, and two half-pipes on Moonshine. Stickline Park between Harrier and Centennial offers a combination of tabletops, banks and log slides. Mystic Isles is a terrain park for begin-ners situated at the top of the Birds of Prey Express. A separate snow-board map at the resort shows riders how to avoid flat paths.

Mountain restaurants

Owing to the well-heeled nature of its clientèle, Beaver Creek takes lunch more seriously than many American resorts – but unfortunately the public are unable to share the best part of it. Beano's Cabin enjoys the pick of the cuisine, but at lunchtime it remains a private club. The same applies to Zach's Cabin and Allie's Cabin. Spruce Saddle Lodge is the main self-service ('great buffalo chilli and a highly acceptable pizza'), while Rafters at Spruce Saddle serves 'good food at reasonable prices. The service is cheerful but desperately slow'. Redtail Camp features an indoor and outdoor barbecue. Gundy's Camp in Bachelor's Gulch also has a barbecue. The Broken Arrow Café in Arrowhead offers 'home-made soup and enormous club sandwiches'.

Accommodation

The Hyatt Regency (☎ 970 949 1234), with its impressive lobby complete with vast log fire and enormous elk horn chandelier, is situated on the edge of the piste in the village centre and caters in style for its opulent guests ('staff put my skis on the snow at the start of the day and took them away when I arrived back in the afternoon.' The Charter at Beaver Creek (☎ 970 949 6660) is equally luxurious, with condominiums as well as rooms. The Inn at Beaver Creek (☎ 970 845 5990) is adjacent to the Strawberry Park Express lift ('great comfort and a wonderful outdoor pool') and Trapper's Cabin (☎ 970 496 4040) is an exclusive hideaway in the woods, reached only on skis or by snowmobile.

Eating in and out

Allie's, Beano's and Zach's, which are closed by day to the public, are open by night to all. In the case of Beano's, dinner involves a sleigh ride behind a diesel-belching snowcat ('the food was at best average'). Splendido at the Chateau is 'the ultimate in fine dining American-style, at a cost you would expect', while Saddle Ridge houses 'an extraordinary museum of Western memorabilia. Lovely atmosphere and setting; shame about the food.' The Mirabelle lies at the entrance to the resort ('best elk I have ever tasted'). Tramoniti serves 'superb lobster ravioli', and Toscani is Italian and 'an altogether less formal and more tasty option in relaxed surroundings'. The Blue Moose is a budget pizzeria.

Après-ski

The Rendezvous Bar and Grill serves 'wicked Martinis'. The Coyote Café, Player's Pub and Dusty Boot Saloon capture the main crowd, along with McCoy's and the Overlook Bar at the Hyatt. Cassidy's Hole in the Wall Saloon at Avon caters to a more culturally and financially diverse clientèle. The Black Family Ice Rink is open until 10pm. All the major hotels have spas, not least Allegria at the Hyatt Regency.

Childcare

Beaver Creek ranks as one of the top US resorts for families ('one of the best resorts we've ever been to with our children'). The Small

Skiing facts: Beaver Creek

TOURIST INFORMATION
PO Box 7, Vail, CO 81658
Tel 1 970 496 4040
(01708 224773 for UK agent)
Fax 1 970 845 2905
(01708 640707 for UK agent)
Email beinfo@vailresorts.com/vailre-sorts@clare.co.uk
Web site www.beavercreek.com

THE RESORT
Airport transfer Eagle Country 45 mins, Denver 2½hrs
Visitor beds 3,430
Transport bus between Beaver Creek, Breckenridge, Keystone and Vail (nominal charge)

THE SKIING
Linked or nearby resorts Arapahoe Basin (n), Breckenridge (n), Copper Mountain (n), Keystone (n), Vail (n)
Number of lifts 13
Total of trails/pistes 1,625 acres (34% easy, 39% intermediate, 27% difficult)
Beginners 3 lifts

LIFT PASSES
Area pass (covers Arapahoe Basin, Breckenridge, Keystone and Vail) $210 for 6 days
Pensioners 70yrs and over

$99 for season
Credit cards yes

TUITION
Skiing Beaver Creek Ski and Snowboard School (☎ 970 845 5325)
Snowboarding as ski school
Other courses bumps, cross-country, powder clinics, race camps, seniors, skiing for the disabled, teen skiing, telemark, women's ski courses
Guiding through ski school

CHILDREN
Lift pass 5–12yrs $126 for 6 days
Ski & board school as adults
Kindergarten (ski) as ski school (non-ski) Small World Playschool (☎ 970 845 5325)

OTHER SPORTS
Basketball, climbing-wall, dog-sledding, hang-gliding, hot-air ballooning, ice-climbing, ice-fishing, ice-hockey, indoor climbing wall, skating, sleigh rides, snowbiking, snowmobiling, snowshoeing, squash, swimming

FOOD AND DRINK
Coffee $2, glass of wine $3–5, small beer $3.50, soft drink $1.5–3, dish of the day $15

World Playschool is the non-skiing kindergarten, while the Children's Ski and Snowboard Center is for three- to 13-year-olds. Arrowhead provides learn-to-ski or -snowboard programmes.

Breckenridge

ALTITUDE 9,600ft (2,927m)

Beginners ✱✱✱ Intermediates ✱✱✱ Advanced ✱✱ Snowboarders ✱✱✱

Breckenridge was the beachhead for the British skiers' invasion of America in the 1980s. In the heart of the Rockies and boasting the infrastructure of a small city as well as the restored charm of an old mining 'boom town', Breckenridge remains a leader in the evolution of American skiing and snowboarding; it was the first resort in Colorado to permit snowboarders. These days Breckenridge is under the same ownership as **Beaver Creek**, **Keystone** and **Vail** – and consequently it has benefited from the huge sums of money that Vail Resorts is continuing to invest in its portfolio of resorts.

- ✔ Good base for visiting other resorts
- ✔ Attractive town centre
- ✔ Choice of dining and après-ski
- ✔ Range of ski-school courses
- ✔ Reliable snow record
- ✗ Peak period overcrowding
- ✗ High altitude may cause sickness

The four resorts share a lift pass, along with nearby **Arapahoe Basin** (A-Basin), and are served by a heavily subsidised shuttle bus. Nearby **Copper Mountain** was not included in the buy-out but was soon snapped up by the Canadian resort developer Intrawest and provides alternative and enjoyable terrain if you can find the time.

Breckenridge is a bustling town that prides itself on accommodating 25,000 snow-users among its 254 downtown restored structures (which date from 1859) and in its self-contained resort/shopping complexes closer to the slopes. It is the oldest continually occupied community in Colorado and has embraced conservation with a fervour that European visitors might regard as verging on the kitsch or over-cute. However, international visitors, who exceed ten per cent of all snow-users, are courted ardently.

The extremely low humidity and altitudes in excess of 12,000ft may cause dehydration and headaches – made worse by exercise – which can be avoided by resting, drinking plenty of water and abstaining from alcohol. 'We were constantly out of breath even though two of us are regular gym users and so pretty fit,' was one comment. Reporters also complained of the cold: 'alternative name could be Breckenfridge'.

Skiing began here in 1961, on Peak 8, and expanded a decade later to Peak 9; Peak 10 opened in 1985 and Peak 7 in 1993. A total of 25 lifts carry more than 25,000 snow-users per hour to 138 well-manicured pistes and half-a-dozen wilderness bowls spread across 2,043 acres. Complaints about both the early closing of the pistes (the

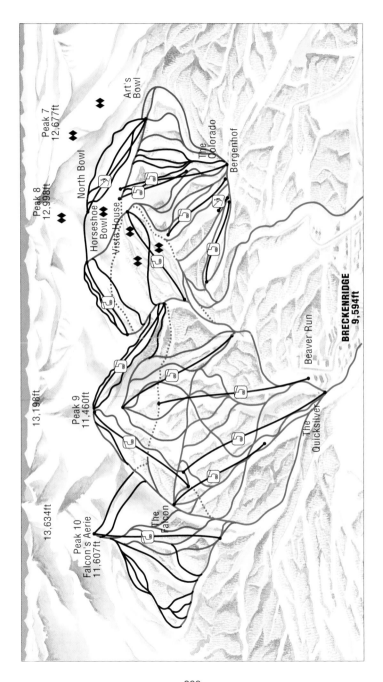

Art's Bowl

Peak 7
12,677ft

Peak 8
12,998ft

North Bowl

Horseshoe Bowl

Vista House

The Colorado

Bergenhof

13,198ft

Peak 9
11,460ft

Beaver Run

BRECKENRIDGE
9,594ft

13,634ft

Peak 10
Falcon's Aerie
11,607ft

The Falcon

The Quicksilver

higher lifts as early as 3.30pm) and overcrowding in town and on the mountain are common: 'the lower runs are mainly green and often get congested in the early morning and in the late afternoon'.

Breckenridge was the first resort in the world to install a high-speed detachable quad chair-lift (it now has six) and it also boasts a double-loading six-person chair-lift. However, one reporter complained that two chair-lifts, including one you have to take to reach Peak 7, provide no safety bar: 'there was no way I could take my fidgety six-year-old, and I have a slight phobia about heights'.

WHAT'S NEW

Peak 7 expansion for 2001–2 season
Additional six-seater chair-lift

The resort has responded to demands from American skiers for more 'European-style off-piste terrain' by opening huge, above-tree-line bowl areas to skiers – who must prove their stamina and determination to ski such steep slopes by first walking uphill, which is not easy at this height. Long criticised for its unchallenging intermediate terrain, the resort now successfully exploits its high altitude and ample natural snow to attract hard-core snowboarders and telemark skiers, as well as the spoilt-for-choice Denver market, who arrive by the thousands with each substantial snowfall.

On the snow
top 12,998ft (3,962m) bottom 9,600ft (2,927m)
Breckenridge's skiing – exceptionally high altitude by Alpine standards – fans out above the town from left to right across four interconnected mountains, numbered from seven to ten, in the Ten Mile Range of the Rockies. Most skiing faces roughly north, exposed to weather that gives the resort its nickname 'Breckenwind'.

Skiing is mostly below tree-level, and Peaks 7 and 8 require 30- to 60-minute climbs to reach their summits. Peaks 8 (intermediate to expert) and 9 (beginner to intermediate) account for most of the resort's groomed skiing, sharing about the same lift capacity and number of runs, though Peak 8 has double the amount of skiing terrain. Peak 10 has only one lift, and until now Peak 7 has had none, thus truly proving the original Edwardian dictum that there is no downhill gain without uphill pain. However, for the 2001–2 season Peak 7 will see an expansion of 165 acres of intermediate terrain, giving six new trails. A new six-seater chair will service the area.

Actual skiing and snowboarding experiences range from 'wide, well-groomed, relatively easy runs' through scenically forested, flat slopes at the resort base to steeps and deeps ('heavily mogulled') in the ample chutes above tree-level – as good as anything in the Alps – on Peaks 7 and 8.

Beginners
Advanced snow-users' dismay is beginner's luck: vast tracts of the lower slopes are as flat as a pancake. At least half of Peak 9 is beginner terrain, with strictly enforced slow-skiing zones. On Peak 8, chairs 5

and 7 access half-a-dozen beginner runs that are effectively barred to faster skiers. All this beginner terrain is beautifully dotted with widely spaced trees.

Intermediates

Peak 9 is medium-standard cruising, marked as blue and green from top to bottom. There is an intermediate way down from everywhere except for the Peak 8 T-bar. Union connects Peak 10 to Peak 9, and subsequently Peak 8, from the top. Four O'Clock and Lehman are long, easy ways home from Peaks 8 and 9 respectively. The six new trails on Peak 7 will add considerable intermediate terrain.

Advanced

The best advanced skiing in Breckenridge is accessed from Chair 6 and the Peak 8 T-bar, both of which offer skiing above 11,480ft. From the T-bar ('some of the best runs in the resort are accessed by this lift') to the skier's right are six black-diamond trails in the North Bowl area. To the skier's left, just past the warming hut, are Horseshoe, Contest and Cucumber bowls, all marked double-black-diamond but all wide open and less than threatening. A dozen marked chutes in the Way Out sector below the Lake Chutes feed into the black Psychopath trail under Chair 6 for a ride up Chair E to the longest-lasting powder on the mountain in the 41 acres of the North Chutes.

Off-piste

Piqued by its reputation for less than adrenaline-inducing skiing, Breckenridge has in the past few years gone to extremes and opened (when safety conditions permit) the Lake Chutes sector, which offers 20 acres of 656-ft vertical pitches of up to 50 degrees. The Lake Chutes can be accessed by climbing some 820ft vertical to the top of Imperial Bowl on Peak 8 from the top of the Horseshoe Bowl T-bar. Less taxing is the climb of 492ft vertical from the same spot to the summit of Peak 7 for the open, untracked Whale's Tail, Peak 7 and Art's Bowls. It is also possible to cheat on the climb by traversing into the lower sectors of these bowls from the T-bar. Forget Me Not black-diamond trail leads you to the Glades, an off-piste area in the trees.

Snowboarding

Freestylers are well served here with two popular terrain parks and half-pipes; of these, the Gold King terrain park on Peak 9 features some impressive jumps. Easily accessed bowls and chutes make Breckenridge hugely popular with boarders, who voted the resort's facilities the best in North America. Away from groomed trails, boarders vastly outnumber skiers, especially on powder days.

Tuition and guiding

Breckenridge Ski School is big – 600 instructors – but diversified, with specialised clinics such as the 50-plus seminars ('taught by oldies for oldies'), women's workshops and teen-only programmes. Instructors try their hardest, as work is assigned according to reports of client satisfaction ('classes were typically small: three students with a maximum of about eight'). However, not all reports are favourable: 'the instructor knew his stuff and was friendly but confused us by throwing too many ideas into the ring'. Snowboarding is big here, and the school teaches everything 'from carving and riding to busting out of the half-pipe'.

Mountain restaurants

Reporters found the mountain restaurants to be 'excellent value for money'. Falcon's Aerie on Peak 10 is little more than a warming hut that serves cold fare for skiers on the move, while Peak 9's eponymous eatery exhausts the shortlist of high-altitude dining spots, as well as the patience of skiers queuing for cafeteria fodder. Vista Haus is on Peak 8, at the bottom of which American blueberry muffins, burritos and 'salads by the pound' are on offer at Bergenhof. Ten Mile Station restaurant ('has a lovely large deck and does BBQs when weather permits') stands at the base of Peak 10.

Accommodation

Nearly all the accommodation in Breckenridge is non-smoking and much of it is within a five-minute walk of the lifts. Most convenient for the lifts are the huge hotel complexes of the Beaver Run Resort (☎ 970 453 6000), the Great Divide Lodge (☎ 970 453 4500) (formerly the Hilton, but now owned by the resort) and the Village at Breckenridge (☎ 970 453 2000), in descending order of altitude. All of these attract large conference groups, as does the Lodge & Spa (☎ 970 453 9300) outside the Breckenridge town limits. Hunt Placer Inn (☎ 970 453 7573) is a European chalet-style B&B, while Muggins Gulch Inn (☎ 970 453 7414) is also praised. Budget accommodation includes the family-oriented Breckenridge Wayside Inn (☎ 970 453 5540) and the old-fashioned Ridge Street Inn (☎ 970 453 4680). The town has a free bus service.

Eating in and out

Breckenridge features a lot of places to eat in (more than 50) but beware of local advice, as Americans often confuse kitsch décor – impossible to escape in Breckenridge – with decent cuisine. Reservations are essential and are unlikely to be honoured if you are so much as 15 minutes late. Casual dining favours Mexican cuisine at Mi-Casa ('lively atmosphere, but the service is a bit familiar'), while spicy Louisiana Cajun fare can be found at Poirrier's. Fatty's and the Village Pasta Company offer exotic pizzas, and the Bamboo Garden provides respectable Szechuan and Mandarin food.

Café Alpine ('a bit of an event') has won several local gourmet awards, yet Pierre's River Walk Café is the sole 'real' French restaurant, eclipsed only by the Top of the World restaurant at the Lodge & Spa, where the red deer carpaccio and buffalo-stuffed pasta are exquisite.

Skiing facts: Breckenridge

TOURIST INFORMATION
PO Box 1058, Breckenridge,
CO 80424
Tel 1 970 453 5000
(01708 224773 for UK agent)
Fax 1 970 496 7138
(01708 640707 for UK agent)
Email breckinfo@vailresorts.com
vailresorts@clara.co.uk
Web site www.breckenridge.com

THE RESORT
Airport transfer Denver International
2hrs, Eagle County 1hr
Visitor beds 25,000
Transport free bus throughout resort.
Shuttle bus to Beaver Creek, Keystone
and Vail

THE SKIING
Linked or nearby resorts Arapahoe
Basin (n), Beaver Creek (n), Copper
Mountain (n), Keystone (n), Vail (n)
Number of lifts 25
Total of trails/pistes 2,043 acres (15%
easy, 28% intermediate, 57% difficult)
Beginners 7 beginner lifts

LIFT PASSES
Area pass (covers Arapahoe Basin,
Beaver Creek, Keystone and Vail)
$174–210 for 6 days

Pensioners 70yrs and over
$99 for season
Credit cards yes

TUITION
Skiing Breckenridge Ski and Snowboard
School (3 centres) (☎ 970 453 3272)
Snowboarding as ski school
Other courses bumps, cross-country,
extreme skiing/boarding, family ski
clinics, moguls, seniors, skiing for the
disabled, teen programmes, telemark,
women's seminars
Guiding none

CHILDREN
Lift pass 5–12yrs $126 for 6 days
Ski & board school as adults
Kindergarten (ski/non-ski) Breckenridge
Children's Centers (☎ 970 453 3258)

OTHER SPORTS
Climbing wall, dog-sledding, horse-
riding, hot-air ballooning, ice-fishing,
indoor tennis, racquet-ball, skating,
ski-jöring, sleigh rides, snowmobiling,
snowshoeing, swimming

FOOD AND DRINK
Coffee $1.50–1.80, glass of wine $3–6,
small beer $2–3, soft drink $2.50,
dish of the day $8–18

Downstairs at Eric's describes itself correctly as 'Breckenridge's most outrageous beer hall and pizza joint', and the Hearthstone is praised for its 'interesting menu'. Bubba Gump's Seafood offers 'a lively, busy atmosphere with food ranging from good to nasty', while Ullr's Sports Grill is said to have 'unpleasant surroundings and poor food'. Spencer's at Beaver Run is 'good for surf and turf, but the wine was disappointing', and Sushi Breck ('the best food in Breckenridge and the cheapest sushi that we have encountered anywhere') is informal and good value.

Après-ski

Breckenridge is renowned as a 'party town'. 'Really friendly, even by American standards' is a frequent comment on the Breckenridge crowd, the rowdier section of which is to be found in the cheerfully seedy surroundings of Shamus O'Toole's Roadhouse Saloon. A reporter who visited Clancy's Irish Bar remarked that 'the beer is terrible but the food was excellent and really tastes home-made like your mum would make it'. The Underworld Club remains popular with snowboarders, and the Gold Pan is a typical 'cowboy' bar. Breckenridge Brewery attracts a tumultuous throng. More sophisticated – and pretentious – is Cecilia's Cigar Parlor, which is the only smoking zone in town. The Back Stage Theater is strictly amateur but entertaining, while Tiffany's Nightclub offers cheap drinks and techno. Sherpa & Yettis presents live reggae, rock and blues acts of some note seven nights a week throughout the season.

The resort is chock-a-block with boutiques, art galleries and ski shops. Scores of designer discount shops can also be found in the nearby factory outlet centres of Frisco and Silverthorne.

Childcare

Advance reservations are advisable for the base-area kindergartens at Peaks 8 and 9. The former accepts infants as young as two months, and the latter children from three years of age. Both have pagers for parents to hire, provide lunches and offer a non-skiing, outdoor snow-play programme. The children's learning area includes two 'magic carpet' conveyor belts. Children from three years old can join the ski school through the Children's Centers, and five-year-olds attend Breckenridge Ski and Snowboard School, which was praised by reporters: 'the ski school was friendly – always a welcoming party for the children before the lesson, therefore no tears' and 'I would definitely recommend Breckenridge to families with children who require warm coaxing into having lessons'. The school also runs a teens-only programme.

The Cottonwood Resorts

ALTITUDE Snowbird 7,740ft (2,359m), Alta 10,550ft (3,216m), Solitude
Mountain Resort 7,988ft (2,435m), Brighton 8,755ft (2,668m)

Beginners ✱✱ Advanced ✱✱✱ Intermediates ✱✱✱ Snowboarders ✱✱
(except Alta)

The best skiing in Utah is to be found up Little Cottonwood Canyon, at **Snowbird** and at the little 1960s-retro resort of **Alta**. Snowbird is rightly considered to be the home of 'champagne powder', a dream-like substance of talcum-type flakes. These have been freeze-dried in their journey over the desert from the distant ocean before being deposited in copious quantities on the steep slopes surrounding Little Cottonwood Canyon. The skiing terrain is more scenic than in many Utah resorts, but at Snowbird the architecture is considerably less attractive.

When Dick Bass, a Texan oilman, built Snowbird 30 years ago this winter, he had apparently fallen under the spell of the latest concrete additions in the French Alps. His argument was that concrete blends with the granite walls of the canyon, and that by adopting the tower block option he fulfilled avalanche safety regulations while avoiding the sprawling condominium suburb of so many of his American competitors. Officially, the heart of the resort is Snowbird Center, the departure point for the cable-car. However, the mirrored walls of the Cliff Lodge, with its 11-storey atrium, dominate the long, narrow swathe of contemporary buildings and car parks. The Snowbird Center comprises the Plaza Deck – an open space surrounded by limited shops on three levels. Outlying buildings house condominiums, and the overall impression is of a single-function resort with few alternatives for non-skiers.

> ✔ Impressive scenery
> ✔ Excellent snow record
> ✔ Short airport transfer
> ✔ Variety of off-piste
> ✔ Late-season skiing
> ✔ Doorstep skiing (Snowbird and Solitude)
> ✗ Limited après-ski
> ✗ Lack of village centre (Snowbird)
> ✗ Few mountain restaurants
> ✗ High-priced accommodation (Alta and Snowbird)

Time ticks in an alternative warp in the neighbouring resort of Alta. While other ski resorts around the world vie with each other to build four-, six- and even eight-person chair-lifts to provide increasingly swifter access to their slopes, Alta makes a fortune out of standing still. The atmosphere is reminiscent of Austria in the 1960s, with cranky lifts leading to uncrowded slopes. Only leather lace-up boots, wooden skis and tea-dancing are missing from the tableau.

Snowboarders, who account for up to 20 per cent of lift tickets sold in other resorts, are banned on the grounds that their behaviour both on and off the mountain might inconvenience the regular visitors. The 'newest' chair-lift celebrates its twenty-first birthday this season. Indeed, the only addition in recent years is a dated rope-tow that ponderously moves skiers from one part of the base area to the other.

The resort is revered both by powder skiers and generations of well-to-do families who return here year after year to stay in expensive and comfortable, but far from luxurious, wooden lodges. Its cheap daily lift ticket makes it extremely popular with local skiers. Alta was here some 30 years before Snowbird and is immensely proud of the fact. It has rather more beginner and lower intermediate terrain, and also phenomenal chutes and secret powder caches reached only by hiking. Devotees refuse to accept that Snowbird is in the same class; realists are thankful that two outstanding powder resorts are so close together.

After years of talks between the rivals the two resorts were tentatively linked during the 2000–1 season. Each afternoon, skiers in Alta were allowed to drop off the shoulder of 11,051ft Sugarloaf and ski down into Snowbird. The agreement has led to the construction of a link chair-lift, and both resorts have announced a joint lift ticket for 2001–2. However, snowboarders will still be excluded from Alta for the foreseeable future. The marketing possibilities of a linked European-style ski circus, the first in the United States, is not lost on either party. The mountain merger has been made possible because of Snowbird's expansion into Mineral Basin, 500 acres of spectacular alpine terrain that adjoins Alta's boundary and is served by a high-speed detachable quad-chair. A new chair-lift built in summer 2001 completes the link.

Just over the western wall of the canyon on skis, but an hour away by car, lies **Solitude**. It is situated 28 miles and 45 minutes' drive from Salt Lake City in the heart of Big Cottonwood Canyon in Utah's Wasatch-Cache National Forest. Solitude is an underrated, little, ski-in ski-out resort that is family owned and full of charm. The resort has existed since 1953 but only in the past half-a-dozen years have its owners, the DeSeelhorst family, found either the money or the planning permission to develop the village. Five apartment blocks and a hotel have followed, including the four-star Inn at Solitude and the Powderhorn Lodge. State-of-the-art machinery ensures that 50 per cent of the mountain is groomed on a rotating basis.

At the top of Big Cottonwood Canyon is **Brighton**, Utah's oldest ski area, which opened in 1936. It remains a small scenic resort.

On the snow
top 11,000ft (3,352m) bottom 7,740ft (2,359m)

Snowbird boasts one of America's few cable-cars, known as the 'tram', which was recently refurbished to carry 125 skiers almost 3,000ft to the top of Hidden Peak in eight minutes. There is only one relatively easy run down: Chips, a three-mile trail back to the base area. Elsewhere, the higher skiing is dominated by bowls, chutes and gullies – an exciting

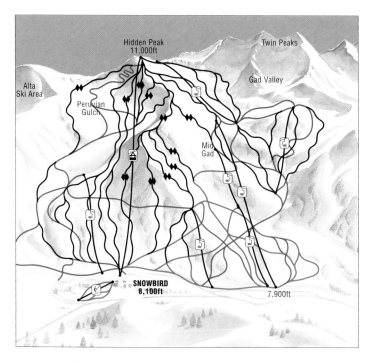

arena for advanced skiers who enjoy powering through steep slopes on ungroomed snow. Intermediates are well catered for, yet there is a shortage of novice skiing. The ski area has recently been expanded by 25 per cent with the development of Mineral Basin. Access is via the tram and return is by a new detachable quad chair-lift. Together they serve 18 trails covering 500 acres with a vertical drop of 1,439ft.

Alta boasts eight fixed chair-lifts and five drag-lifts, and its uphill capacity is limited to 10,750 skiers per hour in order to make the skiing experience more pleasant.

At Solitude, seven lifts serve 1,200 acres of terrain, which was featured in the popular children's film, *The Grinch*. Around 50 per cent of pistes are rated intermediate. Solitude has a hands-free lift pass.

Brighton offers seven lifts, including three high-speed quads, within 850 acres of terrain, comprising 21 per cent easy pistes, 40 per cent intermediate ones and 39 per cent advanced. The resort provides some meticulously groomed trails, of which 18 are floodlit for night-skiing.

An interchangeable ski-lift voucher covers the four Cottonwood Resorts but can be ordered only in advance from the Salt Lake Convention and Visitors Bureau (☎ 801 534 4919 creid@saltlake.org).

Beginners

Snowbird's Baby Thunder lift opens up a network of green (easy) runs as well as the slightly more demanding blue (intermediate) trail, Thunder Alley, all of which end up below the village. Novice skiers and riders should stay away from the top of Hidden Peak unless they really feel they can cope with Chips Run, which is a very long blue. Complete beginners can ski off the Chickadee lift down by the Cliff Lodge. Otherwise, the Mid Gad and Wilbere lifts serve some of Snowbird's least intimidating terrain. This includes Big Emma, which is a wide green (easy) slope, named after the popular *madame* of a mining camp brothel.

The biggest surprise in Alta is that a resort with such a macho reputation for deep powder should have so much easy, groomed skiing. The runs served by the Sunnyside, Albion and Cecret chairs are ideal for novices.

In Solitude, beginners head for the Moonbeam II lift for easy runs such as Little Dollie and Pokey-Pine, whereas in Brighton the easiest run is Main Street from the top of the Evergreen lift.

Intermediates

The ski area at Snowbird offers a number of well-groomed runs best suited to confident parallel skiers. Bassackwards, Election, Bananas and Lunch Run are all straightforward cruising trails. However, the ski area is littered with black-diamond slopes and intimidating double-black-diamond runs; considerable care should be taken to avoid embarking on a slope that may be too testing.

Alta's network of blue trails criss-cross the mountain. Both the Sugarloaf and Supreme lifts provide access to cruising runs such as Rock 'N' Roll and Devil's Elbow.

The mainly benign blues served by the Eagle Express quad at Solitude provide plenty of cruising territory. At Brighton, the Crest Express and Snake Creek Express lifts give access to runs such as Thunder Road, Pioneer and Lone Star.

Advanced

Snowbird's strong skiers are spoilt for choice, with everything from fairly easy, open-bowl skiing to very difficult bump chutes. With the exception of Chips, all the trails off Hidden Peak are classified as either black-diamond or double-black-diamond. Challenging black runs through spruce and lodge-pole pine, such as Gadzooks and Tiger Tail, are reached from the Gad 2 lift. The Road To Provo traverse from Hidden Peak (also reached by the Little Cloud lift) leads to other demanding runs such as Black Forest and Organ Grinder.

In Alta, serious skiers head for the Supreme lift and runs such as Catherine's Area, So Long and Sidewinder. Devil's Castle and East Devil's Castle also provide spectacular skiing in powder conditions.

Honeycomb Canyon in Solitude, reached by a long traverse from the Summit lift, offers a series of short but steep descents down to the Woodlawn and Honeycomb Return black-diamond runs around the shoulder.

In Brighton, the Great Western Express takes you to the top of Clayton Peak for a choice of double-black-diamonds including Endless Winter and Clark's Roost.

Off-piste

Snowbird's off-piste terrain is superb, and the key to it is the Cirque Traverse from Hidden Peak. From this narrow ridge skiers can drop off both sides into a large selection of chutes and gullies. Some are sandwiched between pines, which have been twisted and stunted by blizzards; others are guarded by imposing outcrops of granite. Plunges into Silver Fox, Great Scott and Upper Cirque on one side and Wilbere Chute, Wilbere Bowl, Barry Barry Steep and Gad on the other can be exhilarating in fresh snow but quite frightening in difficult conditions. There is also some awesome back-country skiing below Twin Peaks in Gad Valley.

Likewise Alta becomes one huge powder playground after a fresh fall. It is vital to take local advice on where to find the best and safest runs. Brighton may have a small groomed ski area, but it also boasts some radical skiing off the back of Millicent in the Wolverine Cirque.

Snowboarding

Freeriders at Snowbird enjoy a superb choice of terrain that varies from gentle bowls to extreme chutes from Hidden Peak. Snowboarding is banned at Alta, but welcomed at both Solitude and Brighton – the latter having a half-pipe.

Tuition and guiding

Snowbird Mountain School operates workshops for style, 'Bumps-and-diamonds' and racing, as well as normal lessons. The Mountain Experience clinic gives powder tuition and free guided tours. The Alf Engen Ski School at Alta was named after its founder, who taught skiing here in 1948; children and adults are catered for.

Solitude's Snowsport Ski School, run by a Norwegian Leif Grevle, offers ski and snowboarding lessons for adults, which include mogul clinics, snowblading, extreme skiing and snowboarding, women's clinics and telemark. Back Tracks at Solitude is the off-piste guiding company. The Brighton Ski School teaches all standards.

Mountain restaurants

The only real restaurant on the mountain at Snowbird is at Mid Gad. The Snowbird trail map accurately describes it as a 'fuel stop'. The Peak Express warming hut on Hidden Peak serves coffee and light snacks. Serious lunchers must return to the base area.

Alf's Restaurant and the Collins Grill, which are both on the slopes at Alta, are warmly recommended along with the Albion Grill at Albion base area. Alta Lodge is 'great for a quiet lunch'.

At Solitude the Last Chance Mining Camp is a large and airy self-service on the piste, and the Creekside Restaurant is conveniently set at the base of the lifts and is open for lunch.

At Brighton, the Alpine Rose is a simple slope-side cafeteria, while Molly Green's is a private club.

Accommodation

At Snowbird most people stay at the Cliff Lodge ('much the smartest and most comfortable address here') or at one of the three other condominium lodges nearby: the Lodge at Snowbird, The Inn and the Iron Blosam Lodge (☎ 801 742 2222 for all accommodation).

Alta's oldest and most charming lodge is Alta Lodge (☎ 801 742 3500), which has been attracting visitors since 1939 and was renovated in 1990. Other accommodation includes the Alta Peruvian Lodge (☎ 801 742 3000) and the Rustler Lodge (☎ 801 742 2200), both of which have heated outdoor pools.

All accommodation at Solitude (☎ 801 536 5700 for reservations) is less than seven years old and is consequently of a high standard. There are comfortable and modern ski-in ski-out apartments in the Creekside Lodge and in the new Powderhorn Lodge, as well as at the Inn at Solitude, which contains the St Bernard's restaurant.

Brighton boasts the slope-side Brighton Lodge (☎ 801 532 4731), while the Silver Fork Lodge (☎ 801 533 9977) is in the Wasatch National Forest overlooking Solitude and close to Brighton.

Eating in and out

Snowbird boasts 12 restaurants, including the Aerie at the top of the Cliff Lodge, which is enclosed by glass and provides continental cuisine. The remodelled Sushi Bar requires guests to be 21 or older. Keyhole Junction specialises in South-western cooking, Pier 49 at Snowbird Center serves gourmet pizzas, and the Steakpit offers an all-American menu that includes king crab. The Wildflower Ristorante at the Iron Blosam Lodge features Italian food.

Alta's best food is to be found in the places such as Alta Lodge, where Chef Paul Raddon has presided over the kitchens for 30 years ('extraordinary chilli-rubbed pork in cider bourbon sauce'). Here in the heart of the world's first retro-resort, reservations are chalked on a blackboard and wealthy guests from Boston and New York dine at communal tables. Albion Grill, Alta Java and Goldminer's Daughter are located at Alta's mountain bases.

Solitude's seven restaurants include St Bernard's, which serves a first-rate breakfast and is also the smartest evening venue. The friendly Creekside Restaurant mixes fine dining with family-friendly dishes such as pizza cooked on a wood-burning stove, and creative pasta. The Yurt is a Mongolian-style hut reached in the evening either on snowshoes or cross-country skis through the trees. Brighton has little to offer apart from cafeteria-style food at the Alpine Rose.

Après ski

Snowbird's bars are few in number and formal enough to deter all but the most enthusiastic nightlifers. Immediately after the lifts close, most people gravitate towards the Forklift, just across the plaza from the tram, and the Wildflower Lodge. The Tram Club at Snowbird Center puts on live music and dancing. Later on, the Aerie often has a pianist, but sitting here until closing time at 1am is not particularly exciting. If the roads are clear and no storms are imminent, you could try a night out in Salt Lake City, 25 miles away. The Cliff Lodge houses a comprehensive spa with a rooftop swimming-pool, exercise studios with floor-to-ceiling windows, and a wide choice of health and beauty treatments. Snowbird also offers an indoor climbing wall, indoor tennis and squash, luge, racket-ball, skating and tubing.

In Alta, après-ski entertainment is limited to the slope-side hot-tub or the screening of a black-and-white ski film, followed by drinks around a roaring log fire. Guests at Alta Lodge swop tales in the Sitzmark Club.

The only post-slope entertainment at Solitude is to be found in the Thirsty Squirrel pub.

Childcare

Daycare for children of six weeks to 12 years old is available at Camp Snowbird at the Cliff Lodge. The Mountain School at Camp Snowbird also organises tuition for three- to 12-year-olds. One reporter described Snowbird as 'the most child-friendly resort I have ever been to'.

Alta's Alf Engen Ski School offers children's lessons. The Alta Lodge Kids' Program is aimed at four- to ten-year-olds and it provides transport to and from ski school, as well as après-ski activities.

The Moonbeam Ski and Snowboard Academy for Kids is part of Solitude Ski School and teaches four- to 12-year-old children. In Brighton, the Kinderski and Young Riders cater for children aged four to seven years with all-day lessons including lunch.

Alta Ski Area
Tel 1 801 359 1078
Fax 1 801 799 2340
Email info@altaskiarea.com
Web site www.altaskiarea.com

Snowbird
Tel 1 801 742 2222
Fax 1 801 742 3344
Email cres@snowbird.com
Web site www.snowbird.com

Brighton
Tel 801 532 4731
Fax 435 649 1787
Email info@skibrighton.com
Web site www.skibrighton.com

Solitude Mountain Resort
Tel 1 801 534 1400
Fax 1 801 649 5276
Email info@skisolitude.com
Web site www.skisolitude.com

Jackson Hole

ALTITUDE 6,311ft (1,924m)

Beginners ✱✱ Intermediates ✱✱ Advanced ✱✱✱ Snowboarders ✱✱✱

In this remote corner of Wyoming the snow-capped Tetons rise like jagged shark's teeth from the valley floor with no foothills to reduce their visual impact. Grand Teton, the greatest of these, soars towards the heavens – the equivalent of seven Eiffel Towers stacked one on top of the other. This panorama assails you even before you leave the aircraft at Jackson Hole Airport. What appears to be a toytown landing strip is in fact served by jet airliners from Denver, Salt Lake City, Chicago and Los Angeles.

✔ Cowboy-town atmosphere
✔ Lively nightlife
✔ Ideal for non-skiers
✔ Beautiful scenery
✔ Attractive town
✔ Well-run kindergarten
✘ Distance from town to slopes
✘ Short ski season
✘ Remote location

A 15-minute car ride from the airport takes you into the quaint cowboy town of Jackson. Jet-lagged visitors assume that the steeped groomed trails immediately above it are their ski destination, but this mountain is the small and entirely separate resort of **Snow King**. Jackson Hole Ski Resort is located a further 20-minute drive away at **Teton Village** on the far side of the Snake River, an enticing trout stream that meanders across the valley floor. This leaves you with the dilemma of where to base yourself. Both places have hotels of equal standard, but the convenience of doorstep skiing in Teton Village has to be weighed against the shops, restaurants and nightlife of Jackson. Others have tried, but only Jackson – and **Telluride** on a smaller scale – have succeeded in welding the dusty gun-slinging charisma of a Western frontier town to the high-tech facilities of a modern ski resort. Reporters praised the town as being 'large enough to be interesting but small enough to get around easily'.

In summer Jackson plays host to two million visitors, who arrive by camper-van en route to Yellowstone Park and Old Faithful, the world's largest geyser. In the winter the resort returns to its natural state, an authentic cattle town complete with wooden boardwalks and shops selling Western clothing. The central square is crowned by a triumphal arch made from thousands of naturally discarded elk antlers. Late-night revellers returning from the Million Dollar Cowboy Bar with a skinful of bourbon should not be surprised to happen upon the occasional elk roaming the streets. Working ranches still surround the town, and horses are the secondary means of transport behind the four-wheel-drive.

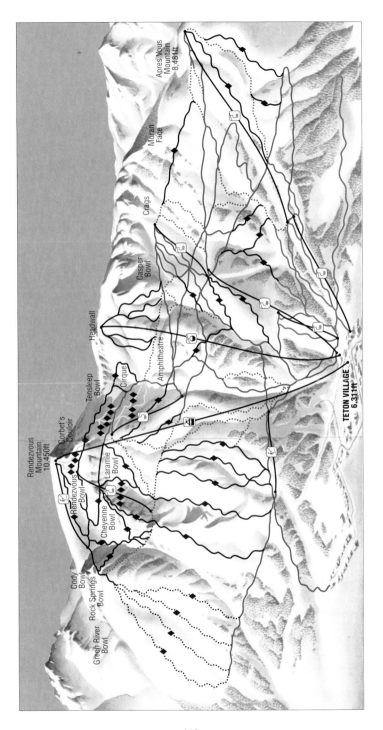

Rendezvous Mountain
10,450ft

Corbet's Couloir

Tensleep Bowl

Cirque

Rendezvous Bowl

Laramie Bowl

Cody Bowl

Cheyenne Bowl

Rock Springs Bowl

Green River Bowl

Headwall

Amphitheatre

Casper Bowl

Crags

Moran Face

Apres Vous Mountain
8,481ft

TETON VILLAGE
6,311ft

413

Teton Village has a few hotels and a couple of ski shops clustered around a picturesque clock tower and the Bridger Center base lodge. A regular 20-minute bus service connects with Jackson.

On the snow
top 10,450ft (3,186m) bottom 6,311ft (1,924m)

Jackson Hole boasts one of the longest continual vertical drops in the USA – the longest now being in **Snowmass**. The skiing takes place on two adjoining mountains: steep Rendezvous and much more benign Apres Vous. In the past you needed to be an expert or complete beginner to enjoy the experience. Anyone in-between risked having their confidence slaughtered by the daunting steepness of the rugged terrain. However, more intermediate trails have been introduced.

While other North American resorts make do with three colour codings for the degree of difficulty of their ski trails, Jackson needs five. Devoted fans around the world see Rendezvous as one of the last wild frontiers of macho mountainside, a place where powderhounds compete for the number of vertical feet they can clock up in a day, in a season or, indeed, in a lifetime. Its ancient lifts, including an antique tram (cable-car), were all part of the legend.

A change of ownership has brought considerable innovations in recent years. The high-speed Bridger gondola up Headwall gives access to 90 per cent of the ski terrain without queuing for the tram that still runs to the top of the mountain. The old, fixed double and triple chair-lifts are gradually being replaced by detachable quads, and planning permission has been granted for a further nine lifts. While Jackson may have been tamed to create wider appeal, it has by no means lost its bite. Most of Rendezvous is given over to black-diamond (difficult) trails, steep chutes and unlimited off-piste. Even some of the blue (intermediate) runs are left ungroomed.

One criticism of Jackson Hole is that for a resort of such international fame the ski area is quite small, and there is little other skiing within driving distance. **Grand Targhee**, 47 miles away, goes some way towards offsetting this disadvantage. The early closure of skiing at the beginning of April is dictated by the elk migration.

Beginners

All the beginner slopes are concentrated at the base of Teton Village, where both the adults' and children's ski schools meet. The nursery slopes are serviced by two short chair-lifts; this allows beginners to start on the easiest slopes and then graduate to steeper gradients. Second-week snow-users can find easier blue runs down Apres Vous Mountain.

Intermediates

As in St Anton and Chamonix, the colour-grading is radical, and you must study carefully the unique colour-coding system, which is explained on the lift map; for most snow-users 'intermediate' means 'difficult', and 'difficult' means 'extreme'. While an acceptable amount of the terrain provides varied skiing for good intermediates, gradients can change suddenly, and in certain conditions unpisted runs are unpredictable and difficult. The friendliest intermediate skiing can be found off Headwall and the Casper Bowl triple-chair. The runs are well marked, but you must pay attention as several blues turn into black-diamond runs on the lower part of the mountain. Only advanced snow-users should stray up the tram.

Advanced
Most of the truly testing terrain can be reached from the top of the gondola – you make your way down Amphitheater to the foot of the Thunder quad-chair. This lift gives access to a series of short but difficult chutes before you ride the lift back up and hop into Laramie Bowl. The steep Alta chutes can then be reached from the Sublette quad-chair. From Rendezvous Trail you can drop off down Central Chute or Bivouac. The possibilities for frightening yourself are endless.

Off-piste
Jackson Hole is one of the few US resorts with unlimited off-piste skiing. Indeed, as grooming is kept to a minimum, it is hard to define what is piste and what is not. Until recently the best powder was to be found in the Hobacks, on the lower section of Rendezvous Mountain. This enormous open area is reached from Rendezvous Trail and is best skied early in the day. However, a further 2,500 acres off the back of Rendezvous has now been opened up to experts ('great care is needed'). Anyone can 'sign out' at various gates of the patrolled ski area, but you are advised to take avalanche transceivers and a guide.

For those with sufficient nerve (and a helmet), Corbet's Couloir, off the top of Rendezvous Mountain and only reached by the tram, is a chute so steep it seems inconceivable that anyone could ski it and survive. It is entered by a 12-ft jump off a cornice; if you manage to control your skis, you will land on a ribbon of snow dropping away at 50 degrees, where you must either turn or fall.

Snowboarding
Riders are catered for by a groomed half-pipe on Apres Vous Mountain, and a natural half-pipe on Dick's Ditch. Nearby Grand Targhee also provides a natural half-pipe for freestylers, but it is the freeriders who will really appreciate the area for its untracked snow.

Tuition and guiding
The ski and snowboard school emphasises having fun and being able to tackle simple slopes in a short time. Group, private and three-day courses are offered in alpine skiing, nordic skiing and snowboarding. The ski school uses video evaluation for many of its classes.

Mountain restaurants

A pizzeria is situated at the top of the gondola, but otherwise mountain eating is limited. The Casper self-service serves both hot food and salads in a pleasant setting with a roaring log fire and Native American memorabilia on the walls, but it tends to get overcrowded. Two small snack bars at the base of the Thunder chair-lift and at the top of the tram provide light refreshment. Most skiers and riders head to the Rocky Mountain Oyster Bar downstairs at the Mangy Moose or to the Alpenhof Lodge, a Tyrolean-style restaurant with waiter service.

Accommodation

The Wort Hotel (☎ 307 733 2190) in Jackson is the original, rebuilt stagecoach inn and is also the most convenient hotel in town. Other hotels include the Forty Niner Inn & Suites (☎ 307 733 7550), The Lodge at Jackson (☎ 307 739 9703) ('pleasant, but inconveniently located') and the Parkway Inn (☎ 307 733 3143) for B&B. The Best Western Inn at Jackson Hole (☎ 307 739 9703) is a four-star hotel at the bottom of the lifts in Teton Village. Self-caterers need to visit Jackson for the supermarkets.

The most luxurious place to stay is the Amangani (☎ 307 734 7333), set in an isolated position between Jackson and Teton Village. From its terraced pool and from every sunken bathtub in the building, guests are treated to a dress circle view of the ski area. Next door, Spring Creek Ranch (☎ 307 733 8833) is another comfortable rural option, where you can stay in the main lodge or in separate self-catering chalets. A Four Seasons Resort hotel with a spa, swimming-pool and two restaurants is due to open at Teton Village in summer 2003.

Eating in and out

The art-deco-style Cadillac Grill in Jackson is one of the few places that accepts children. Sweetwater ('lovely cosy log cabin, interesting menu with well-presented, well-cooked food'), the Snake River Grill and the Blue Lion all offer the American fine-dining experience, but as one reporter commented, 'just because you are paying more for the food doesn't mean it is going to taste any better'. Reporters unanimously praised the Snake River Brewery: 'reasonable prices and sensible portions'. Merry Piglets is a Mexican restaurant that was said to be 'bright, fun, with fast service'. Nani's is an Italian-style eatery: 'moderate prices but the food was good'.

Après-ski

Unless you can prove you are 21 or over, you are not going to enjoy yourself outside skiing hours in Jackson Hole. So strict are Wyoming's licensing laws that even young-looking 30-year-olds should carry identification at all times. The Million Dollar Cowboy Bar and the Silverdollar are the main meeting places along with the Snake River Brewery ('bustling and friendly'). The Cowboy Bar exudes the most atmosphere, with real leather saddles as bar stools and a stuffed grizzly bear in a glass cage.

The Mangy Moose at Teton Village often puts on live music in the evenings and has a video room for those under age, while the Wingback Lounge at the Inn is a quieter option. Teton Village features a skating-rink. Other après-ski activities include sleigh rides through the elk reserve and snowmobile tours of Yellowstone National Park. Shops sell everything from cowboy boots at Corral West to cut-price ski clothing at Gart Sports, and include GAP and Broadway Toys & Togs.

Childcare

Kids' Ranch in the Bridger Center is, in a country of superlative ski kindergartens, one of the best. It boasts a 'magic carpet' conveyor-belt style and its own building called Cody House. Programmes available at the Kids' Ranch are for skiers aged three to five years, while the non-ski kindergarten is for children aged two months to five years. Explorers is a ski course for children aged six to 14; instruction is combined with scouting for moose, porcupines and eagles.

Linked or nearby resorts

Grand Targhee
top 10,230ft (3,118m) bottom 8,000ft (2,438m)

This small resort just inside the Wyoming border and 42 miles from Jackson Hole is blessed with a first-rate snow record, which is why the main attraction is snowcat skiing and boarding in the virgin powder (2,000 acres of it). This is only by previous arrangement, as the cat takes a maximum of ten passengers, plus the guide and a patrolman. If you can't get a booking, the resort's 2,000 skiable acres outside the cat skiing are varied, exciting and served by five lifts. New for the 2001–2 season is a detachable quad and 500 acres of skiing on Peaked Mountain. The resort provides one ski and snowboard school, a kinder-garten, a small shopping centre and limited restaurants. Prices are notably lower than those in Jackson Hole. The Trap offers 'friendly table service, ski videos and a good variety of local beers', and accom-modation (☎ 800 827 4433) includes the Teewinot Lodge, Targhee Lodge and Sioux Lodge Condominiums.

TOURIST INFORMATION
Tel 1 307 353 2300
Fax 1 307 353 8148
Email info@grandtarghee.com
Web site www.grandtarghee.com

Snow King
top 7,808ft (2,380m) bottom 6,237ft (1,901m)

This small ski area is in Jackson town and a free shuttle-bus ride from Teton Village. The ski area with its four lifts and 300 acres of terrain is 'interesting enough for a day's skiing and very quiet'. The lower slopes

Skiing facts: Jackson Hole

TOURIST INFORMATION
PO Box 290, Teton Village, WY 83025
Tel 1 307 733 2292
Fax 1 307 733 2660
Email info@jacksonhole.com
Web site www.jacksonhole.com

THE RESORT
Airport transfer Jackson Airport 15–20 mins from Jackson and Teton Village
Visitor beds 12,000
Transport bus service between Jackson and Teton Village

THE SKIING
Linked or nearby resorts
Grand Targhee (n), Snow King (n)
Number of lifts 11 in Jackson Hole
Total of trails/pistes 2,500 acres (10% easy, 40% intermediate, 50% difficult)
Beginners 3 lifts, reductions available

LIFT PASSES
Area pass $294 for 6 days
Pensioners 65yrs and over $147 for 6 days
Credit cards yes

TUITION
Skiing Jackson Hole Ski & Snowboard School (☎ 307 739 2663)

Snowboarding as ski school
Other courses cross-country, Explorers' ski course for children, extreme skiing/boarding, heli-skiing/boarding, powder clinics, race-training, seniors, skiing for the disabled, steep skiing, teen skiing, telemark, women's clinics
Guiding JHMR Backcountry Guides (☎ 307 739 2663), High Mountain Heli-skiing (☎ 307 733 3274)

CHILDREN
Lift pass 14yrs and under $147 for 6 days. Free for 5yrs and under on Eagle's Rest
Ski & board school as adults
Kindergarten (ski/non-ski) Kids' Ranch (☎ 307 739 2691), (non-ski) Annie's Nannies (☎ 307 733 8086), Babysitting by the Tetons (☎ 307 730 0754)

OTHER SPORTS
Dog-sledding, horse riding, indoor tennis, night-skiing, parapente, skating, sleigh rides, snowcat skiing (Grand Targhee), snowmobiling, snowshoeing, swimming, tubing

FOOD AND DRINK
Coffee $1.75–3, glass of wine $4, small beer $2.75–3, soft drink $2, dish of the day $6.50–8.50

are floodlit, and skating and tubing are also available. Reporters praised the area as 'a good place to learn to ski – the lower slopes are more gentle than at Jackson Hole'. Accommodation is in the Snow King Resort Hotel and Condominiums (☎ 307 733 5200) at the base.

TOURIST INFORMATION
Tel 1 307 733 5200
Fax 1 307 733 4086
Email info@snowking.com
Web site www.snowking.com

Keystone

ALTITUDE 9,300ft (2,835m)

Beginners ✱✱✱ Intermediates ✱✱✱ Advanced ✱✱ Snowboarders ✱✱✱

Set among forests of pine in the heart of the Rocky Mountains in Colorado, Keystone is a modern purpose-built sprawl of multi-level complexes running west to east along Highway 6, 90 miles west of Denver airport. The resort has been almost entirely rebuilt during the past few years, with $700 million spent on new condominiums in the River Run and Ski Tip Ranch sectors of town, together with new shops and restaurants. However, it is essentially a seasonal village, and consequently there is a lack of atmosphere. Bussing from one sector of the resort to another in search of some nightlife becomes tiresome. The high altitude may have adverse effects for some – altitude sickness or headaches brought on by dehydration may persist for days.

Keystone has won numerous awards for its family facilities. Two of its restaurants rate among the best in American ski resorts, though overall standards are unexceptional. Children under 13 stay for free, and children under 5 ski for free. The resort also boasts a superlative range of intermediate terrain and America's most comprehensive snowmaking and night-skiing operations ('it is excellent – enjoy!'). Keystone's three mountains, with 22 lifts and 116 trails, are owned by Vail Resorts, which also owns **Vail**, **Beaver Creek** and **Breckenridge**. The four resorts are connected by shuttle bus, and you can ski all of them on the same lift ticket, though with various restrictions. Nearby **Arapahoe Basin** (A-Basin) is also included in the lift ticket and provides limited, but exciting, advanced skiing.

> ✔ Highly rated restaurants
> ✔ Long ski season
> ✔ Whole ski area covered by snow-cannon
> ✔ Major night-skiing centre
> ✔ Facilities for families
> ✔ Excellent grooming and sign-posting
> ✔ Range of ski school courses
> ✔ Superb facilities for snow-boarders
> ✘ Limited nightlife
> ✘ High altitude may cause sickness
> ✘ Weekend and holiday crowds

On the snow
top 11,980ft (3,652m) bottom 9,300ft (2,835m)

Keystone's skiing is laid out on three interlinked mountains, one behind the other and each progressively more challenging. Facing the resort is Keystone Mountain, with 16 lifts and 55 invitingly easy, meticulously groomed, rolling trails through forest. North Peak's three lifts access 19 shorter, more difficult runs, some of which are left ungroomed in sections. The huge Outback area, the size of both other mountains combined, is protected from the wind and is an excellent introduction to advanced skiing, especially in its two wilderness bowls. Queues used to exceed 15 minutes at weekends, especially on the Skyway Gondola, but the high-speed quad that now runs in tandem has considerably eased congestion. However, the ride can be a cold one. Locals warn of the 'Keystone doughnut' effect: icy slopes whenever nearby Lake Dillon fails to freeze over.

Beginners

Progressing from the Discovery beginner slope, even the most inept snow-user will be flattered by the wealth of ultra-simple green (easy) and blue (intermediate) runs, which comprise almost all of Keystone Mountain's front face. The next step up is Schoolmarm ('extremely long, and narrow in places'), running three miles from top to bottom via a traverse of the resort's western boundary. Ina's Way is a green run to the village.

Intermediates

Intermediates enjoy the run of all three mountains. The Flying Dutchman blue trail takes the most direct line down Keystone Mountain's front face. North Peak boasts five gladed blue runs, with Star Fire taking the most direct and challenging line. In the Outback area, Elk Run is the widest, with Wolverine throwing up more trees to dodge, although it is still graded blue. Mozart, Starfire and East Wall are the longer trails.

Advanced

Keystone's cautious grading puts black-diamond (difficult) runs within the scope of aggressive intermediates, who may first want to test their skills on the short black-diamond sections near Area 51 on Keystone Mountain's west border. North Peak includes six fall-line black-diamond runs tumbling down to the Santiago chair. However, it is the Black Forest in the Outback that is most testing, with four narrow, heavily bumped tree-line runs, particularly adored by snowboarders. Diamond Back is 'usually the only black run at Keystone that is pisted'.

Off-piste

A short hike above the Outback lift at 11,980ft brings you to the North and South bowls, which are within Keystone's boundaries. In powder conditions they provide an exhilarating mix of quite steep, untracked terrain leading down into the trees.

Snowboarding

Keystone offers one of the biggest and best-designed terrain parks in America. Area 51 features numerous pipes in a 20-acre terrain park and is lit at night.

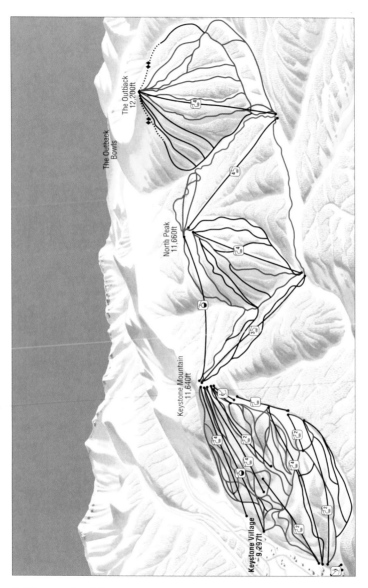

Tuition and guiding

Keystone Ski and Snowboard School is rated among America's top five and features a varied menu of special clinics for women, bump skiers and those convinced they will 'never ever' be able to ski.

Skiing facts: Keystone

TOURIST INFORMATION
PO Box 38, Keystone, CO 80435
Tel 1 970 496 4386
(01708 224773 for UK agent)
Fax 1 970 496 2316
(01708 640707 for UK agent)
Email keystoneinfo@vailresorts.com
vailresorts@clara.co.uk
Web site www.keystoneresort.com

THE RESORT
Airport transfer Vail/Eagle County
1¼hrs, Denver 1½hrs
Visitor beds 5,200
Transport free resort bus service, also to Breckenridge

THE SKIING
Linked or nearby resorts Arapahoe Basin (n), Beaver Creek (n), Breckenridge (l), Copper Mountain (n), Vail (n)
Number of lifts 22
Total of trails/pistes 1,861 acres
(13% easy, 36% intermediate, 51% difficult)
Beginners 1 lift

LIFT PASSES
Area pass (covers Arapahoe Basin, Beaver Creek, Breckenridge and Vail) $174–210 for 6 days

Pensioners 70yrs and over
$99 for season
Credit cards yes

TUITION
Skiing Keystone Ski and Snowboard School (☎ 970 496 4170)
Snowboarding as ski school
Other courses backcountry nature tours, bumps, cross-country, freestyle, powder clinics, seniors, teen programmes, women's clinics
Guiding through ski school

CHILDREN
Lift passes 5–12yrs $126 for 6 days
Ski & board school as adults
Kindergarten (ski) as adults, (ski/non-ski) Keystone Children's Center and Snowplay Programs
(☎ 970 496 4181)

OTHER SPORTS
Dog-sledding, horse-riding, indoor climbing wall, indoor tennis, moonlight cross-country tours, night-skiing, skating, ski-jöring, sleigh rides, snowbiking, snowmobiling, snowshoeing, swimming, tubing

FOOD AND DRINK
Coffee $1.50, glass of wine $5, small beer $2–3, soft drink $1.50, dish of the day $10–18

Mountain restaurants
The Alpenglow Stube is without question the highest – at 11,444ft – haute cuisine in North America. Culinary delicacies served here include tenderloin of wild boar. The Mountain House self-service remains reasonably priced.

Accommodation

The most characterful accommodation is at the Ski Tip Lodge, which used to be an old stagecoach inn and retains the intimate and appealing atmosphere. Keystone Ranch is a hotel with swimming-pool, fitness centre and hot tubs. It is a bus ride away from the skiing and is, according to visitors, 'rather spread out with a long walk to the rooms'. The Inn is closer to the lifts and provides rooms with private hot tubs. The Pines condominiums are recommended: 'well equipped and spacious'. Nearly 1,000 condo flats and private homes of quite luxurious standards are also available. There is central booking (☎ 970 496 4386) for all hotels and condominiums.

Eating in and out

The Edgewater Café and the Bighorn Southwestern Grille at the Keystone Lodge are uninspiring, but reporters praised The Garden Room at the Keystone Lodge for its à la carte menu, and Soda Creek Homestead is a rustic cabin reached by horse-drawn sleigh. Truly memorable dining is reserved for two of the best resort-restaurants in America: the Ski Tip Lodge (Colorado's oldest such establishment) and the Keystone Ranch, which is rated by some US publications as the best resort-restaurant on the continent.

Après-ski

Take a stagecoach to dinner, rip through the Arapahoe National Forest on a snowmobile or ski until 9pm. Apart from America's largest outdoor ice-skating rink and superlative indoor tennis courts, really exuberant nightlife is quashed by the preponderance of families with small children. However, Kichapoo Tavern (with live music), The Great Northern Taverne and Inxpot add atmosphere in the River Run sector, and The Snake River Saloon provides live music and two pool tables. Grassy's Pub and Killian's Bar at the base of the slopes are popular after skiing, as are the nightly bonfires with marshmallow-roasting. Shopping in the resort is limited to a few sports and gift shops, but the factory outlet shopping village at Silverthorne is about 15 minutes' drive from the resort and well worth a visit.

Childcare

The nursery at Keystone Children's Center takes babies from two months old, and Snowplay Programs are for three-year-olds and above. Telephone pagers are available for parents. The Ski and Snowboard School also caters for children aged three to 14. Fort Saw Whiskers is a children-only ski playground.

Killington

ALTITUDE 2,200ft (671m)

Beginners ✱✱✱ Intermediates ✱✱ Advanced ✱✱ Snowboarders ✱✱✱

Killington has the longest season on the East Coast and is a principal component of the giant American Skiing Company, which owns a string of resorts across the USA. The extent of the skiing, coupled with ease of access and an unusually vibrant nightlife, make it one of the most popular US destinations for British visitors. Reporters described the resort as 'big and brash and American. During holiday periods it is full of New Yorkers and Bostonians who want to pack as much as possible into a very short time. However, outside these times there is a real New England feel to the area, particularly if you get off the mountain road and away from the main strip of restaurants, bars and hotels.' A choice of direct seven-hour flights to Boston from Britain, followed by a three-hour transfer journey give Killington a marginal edge over its Colorado rivals. Alternatively, visitors can fly to New York and take the Amtrack rail service to Rutland, a 30-minute drive from the resort.

✔ Easy resort access
✔ Excellent facilities for children
✔ Extensive snowmaking
✔ Modern lift system
✔ Lively nightlife
✔ Wide choice of restaurants
✗ Lack of charm
✗ Straggling layout
✗ Very cold climate

The downside is the New England weather, which is often extremely cold or wet, with low cloud – although 2000–1 was a vintage year for snow cover. To combat the vagaries of nature, all the Vermont resorts invest large amounts of money in snowmaking equipment, and nowhere more so than Killington, where 24 hours a day (temperature permitting), state-of-the-art snow cannons mounted on 15-foot 'giraffe' pylons power out ample quantities of the man-made variety. So sophisticated is the system that the big business of skiing and snowboarding can continue here without weather worries. However, as one reporter put it: 'the snowmaking can become intrusive, as on cold sunny days all you can hear is the roar of cannons'.

Those without a car are tied to the shuttle bus service from their lodging to the mountain or, in many cases, between their lodging and any form of entertainment. Waiting for the bus is a bitterly cold experience. A new slope-side village is on the drawing board but shows no sign of becoming a reality at present. The three-level base-lodge includes a cafeteria, ski rental shop and selection of other retail outlets.

The après-ski starts early, with hot snacks available from 3pm onwards. This sets the tone for the varied nightlife, with a choice of bars

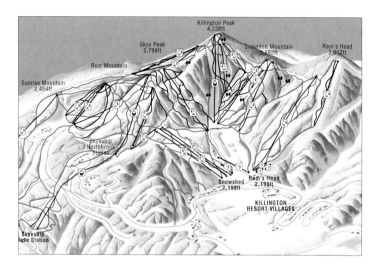

and clubs and cosmopolitan restaurants. Unlike the Rocky Mountain states, Vermont allows older teenagers into bars – but not clubs – provided they do not drink alcohol.

Killington opened for skiing in 1958, when the first tickets were sold out of a ticket booth made from a converted chicken coop. Much has changed since then, although the pedestrianised slope-side village that has been talked about since the early days has still not been realised. The resort lacks a heart, with most of the hotels, condominiums, restaurants and bars lined up on either side of Killington Road, the five-mile link between the ski area and the junction to the main highway.

On the snow
top 4,220ft (1,287m) bottom 1,045ft (319m)
Killington's seven peaks and 32 lifts provide plenty of skiing and riding for all grades, but by European standards the emphasis is on mileage rather than variety. At this low altitude it is inevitable that the runs are glades cut through the all-embracing forest. Although the pitch changes, it is hard to tell one run from the next and piste naming is 'chaotic'. On the plus side, different levels are catered for in separate areas, with beginners safely corralled on their own hill – an arrangement that benefits everyone. The Edge frequent skier card means that skiers and riders can earn points towards free skiing with every lift pass they buy.

A link to neighbouring **Pico** has still not been built, although it is marked on the lift map as a proposal, Pico's chairs were said to be 'starting to show their age'. Another reporter recommended visiting 'the plethora of small ski areas nearby' such as **Okemo**, **Ascutney**, **Suicide Six**, **Sugarbush** and **Mad River Glen**.

Beginners

The beginner slopes on Snowshed are served by a quad-chair and two double-chairs, and encourage a gentle learning curve. The Perfect Turn Discovery Center, Killington's introductory programme for skiing and snowboarding, is located at the Snowshed Base Lodge.

The most comfortable approach to Killington's upper slopes, especially in hostile weather, is via the two-stage Skyship up to Skye Peak. The eight-person gondola is described as the longest and fastest lift in the east of the USA, but more importantly it has heated cabins. Many of the runs from the top are green (easy), with Great Eastern providing a long, gentle return to the base-station.

Intermediates

Once confident on the beginner trails, snow-users can graduate to the three easy blue trails of Timberline, Header and Swirl. Other blue trails to look out for are Needle's Eye, Home Stretch and Cruise Control. Halfway down Great Eastern, you come to the Bear Mountain quad, which opens up another zone, with more black-diamond (difficult) and green runs than blue ones. Snowdon, which is networked with green and blue trails, is also recommended for lower intermediates.

Advanced

Expert snow-users should try the black-diamond runs on Skye Peak or the pistes starting from the complicated junction at the top of the eight-person gondola, although it is necessary to take care when selecting a route there. The most extensive area of double-black-diamond trails is on Killington Peak, with Double Dipper, Cascade, Escapade and Downdraft among the names to look out for. Big Dipper is a gladed trail, but care should be exercised when conditions are icy. Killington's alternative macho challenge is the Outer Limits double-black-diamond mogul slope ('the steepest mogul slope in the East') on Bear Mountain.

Off-piste

'Killington would not suit people who are looking for steep and deep off-piste,' said one reporter. Although there are no powder fields, the resort has created Wild Side and Fusion Zones in the forest by thinning out the trees and clearing away the undergrowth. North Star and West Glade are two of the trails that are left ungroomed. Squeeze Play, off Rams Head, is the logical starting point, with Low Rider on Snowdon and Julio, between Killington and Skye Peaks, providing a sterner test.

Snowboarding

Killington boasts two terrain parks, a half-pipe and a boardercross race-course, as well as a special trail map for snowboarders. The permanent boardercross course is located on Middle Dream Maker, although beginner snowboarders are advised to join a learn-to-ride programme in the enclosed novice area on Snowshed before heading for the beginner-pipe at Highline. Pico provides its own terrain park.

Tuition and guiding

The resort features a Perfect Turn Discovery Center at Snowshed Base Lodge. Reporters praised the ski tuition as 'good value for money. On weekdays, group lessons turned into private lessons as there were so few people'.

Mountain restaurants

Mountain eating is not Killington's strongest point: 'basically geared up to people either bringing packed lunches or burgers/pizzas,' commented one reporter. Killington Peak Restaurant offers views of five US states as well as Canada. The Mahogany Ridge Bar at the Killington base serves a typically limited soup, sandwich and salad menu, but a comprehensive drinks list, with foreign beers, including Newcastle Brown. Its selection of hot alcoholic concoctions is welcome after a morning spent combating the wind-chill factor. Max's Place is said to be civilised, and there is a sushi bar in the Snowshed Base Lodge.

Accommodation

Snowshed base is recommended by reporters as the best place to stay if you don't have a car because it has 'the biggest concentration of restaurants, bars and shops'. The Killington Lodging and Travel Service (☎ 0800 893670 in UK) is the central booking office for accommodation of all types, including condominiums, country inns, lodges and motor inns. The Trail Creek, Whiffletree, Edgemont and Fall Line condominiums are the most conveniently situated, while Cortina Inn, eight miles from the mountain, offers luxurious accommodation. The Inn of the Six Mountains is close to the nightlife and runs its own courtesy bus to the lifts, and the Killington Grand Hotel is a slope-side condominium-hotel with a health club. The Grey Bonnet Inn, six miles from Killington base, has 'a New England atmosphere and extremely welcoming owners'. Its facilities include a swimming-pool.

Eating in and out

The area has a huge choice of restaurants, not least Hemingway's near the Skyship base, which is the only four-star restaurant in Vermont and is reputed to be 'one of the best fine-dining restaurants in America. Food excellent but pricey, service attentive but unobtrusive'. Other eateries include those serving French, Italian, Thai, Japanese (such as Sushi Yoshi), Chinese, Greek, Mexican and American fare. Claude's is known for its European cuisine, while Santa Fe and Casey's Caboose specialise in basic American 'surf and turf'. The Back Behind Saloon at West Bridgewater serves 'delicious steaks, duck and just about every type of meat and fish in a converted railway wagon', while Charity's is popular ('it can be difficult to get a table'). The Garlic offers 'good French food but the service is indifferent – more French than American', and Olivia's in the Grey Bonnet Inn serves 'good American home cooking,' as does Mother Shapiro's. Gaucho's is a reasonably priced Mexican ('does a wonderful Margarita') and The Outback is praised for its oven pizzas. Ppeppers bar and grill is recommended for its 'Eggs 'n' edges' breakfast, whereby the ski shop next door will sharpen your skis for half price while you eat breakfast. The Killington Market sells everything required for self-caterers, including fresh meat, groceries, local cheese and wine.

Après-ski

The base lodges, particularly at Killington base and Snowshed base, are the focus of early-evening après-ski. Later on try the six-mile Killington Road, which is lined with pubs and clubs. The multi-level Pickle Barrel is the centre of the action, with a season-long schedule of big-name bands playing every weekend. The Wobbly Barn attracts a noisy crowd and it combines steakhouse dining with an accompaniment of live rhythm and blues. The Outback and Mother Shapiro's are local bars with pool tables, while the Long Trail Brewery at Bridgewater is recommended, too: 'it serves the range of Long Trail beers and free popcorn'. Teenagers can dance and listen to live music at Bumps, in the Killington Dance Club at the Ram's Head base lodge, on Friday and Saturday evenings. Night-skiing and snowboarding, racquetball, skating, sleigh rides, snowmobiling, snowshoeing and tubing are the alternative activities available in the resort. Excursions can be made to Ben and Jerry's ice-cream factory and the factory outlets at Manchester.

Childcare

The Rams Head area is the ultimate in luxury for families, with four of its own lifts. At the bottom of the hill the flattest slope is designated as a beginners' park and is served by a 'magic carpet' conveyor belt and two hand-tows. However, young snow-users soon graduate to a modern high-speed quad, which gives effortless access to wide descents.

The Perfect Kids programme is divided into sections according to age and skiing ability, with the Friendly Penguin nursery at the Ram's Head Family Center caring for non-skiing children between six weeks and six years old. Ski tuition is available for children from two years of age and snowboarding from four.

TOURIST INFORMATION
Tel 1 802 422 3333 (0800 893670 in UK)
Fax 1 802 422 4391
Email info@killington.com
Web site www.killington.com

Lake Tahoe

ALTITUDE Heavenly 6,500ft (1,982m) Squaw Valley 6,200ft (1,890m)

Beginners ✱✱ Intermediates ✱✱✱ Advanced ✱✱✱ Snowboarders ✱✱✱

California is a world unto itself, so it is not surprising that its ski resorts are also unique. The majority of them – 15 alpine and 8 cross-country – are clustered around the shores of Lake Tahoe, a glimmering stretch of cobalt-blue water that lives up to its reputation as the second largest and most magnificent alpine lake in the world after Lake Titicaca in Peru. **Heavenly** (on the Nevada–California state-line) and **Squaw Valley** (on the north-west shore of the lake) are the main players, but nearly all the other resorts are worth a day's skiing. Transport is easy, and interchangeable lift tickets can be bought through the North Lake Tahoe Resort Association and used at Heavenly, Squaw Valley, **Kirkwood**, **Northstar-at-Tahoe**, **Alpine Meadows** and **Sierra-at-Tahoe**. Kirkwood is a favourite among locals, and one reader described it as 'the star of the show'. Sierra-at-Tahoe features crowd-free trails and some challenging runs for snowboarders, while Alpine Meadows has become one of the most popular resorts in the area for riders.

✔ Spectacular scenery
✔ Diverse resorts share lift pass
✔ Facilities for children
✔ Extensive snowmaking (Heavenly)
✔ Recommended for cross-country
✔ Plenty of tree-level skiing
✔ Lively après-ski (South Lake Tahoe)
✗ No resort centre at Heavenly
✗ Few non-skiing activities

A 13-acre, alpine-style village is being built by the Canadian developer, Intrawest, at the base of Squaw Valley. The first phase, which is now complete, comprises 19 shops and restaurants as well as 139 'designer mountain homes'. The second construction phase began in summer 2001.

Heavenly is part of the American Skiing Company's empire and has consequently also undergone major redevelopment: the Tamarack Express six-person detachable chair-lift was erected as the first stage of a ten-year masterplan of on-mountain improvements, followed by two high-speed quads. Heavenly is a resort of extraordinary contrasts: from the top of the Sky Express chair-lift you can turn left to ski in Nevada, with views of the arid vastness of the Nevada Desert, or turn right to the Californian side overlooking the lush beauty of Lake Tahoe. Off the slopes, in the nearest town of South Lake Tahoe ('zero village feel'), serenity switches to frenzy amid the clunk of one-arm bandits in the 24-hour casinos. Gambling is legal in South Lake Tahoe on the Nevada side of the state-line. Reporters agreed that the view is the best part of Heavenly, which otherwise lacks charm and challenge: 'all in all the ski area has a very commercial feel'. The huge neon signs and monstrous casino complexes are such a contrast to the lake front and its simple, single-storey homes that it takes a while to come to terms with the town of South Lake Tahoe.

Alternatively, you can ignore the tacky glitter ('the main drag through town does have a tired look') and find a small restaurant for an intimate dinner. This is easier in Tahoe City, a ten-minute drive from Squaw Valley. The small town exudes considerable atmosphere and boasts several appealing restaurants on the lakeside. The drive to Squaw Valley from the South Shore along the lake past Emerald Bay is spectacular.

WHAT'S NEW
Further construction for the new pedestrian village at Squaw
50% expansion of terrain parks at Squaw Valley

Squaw Valley, which hosted the 1960 Winter Olympics, provides the steeper and altogether more demanding terrain in a corner of the Sierra Nevada that has a long skiing tradition. As far back as 1856 John 'Snowshoe' Thompson, a Norwegian immigrant, used to carry the mail on skis between the mining camps in these mountains. Until the railway was built in 1872, skiing was the miners' only winter link with the outside world.

On the snow
top 10,100ft (3,079m) bottom 6,200ft (1,890m)

With 29 lifts, Heavenly is one of America's larger ski areas, and almost all of it is below the tree-line. It also features one of America's most extensive snowmaking programmes. The skiing itself is divided between the Nevada and the Californian sides of the mountain. During the 2000–1 season Heavenly opened The Gondola, which takes skiers and snowboarders from the 'casino corridor' to the top of the mountain. The Nevada face consists mainly of blue runs, while the upper Californian side is mainly fast, blue, cruising terrain with more difficult runs higher up. The ski area received criticism: 'it's a drag getting from the California side to the Nevada one for skiers. For snowboarders it's a real pain, too much flat stuff'.

The skiing at Squaw Valley takes place on six peaks: Granite Chief, Snow King, KT-22, Squaw Peak, Emigrant and Broken Arrow. The area is divided into three sectors, but the 30 lifts, rather than the runs, are colour-graded. All the main lifts on KT-22, Squaw Peak and Granite Chief are black-diamond (difficult), while those on Snow King and Emigrant are blue. Intermediates will find a huge amount of skiing – the highlight being a three-mile trail from the High Camp area down to the mountain base. The main mountain access is via the Gold Coast Funitel, the first of its kind in North America. It has an hourly capacity of 4,000 snow-users, and its dual cable allows it to operate in winds of up to 75mph.

Beginners

Heavenly offers three beginner areas: the Enchanted Forest at the California base, Boulder Base Lodge and midway up the mountain on the California side ('wide open pistes, very uncrowded by European standards'). Squaw's main beginner area is located adjacent to the High Camp Bath and Tennis Club at the top of the mountain and accessed by cable-car. This location offers beginners the same mountain experience as more advanced skiers and riders.

Intermediates

Medium-standard skiers will discover that they can explore virtually every run on the mountain at Heavenly. Most of the trails are long cruisers bordered by banks of pine trees and enhanced by the stunning view of the lake. You can take the Sky Express chair and try Liz's or Betty's, then head to Nevada for the Big Dipper, Sand Dunes, Perimeter and Galaxy runs. You should make your way back to the state in which you started by 3.30pm.

Squaw Valley has three main intermediate areas: the off the Squaw Creek and Red Dog lifts, which are best tackled later in the day; the area off the Gold Coast Express chair-lift; and the bowls off Emigrant Peak and the tree runs off the Shirley Lake Express chair-lift.

Advanced

Heavenly's Milky Way Bowl provides challenging skiing, but the most advanced skiing is in Mott Canyon and Killebrew Canyon. Steep chutes are cut through the trees, with runs such as Snake Pit. Heavenly has the odd black-diamond trail – such as Ellie's from the Sky Express and the Face near the California base-lodge – as well as huge areas of tree-level skiing. Gunbarrel, East Bowl and Pistol are said to be 'good long black runs, if boringly straight, usually left mogulled'.

Squaw was the birthplace of the American extreme skiing movement and boasts some seriously steep couloirs as well as open bowl skiing. The most radical terrain is to be found off the KT-22, Headwall, Cornice II and Granite Chief chair-lifts.

Off-piste

Heavenly is reputed to have the best tree skiing in the Tahoe area on a powder day. The Milky Way, Mott Canyon and Killebrew Canyon are large expanses of off-piste; you need to arrive early as they are quickly skied out.

At Squaw Valley, the farther away from the lifts you travel the more likely you are to find good powder snow. Many skiers opt for Headwall, Cornice II and KT-22, but some excellent skiing is also found off Red Dog, Squaw Creek, Granite Chief and Silverado. High Sierra Heli-Skiing offers heli-skiing and heli-boarding.

Snowboarding

Heavenly features two half-pipes, two terrain parks and a boardercross course with huge 'tabletops' and 'rhythm sections' located around the mountain. Squaw Valley has expanded its terrain parks by 50 per cent for the 2001–2 season. The old Riviera terrain park and half-pipe under the chair-lift of the same name is open until 9pm, while the new Mainline Terrain Park (adjacent to the Mainline chair) comes complete with a super-pipe, boardercross course, 'fun boxes', 'volcanoes', a 'triangle jump' and myriad other treats for riders. KT-22 is a particularly good area for freeriders in search of challenge and excitement.

Tuition and guiding

The Perfect Turn ski and snowboard school at Heavenly is identical to the other American Skiing Company schools you will find in **Killington** and **Sunday River**. It offers courses such as race camps, seniors groups, skiing for the disabled, teen skiing and boarding, Mountain Adventure (off-piste) and women's seminars.

The Squaw Valley Ski and Snowboard School puts on programmes for all ages and abilities. Advanced ski clinics, mogul clinics, seniors, skiing for the disabled, telemark, women's clinics and beginner's packages are also available, as well as X-Clinics (tuition in extreme skiing).

Mountain restaurants

Heavenly's restaurants can arrange on-mountain catered picnics, which include a 'snow table' complete with linen tablecloth and a vase of flowers together with a private waiter to serve the food and champagne. The Monument Peak restaurant is in the Top of the Tram complex at Heavenly and boasts a sundeck. You can cook your own food at a barbecue at Sky Meadows on the California side. Boulder Lodge offers a bar, cafeteria and sundeck, while Stagecoach Lodge has a cafeteria. The Slice of Heaven Pizza Pub at the Stagecoach Base Lodge is warmly recommended, while Stagecoach Lodge was said to be 'well worth a visit for the meatball sandwich'.

The Gold Coast, at the top of the Funitel in Squaw Valley, features a barbecue, restaurants and bars on three levels. High Camp boasts five different restaurants and bars, and the main dining-room is open at night. At the base village, dining options range from a hearty breakfast to pizza, burgers, sandwiches and Mexican food.

Accommodation

The ski area of Heavenly and the town of South Lake Tahoe are separate entities, although the Tahoe Seasons Resort hotel complex (☎ 530 541 6700) is close to the lifts at the California base. Harrah's Lake Tahoe (☎ 702 588 6611) and the Lake Tahoe Horizon Casino Resort (☎ 775 588 6211) in South Lake Tahoe are two of the bigger casino-hotels; others include Caesar's Tahoe (☎ 702 588 3515) and Harveys Resort Hotel (☎ 775 588 2411) – all have good spas. The Station House Inn (☎ 530 542 1101) and the Timber Cove Lodge (☎ 530 541

6722) are acceptable motels that have been singled out by reporters. Much of the accommodation is in condominiums.

The Resort at Squaw Creek (☎ 530 583 6300) is a large ski-in ski-out complex near the base of Squaw Valley and offers its own restaurants, bars, fitness centre and ice-skating rink ('I can't imagine why anyone would want to stay anywhere else here'). The recently-expanded Squaw Valley Lodge (☎ 530 583 5500) is close to the base lifts. The Plumpjack Squaw Valley Inn (☎ 530 583 1576) offers some of the most stylish accommodation. Other accommodation is at The Olympic Village Inn (☎ 530 583 1576). Tahoe City and Truckee provide alternative bed bases for visiting resorts in the area.

Eating in and out
In South Lake Tahoe, the Summit in Harrah's is rated one of America's top 100 restaurants. Caesar's contains Planet Hollywood. Harvey's Mexican restaurant is recommended, as is Chevy's. Zachery's and Dixie's specialise in Cajun cooking, the Swiss Chalet receives praise for its fondue, while Red Hute, Ernie's and Heidi's all remain popular for breakfast. The Station House Inn serves reasonably priced meals, and the Chart House is more expensive but affords great views. The Gourmet Café, on the edge of South Lake Tahoe, is highly rated, while The Dory's Oar, just outside Squaw Valley, boasts good seafood.

At Squaw Valley, the Resort at Squaw Creek is warmly praised. Glissandi is a high-priced Italian, and Graham's (in the valley) is cosy. The restaurants in Tahoe City and several in Truckee ('a characterful Wild West town'), half-an-hour away, are more fun. In Tahoe City, Za's is a basic Italian, while upmarket Christy Hill's overlooks the lake. The Cal-Neva Lodge in Crystal Bay on the north shore features two restaurants and an oyster bar.

Après-ski
Heavenly base has no après-ski apart from the California Bar, where there is live music from Wednesday to Saturday. Most of the after-skiing activities take place in South Lake Tahoe, with bars in all the hotels and Vegas-style celebrity shows. The gaming tables attract money, and money attracts the top names in showbusiness. Some excellent cabaret acts and pop concerts are staged here and often feature top artists. McP's is a lively Irish pub, Turtle's puts on dancing, and the Christiania Inn is close to the ski area and creates a good atmosphere.

At Squaw there is music at Gold Coast on the mountain and at Bar One in the base village. Other post-slope options include Salsa, the Plump Jack at Squaw Valley Inn, and the Red Dog Saloon, which is where you will find the locals. The High Camp Bath and Tennis Club is open until 9pm with tubing and ice-skating in winter, and swimming during the spring. Cross-country skiing, sleigh rides, snowshoeing and dog-sled tours are available in the valley. Night-skiing and boarding are included in the daily lift ticket.

Childcare

Heavenly has a Perfect Turn Children's Center along the lines of the other highly successful American Skiing Company resorts. Here childcare is completely flexible, with children dropped off for either half- or full-days, with or without lunch. Parents can rent a Perfect Kid's pager to keep in touch. The Daycare Center is for non-skiers from two months to four years old, while a ski/snowplay combination is also offered. Ski and Snowboard Clinics are for children up to 12 years old.

At Squaw, Children's World is a 12,000-sq-ft complex at the base of the mountain for two- to 12-year-olds, and is convenient for families. Parents can deliver their offspring and buy their tickets at the same time. Toddler Care is a kindergarten that takes two- to three-year-olds for snow play and arts and crafts. At Children's World Ski and Snowboard School, instructors teach children between four and 12 years old.

TOURIST INFORMATION
Tel (Heavenly) 1 775 586 7000/(Squaw) 1 530 583 6985
Fax (Heavenly) 1 775 588 5517/(Squaw) 1 530 581 7106
Email info@skiheavenly.com / squaw@squaw.com
Web site www.skiheavenly.com / www.squaw.com

Linked or nearby resorts

Public transport is efficient and frequent, but a car is useful for exploring the enormous amount of skiing on offer. Alpine Meadows, next to Squaw, has similar steepish terrain and is rated as one of the top US resorts for backcountry (off-piste) skiing in its open bowls. Scott Chute and Hot Wheel Gully were particularly recommended by reporters. Kirkwood enjoys some of the best snow in the area and some advanced terrain, ranging from smooth slopes to sheer cliffs. Sierra-at-Tahoe is the third largest resort around the lake and features three high-speed quad-chairs. Castle, Preacher's Passion and Dynamite are praised as 'good blacks,' and there is 'a little fun snowboard park'.

Donner Ski Ranch, geared mainly towards good intermediates, was linked in January 2000 to the more gentle area of **Boreal** to give a total of 15 chair-lifts, 86 trails and five terrain parks. **Granlibakken**, just outside Tahoe City, is the oldest resort on the lake and is open only at weekends, while **Sugar Bowl** comprises 58 trails and a 1,500-ft vertical drop. Locals' favourite **Mount Rose** has 43 trails and is only 22 miles from Reno. Northstar-at-Tahoe provides five lifts and a cross-country centre, **Diamond Peak** calls itself 'Tahoe's premier family ski resort', and **Ski Homewood** on the West Shore boasts views of the lake on every run and is popular with snowboarders. **Tahoe Donner** and **Soda Springs** are both beginner areas.

TOURIST INFORMATION
Lake Tahoe resorts
Email info@tahoe.com
Web site www.tahoe.com

Mammoth

ALTITUDE 7,800ft (2,377m)

Beginners ✱✱✱ Intermediates ✱✱✱ Advanced ✱✱ Snowboarders ✱✱✱

For the present, the Californian resort of Mammoth still has the family-run feel that it maintained throughout the second half of the twentieth century. Founder Dave McCoy set up the first rope tow here in 1941, bought the resort in 1953 and has spent most winter days on the mountain ever since. But in 1998 he sold out his majority share-holding to the Canadian giant resort developer Intrawest, and Mammoth became the latest ski resort victim of corporate interests. Size-wise it competes favourably with many Alpine resorts. What it might lack in vertical drop it makes up for in altitude and sheer expanse of terrain. New ownership has resulted in major transformations. The resort, together with the nearest town of Mammoth Lakes, is investing more than $830 million to transform the ski region. This includes the development of The Village on Minaret Road, the approach route to the existing resort. In summer 2000 work started on what is conceived as a European-style ski community, eventually to be linked to the main ski area by gondola and a return ski trail. Meanwhile, two new luxury lodges, Juniper Springs and Sunstone, are being built at the Juniper base area. The high-speed Eagle Express six-person chair provides increased mountain access from here.

- ✔ Large ski area
- ✔ Varied terrain including three terrain parks
- ✔ Exceptionally long season
- ✔ Good sunshine and snow records
- ✘ Remote location
- ✘ Spread-out town and lack of ski-village ambience
- ✘ Limited après-ski
- ✘ Shortage of on-mountain restaurants
- ✘ Long airport transfer

First impressions suggest Mammoth was named after the size of its ski area, which is still one of the largest in North America. However, it dates from the Victorian Gold Rush and refers to the consolidation of small operations into one Mammoth Mining Company. The season here is equally mammoth – it officially runs from November to June and sometimes extends to Independence Day in July. The average snowfall of 383 inches is deposited by major storms rolling in from the Pacific.

Getting to this remote corner of the eastern Sierra Nevada is also a herculean task. The resort is situated three hours and 168 miles from Reno, and six hours and 307 miles from Los Angeles. You can stay in condominiums or hotels at the foot of the lifts, but most accommodation is situated four miles away in Mammoth Lakes. A frequent, free town shuttle-bus runs to and from the ski area bases at Main Lodge, Canyon Lodge and Juniper Springs. An airport shuttle bus operates between Reno and Mammoth. The town's small airport is being upgraded, and a scheduled air service is expected to resume in time for the 2002–3 season.

Mammoth Lakes has excellent shopping with numerous sports outlets as well as brand-name factory stores where you can buy clothing and equipment for considerably less than in the UK. The town and the slopes tend to be quiet during the week for much of the winter but become overcrowded at weekends with the influx of Los Angelinos.

> **WHAT'S NEW**
>
> Plans for remodelling of mid-mountain lodge
> Upgrading of Tamarack Cross-country Ski Center

Twenty miles away by road to the north lies its baby sister resort of **June Mountain,** which offers more benign terrain and seven lifts in a spectacular craggy mountain setting.

On the snow
top 11,053ft (3,369m), base 7,953ft (2,424m)

Four separate bases provide access to 30 lifts serving 150 trails set in more than 3,500 skiable acres. The two-stage eight-person Panorama gondola from Main Lodge provides the fastest way to the 11,053-ft (3,369-m) summit and some of the best skiing. This top section gives access to some extremely steep bowls but it is not just for experts – the narrow blue (intermediate) Road Runner provides a gentle cruise around the shoulder of the mountain.

This top section is at the mercy of high winds and prone to avalanche risk, but die-hards line up when it reopens in order to cut fresh tracks in deep powder on the steep faces below the cornice.

Canyon is the sunny side of the mountain, where fresh snow can become heavy. In spring, slushy conditions are offset by the beach atmosphere outside the lodge, with sun loungers, BBQ and bar animated by live bands.

At weekends the slopes immediately above the access points are prone to overcrowding. One reporter suggested heading for the older double- or triple-chairs higher up the mountain where trails are 'nearly always deserted'. Snow-cannon cover 25 per cent of the area.

Beginners

Green (easy) runs surround all the access points, and separate ski and snowboard schools operate from both Main and Canyon Lodge. Students will quickly advance to blue terrain, enabling them to cover the whole mountain.

Intermediates

Mammoth's ski area is littered with intermediate pistes that allow skiers and riders to progress gradually from basic blue to advanced–interme-

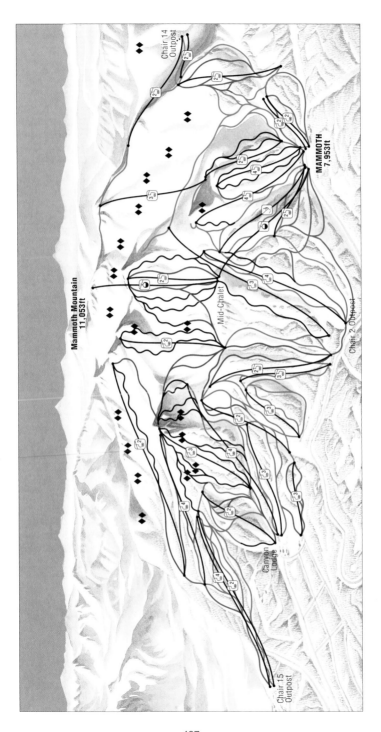

diate terrain (marked blue-black). The familiar black-diamond (difficult) and double black-diamond (very difficult) signs can be offputting.

Chairs 12, 13 and 14 give access to plenty of cruising terrain with runs such as Surprise, Secret Spot and Bristlecone. Broadway at Main Lodge and Stump Alley above The Mill Café are recommended. Gold Rush Express quad gives access to interesting blue runs, such as Lower Dry Creek (a natural half-pipe) and provides liaison with intermediate slopes above Canyon Lodge.

Advanced

The majority of seriously challenging double-black-diamond trails are reached from the top of the Panorama gondola and Chair 23. Seekers of scary steeps are not disappointed. The upper half of the ski area offers open bowls, gullies and tree-skiing. The bumps here are generally considered to be some of the most demanding in California. Few of the black trails are groomed – Cornice Bowl being a regular exception. Face Lift and Chair 5 lead to some black-diamond terrain, including Dry Creek and West Bowl, which tends to develop friendly bumps. Chair 22 gives access to Lincoln Mountain with steep, ungroomed but sheltered runs through the trees.

Off-piste

Skiing and riding are permitted everywhere within the boundary. There are even some out-of-bounds routes, such as Hole in the Wall, down which instructors are allowed to take clients (with permission from the ski patrol). Almost all the expert terrain is left ungroomed, as is enough of the intermediate slopes to allow less accomplished skiers and snowboarders a piece of the action.

Snowboarding

Mammoth is one of the USA's top snowboarding destinations – it now has three terrain parks. The original (best suited to advanced riders) is reached by Thunder Bound Express from Main Lodge and includes a half-pipe, super-pipe, tabletops and other jumps. The two other terrain parks are at Canyon Lodge and below the Roller Coaster chair. The varied trails offer considerable interest. Boardertown at June Mountain has spines, pipes and rails.

Tuition and guiding

Canyon Lodge Sports School and the Main Lodge Sports School offer three-hour group lessons each morning for skiers and riders. The High Alpine Freeride Camp is tailored to advanced skiers seeking to improve their performance on steep terrain and in the most difficult snow conditions. Women's Seminars are perennially popular, or you can fine-tune your slalom skills with the former Olympic downhill racer at AJ Kitt's Ski & Race Camp. Free piste tours are hosted on a daily bases by local volunteers.

Skiing facts: Mammoth

TOURIST INFORMATION
PO Box 24, Mammoth Lakes, CA 93546
Tel 1 760 934 2571
Fax 1 760 934 0761
Email info@mammoth-mtn.com
Web site www.mammothmountain.com

THE RESORT
Airport transfer Mammoth Lakes–June Lake Airport 15 mins, Los Angeles 6hrs, Reno 3hrs
Visitor beds 8,200
Transport free shuttle bus links Mammoth Lakes with ski area

THE SKIING
Linked or nearby resorts June Mountain (n)
Number of lifts 30
Total of trails/pistes 3,500 acres – 30% easy, 40% intermediate, 30% difficult
Beginners 2 lifts

LIFT PASSES
Area pass (covers Mammoth and June Mountain) $293 for 6 days
Pensioners 65–79yrs 50% reduction, free for 80yrs and over
Credit cards yes

TUITION
Skiing Canyon Lodge Sports School, Main Lodge Sports School both
☎ 760 934 2571
Snowboarding as ski schools
Other courses cross-country, extreme skiing/boarding, moguls, powder clinics, race-training, skiing for the disabled, teen skiing, telemark, women's ski seminars
Guiding Mammoth Mountaineering School ☎ 760 924 9100

CHILDREN
Lift pass 7–12yrs, $140, 13–18yrs $213, both for 6 days
Ski & board school Canyon Kids, Woollywood, both ☎ 760 934 2571
Kindergarten (ski/non-ski) as ski and board schools

OTHER SPORTS
Dog-sledding, horse riding, ice-climbing, indoor climbing wall, indoor tennis, skating, night-skiing, snowmobiling, snowshoeing, swimming, tubing

FOOD AND DRINK
Coffee $1.50, glass of wine $4, small beer $3–3.50, soft drink $1.25–2, dish of the day $10.50

Mountain restaurants
Self-service cafeterias are located in both Main and Canyon Lodge and at the mid-station of the gondola. A quick bite can be taken on the run at the BBQ snack bars at the bases of Chairs 14 and Eagle Express. The Mill Café at the bottom of Stump Alley is a cosier and more relaxing alternative, with an open fire, a sunny deck and Californian cuisine. The Mountainside Grill in the Mammoth Mountain Inn and The Yodler Bar & Pub – a Swiss chalet shipped piecemeal from the Alps – are the other culinary options.

Accommodation

Enthusiasts wanting a head start in the mornings should stay at Mammoth Mountain Inn (☎ 760 934 0601) at the Main Lodge base or the Austria Hof Lodge (☎ 760 934 8558) ('good value with good rooms') at Canyon Lodge. Juniper Springs & Sunstone Lodges (☎ 769 924 1102) provide ultimate slope-side self-catering accommodation. The Alpenhof Lodge (☎ 760 934 8558), located in The Village, is within easy access of the skiing and the town, and one reporter described it as 'well above average with friendly staff'. In Mammoth Lakes, the Shilo Inn (☎ 760 934 4500) is warmly recommended. Double Eagle Resort & Spa (☎ 760 648 7004) in June Lake offers a swimming-pool, steam room, whirlpool, fitness classes and a gym. While the Mammoth ski pass covers June Mountain, there is no free bus service between the two resorts.

Eating in and out

Mammoth Lakes has a variety of international cuisine to suit the demanding palates of visiting Los Angelinos. Skadi and Nevados are 'both excellent for a special night out', while Ocean Harvest specialises in seafood. Shogun is the best Japanese restaurant, and Karlotta's and Matsu's both offer an eclectic Far Eastern menu, including Thai and Chinese specialities. The Charthouse and the Mogul are recommended for steaks. Alpenrose provides the inescapable (even here) cheese fondue. Giovanni's is praised for its pizzas, and Roberto's is authentically Mexican. One reporter recommended The Restaurant at Convict Lake, a 20-minute drive away, as 'an absolute must'. Vons supermarket is said to offer the best value in town. Village Market, situated at North Village, is pricier.

Après-ski

Skiers and riders gather at The Yodler when the lifts close. Canyon Lodge regularly has a live band. Later in the evening, The Clocktower pub at the Alpenhof is a popular resort rendezvous along with nearby Whiskey Creek. In town, Grumpy's Sports Bar attracts a young crowd. Shogun has a separate bar serving sushi and Japanese snacks. Ocean Harvest and neighbouring High Sierra Rock and Grill also have night-clubs with dancing and live entertainment. The outdoor skating rink in town is a welcome addition to après-ski activities.

Childcare

Canyon Kids and the Woollywood Sports School offer morning and afternoon lessons for children aged 4 to 14 years as well as daycare for small non-skiers. The Discovery Chair ensures beginners and little children maximum snow time.

Park City Resorts

ALTITUDE Park City Mountain Resort 6,900ft (2,104m), Deer Valley Resort 7,200ft (2,195m), The Canyons 6,800ft (2,071m)

Beginners ✱✱ Intermediates ✱✱✱ Advanced ✱✱✱ Snowboarders ✱✱ (except Deer Valley)

A group of distinctively different resorts make up the Park City ski area, a clutch of three destinations situated side by side, a 40-minute drive from Salt Lake City in Utah, the state that boasts the finest, driest powder snow in the world. In February 2002 the region will be the focus of world attention when Salt Lake plays host to the Winter Olympics. Other equally important destinations (see **The Cottonwood Resorts**) are also within an hour's drive. Although Salt Lake City offers the greatest variety of accommodation, restaurants and entertainment, it is a large, bustling town that lacks the atmosphere of a ski resort. Wherever you choose to stay, a car is essential to explore fully the first-rate skiing.

The focus for the Olympic Alpine events is on **Park City** and **Deer Valley**, 36 miles from Salt Lake City.

✔ Tree-level skiing
✔ Excellent snow record (Park City and Deer Valley)
✔ Short airport transfer
✔ Wide choice of restaurants (Park City)
✔ Activities for non-skiers
✔ Excellent children's ski school (Deer Valley)
✘ Spread-out town and resort (Park City)
✘ No children's daycare (Park City)

The Canyons is North America's newest international ski resort, but it will not host any events. The three resorts are so close together that it is possible to go – illegally – under the ropes from one to another. Talks aimed at linking the three to create the largest and best-equipped single resort in North America continue and there now exists a Silver Passport ticket that is valid at all three for guests staying at least three nights in any one of the resorts. At present the ski areas are under rival ownership, but all three have indicated that lift-linking is a viable possibility. However, Deer Valley is not keen to link because of its exclusive label and ban on snowboarders.

Since mining began here in the mid-nineteenth century, silver to the value of $400 million has been extracted from the hills surrounding Park City, which has artfully converted its mining past into a colourful touristic present. The heart of the town is Main Street, home to the Wasatch Brewery, the Egyptian Theatre and a host of art galleries and boutiques. Among them are numerous bars, coffee shops and restaurants. The ski base area is a moderately well-designed complex on three levels, with shops and cafés set around an open-air ice-skating rink. Both the men's and women's Olympic giant slalom events will take place at Park City.

Today, Park City has a reputation for being rather more than a ski town. Its cultural aspirations have been enhanced by the emergence of the Sundance Film Festival. This event, which takes place over the last ten days in January each year, under the patronage of Robert Redford's Sundance Institute, is now recognised as the premier showcase for independent American films.

Unashamedly luxurious, Deer Valley lies one mile north-east of Park City, up a winding mountain road lined with multi-million-dollar homes. This is a resort where grooming counts, both on the meticulously pisted slopes ('like going skiing at Harrods') and with the clientèle, who are a walking advertisement for Bogner and Prada designer ski clothing. The resort is the venue for the slalom and freestyle events at the 2002 Winter Olympics.

Over the past four years The Canyons, the nearest of the three to Salt Lake City, has been growing from a small, local ski area into what has been planned as the largest ski resort in the United States. It already boasts 15 lifts and a brand new resort village, with the facilities to attract international skiers and snowboarders.

WHAT'S NEW

Legacy Lodge base at Park City
Completion of day lodge at Deer Valley's Empire Canyon

Other notable nearby resorts are Robert Redford's **Sundance**, and **Snowbasin** where the former Swiss champion Bernhard Russi has spent much of his time forging the course for the Olympic Men's Downhill, promised to be the most demanding and dramatic of all time.

Beaver Mountain, **Elk Meadows**, **Nordic Valley Ski Mountain** and **Powder Mountain** are smaller centres. The principal cross-country locations are **Brian Head Resort**, **Homestead**, **Ruby's Inn** and **Sherwood Hills. Soldier Hollow** and **White Pine Touring** are where the cross-country events will be held for the Winter Olympic Games.

The Utah Olympic Park, adjoining The Canyons, is the venue for the bobsleigh, luge, and ski-jumping events.

On the snow

When Park City opened as a ski resort in 1963 it was called Treasure Mountain. Its former life was as a prosperous silver-mining town and the first skiers were taken up through the mountain on a mine train before being raised to the surface on a mine hoist lift. Today there are still over a thousand miles of silver-mine workings and tunnels under the slopes of Park City Mountain Resort. The main skiing at Park City consists of 3,300 acres served by 14 lifts. The terrain ranges from rolling runs to open bowls.

Access to the top of the main ski area is by two detachable six-person chair-lifts, which take 12 minutes from Park City to the Summit House Restaurant. The highest point is Jupiter Bowl. Snow-users of all

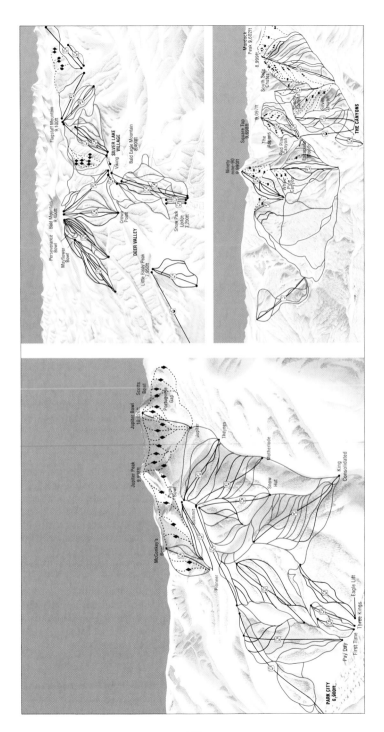

443

standards will find suitable runs from the summit to the bottom of the Silverlode six-person chair. Park City also has floodlit skiing. Reporters praised the trails as 'beautifully groomed and policed'.

Neighbouring Deer Valley is so exclusive that staff, who unload your skis from your car and carry them to the snow for you, won't even accept tips. The 1,750 acres of skiing takes place on four mountains, served by 19 attractive, dark-green-painted lifts, and is constantly being expanded.

Not much of the 3,625 acres of The Canyons ski area can be seen from the base, but a short walk takes guests to the Flight of the Canyons gondola and so to the Red Pine Lodge mid-station, and from here its full magnificence is revealed. A total of 15 lifts give access to skiing on seven peaks.

Beginners

Park City has two beginner areas, one at the base with two lifts and another centred around the Silverlode chair. Novices can profit from a 3.5-mile green (easy) descent from the Summit Smoke House & Grill to the Park City centre, via the top of Claimjumper, Bonanza and Sidewinder. This is broad, flat territory, which is perfect for discovering the pleasures of the beautifully groomed snow. The less experienced should avoid it late in the afternoon, when it becomes a race-track back to base.

Deer Valley has green trails all the way down from three out of its four peaks. Bald Eagle and Flagstaff Mountains offer the best beginner terrain. Only 14 per cent of the terrain at the Canyons is suitable for beginners; most of it is on the Meadows trails above Red Pine.

Intermediates

At Park City, 44 per cent of the trails are listed as intermediate and cover every area of the mountain except Jupiter Bowl. Confident skiers and boarders will not find themselves unduly tested by Hidden Splendour, Mel's Alley, Powder Keg and Assessment. However, Prospector, Single Jack, Sunnyside and Parley's Park take more direct routes down the mountain. Favourite trails include 10th Mountain. The King Con chair-lift is the access point for ten blue runs.

Deer Valley is well suited to moderate skiers with some 50 per cent of the ski area classified as intermediate. Flight of The Canyons gondola at The Canyons gives rapid access to the Saddleback and Tombstone express quads. Both offer long cruisers and short chutes in glades cut through forested hillsides. A choice of Apex Ridge or Upper Boa, two long blue (intermediate) trails from the top of the Super Condo Express, link into a green that takes you back to the resort.

Advanced

The highest point of Park City is Jupiter Bowl, which is reached by the Jupiter and McConkey chairs and is recommended for advanced snow-users only. 'We never saw a queue at the Jupiter chair even in high season when it was busy elsewhere'. Experienced snow-users have a choice of moderate black-diamond runs, including The Hoist, Thaynes, Double Jack, Ford Country and Glory Hole, which all lead into Thaynes Canyon, a blue cruiser that marks the eastern boundary of the ski area. Halfway down, the Motherlode chair-lift takes you back to the Summit Smoke House & Grill. The black-diamond options to the west of Park City are six parallel descents through aspen trees, although these are prone to closure in poor snow conditions.

At Deer Valley the Mayflower and Sultan lifts give access to some steeper terrain including Mayflower Bowl. Daly Chutes and Daly Bowl as well as Anchor Trees at Empire Canyon can be seriously testing in some snow conditions. At the Canyons, the Ninety Nine 90 Express serves an impressive double-black-diamond zone, with open bowls and spectacular views.

Off-piste
Those in search of adventure at Park City should take the Jupiter Access trail from the top of the Pioneer chair-lift to the Jupiter chair-lift. This goes up to the top of the resort, a ridge with a variety of ungroomed options. Shadow Ridge and Fortune Teller go straight down under the chair through sparsely wooded snowfields, but a 10-minute walk along the ridge to the east brings skiers to the top of Scott's Bowl. Further along, Portuguese Gap is a narrow, often heavily mogulled, field between the trees. A 20-minute walk along the ridge to the west leads to Jupiter Peak. Here there is a choice between the steep descent into Puma Bowl via the East Face, or back to the chair-lift via the West Face. All these runs are well worth the walk.

Nearly all of the skiing at The Canyons is below the tree-line, and consequently the resort has some fabulous tree skiing. The Dreamscape chair, which opened in the 2000–1 season, offers some gentle off-piste. The back-country skiing can be accessed from the top of the Crowning Glory and the Ninety Nine 90 Express chairs.

A guided programme called Ski Utah Interconnect is a full-day off-piste adventure that takes you from Park City to **Brighton**, **Solitude** and **Alta**. Park City Powder Cats arranges guided snowcat-skiing or -boarding.

Snowboarding
At Park City the Jupiter Access trail from the top of the Pioneer chair-lift offers some excellent ungroomed riding. Some of the best freeriding, such as Scott's Bowl and Puma Bowl, is accessible only by first walking uphill for about 10 minutes. The resort does not have a terrain park, so freestylers will have to find their own natural hits. Off Payday trail is a half-pipe, which is illuminated at night.

Riders and skiers at The Canyons are served by a terrain park on Saddleback and half-a-dozen natural half-pipes. Deer Valley remains one of the four remaining US resorts that bans snowboarding. The others are **Alta**, **Mad River Glen** in Vermont and **Taos** in New Mexico.

Tuition and guiding

We have enthusiastic reports of the Park City Ski & Snowboard School: 'the ski school is the best we have found anywhere'. Its Mountain Experience programme takes good intermediate to advanced snow-users into the high bowls on Jupiter Peak. The Deer Valley Ski School offers group and private lessons. For adult beginners at The Canyons, the Perfect Turn programme has three-day Learn-to-Ski (using gradu-ated ski lengths to build up confidence) and Learn-to-Ride packages.

Mountain restaurants

The Mid-Mountain Lodge at Park City, a modified version of an old miners' dwelling, offers high-quality fast food ('simply heaven on a sunny day'). Its rivals are the Summit Smoke House & Grill and the Snow Hut at the bottom of the Silverlode lift. The Legacy Lodge fea-tures a day-service restaurant and an international food bar. 'Skiosks' are yurt-style shelters on the mountain where guests can stop for a quick snack or drink.

The Silver Lake Lodge, on the slopes at Deer Valley, is home to three restaurants as well as an outdoor barbecue. The slope outside is aptly nicknamed The Beach. On a fine day the rows of smart deckchairs con-tain more designer-suited sunbathers than you will see in any other ski resort in North America.

The Canyons has three on-mountain restaurants: Red Pine, Lookout Cabin and Sun Lodge. As befits the central link in the lift system, Red Pine is large and busy, with the usual range of Rocky Mountain lunch options: pizza, grill, deli and salad bar. Lookout Cabin is much quieter, with an unexpectedly sophisticated menu and table service. Sun Lodge lives up to its name with a sheltered deck and an open-air grill.

Accommodation

Much of the accommodation in Park City is in condominiums. One of the most convenient places to stay is the Silver King Hotel (☎ 649 5500), a complex offering units ranging from studios to penthouses. Most of the hotels are a few miles from Park City on the free bus route, and include The Radisson Inn (☎ 649 5000) and Yarrow Hotel (☎ 649 7000). The Marriott Summit Watch (☎ 647 4100) on Main Street is central for shopping and eating. At the unusual Angel House Inn (☎ 647 0338) each of the nine rooms is modelled on a different angel. The Best Western Landmark Inn (☎ 649 7300) at Kimball Junction is 6 miles out of town, but good value and with its own sports complex.

Deer Valley does not have a village base as such. Slope-slide accom-modation is in large, luxurious condominiums and smart hotels, includ-ing the Lodges at Deer Valley (☎ 615 2600), the Goldener Hirsch Inn (☎ 649 7770) and the Stein Eriksen Lodge (☎ 649 3700). The mid-mountain Chateaux at Silver Lake (☎ 649 4040) is new.

Plans for The Resort Village at the Canyons include hotels, restau-rants and malls attractively linked to a central forum by walkways and waterways. However, the buildings are of a utilitarian style and the village so far lacks atmosphere. The Grand Summit Resort Hotel (☎ 800 472 6309 for all accommodation) is an impressive slope-side condominium hotel and conference centre, with 365 rooms, a health club and outdoor swimming-pool. The 190-room Sundial Lodge provides accommodation on a rather less grandiose scale, with the addition of a roof-top hot tub and plunge pool.

Eating in and out

Park City is a strong contender for the 'best dining' accolade in a US ski resort, with some 100 restaurants offering a choice of South-western, Thai, Japanese, Chinese and Italian cuisine ('a good variety, but expensive'). A traditional start to an evening on Main Street would be dinner at The Claimjumper Steakhouse, an all-American establishment serving 'surf-and-turf'. Chimayo serves for Mexican and Southwestern cuisine. Mikado boasts a wide selection of sushi. 'Excellent crab and enormous Pacific mussels' can be found at 350 Main. Grappa is classic Tuscan. The Riverhorse Café is American and trendy, while Texas Red's Pit Barbecue is 'cheap and cheerful with great chilli'. Zoom, owned by Robert Redford, is the clear winner with its Californian cuisine with oriental overtones ('The Thai Barbecue Shrimp with a Sesame-Ginger Salad, Rice Noodles and Mango Confetti is to die for'). For those counting their cents, Ruby Tuesday, at Kimball Junction, is a good-value diner that is suitable for families.

The Seafood Buffet at The Snow Park Lodge at Deer Valley is warmly recommended: 'wonderful sushi and crab legs'. The Mariposa at Silver Lake Lodge offers 'American Continental' fine dining.

The Cabin, in the Grand Summit Hotel at The Canyons, with its kitchens under the control of master chef Houman Gohary, is one of the smartest eateries in the region. Alternatives include the Gondola Bar and Lounge and the deli-style Café. Smokey's Smoke House is family-friendly, with a Cajun menu and a barbecue.

Après-ski

During the build-up to the Olympics, Utah's traditionally stiff stance on alcohol consumption has been visibly relaxed. Any establishment serving food is allowed to sell beer and usually wine. Late-night bars must conform to the strictures of a private club licence, but temporary membership is easily obtained. This is done either by paying a nominal fee or being sponsored – in exchange for a drink – by a fellow drinker at the bar. The Alamo Bar displays the local Park City Rugby Club memorabilia on its walls, alongside stuffed moose and elk heads. Legends in Legacy Lodge at the Park City ski base is a licensed club with live music every afternoon and early evening.

The Factory Stores at Kimball Junction, a 4-mile drive from Park City, is a large shopping centre selling end-of-the-line designer clothing such as Polo Ralph Lauren, Banana Republic and GAP at cut prices, and is well worth the visit. In town, Dolly's Bookstore is a charming little bookshop that also sells home-made cookies and ice-cream.

The Après Ski Lounge at the Snow Park Lodge in Deer Valley is popular after skiing, but the best of the nightlife is in Park City.

Doc's at the Gondola is the watering hole of choice for resort staff at The Canyons, but there is a shortage of options by night. Those who are looking for nightlife may prefer to stay in Park City, served by a free shuttle bus between the downtown hotels and The Canyons every 20 minutes. Canyon Mountain Sports, close to the Sundial Lodge, has a good selection of ski clothing and equipment.

The Utah Winter Sports Park, located beside The Canyons resort, is one of the few places in the world offering recreational ski-jumping on three days each week during the mid-winter months as well as bob-sleigh and luge. You can also ice-rocket (on a one-person sled) and ski-jump at night.

Childcare

Although babysitting is available in town through a choice of three companies, Park City Mountain Resort does not have a ski kinder-garten. Families with small children who want to ski would be better off in Deer Valley. The Park City Ski & Snowboard School provides tuition for children aged 3 to 12 years, including lunch and indoor supervision. The Burton Chopper Center (for 7–12-year-olds) allows kids to practise their moves on a training trampoline.

Children aged two months to 12 years are looked after by Deer Valley Children's Center, situated in the base lodge at Snow Lodge. The ski facilities for children receives praise: 'The Children's Centre was a friendly place. My daughter was given one-to-one tuition at no extra cost while the instructor decided which ski school class she should join. The children were taken in for a hot chocolate when they were cold, and spent time drawing or listening to stories when they weren't skiing'. The Deer Valley Children's Ski School takes children from three-and-a-half to 12 years of age, with Teen Equipe lessons for 13- to 17-year-olds.

Perfect Kids, conveniently based at the Grand Summit in the Canyons, offers daycare from 18 months to nine years of age, from 8.30am to 4.30pm, with group ski clinics for four- to 12-year-olds and group snowboard clinics for children aged seven to 12. Skiers in Diapers programme offers private instruction for children aged 18 months to three years.

Linked or nearby resorts

Snowbasin
top 9,288ft (2,831m) bottom 6,291ft (1,914m)

Snowbasin is the venue for the Blue Riband events of the 2002 Winter Olympics, the men's and women's downhills and super-Gs, on a course crafted by the veteran Swiss racer Bernhard Russi. Skiing came to the mountain in 1940. A local entrepreneur bought the little resort in 1984, and in preparation for the Olympics has doubled the ski area from

Skiing facts: Park City Resorts

TOURIST INFORMATION
Park City
1310 Lowell Avenue, PO Box 39, Park City,
UT 84060
Tel 1 435 649 8111 **Fax** 1 435 647 5374
Email pcinfo@pcski.com
Web site www.parkcitymountain.com
Deer Valley Resort
2250 Deer Valley Drive South, PO Box 1525,
Park City, UT 84060
Tel 1 435 649 1000 **Fax** 1 435 645 6939
Email patti@deervalley.com
Web site www.deervalley.com
The Canyons
4000 The Canyons Resort Drive, Park City, UT
84098
Tel 1 435 649 5400 **Fax** 1 435 649 7374
Email info@thecanyons.com
Web site www.thecanyons.com

THE RESORTS
Airport transfer Salt Lake City 45mins
Visitor beds 17,929 Park City, 6,668 Deer
Valley, 718 The Canyons
Transport free ski bus

THE SKIING
Linked or nearby resorts Deer Valley (n),
The Canyons (n)
Number of lifts 48 lifts in area (14 in Park
City, 19 in Deer Valley, 15 in The Canyons)
Total of trails/pistes 3,300 acres Park City
(18% easy, 44% intermediate, 38% difficult),
1,750 acres Deer Valley (15% easy, 50%
intermediate, 25 difficult, 10% very difficult),
3,625 acres The Canyons (14% beginner,
44% intermediate, 42% difficult)
Beginners 2 beginner lifts at Park City, 2
beginner lifts and magic carpet at Deer Valley,
1 beginner lift at The Canyons. Reductions
available

LIFT PASSES
Area pass Park City $210–294, Deer Valley
$324, The Canyons $288. All for 6 days. Silver
Passport (covers all three) $TBA
Pensioners Park City 65–9yrs $105–147,
free for 70yrs and over. Deer Valley 65yrs and
over $222. The Canyons 65yrs and over $144.
All for 6 days
Credit cards yes

TUITION
Skiing Park City Ski & Snowboard School
(☎ 435 649 5496), Deer Valley Ski School
(☎ 435 649 1000), Perfect Turn at
The Canyons (☎ 435 615 3449)
Snowboarding Park City and The Canyons as
ski schools
Other courses cross-country, extreme ski-
ing/boarding, heli-skiing/boarding, men's ski
clinics (Deer Valley), moguls, powder clinics,
race-training, skiing for the disabled, ski
jumping, teen skiing (Deer Valley), telemark,
women's ski clinics
Guiding Ski Utah Interconnect Tour (☎ 801
534 1907) Wasatch Powderbird Guides heli-
skiing (☎ 801 742 2800)

CHILDREN
Lift pass Park City 7–12yrs $108–132 for 6
days, free for 6yrs and under. Deer Valley
3–12yrs $324, 3yrs and under $108. The
Canyons 7–12yrs $144, free for 6yrs and
under. All for 6 days
Ski & board school Deer Valley, Park City and
The Canyons as adults
Kindergarten (Park-City: (non-ski)) Annie's
Nannies (☎ 435 615 1935) Creative
Beginnings (☎ 435 645 7315) Guardian
Angel (☎ 435 783 2662). (**Deer Valley:**
(ski/non-ski)) Children's Ski School (☎ 435
649 1000). (**The Canyons:** (ski)) as ski
school, (non-ski) Daycare (☎ 435 615 8036)

OTHER SPORTS
Bobsleigh, ice-climbing, ice-rocketing, indoor
climbing-wall, indoor tennis, microlighting,
night-skiing, raquetball, skating, ski-jumping,
sleigh rides, snowmobiling, snowshoeing,
swimming, tubing

FOOD AND DRINK
Coffee $1.50–3, glass of wine $4–5,
small beer $3–3.50, soft drink $1.50–2.50,
dish of the day $7–12

1,800 to 3,200 acres, spending $80 million on facilities that include two eight-person gondolas, a high-speed quad, an Olympic tram and a computerised snowmaking system with 40 miles of underground pipes.

The Olympic courses are accessed by the John Paul Express quadchair, named not after the Pope but after a 20-year-old Ogden boy who died with the 10th Mountain Division in Italy in World War II. John Paul is steep, with an average gradient of 34 per cent compared to the 29–30 per cent that is normal for a men's downhill course – so competitors and regular skiers can be sure of a gruelling workout.

Beginner slopes are very limited but the rest of the resort, accessed by the Strawberry Express and the Middle Bowl Express gondolas, is largely intermediate, apart from a small zone of bowls and chutes on De Moisy for experts. The terrain is interestingly varied, with clumps of trees rather than dense forest. The Snowbasin Ski School has daily group lessons for those aged four and over.

TOURIST INFORMATION
Tel 1 801 399 1135
Fax 1 801 399 1138
Email info@snowbasin.com
Web site www.snowbasin.com

Sundance
top 8,250ft (2,515m) bottom 6,100ft (1,859m)

When Sundance was created by the film star Robert Redford in 1969, he visualised a community where the arts, environment and recreation would thrive harmoniously together. The traditional little resort has old boardwalks and an atmosphere of a bygone age. It is 55 minutes' drive from Salt Lake City, or a 40-minute scenic drive through the Heber Valley from Park City. Lift queues are a rarity here, and a variety of terrain – ranging from wide open trails to bowl skiing – is available. Four chair-lifts serve a choice of 41 trails.

The two restaurants, the Tree Room and the Foundry Grill, serve regional dishes and are open for lunch and dinner. The Tree Room has a tree growing through its centre and is decorated with Native American art along with Robert Redford's personal collection of Western memorabilia. The Owl Bar was once frequented by Butch Cassidy's Hole-In-The-Wall Gang in its original location in Wyoming, before being transported to Sundance. Resort accommodation is in the Sundance Cottages (☎ 801 225 4107).

TOURIST INFORMATION
Tel 1 801 225 4107
Fax 1 801 223 4551
Web site www.sundanceresort.com

Smugglers' Notch–Stowe

ALTITUDE Smugglers' Notch 1,030ft (314m), Stowe 1,300ft (396m)

Beginners ✱✱✱ Intermediates ✱✱ Advanced ✱✱ Snowboarders ✱✱

The Smugglers' Notch pass in Vermont was given its name shortly before the American War of Independence, when it was used for the illicit passage of supplies from Canada. Sensibly, given the nature of its mainly gentle, pine-clad slopes, the resort of Smugglers' Notch has not tried to compete with its bigger sisters in Colorado and Utah but has carved a niche that no other resort in the world has so far been able to match. 'Smuggs', as the locals call it, has established itself at the cutting edge of the family market and regularly wins awards for its child-friendly facilities. This is not a resort that attracts couples or singles; in fact you would not choose to come to Smuggs if you did not have small children. The key is convenience, with the lifts and accommodation within a 350-yd radius, and apartments designed with families in mind. Smuggs is a small, unadorned village consisting mainly of condominiums. A single sports shop in the village provides the necessary balaclavas and neoprene face masks, and one small supermarket sells provisions for self-caterers.

> ✔ Superb children's facilities (Smuggs)
> ✔ Lack of queues
> ✔ Outstanding ski school (Smuggs)
> ✔ Attractive village of Stowe
> ✗ Low mid-winter temperatures

In complete contrast, the eighteenth-century town of **Stowe** over the mountain, which can be reached on skis via a tenuous connection, has been a sophisticated tourist centre for more than a century and attracts wealthy Bostonians. It is a typical Vermont town of red-and-white, weather-boarded houses set around a steepled, white church on attractive Main Street, where most of the shops and some of the accommodation are located. Convenience is not a feature here because, as is often the case in US resorts, the village is separated from the skiing base by five miles of winding highway lined with the customary motels, rental shops and restaurants.

On the snow
top 4,393ft (1,339m) bottom 1,030ft (314m)

The skiing at Smugglers' Notch is mainly benign, with 70 trails serviced by nine lifts, although a handful of unpublicised tricky mogul slopes keep competent parents happy. Snow records are good, but patches of unpleasant ice on groomed runs, known locally as 'frozen granular patches', are an all-too-common occurrence. The three mountains – Morse, Madonna and Sterling – are interconnected, and Sterling in turn links with Stowe's Spruce Peak via Snuffy's Trail. This requires a lot of poling in both directions. The old, fixed, double chair-lifts at Smugglers' Notch are in need of upgrading, but their low capacity means that the slopes remain uncrowded even in high season.

The skiing at Stowe lies on two mountains outside the village centre, with 59 per cent of the trails rated intermediate and a possible 73 per cent of the terrain covered by artificial snow. The top of the skiing is Mount Mansfield, Vermont's highest peak, which is reached in comfort by an eight-seater gondola. Although the ForeRunner quad to the Octagon Web Café is considerably more exposed, it opens up a much bigger part of the mountain, with a choice of runs for all standards. Reporters noted that the mountain transport was slow, especially the Easy Mile lift: 'lifts seemed to be a bit antiquated compared with some European resorts. However, the operating staff were always on hand and always cheerful'.

> **WHAT'S NEW**
>
> Additional snowmaking at Smugglers' Notch
> Two more gladed trails on Sterling and Madonna Mountains
> Two additional condominium buildings at Smugglers' Notch

Beginners

Morse is the beginners' mountain, conveniently situated in the village centre of Smugglers' Notch. A new novice area, Morse Highlands, is set halfway up the mountain and is serviced by five trails. From the top of Morse Mountain at 2,250ft you can ski along a green (easy) trail to the base of Madonna Mountain and back again. From the top of the Mountain Triple and Toll House Double lifts at Stowe are a network of blue (intermediate) trails to the Toll House base. Reporters praised Sterling (from Big Spruce), Toll Road and Crossover (from Mansfield): 'a lovely, gentle, three-mile run returning to Spruce base'.

Intermediates

More adept snow-users quickly move on from Morse Mountain in Smuggs to the other two mountains, which are reached by bus or on skis. Madonna Mountain offers some pleasant trails such as the blue (intermediate) Upper and Lower Drifter, and Upper and Lower Chilcoot. From the top of the ForeRunner lift at Stowe there are some good blue cruisers, one of which – Rimrock – connects across to the second half of the mountain. Here the choice of trails back to base lies between three blues.

Advanced

Smugglers' Notch features several sharp double-black-diamond (very difficult) trails, as well as The Black Hole, which is billed as 'the only triple-black-diamond in the east'. The trail directly below the Madonna No. 1 chair-lift is intimidating: 'looking down from the chair at rocks covered in ice, I could hardly believe they were actually skiable'.

The skiing can also be near perpendicular in places at Stowe. It is said that if you can ski Stowe's celebrated Front Four, you can ski anywhere. Starr, Liftline, National and Goat are also ready to test the most proficient of snow-users. Chin Clip is the sole black-diamond (difficult) trail back to base on Mount Mansfield.

Off-piste
There is some unpatrolled skiing through the trees, but those in search of serious powder adventures would be better going elsewhere.

Snowboarding
Madonna at Smuggs boasts a large terrain park for intermediate and advanced skiers and boarders, with a 350-ft half-pipe and music that belts out above your head from speakers that are attached to the lift pylons. A second terrain park is on Morse, which contains 'hips, rolls and spines', and a new park on Sterling is for beginner riders. There are two terrain parks at Stowe.

Tuition and guiding
Smugglers' Snow Sports University is the impressive ski and snowboard school at Smuggs. Special courses include 'Dad & Me' and 'Mom & Me', where you and your child are taught together, with the emphasis on picking up useful tips to teach your child yourself. A vast range of other options are available, including Terrain Park Tactics for skiers, riders and snowbladers.

Stowe's Ski and Snowboard School puts on adult workshops, race clinics, women's clinics, courses for seniors, snowblading, telemark and even Quick Fix, where you 'take a run with a personal ski trainer'. During January one reporter found he was the only pupil in his class.

Mountain restaurants
At Smuggs the only on-mountain eating place is the small, bleak hut called Hearth & Candle At The Top Of The Notch. Although it still provides only self-service drinks and snacks during limited hours, on one evening a week it now also offers gourmet dining (see *Eating in and out*). During the day, most snow-users return to the two bases, where at Morse there is a choice of The Village Lodge, which houses the Green Mountain Café & Bakery, and Rigabello's Pizzeria. At Madonna base you can lunch at the Green Peppers Pub, the Black Bear Lounge, which serves foot-long sandwiches, or the cafeteria.

The Cliff House Restaurant on Mount Mansfield at Stowe features moderately priced food that is well presented. Other eating places include the Fireside Tavern (located at the Inn at the Mountain) for pasta and seafood, the Midway Café for pizzas and soup, and José's Cantina at Midway for Mexican cuisine. The most unusual place to eat is the Octagon Web Café ('food of decent quality') at the top of Stowe's ForeRunner quad, where computer terminals are set up for guests' use and free email postcards can be sent.

Accommodation

The Village at Smugglers' Notch offers a variety of self-catering apartments. The resort's condominiums are highly recommended for families: 'the best two-bedroomed apartment we have ever seen, with a separate 30-ft sitting room and a television in every room, including one angled above the family-sized whirlpool'. Two more condominium buildings, the Falcons and Sycamores Three, are in the process of being built. Reservations for all apartments can be made through the tourist information centre.

Staying in Stowe is civilised rather than riotous, especially at the Trapp Family Lodge (☎ 802 253 8511) four miles out of town. The tone is opulent Austrian-staid, and afternoon tea is a major attraction. Ye Olde England Inne (☎ 802 253 7558) plays heavily on its name, with Laura Ashley fabrics in the bedrooms and a red telephone box outside the door; its architecture is Fawlty Towers–Tudor. The Green Mountain Inn (☎ 802 253 7301) is a no-smoking establishment boasting a health club and heated outdoor swimming-pool, while the Inn at the Mountain (☎ 802 253 3000) is the only slope-side accommodation. Altogether Stowe musters 32 three- and four-diamond lodges and restaurants, which is more than Boston.

Eating in and out

All the restaurants in and around Smugglers' Notch are child-friendly. At the Mountain Grille, children under 12 years old are charged half their age in dollars for all they can eat for breakfast. The Hearth & Candle restaurant is the only eatery that has a separate upstairs section – for adults without children. Hearth & Candle At The Top Of The Notch features gourmet dining on one evening a week; it is reached by snowcat, and is lit entirely by candles. Café Bandito's is recommended for families, and Three Mountain Lodge recreates an authentic Vermont atmosphere.

During the evening at Stowe, Winfield's in the Stoweflake Resort is praised for its fish, as is The Golden Eagle, which specialises in fresh Cape Cod seafood. The Fireside Tavern serves lunch and dinner. Copperfields at Ye Olde England Inne concentrates on game and seafood, while La Toscana and Trattoria La Festa both offer Italian cuisine. The pizzas from The Pie in the Sky in Stowe are recommended, too, and the Whip in the Green Mountain Inn was said to have 'excellent sandwiches' at lunchtime. McCarthy's was commended as 'the best place for breakfast – at about $4 each'.

Après-ski

Nightlife in Smuggs is geared to family entertainment and fun for children of all ages. The atmosphere is more Butlins-on-snow than **Beaver Creek**. After skiing, hot chocolate awaits you as you gather around a camp fire at the foot of Morse Mountain.

Floodlit snowboarding and tubing down Sir Henry's Sliding Hill provide the later evening entertainment. Snowshoeing on Sterling Pond is another popular après-ski adventure. SmuggsCentral comprises a family-friendly swimming-pool, hot tub and FunZone. Art and craft sessions are also available in the resort, as well as an Outer Limits Teen Center, t'ai chi classes and magic shows. The Family Snowmaking Center is an educational experience you can ski to on your way home on the Meadowlark green trail. A self-drive snowmobile tour of the mountain by night and a skating-rink are the other evening activities.

At Stowe, Mr Pickwick's Polo Pub serves international ales, including Youngs and Morland Old Speckled Hen. Next door, the Fox and Hounds provides further evidence that Stowe is an aspiring home from home for visiting Brits. Bars to look out for include the Shed ('good atmosphere and good food'), which has its own micro-brewery, and the Broken Ski. At The Matterhorn you can play pool, eat sushi and enjoy the live music, while the Rusty Nail also provides music and dancing. Other activities at Stowe include night-skiing, sleigh rides, snowmobiling, snowshoeing, squash and swimming. The shops are mainly touristy with 'lots of maple syrup and quilts'. However, the resort verdict from a dedicated snowboarder from Pennsylvania was succinct: 'it's even quieter than back home'.

Childcare

Children are what Smuggs is all about, and everything centres around them. The only disadvantage is the numbingly low temperatures. Little ones from just six weeks of age spend their days at Alice's Wonderland Child Care Center, which includes a children's zoo and an outdoor pirate ship playground in the warmer weather. The ski school ('outstanding and put anything in Europe that we had experienced to shame') takes children to and from the slopes in a tractor-drawn trailer, and in the cold weather classes frequently return to base for hot chocolate, videos and snacks. The timed carving course provides endless on-slope entertainment for more proficient children.

The amenities at Stowe's base include Cub's Daycare for children from six weeks to six years, and the Children's Adventure Center.

TOURIST INFORMATION
Smugglers' Notch
Tel (0800) 169 8219 (*freephone from UK*)
Fax 1 802 644 2713
Email smuggs@smuggs.com
Web site www.smuggs.com

Stowe
Tel 1 802 253 3000
Fax 1 802 253 3439
Email info@stowe.com
Web site www.stowe.com

Tremblant

ALTITUDE 870ft (265m)

Beginners ✷ Intermediates ✷✷ Advanced ✷✷ Snowboarders ✷✷✷

Located in the Laurentian Mountains, 75 miles north-west of Montreal. Tremblant offers skiing in a cold climate, combined with a chance to appreciate Québéçois culture and cuisine. A massive investment of CDN$1 billion over a ten-year period by the owner, Intrawest, has transformed – and is continuing to transform – the traditional ski village into a state-of-the-art resort. Intensive piste-grooming and Canada's largest snowmaking system do much to combat the prevailing icy conditions. The old part of Tremblant has been meticulously restored, and the new section artfully designed to create steeply terraced main streets with painted wooden buildings that are modelled on the old quarter of Montreal. The numerous boutiques in the Place St-Bernard are enticing; the resort boasts a total of 80 shops and restaurants.

- ✔ State-of-the-art lift system
- ✔ Recommended for families
- ✔ Extensive snowmaking
- ✔ Atmospheric village
- ✔ Wide choice of restaurants
- ✔ Car-free centre
- ✔ Short airport transfer
- ✗ Extremely low temperatures
- ✗ Peak-season overcrowding

On the snow
top 3,001ft (914m) bottom 870ft (265m)

Tremblant opened its first chair-lift in February 1939. Today, it features 602 acres of varied pistes and 12 lifts – and it is still growing. The eight-person heated gondola is a welcome addition to the chair-lifts ('pretty uncomfortable in bad weather'). The lifts on both sides of Tremblant – Versant Sud and Versant Nord – meet at Le Grand Manitou Lodge at the top. The Versant Soleil area, on the south side of the mountain, is reached by Le Soleil high-speed quad-chair.

This resort claims to possess Canada's most powerful snowmaking system, with 620 snow-cannon that guarantee season-long snow cover. However, reporters agreed that the snowmaking is 'excessive'. 'On most days up to two-thirds of the runs were impassable and the noise of those infernal machines was deafening. Both views and sunshine were blocked out by the cloud of vapour rising into the sky'. Peak-week queuing is a problem: 'the resort was very, very busy over Easter, with too many skiers for the size of the ski area'.

The piste map indicates a designated 'mogul zone' and a 'blade zone', and there are also 50 miles of cross-country trails. The small neighbouring ski area of **Gray Rocks** at St-Jovite makes an interesting day out when high winds shut the lifts at Tremblant.

Beginners

As much as 16 per cent of the runs are for beginners, so second-weekers and early intermediates are able to go almost anywhere: 'skiing as a family with two small children, we were able to go all over the mountain'. Enchanted Forest is a special beginners' and children's trail on the mountain, which is graded green (easy), and you can also travel from top to bottom of the south face on green trails. However, the downside of the resort is the extreme cold, which can make the first few days in a beginners' class – traditionally spent falling and standing around waiting for others who have fallen – not a lot of fun.

Intermediates

Those keen to bash the pistes will find plenty of scope on both sides of the mountain. Intermediate snow-users have 12 blue (intermediate) trails on the generally easier, south face, while over the top the skiing is more challenging.

Advanced

The ski area on both sides of the mountain is surprisingly demanding, with more than half designated as advanced terrain. Dynamite is a double-black-diamond (very difficult) trail located on the north side of the mountain; it has a 42-degree pitch, making it one of the steepest trails in eastern Canada. Beside it, the legendary Expo piste is for lovers of tricky moguls, and Cossack has been the site of three world freestyle championships.

The Edge is a corner of the mountain that has been set aside for advanced skiers and riders and is served by its own quad-chair. It contains three demanding trails – Emotion, Action and Haute Tension – the difficulty of which is accentuated by the icy, hardpacked snow conditions, which prevail in East Coast resorts.

Off-piste

Three intermediate runs among frozen spruces provide a dramatic introduction to tree-skiing. The Edge sector features some difficult gladed skiing at the sides of its trails.

Snowboarding

Tremblant is excellent for snowboarders, with two terrain parks. These include the large floodlit Xzone on the front (south) face of the mountain, which boasts a half-pipe, jumps and obstacles.

Tuition and guiding

The Tremblant Snow School organises lessons between 10am and midday and between 1.30 and 3pm. The school also offers a choice of courses ('a bewildering variety'). Ladies Love Wednesdays is a crèche-

and lunch-inclusive mid-week package for women skiers with children which can be booked through the ski school. We have, however, received criticism about the ski school during high season: 'the queues for ski lessons were awful. After a long wait we were told that all the classes were full and the next available group lessons would be in a week's time. Even private lessons were scarce'.

Mountain restaurants

Mountain eating opportunities are disappointing – Le Grand Manitou at the summit being the only restaurant. It houses both a self-service restaurant and La Légende, a table-service restaurant that promotes its 'fine-dining experience'. Restaurants near the base are easily accessible at lunchtime and provide more variety. These include Le Shack in the square: 'a good atmosphere at lunchtime and a view of the slopes'.

Accommodation

Of the nine hotels and seven lodges that have been built so far, Fairmont Chateau Tremblant (☎ 819 681 7000) is undeniably the smartest and most comfortable place to stay on the slope side. Other hotels include Le Lodge de la Montagne (☎ 819 681 3000) and La Tour des Voyageurs (☎ 819 681 2000). Newer is Le Westin Resort (☎ 819 681 3000), a five-star hotel containing a spa. Those who prefer self-catering can choose from a dozen condominium buildings.

Eating in and out

In contrast to the better-known Canadian resorts, such as Banff and Lake Louise, restaurant prices in Tremblant are high – indeed they are equivalent to those in any medium-sized French resort. However, the choice of eating places is wide, ranging from pizzerias to atmospheric establishments serving *cuisine québécois*. Le Gascon, a brasserie transported from the foothills of the Pyrenees, boasts 'outstanding cassoulet and robust bottles of *vin rouge*'. Pizzatéria and Ya'ooo Pizza are both lively and busy, and Mexicali Rosa's is recommended for its food and service. Coco Pazzo is an elegant Italian restaurant, while La Grappe à Vin calls itself a 'resto-bar', specialising in 'rare liquors' and wild game. Le Sen Soriel serves 'cuisine fusion' and Soto Sushi is located in Le Westin Resort.

Après-ski

The nightlife is concentrated at Vieux Tremblant, which boasts a growing number of bars and clubs, such as the popular Café de l'Epoque, Le P'tit Caribou and Octobar Rock bars. Le Cirque Blanc is a no-go area for adults, where children up to 18 years of age can play pool and video games, listen to music and enjoy non-alcoholic drinks at the bar. La Source Aquaclub, which features a swimming-pool modelled on a lake with an island in the middle and a 9ft-deep diving area with rocks to jump from, makes good family entertainment. Adults might prefer to relax at Spa Le Scandinave. Other activities include deer observation outings.

Skiing facts: Tremblant

TOURIST INFORMATION
3005 ch. Principal, Mont-Tremblant, QC
J0T 1Z0
Tel 1 819 681 2000
Fax 1 819 681 5996
Email reservations@intrawest.com
Web site www.tremblant.com

THE RESORT
Airport transfer Montreal 1½hrs
Visitor beds 3,000
Transport free bus service

THE SKIING
Linked or nearby resorts Gray Rocks at
St Jovite (n)
Number of lifts 12
Total of trails/pistes 602 acres
(16% easy, 41% intermediate,
32% difficult, 11% very difficult)
Beginners 1 free lift

LIFT PASSES
Area pass CDN$234–312 for 6 days
Pensioners CDN$40 per day for 65yrs
and over
Credit cards yes

TUITION
Skiing Tremblant Snow School
(☎ 888 736 2526)
Snowboarding as ski school
Other courses cross-country,
cybercamps, Discovery Program (for
beginners), moguls, Parallel Perfection,
race-training, seniors, skiing for the
disabled, snowblading, teen
skiing/boarding, telemark,
women's clinics
Guiding through Tremblant Snow School

CHILDREN
Lift pass 6–12yrs CDN$170, 13–17yrs
CDN$220, both for 6 days
Ski & board school as adults
Kindergarten Kidz Club at ski school

OTHER SPORTS
Dog-sledding, horse-riding, ice-climbing,
night-skiing/boarding, skating, sleigh
rides, snowmobiling, snowshoeing,
swimming, tobogganing, tubing

FOOD AND DRINK
Coffee CDN$1.40–2.50,
glass of wine CDN$6, small beer CDN$5,
soft drink CDN$1.25–2.50,
dish of the day CDN$7–18

Childcare
Low temperatures aside, this is an ideal resort for families. At the base
of the slopes is the Kidz Club, which is served by a 'magic carpet' conveyor belt lift. The club organises ski lessons for three- to 12-year-olds
and snowboarding from seven years of age, as well as twice-weekly
après-ski for children (between 5.30 and 9.30pm) including a hot meal.
Also in the evening is 'sliding fun for tots' at the base of the mountain.

Vail

ALTITUDE 8,120ft (2,475m)

Beginners ✱✱✱ Intermediates ✱✱✱ Advanced ✱✱✱ Snowboarders ✱✱✱

Vail is the showcase of American skiing. Other resorts, from Vermont to California, look in the window of this Colorado superstore and then race home to emulate what they have seen. Through massive investment in recent years, Vail has wooed both domestic and international skiers to its immaculately groomed slopes, and now delivers the largest ski area of any US resort, unbeatable service and guaranteed snow. The primping and pampering of an otherwise mediocre stretch of mountainside, dotted with 33 lifts, signals the danger of homogenising the skiing and snowboarding experience to the level of a Disney-style theme park. The Yellow Jackets ski patrol operate speed traps in designated slow skiing zones, and offenders are liable to lose their lift tickets without warning – an unhappy reminder of the real tarmac-and-wheels world from which, on holiday, you may have hoped to escape. However, this cynicism is completely lost on the resort's big-buck owners and its flock of devotees. As one reader put it: 'Vail may not be Chamonix, but it is still enormous fun'.

✔ Favourable snow record
✔ Large ski area
✔ Separate children's ski area
✔ Excellent ski school
✔ Easy introduction to off-piste
✔ Wide choice of resort restaurants
✘ Limited steep terrain
✘ Homogenised skiing
✘ Limited choice of mountain restaurants
✘ High prices

Anyone expecting a classic Rocky Mountain settlement at their journey's end is in for a disappointment. The pedestrianised village centre is built in neo-Tyrolean style with chalets clustered around a central clock tower. Vail's suburbs sprawl for seven miles along the busy I-70 freeway. It shares a lift pass with its sister resort **Beaver Creek**, ten miles to the west, as well as **Arapahoe Basin**, **Breckenridge** and **Keystone**, and there is a regular subsidised shuttle service between them.

Queuing is not a problem except at the main access points during peak-season rush-hour. In the words of one reporter: 'Vail does everything right. It overwhelms you with service and courtesy. Indeed, if you feel it does not, then they want to know about it'.

On the snow
top 11,480 ft (3,499m) bottom 8,120ft (2,475m)

Vail's main skiing takes place on the north-facing side of the mountain above the resort and is reached from three principal access points along

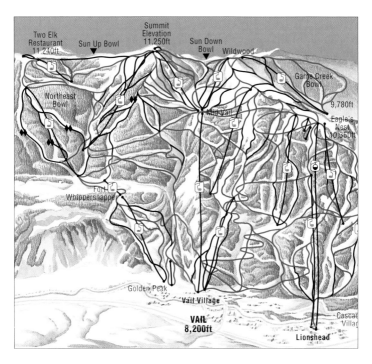

the valley floor: the Vista Bahn in Vail Village, a gondola and high-speed quad in Lionshead, and the Riva Bahn Express at Golden Peak. There is also a slow quad chair-lift at Cascade Village. All these lifts are served by an efficient ski bus system. The backside of the mountain is devoted to the largely unpisted Back Bowls area, renowned for its powder. When the resort is busy you can take the much-underused, detachable quad-chair at Golden Peak, which connects with the Northwoods Express lift and provides direct access to the Back Bowls.

Typical Colorado conditions are on a par with exceptional days in Europe. Ice, crud, bare patches or uncovered rocks are a rarity. Ample fluffy snow and top-to-bottom skiing from mid-November to the end of April is usual. Vail provides state-of-the-art snowmaking. A battalion of snowcats manicures the slopes at the end of each day, all the pistes are well signposted, and any obstacles are marked. One criticism, however, is lack of variety. While many of the runs on the front face are indistinguishable apart from their names, some of the steeper trails are heavily mogulled and some exciting tree-skiing, and plenty of long cruising runs are on offer.

Beginners

The two beginner areas in Vail are at Golden Peak and Eagle's Nest. The former, at the east end of the mountain, includes a number of easy runs and short lifts at the base area. Fort Whippersnapper, at the mid-station of the Riva Bahn lifts, is an extensive ski-in ski-out playground for children. At Eagle's Nest, reached directly by the gondola from Lionshead, are several easy runs and an activity centre that includes tubing, skating and a terrain park. Advanced beginners can find suitable runs on all areas of the mountain by following the green (easy) runs on the piste map.

Intermediates

Vail is essentially an intermediate's mountain. If you want to perfect your turns, the wide open pistes are a perfect training ground. Most skiers head to the top of the mountain via the Vista Bahn to mid-Vail ('worst queues of anywhere in the region'), where two high-speed quads let you explore the central west side of the mountain. The Back Bowls can be reached from the Mountaintop Express or Wildwood Express lifts. Intermediates favour the long, cruising runs from the Northwoods Express or the easier trails off Game Creek Express lift. For fast and smooth cruising you can take the runs off Eagle's Nest Ridge, such as Lodgepole, Berries and Ledges, down to the Avanti chair or all the way to the base. Although the Back Bowls are well-known, off-piste areas, they are not at all steep, with the easier runs offering a gentle introduction to powder skiing. A few runs such as Poppyfields are groomed.

Advanced

Highline and Roger's Run are both double-black-diamond (very difficult) trails, which are steep and heavily mogulled. Skipper, off the Windows Road catwalk, is little skied and can provide considerable challenge, while Ouzo Woods off Faro, Ouzo and Ouzo Glade all offer first-rate tree-skiing. Look Ma and Challenge under the Wildwood Express chair really test skiing technique in good snow. Kangaroo Cornice and North Rim under the Northwoods Express are well worth skiing, too. Most advanced skiers and riders congregate in the Back Bowls, where superb skiing and boarding exists in true powder conditions. However, they can be closed in bad weather or when snow cover is insufficient.

Off-piste

The Back Bowls provide Vail's off-piste skiing and snowboarding, and it is rewarding to make fresh tracks here on a powder day. Chutes, drop-offs and fine tree-skiing are available in the Mongolia Bowls, and Blue Sky Basin, Vail's newest bowl area, adds an impressive 885 acres of off-piste terrain. The Minturn Mile takes you down through some scenic and challenging terrain to the small town of **Minturn**; margaritas or pitchers of beer at The Saloon here provide a pleasant end to the outing.

Snowboarding

Vail has enthusiastically embraced snowboarding and prides itself on the variety and challenge of its riding terrain, which includes dedicated pistes cut through the trees. These are marked on a separate snow-boarding map. Vail boasts three half-pipes, one of which – the Tag Heuer – is said to be the largest in the US. The terrain park is spread over 12 trails, with a combination of natural and man-made features.

Tuition and guiding
The Vail/Beaver Creek Ski and Snowboard School, with a total of 1,300 instructors, is one of the largest in the world. In Vail it has six separate locations: at the base of Golden Peak, Lionshead and in Vail Village, and at Two Elk, Mid-Vail and Eagle's Nest. Reporters continued to comment on the high quality of instruction and the friendly attitude of the teachers: 'what a change from Europe. Our instructor became a real pal, and we learned more from her in a week than in the previous three seasons in France'. The school employs 150 snowboard teachers with dedicated classes in high season for teenagers.

Mountain restaurants
Size rather than intimacy seems to be the priority at most mountain restaurants here. The Two Elk is a cavernous self-service. The smaller Wildwood Smokehouse is renowned for its tuna sandwiches, and Buffalo's at Chair 4 is prized for snacks. All the mountain restaurants are owned by the resort and are geared towards high turnover rather than the leisurely lunching enjoyed by most Europeans – Larkspur at Golden Peak being an exception. Garfinkels and Bart and Yeti's at Lionshead are recommended, as are Pepi's and Los Amigos in Vail Village. The Lodge at Vail serves 'the best-value buffet in the whole resort'.

Accommodation
The Lodge at Vail (☎ 970 476 5011) is now owned by the resort but remains one of the most luxurious hotels in the resort, together with the Sonnenalp Resort (☎ 970 476 5656). Vail Village Inn (☎ 970 476 5622) and Chateau Vail (☎ 970 476 5631) head the second rank. Vail Marriott's Mountain Resort (☎ 970 476 4444) has spent $10 million upgrading its rooms and is warmly praised. Cheaper are Roost Lodge (☎ 970 476 5451), in West Vail, and West Vail Lodge (☎ 970 476 3890). Vail Mountain Lodge and Spa (☎ 970 476 0700) (formerly Vail Athletics Club) has undergone a major renovation, while Antlers at Vail (☎ 970 476 2471) has built new condominiums as part of it is $17-million makeover.

Eating in and out
The Vail Valley features an enormous choice of restaurants, serving food of every nationality from Mexican to Thai and Japanese. Terra Bistro and Sweet Basil are praised for their Californian cuisine. The Wildflower in The Lodge, La Tour and the Left Bank are also strongly recommended for a special night out, as are The Tyrolean and The Lancelot Inn. Montauk in Lionshead features superlative seafood:

Skiing facts: Vail

TOURIST INFORMATION
PO Box 7, Vail, CO 81658
Tel 1 970 496 4040
(01708 640707 for UK agent)
Fax 1 970 845 2905
(01708 640707 for UK agent)
Email vailinfo@vailresorts.com/vailre-sorts@clara.co.uk
Web site www.vail.com

THE RESORT
Airport transfer Eagle County 45mins, Denver 2½hrs
Visitor beds 41,305 in Vail Valley
Transport bus between Beaver Creek, Breckenridge, Keystone and Vail (nominal charge)

THE SKIING
Linked or nearby resorts Arapahoe Basin (n), Beaver Creek (n), Breckenridge (n), Keystone (n)
Number of lifts 33
Total of trails/pistes 5,289 acres (28% easy, 32% intermediate, 40% difficult)
Beginners 2 areas at Golden Peak and top of Eagle's Nest

LIFT PASSES
Area pass (covers Arapahoe Basin, Beaver Creek, Breckenridge and Keystone) $174–210 for 6 days
Pensioners 70yrs and over $99 for season
Credit cards yes

TUITION
Skiing Vail Ski and Snowboard School
(☎ 970 476 3239)
Snowboarding Vail Ski and Snowboard School
Other courses bumps, cross-country, extreme skiing/boarding, powder clinics, race-training, seniors, skiing for the disabled, teen programmes, telemark, women's ski courses
Guiding none

CHILDREN
Lift pass 5–12yrs $126 for 6 days
Ski & board school as adults
Kindergarten (ski) through ski and snowboard school, (non-ski) Small World Playschool (☎ 970 479 3285)

OTHER SPORTS
Climbing-wall, dog-sledding, hang-gliding, horse-riding, hot-air ballooning, ice-climbing, ice-fishing, ice-hockey, indoor climbing wall, indoor tennis and squash, skating, sleigh rides, snowbiking, snowmobiling, snowshoeing, swimming, thrill sledding, tubing

FOOD AND DRINK
Coffee $2, glass of wine $3–5, small beer $3.50, soft drink $1.5–3, dish of the day $15

'quite outstanding, some of the best food in the resort'. The Half Moon Saloon in West Vail is worth a visit, as is The Saloon at Minturn ('try their quail speciality'). Campo de Fiori and Cucina Rustica both offer 'authentic Italian dishes at slightly silly prices'. Up The Creek is praised for its 'excellent duck' and May Palace in the West Vail Mall is a recommended Chinese restaurant. For cheaper food, try the Hubcap Brewery, Kitchen and Pazzo's Pizzeria. Higher up the mountain, the luxurious members-only Game Creek Club is now open to the public at night.

Après-ski

Check out the sunset at the Blue Moon bar at Eagle's Nest, or sip a margarita at Los Amigos at the bottom of the Vista Bahn lift. Mickey's Piano Bar at the Lodge is the place in which to spot celebrities. Other favourite post-ski hang-outs are the deck at Pepi's Bar and the Red Lion. In Lionshead go to Garfinkels, Trail's End or Bart and Yeti's. The Ore House offers après-ski, happy-hour prices. For coffee visit the Daily Grind, and for tea the Alpenrose. Later on, Garton's puts on rock'n'roll and sometimes country and western. Club Chelsea provides a disco, and Bully Ranch at the Sonnenalp is popular, along with The Club. Locals hang out at The George, and riders at Shieka's and Nick's. Silverthorne, 40 minutes away, has factory outlets such as Nike, Osh-Kosh, DKNY, GAP and Levis, all of which offer some great bargains.

Childcare

The Small World Playschool at Golden Peak and at Lionshead is a non-ski kindergarten. The Children's Ski and Snowboard School at both locations is for kids from three to 13 years of age. After-skiing children's and family programmes include Kid's Night Out Goes Western, for children aged five to 13, with music, pizza and a Wild West show. Kids can ski with the Buckaroo Bonanza Bunch, a group of Western characters who tell stories about the Wild West.

Whistler

ALTITUDE 2,214ft (675m)

Beginners **✱✱✱** Intermediates **✱✱✱** Advanced **✱✱✱** Snowboarders **✱✱✱**

In the past, fewer than a dozen resorts (Sun Valley, Cortina d'Ampezzo, Megève, Kitzbühel, Davos, Aspen, St Moritz, St Anton, Chamonix and Val d'Isère) have taken a turn as the acknowledged snow capital of the world, the anvil on which innovation is forged and the standard of excellence to which all serious skiers and snowboarders must aspire. However, for the present and for the foreseeable future this mantle is firmly fixed on Whistler.

> ✔ Long vertical drop
> ✔ Attractive village centre
> ✔ Modern lift system
> ✔ Long ski season
> ✔ Extensive off-piste
> ✘ Harsh maritime climate
> ✘ Peak-season lift queues
> ✘ Short skiing days

This resort in British Columbia provides the most challenging skiing and the most cosmopolitan atmosphere of any in North America. Here you can ski or snowboard your heart out on two adjoining peaks, which offer skiing for all standards, with plunging powder bowls, sheer couloirs and gladed skiing. Down below, the once unconnected villages of Whistler and **Blackcomb** have been skilfully melded into one charismatic resort by the owners, Intrawest, and Blackcomb has been renamed Upper Village.

It is reached from Vancouver airport by a visually intoxicating drive northwards along the Sea-to-Sky highway 'sandwiched between soaring hemlocks on one side and open vistas of the Pacific on the other'. Whistler is prime evidence that a purpose-built resort can be attractive. It is a mixture of chalet-style apartments, inns, lodges and condominiums, with weatherboarding more in evidence than concrete. Its steep rooflines and pastel colours are an alluring contrast against the snow-capped mountains. There are few large buildings, and the biggest hotel, the Fairmont Chateau Whistler, is built in a neo-Gothic style. The centre of Whistler is car-free, and getting from Village Square to Mountain Square at the base of the two gondolas involves a two-minute walk. A third area, Market Place, is the cheaper base, where many of the resort staff shop and stay.

Such has been the scale of development that anyone who has not visited Whistler during the past few years would fail to recognise it. With the addition of new condominiums, hotels, shops and restaurants, the resort has virtually doubled in size. The increased number of tourist beds has encouraged mass-market British tour operators to compete with each other, and the immediate effect has been to lower holiday

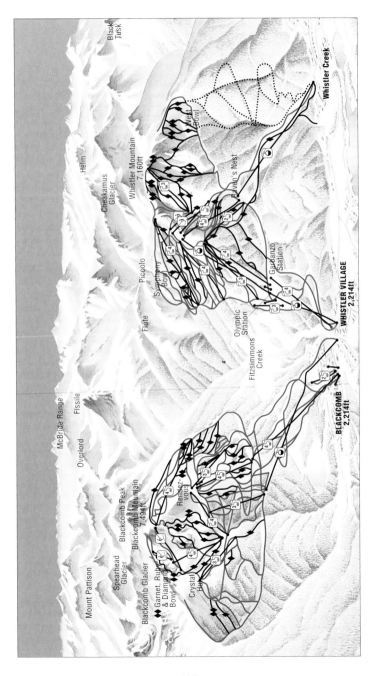

cost. Purists argue that the original rugged character of the resort has already changed irrevocably.

Whistler Mountain stands at only 7,160ft but affords more than 5,020ft of vertical – one of the longest continuous drops in North America. Its equally rugged neighbour, Blackcomb Mountain, was originally developed in 1980 by a breakaway consortium. The contrastingly different, and often more demanding, terrain includes two glaciers and a set of truly awesome couloirs.

Since Whistler and Blackcomb merged in 1997 some CDN$68 million has been spent on improvements to the lift system and mountain facilities in addition to the CDN$500 million investment in the base area. The next construction stage is under way – the development of a completely new village in the satellite of **Whistler Creek**, along with sufficient parking and swift mountain access to absorb the day-visitors from Vancouver, who clog the main resort at weekends. The continued development has met with opposition from permanent residents, who argue that the focus on increased tourism is too intense and that insufficient funds have been set aside for housing, schools and other social structures needed by the locals. However, Whistler has a five-year project in place to restore and protect the mountain and is winner of the *2001 Starfish Award for Environmentally Responsible Tourism (BC)*.

WHAT'S NEW

Development has started on Whistler Creek Village

Whistler may indeed be a winter-sports colossus, but it has one major problem that no amount of investment can solve: its maritime position means that much of the heavy winter precipitation falls as rain in the village and only as powder snow higher up. As one reporter put it: 'there is no denying the damp weather and dreary temperamental skies that are the colour of crude oil. Plan to get wet.' Pack an umbrella. A common fact of life in these high mountains is that you never know until you get up there what awaits you at the top. In the course of a typical day you may encounter rain and light powder interspersed with sunshine and clear blue skies. Days go by without one ray of sunshine, but you don't need to pick sunny days to enjoy the skiing. Whole sunshine days are statistically scarce in comparison with the weather enjoyed by Whistler's Rocky Mountain cousins in the USA. Changes in temperature between village and summit can be frostbitingly dramatic, although not as extreme as in **Banff/Lake Louise**.

High-season queues – particularly at weekends, when the number of snow-users on both mountains is augmented by day-visitors from Vancouver – can be frustrating: 'on one day it was so bad we gave up and got a refund on our lift pass'. However, as another reporter commented: 'if you are in ski school you have priority, so queuing for lifts is not a problem'. The Fitzsimmons Express chair-lift from Whistler base is a swift backdoor into the lift system that is ignored by nearly all but the locals.

Whistler's position on the edge of the Pacific Rim means it attracts visitors from Japan as well as Europe. As a consequence its shops and restaurants display an international ambience that is unusual in a North American ski resort. During February the Japanese can account for nearly as high a percentage of the clientèle as the British, when both seek to escape the rigours of their own respective winters. Australians, New Zealanders and British provide a high proportion of resort workers. Whistler's appeal is multi-faceted, so, unlike other comparable resorts, there is no end-of-term feeling in the post-Easter weeks. As the snow melts the workforce falls by only 25 per cent. For the remainder, it is their home and it is time to oil up the mountain bike. Limited glacier skiing continues on Blackcomb throughout much of the summer.

On the snow
top 7,492ft (2,284m) bottom 2,214ft (675m)

'The variety of skiing is nothing short of startling,' said one reader, 'Whistler stands in a class alone. Be surprised at nothing.' The two mountains of Whistler and Blackcomb stand side by side and share a lift pass, but they are divided by Fitzsimmons Creek and are at present linked only at the foot. Plans to create a mid-mountain gondola link should be realised within four years. For the present, snow-users wanting to cross over from Blackcomb to Whistler have to travel all the way down to the bottom and take a green trail to catch the Whistler Village Gondola or the Fitzsimmons Express chair up the other side. Similarly, Whistler snow-users have to return to the village to take the Excalibur Gondola up Blackcomb. Blackcomb also has its own chair-lift, the Wizard Express, which links to the Solar Coaster Express. This takes you up to the Rendezvous.

Superficially, the two mountains are not dissimilar: each claims more than a hundred runs and each has long cruising trails. But whereas Whistler is known for its bowls, Blackcomb prides itself on its two glaciers and some dramatic couloirs.

Beginners

Both areas have easy trails high on the mountain, so novices can enjoy the wide-open spaces and a vertical drop usually associated with intermediate ambitions. At Whistler, you can ride all the way up to the Roundhouse on the gondola and also access ski trails such as Upper Whiskeyjack and Pony Trail (where packhorses once helped transport lift equipment). Papoose, Bear Cub and Expressway are other options lower down.

On Blackcomb Mountain take the Wizard Express quad-chair and switch to the Solar Coaster Express, which takes you to the easy Expressway link with the Seventh Heaven Express quad and Xhiggy's Meadow – a black-diamond (difficult) run that is also the top of the easy Green Line trail. From here beginners can also ski from the top of Crystal Traverse, which leads to the Jersey Cream and Glacier Express quads, both of which access some easy learner trails. Nursery slopes are also situated around the Olympic Station of the Whistler gondola and at the Blackcomb base area.

Intermediates

Whistler and Blackcomb mountains both offer exhilarating top-to-bottom skiing, much of it below the tree-line. Half of the runs on the two mountains are graded intermediate. Easier access routes to Whistler Bowl and West Bowl have opened up this huge area to less experienced snow-users. Franz's run is a 'good high-velocity cruiser' that drops from the tree-line all the way to Whistler Creek, where a gondola takes you back up to the mid-station in just seven minutes.

On Blackcomb, the Seventh Heaven Express quad-chair and Showcase T-bar to the Blackcomb Glacier serve mainly intermediate terrain at the top of the mountain. The extensive mid-mountain area beneath the Solar Coaster Express quad-chair is dominated by a large number of medium-standard runs, including the long Springboard trail. Zig Zag and Cruiser are also popular pistes. Rock 'n' Roll on Blackcomb is 'a three-mile screamer with relaxing sections punctuated with steeper plunges'.

Advanced

At Whistler, much depends on whether the Peak chair or Harmony Express quad are open. If not, good advanced terrain can be found around Chunky's Choice and GS. Lower down, Seppo's and Raven off the Black chair-lift provide black-diamond skiing, and the Orange chair accesses the long Dave Murray Downhill and two expert cut-offs: Bear Paw and Tokum. Some of Blackcomb's most difficult runs are among the trees in a broad triangle between the lower sections of the Glacier Express and Crystal Chair, which means you can inspect them before you ski. Trapline, Straight Shot, Rock'n Roll and Overbite are Crystal Chair's featured runs, and The Bite, Staircase and Blowdown are on your right as you board the Glacier Express.

Off-piste

Blackcomb's couloirs and Whistler's bowls are the main areas of interest for off-piste snow-users. Couloir Extreme separates the advanced skier from the expert ('nerves of steel are a distinct advantage'). It is the location for an annual extreme ski-race in which more than a hundred competitors, both professional and amateur, take part in a contest described as '2,500ft of thigh-burning hell'. Pakalolo is another couloir that attracts experienced snow-users. It has a fearsome reputation but is not in the same league as Couloir Extreme. A short hike from the top of the Showcase T-bar on Blackcomb gives access to a delightful intermediate off-piste run down the Blackcomb Glacier. Whistler's main lift-served bowls – Symphony, Glacier, Whistler, Harmony and West Bowls – offer a wide spectrum of off-piste challenges. Reporters commended the 'good powder bowl skiing off Flute and Oboe – the former is a reasonable boot hike, the latter is better on skins'. For those prepared to tour, the possibilities are endless. However, it should be noted that couloirs and bowls in the immediate vicinity of the resort that are marked as 'permanently closed' should be avoided. Anyone caught skiing here by the ski patrol is liable to forfeit his or her lift ticket. Five heli-ski companies operate in and around Whistler including Whistler Heli-skiing, which runs daily excursions and a new company, Cayoosh Helisports, which operates out of Pemberton (25 miles away), is a welcome addition, offering heli-skiing. The company also offers heli-hiking and heli-fishing.

Snowboarding

Whistler is the best snowboarding resort in Canada and arguably in the whole of North America. The contours on both mountains are exceptionally well suited to riding, and Blackcomb features a terrain park comprising 16 acres with two half-pipes. Blackcomb also gives riders the choice of an intermediate or expert run. Whistler is less challenging and offers more of a freeride experience – the best freeriding and off-piste snowboarding being accessed by the Peak quad-chair. Expect to find a considerable number of skiers and snowbladers in the terrain park.

Tuition and guiding

Whistler/Blackcomb Ski and Snowboard School (SSS) has an excellent reputation: 'the tuition was so illuminating, with smooth and rapid progress, that I wondered how we had ever skied without it. We never felt rushed and the instructor answered any questions that we had. Any weak areas were pinpointed with the accuracy of a laser'. However, another reporter commented: 'I did feel there was a little too much "Hey, you're doing great!", "Check it out!", "Wow!" and "Brilliant!" – particularly when I knew that it had not gone that well'. The resort's regular free tours of the pistes with some of Canada's greatest skiers are strongly recommended: 'it was an extraordinary experience to ski with someone of world class, and one that I will never forget'. The ski patrol's Avalanche Awareness Course is described as 'a must for all advanced skiers, but you don't need to be an expert to do it'. Extremely Canadian provides lessons in extreme skiing and snowboarding.

Mountain restaurants

These are Whistler's weakest point. They are, as one reporter put it, 'huge, very busy and not terribly appealing' and 'it is hard work finding a place for a group to sit'. On Whistler Mountain, the Roundhouse Lodge promises 'everything from burgers and fries to fresh pasta and Asian cuisine'. However, one reporter found 'the service poor'. An alternative is Steeps Grill, a waiter-service restaurant located inside the Roundhouse. The Raven's Nest at the top of the Creekside gondola specialises in pasta and home-made soup, while the Chick Pea at the top of the Garbanzo chair-lift serves soup and snacks.

On Blackcomb, Christine's Restaurant in the Rendezvous Lodge was described as 'a sad disappointment' by one disgruntled family, although another reporter said the food was 'pretentious, but still the best on the mountain'. The Rendezvous offers more casual but faster service. Crystal Hut at the top of the Crystal chair-lift is 'just like an atmospheric Swiss or Italian alpine hut with the same primitive toilets', and the River Rock Grill, upstairs at the Glacier Creek, is praised for 'a cosmopolitan choice of cuisine with wonderful glacier views'.

Wise snow-users eat at one of the bases, which are easy to reach at lunch-time. Monk's Grill Steak House by the Wizard Express lift at Upper Village base is highly recommended, as is Dusty's Café at Creekside base. At Excalibur Village Station, Essentially Blackcomb features an outdoor barbecue.

Early birds are advised to start the day at the Roundhouse Lodge with the Fresh Tracks programme. You board the Whistler gondola at 7.15am for an all-you-can-eat breakfast before setting off down the mountain as soon as the ski patrol declares it open. Béla's in the Excalibur Base II Day Lodge serves all-day breakfast.

Accommodation
Make sure you know which part of Whistler your accommodation is in (Upper Village, Whistler Village, Village North or **Creekside**) before reserving ski school places. Tour operators have been known to book clients into the least convenient school for a hotel. The 13-storey Fairmont Chateau Whistler (☎ 604 938 8000) sits on the edge of the piste in the lower village and dominates the skyline as you ski down to the resort. It remains one of the truly great ski hotels of the world, with the addition of an innovative spa ('the Ayurvedic treatments and Lomi Lomi Hawaiian massage were blissful'). We also received good reports of the Delta Whistler Resort (☎ 604 932 1982) ('next to the mountain and very convenient'). The Pan Pacific Lodge (☎ 604 905 2999) ('rather noisy') is another convenient and centrally placed hotel for both the skiing and Whistler Village; it also has an outdoor heated swimming-pool. Timberline Lodge (☎ 604 932 5211) is 'comfortable, well situated and friendly,' while the Crystal Lodge (☎ 604 932 2221) ('comfortable, conveniently located and the staff were helpful') and the Listel Whistler Hotel (☎ 604 932 1133) are both popular.

Apartments at the Residence Inn by Marriott (☎ 604 905 3400) in Upper Village were rated as 'extremely spacious for two to three people, and luxuriously comfortable compared with apartments in Europe where they would have been for at least six people'. Whistler Chalets (☎ 604 905 5287) boasts a portfolio of luxury self-catering homes for rental. Westin Resort & Spa (☎ 604 905 5000) at the base of Whistler Mountain is a village in itself containing a shopping mall and a sushi restaurant among its many facilities. Work has started on the new Four Seasons Lodge on the piste near the Fairmont Chateau Whistler. It is planned to be a 273-roomed hotel with a spa opening in 2004. Condominiums at the Blackcomb Lodge and Mountainside Lodge are both recommended.

Alpine Springs B&B (☎ 604 905 2747) and Blue Spruce Lodge (☎ 604 932 3508) have moderate prices, while Haus Stephanie is 'a friendly, little bed-and-breakfast'. Travel firms operate a growing number of catered chalets, but it is worth checking the exact position before booking as many are situated an inconvenient distance from the lifts and village centre.

Eating in and out

You can tell a remarkable amount about a ski resort by its restaurants – in this case 87 of a dozen nationalities. As one reporter put it: 'eating out in Whistler is nothing short of sensational. We ate Japanese, Chinese, Thai, Italian, Greek, French, American and pub food. We did not have one bad or even mediocre meal'. However, reporters also pointed out that 'the resort suffers from serious overcrowding problems in restaurants at weekends, owing to an influx of local skiers from Vancouver, and the service was underwhelming at all times. I would make an exception for the Wildflower in the Fairmont Chateau Whistler, which was excellent with prices surprisingly low'.

Bearfoot Bistro is the crowning glory of Whistler's eateries: it is 'a luxurious candle-lit place with exquisite food and ceremonial lid-lifting'. Trattoria di Umberto ('very fine') and Il Caminetto di Umberto are also praised, along with La Rua. Quattro in the Pinnacle International Resort is a recommended Italian eatery, while Zeuski's Taverna in Village North was said to have 'soundly priced and tasty meals'. Sushi Village ('so popular you should book before you leave home') is one of eight Far-Eastern restaurants. Sushi-Ya in Village North and Teppan Village – 'a stir-fry bar' in Whistler Village – are also excellent. Kypriaki Norte received unfavourable reports. Ristorante Araxi specialises in Mediterranean cuisine and is 'absolutely delightful', Ingrid's Café is 'cheap, cheerful and wholesome', and Citta's is a friendly, little bistro. Monks Grill and Thai One On in Upper Village and the Garibaldi Lift Co. in Whistler Village are all warmly praised. Rim Rock at Whistler Creek was highly commended by reporters, too. Nester's is said to be the best-priced supermarket. For something a little different, you can cook your own dinner at Whistler Cooking School. Students participate in the cooking with the help of a visiting chef and eat the results.

Après-ski

Whistler's nightlife was highly praised by reporters: 'the bars and nightlife were wonderful – no drunks and hooligans, just loads of friendly, happy people telling you their escapades of the day's skiing'. Dubh Linn Gate is an Irish pub described by one reporter as 'a great place to step out of your wet clothes and into a dry Martini'. The Longhorn Saloon at the foot of the slopes catches skiers and snowboarders as they come off the mountain ('beers gush from the tap like oil from a pipeline, a great place for anyone slightly deaf and with a cast-iron liver'). Merlin's Bar at Blackcomb base is lively, and Tapley's Pub

Skiing facts: Whistler

TOURIST INFORMATION
4010 Whistler Way, Whistler,
BC V0N 1B4
Tel 1 604 664 5625
Fax 1 604 932 5758
Email
reservations@tourismwhistler.com
Web site www.tourismwhistler.com

THE RESORT
Airport transfer Vancouver 2hrs,
frequent coach service to resort
Visitor beds 26,541
Transport free shuttle bus within the
village loop

THE SKIING
Linked or nearby resorts Whistler
Creek (l)
Number of lifts 33
Total of trails/pistes 7,071 acres
(20% easy, 55% intermediate,
25% difficult)
Beginners 5 baby lifts
Summer skiing mid-June to mid-August
on Horstman Glacier on Blackcomb
Mountain

LIFT PASSES
Area pass CDN$324 for 6 days
Pensioners 65yrs and over CDN$275 for
6 out of 7 days, 75yrs and over ski free
Credit cards yes

TUITION
Skiing Extremely Canadian (☎ 604 932
4105), Lauralee Bowie Ski Adventures
(☎ 604 689 7444), Whistler/Blackcomb

SSS (☎ 604 932 3434)
Snowboarding as ski school,
Extremely Canadian (☎ 604 938 9656)
Other courses avalanche awareness,
cross-country, heli-skiing/boarding,
race-training, slalom, teen programmes,
women's clinics
Guiding Blackcomb Helicopters
(☎ 604 938 1700),
Cayoosh Helisports (☎ 604 894 1144),
Helico Presto (☎ 604 938 2927),
Spearhead Mountain Guides
(☎ 604 932 8802),
TLH Heliskiing (☎ 250 558 5379),
Whistler Alpine Guides Bureau
(☎ 604 932 4040),
Whistler Heli-skiing (☎ 604 932 4105)

CHILDREN
Lift pass 7–12yrs CDN$162, 13–18yrs
CDN$275, both for 6 out of 7 days
Ski & board school Ski Scamps
(☎ 604 932 3434)
Kindergarten (ski) as ski school, (non-
ski) The Nanny Network
(☎ 604 938 2823)

OTHER SPORTS
Dog-sledding, heli-hiking, heli-fishing,
indoor climbing wall, indoor tennis and
squash, parapente, skating, sleigh rides,
snowmobiling, snowshoeing, swimming

FOOD AND DRINK
Coffee CDN$1.50, glass of wine CDN$7,
small beer CDN$5, soft drink CDN$1.50,
dish of the day CDN$10–22

is 'friendly, cheap and used by the locals'. Garfinkel's, Tommy Africa's and the Savage Beagle Bar are all extremely popular nightclubs, while Blacks Pub employs 'friendly staff and was not too noisy'. One of the 'in' places for riders is the Maxx Fish disco. Whistler offers a choice of

13 spas and health centres, some of them in hotels. Shops stay open until 10pm, and shopping is a core part of the evening entertainment either before or after dinner, with ski clothing such as North Face at approximately half UK prices, plus two Helly-Hansen outlets. Other shops worth visiting include a Guess Jeans shop, GAP and Roots Canada. Lush 'sells unusual unguents for the bath' and Skitch Knicknacks & Paddywacks is for original gifts.

Childcare

Whistler Kids caters for children aged three months to 12 years on both mountains with all-day care and lessons for appropriate ages: 'my four-year-old daughter learned more in a week than she had done in two previous weeks in France. She enjoyed every minute of it and cried when she had to leave'. Whistler/Blackcomb SSS also runs special classes for teenagers. Parents with small children at the kindergarten are given optional pagers so they can be called anywhere on the mountain if their child needs them. Ski Scamps ski and snowboard school is based at Whistler and Blackcomb mountains. The Nanny Network provides babysitters who will come to your lodging during the day or evening ('we booked in the morning during the busiest week of the year and childcare was instantly arranged for that evening').

Round-up

RESORTS COVERED Alaska: Alyeska. Alberta: Jasper. British Columbia: Big White, Fernie, Kicking Horse, Panorama, Red Mountain, Silver Star, Sun Peaks. Colorado: Arapahoe Basin, Copper Mountain, Crested Butte, Durango, Steamboat, Telluride, Winter Park. Idaho: Sun Valley. Maine: Sunday River. Montana: Big Sky. New Mexico: Taos. Quebec: Mont Sainte-Anne

ALASKA

Alyeska
Top 2,750ft (838m) bottom 250ft (76m)

Alaska's Chugach range of steep-sided, deeply furrowed peaks has for some years been the cult destination for extreme skiers and snowboarders. Alyeska, an Aleut name meaning 'vast white wilderness', is a small, family-oriented resort frequented mostly by locals from Anchorage, 40 miles north of the airport on what *National Geographic* magazine has rated one of North America's top ten scenic drives. The resort has only 800 acres of terrain and nine lifts, one of which is a 60-person tram that departs from inside the Alyeska Prince Hotel (☎ 907 754 1111). The base-station is barely above sea level, yet Alyeska enjoys phenomenal snow (a record 782ft during the 2000–1 season) and astonishing scenery. Most resort trails are unthreatening to intermediates. However, Alyeska's North Face couloirs, supervised by the ski patrol, are raw Alaska adventure – inside resort boundaries. Alyeska's lifts are open until 5.30pm from February, and it offers more daylight skiing hours than any North America resort, as well as floodlit skiing and snowboarding two nights per week.

Alyeska boasts a wealth of non-skiing activities including helicopter and snowcat skiing and snowboarding, snowmobiling, husky sleigh rides and day trips to the Columbia Glacier. There are some B&Bs and condominiums (☎ 907 783 2000 for bookings), but the 307-room Alyeska Prince Hotel (☎ 907 754 1111) accommodates most visitors. The tram runs diners to the mountain top for evening meals. Alternatively, the hotel contains a variety of restaurants featuring Alaskan King crab and exotic game specialities, as well as two sushi restaurants. Hotel staff will awaken guests who so request when the fabled Northern Lights make an appearance.

TOURIST INFORMATION
Tel 1 907 754 1111
Fax 1 907 754 2200
Email info@alyeskaresort.com
Web site www.alyeskaresort.co

ALBERTA

Jasper
top 8,533ft (2,601m) bottom 5,640ft (1,719m)

The most northerly and arguably the most beautiful of Canadian resorts is set among the glaciers, forests, frozen lakes and waterfalls of Jasper National Park. The ski area at **Marmot Basin**, a 20-minute drive from the town, is not large but the terrain is extremely varied, with open bowls, steep chutes and glades cut through the trees. The 53 trails are split evenly between green (easy), blue (intermediate) and black-diamond (difficult), and are serviced by seven lifts. The longest run is 3½ miles long. Plans are at an advanced stage for a new quad chair-lift for the 2001–2 season to provide easy access to extensive terrain on Eagle East and Chalet Slope.

Founded by fur traders in 1811, Jasper has developed into a typical Canadian railway town, with a wide choice of restaurants and bars. In spite of the long transfer time (Calgary International Airport is a five-hour drive to the south) visitors say that the resort is an exceptionally good place in which to unwind.

Alpine Sports Training Center organises skiing, snowboarding and tele-mark classes, and children from four years old can take group lessons. Paradise Chalet and Eagle mid-mountain lodge are the places to go for lunch.

A dozen hotels are headed by the Fairmont Jasper Park Lodge (☎ 780 852 3301), a huge hotel on the outskirts of town. It possesses 442 rooms spread out in bungalows and two-storey buildings in the extensive grounds, plus four restaurants, a nightclub, shopping mall and an out-door swimming-pool, and is a resort in its own right. The Royal Canadian Lodge (☎ 780 852 5644) is 'extremely comfortable' too, while the Whistler Inn (☎ 780 852 3361), a budget hotel named after a local mountain, is smaller still and even more central, with its own Italian restaurant, pub and wildlife museum. Other entertainment includes ice-climbing, sleigh rides, snowmobiling and skating on the lake. The ice-covered Maligne Canyon is unique, and heli-skiing/boarding is possible at **Valemount**, an hour's drive away. Wolf Howl is where you are accompanied by a park interpreter to go out and talk to the animals.

TOURIST INFORMATION
Tel 1 780 852 3816
Fax 1 780 852 3533
Email info@skimarmot.com
Web site www.skimarmot.co

BRITISH COLUMBIA

Big White
top 7,606ft (2,319m) bottom 4,950ft (1,508m)

The recipient of lavish funding that many resorts would envy, this

Australian-owned mountain is in the process of transforming itself into a major player in the Okanagan Highlands, to the east of the huge Lake Okanagan. Local lore has it that Big White is named after the cloud that often conceals it. The resulting humidity creates a phantom forest of snow-ghosts: trees frozen into eerie, monster-like formations. The extensive, but predominantly intermediate ski area is better suited to families than radical adventurers but, given sunshine and powder, Big White is a magical place. The snowboarding is spectacular, with two terrain parks, a half-pipe, an illuminated quarter-pipe (for night-riding) and some large powder bowls.

The 13-lift system – including a recently installed gondola – provides high-speed access to 2,150 acres of terrain, of which only 750 acres are groomed. A wide variety of green (easy) and blue (intermediate) trails can be reached via Ridge Rocket Express, Bullet Express and Black Forest Express, while the much shorter Plaza quad-chair gives access to a first-timer's area and children's park below the main village. Advanced skiers must head for less speedy lifts: the Alpine T-bar for steep, open slopes or the Powder Chair for glade-skiing. Advanced terrain has expanded by 25 per cent with the opening of four new trails this winter in the area between Goat's Kick and Serwa's, known as Never-Never Land.

Big White's Ski and Snowboard School employs 60 instructors, who teach children and adults. Tot Town Daycare caters for children aged eighteen months to six years old, and Ski Cubs looks after those aged three to six years.

All the accommodation is ski-in ski-out. Coast Resort (☎ 250 491 0221) is smart and comfortable, while the White Crystal Inn (☎ 250 765 4611) features rooms as big as ballrooms and chilly, but its Grizzly Bear lounge is popular for après-ski. Snowshoe Sam's (famous for its Gunbarrel coffee) is a particularly good example of the one-stop nightlife that is typical of the British Columbian interior: rough-hewn and friendly, with pool tables, a dance area and a restaurant – it is all things to all visitors, which is fortunate because the alternatives are few.

TOURIST INFORMATION
Tel 1 250 765 8888
Fax 1 250 765 8200
Email bigwhite@bigwhite.com
Web site www.bigwhite.com

Fernie
top 6,316ft (1,925m) bottom 3,500ft (1,067m)

Until the mid-1990s Fernie was a little-known and unfashionable resort in the south-east corner of the British Columbian Rockies with unexpectedly good terrain and an exceptional snow record. It has now benefited from a major CDN$100-million expansion – doubling its terrain – having been acquired in 1998 by Charlie Locke, the owner of a portfolio of Canadian resorts including Lake Louise. Fernie now boasts ten lifts serving some 2,504 acres of skiing and claims to be the fourth largest ski resort in Canada. With an extensive array of steeper-than-average terrain, impressive off-piste opportunities in five bowls and challenging snowcat-skiing, it is 'reminiscent of Argentière before it got too busy – some of the best terrain I have ever skied anywhere'. However, another reporter thought the lift system 'pitiful for the cost of the lift ticket, and none of the chair-lifts had covers – in spite of the cold climate. But I have never come across such friendly lift staff.'

The two main peaks tower above the base area of Timberline Villages, giving evocatively named black-diamond (difficult) runs, such as Stag Leap and Sky Dive, and even blue (intermediate) trails the appearance of being so steep as to be scarcely skiable. Fortunately, this transpires to be something of an illusion. Conversely, a few of the many green (easy) trails are quite steep for novices. Fernie is a good resort for learning to snowboard, with plenty of suitable trails.

Snowcat-skiers and -boarders will be in their element. Several companies will arrange trips, including Island Lake Lodge, with 7,000 acres of terrain six miles further along the valley, and Fernie Wilderness Adventures.

The children's programme is extensive: Ski Bunnies for three-year-olds, Ski Wizards And Surfers for children between five and 12 years of age, and a Freeriders Programme for experienced children up to the age of 17.

The somewhat drab town of Fernie, three miles and five minutes' drive to the east, has the potential but as yet little of the glitz of such Rocky Mountain mining-towns-turned-ski-resorts as Telluride or Crested Butte. However, one reporter found that staying here was preferable to staying at the resort.

Accommodation at the rapidly expanding base area includes condominiums and an assortment of brand new chalets and town houses, all of which can be booked through Resorts of the Canadian Rockies (☎ 800 258 7669). Cornerstone Lodge (☎ 403 256 8473) is 'the best location on the mountain'. In town, Park Place Lodge (☎ 403 256 8473) is 'spacious and modern' and serves 'epic breakfasts' but with 'disappointingly impersonal service', while the Old Nurses Residence (☎ 250 423 3091) is a B&B with large Victorian rooms. The Ginger Beef Restaurant is 'to be avoided, greasy platefuls of food pretending to be Chinese', whereas Gabriella's Restaurant at the base area is recommended: 'Italian food with Canadian bonhomie'.

TOURIST INFORMATION
Tel 1 250 423 4655
Fax 1 250 423 6644
Email info@skifernie.com
Web site www.skifernie.com

Kicking Horse
Top 8,037ft (2,450m) bottom 3,902ft (1,190m)

Kicking Horse is the newest major resort to be developed anywhere in the world in the past quarter of a century. The resort is two-and-a-half hours' drive from Calgary airport in the eastern British Columbia Purcell range. It opened in winter 2000–1 with a £11-m investment, which includes the highest mountain peak restaurant and the most hi-tech, eight-person gondola in Canada, as well as a characterful new base-lodge. Kicking Horse expands its terrain for the 2001–2 season to 4,000 acres, almost double the size of the ski area at Breckenridge. Its location was especially chosen for the champagne-quality snow, which at the summit averages 276 inches per winter. The gondola and two chair-lifts access a huge variety of terrain, ranging from chutes and easy bowls to long intermediate trails. One of Canada's oldest heli-skiing companies, Purcell Heli Skiing, is based here.

Kicking Horse lies about 20 minutes' drive by rough road uphill from the mining village of Golden BC. A Whistler-style village with shops, restaurants and hotels, plus condominiums at the resort base, should be finished during the 2001–2 season. Meanwhile, Golden provides a youth hostel, half a dozen B&Bs, and ten motels and lodges. Further away, about 30 miles on the other side of the scenic Kicking Horse Pass, the isolated lakeside cabins of Emerald Lake Lodge (☎ 250 439 5400) are uniquely Canadian. Golden boasts a number of youth-orientated coffee shops and cyber cafés ('exceptional soups at the Dogtooth Café'), while the log cabin Kicking Horse Grill is the best restaurant.

TOURIST INFORMATION
Tel 1 250 439 5400
Fax 1 403 245 8291
Email info@kickinghorseresort.com
Web site www.kickinghorseresort.com

Panorama
top 7,800ft (2,360m) bottom 3,800ft (1,158m)

Panorama lies a two-hour drive to the south-west of **Banff** and is on the edge of the Bugaboos mountain range, best known for its heli-skiing. Ten lifts provide more than 100 trails and 4,000ft of vertical drop, one of the longest in North America. More than half of the 2,847 acres of terrain is intermediate, with long, sweeping runs making the most of the impressive vertical drop. In 2001–2, Panorama extends its black-diamond (difficult) terrain by opening the Outback region in Taynton Bowl. Meanwhile beginners can gain confidence on easy and well-groomed trails. Panorama's RK heli-skiing operation, based in the village, involves an exhaustive instructional preamble, followed by three to four runs and a picnic lunch. Other activities include night-skiing and night-boarding, skating, sleigh rides, snowmobiling, tubing and an outdoor waterpark with swimming-pools and hot tubs. Wee Wascals Childcare looks after children aged 18 months to five years.

This is a family resort with most of the accommodation in condominiums. These include Ski Tip Lodge, Tamarack Lodge, Horsethief Lodge, Toby Creek Lodge, Hearthstone Townhomes and Panorama Springs. The Pine Inn is functional, and breakfast may be included in the price. Bookings for all these are available through Panorama Mountain Village Reservations (☎ 800 663 2929). The Kicking Horse is the liveliest bar, the Jackpine pub is great for a pint and darts, Heliplex offers 'fun food' and Toby Creek leads the way for fine dining.

Panorama's owners, Intrawest, have invested CDN$70 million to date in the resort, which consistently wins awards for its standard of service in North American ski magazines. The resort is part of the Canadian Rockies Super Pass, enabling you to ski at eight other resorts, including Banff/Lake Louise, Fernie, Nakiska, **Kimberley** and Fortress Mountain. The last possesses some excellent tree skiing and is particularly recommended for snowboarders.

TOURIST INFORMATION
Tel 1 250 342 6941
Fax 1 250 341 6262
Email paninfo@panoramaresort.com
Web site www.panoramaresort.com

Red Mountain
top 6,800ft (2,072m) bottom 3,888ft (1,185m)

Rossland, the distressed mining town that serves Red Mountain and Granite Mountain, had its heyday in the 1890s, when the discovery of gold and copper attracted fortune hunters including immigrant Scandinavians, who established the first local ski club in 1896. At first they skied Red Mountain, but later neighbouring Granite Mountain (the main ski area) was developed. Their original rugged view of skiing has, however, been carefully conserved. By refusing to invest in state-of-the-art lifts, the resort has kept the pioneering spirit intact, and the terrain has done the rest. The two mountains share 83 trails, four chair-lifts and a T-bar, and the longest run is an exhilarating roller-coaster, Long Squaw, which continues for four-and-a-half miles.

Located in the Kootenay Mountains, very close to the US border, Rossland enjoys a microclimate with higher temperatures and clearer skies than elsewhere in the Canadian Rockies. It is most readily reached via Spokane in Washington State, a two- to three-hour drive away, although it is also possible to fly into Castelgar via Calgary. Red's hard core is made up of ski bums, many of whom have small incomes and enjoy the machismo that goes with the territory throughout the winter. Most of the passing strangers see their visit as a rite-of-passage pilgrimage to a resort with a reputation for testing the best. Snowboarders view the resort as one of the top two in Canada (the other being Whistler), with especially good terrain for experienced freeriders.

Beginners and intermediates have limited prospects at Red Mountain. However, the old, slow, double chair-lift has been replaced by two triple chair-lifts, which have greatly improved access to some of the less formidable runs. Because everyone who skis Red skis trees, all the trails have sizeable moguls to add to the general sense of challenge. Most of the runs have open bowls interspersed with gladed sections of varying degrees of difficulty. Beer Belly, Short Squaw and Powder Fields are skiable one way or another, but the trees tighten up on Roots and Paleface, while Cambodia, with its 15-ft drops over frozen water-falls, is a stretch too far for most people. **Whitewater**, near Nelson, which has been described as a 'mini Alta', is well worth a visit for those who like their slopes steep and deep.

The main hotel in Rossland is the Uplander (☎ 250 362 7375), which has simple rooms but serves unexpectedly good meals in the Louis Blue Dining Room. The hotel also features the Powder Keg Pub, the town's hot-spot, with pool tables and a video ski game. The Ram's Head Inn (☎ 250 362 9577), a comfortable B&B establishment, is close enough to the slopes to ski back to, but the most convenient place to stay is the family-run Red Shutter Inn (☎ 250 362 5131), right next to the car park. The Swiss Alps Inn (☎ 250 362 7364) serves the best Rösti breakfast in town. The only on-mountain restaurant is at Paradise Lodge, while Rafters, on the third floor of the base-lodge, provides a simple but substantial lunch menu, a well-stocked bar and a cheerful ambience.

TOURIST INFORMATION
Tel 1 250 362 7384
Fax 1 250 362 5833
Email redmtn@ski-red.com
Web site www.ski-red.com

Silver Star
top 6,280ft (1,915m) bottom 3,780ft (1,152m)
The design of Silver Star is a law unto itself – a colourful ski-in ski-out village that is said to be modelled on a typical British Columbian mining town of the 1890s and painted in unexpectedly bright colours. However, the cheerful paint is welcome in a place where temperatures may dip to uncomfortable levels – even though it is said to have some of the best weather in the Canadian Rockies. Silver Star is currently undergoing a CDN$150-million expansion: improvements for 2000–1 included the construction of a new 10,000-sq-ft day-lodge and a slope-side youth hostel.

The most challenging skiing is to be found on the north-facing Putnam Creek side of the mountain, reached by a long, high-speed quad-chair. This area has a 'hike-in adventure skiing area' called Valhalla as well as a network of the highest number of double-black-diamond (very difficult) trails in British Columbia.

The south-facing Vance Creek area overlooking the village possesses long cruises suitable for intermediates: Sundance, Whiskey Jack and Interloper. The Yellow Chair serves a terrain park, and the Silver Queen Chair a beginners' area. In all, Silver Star boasts nine lifts covering 2,600 acres, and a proposed new quad-chair would give access to a further 4,000 acres.

The Craigellachie Room at Putnam Station Inn features beef, salmon and trout, while the Wine Cellar, also at the inn, produces a good selection of wines. Paradise Camp, at mid-mountain, offers a varied menu that includes buffalo burgers. The heart of the village, which attempts to rekindle the Victorian gaslight era, resembles a pedestrianised film set, with horse-drawn sleighs adding a further touch of theatricality. The Silver Star Club Resort (☎ 250 549 5191) is the most prominent hotel, and restaurants include Lucciano's Trattoria and Clementine's Dining Room as well as the Silver Lode Restaurant – a genuine Swiss outpost serving Apfelstrudel and Bratwurst. The town of Vernon is 12 miles away and provides a bigger choice of facilities. Star Kids Centre takes children from 18 months of age with optional ski lessons for those aged over three years.

TOURIST INFORMATION
Tel 1 250 542 0224
Fax 1 250 558 6090
Email reserv@junction.net
Web site www.skisilverstar.com

Sun Peaks
top 6,814ft (2,077m) bottom 3,970ft (1,210m)

Nancy Greene, who became the *grande dame* of Canadian ski-racing after winning the Olympic gold at Grenoble in 1968, came to Sun Peaks via Red Mountain, where she was born and raised, and Whistler, where she played a key role in developing the resort. Now she and her husband, Al Raine, have helped transform Tod Mountain – the local ski hill for the logging town of Kamloops – into Sun Peaks, a modern six-lift resort funded with CDN$150 million of Japanese money. The change of resort name from Tod Mountain was prompted by the need for an international image – Tod meaning 'death' in German.

Sun Peaks is one of the newest resorts in British Columbia and is considered to be one of the most beautiful villages in Canada, with a 3,000-ft vertical drop. It is situated deep in the British Columbian heartland, a four-hour drive east of Whistler. Alternatively, it can be reached by plane to Kamloops, via Vancouver or Calgary. In recent years, Sun Peaks has picked up a number of national accolades including *Ski Canada* magazine's award for Best Grooming, Best Hotel Service and Best Family Features.

The best skiing is on Mount Tod, while the Top of the World area is a steep-sided dome above the tree-line, with advanced skiing in chutes and bowls. The toughest terrain is on the lower half of the Burfield quad chair-lift, and Challenger is one of the steepest marked trails in Canada. Other demanding trails are on the Headwalls, a wide face of short, double-black-diamonds (very difficult) above the main on-mountain pit stop, the Sunburst Lodge. However, a five-mile green (easy) trail leads from the top of the skiing back to the resort, making it user-friendly for all standards.

Below the tree-line, the mountain flattens out progressively, with the easiest slopes just above the resort. This is an excellent arrangement for beginners and lower intermediates, who have their own zone served by the Sundance Express quad. Sun Peaks is an ideal resort for beginner snowboarders, but the more experienced are also well catered for by a vast terrain park boasting half-pipes and its own access lift. The ski area between the tree-line and the village, served by the Sunburst Quad, offers excellent moguls and some of the best advanced cruising terrain in this part of Canada.

The Village Day Lodge, a study in elegant design in local timber and glass, features a gastronomic restaurant and an excellent ski rental shop. Six slope-side hotels include Fireside Lodge (☎ 270 578 7842) and Hearthstone Lodge (☎ 250 578 8588), which both possess luxurious suites. Nancy Greene's Cahilty Lodge (☎ 250 578 7454), in a sheltered position overlooking the valley, offers four-star comfort. Sun Peaks Village is ski-in ski-out, and boasts an array of two dozen shops set in a pedestrian mall and new eateries ranging from steakhouses to a Japanese restaurant. The resort also features two outdoor skating-rinks and an outdoor swimming-pool.

TOURIST INFORMATION
Tel 1 250 578 7842
Fax 1 250 578 7843
Email info@sunpeaksresort.com
Web site www.sunpeaksresort.com

COLORADO

Arapahoe Basin
top 13,050ft (3,967m) bottom 10,780ft (3,283m)
Arapahoe Basin (or A-Basin as it is usually known) is a small, steep ski area that first opened its lift-served skiing in 1948. Its high altitude means that skiing is assured here until June, when **Keystone** and other neighbouring resorts have closed. A-Basin can be skied on the **Vail** lift pass, which also includes **Beaver Creek**, **Breckenridge** and Keystone. From the top of the Lenawee and Norway lifts, almost every run down the middle is intermediate or beginner terrain, and Dercum's Gulch gives access to the long easy trails of Wrangler, Sundance and Chisholm. At the top of the ski area, Palavicinni is one of the longest and steepest bump runs in North America, and the Alleys and East Wall provide some exciting off-piste. Five lifts serve 490 acres of terrain.

A-Basin provides a ski and snowboarding school for adults and children but does not have any of its own accommodation. The nearest is six miles away at Keystone. The Legends Café and the 6th Alley Bar are the two most popular après-ski venues. Kids Room takes children from four months to seven years old with optional one-to-one lessons for older children, while Children's Centre Nursery caters for children from one to three years old.

TOURIST INFORMATION
Tel 1 970 496 7077
Fax 1 970 496 4546
Email abasin@colorado.net
Web site www.arapahoebasin.com

Copper Mountain
top 12,313ft (3,767m) bottom 9,712ft (2,926m)

Copper Mountain, situated on the Denver side of the Vail Pass, has been the subject of a complete $400-million makeover since it was acquired in 1998 by Canadian resort developer Intrawest. The new resort base is slowly emerging from the initial building-site phase, and contractors promise to complete the second construction phase imminently. The car-free village is set around four new lodges and plazas with shops and restaurants. This should be a major improvement on the original village, which was constructed in a style reminiscent of a French purpose-built resort and which may explain the presence of Club Med. One reporter portrayed the resort as 'having all the aesthetic appeal of a North American Les Menuires'. However, the actual skiing is well worth the visit. Copper likes to describe its ski area as one of the best-designed in North America.

There is a natural tendency for the tree-lined trails to become more difficult as you move east (left on the piste map). Thus, advanced skiers and boarders tend to stick to the main face of Copper Peak, and beginners will find little beyond their capabilities on the west side of the resort. In between, the terrain is mainly intermediate. Copper Bowl and Spaulding Bowl provide some of the best off-piste skiing in Colorado, with the latter full of natural jumps and lips for riders. Copper possesses a total of 21 lifts covering 118 groomed trails, and the mountain summit is reached in eight minutes by the six-person detachable Super Bee chair-lift.

Copper Mountain Ski and Snowboard School offers group and private lessons, as well as bumps and powder workshops and beginner packages. Most of the accommodation is in apartments. Copper's nightlife is fairly quiet, with the exception of the popular O'Shea's restaurant. The Double Diamond Grill and good-value Farley's Prime Chop House are recommended. Imperial Palace is an Far-Eastern restaurant that 'does a first-class take-away'. Molly B's serves burgers, steaks and pasta.

The Copper Mountain Racquet and Athletic Club boasts excellent facilities, including a swimming-pool, indoor tennis and racket-ball courts. Belly Button Babies kindergarten accepts children from two months to two years old, and its stablemate, the Belly Button Bakery, caters for children over two and skiers over three years of age. Copper Mountain arranges Junior and Senior ski programmes for children.

TOURIST INFORMATION
Tel 1 970 968 2882
Fax 1 970 968 6227
Email cmr-res@ski-copper.com
Web site www.ski-copper.com

Crested Butte
top 12,162ft (3,707m) bottom 9,100ft (2,774m)

This small, historic town is one of the most attractive ski resorts in Colorado. In the old town's Main Street, 40 of the original nineteenth-century buildings, with their colourful wooden façades, have been converted into shops and restaurants, giving the place a Wild West atmosphere. The town is overlooked by the Butte (pronounced as in 'beaut-iful'), which is a mountain that stands alone. Hotels and guest-houses scattered around the town include the Nordic Inn, a family-run ski lodge that is firmly recommended. The other option is to stay at the Sheraton Resort (☎ 970 349 8000) or at the new Club Med (☎ 020-7348 3333 in UK), which takes children from four years old and is on the site of the old Marriot. Both are at the base of the ski slopes, three miles away from the town. Crested Butte's nightlife has a cowboy atmosphere and is mainly good value. The Idle Spur has live music, steaks and beer, and Talk of the Town is another busy place to try.

Crested Butte is renowned for its steep skiing and each year hosts ski-extreme championships. At the opposite end of the scale, it also has some of the easiest skiing in Colorado. The resort's 14 lifts serve 1,434 acres of ski terrain. A high 58 per cent of the trails are classed as difficult, 29 per cent intermediate and 13 per cent easy. The Extreme Limits area comprises some 550 acres of ungroomed extreme skiing and snow-boarding, which locals claim is some of the most challenging in Colorado. Off-piste enthusiasts would be wise to hire the services of a local mountain guide or at the very least buy The Extreme Limits Guide – a lift and trail guide telling you where it is safe to ride and ski. Crested Butte's terrain park is designated for riders only.

Children under two years old ski free, children under 16 years pay their age in dollars per day. The Baby Bears kindergarten takes potty-trained toddlers. Hot-air balloooning is a popular non-skiing activity here.

TOURIST INFORMATION
Tel 1 970 349 2222 (freephone 0800 894085 in UK)
Fax 1 970 349 2397
Email info@cbmr.com
Web site www.crestedbutteresort.com

Durango
top 10,822ft (3,299m) bottom 8,793ft (2,680m)

This is the new name for the ski resort of **Purgatory**, which has unfortunately succumbed to the machinations of the marketing team employed to give it an interstate and international image. This purpose-built, alpine-style resort 25 miles from Durango Airport received enthusiastic praise from reporters: 'it has an old town feel in an unspoilt forest area of the Rockies. We felt very welcome and shall be endeavouring to make a return visit soon.' The ski area boasts 11 lifts, including a new six-person quad, and 1,200 acres of trails.

Durango's Ski and Snowboard School offers group and private lessons to adults and children, while the kindergarten accepts non-skiing children from two months old, and from three years for skiing. Snowboarders are well catered for with the Pitchfork Snowboard Park. The Adaptive Sports Association provides lessons for disabled skiers and is ranked as one of the best ski schools of its type in the USA.

Powderhouse, which serves pizzas, pasta and salads, and Dante's ('downstairs self-service, upstairs sit-down service') are the only two on-mountain restaurants, while Columbine Station is at the base of the slopes of the same name. Purgy's in the village centre serves pizzas and Purgy's Pale Ale to live music. Powdermonkey Grill is a ten-minute, free shuttle bus ride from the centre and receives favourable reports. Between them the ski area and the town of Durango have more than 50 eateries including Mexican, Far-Eastern and Mediterranean restaurants.

Mountain area hotels include the Purgatory Village Hotel (☎ 970 385 2100) and Sheraton Tamarron Resort (☎ 970 259 2000), and the Twilight View Condos are recommended: 'huge picture windows and balconies overlooking the ski slopes'. Of the nine B&Bs, Apple Orchard Inn (☎ 970 247 0751), Blue Lake Ranch (☎ 970 385 4537), Country Sunshine (☎ 970 247 2853) and River House (☎ 970 247 4775) all boast fireplaces and hot tubs. All bookings can be made through Durango Central Reservations (☎ 800 982 61030).

Other activities in the resort include cross-country, sleigh rides, snowmobiling, tubing and visits to the local hot springs.

TOURIST INFORMATION
Tel 1 970 247 9000
Fax 1 970 385 2131
Email lwright@durangomountain.com
Web site www.durangomountainresort.com

Steamboat
top 10,568ft (3,221m) bottom 6,900ft (2,103m)

Steamboat lies at the foot of Rabbit Ears Pass in north-west Colorado, a 3½-hour drive from downtown Denver. Winter sports started here as long ago as 1912, when a Norwegian, Carl Howelsen, introduced ski-jumping lessons. Downhill skiing took off in the 1960s, triggered by the opening of the first double chair-lift on Storm Mountain. Snowboarders are particularly welcome and account for one in three of the lift tickets sold. The resort is part of the empire of the American Skiing Company and provides 20 lifts serving 2,939 acres of skiing and 142 trails.

Steamboat is a genuine cowboy town and trades heavily on this cowboy motif in its marketing strategy. Each January it hosts The Cowboy Downhill, a unique slalom with roping and saddling elements contested by more than 100 professional rodeo riders in full costume.

The skiing covers three interlinked mountains: Sunshine Peak, Storm Peak and Mount Werner. The area's modern lift system is backed up by extensive snowmaking, and the terrain is famous for its tree skiing. The Silver Bullet gondola takes snow-users up to the Thunderhead mid-station, and two high-speed quads allow them to fan out rapidly over the upper slopes. The development of the Morningside Park bowl off the back of Storm Peak provides gentle terrain and better access to the rugged skiing off the face of Mount Werner. The Pioneer Ridge sector opens up 12 trails mainly for advanced skiers.

The wide, flat area at the base of the gondola is an ideal place to learn to ski or snowboard and is served by six beginner lifts. Steamboat Ski School teaches adults, children and teenagers, while the Billy Kidd Center provides more advanced training in bumps, racing and other disciplines. The Kids Vacation Center takes skiing children from two to six years old, and babies and non-skiing children are looked after at Kiddie Corrall Child Care.

In tune with the current trend in the Rockies, Steamboat features gourmet lunches as a supplement to cafeteria fare. The most sophisticated option is Hazie's at the Thunderhead mid-station. The alternative sit-down choice, Ragnar's at Rendezvous Saddle, specialises in Scandinavian dishes. Both the Thunderhead and Rendezvous self-services have sundeck barbecues.

Visitors stay either at the purpose-built Steamboat base area or four miles away in the town of Steamboat Springs. The Steamboat Grand Resort and Conference Center (☎ 970 871 5500) – the resort's own venture into the hotel business – possesses 328 rooms and 'excellent cuisine' at the Cabin Restaurant. The Sheraton Steamboat (☎ 970 879 222) is recommended, too. But the real action is in the Old Town area of Steamboat Springs, which houses shops that go far beyond the normal range of ski-related goods, as well as the best restaurants. The Harbor Hotel (☎ 970 879 1522) and the Alpiner Lodge (☎ 970 879 1430) are among the most popular hotels.

When the lifts close, beer lovers gather at Slopeside in Ski Time Square and the Steamboat Brewery and Tavern on Lincoln Avenue in Steamboat Springs. Watering-holes include the Hilltop Bar, the Tugboat and Dos Amigos, which are all near the mountain base. In the downtown area, Tap House is for live music, and the Old Town Pub provides pool tables. Cellar Lounge is lively until late, as is Harwigs.

For a resort of this size, the range and quality of the restaurants are impressive. Sevens at the Sheraton represents hotel-chain grandeur and expense, but finer dining can be found at L'Apogee, Antares,

Giovanni's and the Steamboat Yacht Club. Riggio's specialises in cheaper Italian fare, and the Chart House boasts the best salad bar in town. There is Chinese food at the Panda Garden and the Canton, sushi at Yama Chan's and Mexican at La Montana. Another option is a snowcat-ride to Ragnar's for a five-course dinner and live music.

Steamboat offers an interesting variety of other sports ranging from bob-sleigh and bungee-jumping to dog-sledding, hot-air ballooning, ice-driving, night-skiing, skating, ski-jumping, sleigh rides, snowmobiling, swimming and winter fly-fishing. Steamboat Powder Cats runs day snowcat-skiing trips to Buffalo Pass in the Routt National Park, a few miles out of town. The natural springs at Strawberry Park Hot Springs, also a few miles out of town, provide a less stressful alternative.

TOURIST INFORMATION
Tel 1 970 879 6111
Fax 1 970 879 7844
Email info@steamboat-ski.com
Web site www.steamboat.com

Telluride
top 12,247ft (3,734m) bottom 8,725ft (2,660m)

A colourful history surrounds Telluride, an old mining town in a beautiful box-canyon in the San Juan Mountains. At the height of the gold rush, 5,000 prospectors crowded into the town, the name of which derives either from tellurium, a non-metallic element in gold and silver ore, or less probably from 'to hell you ride' – a sobriquet that could apply to Butch Cassidy, who robbed his first bank on Main Street in 1889 before escaping on horseback. In keeping with the rollicking climate of those times, Main Street divided the town, with a residential district on one side and a flourishing red light district on the other.

The wide street, dominated by the New Sheridan Hotel (it was new in the Victorian times) and the original court house, is architecturally little changed today, but over the last decade the nature of the resort has been radically altered by the construction of the Mountain Village Resort. Four miles away by road, it is connected to the town by gondola between 7am and 11pm on weekdays and between 7am and midnight at weekends. The development of condominiums, shops and a golf course triggered a real-estate boom and attracted a number of Hollywood investors. They have now mainly moved on to fresh pastures, although Tom Cruise remains a regular visitor. Both town and mountain village are equally convenient for the skiing, although the delightful town is one of the prime reasons for visiting this remote corner of Colorado.

The backbone of the area is the appropriately named See Forever, a long, rolling blue (intermediate) run from the top of the skiing to the mountain village; it provides encouragement or speed, according to ability and taste. The Galloping Goose area, isolated to one side of the mountain village, is perfect for beginners. The giant terrain park with a half-pipe is the largest in Colorado and was built to the same specifications as the one used in the Nagano Winter Olympics, and Telluride is one of the best places in the state to learn to snowboard. Aggressive skiers and riders head for the double-black-diamond (very difficult) Spiral Stairs or Gold Hill for short but steep off-piste glades.

Having replaced four older chair-lifts with three high-speed quads, Telluride is finally going ahead with its expansion plan at Prospect Bowl. After years on the drawing board, the new area is scheduled to open for 2001–2. Three new, detachable quad chairs will increase the expert terrain, while a large wooded area of 733 acres around Prospect Bowl will open up further intermediate slopes. There will also be a new beginner area. The project, when completed, will almost double Telluride's lift-served terrain.

The choice of where to stay is dictated by the nightlife, which is much better in the downtown area. The New Sheridan Hotel (☎ 800 200 1891) is central and traditional, with a handsome mahogany bar, while the restaurant serves fashionable dishes of elk, venison and ostrich. The Ice House (☎ 800 544 3436) is modern, central, smart and convenient for the Oak Street base-station, while the best placed hotel in town is Camel's Garden (☎ 888 772 2635), right next to the gondola station. The sprawling Peaks Resort (☎ 800 789 2220) at Mountain Village is 'the ultimate in luxury spa hotels', and Club St Sophia offers fine on-mountain dining reached by gondola. Telluride Sports sells an excellent range of ski clothing and equipment.

TOURIST INFORMATION
Tel 1 970 728 3041
Fax 1 970 728 6475
Email skitelluride@telski.com
Web site www.telski.com

Winter Park
top 12,057ft (3,676m) bottom 8,973ft (2,735m)

Winter Park is the nearest recreation ground for the people of Denver, only 67 miles away, and is owned by the city council. A high number of skiers and snowboarders commute here each Saturday and Sunday from Denver by snow train, which conveniently deposits them at the foot of the lifts. An Amtrack rail service stops at nearby Fraser on weekdays. Winter Park has been steadily expanding in recent years with the development of a new base-area village that is three miles from the town. Future plans include a gondola link directly from the town to the ski area, and land has already been purchased to this aim. However, there is now considerable uncertainty over the short-term future of Winter Park. In order to compete with other major Colorado ski areas, a huge level of investment is required that is not available in the public sector. While the city of Denver may be reluctant to sell, it may be faced with little choice. The new base-area village is built around the Zephyr

Mountain Lodge (☎ 970 726 6669), which comprises a restaurant, pub and ski shop as well as 230 condominiums.

The skiing here is excellent, with long, wide trails, challenging mogul fields, few mid-week queues, efficient lifts, perfectly manicured slopes and usually reliable snow conditions. The area is divided into two main sections: Winter Park and Vasquez Ridge, which have mostly intermediate trails; and Mary Jane, which features hard bump-skiing as well as tree-level runs and long blues (intermediates) from the Parsenn Bowl. At present there are 22 lifts, including seven detachable quads, which cover 2,886 acres. Winter Park boasts three terrain parks and a half-pipe for snowboarders, while the children's area has a 'magic carpet' lift where the ski school takes beginners.

Mountain restaurants include the Dining Room at the Lodge at Sunspot, which is on the summit of Winter Park Mountain, as well as several cafeterias and a pizza parlour mid-mountain.

Winter Park's wild neighbour is **Berthoud Pass**, named after a Victorian surveyor. The resort first opened in the 1930s and has since survived a chequered history of openings and closures. What you will find is just two chair-lifts, but with the help of a shuttle-bus service these open up 1,000 acres of some of Colorado's most exciting skiing terrain on both sides of the pass. For the present, the unsophisticated town of Winter Park (two miles from the ski area) provides the main accommodation, with private homes attractively set in the woods above.

Winter Park boasts a separate après-ski 'trail map' dedicated to pubs and eateries. The Black Diamond Nightlife Tour takes in 23 restaurants and bars, kicking off at The Club Car at the base of Mary Jane and ending up at The Crooked Creek Saloon.

TOURIST INFORMATION
Tel 1 970 726 5514
Fax 1 970 726 5823
Email kate_mullany@mail.skiwinterpark.com
Web site www.winterparkresort.com

IDAHO

Sun Valley
top 9,150ft (2,789m) bottom 5,750ft (1,753m)

America's oldest ski resort has been a magnet for the Hollywood élite since it opened in 1936. As with so much of the USA, Sun Valley's rise to prominence was railway-led. Averell Harriman, then the chairman of the Union Pacific Railway, commissioned Count Felix Schaffgotsch to find a place to build a ski resort near a Union Pacific rail terminus. His choice, the mountainside near the dilapidated mining town of Ketchum, was inspired by its terrain and its sunshine records. In August 1936 the world's first chair-lift, adapted from a system for moving stems of bananas in Panama, was installed. However, no allowance was made for the snowfall – by the winter, it had completely ground to a halt.

Today, the skiing is divided between Dollar/Elkhorn, the site of some of the original lifts (the original was on Proctor Mountain) and the much more demanding slopes of Bald Mountain, which has earned a reputation as one of the best single ski mountains in the United States. It provides a 3,400-ft vertical drop, and the whole ski area is covered by a network of 17 lifts. The upmarket clientèle has encouraged the establishment of some excellent restaurants, on and off the mountain. The Soupçon and the Evergreen Bistro offer gourmet dining, while the Pioneer Steakhouse, Clint Eastwood's favourite, is cheerful and much cheaper. Sun Valley's Elkhorne Resort and Sun Valley Resort both contain suites, rooms and condominiums. Bookings should be made through Sun Valley Central Reservations (☎ 800 634 3347).

TOURIST INFORMATION
Tel 1 208 726 3423
Fax 1 208 726 4533
Email svmkting@micron.net
Web site www.visitsunvalley.com

MAINE

Sunday River
top 3,140ft (957m) bottom 800ft (244m)

Sunday River is one of the largest East Coast resorts. It belongs to the American Skiing Company, whose portfolio also includes Steamboat in Colorado, Heavenly in California, and The Canyons in Utah. The picturesque state of Maine suffers at times from sparse natural snow, but given low temperatures this is of little consequence thanks to an arsenal of custom-built cannons that blast out man-made crystals throughout the winter. Unlike European artificial snow, which is harder and more difficult to ski on than the real thing, their recipe feels remarkably natural and can cover up to 92 per cent of the total terrain.

The range and quality of the skiing compares favourably with that of a medium-sized resort in Italy or France. Fortunately, Sunday River is situated in a rural area sufficiently far from New York not to suffer from the overcrowding to which the Vermont resorts are prone. The slopes are uncrowded even during high season ('we had the steeper runs almost entirely to ourselves').

The resort is flanked at one end by the Grand Summit Hotel (☎ 207 824 3500) and at the other by the Jordan Grand Resort (☎ 207 824 5000). In between lies the main base area beneath a ridge of eight peaks offering a variety of terrain, ranging from beginner trails to Chutzpah, one of the ten most extreme trails in eastern USA. A total of 654 acres of skiing is served by a substantial network of 18 lifts, and the two main base areas are also linked by an efficient bus service.

The Perfect Turn ski and snowboard school offers a wide range of tuition. Courses include cross-country, skiing for the disabled and women's ski clinics. Sunday River is an ideal resort for families with children of all ages and for all standards of snow-user. It is also popular with British school groups. Tiny Turns Childcare intersperses play with one-hour private ski lessons until your child is ready for his or her first group ski class. Children aged four to six can join all-day Mogul Munchkins classes and seven- to 12-year olds join the Mogul Meisters.

The resort is rider-friendly ('lift operators slowed down for snowboarders'), with two major terrain parks, a separate mini-pipe for beginners, a floodlit half-pipe and a boardercross course. Yet another half-pipe and a top-to-bottom terrain park opened for the 2000–1 season. Floodlit tubing at the White Cap Fun Center is a popular evening activity, along with skating and night-snowboarding. The nearby small town of Bethel is the quintessential Maine community, complete with a plethora of craft shops and restaurants.

TOURIST INFORMATION
Tel 1 207 824 3000
Fax 1 207 824 5110
Email snowtalk@sundayriver.com
Web site www.sundayriver.com

MONTANA

Big Sky
top 11,150ft (3,399m) bottom 6,970ft (2,125m)

In Montana, big is good but bigger is better, which provides the rationale for the Lone Peak Tram – a tiny cable-car cabin that briefly and slightly dubiously gave Big Sky the right to claim the longest vertical drop in the USA from the previous holder Jackson Hole. (Both resorts have now been upstaged by Snowmass.) Nevertheless, with an impressive 18 lifts and 3,600 skiable acres, Big Sky's skiing is worthwhile and its extensive slopes are among the least crowded in the northern hemisphere. This is not surprising, as it is an hour's drive from Bozeman, the nearest airport, and seven hours from Salt Lake City. However, the wide, open snowscape is attractive, especially to Europeans accustomed to crowds. The runs are on two well-linked mountains: Lone Peak, which has the bulk of the serious skiing, and Andesite, where beginners and intermediates will find plenty to occupy them. Skiers have to hike to reach the A–Z chutes, but all except the most extreme skiers will prefer the bowl off the triple-chair and the glades off the slow, 'experts-only' Challenger chair. Further new trails are served by the triple chair in the new Lone Moose ski sector.

Big Sky was created by Chet Huntley, the late NBC newscaster of the 1960s and a Montana man who wanted to give something back to the state in which he was born. The Huntley Lodge and the Shoshone

Condominium Hotel (☎ 406 995 5000 for central reservations) pro-vide comfortable ski-in ski-out accommodation, but the nightlife is lim-ited to a poker game in Chet's Gaming Parlor and a small assortment of bars, such as Dante's Inferno, Scissorbills, Lolo's Saloon and the Black Bear Bar and Grill. At lunchtime, Mountain Top Pizza, the Lone Peak Café and the Sun Dog Café are the main sources of sustenance.

The road from Bozeman winds along the River Gallatin, where Robert Redford directed *A River Runs Through It*, a taster for the mag-nificent scenery that makes Montana a favoured hideaway for contem-porary Hollywood stars. Andie MacDowell rates the acreage of her ranch as 'too big to count'. There is a sense of history too, with Little Bighorn, the location of Custer's last stand, a mere two-hour drive away. As Montana has abolished the speed limit, however, that may well be quite a distance.

TOURIST INFORMATION
Tel 1 406 995 5000
Fax 1 406 995 5001
Email info@bigskyresort.com
Web site www.bigskyresort.com

NEW MEXICO

Taos
top 11,819ft (3,603m) bottom 9,207ft (2,807m)

Taos likes to describe itself as 'the last bastion of pure skiing – a lot of sun, snow, mountains … and no snowboarders'. Provided you prefer two planks to one, the Taos Valley possesses a charm that is all its own. Although it is at the same latitude as Rome, the snow in a north-facing bowl in the Carson National Forest is surprisingly good. A few miles down the road, the cacti and sagebrushes that characterise the New Mexican desert stretch as far as the eye can see. The town of Taos, an art-led, cosmopolitan melting pot with a dominant Native American culture, is 20 miles away.

The Taos Ski Valley was created by the legendary Ernie Blake, a German-born Swiss who discovered what he recognised as perfect ski-ing terrain while flying over the Rockies in the early 1950s. In 1956 Blake was joined by the French racer Jean Mayer in an enterprise that still combines Teutonic efficiency with Gallic flair. Blake was a firm believer in ski classes, even for cocky Americans who thought that they could ski, and he created the best ski school in the country in his own image. Mayer's interest was also gastronomic, and he indulged it at the slope-side Hotel St Bernard (☎ 505 776 2251), which is usually booked out for the next season by early June.

Blake died in 1989, but Taos continues in the same distinguished tradition under the stewardship of his son Mickey and son-in-law Chris Stagg, the local mayor. The mountain is imposing, especially from the village perspective. Al's Run, the tough mogul field under the lift line, makes such an impression that a notice reassures visitors of easier skiing further up the hill. While this is true, there is also even more difficult skiing, especially off the high traverse, where trails such as Oster, Tresckow and Stauffenberg (German officers who plotted against Hitler) testify to the founder's anti-Nazi stance during World War II. Sir Arnold Lunn, the father of modern European skiing, is also commemorated on the trail map. The key run in the beginner's area is Honeysuckle, while intermediates should head for Porcupine and Powderhorn, both ego-boosting cruisers. Taos has a total of 72 trails covered by 12 chair-lifts. Snowboarding is banned.

Taos Ski Valley is extremely compact, and hotel accommodation is limited. The St Bernard was one of the first hotels to be built here, while the Thunderbird Lodge (☎ 505 776 2280) is comfortable and hosts live jazz. The Sagebrush Inn (☎ 505 758 2254) was built in 1929 and is in Taos town. The other hotels are the Edelweiss (☎ 505 776 2301) and the Rio Hondo Condos (☎ 505 776 2347). The choice of condominiums is wider, with the Kandahar (☎ 505 776 2226) at the top of the list of recommendations. Four miles down the valley, the adobe Quail Inn Ridge Resort (☎ 505 776 2211) features a desert ambience, indoor and outdoor tennis and an outdoor swimming-pool.

TOURIST INFORMATION
Tel 1 505 776 2291
Fax 1 505 776 8596
Email tsv@skitaos.org
Web site www.skitaos.org

QUEBEC

Mont Sainte-Anne
top 2,625ft (800m) bottom 575ft (175m)

With a vertical drop of more than 2,000ft, 56 trails covering 40 miles, 13 lifts (including an eight-person gondola) and skiing on three sides of the mountain, Mont Sainte-Anne is one of the most significant ski and snowboarding areas in eastern Canada. The resort enjoys magnificent views across the drifting ice-pack of the St Lawrence river and Quebec City 25 miles away. Like all destinations in Quebec, Mont Sainte-Anne – nicknamed La Belle et La Bête (Beauty and The Beast) – can be very cold in the depths of winter. In spite of this, 15 trails are open for night-skiing and snowboarding on what is claimed to be the biggest illuminated vertical drop in Canada.

The modern base area, with electronic ticketing, includes four restaurants, with three more on the mountain itself. There is a 282,500-sq-ft terrain park as well as half-pipes. Eighty per cent of the mountain possesses snowmaking capabilities. The Children Center welcomes children from six months to ten years, and Kinderski and Kindersnow programmes mix games with ski or snowboard lessons for children of four and over. Children under seven ski free. A tubing centre has now been opened at the base area, and off-piste skiing and riding are allowed on the previously restricted west side of the mountain.

For convenience, most people stay at the Chateau Mont Sainte-Anne (☎ 418 827 5211), at the base area, or the Chalets Mont Sainte-Anne (☎ 418 827 5776), a condominium complex close by. The Hotel Val des Neiges (☎ 418 827 5711) is at the base area, too. Mont Sainte-Anne claims to have the largest cross-country trail network in Canada, and dog-sledding, parapente, skating, snowmobiling and snowshoeing are also available.

A new Carte-Blanche multipass allows skiers and boarders to visit the nearby resorts of **Stoneham**, **Le Massif** and **Le Relais**. Le Massif, right on the banks of the St Lawrence river boasts a vertical drop of 2,645ft – the biggest in eastern Canada.

TOURIST INFORMATION
Tel 1 418 827 4561
Fax 1 418 827 3121
Email neige@mont-sainte-anne.com
Web site www.mont-sainte-anne.com

Andorra

Beginners ✳✳✳ Intermediates ✳✳ Snowboarders ✳✳

With the steady decline in popularity of eastern Europe as a value-for-money ski destination, Andorra has consolidated its position as the favoured country for those on a tight budget. Unlike Bulgaria and Romania in recent seasons, the tiny Pyrenean principality has been blessed with abundant snow cover, although 2000–1 was poor in comparison with the two previous winters. Even more importantly, while the former Communist states rely on archaic lift systems that date from the Khrushchev era, Andorra has invested £52 million to create a sophisticated network of gondolas and detachable chairs to rival many Alpine resorts. The country's first and only cable-car now provides a welcome link between **Pal** and **Arinsal**. It is a pity that this enormous nationwide makeover is marred by the continuing squabble between Pas and **Soldeu**, which prevents skiers from enjoying their combined area on one weekly lift pass.

> ✔ Low prices
> ✔ Facilities for children
> ✔ Excellent skiing tuition
> ✔ Lively nightlife
> ✘ Few mountain restaurants
> ✘ Lift queues
> ✘ Lack of resort ambience
> ✘ Heavy traffic (Pas de la Casa)

Somehow along the way Andorra has gained the youthful allure of indecent Ibiza and combined it with the comfortable family reliability of opulent Obergurgl to create the 'in' snow destination for Euro-youth. At the same time, a blossoming sense of national identity has led to a cultural renaissance. The 1960s concrete apartment blocks have given way to attractive new buildings of natural stone, which are in keeping with the beauty of their mountain surroundings.

Catalan, once banned by General Franco, is taught in schools along with Spanish and French, and has emerged once again as the national language. Despite their considerable differences, Soldeu and **Pas de la Casa** offer by far the best skiing in the country. Prices are similar, but Soldeu is actively creating a smarter image in contrast to the 'yoof' culture that thrives in Pas de la Casa and, to a lesser extent, in Arinsal. The standard of ski school tuition (particularly in Soldeu–El Tarter) is high, and most of it is provided by native English-speakers. Andorra, where the population is outnumbered six-to-one by seasonal guest-workers, welcomes foreign ski teachers.

The new Andorra is anxious to portray an image that goes beyond wall-to-wall perfume shops, supermarkets and boutiques selling cosmetics, booze, clothing and ski equipment at knock-down prices.

Anyone looking for ski bargains should consider the fact that resort shops are allegedly used as dumping grounds by manufacturers for last year's products. However, reporters complained that 'the value-for-money of shopping has now been eroded almost completely, with bargains few and far between'. As of 1 January 2002 the euro becomes the official currency of Andorra.

The choice of where to stay is expanding each year. The valley town of **Encamp** has a giant gondola financed by Pas de la Casa, which rises to the top of Grau Roig. New hotels are under construction to encourage skiers to base themselves here or in more cosmopolitan **Andorra la Vella** from where they can still enjoy Pas de la Casa's ski area without having to negotiate daily the winding valley road that passes temptingly through Soldeu–El Tarter. These moves have added fuel to a centuries-old vendetta between Pas de la Casa and Soldeu. The latter has responded by building another giant gondola from the neighbouring community of **Canillo** – also on the valley road – to the top of their territory.

Arcalis
top 2,624m (8,609ft) bottom 1,940m (6,363ft)

Arcalis is a ski area without a village, situated at the end of a remote and beautiful valley. It has five chair-lifts and eight drag-lifts serving 26km of piste. In 2000 the sunny Creussans area was incorporated, with a new quad chair-lift taking you up to the ridge at 2,624m for a winding 2km blue (easy) run down past the lake to La Coma restaurant. A timed slalom course has also been introduced. The kindergarten cares for children from 12 months old while Snowgarden looks after children aged four to nine. Visitors are almost exclusively Spanish – few British and hardly any French make their way to this remote location. What they are missing is some of the most challenging terrain in Andorra. The resort is situated 20 minutes' drive from the villages of **Ordino** and **La Massana**, both of which offer a reasonable choice of accommodation. Hotel Rutllan (☎ 83 50 00) in La Massana is described as 'the perfect jumping-off point for Pal–Arinsal and Arcalis'.

TOURIST INFORMATION
Tel 376 73 70 80
Fax 376 83 92 25
Email ito@andorra.ad
Web site www.andorra.ad/comuns/ordino

Pal–Arinsal
top 2,573m (8,442ft) bottom 1,550m (5,084ft)

The separate resorts of Arinsal and Pal have now been linked by a 50-person cable-car to create a single ski area of 30 lifts serving 63km of groomed runs. On the Arinsal side the skiing takes place in a bleak and treeless area enclosed between two ridges that funnel back to the large reception centre above the Arinsal gondola station. This houses restaurants, bars, the ski school and sports shops. The two main pistes –

the black (difficult) La Devesa and the blue (easy) Les Marrades 1 –
drop from the top of the Arinsal gondola down to the resort but are
sometimes closed due to lack of snow. The new cable-car takes skiers
from the top station of Arinsal to Coll de la Botella, where a chair-lift
then gives access to Pal's more intermediate skiing. From the top of the
Pal ski area at the Pic del Cubil you can either return to Coll de la
Botella via two red (intermediate) runs or ski over towards Refugi Pla
de la Cot on a choice of four red pistes. Off to one side is Edifici La
Caubella, where most of the shorter and easier runs are situated.

The Arinsal terrain park, which has a half-pipe, was enlarged during
the 2000–1 season and caters for the high percentage of riders among
the resort's clientèle. Escola d'Esqui d'Arinsal and Escola d'Esqui de
Pal are the ski and snowboard schools, and the two heli-ski companies
are Heliand and Helitrans. Two kindergartens cater for children aged
one to four, and two Snowgardens look after four- to eight-year-olds.

The mountain restaurants in Arinsal serve 'ubiquitous burgers 'n'
beer in surroundings that make up for in price what they lack in charm'.
Quo Vadis is a popular bar with videos. Surf Bar, Cisco's and Bar El
Derbi are the alternatives. Much of the accommodation is cheap and
primitive. The Poblado apartments (☎ 83 51 22) are recommended,
while Hotel Rossell (☎ 83 50 92) has 'basic food'. Attitude and service
at the Grand Hotel Font (☎ 83 52 94) came under fire from reporters.
Residència Daina (☎ 83 60 05), 15 minutes' walk from the centre, is a
newer addition, while Residència Janet (☎ 83 50 88) is a small, family-
run establishment on the outskirts of Arinsal. Recommended restaurants include El Rusc ('excellent food in amicable surroundings')
and La Borda ('authentic Catalan cuisine and a great night out').

TOURIST INFORMATION
Tel (Arinsal) 376 73 70 20 / (Pal) 376 73 70 00
Fax (Arinsal) 376 83 62 42 / (Pal) 376 83 59 04
Email pal@arinsal.ad
Web site www.palarinsal.com

Pas de la Casa–Grau Roig
top 2,580m (8,465ft) bottom 2,095m (6,872ft)
Pas de la Casa is a border town that divides not only countries but cul-
tures; a tawdry small-time Tijuana that promises (but not necessarily
delivers) rock-bottom prices along with a heady release from the strictures of bourgeois existence across the frontier in provincial France.
Every weekend the youth of Toulouse come over the border in search of
day-time snow and night-time action in a town where the pub crawl has
been raised to an art form. They are joined, in coaches from Carcassone,
Toulouse and Barcelona airports, by hordes of Brits in search of holiday
debauchery. 'One of the cheapest places in the world to be sick in', says
one reporter. Snow-users aged between 16 and 25 might find a holiday
here off – and even on – the slopes an enjoyable experience. If you are
older, you might do well to look elsewhere.

The fundamental impression of Pas de la Casa is of a brash city of giant advertising hoardings, scores of tacky shops, crowds of shoppers and choking traffic fumes. The architecture is both higgledy-piggledy and ugly. The town feels like a resort that owes its existence to bargain basements rather than skiing. Supermarket shelves are piled high with cut-price alcohol, much of it produced locally.

The skiing is linked to the neighbouring ski area of **Grau Roig** and jointly they offer 31 lifts and 100km of the pick of Andorra's skiing. This in turn should be connected to the 29 lifts and 86km of piste belonging to Soldeu–El Tarter on the far side of the pass. The lift links are in position, but the two bitter neighbours have for five years promised but failed to agree upon a joint lift pass. Further negotiations were taking place during the summer of 2001 – but don't count on a lasting solution. The rivals originally fell out over common land grazing rights in the eighteenth century, and relationships remain almost comically volatile. Pas de la Casa's brochure and lift map fail to show any lifts at all in Soldeu.

Pas de la Casa's own skiing takes place mainly in two bowls on either side of the 2,600-m pass, making it the highest resort in Andorra. The main slopes are well covered by snow-cannon. The Font Negra piste above the village is floodlit for night-skiing and -snowboarding.

The main access to the pass is via an efficient but usually over-subscribed quad chair-lift. From the top you can return to the resort via a choice of runs, which can be crowded and icy. Alternatively, you can ski on down the gentler but more rewarding pistes to Grau Roig, which is little more than a car park and a hotel on the floor of the adjoining valley. A six-seater chair-lift takes you up from the bottom of the Serrat Pinos red (intermediate) run to the top of the Encamp cable-car.

One major complaint is that beginners are forced to buy a full area lift pass just to use the two short drag-lifts on the nursery slopes. Indeed, none of the ten beginner lifts are free. One reporter griped: 'during February half-term the resort was overcrowded, the ski school overloaded and the lift queues enormous'. Here, as in other Andorran resorts, the standard of English spoken by instructors is high, and many have BASI or similar qualifications.

Pas de la Casa's snowboarders congregate at the terrain park at La Coma III in the Grau Roig area. Both Pas de la Casa and Grau Roig have ski kindergarten for children aged three to six years. Grau Roig has a nursery that accepts children from one to three years.

The six mountain eating-places in the Pas de la Casa/Grau Roig ski area are little more than cheap and functional snack-bars. The Bar El Piolet at the bottom of the Del Clot drag-lift is recommended. Refugi dels Llacs Pessons has 'a log fire and pleasant food and service'.

While Pas de la Casa cannot in any way be called attractive, it does have a large variety of accommodation, which ranges from the comfortable to the very basic. The four-star hotels include the Sporting (☎ 85 54 51), the Grau Roig (☎ 85 55 56) and the Himalaia (☎ 85 62 19). The budget hotel Central (☎ 85 53 75) is recommended by reporters. Much of the resort accommodation is in apartments. 'Many of the younger people choose the apartments close to the slopes, while families and those seeking a quieter life choose the hotels.' Of the many self-catering apartments, neither Paradis Blanc nor Lake Placid seem to have many admirers; reporters complain about their small size and lack of sound-proofing.

The restaurants are cheap and cheerful. The food is mainly Spanish, with fresh seafood and the ubiquitous paella, although some concessions have been made to the French. Nightlife is frenetic and cheap, and even bars with dancing seem to have resisted the urge to charge for entry. The Marseillais 'is the place for a quiet drink and has great lasagne'. The Discoteca Bilboard is popular and is split into two with 'general nightclub music played in one half and house/garage music in the other; there is no entry fee and you are able to roam between the two halves'. Other favourite nightspots include Milwaukee's and KYU. Le Pub has a happy hour each evening and holds weekly theme nights.

TOURIST INFORMATION
Tel 376 80 10 60
Fax 376 80 10 70
Email info.reserves@pasgrau.com
Web site www.pasgrau.com

Soldeu–El Tarter
top 2,560m(8,399ft) bottom 1,800m (5,904ft)

Soldeu and linked El Tarter together provide the best combination of skiing, accommodation, architecture, scenery and ambience of any resort in Andorra. Readers are unanimous in their praise: 'I would recommend Soldeu to anyone. It is especially great for beginners, and the ski school is excellent for all levels. The nightlife is cheap and suitable for anyone of any age'. The ski school has an enduring reputation as one of the best in Europe and is a contributory reason for Andorra's success, based not only on sound technique but also on language ('top marks for organisation, friendliness and teaching'). A startling 110 of its 170 instructors are native English speakers.

An eight-person gondola spearheaded a host of new and mainly high-speed lifts and a major expansion of the area, which now has 29 lifts and 86km of groomed pistes. The gondola emerges from beneath one of the many four-star hotels to whisk skiers across the gorge of the river Valira – formerly negotiated via a rickety Indiana Jones-style bridge – and up to the mid-mountain ski school meeting area at Els Espiolets. At the end of the run a new piste bridge across the river takes you swiftly back up to the gondola station. An alternative route is by chair-lift from El Tarter, 2km down the road.

A second eight-person gondola was added in 1999–2000 from the village of **Canillo** to link with a quad-chair in the El Forn area, which in turn connects with the rest of the ski area. This created what was effectively a new ski resort out of the existing town of Canillo, which now has its own ski school, kindergarten, restaurant and cafeteria. Back in Soldeu the addition of three six-seaters and another quad chair-lift have transformed traffic around Soldeu and largely dispensed with queues even at peak teams, although the runs themselves 'can become saturated with people – especially during February half-term'. Snow-cannon cover 25 per cent of the ski area.

There is little here to attract advanced skiers used to the Alps, but low-cost heli-skiing is available. The area is otherwise highly suited to beginners and second-weekers, although one reporter commented that 'some of the green (beginner) runs are like cross-country runs'. We have good reports of the nursery slopes, which are 'well prepared and fenced off from the rest of the pistes'. Soldeu has an ungroomed snowboard zone. The ski school has a long tradition of teaching British children ('my children were looked after by British instructors with a real empathy for kids'). The Club dels Pinguins kindergarten cares for children aged three to ten, with ski lessons for older children. Non-skiing children are cared for at a choice of two crèches.

Architecturally, Soldeu and El Tarter provide a marked contrast to Pas de la Casa, both consisting of little more than a ribbon of stone-and-wood buildings alongside the main road. Environmentally sympathetic regulations mean that recent constructions are much more attractive than those of their neighbouring town. Mountain restaurants are said to be cheap but offered 'dull but fair-priced food for refuelling'. The Esqui Calbo restaurant is recommended for its service and good value. Xalet Sol I Neu, at the bottom of the mountain at Soldeu, serves 'tasty chicken curry made with better cuts of chicken breast than I have ever experienced in an English curry house'. Both mountain cafeterias are usually overcrowded between 11am and 4pm.

One of the best hotels is the four-star Piolets (☎ 87 17 87). The four-star Sport Hotel (☎ 85 10 51) received some criticism: 'situated at the quiet end of town. However, I would caution against rooms near the Piccadilly Pub due to noise'. The ski room, across the road in another building, was 'very crowded and unpleasant'. The food was said to be disappointing. Hotel Naudi (☎ 85 11 48) is 'very noisy due to the pubs at that end of town'. The newly refurbished Hotel Soldeu (☎ 85 10 35) is said to be 'very comfortable and has reasonable food'. At the foot of the slopes in El Tarter is the conveniently placed Hotel Llop Gris (☎ 85 15 59), which has a swimming-pool and squash courts. Further down the road is Parador Canaro (☎ 85 10 46), which offers an even higher standard of comfort.

Nightlife thrives in Soldeu but does not try to compete with the fleshpots of Pas de la Casa. Discos such as Fat Albert's (a good atmosphere') and the Irish Pub are very busy, while Aspen maintains 'a frenetic pace'). The Esquirol and the Hard Rock Café are also popular.

TOURIST INFORMATION
Tel 376 89 05 00
Fax 376 89 05 09
Email soldeu@soldeu.ad
Web site www.soldeu.ad

Eastern Europe

RESORTS COVERED Bulgaria: Bansko, Borovets, Pamporovo, Vitosha. Romania: Poiana Brasov, Sinaia. Slovenia: Bled, Kranjska Gora

Beginners ✱✱ Intermediates ✱

Most of the mountainous countries of eastern Europe offer skiing in some shape or form and have done so for 40 years, regardless of political orientation. For a while, when the Berlin Wall came down and the Iron Curtain was raised, it looked as if a few of them – led by Bulgaria and Romania – would realise their potential and become serious destinations. However, this was not to be.

The transition to a market economy has so far failed to provide the kind of national or international investment needed to build a serious infrastructure for any of the underdeveloped resorts in these countries. This, coupled with intermittent hostilities in the Balkans, has limited their potential. Furthermore, the snowfall here is by no means reliable.

- ✔ Low prices
- ✔ Fascinating cultural experience
- ✘ Poor-quality food
- ✘ Lack of alpine charm
- ✘ Few consumer goods
- ✘ Uncertain snow cover

The most persuasive reason for choosing this part of the continent remains its value for money. Although we have continuing reports that bars and restaurants in Bulgaria have been adjusting their prices from week to week, depending on the level of demand, it is still true to say that, in general, eastern Europe represents excellent holiday value for visitors on a moderate budget. However, the strength of sterling continues to make Andorra and the rest of the Pyrenees almost as financially attractive – and with far better skiing.

Eastern European countries that offer skiing include the Czech Republic, Poland, Romania, Serbia, Slovakia and Slovenia, as well as Russia, Georgia and a number of smaller states of the former USSR. Here we concentrate on the principal ones. We have not given the telephone numbers of hotels or local tourist offices, because we recommend that you travel through a bonded tour operator or via a country's own state travel agency (see *Skiing by numbers*).

BULGARIA

Bulgaria has been a favourite eastern European destination with British skiers for more than 20 years, with **Borovets** and **Pamporovo** the most popular resorts, and **Vitosha** and **Bansko** the smaller, less sophisticated options. Bulgarian skiing is, by Alpine standards, extremely limited. The largest ski area is not much bigger than a relatively unknown resort in the French Jura. The number of visiting skiers continues to decline and will no doubt continue to do so until the local authorities appreciate the inadequacies of their lift systems. Lengthy queues for single-seater chair-lifts, followed by deeply rutted and ill-prepared slopes, may still be acceptable to first-time skiers on a budget – but the amount of repeat business will inevitably be small. However, we must point out that a hard core of our readers are unstinting in their praise. They shrug off the deprivations, swallow the indifferent food, smile in the endless lift queues, and return for more.

Reports of Bulgarian hospitality are mixed, with opinion split fairly evenly between those who found their hosts brusque and unhelpful, and more positive assessments of an affable people who are keen to please. A turbulent history of occupation by neighbouring powers has left the Bulgarian people unsure of how to deal with foreigners. The political changes of the early 1990s may have led to a progressive thaw in attitudes towards visitors, but there is still some way to go before the country will be fully geared to a tourist industry.

Visitors will find badly maintained roads, sub-standard accommodation and inadequate facilities for exchanging currency. Credit cards are rarely accepted except in the major hotels, and worn foreign banknotes are often refused, even by banks. Journeys by taxi can be unnerving, and public transport is unpredictable.

On the positive side, Bulgaria is a country with a fascinating cultural heritage. The ski resorts are located in areas of considerable natural beauty, close to places of great historical significance. The Rila Monastery, midway between Borovets and Bansko, is one of the most perfectly preserved medieval structures of its type in the world. Equally, the ancient town of Plovdiv has much to recommend it. Shoppers will find a range of goods, from hand-carved music-boxes to pirate CDs, on street-corner stalls and even at the base of the Borovets ski lifts.

Mountain restaurants tend to be temporary-looking – indeed, some are just caravans on the hill. Few serve more than toasted sandwiches and soup, and even fewer have WCs. Those that are provided are in such a sorry state of hygiene that they are to be avoided in all but the direst necessity. The quality and blandness of hotel food is the main complaint, but reporters say that you can eat well at little cost in simple restaurants. The quality of rental equipment is improving, but it is not uncommon to see skis and bindings that are ten to 15 years old. However, if you insist on a higher grade of rental gear, superior skis and boots usually materialise from the back of the hire shop.

Bansko
top 2,000m (6,560ft) bottom 936m (3,079ft)

A little over 160km south from Sofia and about an hour's drive beyond **Borovets**, Bansko is a largely unspoilt – and undeveloped – resort. The town is more famous for its religious icon painting school than for its skiing. It lies in the shadow of the 2,915-m peak of Vihren, the highest mountain in the spectacularly beautiful Pirin range, close to the borders with Macedonia and Greece. There are few shops and no supermarkets, but what the town lacks in retail facilities it more than compensates for in extensive cultural diversions: three museums and a magnificent old church, which is unlikely to have altered much in 500 years.

The main focus of the skiing is located out of town at Shiligarnika, the largest of three ski areas. This is reached by a free, half-hour ski-bus ride along a narrow, picturesque mountain road through dense forest. The base-station at Shiligarnika is little more than a couple of new hotels in the midst of a forest clearing.

The area offers about 20km of mainly wide, tree-lined slopes reached by a modern three-seater chair-lift and two drag-lifts. The Chalin Valog area, a little further down the mountain, offers more difficult skiing. In good snow conditions off-piste opportunities are plentiful and the cost of a local guide is remarkably low. The third ski area of Banderishka Poliana has the best nursery slope.

The Dedo Pene, a converted eighteenth-century town house, and the equally atmospheric Mexana Rumen Baryakov are highly recommended restaurants. The Milush Tavern specialises in local dishes. The Torino cabaret bar is unexpectedly upmarket and popular with prosperous-looking Sofians. Hotel Bansko and The Pirin are both praised along with the Strajite and Pension Sema. Up the mountain, the Hotel Todorka is impressive but isolated; however, it offers free transfers to the town centre three nights a week.

Borovets
top 2,540m (8,333ft) bottom 1,323m (4,339ft)

What started as a hunting lodge for the Bulgarian royal family in the nineteenth century developed in the 1970s into an international ski resort. Borovets is 73km from Sofia and set in the pine forest at the foot of Mount Moussala, the highest peak in the Balkans. But like much of eastern Europe the resort has squandered the natural beauty of its setting by erecting buildings of dubious architectural merit.

The extent of the skiing surpasses anything found elsewhere in the country, but the ancient lift system consists only of an ageing gondola, a quad-chair, an antique single-chair and 13 assorted drag-lifts. The inevitable queues and lack of adequate piste-grooming are a constant source of irritation. The skiing is divided into two separate sectors, linked by a long walk on an ice-rutted road.

Principal access to the main area is by a 20-year-old six-person gondola ('the queue went around the block and seemed to last forever'). The Markoudjik sector above it offers the best of the resort's 40km of skiing, which is mainly above the tree-line with a highest ski point of 2,540m. The separate Martinovi Baraki area has a quad chair-lift and four drag-lifts, but the top section can be reached only by an ancient single chair-lift, which is prone to enormous queues. All the nursery slopes are located at the base of this area.

Both main ski schools are well regarded, and English is widely spoken. Ski classes do not have priority on the lifts. The Peter Popanguelov School for Expert Skiing has ten instructors and offers its services 'for those who want to hone their skiing skills to world champion class'. The Rila Hotel kindergarten takes non-skiers from two years old and skiers aged four to seven.

Accommodation is almost exclusively hotel-based, with the conveniently located Samokov standing out as by far the best example. It offers a range of modern facilities including a swimming-pool and bowling alley, and it also has a nightclub and 'American' bar. The giant Rila Hotel is more basic but of reasonable standard. Hotel Breza is 'quiet, comfortable, and rooms have adequate showers and WCs'. The Hotel Mura has also earned good reports.

Borovets is situated in the heart of Bulgaria's potato-growing region. The approach road to the resort is lined with the cars and carts of hopeful farmers selling souvenir spuds at 10p a pound. These, served boiled or re-presented as salads, form the core of hotel restaurant fare along with greasy soups and stews. Consequently, the motley collection of bars and private restaurants in the surrounding woods do a healthy trade in hamburgers and chicken-and-chips.

Pamporovo
top 1,925m (6,316ft) bottom 1,450m (4,757ft)

Pamporovo is a small resort with the majority of its accommodation in nine hotels strung out between the centre and the lift station, about a ten-minute journey by free ski bus. Most of the hotels face the area's only ski mountain, Snezhanka, the summit of which is crowned by the Bulgarian equivalent of the British Telecom Tower. Pamporovo claims an average of 272 sunny days each year. Unfortunately, it does not always snow on the other days.

There is one black (difficult) run (optimistically called 'The Wall'), which is immediately beneath the summit, and a couple of good-quality red (intermediate) runs on either flank. One of these provides the resort's longest run of 4km. Otherwise, the whole place is mostly geared to novices and lower intermediates. However, the 25km of marked skiing, most of which is on tree-lined runs, is undeniably pretty. One relatively modern three-seater chair links the base and summit, but the remaining lifts comprise a double-chair, three archaic single-seaters and an assortment of four equally ancient drag-lifts. Lift queues are rare, except for a 15-minute spell in the morning when all the ski school classes set off simultaneously.

The locals claim that the Pamporovo Ski School is internationally renowned, although one reporter queried whether this might be for 'the grumpiness of its instructors'. Another, who chose the resort for a week's snowboarding course, reported that her instructor was 'charming, helpful, could board like a dream but, alas, wasn't all that gifted at passing on his undoubted talent'. The ski school kindergarten caters for children aged five to eight.

Of the resort's hotels, the Perelik was described as 'basic but comfortable – unless your room is above the disco that closes at 3am'. The hotel also houses Pamporovo's only swimming-pool and the main shopping centre. Among the competition, the Chevermeto restaurant is recommended for its 'folk' nights, when whole sheep are roasted over open fires, and dancers in traditional dress provide a colourful floor show.

Vitosha
top 2,295m (7,530ft) bottom 1,650m (5,413ft)

Bulgaria's highest resort is on Mount Vitosha, overlooking Sofia, which is 20km away and can be reached by a cheap bus service. The resort consists of a couple of comfortable hotels, old hunting lodges, a hire shop and lift station. A total of 22km of north-facing slopes above the tree-line on Mount Cherni Vrah are served by a small network of lifts. Vitosha is an ideal resort for beginners and early intermediates. The ski school is said to be excellent; however, Vitosha's proximity to the capital means that it is inundated with weekenders.

Hotels include the Hunting Lodge, a unique residence set in its own grounds, 700m from the nearest ski lift. The Prostor is the largest hotel, with facilities including a swimming-pool and the resort's only disco. One reporter commented: 'the view was fabulous, but the maintenance appalling; it was very noisy, and the food was poor'. Hotel Moreni is 'basic, with no frills'. The other main hotels are the Moten, completely renovated in 1999, and the Kremikovtski.

ROMANIA

Prices in Romania are even lower than in Bulgaria. For example, bus and taxi fares can be measured in pence rather than pounds, a three-course dinner with wine costs £6 and a bottle of beer or a soft drink as little as 30p – but this is one of Romania's only attractions as a ski destination. While other former eastern-bloc countries have steadily improved facilities for tourists, Romania seems stuck in a time warp from which it shows no signs of freeing itself. Consumer goods are scarce. Ski lifts are dilapidated, prone to lengthy delays, and the safety of some of them must be seriously questioned. We are promised that major refurbishment – particularly at **Sinaia** – is in hand, but we see no sign of it. However, English is spoken everywhere and the standard of ski tuition is generally high, although classes can be oversized.

Poiana Brasov
top 1,775m (5,823ft) bottom 1,021m (3,350ft)

This is the best-known resort in Romania, located in the attractive Carpathian Mountains, three hours' drive north of Bucharest. Ski racing took place here as early as 1909, but the resort was mainly purpose-built during the 1950s to promote tourism, and resembles an enormous holiday camp rather than a village. A few hotels, restaurants and a large sports centre are set back from the base of the ski area; the furthest hotels are about 2km away.

The 14-km ski area is reached either by gondola, an antiquated open-air affair 'like a series of mop buckets on a string', or by two cable-cars ('do not expect them both to be running at the same time') to the summit. Piste-marking, grooming and artificial snow are non-existent. The nursery slopes are at the bottom of the mountain, but when there is a lack of snow, beginners are taken to a gentle slope at the top of the gondola. Most of the skiing is intermediate, with runs roughly following the line of the lifts. There are two black runs, one of which circumnavigates the mountain and ends at the base.

The ski school is unanimously recommended: 'exceptionally good value'. There is no shortage of ski-school instructors who speak fluent English and are keen to show you a good time. The Hotel Sport is the best-situated place to stay, while The Bradul has a faded air. The Alpin is of a slightly higher standard. Tourist-oriented restaurants include Coliba Haiducilor, Sura Dacilor and Vanatorul.

Après-ski takes place in the hotels, nearly all of which have discos or floor shows. The centre of activity is Vicky's Bar. Festival 39 has '1930s décor and occasional live jazz'. The Britannia Arms Pub 'is as you would expect'. Dinner at The Outlaws Hut is lively, starting with musicians playing around a log fire ('it is OK if you can cope with eating roast bear'). Alternatively, you can take part in a folklore dinner at the Carpathian Stag in Brasov. The main discos are the Blitz Club, Pro Club and the giant Hacienda. There are ten strip clubs including the Aristocrat, President and Scotch Club. Excursions to Dracula's Castle can easily be arranged. Cheap buses and taxis can take you into the town of Brasov for limited shopping.

Sinaia
top 2,219m (7,280ft) bottom 855m (2,805ft)

Sinaia is a spa town where the Romanian royal family used to spend their summers after King Karol I built the beautiful Peles Castle here in the 1870s. Its once-elegant hotels and casinos have an air of faded grandeur. The resort is as popular in summer as in winter, and visitors come here from all over eastern Europe to take the waters, which are said to be particularly favourable for acute gastric and liver problems, as well as for those suffering from high cholesterol.

A two-stage cable-car from the town, its top section duplicated by a chair-lift, serves long intermediate runs down the front of the mountain. These runs are poorly marked and are consequently challenging in uncertain visibility. The main area is on exposed, treeless slopes behind the mountain and on subsidiary peaks beyond. It consists of short intermediate runs with some variety, and plenty of scope for off-piste. Snowboarding is not encouraged. The traditional Hotel Palace overlooks a park and is a short walk from the lifts. Hotel Mara Holiday Inn resort is less convenient. The town is quiet and has just a few bars and restaurants that offer après-ski conviviality.

SLOVENIA

'A poor man's Austria with less skiing and less alpine charm' is how one reporter described Slovenia. Like other eastern European countries, it is reasonably priced – food, drink and internal travel are about one-third of British prices. Reports of the ski schools are generally favourable, with English widely spoken and the video analysis helpful.

Bled
top 1,275m (4,183ft) bottom 880m (2,657ft)

The attractive old spa town of Bled looks on to a seventeenth-century church on an island in the middle of a lake. Its main ski area is 8km away at Zatrnik, where a total of five lifts serve 18km of easy wooded slopes in a bowl; these are ideal for beginners in good snow conditions but provide little challenge for intermediates. Another even smaller area is Straza, which has just two lifts; both areas have artificial snow-making. The Golf, a quiet hotel set slightly away from the main centre, is recommended, while the Lovec is an older, wood-panelled hotel. Hotel Vila Bled is an elegant residence set in its own grounds on the shore of Lake Bled. Grand Hotel Toplice, Golf Hotel Bled and the Park Hotel are the other main options.

Kranjska Gora
top 1,630m (5,348ft) bottom 810m (2,667ft)

This is one of the best-known resorts in the region. Set in a pretty flat-bottomed valley between craggy wooded mountains, it is close to the Italian and Austrian borders and is Austrian in ambience, even down to its domed church. Hotels are improving, although are still not comparable in standard to cosy Austrian gasthofs. The four nursery runs are short, wide and gentle and set at the edge of the village; the transition to real pistes is rather abrupt, with the mountains rising steeply from the valley floor. A total of 30km of pistes, the majority of which are blue (easy), are served by 23 lifts of which 18 are T-bars. The longest run, Vitranc, is reached by chair-lift to the top of the ski area and is graded red (intermediate). The other lifts go only halfway up the small mountain, which means limited skiing and the risk of poor snow cover.

The Alpine Ski Club offers both group and private lessons, although only private lessons are available for snowboarding and cross-country. The Zgornjesavska valley has 40km of langlauf tracks. Children are catered for in the ski school but there is no kindergarten. The Kompass, one of the resort's best hotels, has a swimming-pool and disco. The modern Hotel Larix is recommended for its location and facilities, and Hotel Prisank has a friendly atmosphere. Other options are the HIT Casino and the Hotel Lek as well as the Hotel Spik. The Razor apartments are situated 200m from the lifts.

Scandinavia

RESORTS COVERED Finnish Lapland: Levi. Norway: Geilo, Hemsedal, Lillehammer, Oppdal, Trysil, Voss. Sweden: Åre

Beginners ✱✱✱ Intermediates ✱✱ Snowboarders ✱✱

English is widely spoken in all the Scandinavian resorts, and both Norway and Sweden are particularly welcoming to the British. Finnish Lapland is now also beginning to attract an international market. Visitors are guaranteed their fill of reindeer – both on the hoof and on the plate – and there's always the hope of glimpsing a familiar old man with a long white beard and a red coat bombing down the piste.

✔ Ideal for small children
✔ Extensive cross-country skiing
✔ Few lift queues
✔ Relaxed atmosphere
✔ Reliable snow cover
✔ Good-value lift passes
✔ English widely spoken
✘ Low altitude
✘ Few long runs
✘ High-priced alcohol
✘ Extremely low temperatures

Traditionally, skiers travelling to Norway tend to be beginners, intermediates and cross-country enthusiasts – it is fair to say that this is not the best destination for advanced skiers. The country's mountains have vertical drops of only 300m to 750m, and fewer than a dozen ski areas can truly be called downhill resorts. Alpine skiing is treated as part of an all-round winter holiday.

The Norwegians are justly proud of their ski schools, which are well organised with English-speaking instructors who are described as 'friendly and helpful'. Telemarking is making a big comeback to this, its country of origin. Norway is highly recommended for families, and a keen emphasis is placed on safety. **Hemsedal** and **Geilo** even provide free lift passes along with free helmets for children up to seven years old, provided the helmets are worn. Free lift passes and helmets are also given to children up to age eleven in **Åre** in Sweden, and up to age seven in **Levi** in Finnish Lapland.

Travelling by train in Norway is particularly comfortable, with exemplary restaurant cars and wonderful facilities for small children, including a 'crèche-carriage' on inter-city trains, containing baby-changing and feeding rooms and an indoor play area, complete with climbing frame and Wendy house. Some of the Norwegian resorts offer a Winterlandet card, which allows you to ski other resorts that share a lift pass. For example, Geilo, **Hallingskarvet**, Hemsedal, **Gol** and **Al** offer a total of 74 runs and 45 lifts.

Skiing in Sweden is an altogether more serious affair and is much more comparable to mainstream Europe. Daylight hours are limited in mid-winter, and temperatures can be extreme. The skiing season is a long one in Scandinavia, but nowhere more so than in the resort of **Riksgränsen** in Swedish Lapland on the Arctic Circle. In the late spring the pistes here stay open for night-skiing under the 'midnight sun'. However, even Scandinavia's snow record is now subject to the peaks and troughs experienced in more southerly latitudes. In 2001–2 resorts such as Åre suffered from a severe lack of snow until late January.

Throughout Scandinavia alcohol remains expensive – even more in Sweden than in Norway and Finland. The Swedish government remains the sole retailer of alcohol with its own state shops, and the level of taxation is exorbitantly high. However, lack of price increases in recent years combined with a strong pound have made pubs and restaurants more tourist-friendly. Overall, prices compare favourably with Courchevel 1850 and Zermatt – although that said, the quality and extent of the skiing is not in the same league. Expect to pay the equivalent of £3 for a glass of wine, or £14 to £20 for a bottle. A pint of beer costs £3 to £4, and a simple, two-course dinner for two with wine is £40. Ski and boot rental is marginally cheaper than in the Alps, while £85 for a six-day lift pass is similar.

Swedish food has an international flavour, although reindeer features strongly in the meat section of any menu, while in Norway the buffet is the staple dinner diet, and visitors are pleasantly surprised by the range and quality of dishes on offer – despite the predominance of fresh, smoked and marinated fish.

Other activities available in Scandinavia include dog-sledding, go-karting on ice, hang-gliding, heli-skiing/boarding, ice-climbing, ice-fishing, reindeer sleigh rides, snowbiking (in Sweden), snowmobiling, snow rafting, snowshoeing, telemark, tyre-racing and frozen waterfall-climbing.

FINNISH LAPLAND

Levi
top 725m (2,378ft) bottom 400m (1,312ft)

This small and unusual resort lies in the Arctic Circle, 161km by road north of Rovaniemi but only 15km from Kittilä Airport. It possesses a total of 19 lifts and is at the centre of 270km of cross-country trails. Snow is guaranteed here from mid-October until early June. When we visited at the end of November it was mainly dark and the sun never actually rose. 'Daylight' (you still needed to use car headlights) was restricted to a couple of late-morning hours, but 12 runs covering 25km were floodlit and the ski area remained open until 7.45pm. The Lapps use soft, low-wattage bulbs to light their homes, and the day – whether indoors or outdoors – passes in a gentle twilight. By night, if you are lucky, the Northern Lights provide nature's supreme fireworks display, adding to the surreal atmosphere of the place, which gives it a cult following. The hours of daylight increase each month until the late spring when the ski area is open from 10am to 8pm. A new gondola provides the main uphill transport to a 19-lift system serving 45 runs. Levi boasts two half-pipes – snowboarding being extremely popular in Finland.

It is worth visiting a traditional Lapp farm for a reindeer sleigh ride, and Santapark – an underground theme park with Disney-style rides at Rovaniemi – should not be missed by families with young children.

Recommended hotels include Hullu Poro (Crazy Reindeer), with 'enormous, comfortable apartment rooms with private saunas', and the more luxurious Levitunturi. All accommodation can be booked through a central office (☎ 166 393300). The resort offers a ski- and non-ski kindergarten, and children under seven years old ski and borrow equipment free if they wear the free helmets supplied by the rental shops. Most restaurants are in hotels, and the nightlife is limited to a few bars.

TOURIST INFORMATION
Tel 358 166 43466
Fax 358 166 43469
Email levi.info@levi.fi
Web site www.levi.fi

NORWAY

Geilo
top 1,178m (3,864ft) bottom 800m (2,624ft)

This is a traditional resort midway between Bergen and Oslo and only 30 minutes' drive from Geilo Airport Dagali. It is especially recommended for cross-country skiers as one of the centres on the famous Hardangevidda Plateau. The downhill skiing, which comprises 35 pistes served by 18 lifts, is relaxed and uncomplicated, with several reporters describing the terrain as 'perfect for novice and intermediate skiers'. Although there are seven nominal black (difficult) runs, advanced skiers will quickly run out of steam here. Plans for a major mountain development have so far failed to materialise. The skiing is made up of two areas inconveniently situated on either side of a wide valley, with the resort beside the lake in the middle. However, a free ski bus service now links the two throughout the day.

The Vestlia area, with a vertical drop of 244m, provides the easiest skiing and is where the excellent ski- and non-ski kindergarten, the Troll Club, is based. The highlight of this area is Bjornloypa, a popular, long, green (beginner) run. The main ski area, on the other side of the valley on the slopes of the Geilohovda, has a much wider selection of pistes than Vestlia, including some steeper terrain and a vertical drop of 378m. Apart from its three ski schools, Geilo also hosts Aktivitets Guiding for off-piste skiing. Snowboarding lessons are available, and the largest terrain park in Norway with its own chair-lift is situated at Fugleleiken. There is also a second, much smaller one at Havsdalen. Norway is famous as the home of cross-country skiing and nowhere more so than Geilo, which boasts 220km of loipe, both on the valley floor and on the Hardangevidda Plateau at 1,312m. It also features floodlit tracks.

Six mountain restaurants are scattered around the two ski areas but most of them are soulless cafeterias. The fast-food restaurant at the top of the main area at Geilohovda is popular, and sun-lovers congregate on the terrace of the stately Dr Holms Hotel, one the most famous hotels in Norway ('stylishly furnished and patronised by sleek Scandinavian families exuding wealth and health'). You can ski to the three-star Solli Sportell Hotel, and the Highland Hotel is also recommended. The Vestlia Hotel is 'warm and comfortable, the food was excellent, and we were two minutes' walk from the lifts', while the Usterdalen Hotel received favourable comments: 'friendly owners, an excellent buffet, a crafts club for children and after-dinner live entertainment'. Norwegian resorts also offer an abundance of usually expensive cabins and apartments. All accommodation can be booked through a central number (☎ 320 95940). The Låven bar at the Vestlia Hotel is a popular apres-ski meeting place together with Bukkesspranget, Kammerset and the Skibaren. Highdance and Syndebukken are the discos.

Geilo's Trollia kindergarten is the Troll Inn, where children under three can take part in indoor and outdoor activities, and which is warmly praised. The downside is that lunch is not provided. The children's ski school receives high acclaim: 'the children were very well looked after' and 'the lessons were fun'.

TOURIST INFORMATION
Tel 47 320 95900
Fax 47 320 95901
Email turistinfo@geilo
Web site www.geilo.no

Hemsedal
top 1,497m (4,911ft) bottom 675m (2,214ft)
Although only an hour's drive from Geilo, in the heart of Norway's Winterland region between Oslo and Bergen, Hemsedal's peaks look a lot more mountainous than Geilo's rounded ski hill, giving a much stronger impression of a serious ski resort. Despite the fact that Hemsedal contains fewer runs than Geilo, and **Oppdal** enjoys a larger ski area and more off-piste, Hemsedal boasts the best alpine skiing in Norway, with a long season stretching from mid-November to May. In a country where ski resorts are dominated by the T-bar, Hemsedal also possesses the most modern lift system, with one quad chair-lift and five chair-lifts (four of them high-speed detachables) among its 16 lifts serving 42km of piste.

The resort features a couple of genuinely steep black (difficult) runs and some entertaining tree-level skiing. One snag is that the village is about 3km from the ski area, and the free ski bus service is infrequent (two go from the village in the morning and two return in the afternoon). This means, for example, that guests staying at the Skogstad

Hotel (which serves dinner between 6pm and 8pm), who wish to take advantage of the much-advertised night-skiing, run the risk of missing dinner. Hemsedal offers some interesting off-piste skiing through the trees – known as 'taxi skiing' because you will need to organise transport to get you back to the slopes or to your base. It also has a severe off-piste run called Reidarskaret, which starts with a steep, narrow couloir that is usually too dangerous to attempt unless weather and snow conditions are perfect. Cross-country skiing is possible from December to May on 130km of marked trails.

Hemsedal Aktiv is the ski and snowboard school, and Norske Opplevelser As organises off-piste guiding. Snowboarding is popular in Norway, particularly in Hemsedal, where there is a floodlit terrain park and a self-timing course. The excellent slope-side babysitting service, Trollia Childrenpark, comes free with a lift pass of at least three days.

Two mountain restaurants are near the top of the Hollvinheisen triple-chair. A third, Skistua, is at the base area and offers self- or table-service. A number of new apartments and cabins have been built for 2001–2, while hotels include the Fossheim ('small, family-run and very comfortable'). All accommodation can be centrally booked (☎ 320 55061). Hemsedal has some packed, noisy bars during the busy weekends. The Garasjen (the old bus garage) can become so crowded that skiers overflow on to the street and those left inside have to come to a tacit agreement as to the moment when snatching a quick sip of beer – in unison – is possible. The Skogstad Piano Bar and Hemsedal Café are almost as crowded. You may have more room to breathe at the Kro Bar in the Fanitullen apartment block.

TOURIST INFORMATION
Tel 47 320 55030
Fax 47 320 55031
Email hemsedal@hemsedal.net
Web site www.hemsedal.com

Lillehammer
top 1,050m (3,444ft) bottom 200m (656ft)

Lillehammer resembles an American frontier town, with its clapboard houses and single main street. The nearest skiing is based 15km away at **Hafjell**, which possesses 25km of prepared trails served by 11 lifts. The best pistes are from Hafjelltoppen (1,050m) down either the Kringelas or Hafjell runs. Both are graded black (difficult), and formed part of the 1994 Winter Olympic slalom courses. Night-skiing is also available once a week. **Kvitfjell**, 50km from Lillehammer, was created as the downhill course for the Winter Olympics. Its 4km of skiing is limited but provides a steeper challenge than anywhere else in the region. The Radisson SAS Lillehammer (☎ 612 86000) is reported to be the best hotel in town, with indoor and outdoor swimming-pool. The Rica Victoria (☎ 612 50049) is also recommended.

TOURIST INFORMATION
Tel 47 612 50299
Fax 47 612 56585
Email info@lillehammerturist.no
Web site www.lillehammerturist.no

Oppdal
Top 1,300m (4,265ft) bottom 545m (1,788ft)

Oppdal lies 120km south of Trondheim and is one of Norway's most northerly downhill resorts. It offers 78km of pistes served by 17 lifts – the most challenging marked trails being Bjorndalsloypa, Hovdenloypa and Bjerkeloypa on the front face of Hovden, the central ski area.

The Vangslia area also features a mixture of terrain, while Stolen at the other end of the resort is made up entirely of beginner and inter-mediate pistes. The fourth area, Adalen, is set in a huge bowl behind Hovden and is dominated by long, mainly blue (easy) cruising runs. At 1pm, for a fee, snowcats will take up to 50 skiers at a time to the top of the mountain at Blaoret for sightseeing and an additional 240m vertical of off-piste skiing. Oppdal also boasts 60km of cross-country trails covering a variety of terrain; five of its tracks are floodlit.

The resort possesses six mountain restaurants: one at the bottom of each base area, and two more at the top of the Hovden and Stolen lift complexes. Only the Vangslia lifts are without a mid-mountain restaurant of any description.

The 72-room Quality Hotel Oppdal (☎ 724 00700) is close to the quiet railway station ('cosy and quaint, despite its size'), while the Oppdal Motel (☎ 724 20600) is well-equipped, with three- and six-bed rooms. Vangslia Fjelltun (☎ 724 00801) contains log-built apartments on the edge of the piste. Reporters spoke favourably of the 'Viking evening' (a misnomer) at a timbered roundhouse in the woods, where local stews, pâtés and sausages are served in front of a roaring fire to an accordion accompaniment. Although Oppdal is a fair-sized town, nightlife is limited to a few bars and restaurants.

TOURIST INFORMATION
Tel 47 724 00470
Fax 47 724 00480
Email post@oppdal.com
Web site www.oppdal.com

Trysil
top 1,132m (3,714ft) bottom 600m (1,969ft)

Situated three hours' drive from Oslo, Trysil is reputed to have the most reliable snow cover anywhere in the country. Its 85km of piste, served by 26 lifts, are spread across the wooded slopes of Trysilfjellet with a 685m vertical drop. As with many Norwegian resorts, the lifts are several kilometres from the resort centre. The skiing varies from easy green (beginner) trails to some more challenging red (intermediate) runs, but is criticised for having too many runs graded green: 'cross-country tracks in disguise'. The resort features an impressive terrain park with a half-pipe. Ninety kilometres of cross-country trails (of which 3km are floodlit for night-skiing) wind through the woods on the lower half of the mountain. Accommodation in Trysil is mainly hotel- and apartment-based, although mountain cabins make a pleasant change for hardy self-caterers. Hotel Trysil Gjestegard Panorama, situated 1km to the south of Trysil, is favoured by reporters. The Norlandia Trysil Hotel and Trysil-Knut are in the centre, while the Trysilfjell aparthotel is on the slopes. All accommodation can be centrally booked (☎ 624 50000).

TOURIST INFORMATION
Tel 47 624 50511
Fax 47 624 51164
Email info@trysil.com
Web site www.trysil.com

Voss
top 945m (3,100ft) bottom 91m (300ft)
Despite its low altitude, Voss provides a reasonable ski area for beginners and lower intermediates. The 40km of prepared pistes includes three black (difficult) runs, two of which are reasonably challenging, and some off-piste. The ten lifts (almost one for each run) include a cable-car, and the longest descent is 3km. Enthusiasts of cross-country skiing will certainly not be disappointed with the 60km of prepared loipe that is close to the centre, although more is available in the valleys around the area. The resort's historic hotel is the Fleischer (☎ 565 20500), which is wood-built in traditional style.

TOURIST INFORMATION
Tel 47 565 20800
Fax 47 565 20801
Email vossn@online.no
Web site www.voss-promotion.no

SWEDEN
Åre
top 1,420 (4,659ft) bottom 380m (1,312ft)
Åre is a serious destination for recreational skiers and snowboarders of all standards. A total of 44 lifts including a gondola and cable-car spread across four villages, linked on mountain or by ski bus, serve 93km of piste. The vertical drop of 890m outranks popular Tremblant in Quebec or Sunday River in Maine, yet Åre remains sidelined as a niche destination for British skiers. Those who come here find a charming village of pastel-painted houses and hotels on the shore of an enormous frozen lake. The outlying hamlets of Björnen, Duved and Tegefjäll

are part of a Trois Vallées-style linked ski area with a modern lift system that dates back to 1910. The transfer time is about 90 minutes from Östersund Airport.

The 1,420-m summit of Åreskutan, reached by a tow behind a snow-cat, provides the launching point for one of Europe's most unusual and rewarding off-piste descents. The gradient is such that the lake far below fills your horizon for much of the run. The skiing is certainly comparable to a medium-sized Alpine resort, with enough challenging runs, including the Salombacken and the World Cup runs.

Beginners are equally well served by the Åre ski school, which enjoys a sound reputation and is staffed entirely by fluent English-speakers. Cross-country is also popular here, with 56km of trails of which 13km are floodlit. Children are well catered for, with a free lift pass and free – compulsory – helmets provided for children up to the age of 11. There is a crèche for three- to five-year-olds, and a ski kindergarten with up to five per group. The list of alternative activities includes the usual horse-riding, parapente, and tobogganing, but it also features more exotic pastimes. Here you can join a husky or snowmobile safari, try your hand at ice-climbing, fish for trout through a hole cut into the ice, and even sample 'snowfering' (windsurfing on snow).

The four-star Åregarden is 'much the best and most centrally located place to stay', while the Arefjällby Apartments are 'very pleasant in the new block, but the others are in need of refurbishment'. The Diplomat Ski Lodge is also warmly praised. The Backpackers' Inn ('cheerful') is the budget option. All accommodation can be booked at a central office (☎ 647 17700).

The 50 restaurants offer greater culinary choice than in Kitzbühel or Chamonix, while from early afternoon guttering candles in the snow lead the way to 15 frenetic après-ski haunts. Restaurants include Grill Hörnan and Liten Krog, which 'has the best pizzas you could wish for'. The resort contains an English pub called the White Hart, while the Skier's Bar at the Diplomat Ski Lodge is 'the "in" place after skiing'. Later on the Bygget at Arefjällby puts on the best live music.

TOURIST INFORMATION
Tel 46 647 17700
Fax 46 647 17707
Email bokning@areresort.se
Web site www.areresort.se

Scotland

RESORTS COVERED Cairngorm Mountain (Aviemore), Glencoe, Glenshee, The Lecht, Nevis Range

Beginners ✳✳✳ Intermediates ✳✳ Advanced ✳ Snowboarders ✳

In winter 2001–2 Scotland enjoyed some of the best snow conditions in the northern hemisphere, with the Nevis Range among the handful of resorts in the northern hemisphere that remained open over the May Bank Holiday. To crown it all, the Cairngorm skier Alain Baxter firmly established himself among the world top-ten slalom racers to become a serious contender for a gold medal in Salt Lake City. It was all a glorious advertisement for Scottish ski areas that are so often underrated or dismissed out of hand by other European skiers.

- ✔ Friendly atmosphere
- ✔ Wide range of non-ski activities
- ✔ Late-season skiing
- ✔ BASI tuition
- ✗ Unpredictable weather conditions
- ✗ Lift queues at peak periods
- ✗ Limited skiing

However, Scottish skiing is dependent on the weather and on the type of snow that falls. On the one hand, a sudden temperature rise can bring a rapid thaw, or rain and gale-force winds can make conditions on the mountain extremely unpleasant as well as closing vital access lifts. On the other, you can experience beautiful sunshine and no wind, with temperatures low enough to keep the snow crisp. When this happens, swarms of enthusiastic Scottish skiers clog up the car parks, rental shops and ticket counters. Scotland is keen to update its old skiing image of wind-blown slopes, obsolete lifts, nasty cafeterias and even nastier WCs. Much has been done to improve facilities, but the fickle winter climate remains unchanged.

Because of the weather, it is a constant battle for resort operators to groom the slopes effectively, and they have to erect chestnut paling fences everywhere in an attempt to catch and contain drifting snow. Rapid temperature fluctuations make the manufacture of artificial snow difficult. But as one reader concluded: 'skiing in Scotland is so much more than a week's skiing holiday. Rather, it forms part of an incredibly diverse package where skiing may or may not predominate'.

The five ski centres in the Scottish Highlands are often marketed together. **Nevis Range** is on the west coast, 33 miles from **Glencoe**. **Cairngorm Mountain (Aviemore)** is in Strathspey, in the Central Highlands, and **The Lecht** and **Glenshee** lie to the east.

The achievements of the resort operators and their staff cannot be overstated. That they manage to build and maintain their operations against this background of meteorological unpredictability, while persuading public and private institutions to invest the capital needed to expand and improve the centres, is a testimony to the dedication of the Scottish skiing fraternity.

The area boasts an exceptional number of ski schools, many of them based at or near Cairngorm Mountain. Most offer a high standard of tuition under the auspices of the British Association of Snowsport Instructors (BASI), the teaching methods of which are now internationally accepted. Cairngorm and Nevis Range both have terrain parks and competition-standard jumps. The downside is a distinct lack of bowls or trees, making the area boring for riders. Glencoe and Nevis Range enjoy the superior terrain.

Scotland offers plenty of opportunities for cross-country skiing and ski-mountaineering. However, because of the cold winds, clothing needs to be extra-protective. Most of Scotland's cross-country skiing is along forest trails, which hold the snow better than the more open terrain. The season runs from early January to mid-March on the lower, wooded trails and sometimes until early May higher up the mountain. The most challenging ski-mountaineering routes are on the rounded mountains of the Central and Eastern Highlands.

The changeable snow and weather conditions mean that a Scottish skiing holiday is not suitable for those who like to plan ahead. It also makes sense to be based where you have access to more than one centre, and not to invest in a week's lift ticket for just one resort. Glenshee and Glencoe offer a joint ticket, as do Nevis Range and Glencoe.

It is unrealistic to expect to enjoy the same sort of skiing holiday here as you would in the Alps, but it is possible to have an excellent time simply by keeping an open mind and being flexible. The Highlands are so used to uncertain weather that the range of alternative outdoor pursuits available puts even the world's top ski resorts to shame: these include canoeing, climbing, dog-sledding, fishing, gliding, gorge walking, hang-gliding, skating, off-road driving, shooting, squash, swimming and tennis – and Nevis Range even provides a year-round mountain bike downhill course from the base of the ski area. Readers consistently comment on the warmth of the welcome. As one reader put it: 'Highland service and general friendliness were positively disarming, sharply contrasting with so many experiences in mainland Europe'.

The Scottish ski resorts' collective web site (www.ski-scotland.com) supplies daily snow reports and a snow-alert email service.

Cairngorm Mountain (Aviemore)
top 3,608ft (1,100m) bottom 1,804ft (550m)

Aviemore is located about 120 miles north of Edinburgh and Glasgow on the A9 and is the nearest town to the Cairngorm Mountain ski area, which lies ten miles to the east. Winter 2001–2 sees the opening of the long-awaited Cairngorm Mountain funicular, which has been built at a cost of £14.7 million. It follows the line of the now-defunct White Lady chairs. For much of its length the track is carried on a viaduct to keep it clear of drifting snow, and the final 250m of the funicular goes through a tunnel. The first trains were expected to run in autumn 2001 and the service should be fully operational for the 2001–2 ski season.

The 15 other lifts serve two distinct sectors that are accessed from separate bases at Coire Na Ciste and Coire Cas, meeting below the 4,084ft Cairngorm peak. Head Wall offers challenging skiing, and White Lady poses some excellent moguls. West Wall and Ciste Gully are recommended first thing in the morning. New base- and middle-stations and a new restaurant are in the pipeline, with completion scheduled for autumn 2002. Cairngorm boasts four snack bars: two at the base-lodges, Shieling at the mid-station and the fourth at the panoramic Ptarmigan. The Shieling is one of the only restaurants in Scotland that allows skiers to eat packed lunches at the table.

The Cairngorm Snowsports School has a snowboard section, with an excellent reputation, and the area also boasts a terrain park. Other courses include cross-country, snowblading and telemark. The Uphill Ski Club runs classes for disabled skiers in the resort. Off-piste routes (with a guide) include the East Wall gullies and Coire Laogh Mor; these are reached by a long traverse, which often has wind-broken snow. The ski schools arrange children's tuition on demand ('in good weather', according to the local tourist board). A crèche is available at the Hilton Coylumbridge.

Aviemore is served by rail direct from Inverness and the south. Daily flights operate from Heathrow, Stansted and Luton. In the 1980s Aviemore suffered from having its facilities based around the Aviemore Centre, a hideous 20-year-old concrete development, which has been in a serious state of decay for the last ten years. More recent developments on Aviemore's main street and on the outskirts of the town ('a modern sprawl with large hotels') are a great improvement. Between Aviemore and the Cairngorm slopes lies the Hilton Coylumbridge Hotel (☎ 01479 810661), 'an excellent base for skiers'. Littlejohns restaurant in Aviemore has a friendly atmosphere, with 1930s paraphernalia and copious quantities of American and Mexican food. The Gallery is at Inverdruie, a mile outside Aviemore; readers praised its food. The Taverna Bistro has reasonable prices.

Aviemore used to be known for its rowdy and sleazy nightlife, but most of the bars have been refurbished, and there is now less of the tough, hard-drinking Scottish pub atmosphere. Crofters is one of the most popular of Aviemore's clubs, and the bar at the Highland Hotel is also praised. Non-ski activities include a theatre, cinema, swimming, skating and off-road driving courses. Reporters generally found the nightlife 'disappointing', with the disco stopping at 11pm. Prices for drinks are 'at the usual pub rates but somewhat inflated in the more expensive hotels'.

TOURIST INFORMATION
Tel 01479 861261 for snow info, 01479 810363 for tourist info
Fax 01479 861207
Email info@cairngormmountain.com
Web site www.cairngormmountain.com

Glencoe
top 3,637ft (1,109m) bottom 2,001ft (610m)

Glencoe Ski Centre, 74 miles north of Glasgow, has attracted a dedicated following for four decades (Britain's first chair-lift opened here in 1961), and during the past few seasons there has been considerable investment in infrastructure here.

There are six miles of piste and the seven lifts possess an uphill capacity of 4,300 people per hour. Beginners are catered for on the gentle nursery areas of the Plateau, and intermediates can progress to the long, sweeping descents of Coire Glades. Glencoe boasts the longest single descent and steepest black (difficult) run in Scotland. It has no special facilities for snowboarders but the resort claims that 'Glencoe's diversity of natural terrain featuring jumps, drop-ins and wide open runs means that there is no need to construct a man-made park'. The Glencoe Ski Centre Ski & Snowboard School teaches adults and children.

The Plateau Mountain Café has been upgraded and the Log Cabin Restaurant at the foot of the slopes is 'hugely welcoming in bad weather'. The Centre is open seven days a week and contains a ski and snowboard school as well as a rental shop. Glencoe provides no child-minding facilities, but the ski school can arrange lessons. The resort shares a Monday-to-Friday lift pass with the Nevis Range. Recommended accommodation nearby includes the Macdonald Hotel (☎ 01855 831539), while apartments and cottages can be booked through Invercoe Highland Holidays (☎ 01855 811210).

TOURIST INFORMATION
Tel 01855 851226
Fax 01855 851233
Email glencoe@sol.co.uk
Web site www.ski-glencoe.co.uk

Glenshee
top 3,504ft (1,068m) bottom 2,000ft (610m)

Glenshee operates 'Britain's largest network of ski lifts and tows, covering four mountains and three valleys'. Its 26 lifts boast an uphill capacity of 18,500 people per hour and give access to 25 miles of piste. The centre is on a rather desolate pass on the A93, with the lifts located on both sides of the road. The skiing provides considerable variety and in fine weather it offers plenty of scope for strong intermediate and advanced skiers. A number of reporters rated Glenshee as having the best skiing in Scotland. It annually hosts a successful telemark festival. Tuition can be taken with the Glenshee Ski Centre Ski & Snowboard School, which organises courses such as cross-country, race-training and skiing for disabled people. The resort has a terrain park at Meall Odhar and a dedicated snowboard rental shop with 200 boards and pairs of soft boots. There is a modest licensed café at the base and a better high-altitude restaurant, the Cairnwell. Also on the slopes, Meall Odhar Mountain Café offers a cosy alternative. Callater Lodge Hotel

(☎ 01339 741275) and The Braemar Lodge Hotel at Braemar (☎ 01339 741627) are both recommended, while Dalmunzie House Hotel (☎ 01250 885224) at Glenshee is the closest to the ski area.

TOURIST INFORMATION
Tel 01339 741320
Fax 01339 741665
Email glenshee@sol.co.uk
Web site www.ski-glenshee.co.uk

The Lecht
top 2,600ft (793m) bottom 2,109ft (643m)

The Lecht is Scotland's smallest ski area, a network of a dozen short button-lifts on both sides of the A939 Cockbridge to Tomintoul road, 56 miles west of Aberdeen and about 45 miles from both Glenshee and Cairngorm. One reader said: 'it is hardly mountainous and you could mistake it for a winter scene at various locations in England, but it is friendly and unpretentious'. The area is best suited to beginners and intermediates living within reasonable driving distance – The Lecht could not be described as a destination resort. The longest run is 900m. Extensive snowmaking and a 200-m artificial slope are a precaution against the vagaries of Scottish weather and The Lecht has now introduced a tubing slope and a small terrain park. The rental shop supplies skis and snowboards with soft boots. Parking is free and the single café is licensed. The nearest accommodation is the Allargue Arms (☎ 01975 651410), three miles away at Corgarff; a choice of hotels and B&B options six miles away at Tomintoul includes the 'comfortable and welcoming' Gordon Hotel (☎ 01807 580206).

TOURIST INFORMATION
Tel 01975 651440
Fax 01975 651426
Email info@lecht.co.uk
Web site www.lecht.co.uk

Nevis Range
top 4,006ft (1,221m) bottom 2,148ft (655m)

Nevis Range is Scotland's nearest equivalent to an Alpine resort. It is located seven miles north of Fort William and close to Ben Nevis, Britain's highest mountain. Its own mountain, Aonach Mor, has 11 lifts and 35 runs, reached from the car park by a modern six-seater gondola. This takes you up to the Snowgoose Restaurant, from where a quad-chair and a series of tow-lifts fan out ('the views are stunning, with mouth-watering scenery in every direction'). The longest run is 2km. The Braveheart chair-lift gives easy access to the back bowls of the Coire Dubh, which provide excellent off-piste terrain after a fresh snowfall for skiers and snowboarders alike. Queues for the return gondola journey down the mountain can be huge when the weather is good in high season. Nevis Range possesses a ski and snowboard school with off-piste clinics when conditions are favourable, as well as junior race-training, women's ski clinics and telemark. It boasts a new terrain park with rails, boxes, ramps and a quarter-pipe. The kindergarten accepts children from three years old. There is a restaurant, the Snowgoose, at the top of the gondola and snack bars at the foot of the Goose and Rob Roy T-bars.

The delightful hamlet of Torlundy offers B&B, although most of the accommodation is in Fort William, an old lochside town with strong tourist appeal. It offers a wide choice of hotels and restaurants, and a leisure centre. Nearby hotels include the nineteenth-century Inverlochy Castle (☎ 01397 702177), which is set in 500 acres of grounds and has sumptuous bedrooms. One reader praised The Moorings Hotel (☎ 01397 772797): 'a friendly three-star'. The Milton Hotel (☎ 01397 702331) provides a health club, and the Crannog restaurant enjoys a good reputation for its seafood.

TOURIST INFORMATION
Tel 01397 705825 for snow info, 01397 703781 for tourist info
Fax 01397 705854
Email nevisrange@sol.co.uk
Web site www.nevis-range.co.uk

Further information about accommodation near some of these resorts can be found in *The Which? Hotel Guide 2002* and *The Good B&B Guide*, available from Which? Books.

Spain

Spain does not have a historical connection with skiing, and indeed it may seem surprising that a country associated with beaches and sunshine should possess any skiing at all. However, in recent years the popularity of skiing, and particularly snowboarding, within Spain has greatly increased. The country has two quite separate mountain ranges: the Pyrenees in the north-east and the Sierra Nevada in the south. Both normally receive adequate winter snowfalls, regardless of what is happening in the Alpine countries. Foreigners on the slopes are few, and the Spanish enjoy their skiing and nightlife vociferously, with the same passion they dedicate to other sports. In Spain partying is an even more serious business than skiing or snowboarding, and Anglo-Saxons who stray into this unfamiliar ski-resort environment either adopt local hours or suffer from what quickly develops into a severe Latin mutation of jet-lag.

- ✔ Efficient lift system
- ✔ Typically Spanish nightlife
- ✔ Reasonable prices
- ✘ Lack of resort charm
- ✘ Short runs

Local skiers hit the slopes at a leisurely 10am and ski furiously until lunch at 2pm. They grab a final hour on the piste before the lifts close at 5pm and then head for the tapas bars before an evening snooze. The length of the 7pm ski siesta is largely dependent on the amount of energy expended on skiing, the size of the paella you ate for lunch, and your intake of *calamares* and Rioja at teatime. Nobody (not even families with young children) sits down to dinner before 9pm, and restaurants begin to get busy at 11pm. Dancing does not start before 1pm and can carry on into daylight hours. As one reporter put it: 'if your aim here is to après-ski enthusiastically, then it would be a good idea to book an additional week's holiday on return to recover'.

The high and usually snow-sure resort of **Sierra Nevada** lies in the far south of the country in the mountains of the same name. However, most of the skiing takes place hundreds of kilometres to the north-east in the Pyrenees, which also usually provide reliable snow cover between Christmas and April. **Baqueira–Beret** remains the most important of these Pyrenean resorts – a small but smart development that attracts wealthy skiers from Madrid and Barcelona.

Baqueira–Beret
top 2,510m (8,235ft) bottom 1,500m (4,920ft)

Baqueira-Beret is Spain's answer to Megève – a smart and fashionable resort where not all the designer ski suits you see parading down the main street make it on to the snow. It lies at the head of the beautiful Val d'Aran, near Viella on the northern side of the Pyrenees; access from France is easy, and the drive from Toulouse airport takes two hours. In keeping with its chic status, prices are higher than you might otherwise expect in Spain.

Baqueira is purpose-built in an aesthetically adequate style. The village lies beside the road that leads up to the very high Bonaigua Pass, which is often closed in winter. Recent, more attractive development has increased its appeal as a base, with some good shops, hotels, restaurants and a leisure centre. King Juan Carlos has made the resort 'by Royal Appointment' by setting up a home here. The atmosphere is relaxed and friendly. Beret is the second base area rather than a separate resort, and consists of little more than a car park and a cafeteria. The veteran Olympic skier José Moga, who taught King Juan Carlos to ski and who also runs the main ski shop in town, described it as 'the best-value skiing in a less pretentious atmosphere than you can find anywhere in Europe'.

The skiing day begins with a ride on the Wah-Wah, a decorative road-train that takes skiers to the main lift station. The place seems curiously deserted because the Spanish, who make up 90 per cent of visitors, are still in bed. A bizarre quad-chair, which you ride without skis (you slot them into the back of the chair in front), takes you up to the mid-mountain station at 1,800m. The skiing takes place on four wide, well-linked mountains with a vertical drop of about 1,000m over varied, often exciting terrain that is reminiscent of Squaw Valley in California. Most of it is suited to intermediates, but one icy couloir, evocatively named Where Goats Tumble, poses a real challenge. The opening up of the Bonaigua area has greatly enhanced its appeal to good skiers and boarders. There is a half-pipe at Bonaigua, and the lower slopes are well covered by snow-cannon. Reporters widely praised the standard of piste-grooming and the amount of snow-making. The resort claims only a modest 77km of groomed piste for its 26 lifts. However, opportunities for easy and safe off-piste excursions between the designated runs abound; and effectively double the amount of terrain suggested by the statistics.

The kindergarten accepts children from three months old at three piste-side locations as well as at a crèche in the resort itself. Few of the ski school instructors speak any English. Cap del Port, a gothic folly colloquially known as Dracula's Castle, provides the only setting for a relaxed gastronomic lunch. The alternative is Restaurant 1800: 'wonderful paella for eight, but you must order a day in advance'.

Baqueira is still largely unknown outside Spain, mainly because of the limited rental accommodation available in the resort. Many of its 12,000 beds are owned or rented for the season by Spaniards, who make the journey here every weekend from Barcelona and Madrid. The king, when duties permit, is among them. Royal watchers can peer down on the king's residence – reputedly given to him by a wealthy courtier – from a new five-star boutique hotel and spa, The Melia Royal Tanau (☎ 973 64 44 46).

Less well-heeled visitors choose to stay in the ageing but still acceptable four-star Hotel Montarto (☎ 973 64 44 44), the three-star Tuc Blanc (☎ 973 64 43 500) or the Hotel Val de Ruda (☎ 973 64 52 58) – said to be 'a pleasant three-star in a good position'. Chalet-hotel Salana (☎ 01457 821200 UK) is warmly praised: 'pleasant food, lively bar and comfortable rooms'. Many regular visitors prefer to stay in the more traditional hotels further down the valley, such as Parador de Arties (☎ 973 64 08 01), and dine in an assortment of smart restaurants situated in the quaint medieval villages off the road up to the resort. These include Era Mariqueria in Arties, where you choose and weigh your own fish and seafood before it is cooked to whatever recipe you suggest. Casa Irene boasts 'quite outstanding Aran cuisine in a delightful setting', and Eth Cerer in Uhna is a wine bar with an extraordinary selection of Spanish vintages. El Divino provides late-night but less selective drinking with music. The region is not suited to the culinary squeamish. Borda Lobato in Baqueira specialises in roast suckling pig and whole baby lamb 'carved at the table with garden shears'. Other recommended restaurants include La Perdiu Blanca, La Ticolet for pierrade and Tamarro's for tapas. Tiffany's is the busiest nightclub. The resort's proximity to the border means that French is also widely understood, if not spoken.

TOURIST INFORMATION
Tel 34 973 63 90 00
Fax 34 973 64 44 88
Email viajes@baqueira.es
Web site www.baqueira@baqueira.es

Sierra Nevada
top 3,470m (11,385ft) bottom 2,100m (6,888ft)

Sierra Nevada lies in Andalucia, 32km from the ancient Moorish city of Granada, and offers mainland Europe's most southerly skiing. The presence of a ski resort here seems at complete odds with the nearby resorts of Marbella and Malaga, with their yacht clubs and golf courses. The resort used to be marketed under the name of Sol y Nieve (Sun and Snow), and the purpose-built village in which most skiers stay (at 2,100m) is known as **Pradollano**. The resort has announced that it is bidding, in association with Granada, for the 2010 Winter Olympics despite the fact that its last major foray on to the world stage ended in humiliation. The 1995 World Alpine Skiing Championships had to be put on hold for a year because of lack of snow – cover at such a southerly latitude being unpredictable. The ski area is extremely vulnerable to bad weather and the mountain range as a whole is exposed to high winds. Too much snow is almost as likely to stop you skiing as too little. But when conditions are good, the skiing can be excellent and the views striking; on a clear day you can even see Morocco.

The village is short on alpine charm yet is 'certainly nowhere near as ugly as the Andorran resorts'. Because of its proximity to Granada and the Costa del Sol, it suffers from extreme crowding at weekends and on public holidays: 'on a high-season Monday we queued 50 minutes for the main gondola, but, once you know the lift system, you can avoid this'.

The resort now possesses 19 lifts covering 34 mainly intermediate pistes totalling 62km. Access to the main skiing area is by a choice of three lifts, including a gondola, from the edge of the village. Sierra Nevada provides a choice of three ski schools. In keeping with the Spanish fondness for lunch, the main bowl houses a wide choice of mountain eateries.

The accommodation is mainly in hotels. The Sol Melia Sol y Nieve (☎ 958 48 03 00) and the four-star Sol Melia Sierra Nevada (☎ 958 24 91 11), both near the main square, are convenient and pleasant. The Sol Melia Sol y Nieve puts on a mini-club for children between five and 11 years of age, while Sol Melia Sierra Nevada boasts a swimming-pool, disco and its own shops, and was described by one reporter as 'the best hotel we have been to in 28 years of skiing'. The four-star Hotel Maribel (☎ 958 24 91 11) is also praised. A kindergarten operates at Pradollano for children aged three months to four years.

Most of Pradollano's buildings date from the 1960s and 1970s. It is not an attractive place ('just like Torremolinos with snow and litter'), but the atmosphere is 'quiet, with quite a Spanish feel to the resort'.

Restaurants include the Andalusi, Pizzeria La Bodega and the Monachil. Early evening entertainment centres around the Crescendo bar. Other recommended venues include Sticky Fingers, Soho and Mango. A dozen clubs, such as Sala Muley in the Sol Melia Sierra Nevada, provide dancing.

TOURIST INFORMATION
Tel 34 958 24 91 00
Fax 34 958 24 91 31
Email cetursa@globalnet.es
Web site www.cetursa.es

Offbeat resorts

Glacier skiing in the Alps is not what is used to be. Global warming is the chief suspect, and a number of traditional summer ski destinations are restricting their summertime operations. Increasingly, hardcore European snow-users with sufficient funds are travelling to the southern hemisphere to bridge the gap between spring and winter in the north. Although there are fewer than two dozen mainstream resorts in all of the Andes, New Zealand's Southern Alps and the Snowy Mountains of Australia, these provide exotic alternatives to Europe's glaciers and can be every bit as good as many of their medium-sized European counterparts in winter. Not all offbeat resorts are in the southern hemisphere – Japan also offers some intriguing and picturesque alternatives.

The **Australian Alps** (also known as the Snowy mountains) are worth a visit, particularly for skiers and snowboarders visiting New Zealand – to travel 12,000 miles to the other side of the world without doing so would be rather a waste. Gladed runs in New South Wales and Victoria mean skiing and boarding through 'snow gums', a type of eucalyptus tree. Instead of the ubiquitous alpine chough of the Alps, your avian companions are likely to be Crimson Rosellas – a richly tinted parrot – or Pied Currawongs, famous for their warbling cry. Even on a hot day with no snow on the approach roads, the authorities insist that you carry chains, which can be rented en route to the slopes.

The Southern Alps of **New Zealand** have some quite impressive resorts that offer higher-quality skiing than Australia, as well as numerous club fields, which are much less sophisticated, with awkward rope-tows and, in most cases, no grooming. But the lift tickets are cheap, and, unlike the commercial areas, there is usually on-mountain accommodation. Most snow-users fly to South Island, where they either head for Christchurch on the east coast, or **Queenstown** on the west. Christchurch offers **Mount Hutt** and a cluster of club fields. Queenstown is a bustling and attractive town on the shores of Lake Wakatipu. It is close to both **Coronet Peak**, one of the oldest ski areas in the country, and **The Remarkables**, which is the newest. **Whakapapa**, at **Mount Ruapehu** on the North Island, has some formidable slopes, but to reach them you must first negotiate some hair-raising mountain roads. The absence of on-mountain accommodation means that you must run the gauntlet for a second time at the end of the skiing day. Conditions in the Southern Alps are susceptible to ever faster change than in other major mountain ranges. The southerly latitude creates a mountain weather pattern at 2,400m that you would expect to find at much higher altitudes in the Alps, the Rockies and the Andes. New Zealand claims to have more heli-skiing and heli-boarding than anywhere apart from Canada, and the South Island has a bewildering number of options.

Chile and **Argentina** can both offer good skiing – although snow cover is unpredictable. The winter of 2000 was excellent, while its predecessor was poor. Most of the main resorts have now invested in snowmaking. The mountains are mystically beautiful, and in good conditions the skiing is unusually varied. The most breathtaking scenery and the best slopes do not always go together, however: the further south that you travel down the Andes the more entrancing the scenery becomes, but the skiing is much less extensive.

The winter season in **Japan** corresponds to the Alps and North America. Japan has more than 700 resorts, although many are little more than single-lift ski hills. Notable exceptions are **Happo'one** and **Shiga Kogen**, venues for the 1998 Winter Olympics. Other major resorts include **Nozawa Onsen**, **Zao** and **Naeba**.

We have given web sites addresses rather than telephone numbers for obtaining further information on accommodation and the skiing throughout this chapter. Alternatively, you can contact the countries' tourist information offices (see *Skiing by numbers*).

ARGENTINA

Gran Catedral (Bariloche)
top 2,050m (6,725ft) bottom 1,050m (3,445ft)

San Carlos de Bariloche, in Patagonia, is home to Gran Catedral – Argentina's oldest and most famous ski resort – better known simply as **Bariloche.** It is a large, attractive resort in the south-west, not far from the Chilean border.

Some 20km from the bustling city and perched high above the spectacular lake of Nahuel Huapi, Catedral – so called because of the cathedral-like rock formations high above the resort – is sophisticated, cosmopolitan and vibrant. With 32 lifts, including a small cable-car, 50 runs and a vertical drop of 1,000m, Bariloche is South America's biggest single resort. It offers an expanse of wide-open, largely intermediate slopes with good, high-speed cruising and abundant off-piste. Lado Bueno (Alta Patagonia) and Robles Catedral are the ski schools.

In recent years there has been a major investment in new lifts, including a six-person covered chair. Natural early-season cover can be sparse, and, although the lower slopes around the main chair-lift are now covered by snow-cannon, temperatures can often be too high to allow them to operate. Alternative nursery slopes are situated at the top of the mountain. The scenery is impressive: the three-peaked Tronador

(3,554m) dominates one horizon, Nahuel Huapi the other. The summit of Piedra del Condor is the site of a terrain park with a half-pipe. Bariloche's nightlife is effervescent. Hotels include the five-star Panamericano and the four-stars Hotel Nevada and Hotel Edelweiss.

Web site www.worldski.com.ar/resorts/bariloch/bariloch.htm

Las Leñas
top 3,340m (11,243ft) bottom 2,240m (7,349ft)

Skiers and boarders searching for challenging slopes rank the terrain at Las Leñas above that of Bariloche. Many regard its off-piste potential as the finest in the southern hemisphere. The resort was built in 1983 with the resort planners at Les Arcs in France acting as consultant. It was constructed almost entirely from a brick-red, wood-lookalike material. Hotels, pistes and lifts are named after signs of the zodiac, with trails names such as Venus, Apolo, Neptuno and Mercurio.

Las Leñas is situated 1,000km from Buenos Aires and reached from Mendoza (three-hour transfer) or Malargüe (one-hour transfer) airports. However, the quality of the snow here, which is usually some of the best on the entire continent, is worth the long journey. The skiing is almost all above the tree-line, making it very exposed and windy. The challenging terrain attracts hard-core skiers and boarders from around the globe, and is accessed by the avalanche-prone Marte chair-lift. This feeds what amounts to a separate ski area with 40 challenging chutes. However, when the lift is closed because of high winds, only the less demanding main ski area of ten lifts is accessible. Beginners have a free drag-lift at the base-station. A new tubing park opened in 2001 and more rental equipment is now available. Piscis, at the foot of the Venus trail, is a five-star hotel offering the best accommodation in town. Cheaper lodging is available at nearby Los Molles or in the valley at Malargüe.

Web site www.laslenas.com

AUSTRALIA

Falls Creek and Mount Hotham
top 1,842m (6,043ft) bottom 1,450m (4,757ft)

Falls Creek and **Mount Hotham** are two of Victoria's three major resorts (the other one is **Thredbo**). They are owned by the same company, share a lift pass and are linked by a helicopter service. The six-minute flight is almost two-and-a-half hours quicker than by road. Mount Hotham Airport at Horsehair Plain, 20km from Hotham, opened in 2000.

Falls Creek Alpine Resort is on the edge of the Bogong High Plains, four hours' drive from Melbourne. It is a European-style ski-in ski-out village with a difference – accommodation among gum trees. Parking is at the base of the village, and luggage is transported to your lodge by snowcat. You can ski directly to eight different lifts from every lodge. Altogether there are more than 20 lifts serving 96 trails spread across four distinct areas. Village Bowl has the principal slopes and some long challenging runs, Sun Valley attracts beginners and intermediates, and the Maze area provides attractive tree skiing. The resort has an impressive terrain park. Falls Creek is famous for the bumps under the Summit quad-chair, particularly on Exhibition run, and provides the venue for many of Australia's mogul competitions. Nearby Mount McKay offers 38 hectares of back-country skiing.

Mount Hotham is the highest alpine resort in Victoria, with most of the slopes lying below the village. Runs such as Mary's Slide, the Chute and Gotcha are quite challenging, while intermediates tend to gather in the Heavenly Valley region. Good nursery slopes are served by the Summit quad-chair and T-bar, and the Big D quad at Mount Higginbotham. In all, the area has 13 lifts and a vertical drop of 395m. **Dinner Plain**, Mount Hotham's architect-designed sister village, provides reasonably priced accommodation and is situated 10km from the mountain, linked by an efficient free bus service.

Web sites www.fallscreek.net
www.hotham.net.au

Mount Buller
top 1,804m (5,917ft) bottom 1,390m (4,559ft)
Mount Buller is the principal area for Melbourne-based skiers, situated a three-and-a-half-hour (200-km) drive north-east from Melbourne, through Ned Kelly country. It has the largest lift capacity in Australia, with a comprehensive network of 25 lifts, including 13 chair-lifts, serving 80km of trails. There are some long cruising runs, including Little Buller Spur and Wombats, and trails that run from the high-altitude snow gums through to the snowline. The Buller Chutes behind the Summit are genuine black-diamond (difficult) runs. The scenery is some of the most impressive in the Victorian Alps, with extensive views across the gum forests. Night-skiing takes place two evenings each week. The Schuss Lodge is a small hotel with 27 beds and some magnificent views.

Web site www.skibuller.com.au

Perisher–Blue
top 2,034m (6,672ft) bottom 1,605m (5,264ft)
The linked resorts of **Perisher/Smiggins**, **Blue Cow** and **Guthega** in New South Wales form the largest ski area in Australia. Perisher alone has 20 lifts, and the combined area has 50. The only way to reach the main complex is by train: the modern Ski Tube takes skiers through 10km of tunnels on a 20-minute journey to Perisher and Blue Cow from Bullocks Flat. Blue Cow prides itself on its testing terrain and the high

proportion of black-diamond (difficult) runs. Accelerator is the longest run in the Perisher–Blue area. However, 60 per cent of the terrain is graded intermediate. Guthega has some challenging short, sharp runs such as Parachute, Bloody Mary and Mother-in-Law.

Transport from the Perisher terminal complex to all the lodges is on caterpillar vehicles. The best accommodation is in the Perisher Valley Hotel, which has 31 rooms and suites. The Perisher Manor is a family-run, ski-in ski-out establishment. The Lodge at Smiggins is a no-smoking, Austrian-style hotel with a swimming-pool. Heidi's Chalet is opposite the lifts at Smiggins.

Web site www.perisherblue.com.au

Thredbo
top 2,037m (6,683ft) bottom 1,365m (4,478ft)
This New South Wales resort, 450km from Sydney, has some of the best skiing in the country, laid out around an attractive Alpine-style village. In the 1950s a large number of Austrians came here to work on the Snowy Mountain hydro-electric scheme, stayed on to take an active part in the skiing business, and have left their cultural imprint on the town. Runs such as High Noon Supertrail, Dream Run and the Crackenback Supertrail cut through a forest of the ubiquitous snow gums. Ego Alley and Albert's Amble offer scenic descents, while Cannonball, Funnelweb and Michael's Mistake are the main challenges. The run from Karels T-Bar, Australia's highest lift, down to Friday Flat extends for 6km. The area has a total of 13 lifts serving some 40 runs.

The resort's leading hotel is the Thredbo Alpine Hotel, which adjoins Village Square with its range of shops and cafés. Other accommodation in the area includes the renovated Snowgoose Lodge. Bursills Lodge boasts an indoor swimming-pool, and House of Ullr has a Scandinavian theme.

Web site www.thredbo.com.au

CHILE

El Colorado, La Parva and Valle Nevado
top 3,670m (12,040ft) bottom 2,430m (7,972ft)
Beneath the peak of El Plomo, which soars to 5,428m, three resorts form the biggest linked playground for skiers and snowboarders in South America. **La Parva**, **Valle Nevado** and **El Colorado** are each significant ski areas in their own right. With over 100km of prepared trails and 42 lifts between them they are the closest major slopes to a capital city in the world. Santiago lies only 64km to the south of the resort ('after the smog and pollution of Santiago, the clean mountain air was a joy. However, descending the windy road in the evening it was not a pleasant sight to see a black pall hanging over the city').

El Colorado comprises two resorts – the original ski area of Farellones and the modern and much more extensive slopes of El Colorado. Skiers flock here from Santiago, but only at weekends, leaving the slopes relatively quiet during the week. La Parva, which has the most varied skiing, has no real hotels at present and remains a second- or even third-home resort for affluent Chileans.

Valle Nevado is the only true destination resort of the three ('enjoyable if you happen to be in Chile anyway, but certainly does not warrant a special journey from Europe'). It was purpose-built by the French in the 1980s. In 1999, the resort installed the largest snowmaking system in South America. A high-speed quad, the Andes Express, now reaches the peak of Cerro Negro (the top of the Peña de Aguila), and a new surface lift has been installed in the Valle del Inca close to La Parva. The new lifts and runs have increased the terrain by 25 per cent. First class hotels include the Puerta del Sol and Tres Puntas. There is a new 27-unit condominium complex and six good restaurants. La Fourchette d'Or serves fine French cuisine and the Café de la Plaza offers traditional Chilean dishes.

Web sites (El Colorado) www.andesweb.com/colorado.html
(La Parva) www.andesweb.com/parva.html
(Valle Nevado) www.andesweb.com/valle.html

Portillo
top 3,348m (10,984ft) bottom 2,512m (8,241ft)

Chile's oldest ski area is picturesque but slightly quirky, in a steep-sided valley next to the breathtakingly beautiful Laguna (lake) del Inca. Almost on the Argentine border, Portillo is just under 160km north of Santiago. Access is via the awe-inspiring Uspallata Pass, one of only two passes between Chile and Argentina accessible during the winter. Aconcagua (6,960m), the highest mountain in the western hemisphere, is nearby. The area was first skied by Norwegian and British engineers, who were building the now largely abandoned trans-Andes railway. The Bajada Del Tren run allows you to ski through an old railway tunnel. Most visitors to Portillo stay at the bright yellow Hotel Portillo, which dominates the resort. A quaint colonial atmosphere still pervades, with the red-and-white jacketed waiters hurrying around the vast lakeside dining-room. Low-budget travellers using the bunk beds at the Octagon Lodge still eat at the hotel, while backpackers at the Inca Lodge have access to all hotel facilities.

The resort is run by a veteran American, Henry Purcell, and the grooming and signposting on the 23 trails, served by 12 lifts, are as efficient as you would expect to find in any North American resort. The North American influence is reinforced by a large number of US ski instructors. The resort has a heli-ski operation that departs from the door of the hotel. There are two bizarre but exhilarating *va et vient* lifts, unique to Portillo, designed for accessing the steep chutes in avalanche-prone areas on both sides of the valley, including the celebrated Flying Kilometre run. The larger lift, Roca Jack, hauls five skiers at a time on linked platters at considerable speed to the top of the chute before suddenly coming to a halt; skiers disengage backwards. *Va et vient* lifts have no lift-towers. Should the cable be cut by an overnight avalanche, it remains buried until it can be repaired or replaced. From the Condor lift, Roca Jack's counterpart across the laguna, you can ski down to the frozen lake and skate home.

Web site www.interknowledge.com/chile/portillo

Termas de Chillán
top 2,500m (8,200ft) bottom 1,800m (5,900ft)

For skiers and riders in search of the more offbeat face of the Chilean Andes without sacrificing quality, this spa resort best combines the two. Beware, however – the more exotic the location, the more treacherous the access route is likely to be. Do not attempt to reach Termas de Chillán without a four-wheel-drive vehicle or at least chains; the final 29km of the journey is on an icy, rocky and potholed road.

The resort itself lies 480km south of Santiago and 80km east of Chillán, the birthplace of Chile's first president, Bernardo O'Higgins. There are 28 groomed runs served by nine lifts spread across 10,118 hectares of unusually varied terrain. A vertical drop of 1,100m is possible for those prepared to hike above the lifts. There are eight lifts, of which the Don Otto chair-lift is reputedly the longest on the continent. The excellent off-piste includes the 14-km Shangri-La run, with its volcanic scenery, and Pirigallo – one of the resort's most celebrated itineraries, which comes complete with fumaroles belching sulphur fumes. It is susceptible to avalanche after a storm. Extreme skiers can reach either of the two summits from the top of the chair-lift, with the Volcán offering the largest variety of steep chutes.

Termas de Chillán is popular with snowboarders, who are attracted to the long vertical drop. The resort also contains Chile's first terrain park and half-pipe. The Gran Hotel has expensive ski-in ski-out accommodation. The villages of Las Trancas and Los Lleunques, both within a 30-minute drive, have more reasonably priced accommodation. Another option is the Villa del Bosque Nevado condominiums; these are next to the Pirigallo Hotel and share its restaurant and spring water swimming-pool.

Web site www.andesweb.com/termas.html

JAPAN

Happo'one and Hakuba Valley
top 1,830m (6,007ft) bottom 760m (2,493ft)

Happo'one is the biggest ski area in the **Nagano** prefecture's resort-studded Hakuba Valley and arguably the best single resort in Japan. The Tsugaike Ridge Mountains rise to almost 3,047m and the valley lies 200km from Tokyo. It is linked to the capital by the shinkansen (bullet-train) built for the 1988 Olympics. As well as offering splendid mountain scenery, some challenging terrain and longer-than-average runs, Happo-one is one of the prettiest ski villages in the country. With skiing up to 1,830m, a vertical drop of more than 1,070m, and some 35 lifts, Happo'one has a good mix of terrain. Another plus point is the quick access to other ski areas in the valley, including **Hakuba 47, Iwatake**, **Goryu-Toomi** and **Sunalpina Sanosaka**. Accommodation includes the Omoshiro Hasshinichi hotel at the base of Happo-one. It has four restaurants and a nightclub, as well as indoor and outdoor swimming-pools. The Hotel Ougiya Hakuba is also recommended.

Web site www.skijapanguide.com

Naeba
top 1,800m (5,905ft) bottom 900m (2,953ft)

This bustling ski area in the Niigata prefecture is one of the most frenetic resorts in the northern Japanese Alps. It is dominated by the Naeba Prince, the largest ski hotel in the world, with a shopping arcade, a Sega amusement area, a health centre and more than 40 restaurants, including one that stays open all night. This enables skiers and riders who are anxious to pack in as many hours on the slopes as possible to eat breakfast at 3.30am and ski under floodlights at 4am. There is no need to stop skiing until 11pm, which means that die-hard snow-users can keep going for 19 hours. At weekends, when packed bullet trains and buses disgorge their human cargo, an almost absurd number of skiers floods the slopes – the record stands at 40,000 in one weekend – so at least at 4.30am there is some chance of finding a little space in which to turn. The resort has 28 trails and a terrain park.

Web site www.skijapanguide.com

Shiga Kogen
top 2,305m (7,562ft) bottom 1,228m (4,028ft)

Nagano's largest ski area, Shiga Kogen, was the venue for the majority of the 1998 Winter Olympic events. It is an extraordinary patchwork of 21 different ski bases, served by more than 80 lifts, dotting six inter-linked mountains. None of the sectors is big or particularly difficult; in Alpine terms the whole area would make up just three or four linked resorts of reasonable size. A competent skier or rider could cover all the terrain in a couple of days. The highest point – the 2304-m summit of

Mount Yoketeyama – is not infrequently obscured by freezing mist or blizzards. The Olympic Giant Slalom and Super-G courses were held at Higashitateyama ski base. Accommodation includes Villa Alpen (which has its own ski school and equipment rental shop) in the Sun Valley resort and Hotel Higashikan at Shiga Kogen. Snowscooting is available as an alternative sport.

Web site www.jinjapan.org/atlas/nature/nat25.html

Nozawa Onsen
top 1,650m (5,414ft) bottom 560m (1,837ft)

Nozawa Onsen, Shiga Kogen's neighbour, is refreshingly old-world; a Japanese Mürren with an excellent ski museum. The busy, narrow streets of the picturesque little spa village are marred by traffic and the scent of sulphur from the 13 public hot spring bath-houses. One of the springs produces water at such a high temperature that it is too hot to bathe in – instead, it is used by the locals to boil vegetables. From downtown Nozawa, the slopes are reached in an arduous fashion by a steep walk up narrow streets, followed by two long escalators. The skiing comprises 33km of slopes served by a large network of 29 lifts, including two gondolas. The area is satisfyingly varied with some steep pitches, but, infuriatingly, two of the best runs are reserved for race-training and competitions. Tanuki (Racoon Run) is officially never open. It starts from the top of the Yamabiko Chair and attracts powder enthusiasts who sneak in when the ski patrol is not watching. Mountain restaurants are unusually plentiful but there is little Western food available. Accommodation is mainly ryokans (inns) and small hotels. The central Kameya Ryokan is recommended.

Web site shinshu.online.co.jp/nozawa

Zao
top 1,736m (5,696ft) bottom 780m (2,599ft)

Zao, in the Yamagata region, retains its spa-town charm in spite of its size. The resort is one of the biggest in Japan, with 42 lifts – including three cable-cars – spread across 186 hectares of terrain on Mount Jizo. It is situated two-and-a-half hours from Tokyo by shinkansen (bullet-train). Its slopes (accessed by a rather ancient cable-car) are famous throughout the country because of a huge forest of 'snow-ghosts' – fir trees which, during icy blasts of maritime winds, become encrusted with hoar frost and snow to form vast cohorts of weird monster shapes. To add to the surreal nature of the resort, 50m above the top of the cable-car is a gigantic statue of Zao Zizo, a jizo-bosatsu (guardian-deity), which is said to protect the peak from evil spirits. In winter there is so much snow that only the statue's head and shoulders can be seen.

Web site www.zao-spa.or.jp

NEW ZEALAND

Mount Hutt
top 2,075m (6,808ft) bottom 1,585m (5,200ft)

This most famous of New Zealand's resorts is situated a 35-minute drive from Methven and 70 minutes from Christchurch, and has magnificent views across the Canterbury Plains. Mount Hutt was previously renowned for its access route: 12km of unsurfaced road at the mercy of strong winds, with somewhat alarming drops. However considerable surfacing work was carried out in time for the 2001 season. The skiing can be excellent, although unpredictable weather has given the resort the rather harsh sobriquet of 'Mount Shut'. Mount Hutt has one of the most extensive snow-making systems in the southern hemisphere. The South Face runs, which end up below the base area, account for its advertised 672-m vertical drop. Local heli-skiing is available. The resort now has two half-pipes and the ubiquitous (in New Zealand) bungee jump. The base area has been partially rebuilt and now features a clock tower, café and restaurant. The choice of accommodation is between hotels in Christchurch and farm cottages, or 'homestays', where you stay and eat with a local family.

Web site www.mthutt.co.nz

Mount Ruapehu
top 2,322m (7,618ft) bottom 1,600m (5,249ft)

Whakapapa, built on the flanks of the Mount Ruapehu volcano in central North Island, is the country's largest developed ski area. It has purchased its neighbour **Turoa** on the other side of the volcano and the two areas are now marketed as Mount Ruapehu. Whakapapa has a vertical drop of 675m and a total of 30 trails. These include a wide selection of cruising runs, some exciting off-piste in its Black Magic area, as well some severe terrain below the Pinnacles. The unpredictable weather is frustrating. Storms can move in fast and furiously, bringing white-outs to both resorts. In 1995 and 1996, a series of spectacular volcanic eruptions brought the ski season to a premature close. Normally it is possible to make the three-hour climb to the Ruapehu crater lake and then ski down. Whakapapa is excellent for riders, with its varied terrain of cliffs and gullies, as well as a well-maintained half-pipe.

Turoa, on the south-western face of Mount Ruapehu, offers the biggest vertical drop (720m) in Australasia. The upper slopes, like Whakapapa's, include some of the exotic qualities associated with volcanic terrain. A climb to the summit affords breathtaking views of the Tasman Sea. It is possible to ski down, but snow-users are urged to check with the ski patrol first. Apart from an unusual and exhilarating terraced effect – steep little sections followed by long, flatter sections – the lift-served slopes provide rolling, wide-open and largely uneventful cruising, with a few runs of almost 4km. The Turoa Ski Lodge is a comfortable place to stay, with a restaurant, a bar and roaring log fires.

Web site www.mtruapehu.com

Queenstown (Coronet Peak and The Remarkables)
top 1,957m (6,421ft) bottom 1,200m (3,937ft)

Queenstown is a lively and picturesque lakeside town situated in the south-west of the South Island. It is flanked by two separate resorts which operate interchangeable lift passes. The traditional resort is Coronet Peak, with a vertical drop of 420m. It has been modernised and enlarged and now provides a wide variety of good all-round skiing and a much-improved lift system. The nursery slope now claims the longest magic carpet lift (146m) in the world.

The Remarkables was constructed more recently. It is visually exciting, but has fewer options than Coronet Peak. From Queenstown The Remarkables range seems impossibly steep, with the peaks resembling a set of sharp, pearly-white teeth, dominating the shoreline of Lake Wakatipu. Fortunately, the ski area is on the other side, where gentle bowls belie the severity of the mountains.

Although The Remarkables provides predominantly intermediate terrain for skiers and riders, some short, sharp couloirs, including Escalator and Elevator, add considerable challenge. Among the steep off-piste sections (a hike is required) are the Homeward Runs. These emerge on the access road to the resort, from where a truck takes skiers back up to the base area. Toilet Bowl, which also ends at the road below, is a good long off-piste descent for freeriders. The award-winning Remarkables Lodge is the closest hotel to the Remarkables ski resort.

Web sites (Coronet Peak) www.nzski.com/coronet_peak
(The Remarkables) www.nzski.com/remarkables

Treble Cone
top 1,860m (6,102ft) bottom 1,200m (3,936ft)

The atmosphere at Lake Wanaka is as tranquil as that at Lake Wakatipu is vibrant. This is the idyllic gateway to Treble Cone, one of the country's top resorts, which houses New Zealand's first six-seater chair. Advanced skiers and freeriders can hike for 20 minutes to the 2,100-m summit to enjoy some of the best off-piste in the area. There is good heli-skiing nearby in the Harris Mountains. Treble Cone has exceptional views across picturesque Lake Wanaka and the Matukituki Valley, as well as Mount Aspiring. Outer Limits is the best of the handful of scenic cruising runs. For off-piste enthusiasts, Treble Cone's big attraction is Saddle Basin, with a collection of chutes, including Bullet, Shooter and Super Pipe. There are two half-pipes.

Web site www.new-zealand.com/treblecone

Other winter sports

There is no shortage of things to do in a winter resort. As indolent as sleeping on a sun terrace or as educational as a stroll through one of many Alpine museums (**Chamonix**, **Saas-Fee**, **St Anton**, **Zermatt**), these alternatives to schussing downhill on skis are proliferating as resorts strive to offer something for everybody. In addition to the main activities explained below, other even more offbeat oddities are on offer at specific destinations. In **Les Arcs** you can play paint-ball, while in **Megève** you can drive bumper-cars on ice. You can join a llama trek in **Grindelwald** or bungee-jump in **Les Deux Alpes**. In **Alpe d'Huez**, **Val d'Isère** and **Valmorel** you can view the slopes from a microlight aircraft. And in **Åre** you can windsurf on ice. In **St Moritz**, where the winter-sports holiday was invented, you can toboggan head-first inches off the ice on the Cresta Run, or play polo, golf or cricket on the frozen lake. In **Bad Kleinkirchheim** you can try ice-tennis and in **Courchevel** you can hurtle down the landing zone of the Olympic ski jump in a rubber boat. But beware: it is essential to check your winter-sports insurance cover before taking part in any of these alternative activities – most are not covered by standard policies.

Bob-sleigh

You can ride as a passenger on a real Olympic ice-walled bob-sleigh course in **Cortina d'Ampezzo**, **Igls**, **La Plagne** or **Park City**. No skill is required: just hold on tight and have faith in the driver and brake-person. In a tamer variation, the track can be negotiated on a foam-rubber raft.

Cat skiing

Cat skiing is a variation on heli-skiing in that you are transported to areas that you cannot otherwise reach by ski-lift. The snowcats are usually heated, with seating inside. Your small group is picked up and taken to a point from where to ski or snowboard, before being collected after completing a run. On a good day you can hope to ski or snow-board around a dozen trails. A guide accompanies the group and, as with heli-skiing, safety is paramount due to avalanche danger. Cat skiing is popular in North American resorts such as **Crested Butte** and **Grand Targhee**.

Curling

Curling takes place on a frozen lake or man-made rink and is the ice-born cousin of bowls. The game probably originated in Scotland, but has been played widely throughout the Alps for more than a century. Players bowl heavy 'stones' at the 'tee', the centre of a 2.1-m circle on the ice. Other members of the team vigorously 'soop' the ice in the path of the stone with brooms to aid its passage. Opinion is divided as to the effectiveness of sooping, but it keeps the players warm. **Seefeld** in Austria is a world centre and boasts 40 curling lanes.

Dog-sledding

You can take a back seat and wonder at the awesome pulling power of a team of huskies as the Alpine scenery slips by in a host of resorts including **Avoriaz**, **Courchevel**, **Les Arcs** and **Tignes**. The real thrill, however, is to drive your own sled. This is best achieved in Scandinavia but is also possible in **Banff**, **Breckenridge** and **Jackson Hole**. All you need are nerves of steel and a firm foot on the brake – metal claws that dig deep into the snow. Such is the Herculean strength of a fresh racing team of 16 dogs that the brake will have little positive effect over the first couple of kilometres – other than to leave a neatly ploughed snow-field in your wake.

Hang-gliding

Hang-gliders are known as 'deltas' throughout most of Europe; these fixed-wing personal aircraft successfully exploit the thermals surrounding high Alpine peaks. Pilot and taxi passenger point their skis downhill and the gliders quickly become airborne. This is a high-adrenaline adventure, with inescapable risk, not suitable for children or timid adults. It is available at dozens of resorts – **Tignes**, **Verbier** and **Wengen** among them.

Hot-air ballooning

This is a spectacular and moderately safe way for all the family to get a quiet, bird's-eye view of the resort and surrounding area. Ballooning in the Alps is centred on Switzerland (**Château d'Oex**, **Crans Montana**, **Gstaad**, **St Moritz**) but is also possible in **Aspen**, **Beaver Creek**, **Breckenridge**, **Crested Butte**, **Filzmoos**, **Megève** and **Zell am See**.

Ice-climbing

With an ice-axe in each hand and front-pointing crampons on each foot scaling ice walls is easier than it looks, though a mountain guide to belay you on ropes is always essential. You can climb – or abseil down ('ruissiling') – frozen waterfalls (**Alpe d'Huez**, **Banff**, **Risoul**, **Tignes**) or man-made ice spires erected each winter in a score of Alpine resorts (**Bad Gastein**, **Courchevel**, **Saas-Fee**, **Zermatt**).

Ice-diving

Beginner adults as well as experienced divers can enjoy the beauty that lies beneath the ice-covered lake in **Tignes**, all winter long. The thrill is the kaleidoscopic colours created by refraction of light on the ice. Despite a dry-suit, some *sang froid* is required but there is little real danger, as you are attached by rope to a guide on the surface.

Ice-driving

You can learn practical skills that may spare you an accident and an insurance claim on a country road next winter as well as have tremendous fun skidding a saloon car around dedicated ice circuits at **Les Deux Alpes**, **Flaine**, **Serre Chevalier**, **Steamboat**, **Val d'Isère** or **Val Thorens**. Dual controls and certified instructors ensure avoidance of trees and other obstacles.

Ice-fishing

This is not a sport that involves cardio-vascular exercise. The only attributes required are patience and the ability to stand around for several hours in sub-zero temperatures. You use a saw to cut a hole in the ice on a lake, drop a baited hook or a spinning lure into the depths beneath and wait for the fish to strike. Trout and perch usually come quietly when arrested in somnolent mid-winter. It is to be hoped that this happens before those on the surface succumb to either the cold or the copious quantities of *schnapps*, which are a feature of such outings. Resorts include **Åre**, **Banff and Lake Louise**, **Beaver Creek**, **Breckenridge**, **Vail** and **Whistler**.

Indoor climbing wall

Resort adventurers who don't want to go out in the cold can get high indoors on an indoor climbing wall. These are wooden walls with artificial rock handholds affixed. An experienced person to belay the climber is essential, and trained guides are on hand in most centres. With proper supervision there is no danger and effectively no age limit.

Night-skiing and night-snowboarding

Floodlit piste skiing is becoming an increasingly popular feature in both major and minor resorts throughout Europe and North America. It is prevalent in Scandinavia where 'night' takes up most of 24 hours during the early part of the winter. In Japan the sheer volume of visitors makes the artificially prolonged skiing day a necessity. Most Alpine and North American resorts light up a single slalom slope and a terrain park until 9pm on certain nights each week. **Keystone** in Colorado has a string of sodium lamps stretching across an entire mountainside. Other principal resorts include **Åre**, **Levi**, **Courchevel**, **Morzine** and **Sestriere**.

Parapente

Parapente, or parascending, is the wingless cousin of hang-gliding (see page 540). Instead of a glider you use a specialist sport parachute to ride the thermals. Initially, you travel as a taxi-passenger, strapped in harness in front of or behind your instructor. You stand on skis on a mountain top, the instructor allows the chute to inflate, then you point your skis downhill and take off. The pilot uses toggle strings to control the direction and angle of descent. You land at a suitable point in the resort or down in the valley beneath. When you are more experienced you can go it alone. The sport is popular in almost every European resort though less popular in North America. No experience or skill is necessary apart from the ability to ski in a straight line and to put your faith in fellow humanity.

Reindeer-sledding

This is an activity found only in Northern Scandinavia (and, of course, throughout the world on the night of 24 December). Contrary to popular belief only one reindeer normally takes the traces. The passenger in the two-person sleigh holds the reins, which give some measure of left- and right-control. The driver, standing on the back axle, operates the brake – a rudimentary mat on a short chain. In moments of crisis he drops the mat on to the snow and stands on it while clinging grimly to the sleigh. Reindeer are far from docile animals and lack the obedience traditionally shown to the jolly man in the red coat. Resorts where you can indulge this include **Levi** in Finland and **Åre** in Sweden.

Ski-jöring

Ski-jöring is a traditional means of transport in Alaska and Scandinavia involving a skier being pulled behind a reindeer, horse or dog – any animal weighing more than 16kg can successfully pull an adult. You wear cross-country skis and a padded, nylon waist-belt (with a quick-release) that is attached by a tow-rope to the animal. Few resorts offer the sport to beginners, but **Banff**, **Breckenridge** and **Serre Chevalier** are the exceptions.

Ski-jumping

Eddie the Eagle is forever enshrined in the public consciousness for his extraordinary nerve and lack of ability at the 1988 Calgary Winter Olympics. Participants begin in tamer circumstances with a hop of just a couple of metres on normal alpine skis. The sport is popular in Finland and the other Scandinavian countries, and there are jump centres in **Les Arcs**, **Chamonix**, **Courchevel**, **Kitzbühel** and **St Moritz**. However, some of the best instruction for novices is found at the Utah Olympic Park near **Park City**, which is the jumping venue for the 2002 Winter Olympics.

Snowbiking

A variety of mountain-bike-style 'snowbikes' with oversized tyres have been developed, mostly for use inside terrain parks with prepared trails. **Alpe d'Huez**, **Avoriaz**, **Courmayeur**, **Crans Montana**, **Méribel**, **Vail** and **Verbier** are snowbiking centres. In **Les Arcs** a handful of extremists risk their lives to ride specially built mountain bikes down the speed-skiing course at 160kph. Inside parks, where helmets are worn, the sport poses little danger.

SnowCarting

SnowCarts are go-kart bodies mounted on ski runners. They have steering wheels and brakes – but no motor – and can be found on- or off-piste in a score of resorts (**Chamonix**, **Grindelwald**, **Gstaad**, **Samnaun**, **Seefeld** and **Verbier**). Speed is easily controlled by applying steel claw brakes. Pedal power dictates that SnowCarts are not suitable for children under 140cm tall.

Snowmobiling

Snowmobiling as a sport, rather than a means of transport for piste and other mountain workers, is banned throughout a large part of Europe. This limits holiday-makers to relatively short circuits in France (**Courchevel**, **La Plagne** and **Val d'Isère**). However, in Scandinavia and North America there are few restrictions, with 212,400km of trails in the USA alone. The ability to drive a motorbike is useful but by no means essential. The principal controls are a throttle and a brake. Special thermal clothing is advisable, and helmets are mandatory. Snowmobiling in wilderness areas can be dangerous, with frostbite, collisions and avalanches all taking their toll.

Snowscooting

This is the newest craze in **Les Arcs**. A mountain bike is mounted on to a snowboard and you descend the piste as fast as on a pair of skis. Going up the mountain is easiest by gondola. Other resorts where you can snowscoot include **Avoriaz**, **Les Contamines**, **Pra-Loup** and **Nagano**.

Snowshoeing

Snowshoeing is a North American import that has become a bit of a fad in the Alps, where most resorts now hire the gear and offer accompanied tours. No experience is necessary and, apart from wandering off-piste into avalanche terrain, there is no real risk.

Speed skiing

Recreational skiers can hire helmets and special speed skis to have a go from lower starting gates on the Flying Kilometre course at **Les Arcs**. Speeds of up to 130kph may be reached, so only strong and confident skiers should consider attempting the descent.

Tubing

Safer than conventional tobogganing and fun for children of all ages, tubing takes place on banked courses in fenced-off terrain parks. It is available almost everywhere in North America (notably **Vail**) and in an increasing number of Alpine resorts including **Mayrhofen** and **La Plagne**. The tubes, in reality tyre inner tubes or specially designed rubber creations in animal shapes, are towed by drag-lift to the top of the course.

Heli-skiing and heli-boarding

Helicopter skiing is an exotic, expensive but very rewarding way for accomplished skiers and riders to reach untracked snow in high mountain regions far beyond the scope of ski lifts. In effect, it is no more than a luxury limousine service, and it is important to dispel the popular misconception among non-skiers (and even some skiers) that it involves James Bond-style jumps from a hovering chopper. The pilot lands firmly on the snow and departs before you ski off.

It is possible to heli-ski and heli-board in a variety of countries, including Canada, India, Italy, New Zealand, Sweden, Switzerland, the USA, and even the former Soviet republics of Georgia and Kazakhstan. Heli-skiing is banned in France for environmental reasons, although companies based in France can arrange trips to the Italian Alps. In Austria it is very restricted, with the exception of a few designated 'drop' points around Lech and Zürs. There is a strong movement in Italy to ban the sport on environmental grounds.

Heli-skiers and heli-boarders expect powder snow, and fresh tracks are taken for granted, but inevitably there will be frustrating days when, because of bad visibility or howling winds, it will not be possible for the helicopter to take off. If you are staying at a remote wilderness lodge, this will also mean no skiing or riding. Canadian Mountain Holidays (CMH), which has ten bases in British Columbia, stresses the dangers to its clients: 'there are no guarantees as to what you will encounter during your week. It could be the best skiing of your life, but it could also be poor and very demanding. We want to make it absolutely clear that there are risks beyond our control that you must share with us'. These risks involve both the hazardous operating of helicopters around mountain peaks and the always-present danger of avalanche. Standard winter sports insurance policies do not include heli-skiing or heli-boarding and you should always take out extra cover.

Basics

The helicopters used to transport skiers and boarders to the mountain tops include the Bell 210 and 212 that seat up to 12 passengers, including a guide. The smaller Aerospatiale *Squirrel* (known in North America as the A Star), which can take up to five passengers and a guide, is also popular. The pilot is the most important person in a heli-skiing operation – even outranking the highly trained guide. Mountain pilots will fly in almost all weathers, including lightly falling snow, as long as there is adequate visibility and low to moderate wind speeds.

The heli-ski experience can range from an introductory run or a single-day package in Europe or North America, to a full week in British Columbia or even the Himalayas, with the number of 'drops' per group running into double figures on most days. A 'drop' is equivalent to one long 'run' in a ski resort. A group of skiers or boarders is deposited on the snow by the helicopter in order to ski or ride down. This group is then collected at the bottom of the run by the helicopter.

In Canada, for example, up to 44 clients will spend a week in a ski lodge in the British Columbian mountain wilderness where they are divided into groups according to ability or who they want to ski with.

How good do you have to be?

Generally you should be reasonably fit and of high intermediate standard (i.e. you should be able to do parallel turns and to manage a black (or black-diamond) trail with confidence). The introduction of wide-bodied or 'fat' skis that allow you to 'float' over all types of snow has made skiing in general less tiring and heli-skiing easier and more accessible. Snowboarders should be of a similar standard. There are no age restrictions, but common sense dictates that the experience is too physically demanding for all but the most accomplished of sub-teenage children as well as skiers in the twilight of their sporting prowess.

For skiers or riders wishing to sample the sport before committing themselves to a lodge in the middle of nowhere for an entire week, heli-skiing or heli-boarding for a single day is easily available in Switzerland.

Safety

Before you even get into the helicopter, you will be given a safety briefing and required to learn some basic procedures for avalanche rescue using transceivers, as well as how to move safely in and around the helicopter. There are several vital points to remember:

- Do not ski or ride near the helicopter, regardless of whether or not the rotor-blade is moving.
- Never go round the back of the helicopter.
- Do not ski or ride past your guide. He or she may have stopped because of changing snow conditions, a tricky cliff area or even a crevasse.
- Do not chase loose items of clothing if they blow away.

How much will it cost?

A single drop costs from approximately £80, with a full day of three descents from about £200 in the Alps to £650 in the Himalayas. Three-and five-day packages are also an option in some locations. RK Heli-ski at Panorama in British Columbia specialises in beginner packages: a day's package of three drops and lunch is just over £200, with additional runs at £25 each. If bad weather prevents you taking your minimum weekly 'ration' you should qualify for a refund.

What will you get for your money?

A week-long package would include accommodation, picnic lunches served on the slopes (unless the weather is bad) and substantial dinners. This would be based in a location where there is little else to do but ski, absorb the scenery and enjoy the camaraderie. You can expect to ski or board 30,000m vertical in a week, but some groups manage more.

Heli-ski companies

Listed below are a selection of heli-ski companies from around the world. Others are listed in resorts' *Skiing facts* boxes under *Guiding*. It must be emphasised that we have personal experience of only some of them. You are strongly advised to ask about safety standards with your chosen company before booking.

CANADA

Blackcomb Helicopters (*Whistler*)
Tel 1 604 938 1700
Fax 1 604 938 1706
Email bbheli@direct.ca
Web site
www.blackcombhelicopters.com

Cayoosh Helisports (*Whistler*)
Tel 1 604 894 1144
Fax 1 604 894 1146
Email info@cayooshhelisports.com
Web site
www.cayooshhelisports.com

Helico Presto (*Whistler*)
Tel 1 604 938 2927
Web site helicopresto.com

Purcell Helicopter Skiing Ltd
(*British Columbia*)
Tel 1 250 344 5410
Fax 1 250 344 6076
Email
info@purcellhelicopterskiing.com
Web site
www.purcellhelicopterskiing

RK Heli-ski (*British Columbia*)
Tel 1 250 342 3889
Fax 1 250 342 3466
Email info@rkheliski.com
Web site www.rkheliski.com

Robson Helimagic (*British Columbia*)
Tel 1 250 344 2326
Fax 1 250 566 4333
Email brigitta@robsonhelimagic.com
Web site www.robsonhelimagic.com

Whistler Heli-skiing
Tel 1 604 932 4105
Fax 1 604 938 1225
Email heliski@direct.ca
Web site www.heliskiwhistler.com

FRANCE

Pros-Neige (*based in Val Thorens, to Le Chaud and Ruitor Glacier*)
Tel 33 479 01 07 00
Fax 33 479 01 07 01
Email info@proneige.fr
Web site www.prosneige.fr

Top Ski (*based in Val d'Isère, to Valgrisenche, Val Veny, Monterosa*)
Tel 33 479 06 14 80
Fax 33 479 06 28 42
Email top.ski.val.isere@wanadoo.fr
Web site www.topskival.fr

ITALY

ETI 2000 (*Cervinia, Monterosa*)
Tel 39 0165 765 417
Fax 39 0165 765 418
Email eti2000@netvallee.it
Web site www.eti2000.it

Heliski Europe (*Valgrisenche, Chamonix Valley, Alaska*)
Tel 020-7584 6287 (UK)
Fax 020-7581 9422
Email heliski@aquiver.co.uk

NEW ZEALAND

Alpine Guides (Aoraki) Ltd (*Mount Cook National Park*)
Tel 64 3435 1834 **Fax** 64 3435 1898
Email mtcook@alpineguides.co.nz
Web site www.alpineguides.co.nz

Back Country Helicopters (*Wanaka surroundings*)
Tel 64 3443 1054 **Fax** 64 3443 1051
Email photoshop@xtra.co.nz
Web site www.heliski.net.nz

Harris Mountains Heli-ski (*The Remarkables, Coronet Peak,Treble Cone and Cardrona, The Doolans, Tyndall Glaciers,The Buchanans*)
Tel 64 3442 6722 **Fax** 64 3441 8563
Email hmh@heliski.co.nz
Web site www.heliski.co.nz

The Helicopter Line (*Mount Cook, Queenstown*)
Tel 64 3442 3034 **Fax** 64 4442 3529
Email thizqn@helicopter.co.nz
Web site www.helicopter.co.nz

Methven Heli-ski (*Arrowsmith, Ragged and Palmer Ranges*)
Tel 64 3302 8108 **Fax** 64 3302 8909
Email methven@heliskiing.co.nz
Web site www.heliskiing.co.nz

Queenstown Mountain Guiding Ltd
Tel 64 3441 3400 **Fax** 64 3442 9595
Email info@mountainguiding.co.nz
Web site
www.mountainguiding.co.nz

SnowCam Land (*Coronet Peak*)
Tel 64 3442 6017 **Fax** 64 3442 8342
Email evan@kiwinewz.com
Web site
www.KiwiNewZ.com/html/
snowcam.htm

SWITZERLAND

Air Glaciers (*Saanen near Gstaad*)
Tel 41 33 744 5550
Fax 41 33 744 0141
Email gstaad@airglaciers.ch
Web site www.airglaciers.ch

Bohag (*Bernese Oberland*)
Tel 41 33 828 9000
Fax 41 33 828 9010
Email info@bohag.ch
Web site www.bohag.ch

Heli Chablais (*Leysin*)
Tel 41 24 494 3434
Fax 41 24 494 3030
Email helichablais@romandie.com
Web site www.helichablais.com

Heliswiss (*based in Bern*)
Tel 41 31 818 8888
Fax 41 31 818 8889
Email info@heliswiss.com
Web site www.heliswiss.com

Air Zermatt
Tel 41 27 966 8686
Fax 41 27 966 8685
Email zermatt@air-zermatt.ch
Web site www.air-zermatt.ch

COMPANIES THAT ORGANISE HELI-SKIING

Alpin Travel
Tel 41 81 720 2121
Fax 41 81 720 2120
Email at@alpintravel.ch
Web site www.alpintravel.ch
Gudauri Heli-skiing

Elemental Adventure
Tel (0870) 738 7838
Fax (07092) 387 880
Email info@eladv.com
Web site www.eladv.com
Himachal Heliskiing (India), Valdez Heli-Camps (Alaska), Last Frontier and TLH (BC)

James Orr Heliskiing
Tel 020-7483 0300
Fax 020-7483 3026
Email info@heliski.co.uk
Web site www.heliski.co.uk
British Columbia specialist: Crescent Spur, Great Canadian, Last Frontier, Selkirk Tangiers, TLH

Manfred Agerer
Tel 43 5472 2774
Email wiegele-europa@tirol.com
Mike Wiegele (BC)

Momentum Travel
Tel 020-7371 9111
Fax 020-7610 6287
Email sales@momentum.uk.com
Web site www.momentum.uk.com
TLH (BC)

Powder Skiing in North America
Tel 020-7736 8191
Fax 020-7384 2592
Web site www.cmhski.com
Canadian Mountain Holidays

Ski Club of Great Britain
Tel 020-8410 2022
Fax 020-8410 2001
Email holidays@skiclub.co.uk
Web site www.skiclub.co.uk
Himachal (India), Klondike (Canada), Selkirk Tangiers (Canada), TLH (BC)

Winter sports insurance

Buying travel insurance is the boring part of planning any kind of holiday. Therefore, it can be tempting to take the insurance offered as part of your holiday package or – if you are making your own arrangements – pick up a policy on the high street. But if you would rather not waste money that could be better spent on a slap-up lunch in a mountain restaurant or several well-deserved glasses of *vin chaud*, you would be better off contacting a ski insurance specialist.

As well as saving money, buying from a specialist means that you get better cover with fewer skier-unfriendly exclusions – largely because many specialist policies are designed by people who are keen skiers or snowboarders themselves. Another good reason for avoiding the high street is that – particularly in the case of travel agents – you are likely to be offered insurance for only a single trip. Since many winter sports enthusiasts try to fit in more than one visit to the slopes and will also take a summer holiday, an annual policy that provides cover for a whole year makes economic sense. Annual policies can be particularly good value for couples and families. To avoid unpleasant and expensive surprises when you make a claim, you need to make sure that the limits imposed by the policy cover the activities you plan to indulge in and the value of your ski or snowboard equipment – whether your own or hired.

If you are heading for the mountains you should ensure that your policy covers:

- at least £1 million in medical expenses
- all mountain rescue expenses
- the cost of an air ambulance back to the UK
- at least £1 million (£2 million for a trip to North America) for your personal-liability in case you accidentally injure someone or damage property
- the reimbursement of costs involved in cancelling or cutting short your holiday
- the cost of pre-paid ski or snowboard lessons, lift passes and equipment hire you are unable to use because of illness or injury (if appropriate)
- the costs of travelling to another resort if lack of snow makes this necessary (although you won't need this cover if you have your own transport).

What are you going to get up to?

While it shouldn't be too hard to find a policy that will provide these essential levels of cover (especially if you use any of the companies we have listed), it may take a little more time to find a policy that suits your personal circumstances. You need to be aware that insurers may refuse to pay out if you hurt yourself in any way other than while skiing recreationally on piste.

SNOWBOARDING

Quite surprisingly, a handful of insurance companies do not provide cover for snowboarding. Several others demonstrate their ignorance of the subject by agreeing to cover boarders only if they do not venture away from marked runs.

OFF-PISTE

The off-piste question affects riders and skiers alike. Some insurers take the view that anyone wanting to go off-piste has a death wish, so will not pay out if you have an accident while skiing (or boarding) off-piste. Others cover off-piste only if you are accompanied by a mountain guide. This definition is so vague that it may or may not cover you if you go accompanied by a qualified ski instructor if he or she does not have a separate mountain guide qualification. Most certainly it will not cover you if you are accompanied only by a gung-ho chalet host. If you go to a resort where the dividing line between what is and what is not considered off-piste is rather blurred, you may find yourself skiing off-piste without realising it. For example, in the Arlberg region and in parts of Switzerland, what were once black (difficult) runs have been regraded as unpatrolled 'ski itineraries'. Although they appear on the piste map they could technically be defined as off-piste. Choose a policy that allows you to go off-piste without a guide – and check the insurer's definition of terms.

Skiers planning more intrepid expeditions away from the confines of a resort's ski area need to check cover carefully. Heli-skiing may be covered as standard, but it is unlikely there will be automatic cover for ski-touring with skins (whether it involves climbing or not) unless you pay an extra premium.

OTHER ACTIVITIES

Do not assume that it is only expert skiers and riders who need to worry about their insurance cover. Even beginners will find it worthwhile to quiz a prospective insurer before handing over any money. The insurance world is divided over whether the end-of-week race organised by most ski schools is a bit of harmless fun (and so covered) or whether it is as risky as the racing shown on *Ski Sunday* (and so excluded). The same confusion applies to the popular timed public slalom courses in many resorts where you can compete against friends.

The more cautious insurers will also refuse to pay a claim if you have an accident while taking part in popular après-ski activities such as tobogganing, ice-skating, parapente, dog-sledding or snowmobiling.

INACTIVITY

Most insurers pay a fixed daily allowance of about £20 to £30 if lack of snow or severe weather conditions keep you off the slopes. However, what constitutes 'lack of snow' or 'piste closure' is very carefully defined. The insurer is unlikely to pay out if you can be transported to a neighbouring resort or if a minimal number of lifts are kept open.

Cover for equipment

Many people wrongly assume that, if their skis are damaged or stolen, their insurer will pay to replace them as new. This will happen only if they are insured under your house contents policy (which can be worth doing if your equipment is particularly expensive). Travel insurers take age and wear-and-tear into account when assessing a claim and so will pay out only as much as the equipment would cost to buy second-hand – provided this figure does not exceed the maximum limit given in the policy, which is typically about £500 (although it can be a lot less). It is very unlikely that equipment over five years old will be covered at all.

THEFT OF EQUIPMENT

Unless you are prepared to buy – and use – special ski locks, most insurers will not pay a claim if your skis are stolen while you are having lunch or stopping for a quick drink at a mountain restaurant. These insurers may be prepared to be more lenient if you can show that you took other precautions to prevent theft – such as leaving your skis in mixed pairs. But if you don't want the hassle of proving this, look for one of the handful of insurers who will not penalise you for leaving your skis or board unlocked while on the slopes.

Leaving skis and boards unlocked and unattended *away* from the slopes is a different matter. You are very likely to have a claim refused if equipment is stolen because you failed to lock it away securely. This applies to leaving equipment locked to a car roof rack overnight – although some insurers may cover theft from a car if it happens on your way to and from the slopes.

REPLACEMENT EQUIPMENT

Although you are unlikely to recover the cost of buying new equipment if you are unfortunate enough to lose or damage it, most insurers *will* pay from £100 to £500 (depending on the insurer) towards the cost of hiring replacement kit. You are also likely to find that, within similar limits, your insurer will reimburse you for having to hire equipment if yours failed to arrive at the resort at the same time as you did.

INSURANCE FOR HIRED EQUIPMENT

Check what a policy will pay out if you lose or significantly damage hired skis or a board. If nothing else, it will help you to answer the vexed question of whether or not you should take the usually iniquitously expensive insurance that the hire shop will offer you.

SKI INSURANCE COMPANIES

The following organisations specialise in winter sports cover

American Express
Tel (0800) 700737 **Fax** (01273) 668453
Web site www.americanexpress.co.uk

BIBA
Tel 020-7623 9043 **Fax** 020-7626 9676
Email enquiries@biba.org.uk
Web site www.biba.org.uk

Columbus Direct
Tel 020-7375 0011 **Fax** 020-7375 0022
Email sales@columbusdirect.demon.co.uk
Web site www.columbusdirect.com

Direct Travel Insurance
Tel (01903) 812345 **Fax** (01903) 813555
Email info@direct-travel.co.uk
Web site www.direct-travel.co.uk

Douglas Cox Tyrie Insurance Brokers
Tel (01708) 385500 **Fax** (01708) 385507

Eagle Star
Tel (0800) 333800
Web site www.eaglestar.co.uk

Endsleigh Insurance Services
Tel 020-7436 4451 **Fax** 020-7637 3132
Web site www.endsleigh.co.uk

Europ Assistance
Tel (01444) 442211 **Fax** (00353) 4674511
Web site www.europ-assistance.co.uk

Fogg Travel Insurance
Tel (01623) 631331 **Fax** (01623) 420450
Email col@fogginsure.co.uk
Web site www.fogginsure.co.uk

Hamilton Barr
Tel (01483) 255666
Fax (01483) 255660
Email sales@hamiltonbarr.com
Web site www.hamiltonbarr.com

James Hampden
Tel (01530) 416369 **Fax** (01530) 412424
Email infor@jhampden.com
Web site www.jameshampden.com

PJ Hayman
Tel (0800) 614216 **Fax** (023) 9241 3416
Email travel.insurance@pjhayman.com
Web site www.pjhayman.com

Liverpool Victoria
Tel (0800) 373905 **Fax** (01202) 502287
Web site www.liverpool-victoria.co.uk

Options
Tel (0870) 848 0870 **Fax** (01420) 566321
Web site www.optionsinsurance.co.uk

Primary Direct
Tel (0870) 444 3434 **Fax** (0870) 444 3436
Email enquiries@primarydirect.co.uk
Web site www.primarydirect.co.uk

Snowcard Insurance Services
Tel (01327) 262805 **Fax** (01327) 263227
Email enquiries@snowcard.co.uk
Web site www.snowcard.co.uk

Sportscover Direct
Tel (0117) 922 6222 **Fax** (0117) 922 1666
Email infor@sportscover.co.uk
Web site www.sportscover.co.uk

Touchline Travel Insurance
Tel (0800) 777143 **Fax** 020-8680 2769

Whiteley Insurance Consultants
Tel (01422) 348411
Fax (01422) 330345
Email kingfisher@whiteley-insur.prestel.
co.uk
Web site www.whiteley-insurance.co.uk

Worldwide Travel Insurance
Tel (01892) 833338 **Fax** (01892) 837744
Email sales@worldwideinsurance.com
Web site www.worldwideinsure.com

Safety on the slopes

The mountains, like the sea, are enormously enjoyable but can also be dangerous, and should be treated with the utmost respect at all times. Only when you find yourself in a potentially dangerous situation, or witness an accident at first hand, do you fully appreciate what the risks are.

Occasionally the combination of exceptionally heavy snowfall and high winds in parts of the Alps means that the ever-present threat of avalanches spreads from the off-piste slopes to the villages. Holiday-makers have to make decisions on whether it is prudent to travel to their holiday destinations, let alone to ski when they get there. In such unusual circumstances it is advisable to check not only with your tour operator but also with the resort tourist office and the appropriate avalanche control authority (see *Skiing by numbers*). All the information below applies to both skiers and snowboarders.

Weather, clothing and exposure
Mountain weather can change at a moment's notice and varies dramatically at different altitudes. Always dress with this in mind and be prepared for all conditions. Several layers of clothing are best, and it is always preferable to be too hot rather than too cold. More heat escapes through the head than any other part of the body, and you should never set off without a hat, as well as sunglasses or goggles. In the event of an accident, a 'space blanket' (a metallic sheet that folds to handkerchief-size and can be bought from any reputable ski or mountaineering shop) can save a life.

Exposure to bad weather can result in frostbite or hypothermia. Frostbite is the excessive cooling of small areas of the body, usually the fingers, toes, nose, cheeks or ears. The affected tissue turns white and numb. This is called first-degree frostbite and can be dealt with by immediate, gentle rewarming. In cold conditions, watch out for signs of frostbite in your companions. Hypothermia results from a drop in the body's temperature. It is difficult to diagnose; some of the more obvious symptoms are physical or mental lethargy, sluggishness, slurring of speech, spurts of energy and abnormal vision.

Children
All young children should wear safety helmets when skiing, preferably with chin guards. These can be worn on their own, or over a thin balaclava or hat on extremely cold days. Unfortunately, apart from in a few Scandinavian resorts, helmets are not yet compulsory on the pistes. In the USA, more adults now wear helmets for recreational skiing, and we applaud this trend. Never ski with a baby or small child in a backpack; anyone, however competent, can catch an edge and fall, or someone could crash into you.

Rules of the slopes

The FIS (International Ski Federation) has established rules of conduct for skiers and snowboarders. This is a summary:

Respect Do not endanger others.

Control Adapt the manner and speed of your skiing to your ability and to the general conditions on the mountain.

Choice of route The skier in front has priority – leave enough space between you and the preceding skier or snowboarder.

Overtaking Leave plenty of space when overtaking a slower skier.

Entering and starting a run Look up and down the mountain each time before starting on or entering a marked run.

Stopping Only stop at the edge of a piste or where you can be seen easily by other skiers and snowboarders.

Climbing When climbing up or down, always keep to the side of the piste.

Signs Obey all signs and markers – they are there for your safety.

Assistance In case of accidents, provide help if you can or alert the rescue service.

Identification All those involved in an accident, including witnesses, should exchange names and addresses.

All the above rules are legally binding and apply to both skiers and snowboarders. You could be in serious trouble if you are to blame for an accident while in breach of these rules.

Important guidelines for skiers and snowboarders

- Consider fitness sessions and taking lessons on a dry slope before going on holiday.
- You ski at your own risk.
- Ski on marked runs – these are protected from unexpected mountain dangers.
- Watch out for piste machines.
- Respect nature – take care not to ski in areas where young trees or wildlife will be disturbed and do not drop litter.

Special rules for snowboarders

- Do not attempt the sport without instruction.
- The ability to ski does not automatically mean you have the ability to snowboard.
- The front foot must be firmly tethered to the board by a safety strap.
- It is essential to look carefully to the right and left when changing direction. When starting a turn heelside, look backwards as well.

Off-piste

Outside the marked pistes and itineraries are areas that are NOT protected from mountain dangers.

Only venture off-piste with a fully qualified guide. This rule applies particularly to glacial terrain, where the risk of crevasses is added to that of avalanches. Always wear a recognised avalanche bleeper and take the time to learn how to use it by making a practice grid search before you set off.

Listen to your guide, learn basic snowcraft and how to read a slope. However, it is important to remember that guides can be fallible and that you alone must take responsibility for decisions concerning your safety. In the event of an avalanche, try to ski to the side. If you fall, try to get rid of your skis, poles and backpack. The chances of survival after an avalanche deteriorate rapidly after the first five minutes beneath the surface of the snow. Make swimming motions with your arms and legs and fight to stay on the surface.

Tips to remember when skiing or snowboarding off-piste

- Always ski in a group, never alone.
- Always ski in control behind the guide.
- Always stop behind the guide (there may be cliffs or other hazards ahead).
- Carry a map of the area and a compass. Know how to use both.
- Be wary of slopes where the run-out is not clearly obvious from the start. Following other skiers' or snowboarders' tracks does not necessarily mean the route is safe.

Avalanche danger

Signs and flags around the ski area may warn you when avalanche danger is present, but do not rely on these alone. Take local professional advice. Even when there is no warning of avalanches there could be localised snow slides.

Both the unified European and the North American avalanche risk scales are numbered 1 to 5 and colour-coded. However, not all countries use colours and the colours are not the same on both sides of the Atlantic. Critics argue that the weight of the descriptions varies from language to language.

1 Low (*Europe*: green *North America*: green).
Europe: release of avalanches is possible only on very few and very steep slopes. Only small spontaneous avalanches are to be expected. Off-piste generally good.
North America: avalanches very unlikely. Isolated areas of instability.

2 Moderate (*Europe*: yellow *North America*: yellow).
Europe: larger additional loads (e.g. a group of skiers) may release avalanches, especially on indicated steep slopes. Larger spontaneous avalanches are not to be expected. Off-piste is only moderately stabilised on some steeper slopes, but otherwise generally well-stabilised.
North America: natural avalanches are unlikely. Human-triggered avalanches are possible. Slab avalanches are possible on steep terrain.

3 Considerable (*Europe*: dark yellow *North America*: orange).
Europe: release of avalanches is likely by moderate additional loads (e.g. a jumping skier or a pedestrian) on the steepest slopes. Occasional medium-sized avalanches and also large spontaneous avalanches have

to be expected. The snowpack is only weakly to moderately stabilised on many steep slopes.

North America: natural avalanches possible. Human-triggered avalanches probable. Slabs probable on steep terrain.

4 High (*Europe*: orange *North America*: red).

Europe: avalanches are likely to occur even in the case of low additional loads on most steep slopes. In some cases many medium-sized and sometimes also large natural releases are to be expected. Off-piste is weakly stabilised on the steepest slopes.

North America: widespread natural or human-triggered avalanches certain. Unstable slabs likely on a variety of aspects and slope angles.

5 Very high (*Europe*: red *North America*: black).

Europe: numerous large natural releases are to be expected even in moderately steep terrain. Off-piste generally not possible.

North America: travel in avalanche terrain is not recommended. Extremely unstable slabs certain on most aspects and slope angles. Large, destructive avalanches possible.

Accident procedure

Speed is essential when an accident has occurred:

- **Secure the accident area** – Protect the casualty by planting crossed skis in the snow a little way above the accident. If necessary post someone above the accident site to give warning to other skiers.
- **First aid –** Assess the general condition of the casualty.
- **Airway** – Make sure nothing is obstructing the mouth or throat.
- **Breathing** – If the casualty is not breathing, administer artificial respiration (mouth-to-mouth resuscitation). If the casualty is breathing but unconscious, turn him/her on to his/her side to minimise the risk of choking.
- **Limbs** – Protect any fractured limb from movement. Do not remove the ski boot if there is injury to the lower leg as it acts as a splint.
- **Circulation** – Check for pulse. Cover any wound using a clean handkerchief or scarf and **keep the casualty warm**. Give the casualty nothing to eat or drink, especially alcohol. If the accident victim appears to be in shock (going pale, cold and faint), he/she should be encouraged to lie with his/her head lower than his/her feet.
- **Alert the rescue service** Contact ski patroller, ski teacher or lift attendant. Give the place of accident (piste name and nearest piste-marker), the number of people injured and the types of injury.
- **Establish the facts of the accident** Take the names and addresses of the people involved and of witnesses. Note the place, time and circumstances of the accident; the terrain, snow conditions, visibility, markings and signs.
- **Report the accident to the police as soon as possible.**

Which tour operator?

Below is a list of ski and snowboard operators that offer inclusive holiday packages. All but a handful fully satisfy the government requirements for bonding. Those that do not have been included because their main client-base is not in the United Kingdom. A large number of other companies and individuals offer accommodation-only holidays or have limited bonding (often through 'borrowed' ATOL licences). Many of these firms are well-established and have sound reputations. Our decision to exclude them does not necessarily mean they should be avoided. Before parting with any money, however, it would be wise to satisfy yourself with what would happen in the event of sudden company closure. Payment by major credit card may act as a secure secondary insurance on your investment.

ABERCROMBIE & KENT
Sloane Square House, Holbein Place,
London SW1W 8NS
Tel 020-7371 8659
Fax 020-7730 9376
Email info@abercrombiekent.co.uk
Web site www.abercrombiekent.co.uk
Luxury hotels in the Alps and North America

ACTION VACANCES/UCPA
30 Brackley Road, Stockport, Cheshire
SK4 2RE
Tel/Fax 0161-442 6130
Email av4ucpa@btinternet.com
Web site www.ucpa.co.uk
Budget skiing and snowboarding holidays for the 18–40s

AIRTOURS
Wavell House, Holcombe Road,
Helmshore, Rossendale BB4 4NB
Tel (0800) 028 8844
Web site www.airtours.com
Major tour operator

ALL CANADA SKI
Sunway House, Lowestoft NR32 2LW
Tel (01502) 565176
Fax (01502) 500681
Email ski@all-canada.com
Web site www.all-canada-ski.com
Ski holidays in Canada

ALPINE ACTION
3 Old Salts Farm Road,
Lancing BN15 8JE
Tel (01903) 761986
Fax (01903) 766007
Email sales@alpine-action.co.uk
Web site www.alpine-action.co.uk
Small operator to the Trois Vallées

ALPINE ANSWERS SELECT
The Business Village, 3–9 Broomhill Road,
London SW18 4JQ
Tel 020-8871 4656
Fax 020-8871 9676
Email select@alpineanswers.co.uk
Web site www.alpineanswers.co.uk
Tailor-made hotel holidays worldwide

ALPINE TOURS
54 Northgate, Canterbury CT1 1BE
Tel (01227) 454777
Fax (01227) 451177
Email alpinetoursltd@btinternet.com
Schools and groups

ALPINE TRACKS
40 High Street, Menai Bridge, Anglesey
LL59 5EF
Tel (01248) 717440
Fax (01248) 717441
Email alpinetrac@cs.com
Web site www.alpine-tracks.co.uk
Holidays in Lech, Morzine and Whistler

ALPINE WEEKENDS
95 Dora Road, London SW19 7JT
Tel 020-8944 9762
Fax 020-8947 9552
Email valweekends@btinternet.com
Web site www.val-disere-ski.com
*Small specialist operator in Val d'Isère,
Morzine and Verbier*

A.P.T. HOLIDAYS
PO Box 125, Rayleigh SS6 9SX
Tel (01268) 783878
Fax (01268) 782656
Email apt.holidays@virgin.net
Web site www.ski-express.net
Weekend coach holidays to France

BALKAN HOLIDAYS
Sofia House, 19 Conduit Street, London
W1S 2BH
Tel 020-7543 5555
Fax 020-7543 5577
Email sales@balkanholidays.co.uk
Web site www.balkanholidays.co.uk
Holidays in Bulgaria

BALKAN TOURS
61 Ann Street, Belfast BT1 4EE
Tel (028) 9024 6795
Fax (028) 9023 4581
Email mail@balkan.co.uk
Holidays in Bulgaria and Romania

BEAUMONT HOLIDAYS
Pinnacle House, 17–25 Hartfield Road,
London SW19 3SE
Tel 020-8544 0404
Fax 00 33 450 53 09 32
Email sales@beau-mont.com
Web site www.beau-mont.com
*Weekends and flexible breaks in European
resorts*

BELVEDERE CHALETS
Peach House, Gangbridge Lane, St Mary
Bourne SP11 6EW
Tel (01264) 738257
Fax (01264) 738533
Web site www.belvedere-chalets.co.uk
Luxury chalets in Méribel

BIGFOOT TRAVEL
186 Greys Road, Henley-on-Thames
RG9 1QU
Tel (01491) 579601
Fax (01491) 576568
Email ann@bigfoot-travel.co.uk
Web site www.bigfoot-travel.co.uk
Holidays in the Chamonix Valley

BORDERLINE
Les Sorbiers, 65120 Barèges, France
Tel 00 33 562 92 68 95
Fax 00 33 562 92 83 43
Email sorbiers@sudfr.com
Web site www.borderlinehols.com
Skiing and snowboarding in Barèges

CHALET SNOWBOARD
31 Aldworth Avenue,
Wantage OX12 7EJ
Tel (01235) 767575
Fax (01235) 767576
Email info@chalet-snowboard.co.uk
Web site www.chalet-snowboard.co.uk
Snowboarding in France

CHALET WORLD
PO Box 260, Shrewsbury SY1 1WX
Tel (01952) 840462
Fax (01952) 840463
Email sales@chaletworld.co.uk
Web site www.chaletworld.co.uk
Alpine chalet holidays

CLASSIC SKI
Ober Road, Brockenhurst SO42 7ST
Tel (01590) 623400
Fax (01590) 624387
Email info@classicski.co.uk
Web site www.classicski.co.uk
Holidays in France for mature skiers

CLUB EUROPE
Fairway House, 53 Dartmouth Road,
London SE23 3HN
Tel (0800) 4964996
Fax 020-8699 7770
Email ski@club-europe.co.uk
Web site www.club-europe.co.uk
Schools and groups

CLUB MED
115 Hammersmith Road,
London W14 0QH
Tel 020-7348 3333
Fax 020-7348 3336
Email cmmarketing@compuserve.com
Web site www.clubmed.com
All-inclusive holiday villages, with childcare

CLUB PAVILION
Lynnem House, 1 Victoria Way, Burgess
Hill RH15 9NF
Tel (0870) 2410427
Fax (0870) 2410426
Email sales@paviliontours.com
Web site www.clubpavilion.co.uk
Holidays in Europe and North America

COLLINEIGE SKI
30–32 High Street, Frimley GU16 7JD
Tel (01276) 24262
Fax (01276) 27282
Email info@collineige.com
Web site www.collineige.com
Chalets in Chamonix Valley, with childcare and mountain guides

CONTIKI
Wells House, 15 Elmfield Road,
Bromley BR1 1LS
Tel 020-8290 6422
Fax 020-8225 4246
Email travel@contiki.com
Web site www.contiki.com
Holidays in Hopfgarten for the 18–35s

THE CORPORATE SKI COMPANY
Spectrum House, Bromells Road, London
SW4 0BN
Tel 020-7627 5500
Fax 020-7622 6701
Email sales@vantagepoint.co.uk
Web site www.vantagepoint.co.uk
Corporate ski events

CRYSTAL HOLIDAYS
King's Place, Wood Street, Kingston
KT1 1JY
Tel (0870) 848 7000
Fax (0870) 848 7032
Email skires@crystalholidays.co.uk
Web site www.crystalski.co.uk
Major tour operator

DESCENT INTERNATIONAL
Laverstoke Mill, Laverstoke, Whitchurch
RG28 7NR
Tel 020-7989 8989
Fax 020-7989 8990
Email ski@descent.co.uk
Web site descent.co.uk
Luxury chalet in Méribel

ELEGANT RESORTS
The Old Palace, Little St. John's Street,
Chester CH1 1RB
Tel (01244) 897333
Fax (01244) 897330
Email enquiries@elegantresorts.co.uk
Web site www.elegantresorts.co.uk
Luxury hotels in major resorts

EQUITY TOTAL SKI
Dukes Lane House, 47 Middle Street,
Brighton BN1 1AL
Tel (01273) 298299
Fax (01273) 203212
Email ski@equity.co.uk
Web site www.equity.co.uk
All-inclusive holidays in Europe and North America

ERNA LOW
9 Reece Mews, London SW7 3HE
Tel 020-7584 2841
Fax 020-7589 9531
Email info@ernalow.co.uk
Web site www.ernalow.co.uk
Apartments and hotels in France and Switzerland

EUROTUNNEL MOTORING HOLIDAYS
Charter House, Woodlands Road,
Altrincham WA14 1HF
Tel (0870) 333 2001
Fax (0870) 333 2002
Email ethols@crestaholidays.co.uk
Web site www.eurotunnel.com
Motoring holidays to France

FAIRHAND HOLIDAYS/SKIARUS
216–218 Main Road, Biggin Hill
TN16 3BD
Tel (01959) 540796
Fax (01959) 540797
Email ian.porter@skiarus.com
Web site www.skiarus.com
Tailor-made holidays in France (Fairhand) and North America (Skiarus)

FANTISKI
Warmlake Business Centre, Maidstone
Road, Sutton Valence ME17 3LR
Tel (01622) 844302
Fax (01622) 842458
Email fctravel@dircon.co.uk
Web site www.fantiski.co.uk
*Family-run operator to France and
Colorado, with childcare*

FINLAYS
The Barn, Ancrum, Jedburgh TD8 6XH
Tel (01835) 830562
Fax (01835) 830550
Email finlayski@aol.com
Web site www.finlayski.com
*Chalets in Courchevel and Val d'Isère, also
short breaks*

FIRST CHOICE
Olivier House,18 Marine Parade, Brighton
BN2 1TL
Tel (0870) 754 3477
Fax (0870) 333 0329
Email fcski@lineone.net
Web site www.fcski.co.uk
Major tour operator

FLEXISKI
Olivier House, 18 Marine Parade, Brighton
BN2 1TL
Tel (0870) 909 0754
Fax (0870) 909 0329
Email reservations@flexiski.com
Web site www.flexiski.co.uk
*Holidays of variable length in Austria,
France and Switzerland*

FREEDOM HOLIDAYS
Solar House, Market Square, Petworth
GU28 OAS
Tel (01798) 342034
Fax (01798) 343320
Web site www.freedomholidays.co.uk
*Holidays of variable length in Portes du
Soleil*

FRONTIER SKI
6 Sydenham Avenue, London SE26 6UH
Tel 020-8776 8709
Fax 020-8778 0149
Email info@frontier-travel.co.uk
Web site www.frontier-ski.co.uk
Canadian specialists

HANDMADE HOLIDAYS
The Old Barn, Yew Tree Farm, Thrupp
GL5 2EF
Tel (01453) 885599
Fax (01453) 883768
Email travel@handmade-holidays.co.uk
Web site www.handmade-holidays.co.uk
*Specialist operator to Europe and North
America*

HANNIBALS
Farriers, Little Olantigh Road, Wye,
Ashford TN25 5DQ
Tel (01233) 813105
Fax (01233) 813432
Email sales@hannibals.co.uk
Web site www.hannibals.co.uk
Specialist operator to France

HEADWATER HOLIDAYS
146 London Road,
Northwich CW9 5HH
Tel (01606) 813333
Fax (01606) 813334
Email info@headwater.com
Web site www.headwater-holidays.co.uk
Ski and cross-country holidays

HF HOLIDAYS
Imperial House, Edgware Road, London
NW9 5AL
Tel 020-8905 9558
Fax 020-8205 0506
Email info@hfholidays.co.uk
Web site www.hfholidays.co.uk
Snowshoeing and cross-country holidays

HUSKI CHALET HOLIDAYS
63a Kensington Church Street, London
W8 4BA
Tel 020-7938 4844
Fax 020-7938 2312
Email sales@huski.com
Web site www.huski.com
Specialist chalet operator to Chamonix

INDEPENDENT SKI LINKS
Little Arram Farm, Bewholme Lane,
Seaton, Hull HU11 5SX
Tel (01964) 533905
Fax (01964) 536006
Email info@ski-links.com
Web site www.ski-links.com
Holidays in the Alps and North America

INGHAMS
10–18 Putney Hill,
London SW15 6AX
Tel 020-8780 4433
Fax 020-8780 4405
Email travel@inghams.co.uk
Web site www.inghams.co.uk
Major tour operator

INNTRAVEL
Hovingham, York YO62 4JZ
Tel (01653) 629002
Fax (01653) 628741
Email winter@inntravel.co.uk
Web site www.inntravel.co.uk
Cross-country and snowshoeing operator

INTERHOME
383 Richmond Road, Twickenham
TW1 2EF
Tel 020-8891 1294
Fax 020-8891 5331
Email info@interhome.co.uk
Web site www.interhome.co.uk
Chalets and apartments in the Alps

INTERSKI
Acorn Park, St Peter's Way, Mansfield
NG18 1EX
Tel (01623) 456333
Fax (01623) 456353
Email email@interski.co.uk
Web site www.interski.co.uk
Holidays in Italy, with own ski school and equipment hire

KUONI
Kuoni House, Deepdene Avenue, Dorking
RH5 4AZ
Tel (01306) 742500
Fax (01306) 744222
Email switzerland.sales@kuoni.co.uk
Web site www.kuoni.co.uk
Operator to 20 Swiss resorts

LAGRANGE
168 Shepherds Bush Road, London
W6 7PB
Tel 020-7371 6111
Fax 020-7371 2990
Email info@lagrange-holidays.com
Web site www.lagrange-holidays.com
Self-catering holidays in 118 French resorts

LEISURE DIRECTION SKI
Image House, Station Road, London
N17 9LR
Tel 020-8324 4042
Fax 020-8324 4030
Email sales@leisuredirection.co.uk
Web site www.leisuredirection.co.uk
Ski-drive to 25 French resorts

LE SKI
25 Holly Terrace, Huddersfield HD1 6JW
Tel (0870) 7544444
Fax (0870) 7543333
Email mail@leski.co.uk
Web site www.leski.co.uk
Chalets in French Alps, with own ski school and childcare

LOTUS SUPERTRAVEL
Sandpiper House, 39 Queen Elizabeth
Street, London SE1 2BT
Tel 020-7962 9933
Fax 020-7962 9965
Email ski@lotusgroup.co.uk
Web site www.supertravel.co.uk
Holidays in the Alps and North America, with childcare

MADE TO MEASURE HOLIDAYS
57 East Street, Chichester PO19 1HL
Tel (01243) 533333
Fax (01243) 778431
Email madetomeasure.holidays@which.net
Web site
www.madetomeasureholidays.com
Tailor-made holidays in Europe and North America

MARK WARNER
10 Old Court Place, London W8 4PL
Tel (08708) 480482
Fax (08708) 480481
Email info@markwarner.co.uk
Web site www.markwarner.co.uk
Chalet-hotels with childcare

MERISKI
The Old School, Great Barrington, Burford
OX18 4UR
Tel (01451) 843100
Fax (01451) 844799
Email sales@meriski.co.uk
Web site www.meriski.co.uk
Chalets with childcare in Méribel

MGS SKI
109 Castle Street, Saffron Walden
CB10 1BQ
Tel/Fax (01799) 525984
Email skimajor@aol.com
Web site www.mgsski.com
Holidays in Val Cenis and Big White

MOMENTUM SKI
162 Munster Road, London SW6 6AT
Tel 020-7371 9111
Fax 020-7610 6287
Email sales@momentum.uk.com
Web site www.momentum.uk.com
*Weekend and bespoke ski holiday
specialists*

MOSWIN TOURS
Moswin House, 21 Church Street, Oadby,
Leicester LE2 5DB
Tel (0116) 271 9922
Fax (0116) 271 6016
Email info@moswin.com
Web site www.moswin.co.uk
Holidays in Germany

MOTOURS
Buckingham House, Longfield Road,
Tunbridge Wells TN2 3DQ
Tel (01892) 677777
Fax (01892) 677766
Email admin@motours.co.uk
Web site www.motours.co.uk
Ski-drive to France

NEILSON
120 St Georges Road, Brighton, West
Sussex BN2 1EA
Tel (0870) 3333347
Fax (0870) 3333436
Email sales@neilson.com
Web site www.neilson.com
Major tour operator

**OAK HALL SKIING AND
SNOWBOARDING**
Oak Hall, Otford TN15 6XF
Tel (01732) 763131
Fax (01732) 763136
Email office@oakhall.clara.net
Web site www.oakhall.co.uk
*Christian holidays in the Alps and North
America*

THE OXFORD SKI COMPANY
PO Box 357, Banbury OX15 5XT
Tel (07000) 785349
Fax (07000) 785340
Email info@theoxfordski.com
Web site www.theoxfordski.com
Chalets and hotels in Crans Montana

PANORAMA HOLIDAYS
Panorama House, Vale Road, Portslade
BN41 1HP
Tel (01273) 427070
Fax (01273) 427111
Email panorama@phg.co.uk
Web site www.panoramaholidays.co.uk
*Value holidays in the Alps and the
Pyrenees*

PEAK SKI
White Lilacs House, Water Lane,
Bovington HP3 0NA
Tel (01442) 832629
Fax (01442) 834303
Email peakski@which.net
Web site www.peak-ski.co.uk
Holidays in Verbier

PGL SKI
Alton Court, Penyard Lane, Ross-on-Wye
HR9 5GL
Tel (01989) 768168
Fax (01989) 768376
Email ski@pgl.co.uk
Web site www.pgl.co.uk
Schools and groups

PISTE ARTISTE
128 Old Brompton Road, London
SW7 3SS
Tel 020-7436 0100
Fax 00 41 24 479 3490
Email reserve@pisteartiste.com
Web site www.pisteartiste.com
Holidays in Champéry

PLUS TRAVEL
Swiss Centre, 10th Floor, 10 Wardour
Street, London W1D 6QF
Tel 020-7734 0383
Fax 020-7292 1599
Email Plustravel@stlondon.com
Holidays in Switzerland

POWDER BYRNE
250 Upper Richmond Road, London
SW15 6TG
Tel 020-8246 5300
Fax 020-8246 5322
Email enquiries@powderbyrne.co.uk
Web site www.powderbyrne.com
Luxury holidays in the Alps, with childcare

PYRENEAN MOUNTAIN TOURS
2 Rectory Cottages, Wolverton, Tadley
RG26 5RS
Tel/Fax (01635) 297209
Email pmtuk@aol.com
Web site www.pyrenees.co.uk
*Ski-touring, snowshoeing and ice-climbing
holidays*

RAMBLERS
PO Box 43, Welwyn Garden City
AL8 6PQ
Tel (01707) 331133
Fax (01707) 333276
Email info@ramblersholidays.co.uk
Web site www.ramblersholidays.co.uk
Group cross-country holidays

ROCKY MOUNTAIN ADVENTURES
Charlotte House, 67–83 Norfolk Street,
Liverpool L15 4JN
Tel 0151-706 0344
Fax 0151-706 0350
Email
snowboarding@rockymountain.co.uk
Web site www.rockymountain.co.uk
Snowboarding in Colorado

**SCOTT DUNN SKI/SCOTT DUNN
LATIN AMERICA**
Fovant Mews, 12 Noyna Road, London
SW17 7PH
Tel 020-8767 0202
Fax 020-8767 2026
Email ski@scottdunn.com
*Luxury chalets in the Alps, with childcare.
Also South America*

SEASONS IN STYLE
Telegraph House, 246 Telegraph Road,
Heswall, Wirral CH60 7SG
Tel (0870) 073 2766
Fax 0151 342 0516
Email sales@seasonsinstyle.co.uk
Web site www.seasonsinstyle.co.uk
*Luxury hotels in Europe and North
America*

SILVER SKI HOLIDAYS
Conifers House, Grove Green Lane,
Maidstone ME14 5JW
Tel (01622) 735544
Fax (01622) 738550
Email hazal@silverski.co.uk
Web site www.silverski.co.uk
Catered chalets in France, with childcare

SIMPLY SKI
Kings House, Wood Street, Kingston upon
Thames KT1 1UG
Tel 020-8541 2209
Fax 020-8541 2280
Email ski@simply-travel.com
Web site www.simplyski.com
Catered chalets in the Alps, with childcare

SKI ACTIVITY
Lawmuir House, Methven PH1 3SZ
Tel (01738) 840888
Fax (01738) 840079
Email sales@skiactivity.com
Web site www.skiactivity.com
*Operator to France, Switzerland and North
America*

SKI THE AMERICAN DREAM
1–7 Station Chambers, High Street North,
London E6 1JE
Tel 020-8552 1201
Fax 020-8552 7726
Email holidays@skidream.com
Web site www.skidream.com
North American specialist

SKI AMIS
Alanda, Hornash Lane, Shadoxhurst,
Ashford TN26 1HT
Tel (01233) 732187
Fax (01233) 732769
Email info@skiamis.com
Web site www.skiamis.com
Chalet holidays in the French Alps

SKI ASTONS
Clerkenleap, Broomhall, Worcester
WR5 3HR
Tel (01905) 829200
Fax (01905) 820850
Email ski@astons-coaches.co.uk
Web site www.astons-coaches.co.uk
Coach holidays for schools and groups

SKI BARRETT-BOYCE
Unit 16, Westmead House,
123 Westmead Road, Sutton SM1 4JH
Tel 020-8288 0042
Fax 020-8288 0761
Email kerry@skibb.co.uk
Web site www.skibb.com
*Chalet in Megève, with tuition and
childcare*

SKI BEAT
Metro House, Northgate, Chichester
PO19 1BE
Tel (01243) 780405
Fax (01243) 533748
Email ski@skibeat.co.uk
Web site www.skibeat.co.uk
Chalets in the French Alps, with childcare

SKIBOUND
Olivier House, 18 Marine Parade, Brighton
BN2 1TL
Tel (0870) 900 3200
Fax (0870) 333 2329
Email sales@skibound.co.uk
Web site www.skibound.co.uk
Specialist schools operator

SKI CHAMOIS
18 Lawn Road, Doncaster DN1 2JF
Tel (01302) 369006
Fax (01302) 326640
Email
skichamois@morzine1550.freeserve.co.uk
Chalets in Morzine

SKI CHOICE
27 High Street, Benson, Wallingford
OX10 6RP
Tel (01491) 837607
Fax (01491) 833836
Email info@choicetravel.co.uk
Web site www.choicetravel.co.uk
Tailor-made holidays in the Alps

**SKI CLUB OF GREAT BRITAIN/
FRESH TRACKS**
The White House, 57–63 Church Road,
London SW19 5SB
Tel 020-8410 2022
Fax 020-8410 2001
Email holidays@skiclub.co.uk
Web site www.skiclub.co.uk
*Specialist holidays, weekends and
instruction courses*

THE SKI COMPANY
The Old School, Great Barrington, Burford
OX18 4UR
Tel (01451) 843123
Fax (01451) 844799
Email sales@skicompany.co.uk
Web site www.skicompany.co.uk
Luxury chalets in the Alps, with childcare

SKI EQUIPE
79 London Road, Alderley Edge SK9 7DY
Tel (08704) 445533
Fax (08704) 423555
Email ski@skiequipe.co.uk
Web site www.ski-equipe.com
Chalets in the Alps and North America

SKIERS WORLD
120 St Georges Road, Brighton BN2 1EA
Tel (0870) 333 3620
Fax (0870) 333 3327
Email info@skiersworld.com
Web site www.skiersworld.com
Schools operator and adult groups

SKI ESPRIT
185 Fleet Road, Fleet GU51 3BL
Tel (01252) 618300
Fax (01252) 618528
Email travel@esprit-holidays.co.uk
Web site www.esprit-holidays.co.uk
Specialist family operator

SKI EXPECTATIONS/SKI YOGI
Jasmine Cottage, Manor Lane, Great
Chesterford CB10 1PJ
Tel (01799) 531888
Fax (01799) 531887
Email ski.expectations@virgin.net
*Tailor-made holidays in Europe and North
America*

SKI FAMILLE
Unit 9, Chesterton Mill, French's Road,
Cambridge CB4 3NP
Tel (01223) 363777/568224
Fax (01223) 519314
Email info@skifamille.co.uk
Web site www.skifamille.co.uk
*Specialist operator to Les Gets, with
childcare*

SKI FRANCE
PO Box 371, Bromley BR1 2ZJ
Tel 020-8313 0690
Fax 020-8466 0653
Email ski@skifrance.co.uk
Web site www.skifrance.co.uk
Holidays in France

SKI FREEDOM
PO Box 377, Bromley BR1 1LY
Tel (0870) 606 2222
Fax 020-8313 3547
Email uv.uk@unitedvacations.com
Web site www.unitedvacations.co.uk
Holidays in North America

SKI GOWER
2 High Street, Studley B80 7HJ
Tel (01527) 851411
Fax (01527) 851417
Email louise@gowstrav.demon.co.uk
School and group holidays in Poland and
Switzerland

SKI HILLWOOD
Lavender Lodge, Dunny Lane,
Chipperfield WD4 9DD
Tel (01923) 290700
Fax (01923) 290340
Email sales@hillwood-holidays.co.uk
Specialist operator to Austria and France,
with childcare

SKI HIVER
119a London Road, Waterlooville
PO7 7DZ
Tel (02392) 428586
Fax 00 33 479 07 84 56
Email skihiver@aol.com
Web site www.skihiver.co.uk
Specialist operator to Peisey-Nancroix,
France

SKI INDEPENDENCE
Broughton Market, Edinburgh EH3 6NU
Tel (0870) 5550555 USA &
Canada/(0870) 60001462
Ski Drive France and Switzerland
Fax (0870) 550 2020
Email ski@ski-independence.co.uk
Web site www.ski-independence.co.uk
Holidays in North America and ski-drive to
Europe

SKI MIQUEL
73 High Street, Uppermill, Oldham
OL3 6AP
Tel (01457) 821200
Fax (01457) 821209
Email ski@miquelhols.co.uk
Web site www.miquelhols.co.uk
Operator to the Alps, Spain and Canada

SKI MORGINS HOLIDAYS
The Barn House, 1 Bury Court Barns,
Wigmore HR6 9US
Tel (01568) 770681
Fax (01586) 770153
Email info@skimorgins.co.uk
Web site www.skimorgins.co.uk
Small specialist operator to Morgins

SKI NORWEST
8 Foxholes Cottages, Foxholes Road,
Horwich, Bolton BL6 6AL
Tel (01204) 668468
Fax (01204) 668568
Email enqskinorwest@cs.com
Web site www.skinorwest.com
Self-drive and coach holidays to Scotland

SKI OLYMPIC
PO Box 396, Doncaster DN5 7YS
Tel (01709) 579999
Fax (01709) 579898
Email info@skiolympic.freeserve.co.uk
Web site www.skiolympic.co.uk
Chalets and hotels in France

SKI PARTNERS
Friary House, Colston Street, Bristol
BS1 5AP
Tel 0117-925 3545
Fax 0117-929 3697
Email jmh@skipartners.com
Schools operator to the Alps and North
America

SKI PEAK
Campbell Park, Milland, Nr Liphook
GU30 7LU
Tel (01428) 741144
Fax (01428) 741155
Email info@skipeak.com
Web site www.skipeak.com
Specialist operator to Vaujany, with
childcare

SKI SAFARI
41 Canada Wharf, 255 Rotherhithe Street,
London SE16 5ES
Tel 020-7740 1221
Fax 020-7740 1223
Email info@skisafari.com
Web site www.skisafari.com
Specialist operator to Canada and USA

SKISAFE TRAVEL
Unit 4, Braehead Estate, Old Govan Road,
Renfrew PA4 8XJ
Tel 0141-812 0925
Fax 0141-812 1544
Operator to Scotland and Flaine

SKI SOLUTIONS A LA CARTE
84 Pembroke Road, London W8 6NX
Tel 020-7471 7777
Fax 020-7471 7771
Email alc@skisolutions.com
Web site www.skisolutions.com
Hotels and luxury apartments worldwide

SKI SUPREME
26 Brodick Drive, Stewartfield, East
Kilbride G74 4BQ
Tel (01355) 260547
Fax (01355) 229232
Email info@skisupreme.co.uk
Web site www.skisupreme.co.uk
Self-drive and coach operator to France

SKI TOTAL
3 The Square, Richmond TW9 1DY
Tel 020-8948 3535
Fax 020-8332 1268
Email ski@skitotal.com
Web site www.skitotal.com and
www.skitotalusa.com
*Chalet operator to the Alps, USA and
Canada, with childcare*

SKI VAL
Shortlands, Middlemoor, Tavistock
PL19 9DY
Tel (01822) 611200
Fax (01822) 611400
Email post@skival.co.uk
Web site www.skival.co.uk
*Chalets and chalet-hotels in the French
Alps and Lech*

SKI VERBIER
26 Chesson Road, London W14 9QX
Tel 020-7385 8050
Fax 020-7385 8002
Email info@skiverbier.com
Web site www.skiverbier.com
Holidays in Verbier

SKI WEEKEND
3 Ram Court, Wicklesham Lodge Farm,
Faringdon SN7 7PN
Tel (01367) 241636
Fax (01367) 243833
Email info@skiweekend.com
Web site www.skiweekend.com
Weekend breaks with specialist courses

SKI WORLD
41 North End Road, London W14 8SZ
Tel 020-7602 4826
Fax 020-7371 1463
Email sales@skiworld.ltd.uk
Web site www.skiworld.ltd.uk
Holidays in the Alps and the Rockies

SLOPING OFF
31 High Street, Handley, Salisbury
SP5 5NR
Tel (01725) 552247
Fax (01725) 552489
Email victorytours@dial.pipex.com
Web site www.victorytours.co.uk
Holidays by coach for schools and groups

SNOWBIZZ VACANCES
69 High Street, Maxey PE6 9EE
Tel (01778) 341455
Fax (01778) 347422
Email snowbizz@snowbizz.co.uk
Web site www.snowbizz.co.uk
*Holidays in Puy-St-Vincent, with childcare
and own ski school*

SNOWBOARD LODGE
The Yellow Room, Unit 1a, Franchise
Street, Kidderminster DY11 6RE
Tel (01562) 740240
Fax (0870) 0548543
Email info@snowboardlodge.co.uk
Web site www.snowboardlodge.co.uk
*Chalets for snowboarders in Morzine and
Avoriaz*

SNOWCOACH HOLIDAYS
146–148 London Road, St Albans
AL1 1PQ
Tel (01727) 866177
Fax (01727) 843766
Email info@snowcoach.co.uk
Web site www.snowcoach.co.uk
Value holidays in the Alps and the Pyrenees

SNOWLINE
Collingbourne House,
140–142 Wandsworth High Street,
London SW18 4JJ
Tel 020-8704807
Fax 020-8759236
Email ski@snowline.co.uk
Web site www.snowline.co.uk
Small operator to the French Alps

SNOWPLUS
19 Craigielaw Park, Aberlady,
East Lothian EH32 0PR
Tel (01875) 870005
Fax (0870) 1371080
Email scottfree@compuserve.com
Web site www.snowplus.co.uk
Holidays in Nendaz, Switzerland

SNOWSCAPE
108 Wylds Lane, Worcester WR5 1DJ
Tel (01905) 357760
Fax (01905) 357825
Email skiandboard@snowscape.co.uk
Web site www.snowscape.co.uk
Holidays in Austria

SOLO'S
54–58 High Street, Edgware HA8 7EJ
Tel 020-8951 2800
Fax 020-8951 1051
Email travel@solosholidays.co.uk
Web site www.solosholidays.co.uk
Singles holidays in the Alps and the Rockies

STANFORD SKIING
16 Sherlock Road, Cambridge CB3 0HR
Tel (01223) 477644
Fax (01223) 710318
Email stanskiing@aol.com
Web site www.stanfordskiing.co.uk
Specialist operator to Megève

SWISS TRAVEL SERVICE
Bridge House, 55–59 High Road,
Broxbourne EN10 7DT
Tel (0870) 727 5955
Fax (01992) 448855
Email swissbook@bridge-travel.co.uk
Web site www.bridge-travel.co.uk
Quality holidays in 18 Swiss resorts

TT SKI/TANGNEY TOURS
3 Station Court, Borough Green
TN15 8AF
Tel (01732) 886666
Fax (01732) 886885
Email ttours@cix.co.uk
Web site www.tangney-tours.com
Group operator to Pyrenees

THOMSON SKI & SNOWBOARDING
King's Place, 12–42 Wood Street,
Kingston-upon-Thames KT1 1UG
Tel (0870) 606 1470
Email reservations@thomson-ski.com/reservations@thomson-snowboarding.co.uk
Web site www.thomson-ski.co.uk
Major tour operator

TOP DECK SKI
131–135 Earls Court Road, London
SW5 9RH
Tel 020-7370 4555
Fax 020-7835 1820
Email res@topdecktravel.co.uk
Web site www.topdeckski.co.uk
Holidays in the Alps and the Pyrenees

TOPS TRAVEL
Lees House, 21 Dyke Road, Brighton
BN1 3GD
Tel (01273) 774666
Fax (01273) 734042
Email sales@topstravel.co.uk
Web site www.topstravel.co.uk
Club-hotels and chalets in France, with childcare

VIP
Collingbourne House, 140–142
Wandsworth High Street, London
SW18 4JJ
Tel 020-8875 1957
Fax 020-8875 9236
Email ski@valdisere.co.uk
Web site www.valdisere.co.uk
Specialist operator to Val d'Isère

VIRGIN SKI
The Galleria, Station Road, Crawley
RH10 1WW
Tel (01293) 617181
Fax (01293) 536957
Email brochure.requests@fly.virgin.com
Web site www.virginholidays.co.uk
Hotel holidays in North America

WASTELAND SKI COMPANY
39–43 Putney High Street, London
SW15 1SP
Tel 020-8246 6677
Fax 020-8246 6982
Email ski@wastelandski.co.uk
Web site www.wastelandski.com
Holidays in France and Austria

WAYMARK HOLIDAYS
44 Windsor Road, Slough SL1 2EJ
Tel (01753) 516477
Fax (01753) 517016
Email info@waymarkholidays.com
Web site www.waymarkholidays.com
Cross-country skiing holidays

WHITE ROC SKI
69 Westbourne Grove, London W2 4UJ
Tel 020-7792 1188
Fax 020-7792 1956
Email ski@whiteroc.co.uk
Web site www.whiteroc.co.uk
Weekends and tailor-made holidays in the Alps

WINETRAILS/SKI GOURMET
Greenways, Vann Lake, Ockley, Dorking
RH5 5NT
Tel (01306) 712111
Fax (01306) 713504
Email sales@winetrails.co.uk
Web site www.winetrails.co.uk
Gourmet catered chalet in Filzmoos

YSE
The Business Village, Broomhill Road,
London SW18 4JQ
Tel 020-8871 5117
Fax 020-8871 5229
Email sales@yseski.co.uk
Web site www.yseski.co.uk
Specialist chalet operator to Val d'Isère

Who goes where?

ANDORRA
Arcalis Snowcoach
Arinsal Airtours, Crystal, First Choice, Inghams, Neilson, Panorama, Ski Partners, Snowcoach, Thomson, Top Deck
Encamp First Choice, Ski Partners, Thomson
Grau Roig Panorama
La Massana Snowcoach
Pal Panorama, Snowcoach
Pas de la Casa Airtours, Crystal, First Choice, Inghams, Lagrange, Neilson, Panorama, Thomson, Top Deck
Soldeu/El Tarter Airtours, Club Pavilion, Crystal, First Choice, Independent Ski Links, Inghams, Lagrange, Neilson, Panorama, SCGB/Fresh Tracks, Ski Partners, Thomson, Top Deck

ARGENTINA
Chapelco Scott Dunn Latin America
Gran Catedral (Bariloche) Scott Dunn Latin America
Las Leñas Scott Dunn Latin America

AUSTRALIA
No current tour operator

AUSTRIA
Alpbach Crystal, Equity Total Ski, Inghams, Interhome, Thomson
Altenmarkt Club Europe, Interhome, Sloping Off
Axamer Lizum Club Pavilion, Lagrange, PGL Ski, Ski Partners
Bad Gastein Club Europe, Crystal, Inghams, Made to Measure, Ski Miquel, SkiBound
Bad Hofgastein Crystal, Inghams
Bad Kleinkirchheim Alpine Tours, Crystal, PGL Ski, Ski Partners, Sloping Off, Solo's
Brand Interhome, Inghams
Brixen-im-Thale Alpine Tours
Bruck Crystal
Ellmau Airtours, Crystal, Inghams, Interhome, Motours, Neilson, Thomson
Fieberbrunn Ski Astons, Snowscape
Filzmoos Inghams, Interhome, Winetrails
Finkenberg Crystal, First Choice

Flachau Club Europe, Interhome, Thomson
Fulpmes Crystal
Galtür Inghams, Made to Measure, Ski Choice
Gargellen Made to Measure
Gerlos Interhome
Hintertux Alpine Tours, Lagrange
Hopfgarten Contiki, First Choice
Igls Inghams, Lagrange
Innsbruck Equity Total Ski, Made to Measure, Ramblers
Ischgl Inghams, Made to Measure, Momentum Ski, Ski Solutions
Itter Neilson, Skiers World
Jenbach Ski Astons
Kaprun Club Europe, Crystal, Interhome, Made to Measure
Kirchberg First Choice, Interhome, Lagrange, Ski Partners, Snowscape, Top Deck
Kirchdorf Crystal, HF Holidays, Snowcoach, Thomson
Kitzbühel Airtours, Corporate Ski Company, Crystal, Elegant Resorts, First Choice, Independent Ski Links, Inghams, Interhome, Lagrange, Made to Measure, Neilson, Panorama, PGL Ski, SCGB/Fresh Tracks, Ski Astons, Ski Partners, Ski Solutions, SkiBound, Thomson
Kühtai Inghams
Lech Abercrombie & Kent, Alpine Answers, Alpine Tracks, Corporate Ski Company, Elegant Resorts, Flexiski, Inghams, Momentum Ski, Seasons in Style, Simply Ski, Ski Choice, Ski Expectations, Ski Solutions, Ski Total, Ski Val, White Roc
Leogang Equity Total Ski
Lofer PGL Ski, Ski Partners, Skiers World
Maria Alm PGL Ski, Ski Astons
Mayrhofen Airtours, Crystal, Equity Total Ski, First Choice, HF Holidays, Inghams, Interhome, Neilson, Ski Astons, Snowcoach, Thomson
Nassfeld Sloping Off
Neustift Crystal, Made to Measure
Niederau/Oberau First Choice, Inghams, Neilson, PGL Ski, Ski Partners, Thomson
Obergurgl/Hochgurgl Airtours, Crystal, Inghams, SCGB/Fresh Tracks, Ski Expectations, Ski Solutions, Thomson

Obertauern Club Europe, Inghams, Ski Partners, Thomson
Rauris Crystal
Saalbach-Hinterglemm Airtours, Club Europe, Crystal, First Choice, Inghams, Interhome, Neilson, Panorama, PGL Ski, Ski Partners, SkiBound, Thomson
Scheffau Airtours, Crystal, Ski Astons, Thomson
Schladming Crystal, Equity Total Ski, Interhome, Oak Hall Skiing, PGL Ski, Ski Partners, SkiBound, Sloping Off
Seefeld Airtours, Crystal, Inghams, Interhome, Lagrange, Thomson
Serfaus Alpine Tours, Interhome, Made to Measure
Sölden/Hochsölden Made to Measure
Söll Airtours, Crystal, First Choice, Inghams, Motours, Neilson, Panorama, Ski Astons, Ski Hillwood, Skiers World, Thomson
St Anton Abercrombie & Kent, Airtours, Alpine Answers, Alpine Tours, Chalet World, Corporate Ski Company, Crystal, Elegant Resorts, First Choice, Flexiski, Independent Ski Links, Inghams, Interhome, Lotus Supertravel, Mark Warner, Momentum Ski, Neilson, SCGB/Fresh Tracks, Simply Ski, Ski Activity, Ski Equipe, Ski Expectations, Ski Solutions, Ski Total, Ski Val, Skiworld, Thomson, White Roc
St Christoph Abercrombie & Kent, Elegant Resorts, Flexiski, Momentum Ski, Seasons in Style
St Johann im Pongau Ski Astons
St Johann in Tirol Crystal, Ski Partners, SkiBound, Thomson
St Michael Alpine Tours, Equity Total Ski, Ski Partners
St Wolfgang Airtours, Crystal, Inghams, Thomson
Stuben Ski Total
Wagrain Club Europe, Thomson
Waidring Thomson
Westendorf Inghams, Interhome, Skiers World, Thomson
Wildschönau Interhome, Ski Partners
Zauchensee Sloping Off
Zell am See Airtours, Club Europe, Crystal, Equity Total Ski, First Choice, Independent Ski Links, Inghams, Interhome, Neilson, Panorama, PGL Ski, Ski Astons, Ski Partners, SkiBound, Skiers World, Thomson
Zell am Ziller Equity Total Ski, First Choice, Oak Hall Skiing, PGL Ski, Ski Partners, Skiers World, Sloping Off, Thomson
Zürs Abercrombie & Kent, Corporate Ski Company, Elegant Resorts, Inghams, Made to Measure, Momentum Ski, Powder Byrne, Seasons in Style, Ski Solutions

BULGARIA
Bansko Balkan Holidays
Borovets Airtours, Balkan Holidays, Balkan Tours, Crystal, First Choice, Inghams, Neilson, Ski Partners, SkiBound, Skiers World, Thomson
Pamporovo Balkan Holidays, Balkan Tours, Crystal, First Choice, Neilson, Skiers World, Thomson

CHILE
La Parva/Valle Nevado/Portillo Scott Dunn Latin America
Termas de Chillán Scott Dunn Latin America

FRANCE
Abondance Interhome, Motours
Alpe d'Huez Airtours, Club Med, Crystal, Erna Low, Eurotunnel Motoring Holidays, Fairhand, First Choice, Inghams, Interhome, Lagrange, Leisure Direction, Motours, Neilson, Panorama, SCGB/Fresh Tracks, Ski Expectations, Ski Independence, Ski Miquel, Ski Partners, SkiBound, Skiworld, Thomson, Tops Travel, Wasteland Ski Company
Les Arcs Action Vacances/UPCA, Airtours, Chalet Snowboard, Club Med, Corporate Ski Company, Crystal, Erna Low, Eurotunnel Motoring Holidays, Fairhand, First Choice, Inghams, Interhome, Lagrange, Leisure Direction, Momentum Ski, Motours, Neilson, PGL Ski, SCGB/Fresh Tracks, Ski Amis, Ski Beat, Ski Hiver, Ski Independence, Ski Olympic, Ski Supreme, Skiworld, Thomson, Wasteland
Argentière Bigfoot, Collineige, Crystal, Erna Low, Independent Ski Links, Interhome, Lagrange, Leisure Direction, Motours, Ski Hillwood, Ski Weekend, Snowline, White Roc
Avoriaz Airtours, Chalet Snowboard, Club Med, Crystal, Erna Low, Eurotunnel Motoring Holidays, First Choice, Lagrange, Leisure Direction, Motours, Neilson, Ski France, Ski Independence, Skiworld, Snowboard Lodge, Thomson

Barèges Borderline, Lagrange, Pyrenean Mountain Tours, TT Ski

Brides-les-Bains Crystal, Erna Low, Eurotunnel Motoring Holidays, Inghams, Leisure Direction, Made to Measure, Motours, Ski Activity, Ski France, Snowcoach,

Les Carroz Fairhand, Motours

Cauterets Lagrange, TT Ski

Chamonix Abercrombie & Kent, Airtours, Alpine Answers, Beaumont, Bigfoot, Club Med, Collineige, Corporate Ski Company, Crystal, Elegant Resorts, Erna Low, Eurotunnel Motoring Holidays, Fairhand, First Choice, Fresh Tracks, Handmade Holidays, HuSki, Independent Ski Links, Inghams, Interhome, Lagrange, Leisure Direction, Momentum Ski, Motours, Neilson, PGL Ski, SCGB/Fresh Tracks, Simply Ski, Ski Activity, Ski Esprit, Ski Expectations, Ski France, Ski Independence, Ski Solutions, Ski Weekend, Thomson, White Roc

Champagny-en-Vanoise Fairhand, Handmade Holidays, Lagrange, Leisure Direction, Made to Measure, Motours, Ski Expectations

Chamrousse Lagrange

Châtel First Choice, Freedom Holidays, Interhome, Lagrange, Leisure Direction, Motours, Ski Independence, Ski Partners, SkiBound, Tops Travel

La Clusaz Classic Ski, Crystal, Fairhand, First Choice, Interhome, Lagrange, Leisure Direction, Motours, Simply Ski, Ski Activity, Ski Amis, Ski Partners, Ski Weekend, SkiBound

Les Coches Crystal, Erna Low, Eurotunnel Motoring Holidays, Lagrange, Leisure Direction, Made to Measure

Les Contamines-Montjoie Classic Ski, Club Europe, Fairhand, Interhome, Lagrange, Ski Expectations, Ski Total, Ski Weekend, SkiBound

Le Corbier Equity Total Ski, Interhome, Lagrange, Leisure Direction, Motours

Courchevel Abercrombie & Kent, Airtours, Alpine Answers, Chalet World, Corporate Ski Company, Crystal, Elegant Resorts, Erna Low, Eurotunnel Motoring Holidays, Finlays, First Choice, Flexiski, Independent Ski Links, Inghams, Lagrange, Leisure Direction, Le Ski, Lotus Supertravel, Mark Warner, Momentum Ski, Motours, Neilson, PGL Ski, Powder Byrne, SCGB/Fresh Tracks, Scott Dunn Ski, Seasons in Style, Silver Ski, Simply

Ski, Ski Activity, Ski Amis, Ski Esprit, Ski Expectations, Ski France, Ski Independence, Ski Olympic, Ski Solutions, Ski Val, Skiworld, The Ski Company, Thomson, Tops Travel, Wasteland, White Roc

Les Deux Alpes Action Vacances/UCPA, Airtours, Club Med, Crystal, Equity Total Ski, Fairhand, First Choice, Independent Ski Links, Inghams, Interhome, Lagrange, Leisure Direction, Mark Warner, Neilson, Oak Hall Skiing, Panorama, Ski Independence, Ski Partners, Ski Supreme, SkiBound, Skiworld, Thomson, Tops Travel

Flaine Action Vacances/UCPA, Classic Ski, Club Med, Crystal, Erna Low, Eurotunnel Motoring Holidays, Fairhand, First Choice, Inghams, Lagrange, Leisure Direction, Momentum Ski, Motours, Neilson, SCGB/Fresh Tracks, Ski Independence, Skisafe Travel, Skiworld, Thomson

Les Gets Fairhand, Fantiski, Lagrange, Made to Measure, Motours, Ski Activity, Ski Expectations, Ski Famille, Ski Hillwood, Ski Independence, Ski Total, Ski Weekend, Tops Travel

La Grave Lagrange, Motours, SCGB/Fresh Tracks, Ski Weekend

Les Houches Bigfoot, Erna Low, Interhome, Lagrange, Motours, PGL Ski, Ski Expectations, Ski Weekend

Isola 2000 Club Pavilion, Erna Low, Fairhand, Lagrange

Megève Abercrombie & Kent, Alpine Answers, Beaumont, Classic Ski, Elegant Resorts, Erna Low, Fairhand, Interhome, Lagrange, Momentum Ski, Motours, Seasons in Style, Ski Barrett-Boyce, Ski Expectations, Ski Independence, Ski Solutions, Ski Weekend, Stanford Skiing, White Roc

Les Menuires Club Med, Crystal, Equity Total Ski, Erna Low, First Choice, Interhome, Lagrange, Leisure Direction, Motours, Neilson, PGL Ski, Ski Independence, Ski Olympic, Ski Partners, Ski Supreme, SkiBound

Méribel Airtours, Alpine Action, Alpine Answers, Belvedere Chalets, Chalet World, Club Med, Corporate Ski Company, Crystal, Descent International, Erna Low, Eurotunnel Motoring Holidays, Fairhand, First Choice, Independent Ski Links, Inghams, Interhome, Lagrange, Leisure Direction, Lotus Supertravel, Mark

Warner, Masterski, Meriski, Momentum Ski, Motours, Neilson, Panorama, SCGB/Fresh Tracks, Scott Dunn Ski, Silver Ski, Simply Ski, Ski Activity, Ski Expectations, Ski France, Ski Independence, Ski Olympic, Ski Solutions, Ski Total, Ski Weekend, Skiworld, Snowline, The Ski Company, Thomson, Tops Travel, Wasteland, White Roc

La Mongie Borderline, Lagrange, Pyrenean Mountain Tours, TT Ski

Montalbert Interhome

Montchavin Crystal, Fairhand, Leisure Direction, Made to Measure

Montgenèvre Airtours, Crystal, Equity Total Ski, Erna Low, Fairhand, First Choice, Lagrange, Made to Measure, Neilson, Ski France, SkiBound, Thomson

Morillon Lagrange, Motours

Morzine Airtours, Alpine Tracks, Alpine Weekends, Chalet Snowboard, Corporate Ski Company, Crystal, Fairhand, First Choice, Independent Ski Links, Inghams, Interhome, Lagrange, Motours, PGL Ski, Simply Ski, Ski Activity, Ski Chamois, Ski Esprit, Ski Expectations, Ski Partners, Ski Weekend, SkiBound, Snowboard Lodge, Snowline, Solo's, Thomson, White Roc

La Norma Fairhand, Interhome

Nôtre-Dame-de-Bellecombe SkiBound

Orcières Merlette Club Europe, Motours

La Plagne Action Vacances/UCPA, Airtours, Chalet World, Club Med, Crystal, Erna Low, Eurotunnel Motoring Holidays, First Choice, Handmade Holidays, Independent Ski Links, Inghams, Interhome, Lagrange, Leisure Direction, Mark Warner, Momentum Ski, Motours, Neilson, SCGB/Fresh Tracks, Silver Ski, Simply Ski, Ski Activity, Ski Amis, Ski Beat, Ski Esprit, Ski Expectations, Ski France, Ski Independence, Ski Olympic, Ski Partners, Ski Supreme, Skiworld, Solo's, Thomson, Top Deck, Tops Travel

Pra Loup Club Europe, Equity Total Ski, Lagrange, SkiBound

Puy-St-Vincent Equity Total Ski, Fairhand, Interhome, Lagrange, Motours, Snowbizz Vacances

Risoul/Vars Action Vacances, Crystal, Erna Low, Fairhand, First Choice, Interhome, Lagrange, Made to Measure, Motours, Neilson, Ski Astons, Ski Independence, SkiBound, Thomson, Tops Travel

La Rosière Crystal, Erna Low, Fairhand, Interhome, Lagrange, Ski Esprit, Ski Olympic

Sainte-Foy Independent Ski Links

Les Saisies Classic Ski, Erna Low, Inntravel, Motours

Samoëns Fairhand, Inntravel, Interhome, Motours

Serre Chevalier/Briançon Airtours, Alpine Answers, Club Med, Crystal, Equity Total Ski, Erna Low, Fairhand, First Choice, Handmade Holidays, Hannibals, Independent Ski Links, Inghams, Lagrange, Leisure Direction, Motours, Neilson, PGL Ski, Ski Expectations, Ski France, Ski Independence, Ski Miquel, SkiBound, Skiworld, Sloping Off, Solo's, Thomson, Tops Travel

St-Gervais APT Holidays, Fairhand, Interhome, Lagrange, PGL Ski, Simply Ski, Snowcoach

St-Martin-de-Belleville Equity Total Ski, Independent Ski Links, Made to Measure, Ski Total, Thomson

Superdevoluy Lagrange, Motours

La Tania Airtours, Alpine Action, Crystal, Erna Low, Eurotunnel Motoring Holidays, Fairhand, First Choice, Independent Ski Links, Lagrange, Leisure Direction, Le Ski, Neilson, Silver Ski, Simply Ski, Ski Amis, Ski Beat, Ski France, Ski Independence, Snowline, Thomson

Tignes Action Vacances/UCPA, Airtours, Club Med, Corporate Ski Company, Crystal, Erna Low, Fairhand, First Choice, Independent Ski Links, Inghams, Interhome, Lagrange, Leisure Direction, Masterski, Momentum Ski, Motours, Neilson, SCGB/Fresh Tracks, Silver Ski, Ski Activity, Ski Amis, Ski Beat, Ski Choice, Ski Expectations, Ski France, Ski Independence, Ski Olympic, Ski Solutions, Ski Supreme, Ski Total, SkiBound, Skiworld, Thomson

La Toussuire Club Europe, Equity Total Ski

Val Cenis Erna Low, Inghams, Lagrange, MGS Ski, Motours, Ski France, Snowcoach

Val d'Isère Abercrombie & Kent, Action Vacances/UCPA, Airtours, Alpine Answers, Alpine Weekends, Chalet World, Club Med, Corporate Ski Company, Crystal, Elegant Resorts, Erna Low, Eurotunnel Motoring Holidays, Fairhand, Fantiski, Finlays, First Choice, Handmade Holidays, Independent Ski Links, Inghams,

Interhome, Lagrange, Leisure Direction, Le Ski, Lotus Supertravel, Mark Warner, Momentum Ski, Motours, Neilson, SCGB/Fresh Tracks, Scott Dunn Ski, Silver Ski, Simply Ski, Ski Activity, Ski Amis, Ski Beat, Ski Choice, Ski Expectations, Ski France, Ski Independence, Ski Solutions, Ski Supreme, Ski Total, Ski Val, Ski Weekend, SkiBound, Skiworld, The Ski Company, Thomson, VIP, Wasteland, White Roc, YSE

Val Thorens Action Vacances/UCPA, Airtours, Club Med, Crystal, Erna Low, Equity Total Ski, Eurotunnel Motoring Holidays, First Choice, Independent Ski Links, Inghams, Interhome, Lagrange, Leisure Direction, Motours, Neilson, Panorama, SCGB/Fresh Tracks, Ski Activity, Ski Amis, Ski Choice, Ski Expectations, Ski France, Ski Independence, Ski Supreme, Skiworld, Thomson, Wasteland

Valfréjus Lagrange, Made to Measure, Motours, SkiBound

Vallandry Independent Ski Links

Valloire/Valmeinier Club Europe, Club Med, Erna Low, Fairhand, First Choice, Lagrange, Leisure Direction, Motours, Savoie Ski, Ski Partners, SkiBound, Snowcoach

Valmorel/St-François/Longchamp Airtours, Club Europe, Crystal, Erna Low, Fairhand, Interhome, Lagrange, Leisure Direction, Made to Measure, Motours, Neilson, PGL Ski, Ski Independence, Ski Partners, Ski Supreme, Thomson

Vaujany Erna Low, Lagrange, Motours, Ski Independence, Ski Peak

Villard-de-Lans Lagrange

GERMANY
Garmisch Partenkirchen Moswin Tours

ITALY
Abatone Alpine Tours, Ski Partners

Alagna Crystal, SCGB/Fresh Tracks, Ski Weekend

Alleghe Crystal

Andalo Airtours, Equity Total Ski, PGL Ski, Ski Partners, Skiers World, Sloping Off

Aprica Interhome, PGL Ski, Ski Partners, Thomson

Arabba Crystal, Inghams, Neilson, Pyrenean Mountain Tours, Ski Yogi

Bardonecchia Crystal, Equity Total Ski, Interhome, Motours, Neilson, Thomson

Bormio Airtours, Inghams, Interhome, PGL Ski, Sloping Off, Thomson

Campitello Crystal, First Choice, Neilson, Thomson

Canazei Crystal, First Choice, Inghams, Neilson, Thomson

Cavalese Alpine Tours

Cervinia Abercrombie & Kent, Airtours, Beaumont, Club Med, Crystal, Elegant Resorts, Equity Total Ski, First Choice, Inghams, Interhome, Momentum Ski, Ski Solutions, Ski Weekend, Thomson, White Roc

Cesana Torinese First Choice, Ski Partners, SkiBound

Champoluc Crystal, Handmade Holidays, Thomson

Clavière Crystal, Equity Total Ski, SkiBound

Colfosco Pyrenean Mountain Tours

Cortina d'Ampezzo Abercrombie & Kent, Alpine Answers, Corporate Ski Company, Crystal, Momentum Ski, SCGB/Fresh Tracks, Ski Equipe, Ski Solutions, Ski Yogi, Solo's, White Roc

Corvara Inghams, Pyrenean Mountain Tours

Courmayeur Abercrombie & Kent, Airtours, Alpine Answers, Corporate Ski Company, Crystal, First Choice, Independent Ski Links, Inghams, Interski, Lagrange, Mark Warner, Momentum Ski, Ski Solutions, Ski Weekend, Ski Yogi, Thomson, White Roc,

Dobbiaco Waymark

Folgaria Alpine Tours, PGL Ski, SkiBound,

Folgarida Club Europe, Equity Total Ski, PGL Ski, Skiers World, Sloping Off

Foppolo Equity Total Ski, PGL Ski, Ski Partners, SkiBound

Gressoney Crystal, Motours

Kronplatz Equity Total Ski

Livigno Airtours, Crystal, First Choice, Inghams, Neilson, Panorama, Thomson

Macugnaga Interhome, Neilson, Skiers World

Madesimo Inghams, Thomson

Madonna di Campiglio Airtours, Alpine Tours, Corporate Ski Company, Crystal, Equity Total Ski, Inghams, Interhome, SCGB/Fresh Tracks, Solo's, Ski Yogi, Thomson

Marilleva Alpine Tours, Club Europe, Interhome

Monte Campione Equity Total Ski
Ortisei Inghams
Passo Tonale Airtours, Alpine Tours, Club Europe, Crystal, Equity Total Ski, First Choice, Inghams, PGL Ski, Ski Partners, SkiBound, Skiers World, Thomson
Pila Crystal, Interhome, Interski
Pinzolo Alpine Tours, Ski Partners, Sloping Off
Sansicario Equity Total Ski
Santa Caterina Airtours, Thomson
Sauze d'Oulx Airtours, Crystal, Equity Total Ski, First Choice, Independent Ski Links, Inghams, Neilson, Panorama, Thomson
Selva/Val Gardena Crystal, Independent Ski Links, Inghams, Momentum Ski, Pyrenean Mountain Tours, Thomson, Waymark
Sestriere Club Med, Equity Total Ski, Interhome, Motours, Neilson, Thomson
La Thuile Crystal, First Choice, Independent Ski Links, Inghams, Interski, Momentum Ski, Neilson, Thomson
Val di Fassa Crystal, Equity Total Ski, Independent Ski Links
Val Senales Inghams

JAPAN
Sahoro Club Med

LAPLAND (FINNISH)
Levi Inghams
Yllas Inghams

NEW ZEALAND
No current tour operator

NORTH AMERICA
Alpine Meadows (Lake Tahoe) Virgin Ski
Alta Club Pavilion, Ski the American Dream, Ski Safari, Ski Total
Alyeska Frontier Ski, Inghams
Apex Frontier Ski, Ski Safari, Skiarus
Aspen/Snowmass Abercrombie & Kent, Crystal, Elegant Resorts, Fantiski, Independent Ski Links, Lotus Supertravel, Momentum Ski, SCGB/Fresh Tracks, Seasons in Style, Ski Activity, Ski the American Dream, Ski Expectations, Ski Freedom, Ski Independence, Ski Safari, Ski Total, Skiarus, Skiworld, Thomson
Attitash Bear Peak Crystal, Skiers World, Virgin Ski
Banff/Lake Louise Airtours, All Canada Ski, Crystal, Elegant Resorts, First Choice, Frontier Ski, Independent Ski Links,

Inghams, Kuoni, Lotus Supertravel, Neilson, PGL Ski, SCGB/Fresh Tracks, Seasons in Style, Ski Activity, Ski the American Dream, Ski Freedom, Ski Independence, Ski Safari, Skiarus, SkiBound, Skiers World, Skiworld, Solo's, Thomson
Big Mountain Inghams, Ski Independence, Skiarus
Big Sky Ski Activity, Ski the American Dream, Ski Independence, Skiarus
Big White All Canada Ski, Frontier Ski, Independent Ski Links, Made to Measure, MGS Ski, Ski Activity, Ski the American Dream, Ski Independence, Ski Safari, Skiarus, Solo's
Black Mountain Crystal
Breckenridge Crystal, Handmade Holidays, Independent Ski Links, Inghams, Neilson, Rocky Mountain Adventures, Ski Activity, Ski the American Dream, Ski Expectations, Ski Freedom, Ski Independence, Ski Safari, Ski Total, Skiarus, Skiworld, Thomson
Canmore Crystal
Cannon Mountain Crystal, Virgin Ski
The Canyons Crystal, Ski the American Dream, Ski Freedom, Ski Independence, Ski Safari, Skiarus, Virgin Ski
Copper Mountain Club Med, Independent Ski Links, Ski the American Dream, Ski Freedom, Ski Independence, Skiarus, Solo's
Crested Butte Club Med, Fresh Tracks, Made to Measure, Ski Activity, Ski the American Dream, Ski Freedom, Ski Independence, Ski Safari, Ski Total, Skiarus
Deer Valley Made to Measure, Ski the American Dream, Ski Freedom, Ski Independence, Ski Safari
Durango Ski Independence, Skiarus
Fernie Airtours, All Canada Ski, Crystal, Frontier Ski, Independent Ski Links, Inghams, Ski Activity, Ski Independence, Ski Safari, Skiarus, Thomson
Grand Targhee Ski Activity, Skiarus
Gunstock Crystal
Heavenly (Lake Tahoe) Crystal, Independent Ski Links, Inghams, Neilson, Ski Activity, Ski the American Dream, Ski Freedom, Ski Independence, Ski Partners, Ski Safari, Skiers World, Ski Total, Ski World, Thomson, Virgin Ski
Jackson Hole Abercrombie & Kent, Crystal, Elegant Resorts, Independent Ski Links, Inghams, Lotus Supertravel,

Momentum Ski, Neilson, Ski Activity, Ski the American Dream, Ski Freedom, Ski Independence, Ski Safari, Skiarus, Skiworld

Jasper All Canada Ski, Crystal, Elegant Resorts, Frontier Ski, Independent Ski Links, Inghams, Neilson, Ski the American Dream, Ski Independence, Ski Safari, Skiarus, Skiers World, Thomson

Keystone Crystal, Handmade Holidays, Ski Activity, Ski the American Dream, Ski Freedom, Ski Independence, Ski Safari, Ski Total, Skiarus, Thomson

Kicking Horse Crystal, Ski Independence, Thomson

Killington Crystal, First Choice, Independent Ski Links, Inghams, Neilson, Ski Activity, Ski the American Dream, Ski Freedom, Ski Independence, Ski Partners, Ski Safari, SkiBound, Skiers World, Thomson, Virgin Ski

Kimberley Airtours, Crystal, Frontier Ski, Inghams, Ski Independence, Ski Safari, Thomson

Kirkwood (Lake Tahoe) Virgin Ski

Lake Tahoe (see Alpine Meadows, Heavenly, Kirkwood, Northstar and Squaw Valley)

Lincoln Crystal

Loon/Bretton Woods Crystal, PGL Ski, Skiers World, Virgin Ski

Mammoth Crystal, Independent Ski Links, Ski Activity, Ski the American Dream, Ski Freedom, Ski Independence, Ski Safari, Ski Total, Skiarus, Skiers World, Virgin Ski

Mont Sainte-Anne Frontier Ski, Inghams, Ski Partners, Ski Safari, SkiBound, Skiers World

Mount Bachelor Skiarus

Northstar (Lake Tahoe) Ski Freedom, Virgin Ski

North Woodstock Crystal

Panorama All Canada Ski, Frontier Ski, Inghams, Oak Hall Skiing, Ski Activity, Ski Safari

Park City Crystal, Independent Ski Links, Momentum Ski, Club Pavilion, Ski Activity, Ski the American Dream, Ski Freedom, Ski Independence, Ski Safari, Ski Total, Skiarus, Skiworld

Pico Virgin Ski

Red Mountain Frontier Ski, Ski Safari, Skiarus

Silver Star Frontier Ski, Made to Measure, Ski Activity, Ski the American Dream, Ski Independence, Ski Safari, Skiarus

Smugglers' Notch Ski the American Dream, Ski Safari, Skiarus

Snowbird Club Pavilion, Crystal, Made to Measure, Ski the American Dream, Ski Freedom, Ski Independence, Ski Safari, Ski Total, Skiarus

Squaw Valley (Lake Tahoe) Crystal, Ski the American Dream, Ski Freedom, Ski Independence, Ski Safari, Ski Total, Virgin Ski

Steamboat Crystal, Independent Ski Links, Inghams, Lotus Supertravel, Neilson, Ski Activity, Ski the American Dream, Ski Freedom, Ski Independence, Ski Safari, Ski Total, Skiarus, Skiers World, Skiworld, Thomson

Stoneham Inghams, Ski Partners, Ski Safari, SkiBound, Skiers World

Stowe Crystal, Elegant Resorts, Independent Ski Links, Inghams, Made to Measure, Neilson, Ski the American Dream, Ski Freedom, Ski Independence, Ski Partners, Ski Safari, SkiBound, Skiers World, Thomson, Virgin Ski

Sugarbush Made to Measure, Ski Safari, SkiBound, Solo's

Sugarloaf First Choice, Ski Partners, SkiBound, Skiers World

Sun Peaks All Canada Ski, Frontier Ski, Made to Measure, Ski Activity, Ski the American Dream, Ski Independence, Ski Safari, Skiarus

Sun Valley Ski Activity, Ski the American Dream, Skiarus

Sunday River First Choice, Neilson, Ski Independence, Ski Partners, Ski Safari, Skiarus, SkiBound, Skiers World, Virgin Ski

Taos Ski Activity, Ski the American Dream, Ski Independence, Skiarus

Telluride Elegant Resorts, Ski Activity, Ski the American Dream, Ski Freedom, Ski Independence, Ski Safari, Skiarus, Skiworld

Tremblant All Canada Ski, Club Pavilion, Crystal, Elegant Resorts, First Choice, Frontier Ski, Independent Ski Links, Inghams, Made to Measure, Neilson, Ski the American Dream, Ski Independence, Ski Safari, Skiers World, Thomson

Vail/Beaver Creek Abercrombie & Kent, Crystal, Elegant Resorts, Independent Ski Links, Inghams, Lotus Supertravel, Momentum Ski, Neilson, SCGB/Fresh Tracks, Seasons in Style, Ski Activity, Ski the American Dream, Ski Expectations, Ski Freedom, Ski Independence, Ski

Safari, Ski Total, Skiarus, Skiworld, Thomson
Waterville Valley Crystal, Virgin Ski
Whistler/Blackcomb Abercrombie & Kent, All Canada Ski, Alpine Tracks, Club Pavilion, Crystal, Elegant Resorts, First Choice, Flexiski, Frontier Ski, Handmade Holidays, Independent Ski Links, Inghams, Kuoni, Lotus Supertravel, Momentum Ski, Neilson, SCGB/Fresh Tracks, Seasons in Style, Simply Ski, Ski Activity, Ski the American Dream, Ski Expectations, Ski Freedom, Ski Hillwood, Ski Independence, Ski Miquel, Ski Safari, Ski Total, Skiworld, Thomson
Wildcat Crystal
Winter Park Crystal, Lotus Supertravel, Made to Measure, Neilson, Oak Hall Skiing, Ski Activity, Ski the American Dream, Ski Freedom, Ski Independence, Ski Safari, Skiarus, Skiers World, Skiworld, Thomson

NORWAY
Geilo Crystal, HF Holidays, Independent Ski Links, Inntravel, Neilson, Skiers World, Solo's, Thomson, Waymark
Hemsedal Crystal, Independent Ski Links, Neilson, Skiers World, Thomson
Lillehammer Neilson, Skiers World

POLAND
Sklarska Poremba Ski Gower

ROMANIA
Poiana Brasov Balkan Holidays, Balkan Tours, Inghams, Neilson, Skiers World

SCOTLAND
Cairngorm Mountain (Aviemore) Ski Norwest Ski Supreme, SkiSafe Travel
Glencoe Ski Supreme, SkiSafe Travel
Glenshee Ski Supreme, SkiSafe Travel
The Lecht Ski Supreme, SkiSafe Travel
Nevis Range (Aonach Mor) Ski Norwest, Ski Supreme, SkiSafe Travel

SLOVAKIA
High Tatras Inghams

SLOVENIA
Bled Alpine Tours, Balkan Holidays, Crystal, Thomson
Bohinj Alpine Tours, Balkan Holidays, Crystal, Thomson

Kranjska Gora Alpine Tours, Balkan Holidays, Crystal, Inghams, Solo's, Thomson

SPAIN
Alp 2500 Club Pavilion
Baqueira-Beret Ski Miquel
Sierra Nevada First Choice, Neilson, Solo's, Thomson

SWEDEN
Åre Independent Ski Links, Neilson

SWITZERLAND
Adelboden Interhome, Kuoni, Plus Travel, Swiss Travel Service
Andermatt Made to Measure, Ski Weekend
Anzère Interhome, Lagrange, Made to Measure
Arosa Inghams, Interhome, Kuoni, Plus Travel, Powder Byrne, Ski Choice, Ski Solutions, Ski Weekend, Swiss Travel Service, White Roc
Celerina Made to Measure
Champéry Alpine Answers, Corporate Ski Company, Piste Artiste, Plus Travel, Scott Dunn Ski, Ski Weekend, White Roc
Château d'Oex Alpine Tours, Crystal, Inghams
Crans Montana Corporate Ski Company, Crystal, Elegant Resorts, Erna Low, First Choice, Independent Ski Links, Inghams, Interhome, Kuoni, Lagrange, Momentum Ski, Motours, Oak Hall Skiing, Oxford Ski Company, PGL Ski, Plus Travel, SCGB/Fresh Tracks, Ski Solutions, Ski Weekend, Swiss Travel Service, Thomson
Davos Alpine Answers, Beaumont, Corporate Ski Company, Crystal, Elegant Resorts, Independent Ski Links, Inghams, Interhome, Kuoni, Momentum Ski, Plus Travel, SCGB/Fresh Tracks, Ski Choice, Ski Expectations, Ski Gower, Ski Weekend, Swiss Travel Service, White Roc
Les Diablerets Crystal, Interhome, Lagrange, Made to Measure, Momentum Ski, Plus Travel, Ski Gower, Solo's
Engelberg Corporate Ski Company, Crystal, Inntravel, Interhome, Kuoni, Made to Measure, Ski Gower, Swiss Travel Service
Fiesch Ski Gower
Flims/Laax Alpine Answers, Corporate Ski Company, Inghams, Interhome, Kuoni, Plus Travel, Powder Byrne, Ski Weekend, Swiss Travel Service, White Roc

Grächen Interhome
Grindelwald Corporate Ski Company, Crystal, Elegant Resorts, Independent Ski Links, Inghams, Interhome, Kuoni, Momentum Ski, Plus Travel, Powder Byrne, Ski Astons, Ski Gower, Swiss Travel Service, Thomson, White Roc
Gstaad Abercrombie & Kent, Corporate Ski Company, Crystal, Elegant Resorts, Inghams, Interhome, Momentum Ski, Seasons in Style, Ski Expectations, Ski Gower, Ski Solutions, White Roc
Interlaken Kuoni, Ski Astons, Ski Gower
Kandersteg Headwater, HF Holidays, Inghams, Inntravel, Kuoni, Waymark
Klosters Alpine Answers, Elegant Resorts, Inghams, Interhome, Kuoni, Momentum Ski, Plus Travel, Powder Byrne, SCGB/Fresh Tracks, Ski Expectations, Ski Gower, Ski Weekend, The Ski Company, White Roc
Lauterbrunnen Oak Hall Skiing, Ski Miquel, Top Deck
Lenk Made to Measure, Swiss Travel Service
Lenzerheide/Valbella Interhome, Kuoni, Plus Travel, Ski Choice
Leysin Club Med, Crystal, Plus Travel, Skiers World
Meiringen Hasliberg PGL Ski
Morgins Ski Morgins
Mürren Inghams, Kuoni, Plus Travel, SCGB/Fresh Tracks, Ski Astons, Ski Solutions, Swiss Travel Service, Thomson, Top Deck
Nendaz/Siviez Interhome, Snowplus
Pontresina Club Med, Made to Measure
Saas-Fee Crystal, Erna Low, First Choice, Independent Ski Links, Inghams, Interhome, Kuoni, Made to Measure, Momentum Ski, Oak Hall Skiing, PGL Ski, Plus Travel, Powder Byrne, SCGB/Fresh Tracks, Ski Choice, Ski Gower, Ski Independence, Ski Solutions, Swiss Travel Service, Thomson
Saas-Grund Ski Gower
Schönried Interhome
Sils Maria/Silvaplana Interhome
St Moritz Abercrombie & Kent, Club Med, Corporate Ski Company, Crystal, Elegant

Resorts, Flexiski, Independent Ski Links, Inghams, Interhome, Kuoni, Momentum Ski, Oak Hall Skiing, Plus Travel, SCGB/Fresh Tracks, Seasons in Style, Ski Gower, Ski Solutions, Swiss Travel Service
Torgon Interhome
Valbella Club Med
Verbier Abercrombie & Kent, Airtours, Alpine Answers, Alpine Weekends, Chalet World, Corporate Ski Company, Crystal, Descent International, Elegant Resorts, Erna Low, First Choice, Flexiski, Fresh Tracks, Independent Ski Links, Inghams, Interhome, Momentum Ski, Motours, Peak Ski, Plus Travel, SCGB/Fresh Tracks, Simply Ski, Ski Activity, Ski Astons, Ski Esprit, Ski Expectations, Ski Solutions, Ski Total, Ski Weekend, Skiworld, Swiss Travel Service, The Ski Company, Thomson, White Roc
Villars Club Med, Corporate Ski Company, Crystal, Erna Low, Inghams, Interhome, Kuoni, Lagrange, Made to Measure, Momentum Ski, Plus Travel, Powder Byrne, Ski Independence, Ski Solutions, Ski Weekend, Swiss Travel Service
Wengen Club Med, Corporate Ski Company, Crystal, Independent Ski Links, Inghams, Interhome, Kuoni, Made to Measure, Momentum Ski, PGL Ski, Plus Travel, SCGB/Fresh Tracks, Ski Astons, Ski Expectations, Ski Gower, Ski Solutions, Swiss Travel Service, Thomson
Zermatt Abercrombie & Kent, Alpine Answers, Corporate Ski Company, Crystal, Elegant Resorts, Erna Low, Independent Ski Links, Inghams, Interhome, Kuoni, Lotus Supertravel, Momentum Ski, Plus Travel, Powder Byrne, SCGB/Fresh Tracks, Scott Dunn Ski, Seasons in Style, Ski Choice, Ski Expectations, Ski Gower, Ski Independence, Ski Solutions, Ski Total, Swiss Travel Service, Thomson, Trail Alpine, White Roc
Zinal Interhome

TURKEY
Palandöken Ingharus

Skiing by numbers

Contents

NATIONAL TOURIST OFFICES

American Travel & Tourism Service
Tel (09065) 508972 (recorded message)

Andorran Delegation
63 Westover Road, London SW18 2RF
Tel/Fax 020-8874 4806
Web site www.andorraonline.ad

Argentinian Consulate
27 Three Kings Yard, London W1Y 1FL
Tel 020-7318 1340 **Fax** 020-7318 1349

Australian Tourist Commission
Gemini House, 10–18 Putney Hill, London
SW15 6AA
Tel 020-8780 2229 **Fax** 020-8780 1496
Email Europe_helpline@atc.gov.au
Web site www.australia.com

Austrian National Tourist Office
PO Box 2363, London W1A 2QB
Tel 020-7629 0461 **Fax** 020-7499 6038
Email info@anto.co.uk
Web site www.austria-tourism.at

Bulgaria, Embassy of the Republic of
186–188 Queensgate, London SW7 5HL
Tel 020-7589 8402 **Fax** 020-7589 4875

Canada, Visit
PO Box 5396, Northampton NN1 2FA
Tel (0906) 871 5000 (premium rates
at all times)
Email visitcanada@dial.pipex.com
Web site www.travelcanada.ca

Chile, Consulate of
Tourist Information, 12 Devonshire Street,
London W1G 7DS
Tel 020-7580 1023 **Fax** 020-7323 4294
Email
cglonduk@congechileuk.demon.co.uk
Web site www.visitchile.org

Czech Tourist Authority
95 Great Portland Street, London
W1W 7NY
Tel (09063) 640641 **Fax** 020-7436 8300
Email cta@inform.demon.co.uk
Web site www.tourist-offices.org.uk

Finnish Tourist Board
PO Box 33213, London W6 8JX
Tel 020-7365 2512 **Fax** 020-7321 0696
Email finlandinfo.lon@mek.fi
Web site www.finland-tourism.com

French Government Tourist Office
178 Piccadilly, London W1J 9AL
Tel (09068) 244123 **Fax** 020-7493 6594
Email info@mdlf.co.uk
Web site www.franceguide.com

German National Tourist Office
PO Box 2695, London W1A 3TN
Tel 020-7317 0908 **Fax** 020-7495 6129
Email gntolon@d-z-t.com
Web site www.germany-tourism.de

Italian State Tourist Office
1 Princes Street, London W1R 8AY
Tel 020-7408 1254 **Fax** 020-7493 6695
Email enitlond@globalnet.co.uk
Web site www.enit.it

Japanese National Tourist Organisation
Heathcoat House, 20 Savile Row, London
W1S 3PR
Tel 020-7734 9638 **Fax** 020-7734 4290
Email info@jnto.co.uk
Web site www.jnto.go.jp

New Zealand Tourism Board
New Zealand House, Haymarket, London
SW1Y 4TQ
Tel (09069) 101010 **Fax** 020-7839 8929
Email annied@nztb.govt.nz
Web site www.purenz.com

Norwegian Tourist Board
5th Floor, Charles House, 5 Lower Regent
Street, London SW1Y 4LR
Tel 020-7839 6255 **Fax** 020-7839 6014
Email infouk@ntr.no
Web site www.visitnorway.com

Romanian National Tourist Office
22 New Cavendish Street, London
W1G 8TT
Tel 020-7224 3692 **Fax** 020-7935 6435
Email uktouroff@romania.freeserve.co.uk
Web site www.romaniatravel.com

Scottish Tourist Board
23 Ravelston Terrace, Edinburgh
EH4 3EU
Tel 0131-332 2433 **Fax** 0131-343 1513
Email info@stb.gov.uk
Web site www.visitscotland.com

Slovenian Tourist Office
49 Conduit Street, London W1 9FB
Tel 020-7287 7133 **Fax** 020-7287 5476
Email slovenia@cpts.fsbusiness.co.uk
Web site www.slovenia-tourism.si

Spanish Tourist Office
22–23 Manchester Square, London
W1M 5AP
Tel 020-7486 8077 **Fax** 020-7486 8034
Email info.londres@tourspain.es
Web site www.tourspain.es

Swedish Travel & Tourism Council
11 Montagu Place, London W1H 2AL
Tel 020-7870 5600 **Fax** 020-7724 5872
Email info@swetourism.org.uk
Web site www.visit-sweden.com

Switzerland Travel Centre
Swiss Centre, 10 Wardour Street,
London W1D 6QF
Tel 00800 100 200 30
Fax 00800 100 200 31
Email stc@stlondon.com
Web site www.MySwitzerland.com

SKI TRAVEL AGENTS

Alpine Answers
The Business Village, 3–9 Broomhill Road,
London SW18 4JQ
Tel 020-8871 4656 **Fax** 020-8871 9676
Email ski@alpineanswers.co.uk
Web site www.alpineanswers.co.uk

Avant-Ski
4 Mildmay Road, Jesmond, Newcastle
Upon Tyne NE2 3DU
Tel/Fax 0191-212 1173
Web site www.avant-ski.com

Erna Low
9 Reece Mews, London SW7 3HE
Tel 020-7584 2841 **Fax** 020-7589 9531
Email info@ernalow.co.uk
Web site www.ernalow.co.uk

Independent Ski Links
Little Arram Farm, Bewholme Lane,
Seaton, Nr Hull HU11 5SX
Tel (0870) 747 9721
Email info@ski-links.com
Web site www.ski-links.com

Skibookers
16 Brook Parade, Chigwell IG7 6PF
Tel 020-8500 9191 **Fax** 020-8500 2593
Email sales@skibookers.co.uk
Web site www.skibookers.co.uk

Ski McNeill
421 Lisburn Road, Belfast BT9 7EW
Tel (02890) 666699
Fax (02890) 683888
Email queries@skimcneill.com
Web site www.skimcneill.com

Ski Solutions
84 Pembroke Road, London W8 6NX
Tel 020-7471 7700 **Fax** 020-7471 7701
Email skihols@skisolutions.com
Web site www.skisolutions.com

Ski Travel Centre
1100 Pollokshaws Road, Shawlands,
Glasgow G41 3NJ
Tel 0141-649 9696 **Fax** 0141-649 2273
Email snow@skitravelcentre.com
Web site www.skitravelcentre.co.uk

Skiers Travel
Fountain Court, High Street, Market
Harborough LE16 7AF
Tel (0113) 292 0893 **Fax** (01858) 828130
Email sales@skiers-travel.co.uk
Web site www.skiers-travel.co.uk

Ski Line
12 Blakeney Road, Beckenham BR3 1HD
Tel 020-8777 0440
Email angus@skiline.co.uk
Web site www.skiline.co.uk

Ski & Surf
37 Priory Field Drive, Edgware HA8 9PT
Tel 020-8958 2418 **Fax** 020-8905 4146
Email janm@skisurf.com
Web site www.skisurf.com

Snow Line
1 Angel Court, High Street, Market
Harborough LE16 7NL
Tel (01858) 828000 **Fax** (01858) 828020
Email sales@snow-line.co.uk
Web site www.snow-line.co.uk

AIRLINES

The main airlines listed below offer international scheduled flights to airports close
to ski areas

Air Canada
Tel (0870) 524 7226
Web site www.aircanada.ca
Air France
Tel (0845) 084 5111
Web site www.airfrance.co.uk
Air New Zealand and Ansett Australia
Tel 020-8741 2299
Web site www.airnewzealand.com
www.ansettaustralia.com
Alitalia
Tel (0870) 544 8259
Web site www.alitalia.co.uk
American Airlines
Tel 020-8572 5555
Web site www.aa.com
Austrian Airlines
Tel (0845) 6010948
Web site www.aua.com
Braathens/Malmo
Tel 0191-214 0991
Web site www.braathens.no
British Airways
Tel (0845) 722 2111
Web site www.britishairways.com
buzz
Tel (0870) 240 7070
Web site www.buzzaway.com
Continental Airlines
Tel (01293) 776464
Web site www.continental.com
Crossair
Tel (0845) 607 3000
Web site www.crossair.com
Delta Airlines
Tel (0800) 414767
Web site www.delta.com
easyJet
Tel (0870) 600 0000
Web site wwweasyjet.com
Finnair
Tel 020-8759 1258
Web site www.finnair.co.uk
go
Tel (0845) 605 4321
Web site www.gofly.com
Iberia Airlines
Tel 020-7830 0011
Web site www.iberiaairlines.co.uk

KLM Direct/Air Engiadina
Tel (0870) 507 4074
Web site www.klm.com
Lauda Air
Tel (0845) 601 0934
Web site www.laudaair.com
Lufthansa
Tel (0845) 773 7747
Web site www.lufthansa.co.uk
Monarch Airlines
Tel (01582) 400000
Web site www.fly-crown.com
Qantas Airways
Tel (0845) 774 7767
Web site www.qantas.com.au
Ryanair
Tel (0870) 156 9569
Web site www.ryanair.com
SAS
Tel (0845) 607 2772
Web site www.scandinavian.net
Swissair
Tel (0845) 601 0956
Web site www.swissair.com
United Airlines
Tel (0845) 844 4777
Web site www.unitedairlines.co.uk
Virgin Atlantic Airways
Tel (01293) 747747
Web site www.virgin.com

UK AND IRISH AIRPORTS
Aberdeen
Tel (01224) 722331
Web site www.baa.co.uk
Belfast
Tel (02894) 422888
Web site www.belfastairport.com
Birmingham
Tel 0121-767 5511
Web site www.bhx.co.uk
Bournemouth
Tel (01202) 364235
Web site www.flybournemouth.com
Bristol
Tel (01275) 474444
Web site www.bristolairport.co.uk
Cardiff
Tel (01446) 711111
Web site www.cial.co.uk
Dublin
Tel 00 353 1 814 1111
Web site www.aer_rianta.ie

East Midlands
Tel (01332) 852852
Web site www.eastmidlandsairport.com
Edinburgh
Tel 0131-333 1000
Web site www.baa.co.uk
Exeter
Tel (01392) 367433
Web site www.exeter-airport.co.uk
Glasgow
Tel 0141-887 1111
Web site www.baa.co.uk
Leeds Bradford
Tel (0113) 250 9696
Web site www.lbia.co.uk
London City
Tel 020-7646 0000
Web site www.londoncityairport.com
London Gatwick
Tel (0870) 000 2468
Web site www.baa.co.uk
London Heathrow
Tel (0870) 000 0123
Web site www.baa.co.uk
London Luton
Tel (01582) 405100
Web site www.london-luton.co.uk
London Stansted
Tel (0870) 000 0303
Web site www.baa.co.uk
Manchester
Tel 0161-489 3000
Web site www.manchesterairport.co.uk
Newcastle
Tel 0191-286 0966
Web site www.newcastleairport.com
Teesside
Tel (01325) 332811
Web site www.teesideairport.com

CAR HIRE
Alamo
Tel (0870) 400 4580
Web site www.alamo.com
Avis
Tel (0870) 590 0500
Web sites www.avisworld.com
www.avis.co.uk
Budget
Tel (0800) 181181
Web site www.go-budget.co.uk
Europcar
Tel (0113) 242 2233
Web sites www.europcar.com
www.europcar.co.uk

Hertz
Tel (0870) 599 6699
Web site www.hertz.com
Holiday Autos
Tel (0870) 530 0400
Web site www.holidayautos.com
Suncars
Tel (0870) 500 5566
Web site www.suncars.com

BREAKDOWN INSURANCE

AA Five Star Services
Tel (0800) 444500
Autohome
Tel (01604) 232336
Britannia Rescue
Tel (01484) 514848
Direct Line Rescue
Tel (0845) 246 8999
Europ Assistance
Tel (01444) 442211
First Assist
Tel 020-8763 1550
Green Flag National Breakdown
Tel (0345) 670345
Key Connect
Tel (01924) 207000
Leisurecare Insurance Services
Tel (01793) 750150
Mondial Assistance
Tel 020-8681 2525 1
RAC Travel Services
Tel (0800) 550055

CHANNEL CROSSINGS

Brittany Ferries *(Portsmouth–Caen)*
Tel (0990) 360360
Eurotunnel *(Folkestone–Calais)*
Tel (0990) 353535
Hoverspeed *(Dover–Calais,Dover–Ostend,*
Newhaven–Dieppe
Tel (0990) 240241
P & O European Ferries *(Portsmouth–*
Le Havre, Portsmouth–Cherbourg)
Tel (0870) 2424999
P & O North Sea Ferries *(Hull–Zeebrugge,*
Hull–Rotterdam)
Tel (0870) 1296002
P & O Stena Line *(Dover–Calais)*
Tel (0870) 600 0600
Seafrance *(Dover–Calais)*
Tel (0990) 711711
Stena Line *(Harwich–Hook)*
Tel (0990) 707070

WEATHER AND SNOW

Terradat
Web site www.snow-forecast.com
Worldwide snow data
The First Resort
Web site www.thefirstresort.com
On-line holiday booking and information
for snow-users
Austrian snow conditions
Tel 00 43 11585 *(Tyrol and Vorarlberg)*
Tel 00 43 11584 *(Salzburgerland)*
Tel 00 43 11590 *(road conditions)*
Met-Call Ski Scotland
Tel (0336) 405 400
Information on Scottish ski resorts
Metéo-France (Savoie)
Tel 00 33 836 68 02 73 *2
Detailed forecast for French Alps (in
French only)
Ski Club Snowline
Tel (0906) 951 9191
24-hr snow and weather information on
more than 200 resorts in 10 countries in
Europe and North America
Swiss Automobile Club
Tel 00 41 31 311 7722 *(road conditions)*
Swiss Touring Club
Tel 00 41 22 417 2727 *(road conditions)*

SKI ROOF BOXES

Kar Rite Europe
Tel (01440) 760000
The Roof Box Company
Tel (01539) 621884
Thule
Tel (01275) 340404

SNOW CHAINS

AA
Tel (0990) 500600
Brindley Chains
Tel 01925 825555
RAC
Tel (0800) 550055
Rudd Chains
Tel (01227) 276611
Snowchains
Tel (01732) 884408

GOING BY RAIL

Rail companies (for Alps)
Austrian Federal Railways
Tel (0906) 851 7175
Eurostar
Tel (0990) 186 186

German Rail
Tel (0870) 243 5363
Motorail
Tel (0870) 241 5415
Rail Europe *(for European rail bookings)*
Tel (0990) 848 848
Swiss Federal Railways
Tel 020-7734 1921
Gatwick Express *(from Victoria)*
Stansted Sky Train *(from Liverpool Street)*
Heathrow Express *(from Paddington)*
Tel (0845) 7484950 (all)

AVALANCHE WARNINGS

Austria
Tel 00 43 5522 1588
Web site: www.lawine.at
Canada
Tel 001 250 837 2435
Web site www.avalanche.ca
France
Web site www.meteo.fr
Germany
Web site
www.lawinenwarndienst.bayern.de
Italy
Tel 00 39 0461 230305
Web site www.aineva.it
Scotland
Tel (0800) 096 0007
Web site www.sais.gov.uk
Spain
Tel 00 34 934 232 967/572
Web site www.icc.es/allaus
Switzerland
Tel 00 41 81 417 0151
Web site www.slf.ch
USA
Web site www.csac.org

SKI-TOURING

The Alpine Ski Club
Tel (01753) 886665 **Fax** (01753) 880305
Email whmann@btinternet.com
Web site www.alpineskiclub.org.uk
*Ski-mountaineering – avalanche
transceivers available for hire*

The Eagle Ski Club
Tel 020-8959 2214 **Fax** 020-8959 4145
Email info@eagleskiclub.org.uk
Web site www.eagleskiclub.org.uk
Uk's largest ski-touring club
Eclipse Mountain Guiding

Tel (01539) 444033 **Fax** (01539) 442145
Email philip@eclipse-outdoor.co.uk
Web site www.eclipse-outdoor.co.uk
*Ski-tours in France and Switzerland with
qualified guides*

Mountain Experience
Tel/Fax (01663) 750160
Email info@mountainexperience.co.uk
Web site www.mountainexperience.co.uk
*Private guiding and courses. Off piste and
ski-touring in France, Italy and Switzerland*

SKI COURSES

The organisations listed below specialise in
ski clinic holidays. Note that several of the
companies in *Which tour operator?* also
offer ski clinics

Ali Ross (through Ski Solutions)
Tel 020-7471 7777 **Fax** 020-7471 7771
Email alc@skisolutions.com
Specialist ski courses in Tignes

The International Academy
Tel (02920) 672500
Fax (02920) 672510
Email info@international-academy.com
Web site www.international-academy.com
*Professional ski and snowboard instruc-
tors' courses in USA, New Zealand,
Canada, Switzerland and Chile*

Lauralee Bowie Ski Adventures
Tel 001 604 689 7444
Fax 001 604 689 7489
Email llbski@canuck.com
Web site www.skiadventures.net
*Personalised instruction in Lake Louise
and Whistler*

McGarry The Ski System
5 Barnhill Road, Dalkey, Co. Dublin
Tel/Fax 00 353 1 285 9139
Specialist courses in Châtel

Optimum Ski Courses
Tel (01992) 561085
Fax 00 33 479 06 93 56
Email info@optimumski.com
Web site www.optimumski.com
*Ski clinics in Les Arcs and Tignes with
BASI trainer*

Ski Club of Great Britain
Tel 020-8410 2000 **Fax** 020-8410 2001
Email info@skiclub.co.uk
Web site www.skiclub.co.uk
Ski courses for all standards

The Ski Company
Tel (0870) 241 2085 **Fax** (01288) 352306
Email sally@theskicompany.co.uk
Web site www.theskicompany.co.uk
*Year-round ski courses in Canada
and France*

The Telemark Ski Company
Tel/Fax (01535) 644069
Email ski@telemarkskico.com
Web site www.telemarkskico.com

Thomson British Ski Academy
Tel/Fax (01932) 242882
Email admin@britskiacad.org.uk
Web site www.britskiacad.org.uk
*Racing courses combined with academic
study for 8–18-year-olds*

Top Ski
Tel 00 33 612 69 81 82
Fax 00 33 479 06 28 42
Email top.ski.isere@wanadoo.fr
Web site www.topskival.com
Ski clinics in Val d'Isère and Tignes

SKI RECRUITMENT AGENCY

Voovs.com Ltd
Tel (01707) 396511
Fax (0870) 1215436
Email info@voovs.com
Web site www.findaskijob.com

TRADE ORGANISATIONS

Artificial Slope Ski Instructors (ASSI)
Tel 0121-501 2314 **Fax** 0121-585 6448
Email esc@englishski.org
Web site www.englishski.org

**Association of British Travel Agents
(ABTA)**
Tel 020-7637 2444 **Fax** 020-7637 5626
Email abta@abta.co.uk
Web site www.abta.com

**Association of British Tour Operators to
France (ABTOF)**
Tel (01989) 769140 **Fax** (01989) 769066
Email abtof@aol.com
Web site www.holidayfrance.org.uk

**Association of Independent Tour
Operators (AITO)**
Tel 020-8744 9280
Brochure line 020-8607 9080
Fax 020-8744 3187
Email info@aito.co.uk
Web site www.aito.co.uk

**British Association of Snowsport
Instructors (BASI)**
Tel (01479) 861717 **Fax** (01479) 861718
Email basi@basi.org.uk
Web site www.basi.org.uk

British Association of Ski Patrollers
Tel/Fax (01855) 811443
Email skipatrol@basp.org.uk
Web site www.basp.org.uk

British Bobsleigh Association
Tel/Fax (01225) 826802
Email bba@dial.pipex.com
Web site www.british-bobsleigh.com

British Bobskeleton Association
Tel (01225) 323696
Fax (01225) 323697
Email bbaska@dial.pipex.com
Web site www.british-bobsleigh.com

British Mountain Guides
Tel (01690) 720386 **Fax** (01690) 720248
Email bmg@mltb.org
Web site www.bmg.org.uk

British Mountaineering Council
Tel 0161-445 4747 **Fax** 0161-445 4500
Email office@thebmc.co.uk
Web site www.thebmc.co.uk

British Ski Slope Operators' Association
Tel/Fax (01928) 710009
Web site www.bssoa.co.uk

British Ski and Snowboard Federation
Tel 0131-445 7676 **Fax** 0131-445 7722
Email britski@easynet.co.uk
Web site www.ifyouski.com

British Snowboard Association
Tel (0700) 036 0540 **Fax** (0700) 072 0540
Email sbba@yahoo.co.uk
Web site www.snowboardbritain.com

Snowsport Industries of Great Britain
Tel 0131-557 3012 **Fax** 0131-557 9466
Email sigb@raremanagement.co.uk
Web site www.snowlife.org.uk

INDOOR SLOPES (ARTIFICIAL SNOW)
Xcape Snozone
Milton Keynes
Tel (01908) 230260 **Fax** (01908) 230270
Web site www.snozonenk.co.uk

Tamworth SnowDome
Tamworth, Staffordshire B79 7ND
Tel (01827) 67905 **Fax** (01827) 62549

SKI COUNCILS
These bodies govern the sport as a whole,
taking responsibility for promoting and
developing snowsports with the aid of
grants from the Sports Council

English Ski Council
Tel 0121-501 2314 **Fax** 0121-585 6448
Email esc@englishski.org
Web site www.englishski.org

Snowsport Scotland
Tel 0131-445 4151 **Fax** 0131-445 4949
Email snowsport@snsc.demon.co.uk
Web site www.snsc.demon.co.uk

Ski Council of Wales
Tel (02920) 561904 **Fax** (02920) 561924
Email robin.snowsportwales@virgin.net
Web site www.snowsportwales.net

SKI CLUBS
Alpbach Visitors Ski Club
Tel 00 43 5336 5282
Fax 00 43 5336 5073
Individual and package holidays

Bearsden Ski Club
Tel 0141-943 1500 **Fax** 0141-942 4705
Email info@skibearsden.co.uk
Web site www.skibearsden.co.uk
Ski club with artificial slope

British Ski Club for the Disabled
Tel/Fax (01747) 828515
Email edski@bscd.org.uk
Web site www.bscd.org.uk

Downhill Only Club
Tel/Fax (01825) 840043
Email ingrid@connectfree.co.uk
Web site www.ukonline.co.uk/dho/
*Ski club with junior racing, based in
Wengen, Switzerland*

Kandahar Ski Club
Tel 020-8878 3445
Email hon.secretary@kandahar.org.uk
Web site www.kandahar.org.uk
*Ski club with junior racing, based in
Mürren, Switzerland*

Ladies Ski Club
Tel (01787) 313923 **Fax** (01787) 375497
Ski racing club

Marden's Club
Tel (01223) 893063 **Fax** (01223) 890846
Web site www.mardensclub.co.uk
Ski club based in Klosters, Switzerland

Scottish Ski Club
Tel 0131-477 1055
Email info@scotski.org.uk
Web site www.scotski.org.uk

Ski Club of Great Britain
Tel 020-8410 2000 **Fax** 020-8410 2001
Email info@skiclub.co.uk
Web site www.skiclub.co.uk
*The leading club for British skiers (see
page 11 for details)*

Thomson British Ski Academy
Tel/Fax (01932) 242882
Email admin@britskiacad.org.uk
Web site www.britskiacad.org.uk
Children's racing club

The Uphill Ski Club of Great Britain
Tel/Fax (01799) 525406
Email Isabel@uphill-ski-club.demon.co.uk
Web site www.ccksb.freeserve.co.uk
Organisation for disabled skiers

World Ski & Snowboard Association
Tel (0114) 279 7300
Fax (0114) 276 2348
Email info@worldski.co.uk
Web site www.worldski.co.uk
Wide range of discounts for members

ON-LINE RETAIL OUTLETS

The following outlets supply skiwear and equipment

Beater Outdoor Adventure Wear
Web site www.beater.com
Factory-direct skiwear

Ellis Brigham
Web site www.ellis-brigham.com
UK clothing and equipment brochure

Finches
Web site www.finches-ski.com
UK clothing brochure

Mountain Equipment Co-op
Web site www.mec.ca
Canadian outdoor gear

mySimon
Web site www.mysimon.com
Ski clothing and equipment on-line

REI
Web site www.rei.com
American co-operative that will ship orders to the UK

REI Outlet
Web site www.rei-outlet.com
Separate discount site

Snow + Rock
Web site www.snowandrock.com
UK clothing and equipment brochure

ON-LINE RESOURCES

Dedicated ski and snowboarding web sites

Ifyouski.com.
Web site www.ifyouski.com
Comprehensive information for snow-users

Iglu.com
Web site www.iglu.com
All-round ski information

Liveski.com
Web site www.liveski.com
All-inclusive ski magazine

Ski Hotline
Web site www.born2ski.com

Ski Web
Web site www.skiweb.co.uk

Reporting on the resorts

Keep sending us your resort reports; they are an invaluable contribution to the essence of the book. Writers of the most informative reports win a free copy of the next edition of the Guide.

Use the structure set out below and send your reports to: Dept CD, Consumers' Association, FREEPOST, 2 Marylebone Road, London NW1 1YN. No stamp is needed. Please type or print your reports. A separate sheet must be used for each resort, however short the report. You can also contact us via email: goodskiandsnowguide@which.net

To use your reports we must have them by **30 April 2002**.

Resort report checklist:

BASICS
Your name
Your address
Your skiing background (experience, competence)
Resort name/country
Date of visit
Tour operator used; service from rep
Hotel/chalet/apartment block in which you stayed

VERDICTS
Your response to our 'ticks' and 'crosses' verdicts on the resort

OPERATION OF LIFTS
Remarks on lift system, queues, new lifts, upgraded lifts, lift passes

OPERATION OF RUNS
Remarks on piste-grooming and accuracy of piste-map. Name any favourite runs and interesting off-piste descents

MOUNTAIN RESTAURANTS
Named establishments only; type and quality of food, the atmosphere

SKI SCHOOLS
Name the school on which you are commenting. Remarks on organisation, tuition, language, use of time, allocation of pupils to classes, group size, etc. Cover private lessons, guiding and special courses

SNOWBOARDING
How user-friendly is the resort for snowboarders? Tuition, terrain, facilities, terrain parks

CHILDREN'S FACILITIES
Name the school, ski- and/or non-ski kindergarten on which you are commenting. Remarks on facilities, staff competence and attitude, language, approach to tuition, meals

LOCAL TRANSPORT
Transport within the resort: frequency, reliability, convenience, cost, crowding. Parking, value of having a car

SHOPPING
Food shops and supermarkets; prices compared to valley town and home

NON-SKIING FACILITIES
Range, quality, convenience and price of non-skiing facilities; excursion possibilities

EATING OUT
Specific establishments, type and quality of food, atmosphere, service

APRÈS-SKI
Range, style and prices in bars, restaurants, discos; what happens in the resort after skiing until the small hours (names of venues are essential)

ACCOMMODATION
Named apartments, chalets or hotels. Advise on comfort, service, atmosphere, food, convenience of location

PRICES
General observations on the cost of meals and drinks. Examples should include a beer, soft drink, house wine, cup of coffee, dish of the day

SUMMARY
What did you particularly like or dislike about the resort? What aspect of the resort came as a surprise (pleasant or otherwise)? Who does the resort suit? And who does it not suit? Would you go back to the resort?

AIRPORTS
Which airport did you fly to and from? How did you find the facilities? Which airline did you travel with and how would you rate it for comfort of seating, staff and food provided?

And finally . . .

THE GUIDE
We would welcome your views on the layout and contents of *The Good Skiing & Snowboarding Guide*. Is there anything more you would like to see included?

Resort index